Employee Training and Development

Employee Training and Development

Seventh Edition

Raymond A. Noe
The Ohio State University

Mc
Graw
Hill
Education

EMPLOYEE TRAINING AND DEVELOPMENT, SEVENTH EDITION

Published by McGraw-Hill Education, 2 Penn Plaza, New York, NY 10121. Copyright © 2017 by McGraw-Hill Education. All rights reserved. Printed in the United States of America. Previous editions © 2013, 2010, and 2008. No part of this publication may be reproduced or distributed in any form or by any means, or stored in a database or retrieval system, without the prior written consent of McGraw-Hill Education, including, but not limited to, in any network or other electronic storage or transmission, or broadcast for distance learning.

Some ancillaries, including electronic and print components, may not be available to customers outside the United States.

This book is printed on acid-free paper.

1 2 3 4 5 6 7 8 9 0 DOC/DOC 1 0 9 8 7 6

ISBN 978-0-07-811285-0
MHID 0-07-811285-0

Senior Vice President, Products & Markets: *Kurt L. Strand*
Vice President, General Manager, Products & Markets: *Marty Lange*
Vice President, Content Design & Delivery: *Kimberly Meriwether David*
Managing Director: *Susan Gouijnstook*
Director: *Michael Ablassmeir*
Brand Manager: *Laura Hurst Spell/Anke Weekes*
Director, Product Development: *Rose Koos*
Product Developer: *Laura Hurst Spell*
Marketing Manager: *Michael Gedatus*
Director of Digital Content: *Sankha Basu*
Director, Content Design & Delivery: *Linda Avenarius*
Program Manager: *Faye M. Herrig*
Content Project Managers: *Jessica Portz, Evan Roberts, Karen Jozefowicz*
Buyer: *Susan K. Culbertson*
Content Licensing *Specialists: DeAnna Dausener*
Cover Image: From left to right: © Frederic Cirou/PhotoAlto/Corbis; Sam Edwards/Getty Images; Ingram Publishing, Purestock/Superstock; © John Lee/Blend Images LLC; © Frederic Cirou/PhotoAlto/Corbis
Compositor: *Lumina Datamatics, Inc.*
Printer: *R. R. Donnelley*

All credits appearing on page or at the end of the book are considered to be an extension of the copyright page.

Library of Congress Cataloging-in-Publication Data

Noe, Raymond A., author.
  Employee training and development / Raymond A. Noe, The Ohio State University. -- Seventh edition.
    pages cm
  ISBN 978-0-07-811285-0 (acid-free paper)
  1. Employees--Training of. I. Title.
  HF5549.5.T7N59 2016
  658.3'124--dc23

                            2015027006

The Internet addresses listed in the text were accurate at the time of publication. The inclusion of a website does not indicate an endorsement by the authors or McGraw-Hill Education, and McGraw-Hill Education does not guarantee the accuracy of the information presented at these sites.

mheducation.com/highered

This book is dedicated to family, friends, colleagues, and all of the current and past hard-working people at McGraw-Hill who have supported and contributed to making seven editions of this book possible.

Preface

Traditionally, training and development were not viewed as activities that could help companies create "value" and successfully deal with competitive challenges. Today, that view has changed. Companies that use innovative training and development practices are likely to report better financial performance than their competitors that do not. Training and development also help a company develop the human capital needed to meet competitive challenges. Many companies now recognize that learning through training, development, and knowledge management helps employees strengthen or increase their skills in order to improve or make new products, generate new and innovative ideas, and provide high-quality customer service. Also, development activities and career management are needed to prepare employees for managerial and leadership positions and to attract, motivate, and retain talented employees at all levels and in all jobs. An emphasis on learning through training, development, and knowledge management is no longer in the category of "nice to do"—they are a "must do" if companies want to gain a competitive advantage and meet employees' expectations.

Businesses today must compete in the global marketplace, and the diversity of the workforce continues to increase. As a result, companies need to train employees to work with persons from different cultures, both within the United States and abroad. Technologies, such as social media, and tablet computers, such as the iPad, reduce the costs associated with bringing employees to a central location for training. At the same time, the challenge is ensuring that these training methods include the necessary conditions (practice, feedback, self-pacing, etc.) for learning to occur. Through the blended learning approach, companies are seeking the best balance between private, self-paced, technology-based training (such as online learning), and methods that allow interpersonal interaction among trainees (such as classroom instruction or active learning). Employees from the millennial generation are well versed in informal learning, especially through collaboration facilitated by social media such as Facebook and Twitter. Also, their gaming experiences lead them to expect that learning experiences will be fun, multidimensional, challenging, and provide immediate feedback and rewards.

The role of training has broadened beyond training program design. Effective instructional design remains important, but training managers, human resource experts, and trainers are increasingly being asked to create systems to motivate employees to learn, not only in programs but informally on the job; create knowledge; and share that knowledge with other employees in the company. Training has moved from an emphasis on a one-time event to the creation of conditions for learning that can occur through collaboration, online learning, traditional classroom training, or a combination of these methods. There is increased recognition that learning occurs informally, outside the boundaries of a formal training course.

Also, the employee-employer relationship has changed. Due to rapidly changing business environments and competition that can quickly cause profits to shrink and skill needs to change, companies are reluctant to provide job security to employees. At the same time, many employees are job hopping to find more challenging and interesting work or to maximize the value that they can get for their skills in the job market, and not making a long-term commitment to any company. As a result, both employees and companies are concerned with developing future skills and managing careers. Companies want a workforce that is motivated and productive, has up-to-date skills, and can quickly learn new skills to meet changing customer and marketplace needs. Despite the prevalence of job hopping, companies want to provide a work environment and training and development opportunities that will them the employer of choice for talented employees. Employees want to develop skills that not only are useful for their current jobs, but also are congruent with their personal interests and values. Given the increasing time demands of work, employees are also interested in maintaining balance between work and non work interests.

The chapter coverage of *Employee Training and Development* reflects the traditional as well as the broadening role of training and development in organizations. Chapter One, "Introduction to Employee Training and Development," covers the role of training and development in companies. Chapter Two, "Strategic Training," discusses how training practices and the organization of the training function can support business goals. Because companies are interested in reducing costs, the amount of resources allocated to training is likely to be determined by the extent that training and development activities help the company reach business goals. Topics related to designing training programs are covered in Chapters Three through Six. Chapter Three, "Needs Assessment," discusses how to identify when training is appropriate. Chapter Four, "Learning and Transfer of Training," addresses the learning process and characteristics of a learning environment. The chapter also emphasizes what should be done in the design of training and the work environment to ensure that training is used on the job. Chapter Five, "Program Design," provides practical suggestions regarding what can be done to facilitate learning and transfer of training before, during, and after a course or program. The role of knowledge management in facilitating learning and transfer of training is also discussed. Chapter Six, "Training Evaluation," discusses how to evaluate training programs. Here, the student is introduced to the concepts of identifying cost-effective training, evaluating the return on investment of training and learning, and determining if training outcomes related to learning, behavior, or performance have been reached. Chapters Seven and Eight cover training methods. Chapter Seven, "Traditional Training Methods," discusses presentational methods (e.g., lecture), hands-on methods (e.g., on-the-job training and behavior modeling), and group methods (e.g., adventure learning). Chapter Eight, "Technology-Based Training Methods," introduces new technologies that are being used in training. These technology-based training methods include e-learning, mobile learning, social media, simulations, serious games, massive open online courses (MOOCs), virtual worlds, and blended learning. Chapters Seven and Eight both conclude by comparing training methods on the basis of costs, benefits, and learning characteristics.

Chapter Nine, "Employee Development and Career Management," introduces developmental methods (assessment, relationships, job experiences, and formal courses). In addition, the use of development plans to help employees succeed in their self-directed or protean careers is highlighted. Topics such as succession planning and on boarding are discussed. Chapter Ten, "Social Responsibility: Legal Issues, Managing Diversity, and Career Challenges," emphasizes the role that training plays in helping companies improve the communities where they are located by increasing the skill level of the workforce, helping provide jobs, and taking actions to help all employees grow and develop, regardless of their personal characteristics or career challenges. The chapter also discusses compliance with laws that affect training and development, training partnerships, managing diversity, cross-cultural preparation, and how companies can help employees deal with career challenges such as balancing work and life, coping with career breaks such as taking time off for family or required military service, job loss, and retirement. Finally, Chapter Eleven, "The Future of Training and Development," looks at how training and development might be different ten or twenty years from now.

Employee Training and Development is based on my more than twenty-five years of teaching training and development courses to both graduate and undergraduate students. From this experience, I have realized that managers, consultants, trainers, and faculty working in a variety of disciplines (including education, psychology, business, and industrial relations) have contributed to the research and practice of training and development. As a result, the book is based on research conducted in several disciplines, while offering a practical perspective. The book is appropriate for students in a number of programs. It suits both undergraduate and master's-level training courses in a variety of disciplines.

DISTINCTIVE FEATURES

This book has several distinctive features. First, my teaching experience has taught me that students become frustrated if they do not see research and theory in practice. As a result, one distinctive feature of the book is that each chapter begins with a real-life vignette of a company practice that relates to the material covered in the chapter. Many examples of company practices are provided throughout the chapters. Each chapter ends with a real-life case and related questions that give students the opportunity to apply the chapter's content to an actual training or development issue.

A second distinctive feature of the book is its topical coverage. The chapters included in Part Two, "Designing Training," relate to training design (needs assessment, training methods, learning and transfer of training, and program design and evaluation). Instructional design is still the "meat and potatoes" of training. Part Three, "Training and Development Methods," covers the more exciting part of training and development—that is, training and development methods. But as the role of managers and trainers broadens, they are increasingly involved in helping all employees grow, develop, and cope with career challenges, as well as preparing high-potential employees for leadership positions. For example, managers and trainers need to understand generational differences in employees' career needs, career paths, cross-cultural training, diversity, outplacement, and succession planning—topics that fall outside the realm of instructional design. These topics are covered in Part Four, "Social Responsibility and the Future."

The book begins with a discussion of the context for training and development. Part One includes chapters that cover the economic and workplace factors that are influencing trends in the training profession. One of these trends is that companies are emphasizing learning through formal training and development, knowledge management, and informal learning. In addition, these chapters discuss the need for training, development, and learning to become strategic (i.e., to contribute to business strategy and organizational goals). Why? In successful, effective training, all aspects of training—including training objectives, methods, evaluation, and even who conducts the training—relate to the business strategy. More and more companies are demanding that the training function and training practices support business goals; otherwise, training may be outsourced or face funding cuts. Although students in business schools are exposed to strategic thinking, students in psychology and education who go on to become trainers need to understand the strategic perspective and how it relates to the organization of the training function and the type of training conducted.

Not only has technology changed the way we live and the way work is performed, but it also has influenced training practice. As a result, one chapter of the book is devoted entirely to the use of technologies for training delivery and instruction, such as online learning, social media, mobile learning, gamification, and virtual worlds.

The book reflects the latest "hot topics" in the area of training and development. Some of the new topics discussed in the book are "flipped classroom," adaptive training, big data and workforce analytics, learning management systems, competencies, knowledge management, massive open online courses (MOOCs), mobile learning (using smartphones), reverse mentoring iPads and other tablet computers, social media such as blogs, wikis, and social networks, and virtual worlds (such as Second Life) for training. Each chapter contains the most recent academic research findings and company practices.

FEATURES DESIGNED TO AID LEARNING

Employee Training and Development provides several features to aid learning:

1. Each chapter lists objectives that highlight what the student is expected to learn in that chapter.

2. In-text examples and chapter openers feature companies from all industries, including service, manufacturing, retail, and nonprofit organizations.

3. Discussion questions at the end of each chapter help students learn the concepts presented in the chapter and understand potential applications of the material.

4. Important terms and concepts used in training and development are boldfaced in each chapter. Key terms are identified at the end of each chapter. These key terms are important to help the student understand the language of training.

5. Application assignments are useful for the students to put chapter content into practice. Most chapters include assignments that require the student to use the World Wide Web.

6. Cases at the end of each chapter and at the end of each of the four parts of the book help students apply what they have learned to training and development issues faced by actual companies.

7. Name and subject indexes at the end of the book help in finding key people and topics.

WHAT'S NEW IN THE SEVENTH EDITION

I want to personally thank all of you who have adopted this book! Based on the comments of the reviewers of the fifth edition and training research and practice, I have made several improvements. Some important changes in the sixth edition of *Employee Training and Development* stand out:

• Each chapter has been updated to include the most recent research findings and new best company practices. New examples have been added in each chapter's text.

• All the chapter opening vignettes are new. For example, the opening vignette for Chapter Eight highlights how Nissan is using e-learning that includes a virtual classroom, social collaboration, and virtual learning lab for skills practice to its geographically dispersed workforce.

- This edition offers new and expanded coverage of topics related to learning, program design, training methods, evaluation, development, and the future of training. From the learning and program design perspective expanded and new coverage is provided on the 70-20-10 learning model, adaptive training, the importance of stakeholder involvement in needs assessment and program design, the use of boosters, reflection, and discussion to enhance learning, how to design training from a project management perspective, and the use of incentives and badges to motivate and reinforce learning. The use of new and increasingly popular training delivery and instructional methods, including massive open online courses (MOOCs), the flipped classroom, serious games and gamification, and mobile learning, is discussed. From a development and career perspective, this edition provides new and expanded coverage of career paths that are more common today, including horizontal and cross-functional career paths, reverse mentoring, stretch assignments, and using succession planning to develop bench strength. In training evaluation, the fundamentals remain important but there is also an increased interest in and use of big data and workforce analytics to show how learning, training, and development contribute to talent management and the company's "bottom line." As a result, in the evaluation chapter we discuss big data and how companies are using it to answer important questions. Finally, new technologies have the potential to radically alter how and when we learn and substitute performance support for learning. As a result, in the last chapter of the book, we discuss the implications of wearables, artificial intelligence, Tin Can API, and neuroscience research for the future of training and development. The implications of the needs and learning preferences of the multigenerational workforce, especially the millennials, for training and development are discussed throughout the book (e.g., reverse mentoring, increased use of games and social collaboration for learning).
- Each chapter ends with application assignments, including new program design and updated web-based exercises. These assignments are also found on the book's website.
- Each chapter concludes with new or updated brief cases that illustrate a training, development, or learning issue faced by a company. The case questions ask students to consider issues and make recommendations based on the chapter content.
- To help students better understand the connections between topics, the book is organized into four different parts. Part One focuses on the context for training and development and includes a chapter devoted to strategic training. Part Two includes coverage related to the fundamentals of designing training programs. Chapters in Part Two focus on needs assessment, learning theories and transfer of training, program design, and training evaluation. Part Three focuses on training and development methods and includes chapters devoted to traditional training methods, e-learning, and the use of new training technologies such as social media and mobile learning. The chapters in Part Four cover employee development and career management and the role of training and learning in helping companies increase their social responsibility. This includes following laws and regulations that relate to training, as well as managing diversity and helping employees cope with career challenges such as balancing work and life, career breaks, identifying and moving along a career path, preparing for retirement, and coping with job loss. Finally, this part provides a look at the future of training and development.

INSTRUCTOR AND STUDENT RESOURCES

McGraw-Hill Connect®: connect.mheducation.com

Continually evolving, McGraw-Hill Connect® has been redesigned to provide the only true adaptive learning experience delivered within a simple and easy-to-navigate environment, placing students at the very center.

- Performance Analytics—Now available for both instructors and students, easy-to-decipher data illuminates course performance. Students always know how they're doing in class, while instructors can view student and section performance at a glance.
- Mobile—Available on tablets, students can now access assignments, quizzes, and results on the go, while instructors can assess student and section performance anytime, anywhere.
- Personalized Learning—Squeezing the most out of study time, the adaptive engine within Connect creates a highly personalized learning path for each student by identifying areas of weakness and providing learning resources to assist in the moment of need. This seamless integration of reading, practice, and assessment ensures that the focus is on the most important content for that individual.

LearnSmart®

LearnSmart, the most widely used adaptive learning resource, is proven to improve grades. By focusing each student on the most important information they need to learn, LearnSmart personalizes the learning experience so they can study as efficiently as possible.

SmartBook®

An extension of LearnSmart, SmartBook is an adaptive eBook that helps students focus their study time more effectively. As students read, SmartBook assesses comprehension and dynamically highlights where they need to study more.

Instructor Library

The Connect Management Instructor Library is your repository for additional resources to improve student engagement in and out of class. You can select and use any asset that enhances your lecture.

The Connect Instructor Library includes:

- Instructor Manual
- PowerPoint files
- Test Bank

Manager's Hot Seat: Now instructors can put students in the hot seat with access to an interactive program. Students watch real managers apply their years of experience when confronting unscripted issues. As the scenario unfolds, questions about how the manager is handling the situation pop up, forcing the student to make decisions along with the manager. At the end of the scenario, students watch a post-interview with the manager, view how their responses matched up to the manager's decisions. The Manager's Hot Seat videos are now available as assignments in Connect.

Acknowledgments

The author is only one of many important people involved in writing a textbook. The seventh edition of this book would not have been possible without the energy and expertise of several others from McGraw-Hill Education and Editors Inc. Diana Murphy, developmental editor, and project managers Jessica Portz and Gunjan Chandola deserve my gratitude and thanks for their patience and expertise in following the insertions and changes I made, and for ensuring that my ideas made sense and my writing was clear, concise, and easy to understand.

I take full responsibility for any errors, omissions, or misstatements of fact in this book. However, regardless of your impression of the book, it would not have been this good had it not been for the manuscript reviewers. Special thanks to these people, who provided me with detailed comments that helped improve the seventh edition of the book for students and instructors. These reviewers include

Rebecca Bryant
Texas Woman's University Denton Campus

Edward Steve Eidson
Albany Technical College

John R. Knue
Baylor University

Liliana Meneses
University of Maryland University College

About the Author

Raymond A. Noe *The Ohio State University*

Raymond A. Noe is the Robert and Anne Hoyt Designated Professor of Management at The Ohio State University. He has taught for more than twenty-five years at Big Ten universities. Before joining the faculty at Ohio State, he was a professor in the Department of Management at Michigan State University and the Industrial Relations Center of the Carlson School of Management, University of Minnesota. He received a B.S. in psychology from The Ohio State University and M.A. and Ph.D. degrees in psychology from Michigan State University. Professor Noe conducts research and teaches all levels of students—from undergraduates to executives—in human resource management, training and development, performance management, and talent management. He has published articles in the *Academy of Management Annals, Academy of Management Journal, Academy of Management Review, Human Resource Development Quarterly, Journal of Applied Psychology, Journal of Management, Journal of Occupational and Organizational Psychology, Journal of Vocational Behavior,* and *Personnel Psychology.* Professor Noe is currently on the editorial boards of several journals, including *Journal of Applied Psychology, Personnel Psychology,* and *Journal of Management.* He is the lead author of "Learning in the 21st century workplace" recently published in the *Annual Review of Organizational Psychology and Organizational Behavior.* Besides *Employee Training and Development,* he has co-authored two other textbooks: *Fundamentals of Human Resource Management* and *Human Resource Management: Gaining a Competitive Advantage,* both published by McGraw-Hill/Irwin. Professor Noe has received awards for his teaching and research excellence, including the Herbert G. Heneman Distinguished Teaching Award, the Ernest J. McCormick Award for Distinguished Early Career Contribution from the Society for Industrial and Organizational Psychology, and the ASTD Outstanding Research Article of the Year Award. He is also a fellow of the Society of Industrial and Organizational Psychology.

Brief Contents

Contents

PART TWO
DESIGNING TRAINING 115

Chapter 3
Needs Assessment 116

Chapter 4
Learning and Transfer of
Training 157

Chapter 5
Program Design 201

ORGANIZATION OF THIS BOOK

This book is organized into five parts. Part One focuses on the context for training and development and includes this chapter, which offered a broad perspective on training and helped answer questions such as: What is training? Why is it important? Who is receiving training? How much money is spent on training? How should training be designed? Part One also includes Chapter Two, which discusses the strategic training and development process. In Chapter Two, you will see how a company's business strategy influences training practices and the organization of the training department. Chapters Three through Six make up Part Two. These chapters discuss the fundamentals of training design and address different aspects of the ISD model, the model used to guide the development of training (see Figure 1.1). Chapter Three deals with how to determine training needs. Chapter Four discusses the important issue of learning—specifically, the importance of learning and transfer of training. The chapter emphasizes what we learn, how we learn, and how to create an environment conducive to learning within a training session. The chapter also discusses what needs to be considered for transfer of training, i.e., ensuring that skills emphasized in training are used on the job. Chapter Five provides insights into the specific of how training programs should be designed to facilitate learning and transfer. The chapter covers the importance of room design, learning objectives, selecting and preparing trainers, and course planning for learning, as well as how managers, trainers, learners, and knowledge management can facilitate transfer of training. Chapter Six explains how to evaluate a training program. Part Three focuses on training and development methods. Chapter Seven looks at traditional training methods such as lecture, behavior modeling simulation, and role-play. Chapter Eight examines e-learning and methods that have developed from applications of new technology, for example, web-based training, virtual reality, mobile learning, and social collaboration.

Chapter Nine addresses the important issue of employee development and career management; it discusses four approaches used to develop employee assessments, assignments, relationships, courses, and formal programs. Part Five considers training's role in social responsibility and the future of training and development. Chapter Ten deals with legal issues and diversity. Topics covered include ethics and legal issues, managing diversity, cross-cultural training, and issues relevant to certain employee groups, such as coping with career breaks and melting the "glass ceiling." Chapter Eleven discusses how new technologies may influence training and how its role may change in the future.

Students should be aware of several important features of the book. Each chapter begins with chapter objectives. These objectives (1) highlight what the student should learn from each chapter and (2) preview the topics. Next comes an opening vignette—an example of a company practice related to the chapter topics. Company examples are liberally used throughout each chapter to help students see how theory and research in training are put into practice. Each chapter ends with key terms, discussion questions, application assignments, and a short case. Key terms are related to important concepts emphasized in the chapter. Discussion questions and application assignments can facilitate learning through interacting with other students and actually trying to develop and conduct various training applications. Many application assignments require the use of the web, a valuable source of information on training practices. Each of the parts concludes with a case that highlights a company's training and development practices. These cases include questions asking you to apply what you have learned in the chapters.

The Context for Training and Development

Part One focuses on issues related to the context for training and development. Chapter One, "Introduction to Employee Training and Development," discusses why training and development are important to help companies successfully compete in today's business environment. The chapter provides an overview of training practices, the training profession, and how to design effective training (a topic that is covered in detail in Part Two, "Training Design"). Chapter Two, "Strategic Training," discusses the strategic training and development process, organizational characteristics that influence training, various models for organizing the training department, how to brand training and market it to the rest of the company, and the advantages and disadvantages of outsourcing training.

Part One concludes with a case that highlights how Dow Chemicals is using training to cope with competitive challenges, reach business goals, and expand learning beyond the classroom and boardroom.

Chapter One

Introduction to Employee Training and Development

Objectives

After reading this chapter, you should be able to

1. Discuss the forces influencing the workplace and learning, and explain how training can help companies deal with these forces.

2. Draw a figure or diagram and explain how training, development, informal learning, and knowledge management contribute to business success.

3. Discuss various aspects of the training design process.

4. Describe the amount and types of training occurring in U.S. companies.

5. Discuss the key roles for training professionals.

6. Identify appropriate resources (e.g., journals, websites) for learning about training research and practice.

Forces Affecting the Workplace Make Training a Key Ingredient of Company Success

Customer service, productivity, safety, employee retention and growth, uncertainty in the economy, extending learning beyond the classroom, the use of new technology—these are just some of the issues affecting companies in all industries and sizes and influencing training practices.

The examples presented below show how these concerns have affected companies in several different business sectors and how training has helped them succeed.

Many companies, recognizing that learning goes beyond typical face-to-face classes, are using technology to make it easier for employees in different locations to learn and share knowledge through formal courses, as well as through collaboration. For example, GameStop, the retailer of new and used video games, hardware, entertainment software, and accessories, has 18,000 employees in more than 6,600 locations in the United States, Australia, Canada, New Zealand, and Europe. Who doesn't like to play video games like Super Mario, Borderlands, or DragonBall XenoVerse! Its customers can get games from GameStop that they can't get anywhere else, and it allows customers to buy, sell, or trade games unlike many of its competitors. GameStop serves a variety of customers, including five-year-olds and their parents who are looking for Nintendo games to adult gamers who want to buy the latest gaming equipment. Most GameStop employees (called game-associates) hold part-time, entry-level jobs, requiring working several shifts during the week. They often leave for other jobs or opportunities such as going back to school. Training helps GameStop successfully deal with turnover by ensuring new employees provide consistent customer service that translates into satisfied customers and return business. Most new employees who join GameStop are expert gamers, have expertise about the technology and trends influencing the gaming market, and were loyal customers. As a result, GameStop's training doesn't focus on teaching employees about video games but instead emphasizes how to interact with customers and understand their gaming needs. Also, the training helps employees become ambassadors for the company by sharing their knowledge and passion for gaming with customers. The LevelUp program is an online program that enables employees to complete training on their own time and at their own pace, scoring points based on achieving different skills and advancing to the next level. Training content varies based on the employees' needs; it allows them to log in and out of training at any time and skip sections they already know. The LevelUp program helps prepare new game-associates as well as provide training for more experienced game-associates who may be more interested in a retail career and want to gain the knowledge and skills necessary to become assistant managers and store managers.

McAfee, part of Intel Security, is the world's largest dedicated security technology company. McAfee protects consumers and businesses from the malware and emerging online threats. Sixty percent of employees use social networking tools that support learning and 50 percent of training content is delivered using self-paced online instruction. McAfee also encourages knowledge sharing. Employees can connect online with potential mentors and mentees based on the personal profiles they create. A career development group helps employees collaborate and share ideas about their personal development. A language learning community is available for employees around the world to talk to each other to improve their language skills.

Blue Cross and Blue Shield of Michigan uses KnowIt and MISource to reach employees at forty different locations. KnowIt includes wikis, web courses, podcasts, discussion boards, and e-learning to provide information on more than eighty business topics. MISource gives claims and customer service employees access to information they need to better serve customers. Scotiabank Group, with operations in more than fifty companies, developed an internal social networking application, FaceForward, which includes user profiles, blogs, wikis, and social bookmarks.

US Airways provides extensive training for flight attendants and pilots. Newly hired flight attendants receive five weeks of training, including an introduction to the aviation industry, and Airbus cabin simulators include "door trainers" to practice opening emergency exits under difficult evacuation conditions, such as total darkness and billowing smoke. Training also includes jumping into a pool and inflating a life raft and helping passengers into and out of a raft. Federal law requires annual classroom safety training for flight attendants, and performance drills every two years. Pilot training includes practicing skills in a simulator that presents many different scenarios, such as both engines failing, and re-creates the feelings and sounds experienced in flight, including turbulence. Forced landings and water ditchings are taught in the classroom. The payoff for this type of extensive training was most evident in the spectacularly safe landing of US Airways Flight 1549 and its 155 passengers and flight crew in the Hudson River in 2009. Based on their almost automatic responses developed through years of training, flight attendants were able to calm passengers, prepare them for a crash landing, and open doors and inflate life rafts to assist in the orderly but quick exit of the slowly sinking airplane. The cockpit crew followed the training they received in how to cope with engine failure and successfully conducted a water landing.

Sources: Based on M. McGraw, "Staying Power," *Human Resource Executive* (January/February 2015): 39–41; "McAffee. Part of Intel Security," *TD* (October 2014): 98. Training Top 125, *training* (January/February 2011): 54–93. 36; S. McCartney, "Crash Courses for the Crew," *The Wall Street Journal* (January 27, 2009): D1, D8.

INTRODUCTION

The examples discussed in the chapter opener illustrate how training can contribute to companies' competitiveness. **Competitiveness** refers to a company's ability to maintain and gain market share in an industry. Although they are different types of businesses, these four companies have training practices that have helped them gain a **competitive advantage** in their markets. That is, the training practices have helped them grow the business and improve customer service by providing employees with the knowledge and skills they need to be successful.

Companies are experiencing great change due to new technologies, rapid development of knowledge, globalization of business, and development of e-commerce. Also, companies have to take steps to attract, retain, and motivate their workforces. Training is not a luxury; it is a necessity if companies are to participate in the global and electronic marketplaces by offering high-quality products and services. Training prepares employees to use new technologies, function in new work systems such as virtual teams, and communicate and cooperate with peers or customers who may be from different cultural backgrounds.

Human resource management refers to the policies, practices, and systems that influence employees' behavior, attitudes, and performance. Human resource practices play a key role in attracting, motivating, rewarding, and retaining employees. Other human resource management practices include recruiting employees, selecting employees, designing work, compensating employees, and developing good labor and employee relations. Chapter Two, "Strategic Training," details the importance placed on training in comparison to other human resource management practices. To be effective, training must play a strategic role in supporting the business.

Human resource management is one of several important functions in most companies. Other functions include accounting and finance, production and operations, research and development, and marketing. Keep in mind that although human resource management practices (such as training) can help companies gain a competitive advantage, the company needs to produce a product or provide a service that customers value. Without the financial resources and physical resources (e.g., equipment) needed to produce products or provide services, the company will not survive.

This chapter begins by defining training and development and discussing how the training function has evolved. Next, the forces that are shaping the workplace and learning are addressed. These forces influence the company's ability to successfully meet stakeholders' needs. The term **stakeholders** refers to shareholders, the community, customers, employees, and all the other parties that have an interest in seeing that the company succeeds. The discussion of the forces shaping the workplace (including technology, globalization, and attracting and winning talent) highlights the role of training in helping companies gain a competitive advantage.

The second part of the chapter focuses on current trends in the training area. This section also introduces you to the trainer's role in a business and how the training function is organized. This section should help you understand current training practices, the types of jobs that trainers may perform, and the competencies needed to be a successful trainer (or, if you are a manager, to identify a successful trainer). The chapter concludes with an overview of the topics covered in the book.

TRAINING AND DEVELOPMENT: KEY COMPONENTS OF LEARNING

Our focus in this book is to help you understand the role of training and development in today's organizations. To do this, it is important for you to understand what training and development means in the broader business context. Figure 1.1 shows the role of training and development for the business. The overall goal of training and development is learning. **Learning** refers to employees acquiring knowledge, skills, competencies,

FIGURE 1.1
The Business Role of Training and Development

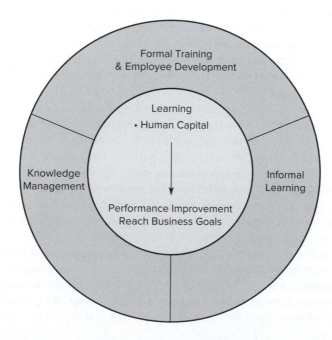

attitudes, or behaviors. But the focus of training and development is not just on employees learning for its own sake. Today, merely offering training programs is not enough to get support and funding from executives and to establish the credibility of the training and development function to managers and employees. Learning needs to demonstrate how it contributes to the company's competitive advantage through improving employee performance, supporting the business strategy (such as growing the business), and contributing positively to business outcomes such as quality, productivity, development of new products, and retaining key employees. From a company's perspective, what employees learn contributes to the development of intangible assets such as human capital. **Human capital** refers to knowledge (know what), advanced skills (know how), system understanding and creativity (know why), and motivation to deliver high-quality products and services (care why).[1] Human capital may be more valuable than physical capital (equipment or technology) or financial capital (monetary assets, cash) for providing a company with an advantage over its competitors, because it is difficult to imitate or purchase and it is unique to the company.

There are a number of different ways that learning occurs in a company. They are represented on the outside of the circle in Figure 1.1. **Training** refers to a planned effort by a company to facilitate learning of job-related competencies, knowledge, skills, and behaviors by employees. The goal of training is for employees to master the knowledge, skills, and behaviors emphasized in training and apply them to their day-to-day activities. Traditionally, companies have relied on formal training through a course, program, or "event" to teach employees the knowledge, skills, and behaviors they need to successfully perform their job. Development is similar to training, except that it tends to be more future-focused. **Development** refers to training as well as formal education, job experiences, relationship, and assessments of personality, skills, and abilities that help employees prepare for future jobs or positions. We will discuss development in more detail in Chapter Nine, "Employee Development and Careers." **Formal training and development** refers to training and development programs, courses, and events that are developed and organized by the company. Typically, employees are required to attend or complete these programs, which can include face-to-face training programs (such as instructor-led courses) as well as online programs. As you will see later in the chapter, U.S. companies invest billions of dollars in formal training.

Informal learning is also important for facilitating the development of human capital.[2] **Informal learning** refers to learning that is learner initiated, involves action and doing, is motivated by an intent to develop, and does not occur in a formal learning setting.[3] Informal learning occurs without a trainer or instructor, and its breadth, depth, and timing is controlled by the employee. It occurs on an as-needed basis and may involve an employee learning either alone or through face-to-face or technology-aided social interactions. Informal learning can occur through many different ways, including casual unplanned interactions with peers, e-mail, informal mentoring, or company-developed or publically available social networking websites such as Twitter or Facebook. The application of social media from a marketing strategy to a learning strategy and the availability of Web 2.0 technologies such as social networks, microblogs, and wikis allow employees easy access to social learning or learning through collaboration and sharing with one or two or more people.[4] One estimate is that informal learning may account for up to 75 percent of learning within organizations.

One reason why informal learning may be especially important is that it may lead to the effective development of *tacit* knowledge, which can be contrasted with *explicit* knowledge.[5] **Explicit knowledge** refers to knowledge that is well documented, easily articulated, and easily transferred from person to person. Examples of explicit knowledge include processes, checklists, flowcharts, formulas, and definitions. Explicit knowledge tends to be the primary focus of formal training and employee development. **Tacit knowledge** refers to personal knowledge based on individual experiences that is difficult to codify. The characteristics of formal training and development programs, such as the relatively short duration of classroom or online training and limited opportunities for practice, may limit the extent to which tacit knowledge can be acquired. Thus, informal learning is central to the development of tacit knowledge because it involves employee interactions in personal relationships with peers, colleagues, and experts through which tacit knowledge is shared. It is important to recognize, however, that informal learning cannot replace formal training and employee development. Formal training and development are still needed to prepare employees for their jobs and to help them advance to future positions. Informal learning complements training by helping employees gain tacit knowledge that formal training cannot provide.

Knowledge management refers to the process of enhancing company performance by designing and implementing tools, processes, systems, structures, and cultures to improve the creation, sharing, and use of knowledge.[6] Knowledge management contributes to informal learning. G4S Secure Solutions provides security solutions around the world.[7] Its employees are spread across field offices and client locations. Most G4S security officers don't have computer access or are restricted by client firewalls. But security officers need timely information in order to protect clients and property. Seeking and sharing knowledge can help save lives. As a result, the company developed an Internet and social networking solution. It provides access to company materials, announcements, policies and procedures, training manuals, operational and support tools, and best practice forums. It can be accessed from anywhere, giving employees the ability to ask questions across the company as well as within their office, location, or work team. The solution includes social networking features similar to Facebook. Employee can create profiles that have their skills, interests, achievements, projects, and contact information. They can participate in threaded discussions. Tags can be used to identify similar documents or discussions on the same topic. Caterpillar Inc. moved toward becoming a continuous learning organization with the help of knowledge management.[8] Thirty years ago, Caterpillar Inc., a manufacturer of construction and mining equipment, engines, and gas turbines, had most of its value in its plant and equipment. Today, intangible assets account for most of the company's value. Caterpillar's web-based knowledge management system, known as Knowledge Network, has thousands of communities of practice. They range in size from small teams to hundreds of employees worldwide. The communities of practice are useful for employees to gain both explicit and tacit knowledge. They are used to distribute information, post questions, and provide space for reference materials. One community of practice focused on bolted joints and fasteners. This gives specialized engineers who generally work alone in manufacturing facilities the ability to ask other engineers questions or get second opinions on designs and problems. The community of practice has resulted in improved decision making, increased collaboration and teamwork, and better product design and development. For example, members of the Bolted Joints and Fastener community and the Dealer Service Training Community saved more than $1.5 million from online discussions.

Many companies who recognize the value of learning have taken steps to ensure that formal training and employee development is linked to strategic business objectives and goals, use an instructional design process to ensure that these programs are effective, and compares or benchmarks the company's programs against its competitors or other companies in the industry.[9]

Consider the role of learning at PricewaterhouseCoopers.[10] Its Learning and Education (L&E) team was restructured to better link it to the business goals related to value and impact. L&E works with the business to understand what it wants education to be. It ensures ongoing innovation in training delivery and instructional methods by evaluating emerging technologies and using them in small pilot projects. The chief learning officer in charge of L&E is a member of the company's leadership team, which gives that individual the opportunity to discuss ideas regarding training methods, delivery, and content with other top-level managers. L&E sponsors traditional and virtual classroom courses, self-study, team-based learning, action learning projects, coaching and mentoring, and conferences, and it has served more than 150,000 users each year, with over 6,000 courses, 12,000 classroom-based training sessions, and 19,000 web-based training sessions.

PricewaterhouseCoopers uses a learning management system to create a single access point for training activities. To help employees learn on an as-needed basis, the company's e-learning includes video and audio conferencing, virtual classrooms, and webcasting. To evaluate the success of training, L&E considers its influence on outcomes, such as retention of top people. Also, focus groups are used to determine whether trainees and managers are satisfied with the training. A program on sustainability was designed to help partners understand how to provide solutions for their clients. The company's investment in the program has paid off. The company believes that it has achieved a return on investment of more than 1,000 percent in new business sold and reputation gains in the marketplace. In the future, L&E plans to further strengthen the relationship between training, development, and the business by focusing on how it can make learning even more accessible and closer to the point where employees need it. L&E wants to integrate learning and knowledge to speed employees' development and improve their competencies.

This discussion is not meant to underestimate the importance of "traditional training" (a focus on acquisition of knowledge, skills, and abilities), but it should alert you that for many companies, training is evolving from a focus on skills to an emphasis on continuous learning and creating and sharing knowledge. This evolution of training is discussed in Chapter Two.

DESIGNING EFFECTIVE TRAINING

The **training design process** refers to a systematic approach for developing training programs. Figure 1.2 presents the seven steps in this process. Step 1 is a needs assessment, which is necessary to identify whether training is needed. Step 2 is to ensure that employees have the motivation and basic skills necessary to master the training content. Step 3 is to create a learning environment that has the features necessary for learning to occur. Step 4 is to ensure that trainees apply the training content to their jobs. This step

FIGURE 1.2   **Training Design Process**

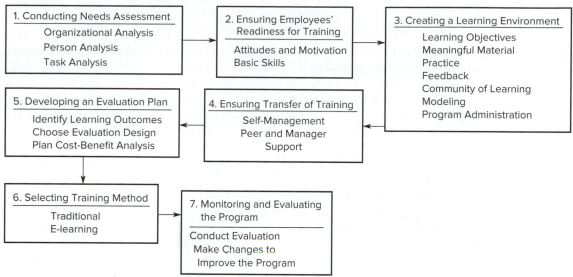

involves having the trainee understand how to manage skill improvement, as well as getting co-worker and manager support.

Step 5 is to develop an evaluation plan. Developing an evaluation plan includes identifying what types of outcomes training is expected to influence (for example, learning, behavior, or skills), choosing an evaluation design that allows you to determine the influence of training on these outcomes, and planning how to demonstrate how training affects the "bottom line" (that is, using a cost-benefit analysis to determine the monetary benefits resulting from training). Step 6 is to choose the training method based on the learning objectives and learning environment. This step may include a traditional training method of face-to-face interaction with a trainer or e-learning using web-based training or mobile learning. Step 7 is to evaluate the program and make changes in it or revisit any of the earlier steps in the process to improve the program so that learning, behavior, change, and other learning objectives are obtained.

The training design process shown in Figure 1.1 is based on principles of Instructional System Design. **Instructional System Design (ISD)** refers to a process for designing and developing training programs. There is not one universally accepted instructional systems development model. The training design process sometimes is referred to as the *ADDIE model* because it includes analysis, design, development, implementation, and evaluation.[11] In Figure 1.1, Step 1, conducting needs assessment, and Step 2, ensuring employees' readiness for training, are related to analysis. The next three steps—creating a learning environment, ensuring transfer of training, and developing an evaluation plan—are design issues. Step 6, selecting and using a training method, relates to implementation. Step 7, monitoring and evaluating the program, relates to evaluation. Regardless of the specific ISD approach used, all share the following assumptions:[12]

- Training design is effective only if it helps employees reach instructional or training goals and objectives.

- Measurable learning objectives should be identified before the training program begins.
- Evaluation plays an important part in planning and choosing a training method, monitoring the training program, and suggesting changes to the training design process.

Trainers for AbsorbU, the internal college for ITU AbsorbTech, an industrial laundry service company, design courses using the ADDIE model.[13] AbsorbU focuses on learning needs related to customer service, production, leadership, and sales. They find that using the ADDIE model helps them to identify training needs and desired results and focus attention on knowledge transfer or behavior change. Also, they use ADDIE when they are revisiting courses to review them and ensure that the content remains useful.

Overcoming the Flaws of the ISD Model

Some training professionals argue that the ISD model is flawed for several reasons.[14] First, in organizations, the training design process rarely follows the neat, orderly, step-by-step approach of activities shown in Figure 1.1. Second, in trying to standardize their own ISD method used in the training function, some organizations require trainers to provide detailed documents of each activity found in the model. This adds time and cost to developing a training program. Third, the ISD implies an end point: evaluation. However, good instructional design requires an iterative process of design, execution, evaluation, and reconsideration of the needs that the program was designed to meet, as well as the learning environment, the transfer of training, and all the other activities in the ISD process. Fourth, many companies claim to use an instructional design approach but dilute its application.[15] This might include assuming that training is the best solution without investigating other causes for performance gaps, failing to identify training objectives and results, focusing too much on the training method while ignoring the role of the work environment in transfer of training, and concentrating evaluation on whether trainees liked the program rather than on measuring the impact of training on job performance or business results. Despite these criticisms, use of the ISD process is the best way to help ensure the effectiveness of training and development.

The training design process should be systematic, yet flexible enough to adapt to business needs. Different steps may be completed simultaneously. For example, a business leader who was an important stakeholder at Deloitte wanted a training module for new employees on how to deliver exceptional customer service to be quickly redesigned.[16] The fast turn-around time was necessary because of its business implications. Many new employees hired each week needed to understand how to provide customer service the Deloitte way. Three teams of talent development professionals were each given the same set of learning objectives to create a revised program. Throughout the process they exchanged and critiqued each other's ideas. At the end of the day the ideas for the revised program were presented to the business leader. The business leader reviewed the teams' recommendations and agreed that hybrid course design based on two of the teams' recommendations would be the best solution. Keep in mind that designing training unsystematically will reduce the benefits that can be realized. For example, choosing a training method before determining training needs or ensuring employees' readiness for training increases the risk that the method chosen will not be the most effective one for meeting training needs. Also, training may not even be necessary and may result in a waste of time and money. Employees may have the knowledge, skills, or behavior they need but simply not be motivated to use them.

The introduction of new technologies such as mobile learning (discussed in Chapter Eight) highlights a shift from trainees having to learn from an instructor in one location to trainees learning independently and not being bound to learn in the workplace. Still, good training design requires determining the trainees' needs, identifying resources so that trainees can learn what they need to know, and providing them with access to reference materials and knowledge bases when they encounter problems, issues, or questions on the job.[17]

The development of a web-based training program focused on teaching managers the skills needed to run effective business meetings provides a good example of the instructional design process. The first step of the process, needs assessment, involved determining that managers lacked skills for conducting effective meetings and helped to identify the type of meetings that managers were involved in. The needs assessment process involved interviewing managers and observing meetings. The needs assessment process also identified the most appropriate training method.

Because the managers were geographically dispersed and had easy access to computers, and because the company wanted a self-directed, self-paced program that the managers could complete during free time in their work schedule, the training designers and company management decided that web-based training was the appropriate method. Because training was going to be conducted over the web, the designers had to be sure that managers could access the web and were familiar with tools for using it (e.g., web browsers). This relates to determining the managers' readiness for training.

The next step was to create a positive learning environment on the web. Designers made sure that the program objectives were clearly stated to the trainees and provided opportunities within the program for exercises and feedback. For example, trainees were asked to prepare an outline for the steps they would take to conduct an effective meeting. The designers built into the program a feedback system that indicated to the managers which of the steps they outlined were correct and which needed to be changed. The designers also included assessment tests that allowed the trainees to receive feedback through the program and to skip ahead or return to earlier material based on their scores on the tests. The assessment included a test of meeting skills that the managers completed both prior to and after completing the program. The assessment tests were stored in a data bank that the company could use to evaluate whether trainees' meeting skills improved from pretraining levels.

THE FORCES INFLUENCING WORKING AND LEARNING

Table 1.1 illustrates the forces that are influencing working and learning. Globalization of business, demographic changes, new technologies, and economic changes are several of the forces shown in Table 1.1 that influence all aspects of our lives: how we purchase products and services, how we learn, how we communicate with each other, and what we value in our lives and on the job.[18] These forces are affecting individuals, communities, businesses, and society. To survive, companies must address these forces—with training playing an important role.

TABLE 1.1
Forces
Influencing
Working and
Learning

Economic cycles
Globalization
Increased value placed on intangible assets and human capital
Focus on link to business strategy
Changing demographics and diversity of the workforce
Talent management
Customer service and quality emphasis
New technology
High-performance work systems

Economic Cycles

It is important to recognize that regardless of the current economic cycle, training has been shown to positively contribute to the company's performance. For example, companies that used more selective staffing and training before the recession outproduced and had better performance than competitors before the economic recession of 2009 and recovered more quickly.[19]

Today, there are many positive signs that the U.S. economy is experiencing positive momentum.[20] Employers are adding jobs at the fastest rate since the late 1990s. The unemployment rate was 5.5 percent in February 2015, the lowest in seven years. Consumer spending benefited from steady job growth, and lower gasoline prices rose in the fourth quarter of 2014 at the fastest rate since the first quarter of 2006.[21] Growth in the gross domestic product (GDP) was 2.4 percent higher than the increase in 2013, and U.S. manufacturing output moved past its prerecession levels. Surveys suggest that company CEOs are optimistic about the U.S. economy's growth prospects.[22] Hiring continues to be a priority for CEOs with two-thirds planning to add new employees in the next year.

However, there are several threats to continued economic growth.[23] Despite the low unemployment rate, employee's pay is slowly increasing, which can ultimately result in reduced consumer spending. Broader measures of unemployment including the numbers of involuntary part-time employees and long-term unemployed were down during 2014, but still higher than before the recession. Also, there are concerns that the Federal Reserve Bank will begin to raise the borrowing rate for federal funds, which has been near zero since the end of 2008. The lowest fund rate in history was provided as an emergency measure during the financial crisis several years ago, but the economy hasn't shown that it can grow without it. A fund rate hike could affect growth, inflation, and exchange rates throughout the world.

Despite companies looking to add new employees to expand operations, replace retiring employees, or keep up with increased demand for their products and services, many companies may be unable to find new employees with the skills they need.[24] Also, valuable high-performing employees may be looking to change jobs for higher wages or better career opportunities. As a result, companies are having problems attracting and retaining talented employees and are looking to training as part of the solution. For example, Panera Bread, Walmart, Starbucks, and Aetna all raised employees' pay.[25] In addition to raising pay, Starbucks has focused on learning as a way to attract and retain employees and show it is committed to their success. Starbucks College Achievement Plan pays employees' tuition for an online bachelor's degree from Arizona State University. Employees can choose from forty degree programs. The only requirements are that employees have to be working at least twenty hours each week; are U.S.-based working in support centers, plants, or at any of company-operated stores (including Teavana, La Boulange, Evolution Fresh, and Seattle's Best Coffee stores); and do not yet have a bachelor's degree. Employees admitted to Arizona State as a junior or senior will earn full tuition reimbursement for each year of coursework they complete toward a bachelor's degree. Those admitted as freshmen and sophomores will receive a partial scholarship and need-based financial aid toward the completing their degree. Employees have no commitment to remain at Starbucks after they graduate.

Globalization

Every business must be prepared to deal with the global economy. Global business expansion has been made easier by technology. The Internet allows data and information to be instantly accessible and sent around the world. The Internet, e-mail, and video conferencing enable business deals to be completed between companies thousands of miles apart.

Globalization is not limited to any particular sector of the economy, product market, or company size.[26] Companies without international operations may buy or use goods that have been produced overseas, hire employees with diverse backgrounds, or compete with foreign-owned companies operating within the United States. Globalization is also likely to increase as major opportunities to expand into new markets grow due to the increasing number of consumers overseas who have products and services and the income to buy them.

One estimate is that developing economies and emerging markets such as those found in the BRIC nations (Brazil, Russia, India, and China) are responsible for 19 percent of the world's economy.[27] Other countries such as Indonesia, Malaysia, Kenya, Columbia, and Poland which have a growing middle class, strong infrastructure, business-friendly regulations, and stable governments are likely new emerging markets. The importance of globalization is seen in recent hiring patterns of large U.S. multinational corporations who have increased their overseas workforce, particularly in Asia.[28] For example, Oracle, the business hardware and software developer, added workers overseas resulting in over 60 percent of its employees located outside the United States. Markets in Brazil, China, and India have resulted in 60 percent of General Electric's business outside the United States, with over half of its employees being located overseas. Clothing retailer Gap Inc Clothing retailer Gap Inc., opened its first company-owned store in China in 2010.[29] It has stores in forty-eight countries, including Asia, Australia, Eastern Europe, Latin America, the Middle East, and Africa. Banana Republic, a Gap Inc. company, recently expanded to important cities for fashions, including Ginza, Paris, and Milan. Coca-Cola operates in more than two hundred countries. Coke recently opened its forty-third production facility in China and plans to invest $5 billion in Africa over the next six years.[30] Coke also plans to open its first bottling plant in Myanmar, which will create thousands of jobs over the next five years. Gap believes it needs to continue to expand its international presence because the U.S. market is maturing and has many competitors. Yum! Brands, the parent company of KFC, Pizza Hut and Taco Bell, has over 6,200 stores in China contributing over 50 percent of the company's profits.[31]

Global companies are struggling both to find and retain talented employees, especially in emerging markets. Companies are moving into China, India, Eastern Europe, the Middle

East, Southeast Asia, and Latin America, but the demand for talented employees exceeds the supply. Also, companies often place successful U.S. managers in charge of overseas operations, but they lack the cultural understanding necessary to attract, motivate, and retain talented employees. To cope with these problems, companies are taking actions to better prepare their managers and their families for overseas assignments and to ensure that training and development opportunities are available for global employees. Cross-cultural training prepares employees and their families to understand the culture and norms of the country to which they are being relocated and assists in their return to their home country after the assignment. Cross-cultural training is discussed in Chapter Ten.

McDonalds continues to open new stores throughout the world.[32] It opened its first restaurant in Vietnam in 2014 and is planning to open a store in Kazakhstan in 2015. The Vietnam store is the 10,000th restaurant for McDonalds in Asia, Pacific, Middle East, and Africa. Kazakhstan is McDonalds 120th global market! To train future managers in store operations, leadership, and staff management skills needed for global expansion to be successful, McDonalds has seven Hamburger Universities in the United States and abroad, including campuses at Oak Brook, Illinois; Sydney; Munich, Germany; London, England; Tokyo, Japan; São Paulo, Brazil; and Shanghai, China. All provide training materials and tools that can be used in different languages and cultures.

IBM obtains more than two-thirds of its revenue from outside the United States and is seeking to build team leadership in order to compete in emerging markets around the world. IBM's Corporate Service Program has donated the time and services of about 600 employees for over 1,000 projects in countries such as Turkey, Romania, Ghana, Vietnam, the Phillipines, and Tanzania.[33] The goal of the program is to develop a leadership team to learn about the needs and the culture of these countries while at the same time providing valuable community service. For example, eight IBM employees from five countries traveled to Timisoara, Romania. Each employee was assigned to help a different company or nonprofit organization. One software-development manager helped GreenForest, a manufacturer of office, hotel, school, and industrial furniture, reach its goal of cutting costs and becoming more efficient by recommending the computer equipment and systems needed to increase production and exports to Western Europe. Another employee worked with a nonprofit organization that offers services to disabled adults. Besides benefiting the companies, the employees also found that the experience helped them understand cultural differences, improve their communication and teamwork skills, and gain insight into global marketing and strategy.

Globalization also means that employees working in the United States will come from other countries. One estimate is that immigrants, some of whom are illegal, will account for an additional million persons in the workforce.[34] Immigrants provide scientific talent and also sometimes fill low-wage jobs. The impact of immigration is especially large in certain areas of the United States, including the states on the Pacific Coast, where 70 percent of new entrants to the workforce are immigrants.[35] U.S. colleges cannot keep up with the demand for engineers. To find engineers, companies have to look overseas to China, Japan, Korea, and India to hire them.[36] The H-1B visa program is for persons in highly skilled and technical occupations requiring completion of higher education. New visas are capped at 65,000 per year, 20,000 of which are reserved for employees with U.S. master's degrees. There is no cap on H-1Bs for employees working for the government, universities, and other nonprofit institutions. The largest number of H1-B visas are issued for computer-related occupations (43 percent). U.S.-based Microsoft and Intel are two of the top ten companies using H-1B visas, but most are used by Indian companies such as Tata Consultancy Services and Wipro Ltd.[37] Other visa programs are available for lower-skilled temporary or seasonal workers (H2-A, H2-B). Many of these immigrants will have to be trained to understand the U.S. culture. U.S. employees will need skills to improve their ability to communicate with employees from different cultures.

Globalization also means that U.S. companies have to carefully consider the costs and benefits of moving jobs overseas or using foreign suppliers. The United States lost six million factory jobs between 1998 and 2010. However, since 2010 the United States has added millions of factory jobs.[38] **Offshoring** refers to the process of moving jobs from the United States to other locations in the world. The reasons given for offshoring factory and other jobs often include lower labor costs and the availability of a skilled workforce with a strong work ethic. However, many companies are deciding to keep their factory work in the United States rather than send it offshore. This is occurring for several reasons, including higher product shipping costs, fear of supply chain disruptions due to natural disasters and political instability, quality concerns, and customer preference for U.S.-made products.[39] Also, rising labor costs in some countries, such as China, are becoming more comparable to those in the United States. Finally, some countries' local standards for safety, health, and working conditions may be substantially lower than in the United States, resulting in negative publicity and turning off potential customers. For example, Hanesbrands has added workers to a plant in North Carolina.[40] The socks are knitted there and then sent to a plant in El Salvador that sews, dyes, and packages the socks. Although El Salvador has the advantage on labor costs, electricity costs in North Carolina were much less. Also, having plants in both places also provides a backup in case of problems. Peds Legwear also makes socks in North Carolina allowing the company to avoid import taxes, cut shipping costs, and respond faster to shifts in demand. Plus, selling socks made in the United States was a major reason why Walmart contracted with the company. Apple is known for introducing revolutionary and functional products such as the iPhone, Mac Air computers, and the iPad.[41] Apple relies on manufacturing partners in Asia to build its products. Apple Inc. has been criticized by labor groups who have challenged how its manufacturing partners in Asia have treated their employees. Apple has taken these criticism seriously and is auditing its suppliers and manufacturing facilities to take steps to reduce, if not eliminate, illegal and poor treatment of workers who assemble or provide materials for any of its products. Apple is especially focused on ensuring that its partners don't hire underage workers, provide adequate training, and pay fair wages. In those cases in which Apple's recommendations based on its audits were not adopted, the company terminated its relationship with the supplier.

Increased Value Placed on Intangible Assets and Human Capital

Training and development can help a company's competitiveness by directly increasing the company's value through contributing to intangible assets. A company's value includes three types of assets that are critical for the company to provide goods and services: financial assets (cash and securities), physical assets (property, plant, equipment), and intangible assets. Table 1.2 provides examples of intangible assets, which consist of human capital, customer capital, social capital, and intellectual capital. Human capital refers to

TABLE 1.2

Examples of Intangible Assets

Sources: Based on L. Weatherly, *Human Capital—The Elusive Asset* (Alexandria, VA: SHRM Research Quarterly, 2003); E. Holton and S. Naquin, "New Metrics for Employee Development," *Performance Improvement Quarterly* 17 (2004): 56–80; M. Huselid, B. Becker, and R. Beatty, *The Workforce Scorecard* (Boston, MA: Harvard University Press, 2005).

Human Capital
- Tacit knowledge
- Education
- Work-related know-how
- Work-related competence

Customer Capital
- Customer relationships
- Brands
- Customer loyalty
- Distribution channels

Social Capital
- Corporate culture
- Management philosophy
- Management practices
- Informal networking systems
- Coaching/mentoring relationships

Intellectual Capital
- Patents
- Copyrights
- Trade secrets
- Intellectual property

the sum of the attributes, life experiences, knowledge, inventiveness, energy, and enthusiasm that the company's employees invest in their work.[42] **Intellectual capital** refers to the codified knowledge that exists in a company. **Social capital** refers to relationships in the company. **Customer capital** refers to the value of relationships with persons or other organizations outside the company for accomplishing the goals of the company (e.g., relationships with suppliers, customers, vendors, and government agencies). Intangible assets are equally as valuable as financial and physical assets, but they are not something that can be touched and they are nonmonetary.

Intangible assets have been shown to be responsible for a company's competitive advantage. Several studies show that investments in training and development lead to increases in financial performance, productivity, and innovation.[43] The American Society for Training and Development (ASTD) found that companies that invested the most in training and development had a shareholder return that was 86 percent higher than companies in the bottom half and 46 percent higher than the market average.[44] Training and development have a direct influence on human and social capital because they affect education, work-related know-how and competence, and work relationships. Training and development can have an indirect influence on customer and social capital by helping employees better serve customers and by providing them with the knowledge needed to create patents and intellectual property.

As mentioned earlier in the chapter, intangible assets such as human capital also contribute to a company's competitive advantage because they are difficult to duplicate or imitate.[45] For example, consider companies in the airline industry. Southwest Airlines is consistently profitable and usually ranks high in on-time arrivals and other indicators of airline success.[46] One of the distinctions between Southwest Airlines and its competitors is how it treats its employees. For example, Southwest has a policy of no layoffs and was able to maintain this record even during the difficult time for airlines following 9/11. Southwest also emphasizes training and development, which provide its employees with skills to perform multiple jobs. This benefit allows Southwest airplanes to be cleaned and serviced at airports quickly because employees have multiple skill sets that can be applied to various aspects of readying an aircraft for departure. As a result of these human resource policies, Southwest employees are loyal, productive, and flexible (which contributes to the success of the airline). Other airlines may have similar or greater levels of financial assets and may have physical assets that are comparable to Southwest's (e.g., same type of airplanes, similar gates), but what contributes to Southwest's success and gives the company a competitive advantage are its intangible assets in the form of human capital. American Airlines and United Airlines have similar (or greater!) financial and physical assets but have not been successful in competing with Southwest by offering flights on the same routes.

Consider the effort that Macy's is undertaking to develop human capital, social capital, and customer capital.[47] Almost half of customer complaints at Macy's department stores are focused on interactions with sales associates. To cut costs to survive during the recession, Macy's closed stores and invested in technology to improve efficiency, which diverted attention away from customer service. But now Macy's is making a considerable investment in training its sales associates to provide better customer service and to help the company to meet sales growth targets. The new training program requires new sales associates to attend a three-hour training session and includes refresher courses and coaching from managers when they are working on the sales floor. The "MAGIC Selling Program" ("MAGIC" stands for meet and make a connection, ask questions and listen, give options and advice, inspire to buy, and celebrate the purchase) is designed to help sales associates make more personal connections with shoppers. Positive interactions with sales associates contribute to the number of items that a customer purchases and can help enhance Macy's service reputation as customers share experiences on social network sites such as Twitter and Facebook.

Chapters Seven, Eight, and Nine discuss specific training and development activities that contribute to the development of human and social capital. How to measure human capital is explained in Chapter Six, "Training Evaluation." The value of intangible assets and human capital has three important implications:

1. A focus on knowledge workers,
2. Employee engagement, and
3. An increased emphasis on adapting to change and continuous learning.

Focus on Knowledge Workers

One way that a company can increase its intangible assets, specifically human capital, is by focusing on attracting, developing, and retaining knowledge workers. **Knowledge workers** are employees who contribute to the company not through manual labor, but through what they know, perhaps about customers or a specialized body of knowledge. Employees cannot simply be ordered to perform tasks; they must share knowledge and collaborate on solutions. Knowledge workers contribute specialized knowledge that their managers may not have, such as information about customers, and managers depend on these knowledge workers to share that information. Knowledge workers have many job opportunities. If they choose, they can leave a company and take their knowledge to a competitor. Knowledge workers are in demand because of the growth of jobs requiring them.

Employee Engagement

To fully benefit from employee knowledge requires a management style that focuses on engaging employees. **Employee engagement** refers to the degree to which employees are fully involved in their work and the strength of their commitment to their job and the company.[48] Employees who are engaged in their work and committed to their companies give those companies a competitive advantage, including higher productivity, better customer service, and lower turnover.

Perhaps the best way to understand engagement is to consider how companies measure employee engagement. Companies measure employees' engagement levels with attitude or opinion surveys. Although the types of questions asked on these surveys vary from company to company, research suggests the questions generally measure themes such as pride in the company, satisfaction with the job, prospects for future growth with the company, and opportunity to perform challenging work.[49] How do we know if an employee is engaged? An engaged employee is passionate about their work, is committed to the company and its mission, and works hard to contribute. Engagement survey results show that only 30 percent of U.S. employees are engaged in their work, 52 percent are not engaged, and 18 percent are actively disengaged.[50] Actively disengaged employees cost the United States billions of dollars every year in lost productivity.

For example, Bridgepoint Education, a for-profit education services holding company, recognizes that employee engagement is necessary for success.[51] To increase employee engagement, the company uses events, celebrations, and a social learning platform to facilitate conversations between employees and their managers. For example, company leaders host discussions with employees, communicate goals, and give employees a chance to ask questions. The results of Satellite Healthcare's, a renal care provider, engagement survey showed that employees want more resources supporting their career development.[52] As a result, Satellite developed a Career Pyramid that defines the positions within a dialysis career category including the position titles from entry-level jobs to top management. The education, experience, and competencies for each position are listed. Standards for promotion and development to advance to each level on the pyramid are provided. The Career Pyramid is especially useful for employees in entry-level jobs such as patient care technicians because it provides a clear structure on possible career moves and the skills that employees need to develop. Employee engagement scores collected after the Career Pyramid was implemented have improved and 92 percent of employees report they expect to have a long-term career with Satellite. At Mohawk Industries, a company that provides carpet and rugs for residential and commercial customers, each employee has a card that lists their development goals and the business goals. These cards help employees have conversations with their managers to ensure personal and business goals are aligned.[53] At LifeGift, a Houston-based nonprofit that recovers human organs and tissues from recently deceased donors and matches them to transplant recipients across the United States, engagement means having employees who never give up on finding a donor.[54] LifeGift's CEO, made employee engagement a priority and started measuring engagement annually starting in 2008. When engagement fell in the last survey, Holtzman required the company managers to hold quarterly one-on-one discussions with each of their employees, separate from annual evaluations. Results from the surveys and discussions ensure that employees receive the training, emotional support, and other resources needed to deal with the demands of the job. Most companies do not deal with life-or-death issues as LifeGift does, but focusing on employee engagement can ensure that employees are satisfied and productive.

Change and Continuous Learning

In addition to acquiring and retaining knowledge workers, companies need to be able to adapt to change. **Change** refers to the adoption of a new idea or behavior by a company. Technological advances, changes in the workforce or government regulations, globalization, and new competitors are among the many factors that require companies to change. Change is inevitable in companies as products, companies, and entire industries experience shorter life cycles.[55] For example, every aspect of Capital BlueCross is changing due to health-care reform.[56] The company's leadership development curriculum helps prepare leaders at all levels of the company to deal with these changes. It includes providing each leader with a coach who reinforces what was learned in the curriculum and tailors it to the individual strengths and challenges of each learner. Each leader also shares what they learned with the employees who report to them. Hu-Friedy, a company that manufactures dental instruments, employs 750 employees.[57] Hu-Friedy is spending $60,000 on an apprenticeship program to develop its employees' skills. Many of employees have worked on the factory floor making instruments for years but don't have the complex understanding of heat treatment, metallurgy, and metal composition necessary for making improvements to the company's products and production processes. Hu-Friedy hopes the apprenticeship program will help keep production work in the United States and keep the company competitive. The characteristics of an effective change process are discussed in Chapter Two, "Strategic Training."

A changing environment means that all employees must embrace a philosophy of learning. A **learning organization** embraces a culture of lifelong learning, enabling all employees to acquire and share knowledge continually. Improvements in product or service quality do not stop when formal training is completed.[58] Employees need to have the financial, time, and content resources (such as courses, experiences, and development opportunities) available to increase their knowledge. Managers take an active role in identifying training needs and helping to ensure that employees use training in their work. Also, employees are actively encouraged to share knowledge with colleagues and other work groups across the company using e-mail and the Internet.[59] At The Cheesecake Factory Inc., which operates about 160 restaurants in the United States, learning is less about formal programs and courses and more about being available on an as-needed basis, driven by employees.[60] The company is focused on fostering continuous learning related to guest satisfaction and perfect execution of the many dishes on its menu. To do so, the company is creating interactive learning content that employees access at work. Through the VideoCafe, employees can upload and share short videos on topics such as customer greetings and food preparation. The company plans to develop interactive games, including a simulation for building the perfect hamburger. Hands-on, employee-driven learning is supported by managers observing employees and providing coaching and feedback to help develop new skills and reinforce their use in the workplace. Chapter Five, "Program Design," discusses learning organizations and knowledge management in detail. For a learning organization to be successful, teams of employees must collaborate to meet customer needs. Managers need to empower employees to share knowledge, identify problems, and make decisions, which allows the company to experiment and improve continuously.

Social collaboration and social networking technology are helping employees share knowledge and contribute to the development of a learning organization.[61] CareSource uses wikis, websites with content created by users, and discussion boards to encourage employees to engage in critical thinking and learn from each other by sharing ideas about how to apply skills that they have acquired in formal training programs. Coldwell Banker encourages its real estate professionals to develop and share videos of the best sales techniques using the company's video portal. Coldwell Banker also uses communities of practice to encourage employees to share best practices and provide insights on how to best approach specific types of job assignments. inVentiv Health, Inc. uses tools on Facebook to help sales employees share information and update lessons learned.

Focus on Links to Business Strategy

Given the important role that intangible assets and human capital play in a company's competitiveness, managers are beginning to see a more important role for training and development as a means to support a company's business strategy; that is, its plans for meeting broad goals such as profitability, market share, and quality. Managers expect training and development professionals to design and develop learning activities that will help the company successfully implement its strategy and reach business goals. Strategic training will be discussed in greater detail in Chapter Two.

Changing Demographics and Diversity of the Workforce

In the United States the Bureau of Labor Statistics (BLS), an agency of the Department of Labor, tracks changes in the composition of the U.S. labor force and forecasts trends. Companies face several challenges as a result of increased demographics and diversity of the workforce. Population is the single most important factor in determining the size and composition of the labor force, which is composed of people who are either working or looking for work. The civilian labor force is projected to increase by 18 million between 2012 and 2022, reaching 163 million by 2022.[62] The workforce will be older and more culturally diverse than at any time in the past 40 years.

Increase in Ethnic and Racial Diversity

Between 2012 and 2022, the U.S. labor force will continue to grow more ethnically and racially diverse due to immigration, increased participation of minorities in the workforce, and higher minority fertility rates. Between 2012 and 2022, the projected annual growth rates for Hispanics (2.5 percent) and "other groups" (which includes individuals of multiple racial origin, American Indians and Alaska Natives, and Native Hawaiians) (2.7 percent) are higher than for African Americans and other groups.[63] By 2022, the workforce is projected to be 78 percent white, 12 percent African American, and 6 percent Asian and 2 percent other ethnic or cultural groups. By 2022, 53 percent of the labor force will be men and 47 percent will be women. Not only must companies face the issues of race, gender, ethnicity, and nationality to provide a fair workplace, but they must also develop training programs to help immigrants acquire the technical and customer service skills required in a service economy.

FIGURE 1.3
Comparison of the Age of the 2012 and 2022 Labor Force.

Source: Based on Bureau of Labor Statistics, U.S. Department of Labor, Employment Projections: 2012–2022, News Release, December 19th, 2013, from *www.bls.gov/emp*, accessed February 25, 2015.

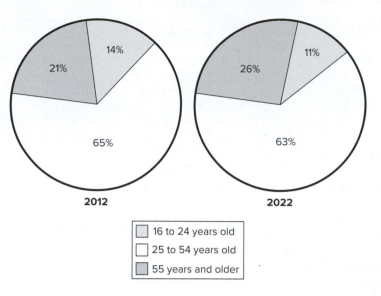

Aging Workforce

Figure 1.3 compares the projected distribution of the age of the workforce in 2012 and 2022. In 2018, baby boomers will be 57 to 70 years old, and this age group will grow significantly between 2012 and 2022. The labor force will continue to age. The 55-and-older age group is expected to grow by approximately 12 million to 42 million in 2022, representing a 29 percent increase between 2012 and 2022. This 12 million is nearly all of the 8.5 million workers who are projected to be added to the workforce by 2022.[64] The labor force participation of those 55 years and older is expected to grow because older individuals are leading healthier and longer lives than in the past, providing the opportunity to work more years. In addition, the high cost of health insurance and decrease in health benefits will cause many employees to keep working to maintain their employer-based insurance or will prompt them to return to work after retirement to obtain health insurance through their employer. Also, the trend toward pension plans based on individuals' contributions to them rather than on years of service, will provide yet another incentive for older employees to continue working.

The aging population means that companies are likely to employ a growing share of older workers—many of them in their second or third careers. Older people want to work, and many say they plan a working retirement. Despite myths to the contrary, worker performance and learning in most jobs is not adversely affected by aging.[65] Older employees are willing and able to learn new technology. An emerging trend is for qualified older employees to ask to work part-time, or for only a few months at a time, as a means of transitioning to retirement. Employees and companies are redefining what it means to be retired to include second careers, as well as part-time and temporary work assignments.

Generational Differences

Five generations are represented in the workforce, each one with unique and similar characteristics to the others. In Table 1.3, the year born, nicknames, and ages of each generation are shown. Consider some of the attributes that are believed to characterize each

TABLE 1.3
Generations in the Workforce

Year Born	Generation	Ages
1925–45	Traditionalists Silent generation	>69
1946–64	Baby boomers	51–69
1965–80	Generation X	35–50
1981–95	Millennials Generation Y Echo boomers	20–34
1996–	Generation Z Digital natives	<20

generation.[66] For example, millennials also known as Generation Y or Echo Boomers, grew up with access to computers at home and school and access to the Internet. They grew up with diversity in their schools and were coached, praised, and encouraged for participation rather than accomplishment by their baby boomer parents. Millennials are characterized as being optimistic, willing to work and learn, eager to please, self-reliant, globally aware, and value diversity and teamwork. They are also believed to have high levels of self-esteem, to the point of narcissism sometimes.

Generation Xers grew up during a time when the divorce rate doubled, the number of women working outside the home increased, and the personal computer was invented. They were often left to their own devices after school (latchkey kids). They value skepticism, informality, and practicality, seek work-life balance, and dislike close supervision. They tend to be impatient and cynical. They have experienced change in all of their lives (in terms of parents, homes, and cities).

Baby boomers, the "Me" generation, marched against the "establishment" for equal rights and an end to the Vietnam War. They value social conscientiousness and independence. They are competitive, hardworking, and concerned with the fair treatment of all employees. They are often considered to be workaholics and rigid in conforming to rules.

Traditionalists or the Silent Generation grew up during the Great Depression and lived during World War II. They tend to value frugality, are patriotic and loyal, adhere to rules, loyal to employers, and take responsibility and sacrifice for the good of the company.

It is important to note that although generation differences likely exist, members of the same generations are no more alike than members of the same gender or race. Research suggests that different generations of employees have similarities as well as differences.[67] Differences in work ethic have been found between baby boomers, Generation Xers, and millennials. However, millennial employees are more similar than different from other generations in their work beliefs, job values, and gender beliefs. The lack of study of generational differences over time, the inability of most studies to separate generational effects from age or life stage, and possible differences across generation in how they interpret survey items used in studies means that you should be cautious in attributing differences in employee behaviors and attitudes to generational differences.[68] Also, treating employees differently based on their age, such as only inviting younger employees to attend training or development programs, may result in adverse legal consequences (e.g., employees forty years or older are covered by the Age Discrimination in Employ-ment Act).

Nonetheless, members of each generation may have misperceptions of each other, causing tensions and misunderstanding in the workplace.[69] For example, millennials may think Generation X managers are bitter, jaded, abrasive, uninterested in them, and poor delegators. In turn, their Generation X managers consider millennials too needy for atten-tion, demanding, and overly self-confident. Millennials might believe that baby boomers are too rigid and follow company rules too closely. They believe that employees in the older generations have been too slow to adopt social media tools and value tenure over knowledge and performance. Traditionalists and baby boomers believe that millennials don't have a strong work ethic because they are too concerned with work-life balance. Also, members of the younger generations may resent baby boomers and traditionalists who are working longer before retiring, thus blocking promotions and career moves for younger workers. We will discuss the potential implications of generational differences for training and development in Chapters Four and Five.

Companies can use increased diversity to gain a competitive advantage. A Society for Human Resource Management (SHRM) survey of its members showed that 68 percent have practices to address workplace diversity.[70] Important outcomes expected from diver-sity practices included improved public image of the company, improved financial bot-tom line, decreased complaints and litigation, and retention and recruitment of a diverse workforce.

Training plays a key role in ensuring that employees accept and work more effectively with each other. To successfully manage a diverse workforce, managers and employees must be trained in a new set of skills, including:

1. Communicating effectively with employees from a wide variety of backgrounds
2. Coaching, training, and developing employees of different ages, educational back-grounds, ethnicities, physical abilities, and races
3. Providing performance feedback that is free of values and stereotypes based on gender, ethnicity, or physical handicap
4. Training managers to recognize and respond to generational differences
5. Creating a work environment that allows employees of all backgrounds to be creative and innovative.[71]

Consider the programs that several companies are offering to capitalize on older employees' skills and accommodate their needs, provide training and development oppor-tunities that appeal to a diverse workforce, and cope with generational differences.[72] Many of these programs are a part of companies' efforts to manage diversity, which we will discuss in more detail in Chapter Ten. S.C. Johnson offers retirees temporary work assign-ments, consulting and contract work, telecommuting, and part-time work. Centegra Health System's phased retirement program offers flexible scheduling, including part-time work, compressed workweeks, job sharing, summers off, and long-distance contract work.

CVS/pharmacy has stories in every climate and region in the United States. CVS created its Snowbirds Program to allow older employees to move among locations according to their preferences. This is especially important for older employees who spend winters in the southern states and summer in the northern states. More than 1,000 employees, including retail clerks, pharmacists, and managers, have participated in the program.

Johnson & Johnson's analysis of women's leadership programs showed that, although the company was not experiencing greater turnover of women, it had been ineffective in reaching multicultural women and women of color.[73] The company has since created a program, titled "Crossing the Finish Line," for high-performing, high-potential multicultural women and women of color. The program includes a two-and-a-half day project in which participants have open conversations with their managers and with executives, including the CEO and the vice chair of the company. The program helps Johnson & Johnson identify women who should be given new development opportunities, as well as help them understand that they must be visible, establish networks, and take the initiative to ask for development assignments. Also, the program educates managers about cultural differences and creates an awareness of how an employee's culture might affect his or her career.

Dell Inc., a technology company, provides a course for all of its new managers that includes topics such as leading multigenerational teams and developing connections with the employees who report to them.[74] All successful managers at Dell must have the ability to relate to and motivate a multigenerational workforce, to create teams to work together, and to encourage an entrepreneurial spirit, regardless of what generation the managers come from. Dell also uses employee resource groups for employees to connect, build relationships, and network. For example, the resource group for millennials is called "GenNext." Dell also encourages employees to participate in discussion with managers about new ways to consider where and how work gets done. This allows employees to choose to work remotely and telecommute, which helps them meet their personal needs, yet successfully complete their work.

MasterCard Inc., the credit card company, is now focusing on developing payment and security innovations.[75] The percentage of MasterCard's employees from the millennial generation has grown from 10 percent in 2010 to 38 percent in 2014. As a result, MasterCard created learning programs that are more appealing to the ways that millennials want to learn. For example, an e-learning program that uses gamification and animation was developed to make required information security and compliance training more fun and less dull and boring. Employees take the roles of "superheroes" to prevent security issues such as not opening e-mails that might contain malware. Within the experience employees become characters in the scenario and they have to make important decisions.

Talent Management

Talent management refers to the systematic, planned, and strategic effort by a company to use bundles of human resource management practices, including acquiring and assessing employees, learning and development, performance management, and compensation to attract, retain, develop, and motivate highly skilled employees and managers. Talent management is becoming increasingly more important because of changes in demand for certain occupations and jobs, skill requirements, the anticipated retirement of the baby boomer generation, and the need to develop managerial talent and skills of the next generation of company leaders. Also, the results of surveys suggest that opportunities for career growth, learning, and development, and the performance of exciting and challenging work are some of the most important factors in determining employees' (especially millennials) engagement and commitment to their current employer.[76]

For Cognizant, a global technology solutions company, business is based on knowledge which depends on the skills of its workforce.[77] Talent development is seen as a strategic business driver. To develop talent, all employees have individual development plans that support their career goals. Learning at Cognizant focuses on building both technical and leadership talent to ensure employees help improve their clients' businesses. Cognizant has several programs to build talent. The Career Architecture program helps employees choose a career track that matches their interests and skills. It helps identify training courses and job rotations that can help employees move along their career track. The Emerging Partners program develops senior account managers and senior delivery managers. The program includes case studies, role-plays, and simulations. More than 100 managers have completed the program and 45 percent have moved within six months into leadership roles involving interactions with clients. Approximately 50.6 million job openings are expected, more than two-thirds from the need to replace workers who retire or leave. Most of the employment growth between 2012 and 2022 is expected to be in service-providing occupations. Employment in construction is the second highest projected employment increase, resulting in 1.6 million new jobs between 2012 and 2022.[78]

Health care and social assistant services, are expected to be one-third of the total projected increase in total employment from 2012 to 2022. This will add 5 million jobs. On the other hand, employment in manufacturing, federal government information, utilities farming, fishing, and forestry occupations is expected to decline. Keep in mind that there are likely some exceptions to these projected trends. Companies that require specialized labor to make industrial lathes, computer chips, and health-care products requiring specialized skills, plan to expand and locate near towns and cities that have such an available workforce.[79] For example, Greatbatch Inc., which makes medical products, has expanded near Fort Wayne, Indiana, to take advantage of the local workforce's specialized skills.

Table 1.4 shows ten of the thirty fastest-growing occupations projected between 2012 and 2022. Of the thirty fastest-growing occupations, fourteen are related to health care (such as personal care aids, home health aides, genetic counselors, and physical therapists) and five are related to construction (insulation workers, brickmasons and blockmasons, electrical, tile, and marble setters' helpers). The growth in health care reflects the inpatient and outpatient medical care that is needed for the aging U.S. population. The growth in the construction occupation is related to replacement needs, growth in the economy, and the need to repair the aging U.S. infrastructure. Slightly less than two-thirds of the thirty fastest-growing occupations require education beyond high school, i.e., at least an associate's degree or higher. Occupations requiring education beyond high school are expected to grow faster and pay more per year (an estimated $30,000) than those requiring a high school diploma or less. Occupations that require an apprenticeship for training, including many construction jobs, are projected to grow approximately 22 percent between 2012 and 2022, which is faster than for jobs requiring any other type of on-the-job training.

Retirement of Baby Boomers

As the oldest baby boomers continue to retire in the next several years, the implications for the workforce could be enormous.[80] This could hinder prospects for economic growth and

TABLE 1.4 **Examples of the Fastest-Growing Occupations**

| Occupation | Employment Change 2012–2022 | | Most Significant Education or Training |
	Number (in thousands)	Percent	
Industrial-organizational psychologists	1	53	Master's degree
Personal care aids	581	49	Short-term, on-the-job training
Home health aids	424	49	Short-term, on-the-job training
Insulation workers	14	47	Short-term, on-the-job training
Interpreters and translators	29	46	Bachelor's degree
Diagnostic medical sonographers	27	46	Associate's degree
Helpers – Brick, block, and stone masons, tile and marble setters	11	43	Associate's degree
Occupational therapy assistants	13	43	Associate's degree
Genetic counselors	1	41	Master's degree
Physical therapy assistants	29	41	Associate's degree

Sources: Based on Bureau of Labor Statistics, U.S. Department of Labor, "Employment projections: 2012–2022," News Release, December 19, 2013, from *www.bls.gov/emp*, accessed February 25, 2015.

put a greater burden on those remaining in the workforce, perhaps forcing them to work longer hours. Especially in occupations with functions less conducive to technology-driven productivity innovations—many jobs in health services and educational services, for example—quality of service may suffer and needs could go unmet unless older workers can be retained or other sources of workers can be found. Even in occupations in which technological innovations have produced relatively large productivity gains—many of the more complex machining jobs in manufacturing, for example—the learning curves often are steep, meaning that new workers need to enter these occupations soon, so they can become proficient in the necessary skills by the time the baby boomers begin leaving the labor force.

It is also important for companies to try to capture the valuable knowledge that is leaving.[81] Consider how Asian Paints and ConocoPhillips try to capture knowledge.[82] Asian Paints, a paint company in India, encourages employees to use their social network to share best practices and new ways to support dealers. The sales team uses this information to find and apply these practices to current challenges they are facing. This means that when an experienced salesperson retires or leaves the company their knowledge is not lost. ConocoPhillips, a multinational petrochemical company, uses wikis to capture knowledge from all employees including retirees. Many of the company's retirees come back to work part-time. They review the information on the company wiki, identify gaps in missing knowledge, and provide content. Their experiences provide the "how," "what," and "why" that gives context to the wiki content. ConocoPhillips also uses mentoring programs pairing up less-experienced employees with more senior employees to facilitate knowledge sharing.

Skill Requirements

As the occupational structure of the U.S. economy has shifted, skill requirements have changed.[83] The demand for specific skills is being replaced by a need for cognitive skills—mathematical and verbal reasoning ability—and interpersonal skills related to being able to work in teams or to interact with "customers" in a service economy (e.g., patients, students, vendors, and suppliers). Cognitive and interpersonal skills are important because in the service-oriented economy, employees must take responsibility for the final product or service. Variety and customization require employees to be creative and good problem solvers. Continuous innovation requires the ability to learn. To offer novelty and entertainment value to customers, workers must be creative. Most companies relate these skills with educational attainment, so many firms use a college degree as a standard to screen prospective employees. Companies also need employees with STEM skills. **STEM skills** refer to skills in science, technology, engineering, and math.

However, new entrants to the workplace, as well as the unemployed, lack the skills needed for companies to compete in the global economy. Several studies illustrate the skill deficit that U.S. companies are experiencing.[84] Nearly half of CEOs of U.S. businesses believe that a significant skills gap exists that will result in loss of business, revenue, decreased customer satisfaction, or a delay in new products or services. A survey by the Organization for Economic Cooperation and Development found that the United States ranked twenty-one out of twenty-three countries in math and seventeen out of nineteen countries in problem solving. A study by the Manufacturing Institute found that 80 percent of manufacturers report a moderate or serious shortage of qualified applicants for skilled and highly skilled production positions. Skill deficits are not just a problem facing U.S. companies.[85] In Italy and Spain nearly three out of ten adults perform at or below the lowest level of proficiency in both literacy and numerical ability. Countries with developing economies such as India and Russia, as well as Japan and Western Europe, are experiencing difficulties in finding workers for the skilled trades, sales, technicians, engineers, and managers.

Although many businesses plan to hire new employees, they are concerned that they will not be able to find the talent needed to capitalize on investments they are making in new technology and other strategic capabilities. Skill deficits are not limited to any one business sector, industry, or job. As result, companies are partnering with unions, elementary and secondary schools, and colleges and universities to develop these skills in the workforce. For example, an upturn in the construction industry following the recession has resulted in contractors having a difficult time finding the skilled workers they need.[86] As result, local trade unions are advertising apprenticeship programs, which can help train much-needed electricians, plumbers, iron workers, roofers, and pipefitters.

Consider the efforts that Intel, Siemens, and Microsoft are making to develop STEM skills.[87] Intel dedicated $300 million to sponsor classes in schools and universities, with a focus on underserved regions. The money is part of an effort to boost diversity in its workforce and fund recruiting, training, and investments in female and minority start-up businesses. Siemens AG, an engineering company and manufacturer of medical equipment, wanted to expand its energy plant in Charlotte, North Carolina, which would require hiring an additional 1,500 employees. Although over 10,000 job applications were received, most did not have the required STEM skills. As a result, Siemens partnered with a community college in the area to develop a specialized course to prepare potential employees for jobs in the energy plant. Siemens put 3,500 of the 10,000 job applicants through the program. Four hundred were employed by Siemens and the others were encouraged to use their new STEM skills to find jobs with other companies. Microsoft is developing STEM skills through efforts to ensure that teachers are trained to use technology in the classroom and using Microsoft employees as part-time co-teachers. Microsoft IT Academy provides teachers and students with opportunities to become certified in different types of software, such as Microsoft Office. The exposure the program exposes students to STEM careers that they might not have considered.

Developing Leadership

Companies report that the most important talent management challenges they face are identifying employees with managerial talent and training and developing them for managerial positions.[88] This is attributed to the aging of the workforce, globalization, and the need for managers to contribute to employee engagement. Executive, administrative, and managerial occupations will experience the greatest turnover due to death or retirement.[89] Also, many companies do not have employees with the necessary competencies to manage in a global economy.[90] To successfully manage in a global economy, managers need to be self-aware and be able to build international teams, create global management and marketing practices, and interact and manage employees from different cultural backgrounds. Managers contribute to employee engagement by performing basic management functions (planning, organizing, controlling, leading) but also through using good communication skills, helping employees develop, and working collaboratively with employees.

A number of surveys suggest that millennials are interested in opportunities for career progression, including becoming managers and leaders, and they are significantly more likely to want formal leadership development opportunities than employees from other generations.[91] Employees from all generations have strengths and weaknesses in management skills. Millennials are strong in adaptability and customer focus. They are similar to Generation Xers in important leadership and interpersonal skills, including developing others, gaining commitment, and communication. To be effective mangers and leaders, millennials need to develop decision-making and planning and organizing skills and learn how to set high work standards.

As result, many companies including General Electric and Sherwin-Williams are taking steps to retain talented millennials and develop their management skills.[92] For example, General Electric provides job rotation for managers, which helps them gain experience working with different senior managers and different business units. This meets millennials' needs for growth experience and networking while developing skills needed to successfully respond to different types of customers and job challenges. Similarly, Sherwin-Williams, a company that manufactures paint and sells it through its retail stores, recognized that it had been losing its manager trainees at a high rate. Using data collected from surveys and interviews, they found that trainees did not feel included and engaged. To solve this problem, Sherwin-Williams developed a new career-progression model. Performance reviews with manager trainees will occur every six months instead of once at the end of the year, which helps provide them with more feedback and the opportunity to receive pay raises every six months. Also, district managers will conduct regular career discussions with trainees to discuss their long-term goals. During their initial two-year training period new employees will have more opportunities to try different roles in the company, including working with sales representatives and different types of stores, such as those specializing in floor coverings and providing commercial services for building contractors.

Customer Service and Quality Emphasis

A company's customers judge its quality and performance. As a result, customer excellence requires attention to product and service features, as well as to interactions with customers. Customer-driven excellence includes understanding what the customer wants, anticipating future needs, reducing defects and errors, meeting specifications, and reducing complaints. How the company recovers from defects and errors is also important for retaining and attracting customers.

Due to increased availability of knowledge and competition, consumers are very knowledgeable and expect excellent service. This presents a challenge for employees who interact with customers. The way in which clerks, sales staff, front-desk personnel, and service providers interact with customers influences a company's reputation and financial performance. Employees need product knowledge and service skills, and they need to be clear about the types of decisions they can make when dealing with customers. Customer service as a strategic training and development initiative is discussed in Chapter Two.

To compete in today's economy, whether on a local or global level, companies need to provide a quality product or service. If companies do not adhere to quality standards, their ability to sell their product or service to vendors, suppliers, or customers will be restricted. Some countries even have quality standards that companies must meet to conduct business there. **Total Quality Management (TQM)** is a companywide effort to continuously improve the ways people, machines, and systems accomplish work.[93] Core values of TQM include the following:[94]

- Methods and processes are designed to meet the needs of internal and external customers.
- Every employee in the company receives training in quality.
- Quality is built into a product or service so that errors are prevented from occurring rather than being detected and corrected.
- The company promotes cooperation with vendors, suppliers, and customers to improve quality and hold down costs.
- Managers measure progress with feedback based on data.

There is no universal definition of quality. The major differences in its various definitions relate to whether the customer, product, or manufacturing process is emphasized. For example, quality expert W. Edwards Deming emphasizes how well a product or service meets customer needs. Phillip Crosby's approach emphasizes how well the service or manufacturing process meets engineering standards.

The emphasis on quality is seen in the establishment of the **Malcolm Baldrige National Quality Award** and the **ISO 9000:2000** quality standards. The Baldrige award, created by public law, is the highest level of national recognition for quality that a U.S. company can receive. The award is given annually. To become eligible for the Baldrige, a company must complete a detailed application that consists of basic information about the firm and an in-depth presentation of how it addresses specific criteria related to quality improvement. The categories and point values for the Baldrige award are found in Table 1.5.

TABLE 1.5
Categories
and Point
Values for
the Malcolm
Baldrige
National
Quality Award
Examination

Source: Based on
"2013–2014 Criteria
for Performance
Excellence" from
the website for the
National Institute of
Standards and Tech-
nology, *www.nist/gov/
baldrige.*

Leadership	**120**
The way senior executives create and sustain vision, values, and mission; promote legal and ethical behavior; create a sustainable company; and communicate with and engage the workforce	
Measurement, Analysis, and Knowledge Management	**90**
The way the company selects, gathers, analyzes, manages, and improves its data, information, and knowledge assets	
Strategic Planning	**85**
The way the company sets strategic direction, how it determines action plans, how it changes strategy and action plans if required, and how it measures progress	
Workforce Focus	**85**
Company's efforts to develop and utilize the workforce to achieve high performance; how the company engages, manages, and develops the potential of the workforce in alignment with company goals	
Operations Focus	**85**
Design, management, and improvement of work systems and work processes to deliver customer value and achieve company success and sustainability	
Results	**450**
Company's performance and improvement in key business areas (product, service, and supply quality; productivity; and operational effectiveness and related financial indicators)	
Customer Focus	**85**
Company's knowledge of the customer, customer service systems, current and potential customer concerns, customer satisfaction and engagement	
Total Points	**1,000**

The award is not given for specific products or services. Organizations can compete for the Baldrige award in one of six categories: manufacturing, service, small business, education, health care, and nonprofit. All applicants for the Baldrige Award undergo a rigorous examination process that takes from 300 to 1,000 hours. Applications are reviewed by an independent board of about 400 examiners who come primarily from the private sector. Each applicant receives a report citing company strengths and opportunities for improvement.

The Baldrige Award winners usually excel at human resource practices, including training and development. For example, consider PricewaterhouseCoopers Public Sector Practice (PwC PSP), a 2014 award winner and MESA Products Inc., a 2012 award winner.[95] PwC PSP provides risk, management, and technology consulting to state, local, and federal governments. Contractor performance assessment reports have been nearly 100 percent "exceptional" or "very good" from 2010 to 2014. PwC PSP scores on a tool used to assess customer engagement and loyalty has been equal to or better than scores from other U.S. consulting companies. An important reason for its customer satisfaction and loyalty is that PwC PSP makes extensive use of knowledge management to help employees learn and to serve clients. It collects knowledge through the Knowledge Gateway where it is reviewed by knowledge management team members and content experts. The knowledge is then shared through a web-based tool designed to help employees collaborate with each other. Employees use this tool to share and find knowledge, exchange ideas, and seek developmental opportunities. Senior leaders at PwC PSP identify high-performing operations and invite them to present their practices at managing partner meeting. The practices are also shared on the Knowledge Gateway. MESA Products Inc. installs protective systems that control metal erosion in underground and submerged pipes and tanks. MESA's culture supports employees in developing or changing their career path. Employees are cross trained, providing them with opportunities to change jobs. MESA's managers place a large emphasis on workforce learning and development.

The International Organization for Standardization (ISO), a network of national standards institutes that includes 160 countries and has a central governing body in Geneva, Switzerland, is the world's largest developer and publisher of international standards.[96] The ISO develops standards related to management as well as a wide variety of other areas, including education, music, ships, and even protecting children. ISO standards are voluntary, but countries may decide to adopt ISO standards in their regulations; and as a result, they may become a requirement to compete in the market. The ISO 9000 is a family of standards related to quality (ISO 9000, 9001, 9004, and 10011). The ISO 9000 quality standards address what the company does to meet regulatory requirements and the customer's quality requirements while striving to improve customer satisfaction and continuous improvement. The standards represent an international consensus on quality management practices. ISO 9000:2000 has been adopted as the quality standard in nearly 100 counties around the world, meaning that companies have to follow these standards to conduct business in those countries. The quality management standards of the ISO 9000 are based on eight quality management principles, including customer focus, leadership, people involvement, a process approach, a systems approach to management, continuous improvement, using facts to make decisions, and establishing mutually beneficial relationships with suppliers. ISO 9001:2008 is the most comprehensive standard because it provides a set of requirements for a quality management system for all organizations, both private and public. The ISO 9001:2008 has been implemented by more than 1 million organizations in 176 countries. ISO 9004 provides a guide for companies that want to improve.

Why are standards useful? Customers may want to check that the product they ordered from a supplier meets the purpose for which it is required. One of the most efficient ways to do this is when the specifications of the product have been defined in an international standard. That way, both supplier and customer are on the same wavelength, even if they are based in different countries, because they are both using the same references. Today, many products require testing for conformance with specifications, compliance with safety, or other regulations before they can be put on many markets. Even simpler products may require supporting technical documentation that includes test data. With so much trade taking place across borders, it is more practical for these activities to be carried out not by suppliers and customers, but by specialized third parties. In addition, national legislation may require such testing to be carried out by independent bodies, particularly when the products concerned have health or environmental implications. One example of an ISO standard is on the back cover of this book and nearly every other book. On the back cover is something called an International Standard Book Number (ISBN). Publishers and booksellers are very familiar with ISBN numbers, since these numbers are the method through which books are ordered and bought. Try buying a book on the Internet, and you will soon learn the value of the ISBN number—there is a unique number for the book you want. And it is based on an ISO standard.

In addition to competing for quality awards and seeking ISO certification, many companies are using the Six Sigma process. The **Six Sigma process** refers to a process of measuring, analyzing, improving, and then controlling processes once they have been brought within the narrow Six Sigma quality tolerances or standards. The objective of Six Sigma is to create a total business focus on serving the customer; that is, to deliver what customers really want when they want it. For example, at General Electric (GE), introducing the Six Sigma quality initiative meant going from approximately 35,000 defects per million operations—which is average for most companies, including GE—to fewer than 4 defects per million in every element of every process GE businesses perform—from manufacturing a locomotive part to servicing a credit card account to processing a mortgage application to answering a phone.[97] Training is an important component of the process. Six Sigma involves highly trained employees known as Champions, Master Black Belts, Black Belts, and Green Belts, who lead and teach teams that are focusing on an ever-growing number of quality projects. The quality projects focus on improving efficiency and reducing errors in products and services. The Six Sigma quality initiative has produced more than $2 billion in benefits for GE.

Training can help companies meet the quality challenge by teaching employees a concept known as "lean thinking." **Lean thinking** is a way to do more with less effort, equipment, space, and time, but still provide customers with what they need and want. Part of lean thinking includes training workers in new skills or teaching them how to apply old skills in new ways so they can quickly take over new responsibilities or use new skills to help fill customer orders. Baylor Health Care System wanted to decrease waste and improve patient satisfaction and outcomes through implementing lean thinking and process improvements in several of its hospitals.[98] This included training employees for how to make changes to work processes. Lean thinking and process improvement supported by training provided significant value. For example, The Corporate Supply Management team eliminated two-thirds of the time for completing contracts, developed a decision tree for different types of projects, and reduced errors saving $10 million. A hospital re-admission team redesigned the patient discharge process to reduce the chances of patients returning within thirty days. They realized a 44 percent decrease in readmissions over a six-month period, which improved the quality of life for patients and Baylor's ability to receive Medicare/Medicaid payments from the government.

A group within the ISO has drafted a standard for employee training. **ISO 10015** is a quality management tool designed to ensure that training is linked to company needs and performance. ISO 10015 has two key features.[99] First, companies have to determine the return on investment of training to company performance. Second, ISO 10015 requires companies to use appropriate design and effective learning processes. ISO 10015 defines training design as analyzing, planning, doing, and evaluating (recall the discussion of the Instructional System Design model earlier in this chapter).

New Technology

Technology has reshaped the way we play, communicate, plan our lives, and work. Many companies' business models includes e-commerce, which allows consumers to purchase products and services online. The Internet is a global collection of computer networks that allows users to exchange data and information. Roughly 84 percent of U.S. households have a computer (desktop, laptop, tablet, or smart phone) and 75 percent have Internet access. A total of 60 percent of Americans visit Google during the week, and 43 percent have a Facebook page.[100] Using Facebook, Twitter, LinkedIn, and other social networking tools available on the Internet accessed through smart phones, notebooks, or personal computers, company managers can connect with employees and employees can connect with friends, family, and co-workers.

Influence on Training

Advances in sophisticated technology along with reduced costs for the technology are changing the delivery of training, making training more realistic, and giving employees the opportunity to choose where and when they will work. New technologies allow training to occur at any time and any place.[101]

Technological advances in electronics and communications software have made possible mobile technology such smart phones, notebook computers, and iPads, and enhanced the Internet through developing the capability for social networking. Social networking refers to websites such as Facebook, Twitter, and LinkedIn, wikis, and blogs that facilitate interactions between people, usually around shared interests. Table 1.6 shows how social networks can be used for training and development.[102]

In general, social networking facilitates communications, decentralized decision making, and collaboration. Social networking can be useful for busy employees to share knowledge and ideas with their peers and managers, with whom they may not have much time to interact in person on a daily basis. Employees, especially young workers from the millennial or Gen-Y generations, have learned to use social networking tools such as

TABLE 1.6 Potential Uses of Social Networking for Training and Development

Issues	Uses
Loss of expert knowledge due to retirement	Knowledge sharing, capturing, and storing
Employee engagement	Collect employee opinions
Identify and promote employee expertise	Create online expert communities
Promote innovation and creativity	Encourage participation in online discussions
Reinforce learning	Share best practices, applications, learning, points, links to articles and webinars
Employees need coaching and mentoring	Interact with mentors and coaching peers

Sources: Based on P. Brotherson, "Social Networks Enhance Employee Learning," *T+D* (April 2011): 18–19; T. Bingham and M. Connor, *The New Social Learning* (Alexandria, VA: American Society for Training & Development, 2010); M. Weinstein, "Are You Linked In?" *training* (September/October 2010): 30–33; S. Gilbert & A. Silvers, "Learning Communities With Purpose", TD (January 2015): 48–51.

Facebook throughout their lives and see them as valuable tools for both their work and personal lives.

Despite its potential advantages, many companies are uncertain as to whether they should embrace social networking.[103] They fear, perhaps correctly, that social networking will result in employees wasting time or offending or harassing their co-workers. But other companies believe that the benefits of using social networking for human resource practices and allowing employees to access social networks at work outweigh the risks. They trust employees to use social networking productively and are proactive in developing policies about personal use and training employees about privacy settings and social network etiquette. They realize that employees will likely check their Twitter, Facebook, or LinkedIn accounts, but they ignore it unless productivity is decreasing. In some ways, social networking has become the electronic substitute for daydreaming at one's desk or walking to the break room to socialize with co-workers.

Robotics, computer-assisted design, radio-frequency identification, and nanotechnology are transforming work.[104] Technology has also made it easier to monitor environmental conditions and operate equipment. For example, consider working a grader construction vehicle (which is used to smooth and level dirt on roadways and other construction projects). Older vehicle models required operating as many as fifteen levers in addition to a steering wheel and several foot pedals. As a result, working the grader usually left operators with sore backs and shoulders at the end of the day. Caterpillar's latest version of the grader includes redesigned controls that use only two joysticks and eliminate the physical demands of pushing pedals and turning a steering wheel. Besides reducing the physical demands, the redesign of the grader without a steering wheel resulted in operators having better visibility of the steel blade, and switches for lights, windshield wipers, and the parking brake could be grouped together in one place in the cab. A Japanese commercial farm, Shinpuku Seika, relies on computer readings from monitors placed out in the fields that report temperature, soil, and moisture levels to the farmers.[105] Computer analysis of these data alerts farmers when to start planting or identifies specific crops that may grow best in each field. Farmers can use cameras in the fields to examine crops. Farm workers can also use their mobile phones to take pictures of potential diseased or infected crops that are uploaded to the computer for diagnosis by crop experts. The workers' phones also include a global positioning system, allowing the company to determine if workers are taking the most efficient routes between fields or slacking off on the job.

Technology has many advantages, including reduced travel costs, greater accessibility to training, consistent delivery, the ability to access experts and share learning with others, and the possibility of creating a learning environment with many positive features such as feedback, self-pacing, and practice exercises. While trainer-led classroom instruction remains the most popular way to deliver training, companies report that they plan on delivering a large portion of training through learning technologies such as intranets and iPods. For example, consider how training at Verizon, the telecommunications company, has changed.[106] Some training programs at Verizon still include face-to-face instructor-led courses. But to improve both employees' accessibility to training and customer service, Verizon has deployed tablets to retail store employees. Employees can use these tablets to get access to information about devices, service plans, product promotions, processes, and procedures. They can share this information with the customer during their interactions. The tablets are also used to deliver e-learning. Learning and development at Verizon is evaluated based on its contribution to both employee and business performance. Verizon also uses social networking tools to train employees to support new products and devices. Device Blog, Device Forum, and Learning Communities help to ensure that employees are ready to support customers when new products and devices are introduced to the market, engages Verizon's multigenerational workforce, and facilitates peer-to-peer learning. Device Blog makes available information and updates on wireless devices (such as DROID), FAQ's (frequently asked questions), how-to-videos, and troubleshooting tips. Device Forums enable retail employees to learn from peers and product manufacturers. Employees can ask each other questions, share issues, post tips, make suggestions, and access product experts. Learning communities are accessed through the Device Blog. They include video blogs, message boards, links to online training modules, and product demonstrations. In addition to these tools, employees have access to My Network for collaborating with their peers, knowledge and document sharing, and creating working groups. Some trainers also use it for posting supplemental content for learners' use.

Technology is pushing the boundaries of artificial intelligence, speech synthesis, wireless communications, networked virtual reality and adaptive learning.[107] Realistic graphics, dialogue, and sensory cues can now be stored onto tiny, inexpensive computer chips. For example, Second Life is an online virtual world that allows members to develop fictional lives. In Second Life, members can run a business, take a date to a dance club, or visit a training center. Virtual sensations (vibrations and other sensory cues) are being incorporated into training applications. For example, in medical training, machines can replicate the feeling of pushing a needle into an artery and use sound and motion to simulate different situations such as a baby crying or a patient in pain.

Flexibility in Where and When Work Is Performed

Advances in technology, including more powerful computer chips and increased processing power of PDAs, notebooks, and iPhones have the potential for freeing workers from going to a specific location to work and from traditional work schedules. One estimate is that 9.5 percent or 13.4 million U.S. employees are working at home at least one day a week.[108] One in four home-based employees are working in management, business, and finance jobs and half are self-employed. Employees in health care and installation, maintenance, and repair occupations are the least likely to work from home. Telecommuting has been shown to increase employee productivity, encourage family-friendly work arrangements, and help reduce traffic and air pollution.[109] Employees at Salesforce.com Inc. can work from home and use Chatter, a Facebook-type application, to coordinate projects.[110] Managers can monitor whether employees working at home have answered clients' questions and finished reports.

At Delta Air Lines, more than 570 of the 5,000 agents work from home full time.[111] To strengthen their commitment and understanding of the company, each agent works in a call center for six months before working from home. While working at home, they can contact a team leader with questions. They also have monthly meetings. Delta spends $2,500 to purchase a computer and software for each reservation agent who works at home. The costs are offset by the lower hourly wage these agents receive compared to agents who work in the office. However, working at home reduces the agents' costs for gasoline and gives them more flexibility to balance their work and personal lives. The company has realized savings in rent and upkeep of office space, and the offsite agents have helped meet customer service demands due to bad weather by volunteering for more overtime than agents working in offices.

Technology also allows companies greater use of alternative work arrangements. **Alternative work arrangements** include independent contractors, on-call workers, temporary workers, and contract company workers. The Bureau of Labor Statistics estimates that alternative work arrangements make up 11 percent of total employment.[112] There are 10.3 million independent contractors, 2.5 million on-call workers, 1.2 million temporary help agency workers, and approximately 813,000 workers employed by contract firms. Use of alternative work arrangements allows companies to adjust staffing levels more easily based on economic conditions and product and service demand. And when a company downsizes by laying off workers, the damage to the morale of full-time employees is likely to be less severe. Alternative work arrangements also provide employees with flexibility for balancing work and life activities. For example, Verigy, a semiconductor manufacturer in California, employs only a small number of permanent employees, and nonessential jobs are outsourced. When demand for its products increases, engineers and other high-tech employees are hired through staffing companies or as independent contractors.[113] Also, the use of alternative work arrangements has resulted in the development of co-working sites where diverse workers such as designers, artists, freelancers, consultants, and other independent contractors pay a daily or monthly fee for a guaranteed work space.[114] The co-working site is equipped with desks and wireless Internet, and some provide access to copy machines, faxes, and conference rooms. Co-working sites help facilitate independent contractors, employees working at home, traveling, or telecommuting, combat their possible feelings of isolation, give them the ability to collaborate and interact, provide a more professional working atmosphere than coffee shops (and similar public locations where such employees often work off-site), and help to decrease traffic and pollution.

A key training issue that alternative work arrangements present is to prepare managers and employees to coordinate their efforts so that such work arrangements do not interfere with customer service or product quality. The increased use of alternative work arrangements means that managers need to understand how to motivate employees who may actually be employed by a third party such as a temporary employee service or leasing agency.

High-Performance Models of Work Systems

New technology causes changes in skill requirements and work roles and often results in redesigned work structures (e.g., using work teams).[115] For example, computer-integrated manufacturing uses robots and computers to automate the manufacturing process. The computer allows the manufacture of different products simply by reprogramming the computer. As a result, laborer, material handler, operator/assembler, and maintenance jobs may be merged into one position. Computer-integrated manufacturing requires employees to monitor equipment and troubleshoot problems with sophisticated equipment, share information with other employees, and understand the relationships among all components of the manufacturing process.[116]

Through technology, the information needed to improve customer service and product quality becomes more accessible to employees. This means that employees are expected to take more responsibility for satisfying the customer and determining how they perform their jobs. One of the most popular methods for increasing employee responsibility and control is work teams. **Work teams** involve employees with various skills who interact to assemble a product or provide a service. Work teams may assume many of the activities usually reserved for managers, including selecting new team members, scheduling work, and coordinating activities with customers and other units in the company. To give teams maximum flexibility, cross training of team members occurs. **Cross training** refers to training employees in a wide range of skills so they can fill any of the roles needed to be performed on the team.

Consider the high-performance work system at the Chrysler Dundee Engine Plant in Dundee, Michigan.[117] Compared to most engine plants, this plant is more automated and has fewer employees—709 compared to 600–2,000. The goal of the plant is to be the most productive engine plant in the world. The plant's hourly employees rotate jobs and shifts, giving the company greater flexibility and employees more family time. The plant's culture emphasizes problem solving and the philosophy that anyone can do anything, anytime, anywhere. Every employee is either a team member or a team leader. By rotating jobs, the plant keeps workers motivated and avoids injuries. Team leaders and engineers don't stay in their offices—they are expected to work on the shop floor as part of six-person teams. Contractors are also seen as part of the team, working alongside assembly workers and engineers and wearing the same uniforms. The plant gives employees access to technology that helps them monitor productivity. Large electronic screens hanging from the plant ceiling provide alerts of any machinery parts that are ending their lifespan and need to be replaced before they malfunction. A performance management system, available on personal computers as well as a display board, alerts employees to delays or breakdowns in productivity. This is different than in most engine plants, where only the managers have access to this information. The technology at the plant empowers all employees to fix problems—not just managers or engineers.

Use of new technology and work designs such as work teams needs to be supported by specific human resource management practices. These practices include the following actions:[118]

- Employees choose or select new employees or team members.
- Employees receive formal performance feedback and are involved in the performance improvement process.
- Ongoing training is emphasized and rewarded.
- Rewards and compensation are linked to company performance.
- Equipment and work processes encourage maximum flexibility and interaction between employees.
- Employees participate in planning changes in equipment, layout, and work methods.
- Employees understand how their jobs contribute to the finished product or service.

What role does training play? Employees need job-specific knowledge and basic skills to work with the equipment created by the new technology. Because technology is often used as a means to achieve product diversification and customization, employees must have the ability to listen and communicate with customers. Interpersonal skills, such as negotiation and conflict management, and problem-solving skills are more important than physical strength, coordination, and fine-motor skills—previous job requirements for many manufacturing and service jobs. Although technological advances have made it possible for employees to improve products and services, managers must empower employees to make changes.

Besides changing the way that products are built or services are provided within companies, technology has allowed companies to perform work using **virtual teams**. **Virtual teams** refer to teams with members that are separated by time, geographic distance, culture, and/or organizational boundaries and that rely almost exclusively on technology (such as e-mail, Internet, and video conferencing) to interact and complete their projects. Virtual teams can be formed within one company, whose facilities are scattered throughout the country or the world. A company may also use virtual teams in partnerships with suppliers or competitors to pull together the necessary talent to complete a project or speed the delivery of a product to the marketplace. The success of virtual teams requires a clear mission, good communications skills, trust between members that they will meet deadlines and complete assignments, and an understanding of cultural differences (if the teams have global members).

For example, Art & Logic software developers all work remotely from across the United States and Canada from home offices, rented office space or at a co-working facility.[119] Their clients represent a diverse set of industries, including education, aerospace, music technology, consumer electronics, entertainment, and financial services. The project teams work on the most unusual and difficult problems that developers at other companies have failed to solve. Art & Logic tries to accommodate the unique schedule and work-style requirements of its developers, but its work is highly collaborative within project teams. Every project consists of at least a project manager/developer and has a maximum of five to seven developers. Teams use Google Apps for Business for sharing documents and communicating (both within the team and with clients).

SNAPSHOT OF TRAINING PRACTICES

Training can play a key role in helping companies gain a competitive advantage and successfully deal with competitive challenges. Before you can learn how training can be used to help companies meet their business objectives, and before you can understand training design, training methods, and other topics covered in the text, you need to become familiar with the amount and type of training that occurs in the United States. Also, you must understand what trainers do. The next sections of this chapter present data regarding training practices (e.g., how much companies spend on training, what type of training is occurring, and who is being trained), as well as the skills and competencies needed to be a trainer.

Training Facts and Figures

The snapshot of training practices provided in this section is based on data and collected from a number of sources, including surveys conducted by *Training* magazine and the ATD. (Association for Talent Development, previously known as the American Society for Training and Development).[120] For several reasons, these data should be viewed as reasonable estimates of practices rather than precise facts. One is that the samples may not be representative of all size or types of companies. For example, the *Training* survey was conducted by a research firm that e-mailed invitations to subscribers to participate in an online survey. The response rate ranged from 31 percent for large firms to 28 percent

TABLE 1.7
Questions and Answers about Training Practices

Source: L. Miller, "2014 State of the Industry" (Alexandria, VA: Association for Talent Development, 2013); "2014 Industry Report," *training* (November/December 2014):16–29.

Investment and Distribution of Expenditures

Q: How much do U.S. organizations spend on employee learning and development?
A: Approximately $161.8 billion
Q: How much is spent per employee?
A: $1,208
Q: What is the percentage of dollars spent on training and development as a percentage of payroll?
A: 3.4 percent
Q: How much is spent as a percentage of profit?
A: 7.5 percent
Q: How much time do employees spend in formal training each year?
A: 31.5 hours
Q: Who receives most of the training?
A: 40 percent of training budgets and dollars are spent on nonexempt employees, 26 percent on exempt employees, 24 percent on managers, and 10 percent on executives

Efficiency

Q: What percent of total expenses go to tuition reimbursement?
A: 10 percent
Q: How many training staff members are there for each employee?
A: 16 staff members for every 1,000 employees
Q: What is the average cost for providing one learning hour to one employee?
A: $74
Q: What is the average cost of producing one hour of formal training?
A: $1,798
Q: What is the ratio of learning hours used to learning hours available?
A: 46 to 1

Delivery Methods

Q: How is training delivered?
A: 47 percent by a instructor in a classroom, 29 percent via blended learning (including both face-to-face and technology delivery), 29 percent online, 1 percent mobile devices, 4 percent social learning
Q: What percentage of direct learning expenditures are allocated to outside providers (i.e., outsourced)?
A: 28 percent

for small firms. The ATD annual *State of the Industry Report* includes hundreds of organizations across all major industries grouped into three categories: companies who have received awards for training, ATD BEST Award winners, Fortune Global 500 companies, and consolidated responses.

You may be asking yourself questions such as, "How much time and money do companies spend on training?" or "Is instructor-delivered training obsolete?" Table 1.7 provides a snapshot of trends in workplace learning. U.S. organizations continue to invest large amounts of money in learning initiatives. Here is an overview of some key trends in these investments:

• Direct expenditures, as a percentage of payroll and learning hours, have remained stable over the last several years.

- There is an increased demand for specialized learning that includes manager, professional, and industry-specific content.
- The use of technology-based learning delivery has increased from 33 percent in 2010 to 39 percent in 2012.
- Self-paced online learning is the most frequently used type of technology-based learning.
- Technology-based learning has helped improve learning efficiency, as shown by decrease in the reuse ration since 2010. (The "reuse ratio" is defined as how much learning content is used or received for every hour of content.) The reuse ratio dropped by 6 percent to 48 hours in 2013. This means that every hour of learning content available was received by about 46 employees. This decrease means that each hour of content was delivered fewer times. A low reuse ratio means new content is being created but not distributed.
- Technology-based learning has resulted in a larger employee–learning staff member ratio.
- The percentage of services distributed by external providers (e.g., consultants, workshops, and training programs) has remained about the same since 2010.
- A high ratio indicates programs being used by more employees, but there are fewer new courses.
- Traditional, instructor-led classroom training continues to be the most popular method.

Of the $61.8 billion spent on training, 63 percent is for internal costs such as training-staff salaries and course development, and 27 percent is for services by external providers (such as consultants, workshops, or training programs outside the company) and 10 percent on tuition reimbursement. After several years of increases in cost per learning hour it fell in 2013, suggesting that companies are more effectively distributing training to employees.

Figure 1.4 shows the different types of training provided by companies. Profession or industry-specific content, managerial and supervisory, and mandatory and compliance account for 34 percent of learning content. The least amount of learning content concerns basic and other skills.

Training Investment Leaders

The chapter's opening vignette illustrates how training can be used by companies to gain a competitive advantage. Higher investment in training by companies in the United States is related to use of innovative training practices and high-performance work practices such as teams, employee stock ownership plans, incentive compensation systems (profit sharing), individual development plans, and employee involvement in business decisions. This spending (along with the use of high-performance work practices) has been shown to be related to improved profitability, customer and employee satisfaction, and the ability to retain employees. For example, companies including Grant Thornton LLP, Wipro Technologies, Steelcase, and InterContinental Hotels Group have recognized that training contributes to their competitiveness. They make a substantial financial investment in training and use it to drive productivity, customer service, and other results important to business. Chapter Two discusses how training can help companies meet their business goals.

FIGURE 1.4 **Different Types of Training Provided by Companies**

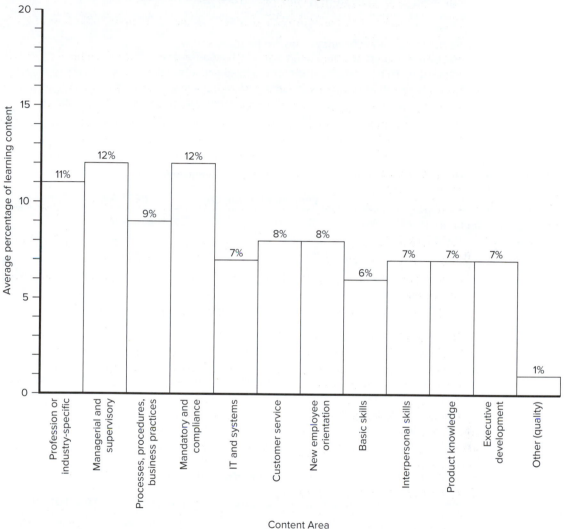

Content Area

Note: Data from consolidate d responses (companies that submitted their annual data as part of ASTD's benchmarking programs).
Source: Based on L. Miller, "2014 State of the Industry" (Alexandria, VA: Association for Talent Development, 2014).

How do the training practices of companies that have recognized training's importance in gaining a competitive advantage differ from other companies? ATD's *State of the Industry Report, 2013* compares the training practices of companies that were part of the ATD Benchmarking program with companies that received ATD BEST Awards (recognizing companies that show a clear link between learning and performance).[121] Benchmarking program companies provided ATD with a standard set of information on their training practices (e.g., number of hours spent on training); these included 340 companies with an average of 16,719 employees. Table 1.8 shows the characteristics of BEST Award–winning

TABLE 1.8
Characteristics of BEST Award Winners

Source: L. Miller, "2014 State of the Industry" (Alexandria, VA: Association for Talent Development, 2014).

Alignment of business strategy with training and development
Learning is valued as part of the culture and supported by executive leaders and top managers
Effectiveness and efficiency of learning is measured
Investment in training and development
Different learning opportunities are provided and all employees have access to them
Measurement of effectiveness and efficiency of training and development activities
Non-training solutions for performance improvement used, including organization development and process improvement

TABLE 1.9   **Comparison of BEST Award Winners and Benchmark Companies**

	Benchmark Company	BEST Award Winner
Amount of training received per employee	32 hours	36 hours
Average cost per learning hour available	$1,798	$1,459
Amount spent on training per employee	$1,208	$1,296
Ratio of learning hours used to learning hours available (reuse ratio)	46.0	78.3

Source: L. Miller, "2014 State of the Industry" (Alexandria, VA: Association for Talent Development, 2014).

companies. As will be discussed in Chapter Two, the BEST Award winners are engaging in strategic training and development—training and development that supports the business's strategies and has measurable outcomes. The BEST Award winners included thirty-three companies with an average of 51,809 employees. Table 1.9 compares the BEST Award winners with the Benchmark companies. As the table shows, companies that were BEST Award winners were able to more efficiently deliver training (less cost, higher reuse ratio) than Benchmark firms. Also, at BEST Award–winning companies employees on average engaged in more learning hours than employees at Benchmark companies.

Roles, Competencies, and Positions of Training Professionals

Trainers can typically hold many jobs, such as instructional designer, technical trainer, or needs analyst. Each job has specific roles or functions. Table 1.10 provides examples of the roles that training and development professionals might take in their jobs. These roles are included in jobs such as organizational change agent, career counselor, instructional designer, and classroom trainer. Training department managers devote considerable time to the roles of business partner and learning strategist. Training department managers may be involved in the project management role, but, because of their other responsibilities, they are involved to a lesser extent than are specialists who hold other jobs. Human resource managers may also be required to complete many of the training roles, although their primary responsibility is in overseeing the human resources functions of the division, department, or company (e.g., staffing, recruiting, compensation, benefits). Special knowledge, skills, or behaviors—also called competencies—are needed to perform each role successfully.

TABLE 1.10 **Training and Development Roles**

Learning Strategist	Determines how workplace learning can be best used to help meet the company's business strategy
Business Partner	Uses business and industry knowledge to create training that improves performance
Project Manager	Plans, obtains, and monitors the delivery of learning and performance solutions to support the business
Professional Specialist	Designs, develops, delivers, and evaluates learning and performance solutions.

Source: Based on M. Allen and J. Naughton, "Social Learning: A Call to Action for Learning Professionals," *T+D* (August 2011): 50–55.

FIGURE 1.5
The ATD Competency Model

Source: From J. Arneson, W. Rothwell, and J. Naughton, "Training and Development Competencies, Redefined to Create Competitive Advantage," *T+D* (January 2013): 42–47.

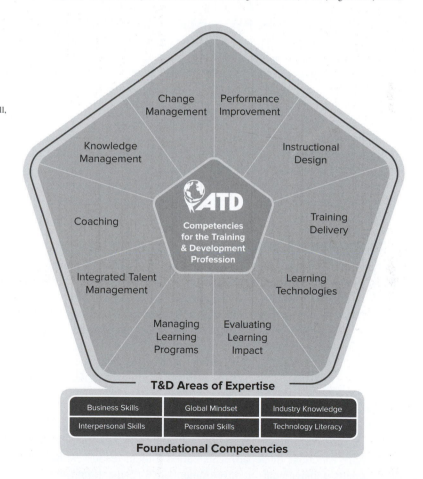

The most comprehensive study of training professionals has been conducted by the ATD.[122] Figure 1.5 shows the ATD competency model. The model describes what it takes for an individual to be successful in the training and development field. It includes specific areas of expertise and foundational competencies. The areas of expertise include knowledge and behaviors required by different roles (e.g., change management, learning technologies, training delivery). Although training professionals spend most of their time designing learning (instructional design), delivering training, managing learning programs, identifying, selecting, and using learning technologies, and coaching (working one-on-one with employees to help them develop), they do spend time in other areas as well. The model recognizes that performance improvement (designing and developing solutions to close performance gaps), talent management (including talent acquisition, development, and retention), and knowledge management are other important areas of expertise.

The foundational competencies anchor the competency model. The foundational competencies include interpersonal skills, business skills, personal skills, global mindset, industry knowledge, and technology literacy. The foundational competencies are important regardless of a trainer's area of expertise or role but are used to a different extent in each role or specialization.

Traditional narrow jobs in the training department focusing on one type of expertise (e.g., instructional designer and technical writer) are changing; having multiple areas of expertise becomes more necessary for training and development to contribute to the business. Project management requires the knowledge of new training technologies (e.g., web-delivered learning, mobile learning, and knowledge management systems) and the ability to manage managers, engineers, scientists, and others who may have more experience, knowledge, or technical savvy than the trainer.

To provide you with an idea of the variety of responsibilities and expertise required for training professional jobs, Table 1.11 provides an example of an instructional system designer job that was posted on the ATD website.

Table 1.12 shows median salaries for training professionals. Keep in mind that very rarely does anyone hold the highest-paying jobs (training manager, executive-level manager) without having developed competencies in a number of training roles.

Who Provides Training?

In most companies, training and development activities are provided by trainers, managers, in-house consultants, and employee experts. However, as the snapshot of training practices suggests, training and development activities are also outsourced. **Outsourcing** means that training and development activities are provided by individuals outside the company. Training providers outside the company include colleges and universities, community and junior colleges, technical and vocational institutions, product suppliers, consultants and consulting firms, unions, trade and professional organizations, and government organizations. Outsourcing is discussed in greater detail in Chapter Two.

Who Is in Charge of Training?

Training and development can be the responsibility of professionals in human resources, human resource development, or organizational development.[123] Companies may also have entire functions or departments called human resources, human resource development, talent management or development, or organizational development that provide training and development.

In small companies, training is the responsibility of the founder and all the employees. When organizations grow to 100 employees, typically someone within the company is in charge of human resources, either as part of that person's job or as his or her sole responsibility. At this point, training becomes one of the responsibilities of the employee in charge

TABLE 1.11
**Example of
Jobs Posted
on the ATD
Website**

Instructional Systems Designer/Developer/Trainer
Role Overview: The job incumbent serves as a consultant and provides hands-on expertise in the areas of adult education methodologies, leadership development, leadership/management training, course design, e-learning, and organizational development. The incumbent of this position is responsible for the performance of duties involved in carrying out the functional responsibilities.

Responsibilities
- Design, develop, and deliver instructor-led, e-learning, or blended training programs, courses, seminars, workshops, and presentations on leadership and management.
- Provide training expertise related to topics such as leadership development, management skills, supervisory training, performance and productivity, conflict management, team building, project teams, business communications, career planning, diversity and inclusion, and interpersonal effectiveness.
- Conduct stand-up training, facilitate learning activities, employ adult learning principles, deliver sessions, provide resources, and advise students.
- Research, design, and evaluate programs, courses, and activities, including selection of media products and animation.
- Design new courses and update existing course designs and training programs.
- Contribute actively to a standard of excellence in carrying out our mission of promoting learning and self-development.
- Serve as facilitator and consultant.
- Lead talent to the highest level of performance and productivity through the creation and use of innovative best practice training and professional development systems, policies, processes, and procedures.

Desired Qualifications
- Master's degree in Instructional Technology, Education, Organization Development, Human Resource Development, Adult Learning, or other related areas.
- Knowledge of and experience in applying Adult Learning Principles.
- Certification and experience in applying one or more assessments (e.g., 5 Dynamics, Myers Briggs, DiSC, StrengthsFinder, Thomas-Kilmann) are highly desired.
- Membership and/or certification in professional organizations are highly desired (e.g., ATD, SHRM, NBCC)

Skills
- Proficient using Adobe tools—eLearning Suite and Master Collection, Camtasia, Adobe Catalyst, Captivate, Photoshop, Illustrator, Macromedia Flash, Premier Pro, and Open Source tools.
- Develop e-learning programs that are SCORM/AICC/Section 508 compliant.
- Experience developing Microsoft SharePoint sites and administration.
- Proficient working with most LMSs and LCMSs.
- Advanced working knowledge using Microsoft Word and PowerPoint, Publisher, Excel, and Outlook.

Experience
- Five plus years of related experience. Diverse work experiences including small and large employer work environments are essential.
- Experience in designing courses, modules, and workshops that incorporate adult education principles and experiential learning techniques; delivering training on supervision and performance management; delivering multiday training programs on leadership

and management topics; writing course designs, course materials, student resource materials, educational aids, and similar educational materials; facilitating discussions, meetings, and training group activities; actively collaborating and contributing to effective teamwork as part of a training team.

Desired Personal Characteristics
- Must be able to function in a multitask environment, as part of a team and individually.
- Must have integrity and high level of interpersonal skills to handle sensitive and confidential issues involving all internal and external customers.
- Work requires continual attention to detail in creating and proofing materials, establishing priorities and meeting deadlines.

Source: From ATD Job Bank http://jobs.td.org/jobs/, accessed March 3, 2015.

TABLE 1.12
Average Salaries for Training Professionals

Source: Based on "Going Up!" *training* (November/December 2014): 34–41.

Executive-Level Training/Human Resource Development Manager	$112,245
Executive-Level Manager	129,053
Training Department Manager (1–5 trainers report to you)	88,658
Training Department Manager (more than 5 trainers report to you)	91,287
One-Person Training Department	68,858
Classroom Instructor/Trainer	68,482
Instructional Designer	71,901
CBT/Web/Multimedia Programmer Designer/Manager	75,432
Management/Career/Organization Development Specialist	81,137
Human Resource Manager/Specialist	75,048

of human resources. In mid-sized to large organizations, training can be the responsibility of human resource professionals, or it can come from a separate function known as human resource development, talent management, development, learning, or organizational development.

Human resource development refers to the integrated use of training and development, organizational development, and career development to improve individual, group, and organizational effectiveness. Human resource development professionals might be involved in job and task analysis, instructional systems design, on-the-job training, and individual performance improvement. Organizational development professionals might focus on training as well as team building, conflict avoidance, employee development, and change management. Talent management professionals might focus on identifying the top talent in the company and ensuring that they get the training and development needed to promote them or prepare them for new positions. Learning professionals might focus on formal training and development activities as well as ensuring that informal learning and knowledge sharing occurs through use of social networking tools. As you can see from these descriptions, training and development activities can be the responsibility of human resource management, human resource development, and organizational development professionals or departments. Keep in mind that regardless of what individual, department, or function is responsible, for training and development to succeed, employees, managers, training professionals, and top managers all have to take ownership for them. Throughout this book, the point is made that although training may be a formal responsibility of someone's job, employees at all levels of the company play a role in the success of training. Also, regardless of which function or department is responsible for training and development, it must be aligned with the business strategy and must support business needs. Professionals who are responsible for training and development may have specialized areas of expertise, such as change management for organizational development specialists, but they may also have training and development responsibilities. As shown in Figure 1.5, to perform workplace learning and performance roles successfully, professionals must understand the business and must master the competencies and areas of expertise.

As companies grow and/or recognize the important role of training for business success, they form an entire training or learning function (how training functions can be organized is discussed in Chapter Two). The training function may include instructional designers, instructors, technical training, and experts in instructional technology.

The reporting relationship between human resource management and the training function varies across companies.[124] Some organizations include training as part of the human resource function, believing that this provides strategic partnerships with other business functions and consistent companywide training. For example, at Life Care Centers of America, a Tennessee-based company that operates elder care facilities, training is included in the human resource department because the company believes that training is part of human resource expertise, including the ability to write training curriculum and evaluate learning. Being centrally located in the human resource department makes the best use of resources and helps communicate a common management culture.

Other companies separate training from the human resource function because it allows the training function to be decentralized to better respond to unique needs in different business units. The training and development department at A. G. Edwards has a learning center and develops training programs for its financial consultants and employees.[125] Representatives of the training department regularly meet with the company's management committee at corporate headquarters, as well as with regional officers and branch managers to help them understand how training can support business objectives. A new branch manager certification program succeeded because the branch managers were involved in identifying skill gaps and their suggestions were used in the program design. The branch managers took ownership of the program and helped develop the program proposal that they then presented to corporate managers to receive funding and approval for the program. Regardless of the organizational approach used for the training function, it must help meet the training needs of the business.

Preparing to Work in Training

Everyone is a trainer at some point in his or her life. Consider the last time you had to teach some skill to a peer, sibling, spouse, friend, or even your boss. Although some people learn to train by trial and error, the best way is to take courses in training and development, or even choose an academic major related to training. For example, training and development courses are usually found in education, business and management, and psychology departments at colleges and universities. Business schools may offer undergraduate and graduate degrees in human resource management with courses in training and development, talent management, and organizational development. Education departments may have undergraduate and graduate degrees in human resource development and learning. Courses offered with such degrees include instructional design, curriculum development, adult learning, evaluation, and on-the-job training. Psychology departments offer courses in training and development as well. These courses can be part of a degree program in industrial and organizational psychology. If you are fortunate enough to be at a large university, you may have the opportunity to take courses from education, business/management, and the psychology departments that relate to training and development. Also, you should consider the competencies you want to focus on and think about how you will master them (courses, work experience, ATD certification).

To be a successful training professional requires staying up-to-date on current research and training practices. The primary professional organizations for persons interested in training and development include ATD, the Academy of Human Resource Development (AHRD), the SHRM, the Society for Industrial and Organizational Psychology (SIOP), the Academy of Management (AOM), and the International Society for Performance Improvement (ISPI). The web addresses for these organizations are listed inside the front cover of this book. Articles about training practices can be found in the following journals: *Training, T+D, Training and Development, Chief Learning Officer, Workforce Management, HR Magazine, Academy of Management Executive,* and *Academy of Management Learning and Education.* Training and development research can be found in the following journals: *Human Resource Development Quarterly, Human Resource Development Review, Performance Improvement, Personnel Psychology, Journal of Applied Psychology, Academy of Management Journal,* and *Human Resource Management.*

Key Terms

competitiveness, *6*
competitive advantage, *6*
human resource management, *6*
stakeholders, *7*
learning, *7*
training, *8*
human capital, *8*
development, *8*
formal training and development, *8*
informal learning, *8*
explicit knowledge, *9*
knowledge management, *9*
tacit knowledge, *9*

training design process, *10*
Instructional System Design (ISD), *11*
offshoring, *17*
intellectual capital, *18*
social capital, *18*
customer capital, *18*
knowledge workers, *19*
employee engagement, *20*
change, *21*
learning organization, *21*
talent management, *26*
STEM, *29*

Total Quality Management (TQM), *31*
Malcolm Baldrige National Quality Award, *31*
ISO 9000:2000, *31*
Six Sigma process, *34*
lean thinking, *34*
ISO 10015, *34*
alternative work arrangements, *38*
work teams, *39*
cross training, *39*
virtual teams, *40*
outsourcing, *46*
human resource development, *48*

Discussion Questions

1. Describe the forces affecting the workplace and learning. How can training help companies deal with these forces?

2. Discuss the relationship between formal training and development, informal learning, and knowledge management. How are they related to learning and creating a learning organization?

3. What steps are included in the training design model? What step do you think is most important? Why?

4. What are intangible assets? How do they relate to training and development?

5. How are companies using training and development to benefit them in today's economy?

6. Training professionals continue to debate whether the ISD model is flawed. Some argue that ISD should be treated as a project management approach rather than a step-by-step recipe for building training programs. Others suggest that ISD is too linear and rigid a process—that it is the primary reason training is expensive, and that it takes too long to develop. ISD focuses on inputs; management wants outputs. Businesses want results, not the use of a design technology. Do you believe that ISD is a useful process? Why or why not? Are there certain situations when it is a more (or less) effective way to design training?

7. Which of the training professionals' roles do you believe is most difficult to learn? Which is easiest?

8. How might technology influence the importance of training professionals' roles? Can technology reduce the importance of any of the roles? Can it result in additional roles?

9. Describe the training courses that you have taken. How have they helped you? Provide recommendations for improving the courses.

10. How does training differ between companies that are considered BEST Award winners and those that are not?

11. What are the implications of generational differences in the workforce? What strategies should companies consider from a training and development perspective to cope with generational differences and use them to benefit the company?

12. How has new technology improved training and development? What are some of the limitations of using smart phones or notebooks for training?

13. Explain how training relates to attracting new employees, employee retention, and motivation.

14. What is the relationship between talent management and employee engagement? What role can training and development practices play in keeping employee engagement high? Explain.

15. How can training, informal learning, and knowledge management benefit from the use of social collaboration tools like Twitter and Facebook? Identify the social collaboration tool and explain the potential benefits gained by using it.

Application Assignments

1. Go to the Association for Talent Development (ATD) home page on the World Wide Web. The address is *www.td.org*. Review the jobs found under "Featured Jobs." Choose a job that interests you and explain why. Based on the ATD competency model presented in the chapter, discuss the roles, areas of expertise, and competencies needed in this job.

2. Go to *www.nist.gov/baldrige/* the website for the National Institute of Standards and Technology (NIST). NIST oversees the Malcolm Baldrige Quality Award. Click on "Learn the Value." Watch the "Getting Results" video. How do companies benefit from winning the Baldrige Quality Reward? What value could a company get from competing for the award even if they don't win it?

3. NewBarista has created a barista skills training program. Go to *www.newbarista.com*. Click on "About Us" to learn about NewBarista. Next click on "Features," and watch the video "Online Barista Training." What technologies does this program use for training delivery and instruction? How do they contribute to helping baristas learn the skills needed to make a great cup of coffee?

4. Conduct a phone or personal interview with a manager or training manager. Ask this person to describe the role that training plays in his or her company; changes, if any, they have seen in training in the past five years; and how they believe it will change in the future.

5. In January 2015, Training identified the Top 125 companies for training. The top 10 ranked companies were:

   1. Keller Williams Realty Inc.
   2. Jiffy Lube International
   3. Capital BlueCross
   4. CHG Health Services
   5. Blue Cross Blue Shield of Michigan
   6. ABF Freight Systems
   7. McCarthy Building Companies Inc.
   8. Wequassett Resort and Golf Club
   9. Capital One
   10. Nationwide Mutual Insurance Company

Choose one of these companies to research. Visit the company's website, use a web search engine, or look for references to the company in publications such as *training, T + D, Workforce*, or *HR Magazine*. Prepare a report (not to exceed three pages) based on your research (a) describing why you believe the company was ranked in the top 10, and (b) explaining the relationship between training and the company's competitiveness, business goals, and objectives. Your instructor will advise you on whether the report should be submitted electronically or on hard copy. (Hint: Possible reasons a company might be ranked include the amount of money it devotes to training, the level of employee involvement in training, and the type of training used.)

Case

Zappos: *Facing Competitive Challenges*

Zappos, based in Las Vegas, is an online retailer. Its initial goal has been to be the best website for buying shoes, offering a wide variety of brands, styles, colors, sizes, and widths. The zappos.com brand has grown to offer shoes, handbags, eyewear, watches, and accessories for online purchase. Zappos's vision is that in the future, online sales will account for 30 percent of all retail sales in the United States, and Zappos will be the company with the best service and selection. As a result, Zappos believes that it can become the online service leader, drawing customers and expanding into selling other products. Zappos believes that the speed at which a customer receives an online purchase plays a critical role in how that customer thinks about shopping online again in the future, so it focuses on making sure that items get delivered to customers as quickly as possible.

In 2009, Zappos was acquired by the Amazon.com, Inc. family of companies, which share a strong passion for customer service. In 2010, Zappos had experienced tremendous growth, resulting in the need to restructure the company. Zappos was restructured into ten separate companies under the Zappos family umbrella, including Zappos.com, Inc. (the management company) and companies devoted to retail, gift cards, merchandising, and order fulfillment. Zappos has received many awards for its workplace culture and practices, including being recognized by *Fortune* magazine in 2013 as the #31 Best Company to Work For.

Zappos CEO Tony Heish has shaped the company's culture, brand, and business strategy around 10 core values:

1. Deliver WOW Through Service
2. Embrace and Drive Change
3. Create Fun and a Little Weirdness
4. Be Adventurous, Creative, and Open-Minded
5. Pursue Growth and Learning
6. Build Open and Honest Relationships with Communication
7. Build a Positive Team and Family Spirit
8. Do More with Less
9. Be Passionate and Determined
10. Be Humble

Deliver WOW Through Service means that call center employees need to provide excellent customer service. Call center employees encourage callers to order more than one size or color because shipping and return shipping are free. They are also encouraged to use their imaginations to meet customer needs.

Zappos's employment practices help to perpetuate its company culture. For example, the HR team uses unusual interview questions, such as "How weird are you?" and "What's your theme song?" to find employees who are creative and have strong individuality. Zappos provides free breakfast, lunch (cold cuts) and snacks, and a full-time life coach (employees have to sit on a red velvet throne to complain). Managers are encouraged to spend time with employees outside the office, and any employee can reward another employee a $50 bonus for good performance. Most employees at Zappos are hourly. All new hires complete four weeks of training, including two weeks working the phones. New recruits are offered $2,000 to leave the company during training—an unusual practice designed to weed out individuals who will not be happy working at the company.

To reinforce the importance of the ten core values, Zappos performance management system asks managers to evaluate how well employee behavior demonstrates the core values, such as acting humble or expressing their personality. To evaluate task performance, managers are asked to provide employees with regular status reports on such things as how much time they spend on the telephone with customers. The status reports and evaluations of the core values are informational or used to identify training needs. Zappos believes in helping others understand what inspired the company culture. The company created the Zappos.com library, which provides a collection of books about creating a passion for customer service, products, and local communities. These books can be found in the front lobby of Zappos offices and are widely read and discussed by company employees.

Zappos also believes that its culture is enhanced through use of social media, including blogs and Twitter, that links employees with one another and with the company's customers. Also, Zappos takes the pulse of the organization monthly, measuring the health of the culture with a happiness survey. Employees respond to such unlikely questions as whether they believe that the company has a higher purpose than profits, whether their own role has meaning, whether they feel in control of their career path, whether they consider their co-workers to be like family and friends, and whether they are happy in their jobs. Results from the survey are broken down by department, and opportunities for development are identified and acted upon. For example, when it was clear from the survey that one department had veered off course and felt isolated from the rest of the organization, a program was instituted that enabled individuals in the group to learn more about how integral their work was. To keep the company

vibrant, CEO Tony Hsieh is spending $350 million to develop a neighborhood in downtown Las Vegas, which will be the home of Zappos.Com new headquarters. Hseih wants to provide employees with a great place to work as well as to live and socialize.

Visit the Zappos website at *www.zappos.com*. Go to the bottom of the page under "About" and click on "about." Review the videos, the media kit, and the information provided about customer service, the family story, the culture, and the values. Review the Tweets especially those focusing on training, learning, and development.

What challenges is Zappos facing that may derail its attempt to be the best online retailer? How can training and development help Zappos meet these challenges? Do you think that employees at Zappos have high levels of engagement? Why? Which of Zappos's ten core values do you believe training and development can influence the most? The least? Why?

Sources: Based on the Zappos website, *www.zappos.com*; J. O'Brien, "Zappos Knows How to Kick It," *Fortune* (February 2, 2009): 55–66; M. Moskowitz and R. Levering, "The 100 Best Companies to Work For," *Fortune* (February 4, 2013): 85–96; D. Richard, "At Zappos, Culture Pays," *strategy+business* (August 2010): 60, accessed from *www.strategy-business.com*, March 15, 2013; K. Gurchiek, "Delivering HR at Zappos," *HR Magazine* (June 2011): 44; R. Pyrillis, "The reviews are in," *Workforce Management* (May 2011): 20–25.

Endnotes

1. R. Ployhart, T. Moliterno, "Emergence of the human capital resource: A multilevel model," *Academy of Management Review*, 36 (2011): 127–150; B. Campbell, R. Coff, and D. Kryscynski, "Rethinking sustained competitive advantage from human capital," *Academy of Management Review*, 37 (2010): 376–395; T. Crook, S. Todd, J. Combs, D. Woehr, and D. Ketchen, Jr., "Does human capital matter? A meta-analysis of the relationship between human capital and firm performance," *Journal of Applied Psychology*, 96 (2011): 443–456.

2. J. Roy, "Transforming informal learning into a competitive advantage," *T+D* (October 2010): 23–25; P. Galagan, "Unformal, the new normal," *T+D* (September 2010): 29–31.

3. S. I. Tannenbaum, R. Beard, L. A. McNall, and E. Salas, "Informal Learning and Development in Organizations," in *Learning, Training, and Development in Organizations,* eds. S.W.J. Kozlowski and E. Salas (New York: Routledge, 2010); D. J. Bear, H. B. Tompson, C. L. Morrison, M. Vickers, A. Paradise, M. Czarnowsky, M. Soyars, and K. King, 2008. *Tapping the Potential of Informal Learning: An ASTD Research Study* (Alexandria, VA: American Society for Training and Development).

4. T. Bingham and M. Conner, *The New Social Learning* (Alexandria, VA: ASTD Press, 2010).

5. I. Nonaka and H. Takeuchi, *The Knowledge-Creating Company: How Japanese Companies Create the Dynamics of Innovation* (New York: Oxford University Press, 1995).

6. D. DeLong and L. Fahey, "Diagnosing cultural barriers to knowledge management," *Academy of Management Executive*, 14 (2000): 113–117; A. Rossett, "Knowledge management meets analysis," *Training and Development* (May 1999): 63–68.

7. J. Salopek, "Where training can make the difference between life and death," *T+D* (October 2014): 80–82.

8. V. Powers, "Virtual communities at Caterpillar foster knowledge sharing," *T+D* (June 2004) : 40–45.

9. M. Green and E.McGill, *State of the Industry*, 2011 (Alexandria, VA: American Society for Training and Development, 2011); M. Weinstein, "Long-range learning plans," *training* (November/December 2010): 38–41.

10. L. Freifeld, "PWC does it again," *training* (February 2009): 24–28.

11. M. Molenda, "In search of the elusive ADDIE model," *Performance Improvement* (May/June 2003): 34–36; C. Allen (ed.), "ADDIE training system revisited," *Advances in Developing Human Resources,* 8 (2006): 427–555.

12. G. Snelbecker, "Practical Ways for Using Theories and Innovations to Improve Training," in *The ASTD Handbook of Instructional Technology,* ed. G. Piskurich (Burr Ridge, IL: Irwin/McGraw-Hill, 1993): 19.3–19.26.

13. "ITU AbsorbTech" *T+D* (October 2014): 97.

14. R. Zemke and A. Rosett, "A hard look at ISD," *training* (February 2002): 26–34; R. Brinkerhoff and A. Apking, *High-Impact Learning.* (Perseus Publishing, 2001)

15. R. Chevalier, "When did ADDIE become addie?" *Performance Improvement* (July 2011):10–14.

16. M. Andrade, "Crowdsource your next program design," *T+D* (March 2012): 52–56.

17. H. Dolezalek, "Who has the time to design?" *training* (January 2006): 25–28.

18. "Action items: 42 trends affecting benefits, compensation, training, staffing, and technology," *HR Magazine* (January 2013): 33–35; "2015 State of Talent Management Research Report" (February 10, 2015), *Human Resources Executive*, from *www.hreonline.com*; *SHRM Workplace Forecast* (Alexandria, VA: Society for Human Resource Management, 2013).

19. Y. Kim and R. E. Ployhart, "The effects of staffing and training on firm productivity and profit growth before, during, and after the great recession," *Journal of Applied Psychology*, 99, 361–389.

20. U.S. Bureau of Labor Statistics, "Productivity and costs, fourth quarter and annual averages 2014, preliminary," February 5, 2015, from http://data.bls.gov, accessed February 20, 2015; J. Sparshott, "Hiring booms but soft wages linger," *Wall Street Journal* (January 10–11, 2015), A1–2; E. Morath, "Brisk jobs growth puts Fed on notice," *Wall Street Journal* (March 7–8, 2015), A1–2.

21. "Optimism about US economy driving private-company expansion plans, according to latest PwC survey," April 29, 2014, from *www.pwc.com/us/en/press-releases*, accessed February 20, 2015.

22. "Good to grow: 2014 US CEO Survey," PricewaterhouseCoopers LLP, from *www.pwc.com*, accessed February 20, 2015.

23. U.S. Bureau of Labor Statistics, "Employment situation summary" (February 6, 2015), from http://data.bls.gov, accessed February 20, 2015; P. Coy, "2015: A Users Guide," *Bloomberg Business Week* (November 10, 2014–January 6, 2015): 22–28; R. Neate, "US Growth Rate Slips to 2.6% Raising Doubts About the Strength of Economy," *www.the guardian.com/business*, accessed February 20, 2015.

24. "Good to Grow: 2014 US CEO Survey," PricewaterhouseCoopers LLP, from *www.pwc.com*, accessed February 20, 2015.

25. "The Starbucks college achievement plan," from http://www.starbucks.com/careers/college-plan, accessed February 20, 2015; Starbucks, Magna Cum Grande, Bloomberg Business Week (June 23, 2014): page 14; P. Ziobro and E. Morath, "Wal-Mart lifts pay as market gets tighter," *Wall Street Journal* (February 20, 2015): A1–2.

26. "Manufacturing: Engine of U.S. innovation," *National Association of Manufacturing* (October 4, 2006), available at website *www.nam.org* (January 21, 2009).

27. I. Bremmer, "The new world of business," *Fortune* (February 1, 2015): 86–92.

28. D. Wessel, "Big U.S. firms shift hiring abroad," *The Wall Street Journal* (April 19, 2011): B1–B2.

29. "Gap Inc. has continued to grow around the world" (October 2014), from *www.gapinc.com*, accessed February 27, 2015.

30. "2013 Annual Review," from *www.coca-cola.com*, accessed February 26, 2015; "Coca-Cola invests an additional US$5 billion for long-term sustainable growth in Africa," August 5, 2014, from *www.coca-cola .com /press-center/press-releases,* accessed February 26, 2015.

31. "2013 Yum! Brands Annual Report," from http://www.yum.com/annualreport/, accessed February 27, 2015; A Gasparro, "Yum sees rise in international earning" (December 9, 2011), from http://*www.market watch.com/story/yum-brands-sees-rise-in-international-earnings-2011-12-09*, accessed February 27, 2015.

32. "McDonald's to enter new market of Kazakhstan in 2015," press release (November 12, 2014); "McDonald's announces official opening of first restaurant in Vietnam," press release (February 10, 2014) from http://*news.mcdonalds.com/Corporate/Press-Releases*, accessed February 27, 2015; "Our facility," from *www.aboutmcdonalds.com/mcd/corporate_careers/training_and_development/hamburger_university /our_faculty.html*, accessed February 27, 2015.

33. C. Hymowitz, "IBM combines volunteer service, teamwork to cultivate emerging markets," *The Wall Street Journal* (August 4, 2008): B6, "Corporate Service Corps," *www.ibm.com*, accessed March 3, 2015.

34. M. Horrigan, "Employment projections to 2012: Concepts and contexts," *Monthly Labor Review,* 127 (February 2004): 3–22.

35. "The people problem," *Inc.* (May 29, 2001): 84–85.

36. "Manufacturing: Engine of U.S. innovation." *National Association of Manufacturing* (October 4, 2006), available at website *www.nam.org* (January 21, 2009).

37. R. Zeidner, "Does the United States need foreign workers?" *HR Magazine* (June 2009): 42–47; U.S. Department of Homeland Security, *Yearbook of Immigration Statistics: 2009*. Washington, D.C.: U.S. Department of Homeland Security, Office of Immigration Statistics, 2010.

38. J. Hagerty and M. Magnier, "Companies tiptoe back toward 'Made in America,'" *Wall Street Journal* (January 14, 2015): A1, A12.

39. J. Hagerty and M. Magnier, "Companies tiptoe back toward 'Made in America,'" *Wall Street Journal* (January 14, 2015): A1, A12.

40. J. Hagerty, "Decimated U.S. industry pulls up its socks," *Wall Street Journal* (December 26, 2014): B6.

41. I. Sherr, "Apple says China partner made changes for workers," *The Wall Street Journal* (February 15, 2011): B5.

42. L. Weatherly, *Human Capital—The Elusive Asset* (Alexandria, VA: SHRM Research Quarterly, 2003).

43. S. Sung and Choi, "Do organizations spend wisely on employees? Effects of training and development investments on learning and innovation in organizations," *Journal of Organizational Behavior,* 35 (2014): 393–412; H. Aguinis, and K. Kraiger, "Benefits of training and development for individuals, teams, organizations, and society," *Annual Review of Psychology,* 60 (2009): 451–474.

44. L. Bassi, J. Ludwig, D. McMurrer, and M. Van Buren, *Profiting from Learning: Do Firms' Investments in Education and Training Pay Off?* (Alexandria, VA: American Society for Training and Development, September 2000).

45. J. Barney, *Gaining and Sustaining Competitive Advantage* (Upper Saddle River, NJ: Prentice Hall, 2002).

46. W. Zeller, "Southwest: After Kelleher, more blue skies," *BusinessWeek* (April 2, 2001): 45; S. McCartney, "Southwest sets standards on costs," *The Wall Street Journal* (October 10, 2002): A2; S. Warren and M. Trottman, "Southwest's Dallas duel," *The Wall Street Journal* (May 10, 2005): B1, B4.

47. R. Dodes, "At Macy's, a makeover on service," *The Wall Street Journal* (April 11, 2011): B10.

48. R. Vance, *Employee Engagement and Commitment* (Alexandria, VA: Society for Human Resource Management (SHRM) Foundation, 2006).

49. Ibid.

50. Gallup, "State of the American Workplace: Employee Engagement Insights for US Business Leaders" (Washington, DC: Gallup, Inc. 2013); "American employees hold back their full potential," *T+D* (September 2013): 17.

51. "Bridgepoint Education," *T+D* (October 2014): 87.

52. B. Ware, "Stop the Gen Y revolving door," *T+D* (May 2014): 58–63.

53. M. Weinstein, "Mohawk's training floors the competition," *training* (January/February 2014): 52–55.

54. M. Ciccarelli, "Keeping the Keepers," *Human Resource Executive* (January/February 2011): 1-20–1-23.

55. J. Meister and K. Willyerd, *The 2020 Workplace* (New York: HarperCollins, 2010).

56. M. Weinstein, "Capital BlueCross Rx for change," *training* (January/February 2014): 44–46.

57. L. Weber, "Just Whose Job Is It To Train Workers," *Wall Street Journal* (July 17, 2014): B1, B5.

58. D. Senge, "The learning organization made plain and simple," *Training and Development Journal* (October 1991): 37–44.

59. L. Thornburg, "Accounting for knowledge," *HR Magazine* (October 1994): 51–56.

60. G. Kranz, "More to learn," *Workforce Management* (January 2011): 27–30.

61. M. Weinstein, "Are you linked in?" *training* (September/October 2010): 30–33.

62. Bureau of Labor Statistics, U.S. Department of Labor, "Employment projections: 2012–2022," News Release, December 19, 2013, from *www.bls.gov/emp*, accessed February 25, 2015.

63. Bureau of Labor Statistics, U.S. Department of Labor, "Employment projections: 2012–2022," News Release, December 19, 2013, from *www.bls.gov/emp*, accessed February 25, 2015.

64. Bureau of Labor Statistics, U.S. Department of Labor, "Employment projections: 2012–2022," News Release, December 19, 2013, from *www.bls.gov/emp*, accessed February 25, 2015.

65. N. Lockwood, *The Aging Workforce* (Alexandria, VA: Society for Human Resource Management, 2003). S. Milligan, "Wisdom of the Ages," *HR Magazine* (November 2014): 22–27.

66. S. Hewlett, L. Sherbin, and K. Sumberg, "How Gen Y and Boomers will reshape your agenda" *Harvard Business Review* (July–August 2009): 71–76; A. Fox, "Mixing it up," *HR Magazine* (May 2011): 22–27; K. Ball and G. Gotsill, *Surviving the Baby Boomer Exodus* (Boston: Cengage, 2011). K. Tyler, "New Kids on the Block," *HR Magazine* (October 2013): 35–40; S. Mulligan, "Wisdom of the Ages," *HR Magazine* (November 2014): 23–27.

67. J. Meriac, D. Woehr, and C. Banister, "Generational differences in work ethic: An examination of measurement equivalence across three cohorts," *Journal of Business and Psychology*, 25 (2010): 315–324; K. Real, A. Mitnick, and W. Maloney, "More similar than different: Millennials in the U.S. building trades," *Journal of Business and Psychology*, 25 (2010): 303–313. S. Lyons and L. Kuron, "Generational differences in the workplace: A review of the evidence and directions for future research," *Journal of Organizational Behavior*, 35 (2013): 139–157.

68. J. Deal, D. Altman, and S. Rogelberg, "Millennials at work: What we know and what we need to do (if anything)," *Journal of Business and Psychology*, 25 (2010): 191–199.

69. A. Fox, "Mixing it up," *HR Magazine* (May 2011): 22–27.

70. 2010 Society for Human Resource Management Workplace Diversity Practices study. Available at *www.shrm.org*, website for the Society for Human Resource Management.

71. M. Toosi, "Labor force projections to 2018: Older workers staying more active" *Monthly Labor Review* (November 2009): 30–51; M. Loden and J. B. Rosener, *Workforce America!* (Burr Ridge, IL: Business One Irwin, 1991); N. Lockwood, *The Aging Workforce* (Alexandria, VA: Society for Human Resource Management, 2003).

72. AARP website, *www.aarp.org*, "2009 AARP Best Employers for Workers Over 50," accessed May 6, 2011; S. Hewlett, L. Sherbin, and K. Sumberg, "How Gen Y and Boomers will reshape your agenda," *Harvard Business Review* (July–August 2009): 71–76; A. Ort, "Embrace differences when training intergenerational groups," *T+D* (April 2014): 60–65; S. Milligan, "Wisdom of the ages," *HR Magazine* (November 2014): 22–27.

73. J. Salopek, "Retaining women," *T+D* (September 2008): 24–27.

74. A. McIlvaine, "Millennials in charge," *Human Resource Executive* (January/February 2015): 12–14.

75. K. Kuehner-Hebert, "Teaching collaboration at MasterCard: Priceless," *Chief Learning Officer* (November 2014): 24–27.

76. M. O'Brien, "What's keeping you up now?" *Human Resource Executive* (September 2, 2011): 30–33; re:SEARCH, "Want to keep employees happy? Offer learning and development," *T+D* (April 2005): 18; P. Cappelli, "Talent management for the twenty-first century," *Harvard Business Review* (March 2008): 74–81.

77. K. Fyfe-Mills, "Committed to talent development excellence," *T+D* (October 2014): 38–41.

78. R. Woods, "Industry output and employment projections to 2018" *Monthly Labor Review* (November 2009): 52–81. Bureau of Labor Statistics, U.S. Department of Labor, "Employment projections: 2012–2022," News Release, December 19, 2013, from *www.bls.gov/emp*, accessed February 25, 2015.

79. P. Wiseman, "U.S. a lean, mean factory machine," *Columbus Dispatch* (January 31, 2011): A3.

80. Bureau of Labor Statistics, U.S. Department of Labor, "Employment projections: 2012–2022," News Release, December 19, 2013, from *www.bls.gov/emp*, accessed February 25, 2015; S. Milligan, "Wisdom of the ages," *HR Magazine* (November 2014): 22–27; C. Paullin, *The Aging Workforce: Leveraging the Talents of Mature Employees* (Alexandria, VA, SHRM Foundation, 2014).

81. J. Salopek, "The new brain drain," *T+D* (June 2005): 23–25; P. Harris, "Beware of the boomer brain drain!" *T+D* (January 2006): 30–33; M. McGraw, "Bye-bye boomers," *Human Resource Executive* (March 2, 2006): 34–37; J. Phillips, M. Pomerantz, and S. Gully, "Plugging the boomer drain," *HR Magazine* (December 2007): 54–58.

82. K. Cavanaughon, "The brain drain: Using technology to capture retiring boomer knowledge," from *www.tlnt.com*, accessed March 4, 2015; M. Harper, "Ways ConocoPhillips created a wiki that people actually use," from *www.apqc.org/blob*, accessed March 4, 2015.

83. R. Davenport, "Eliminate the skills gap," *T+D* (February 2006): 26–34; M. Schoeff Jr., "Amid calls to bolster U.S. innovation, experts lament paucity of basic math skills," *Workforce Management* (March 2006): 46–49.

84. "Good to grow: 2014 US CEO Survey," PricewaterhouseCoopers LLP, from *www.pwc.com*, accessed February 20, 2015; P. Gaul, "Nearly half of U.S. executives are concerned about skills gap," *T+D* (February 2014): 18; "2014 Accenture manufacturing skills & training study," from *www.themanufacturinginstitute.org*, accessed March 2, 2015; Organization for Economic Cooperation and Development (OECD), "Survey of Adult Skills," 2013, from http://*skills.oecd.org*, accessed February 20, 2015.

85. E. Krell, "The global talent mismatch," *HR Magazine* (June 2011): 68–73. Organization for Economic Cooperation and Development (OECD), "Skilled for life? Key findings from the Survey of Adult Skills," 2013, from http://*skills.oecd.org*, accessed February 20, 2015.

86. S. Wartenberg, "No snow days," *Columbus Dispatch* (February 22, 2015): D3.

87. M. Lev-Ram, "The business case for STEM," *Fortune* (February 1, 2015): 20; J. Cook-Ramirez, "STEM-ing the tide," *Human Resource Executive* (September 2014): 27–31.

88. Towers-Perrin, *Talent Management: The State of the Art* (Towers-Perrin, Chicago, IL, 2005).

89. A. Dohm, "Gauging the labor force effects of retiring babyboomers," *Monthly Labor Review* (July 2000): 17–25.

90. C. Paullin, *The Aging Workforce: Leveraging the Talents of Mature Employees* (Alexandria, VA, SHRM Foundation, 2014).

91. "Millennials: From generational differences to generating growth," from Development Dimensions Inc., http://www.ddiworld.com/DDI/media/trend-research/glf2014-findings/millennials_glf2014_ddi.pdf, *accessed February 20, 2015; "Millennials at work: Reshaping the workplace in financial services,"* from *www.pwc.com/financial services*, accessed February 26, 2015; E. Sinar, "Perspective: Are millennials ready to lead," from *GOMagazine*, http://www.ddiworld.com/go/archive/2012-issue-1/perspective-millennials-are-ready-to-lead, accessed February 20, 2015.

92. A. McIlvaine, "Millennials in charge," *Human Resource Executive* (January/February 2015): 12–14.

93. J. R. Jablonski, *Implementing Total Quality Management: An Overview* (San Diego: Pfeiffer, 1991).

94. R. Hodgetts, F. Luthans, and S. Lee, "New paradigm organizations: From total quality to learning to world-class," *Organizational Dynamics* (Winter 1994): 5–19.

95. "Malcolm Baldrige National Quality Award 2014 Award Recipient, Service Category, PricewaterhouseCoopers Public Sector Practice," from *www.nist.gov/baldrige/award_recpients*, accessed February 24, 2015; "Malcolm Baldrige National Quality Award 2012 Award Recipient, Small Business Category, MESA Products, Inc.," from *www.nist.gov/baldrige/award_recpients*, accessed February 24, 2015.

96. "ISO in One Page," "Quality Management Principles," "ISO 9000 Essentials," and "Management and Leadership Standards," from *www.iso.org*, accessed April 9, 2011.

97. General Electric 2014 Annual Report. Available at *www.ge.com*. "What is Six Sigma?" from http://www.ge.com/en/company/companyinfo/quality/whatis.htm, accessed March 3, 2015.

98. "Baylor Health Care System: Lean and process improvement training," *training* (January/February 2014): 106.

99. L. Yiu and R. Saner, "Does it pay to train? ISO 10015 assures the quality and return on investment of training," *ISO Management Systems* (March–April 2005): 9–13.

100. L. Morales, "Google and Facebook users, skew young, affluent, and educated," February 17, 2011, *www.gallup.com*. "Census Bureau's American Community Survey provides new state and local income, poverty, health insurance statistics," September 18, 2014, from http://www.census.gov/newsroom/press-releases/2014/cb14-170.html, accessed February 27, 2015.

101. D. Gayeski, "Goin' mobile," *T+D* (November 2004): 46–51; D. Hartley, "Pick up your PDA," *T+D* (February 2004): 22–24.

102. M. Derven, "Social networking: A frame for development," *T+D* (July 2009): 58–63; J. Arnold, "Twittering and Facebooking while they work," *HR Magazine* (December 2009): 53–55.

103. C. Goodman, "Employers wrestle with social-media policies," *The Columbus Dispatch* (January 30, 2011): D3.

104. "Manufacturing: Engine of U.S. Innovation," *National Association of Manufacturing* (October 4, 2006). Available at *www.nam.org* (January 21, 2009).

105. D. Wakabayashi, "Japanese farms look to the 'cloud,'" *The Wall Street Journal* (January 18, 2011): B5.

106. L. Freifeld, "Verizon's #1 calling," *training* (January/February 2013): 26–32; J. J. Salopek, "Good connections," *T+D* (October 2014): 48–50; "Verizon," *training* (January/February 2014): 58.

107. A. Weintraub, "High tech's future is in the toy chest," *BusinessWeek* (August 26, 2002): 124–126.

108. N. Shah, "More Americans are working remotely," *Wall Street Journal* (March 6, 2013): A3.

109. P. Marinova, "Who works from home and when," (February 28, 2013), from *www.cnn.com*, accessed February 28, 2013; C. Suddath, "Work-from-home truths, half-truths, and myths," *Bloomberg Business Week* (March 4–March 10, 2013): 75; R. Silverman and Q. Fottrell, "The home office in the spotlight," *Wall Street Journal* (February 27, 2013): B6; N. Shah, "More Americans working from home remotely," *Wall Street Journal* (April 6, 2013): A3.

110. R. Silverman and Q. Fottrell, "The home office in the spotlight," *Wall Street Journal* (February 27, 2013): B6.

111. D. Meinert, "Make telecommuting pay off," *HR Magazine* (June 2011): 32–37.

112. Bureau of Labor Statistics, "Contingent and Alternative Employment Arrangements, February 2005" from *www.bls.gov*, the website for the Bureau of Labor Statistics (accessed January 21, 2009).

113. R. Zeidner, "Heady debate," *HR Magazine* (February 2010): 28–33.

114. A. Fox, "At work in 2020," *HR Magazine* (January 2010): 18–23.

115. P. Choate and P. Linger, *The High-Flex Society* (New York: Knopf, 1986); P. B. Doeringer, *Turbulence in the American Workplace* (New York: Oxford University Press, 1991).

116. K. A. Miller, *Retraining the American Workforce* (Reading, MA: Addison-Wesley, 1989).

117. J. Marquez, "Engine of change," *Workforce Management* (July 17, 2006): 20–30. Global Engineering Manufacturing Alliance website at *www.gemaengine.com*, "Dundee Engine Plant" from *www.media.chrysler.com/newsrelease*, accessed March 3, 2015.

118. J. Neal and C. Tromley, "From incremental change to retrofit: Creating high-performance work systems," *Academy of Management Executive,* 9 (1995): 42–54; M. Huselid, "The impact of human resource management practices on turnover, productivity, and corporate financial performance," *Academy of Management Journal,* 38 (1995): 635–72.

119. B. Reynolds, "Twenty-six companies that thrive on remote work" (March 14, 2014), from http://www.flexjobs.com, accessed March 3, 2015; Art & Logic company website at http://www.artandlogic.com/about, accessed March 3, 2015.

120. L. Miller, "2014 State of the Industry" (Alexandria, VA: American Society for Training & Development, 2013); "2014 Industry Report," *training* (November/December 2014): 16–29.

121. "2014's very best learning organizations," *T+D* (October 2014): 34–98.

122. J. Arneson, W. Rothwell, and J. Naughton, "Training and development competencies redefined to create competitive advantage," *T+D* (January 2013): 42–47.

123. "SHRM Elements for HR Success Competency Model, 2012," from *www.shrm.org*, accessed March 21, 2012.

124. J. Schettler, "Should HR control training?" *training* (July 2002): 32–38.

125. K. Ellis, "The mindset that matters most: Linking learning to the business," *training* (May 2005): 38–43.

Chapter **Two**

Strategic Training

Objectives

After reading this chapter, you should be able to

1. Discuss how business strategy influences the type and amount of training in a company.
2. Describe the strategic training and development process.
3. Discuss how a company's staffing and human resource planning strategies influence training.
4. Explain the training needs created by concentration, internal growth, external growth, and disinvestment business strategies.
5. Discuss the advantages and disadvantages of centralizing the training function.
6. Explain a corporate university and its benefits.
7. Discuss the strengths of a business-embedded learning function.
8. Discuss how to create a learning or training brand and why it is important.
9. Develop a marketing campaign for a training course or program.

Selling Real Estate Is All About Location (and Training) at Keller Williams

The vision of Keller Williams, the largest real estate franchise in North America, is to be the real estate company of choice for agents, franchisees, and customers. The company has started to expand outside of North America adding sales regions, including Dubai, Mexico, and Portugal. Keller Williams strives to train its agents better than any other company in the world so they can delight customers, build their business, and have financial success. Just as location is a key factor in attracting buyers to purchase a home or commercial property, training is a reason for Keller Williams's ability to reach its business goals, which in 2013 included adding 8,000 agents, increasing agent's commissions by 20 percent, and ensuring that over 90 percent of its franchise offices were profitable. Keller Williams's CEO believes that training is critical for the company to attract new agents because it helps them quickly become productive, resulting in sales and commissions. Training involves both online and classroom instruction where learning occurs through interacting with instructors and coaching and opportunities for agents to collaborate, which helps them learn from each other by sharing knowledge and practices. Keller Williams's commitment to training and its role in the success of the business was recognized by its top ranking received in back-to-back years in *training* magazine's Top 125. The company earned the distinction of being ranked #1 in 2015 and #2 in 2014.

Keller Williams has several different training programs that support agents and the business. Business Objective: A Life By Design (BOLD) is a seven-week training program during which agents are taught mindset exercises, language techniques, and participate in lead generation activities. The course focuses on personal well-being as well as business skills. During some classes in the program agents engage in "real play," calling customers with instructors providing guidance and support. This allows the agents to generate business while learning. BOLD graduates have increased sales volumes by 80 percent, closed sales by 86 percent, and increased commission by 118 percent compared to agents who haven't taken the program. Mega Agent Expansion (MAE) helps top-performing agents understand how and when to expand into new markets. MAE includes instructor-led classes, webinars, expert interviews, productivity resources, and coaching. The program helps participants understand all aspects of expanding their business, including how to centralize lead generation and administration and develop a workable business plan. They have access to a social media network for learning and sharing as well as monthly opportunities to ask questions of Keller Williams top expansion agents. Growth Initiative (GI) is a distant learning and consulting program that trains managers how to effectively recruit and retain agents. The program includes weekly one-hour seminars, requires managers to make two recruiting appointments each day, five days a week, and helps managers share best practices through an online community, and a dedicated Facebook page. In addition to its training programs Keller Williams invested in building a training and education center at its corporate headquarters in Austin, Texas. The center manages all aspects of learning and develops new courses, learning tools, and videos. Recently, the center developed apps that provide short training opportunities that agents can access anytime and anywhere through their smartphone, laptop, or notebook.

Keller Williams doesn't just invest time and money into training, it also takes steps to assure its effectiveness. To keep training standards high and improve learning every trainer and instructor must take several "Train the Trainer" courses before they can teach any courses. Different types of evaluation data are collected and shared with agents and managers. Because all of training is voluntary, one measure of its value is participation. This includes tracking how much time employees spend in training (82 average per person hours of formal, planned training) and the number of employees and franchisees trained each year in instructor-led courses (100,000) and online courses (26,000). The return on investment (ROI) of many courses is calculated. For example, BOLD costs $799 per student but the average agent who participated in the course earned an additional $55,000 for the year. Keller Williams also tracks metrics such as the average days a property is on the market. The average days on the market is lower than their competitors, providing evidence that training is helping agents close deals quicker and provide better service.

The company anticipates it will continue to grow at a rapid pace, but recognizes that real estate is a local business based on agents and their relationships. Training is likely to continue to play a key role in helping agents become successful, which in turn means success for Keller Williams. One of CEO Chris Heller's "dreams" is to provide every employee with a coach and provide daily access to world-class trainers.

Sources: L. Freifeld, "Keller Williams Is at Home at No. 1," *training* (January/February 2015): 28–34; L. Freifeld, "Keller Williams Is On the Move," *training* (January/February 2014): 40–42.

INTRODUCTION

As the chapter's opening vignette shows, training at Keller Williams support the business strategy. Recognizing that learning is part of all employees' responsibilities, both managers and peers, along with training professionals, are actively involved in helping other employees gain new skills and perspectives. This helps to reinforce the value of learning and its importance for the business. Keller Williams recognizes that learning through training and development is critical for winning in the marketplace.

Why is the emphasis on strategic training important? Companies are in business to make money, and every business function is under pressure to show how it contributes to business success or else it faces spending cuts and even outsourcing. To contribute to a company's success, training activities should help the company achieve its business strategy. A **business strategy** is a plan that integrates the company's goals, policies, and actions.[1] The strategy influences how the company uses physical capital (e.g., plants, technology, and equipment), financial capital (e.g., assets and cash reserves), and human capital (employees). The business strategy helps direct the company's activities (production, finance, marketing, and human resources) to reach specific goals. The goals are what the company hopes to achieve in the medium- and long-term future. Most companies' goals include financial goals, such as to maximize shareholder wealth. But companies have other goals related to employee satisfaction, industry position, and community service.

There are both direct and indirect links between training and business strategy and goals. Training that helps employees develop the skills needed to perform their jobs directly affects the business. Giving employees opportunities to learn and develop creates a positive work environment, which supports the business strategy by attracting talented employees, as well as motivating and retaining current employees.

Consider the relationship between business strategy and learning at United Parcel Service (UPS), the world's largest package delivery company and provider of specialized transportation and logistics services.[2] Beginning in 2010 UPS changed its business strategy to refocus the company's approach to profitability. This includes considering the role that employees, facilities, and vehicles have in meeting market needs. From a strategic perspective, e-business has shifted more and more of UPS's delivery stops to residences, which are projected to make up half of all deliveries by 2018. Also, pay and benefit costs are higher for UPS's unionized workforce compared to competitors, such as FedEx who use an independent contractor model for deliveries. This means the business has tight profit margins in an increasingly competitive business. UPS Strategic Enterprise Fund is an investment that the company has made to explore emerging markets and technologies that can help the business. For example, UPS has spent millions of dollars developing software called "Orion" to provide its delivery drivers with the most consistent and efficient delivery route. More than 40 percent of company's routes using the software have seen travel distances reduced between seven and eight miles. UPS CEO expects the software to enhance the "bottom line" by saving the company up to $400 million a year once it is fully implemented in 2017. Investing in training, learning, and development is an expense that UPS believes are critical to its success. For example, implementing Orion requires seven hundred trainers working on deploying the software all the way through each of UPS 55,000 U.S. routes by the end of the 2015. Training involves balancing Orion's logic with each driver's experience. It takes about six days to train each driver. Trainer and drivers review satellite images and route details and ride the routes together to make sure the software "understands" the route.

Additionally, learning at UPS has been transformed from classroom instructor–led training to a more blended approach, including virtual instructor–led training, e-learning, and on-the-job training. UPS expanded the reach of UPS University from 67,000 managers in 2012 to more than 104,000 in 2013. The goal is to expand its reach to all of UPS administrative and technical employees. The UPS learning and development team report every business quarter to the company's talent management committee, which includes the highest-level senior leaders responsible for employee development throughout UPS. The learning and development team is responsible for showing the impact and value of learning initiatives to the committee, which ensures that UPS business strategy, talent, performance, and learning are closely linked.

Business strategy has a major impact on the type and amount of training that occurs and whether resources (money, trainers' time, and program development) should be devoted to training. Also, strategy influences the type, level, and mix of skills needed in the company. Strategy has a particularly strong influence on determining the following:

1. The amount of training devoted to current or future job skills
2. The extent to which training is customized for the particular needs of an employee or is developed based on the needs of a team, unit, or division
3. Whether training is restricted to specific groups of employees (such as persons identified as having managerial talent) or open to all employees
4. Whether training is planned and systematically administered, provided only when problems occur, or developed spontaneously as a reaction to what competitors are doing
5. The importance placed on training compared to other human resource management (HRM) practices such as selection and compensation[3]

This chapter begins with a discussion of how training is evolving. Traditionally, training has been seen as an event or program designed to develop specific, explicit knowledge and skills. But managers and trainers and human resource professionals have begun to recognize the potential contribution to business goals of knowledge that is based on experience, which is impossible to teach in a training program, and they have broadened the role of training to include learning and designing ways of creating and sharing knowledge. The chapter goes on to discuss the process of strategic training and development, including identifying business strategy, choosing strategic training and development initiatives that support the strategy, providing training and development activities that support the strategic initiatives, and identifying and collecting metrics to demonstrate the value of training.

The chapter next describes organizational factors that influence how training relates to the business strategy. These include the roles of employees and managers, top management support for training, integration of business units, staffing and human resource planning strategy, degree of unionization, and manager, trainer, and employee involvement in training. The chapter addresses specific strategic types and their implications for training. Then the chapter emphasizes that for strategic learning, training, and development to be adopted, accepted, and used by managers and employees, it is important to consider it from a change model and marketing perspective. The chapter ends with a description of several different ways of organizing the training function, emphasizing that the business-embedded and corporate university models are gaining in popularity as companies are aligning training activities with business goals.

The Evolution of Training: From an Event to Learning

As more companies such as Keller Williams recognize the importance of learning for meeting business challenges and providing a competitive advantage, the role of training in companies is changing.

Recall the discussion in Chapter One, "Introduction to Employee Training and Development," of the different ways that learning can occur in a company. Learning occurs through training, development, informal learning, and knowledge management. Training and development programs that are organized and created by the company, i.e., formal training and development programs, are one way to ensure that employees learn. In less strategic approaches, training involves a series of programs or events that employees are required to attend. After attending the training program, employees are responsible for using what they learned in training on the job, and any support they might receive is based on the whims of their manager. Also, training provides no information that would help employees understand the relationship between the training content and their job performance, development objectives, or business goals. This type of training usually fails to improve workplace performance and meet business needs. The role of training as a program or event will continue into the future because employees will always need to be taught specific knowledge and skills. This approach assumes that business conditions are predictable, they can be controlled by the company, and the company can control and anticipate the knowledge and skills that employees need in the future. These assumptions are true for certain skills, such as communication and conflict resolution. However, these training events or programs will need to be more closely tied to performance improvement and business needs to receive support from top management. The training design model, presented in Chapter One, and the different aspects of the model, discussed in Chapters Three through Eight, will help you understand how to design training programs that can improve employee performance and meet business needs.

LEARNING AS A STRATEGIC FOCUS

The Learning Organization

Many companies, recognizing the strategic importance of learning, have strived to become learning organizations. As discussed in Chapter 1, a **learning organization** is a company that has an enhanced capacity to learn, adapt, and change.[4] Training processes are carefully scrutinized and aligned with company goals. In a learning organization, training is seen as one part of a system designed to create human capital. ARI's president is the company's biggest cheerleader for learning and development.[5] His vision is that all ARI employees are lifelong learners. To foster a learning culture, ARI emphasizes choosing new employees who have a desire for personal and professional development and providing an environment that fosters learning. Interview questions for job candidates focus not only on the match between their abilities, experiences, and job requirements, but also on their desire for personal and professional development. All employees have individual development plans that match career goals with learning objectives. Every employee needs a development plan to be considered for promotion. The company sets goals for average training hours for employees each year. If those goals are reached, nonmanagement employees receive a bonus of one day's pay. ARI has a corporate university but they also support employees interested in other types of learning by providing complete tuition reimbursement from the first day employees join the company.

The essential features of a learning organization appear in Table 2.1. Note that the learning organization emphasizes that learning occurs not only at the individual employee level (as we traditionally think of learning), but also at the group and organizational levels. The learning organization emphasizes knowledge management.

One of the most important aspects of a learning organization is the ability for employees to learn from failure and from successes. That is, learning includes understanding why things happen and why some choices lead to outcomes.[6] Both success and failure trigger investigation, which help employees revise assumptions, models, and theories. For example, Apple's Newton tablet failed miserably when it was introduced in 1990. However, the failure caused Apple to reexamine its theories about what makes successful products. As a result, Apple recognized that a touchphone would be accepted more easily by consumers

TABLE 2.1   **Key Features of a Learning Organization**

Supportive Learning Environment
- Employees feel safe expressing their thoughts about work, asking questions, disagreeing with managers, and admitting mistakes.
- Different functional and cultural perspectives are appreciated.
- Employees are encouraged to take risks, innovate, and explore the untested and unknown, such as trying new processes and developing new products and services.
- Thoughtful review of the company's processes is encouraged.

Learning Processes and Practices
- Knowledge creation, dissemination, sharing, and application are practiced.
- Systems are developed for creating, capturing, and sharing knowledge.

Managers Reinforce Learning
- Managers actively question and listen to employees, encouraging dialogue and debate.
- Managers are willing to consider alternative points of view.
- Time is devoted to problem identification, learning processes and practices, and post-performance audits.
- Learning is rewarded, promoted, and supported.

Sources: A. Edmonson, "Strategies for Learning from Failure", Harvard Business Review (April 2011): 48–55; F. Gino and G. Pisano, "Why Leaders Don't Learn From Success," *Harvard Business Review* (April 2011): 68–74. Based on D. Garvin, A. Edmondson, and F. Gino, "Is Yours a Learning Organization?" *Harvard Business Review* (March 2008): 109–116.

because of the existing smartphone market. Subsequently, using what they learned about the iPhone helped develop a more successful tablet, the iPad. Pixar, which has created a number of successful and acclaimed animated films, still conducts reviews of the process used to make each of its films. For example, Pixar asks employees the top five things they would do and not do again. This is important to gain a better understanding of the reasons behind successful performance so they can be shared by others. To learn from failure and success requires providing employees with the opportunity to experiment with products and services similar to what happens in engineering and scientific research. Some of the conditions necessary for successful experimentation include that it involves genuine uncertainty, the cost of failure is small and contained, the risks of failure are understood and eliminated if possible, there is an understanding that failure still provides important information, success is defined, and the opportunity is significant.

At Walt Disney Company over the last ten years, training has evolved to include flexible learning delivery, customized learning experiences, and collaborative development with internal training customers.[7] Disney has moved from an instructor-led training approach to an approach that uses face-to-face instruction (either in a classroom or on the job) combined with online instruction (game simulation, e-learning). This suits Disney's business strategy, which has always emphasized matching the appropriate technology and methods to the audience regardless of whether the audience is a guest or an employee (cast member).

A single training event or program is not likely to give a company a competitive advantage because explicit knowledge is well known and programs designed to teach it can be easily developed and imitated. However, tacit knowledge developed through experience and shared through interactions between employees is impossible to imitate and can provide companies with a competitive advantage. Pixar's development of successful computer-animated films such as *WALL-E* (a robot love story set in a post-apocalyptic world of trash) and *Inside Out* (the story about emotions, change, and growing up) required the cooperation of a team of talented directors, writers, producers, and technology artists who were located in different buildings, have different priorities, and speak different technical languages.[8] Pixar follows three operating principles: (1) all employees must have the freedom to communicate with other employees, regardless of their position or department; (2) it must be safe for everyone to offer ideas; and (3) the company must maintain awareness of innovations occurring in the academic community. Pixar University offers a collection of in-house courses for training and cross-training employees within their specialty areas. But it also offers optional classes that provide opportunities for employees from different disciplines to meet and learn together. Screenplay writing, drawing, and sculpting are directly related to the business, while courses in Pilates and yoga are not. The courses are attended by employees with all levels of expertise—from novices to experts—which reinforces the idea that all employees are learning and it is fun to learn together.

Implications of Learning for Human Capital Development

The emphasis on learning has several implications. First, there is a recognition that to be effective, learning has to be related to helping employee performance improve and the company achieve its business goals. This connection helps ensure that employees are motivated to learn and that the limited resources (time and money) for learning are focused in areas that will directly help the business succeed. Second, unpredictability in the business environment in which companies operate will continue to be the norm. Because problems cannot be predicted in advance, learning needs to occur on an as-needed basis. Companies need to move beyond the classroom and instead use job experiences, online learning, and mobile learning to help employees acquire knowledge and skills while they focus on business problems. Third, because tacit knowledge is difficult to acquire in training programs, companies need to support informal learning that occurs through mentoring, social networks, and job experiences. Fourth, learning has to be supported not only with physical and technical resources but also psychologically. The company work environment needs to support learning, and managers and peers need to encourage learning and help employees find ways to obtain learning on the job. Also, managers need to understand employees' interests and career goals to help them find suitable development activities that will prepare them to be successful in other positions in the company or deal with expansion of their current job. Chapter Five, "Program Design," discusses how to create a work environment that supports training and learning.

Creating and sharing knowledge refers to companies' development of human capital. As discussed in Chapter One, human capital includes cognitive knowledge (know what), advanced skills (know how), system understanding and creativity (know why), and self-motivated creativity (care why).[9] Traditionally, training has focused on cognitive and advanced skills. But the greatest value for the business may be created by having employees understand the manufacturing or service process and the interrelationships between departments and divisions (system understanding), as well as motivating them to deliver high-quality products and services (care why). To create and share knowledge, companies have to provide the physical space and technology (e-mail, websites, social networks) to encourage employee collaboration and knowledge sharing. Ford Motor Company has communities of practice organized around functions.[10] For example, all the painters in every Ford assembly plant around the world belong to the same community. At each plant, one of the painters serves as a "focal point." If a local painter discovers a better way to improve one of the sixty steps involved in painting, the focal person completes a template describing the improvement and its benefits. The template then is submitted electronically to a subject-matter expert located at Ford headquarters, who reviews the practice and decides whether it is worth sharing with other assembly plants. If so, the practice is approved and sent online to the other assembly plants. Ford has collected $1.3 billion in projected value for the company and has realized over $800 million of actual value from its communities of practice.

As companies recognize the value of training and development and view them as part of a broader learning strategy, seven key capabilities are needed.[11] These capabilities are:

1. Alignment of learning goals to business goals
2. Measurement of the overall business impact of the learning function
3. Movement of learning outside the company to include customers, vendors, and suppliers
4. A focus on developing competencies for the most critical jobs
5. Integration of learning with other human resource functions, such as knowledge management, performance support, and talent management
6. Delivery approaches that include classroom training as well as e-learning
7. Design and delivery of leadership development courses

These capabilities are part of the strategic training and development process, which is discussed next.

THE STRATEGIC TRAINING AND DEVELOPMENT PROCESS

Now that you understand how training is evolving in companies and have been introduced to the concept of business strategy and how training can support a business strategy, you are ready to study the process of strategic training and development. Figure 2.1 shows a model of the strategic training and development process with examples of strategic initiatives, training activities, and metrics.

The model shows that the process begins with identifying the business strategy. Next, strategic training and development initiatives that support the strategy are chosen. Translating these strategic training and development initiatives into concrete training and development activities is the next step of the process. The final step involves identifying measures or metrics. These metrics are used to determine whether training has helped contribute to goals related to the business strategy. The following sections detail each step in the process.

Business Strategy Formulation and Identification

Five major components are part of developing a new business strategy or changing an existing one.[12] Figure 2.2 shows the components. The first component is the company **mission,** which is a statement of the company's reason for existing. Company missions vary, but they typically include information on the customers served, why the company exists, what the company does, the value received by the customers, and the technology used. The mission statement is often accompanied by a statement of the company's vision or values. The **vision** is the picture of the future the company wants to achieve, while **values** are what the company stands for. The second component is the company **goals,** which are what the company hopes to achieve in the medium to long term; they reflect how the mission will be carried out. Training can contribute to a number of different business goals, as shown in Table 2.2. Both for-profit and not-for-profit companies often include goals related to satisfying stakeholders. The term *stakeholders* refers to shareholders (if the company is publically traded and for-profit), the community, customers, employees, and all the other parties that have an interest in seeing that the company succeeds.

FIGURE 2.1
The Strategic Training and Development Process

FIGURE 2.2
Formulating the Business Strategy

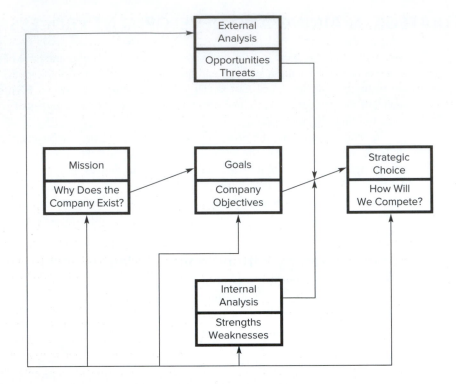

TABLE 2.2
Possible Business Goals Influenced by Training

Sources: Based on R. Rivera, "How to Demonstrate Value: Key Measures Every Learning Professional Should Know," in *WLP Scorecard: Why Learning Matters* (pp. 17–24). Alexandria: VA: ASTD Press.

Productivity
Reduced scrap and rework
Increased customer satisfaction
Reduced operational risks and accidents due to employee carelessness
Increased employee satisfaction and retention
Increased time and value-producing goods, such as increase in billable project time hours
Better management decisions
Increased development of human capital
Succession planning needed for competitive advantage and growth.

The third and fourth components, external and internal analysis, are combined to form what is called a SWOT analysis. A **SWOT analysis** consists of an internal analysis of strengths and weaknesses and an external analysis of opportunities and threats to the company that currently exist or are anticipated. **External analysis** involves examining the operating environment to identify opportunities and threats. The business challenges identified in Chapter One can represent opportunities (or threats) to the company. Examples of opportunities include customers and global markets who are not being served, technology that can help the company, and unused or underutilized potential sources of talented employees. Threats might include changes in the economy, talent, and leadership shortages, new competitors, and changes in legislation that can adversely affect the company. **Internal analysis** attempts to identify the company's strength and weaknesses. It focuses

TABLE 2.3
Decisions a Company Must Make About How to Compete to Reach Its Goals

Source: "Strategy—Decisions About Competition," in *Human Resource Management: Gaining a Competitive Advantage,* 9th ed, R. Noe, J. Hollenbeck, B. Gerhart, and P. Wright. (Burr Ridge, IL: Irwin/McGraw-Hill, 2013): 77.

1. **Where to compete?**
   In what markets (industries, products, etc.) will we compete?
2. **How to compete?**
   On what outcome or differentiating characteristic will we compete? Cost? Quality? Reliability? Delivery? Innovativeness?
3. **With what will we compete?**
   What resources will allow us to beat the competition? How will we acquire, develop, and deploy those resources to compete?

on examining the available quantity and quality of financial, physical, and human capital. The last component is strategic choice. After completing the SWOT analysis, the company (usually managers involved in strategic planning) has all the information it needs to consider how to compete, generate several alternative business strategies, and make a strategic choice. The decisions that a company has to make regarding how to compete are shown in Table 2.3. The possible alternative strategies are compared based on the ability to achieve the company goals. The **strategic choice** represents the strategy believed to be the best alternative to achieve the company goals.

Consider the role of SWOT analysis at CarMax, used car stores located across the United States with low, no haggle pricing, and DPR Construction.[13] Understanding the skills its employees need to succeed is an important part of the long-range strategy at CarMax. CarMax considers what skills employees need to both support its fundamental business principle of integrity as well as company performance. It emphasizes the importance of competencies that drive behavior and influence employee performance. CarMax training programs are based on both internal and external evaluations. Internal evaluations include input from managers about competency needs and gaps, as well as surveys of employees asking them what they need to improve their performance. External analysis includes monitoring trends and new practices in talent management, human resources, and broader society. For example, the emerging use of social networking technology convinced CarMax to incorporate it into its training programs.

DPR Construction's overall learning mission is "We create and provide learning opportunities to enhance the potential of our employees in support of our business objectives." At planning sessions for the next year that take place in the fall, DPRs global learning group meets. This group includes individuals from different offices and roles who focus on training initiatives, as well as company leaders. The global learning group discusses best practices, needs assessment data, and the business strategy. A summary of the meeting is presented to the Management Committee, which is responsible for operations across DPR. Subject matter experts are asked to help with the design and delivery of new training initiatives to meet identified training needs. Employee feedback is also taken into account when considering new training initiatives. For example, when DPR was interested in how new technology such as e-learning could be used in its training programs, they developed and administered an employee survey which included a list of courses and asked to choose which ones they preferred to be delivered in the classroom or via e-learning.

Although these decisions are equally important, companies often pay less attention to the "With what will we compete?" issue, resulting in failure to reach the goals. This decision includes figuring out how human, physical, and financial capital will be used. To use human capital to gain a competitive advantage requires linking the company's human resources practices (such as training and development) to the business strategy.

Identify Strategic Training and Development Initiatives That Support the Strategy

Strategic training and development initiatives are learning-related actions that a company should take to help it achieve its business strategy.[14] The strategic training and development initiatives vary by company depending on a company's industry, goals, resources, and capabilities. The initiatives are based on the business environment, an understanding of the company's goals and resources, and insight regarding potential training and development options. They provide the company with a road map to guide specific training and development activities. They also show how the training function will help the company reach its goals (and in doing so, show how the training function will add value).

There is a tendency to have a disconnect between the strategy and execution of the strategy. To avoid this, learning professionals need to reach out to managers to ensure that the strategic training initiatives and training activities are aligned with the business strategy and that the necessary financial resources and support are provided to carry out the training activities.[15]

To contribute to a company's business strategy, it is important that the training function understand and support it and provide value to its customers. Linking training plans to business plans is important because business plans describe company priorities (plans or initiatives) and include descriptions of who will be involved, the context and how it might affect the plan, how the plan will be carried out (operations), and what decisions have to be made, including those involving training and development, to increase the likelihood that the plan will succeed. To help ensure that its training and development initiatives support the business strategy, CA, a software company, builds training plans and establishes priorities for separate business plans for nonmanagers, managers, and executives during the budget planning process each fiscal year.[16] Training plans include both the technical and interpersonal skills required for each group and how those skills will be developed. To ensure that the training plans help meet business needs, they are updated on a quarterly basis and monthly meetings are held that include both training staff and business leaders who review training needs and discuss future business plans. The training staff focuses on identifying the three to five initiatives that are most important to support the business strategy.

Table 2.4 shows strategic training and development initiatives and their implications for training practices. *Diversify the learning portfolio* means that companies may need to provide more learning opportunities than just traditional training programs. These learning opportunities include informal learning that occurs on the job through interactions with peers; new job experiences; personalized learning opportunities using mentors, coaches, and feedback customized to employee needs; and the use of technology (including web-based training). Such training is self-paced and available outside a formal classroom environment (these learning opportunities are discussed in Chapters Seven, Eight, and Nine).

Reliance Industries Ltd., an Indian company with businesses in energy and petrochemicals and polyester products, employs a wide variety of learning initiatives using different methods.[17] For example, to increase the opportunities for plant employees to

TABLE 2.4 **Strategic Training and Development Initiatives and Their Implications**

Strategic Training and Development Initiatives	Implications
Diversify the Learning Portfolio	• Use technology, such as the Internet, for training • Facilitate informal learning • Provide more personalized learning opportunities
Expand Who Is Trained	• Train customers, suppliers, and employees • Offer more learning opportunities to nonmanagerial employees
Accelerate the Pace of Employee Learning	• Quickly identify needs and provide a high-quality learning solution • Reduce the time to develop training programs • Facilitate access to learning resources on an as-needed basis
Improve Customer Service	• Ensure that employees have product and service knowledge • Ensure that employees have skills needed to interact with customers • Ensure that employees understand their roles and decision-making authority
Provide Development Opportunities and Communicate with Employees	• Ensure that employees have opportunities to develop • Ensure that employees understand career opportunities and personal growth opportunities • Ensure that training and development addresses employees' needs in current job as well as growth opportunities
Capture and Share Knowledge	• Capture insight and information from knowledgeable employees • Organize and store information logically • Provide methods to make information available (e.g., resource guides, websites)
Align Training and Development with the Company's Direction	• Identify needed knowledge, skills, abilities, or competencies • Ensure that current training and development programs support the company's strategic needs
Ensure that the Work Environment Supports Learning and Transfer of Training	• Remove constraints to learning, such as lack of time, resources, and equipment • Dedicate physical space to encourage teamwork, collaboration, creativity, and knowledge sharing • Ensure that employees understand the importance of learning • Ensure that managers and peers are supportive of training, development, and learning

Source: Based on S. Tannenbaum, "A Strategic View of Organizational Training and Learning," in *Creating, Implementing, and Managing Effective Training and Development*, ed. K. Kraiger (San Francisco: Jossey-Bass, 2002): 10–52.

train for emergencies and malfunctions, Reliance invested in simulator training at more than 185 facilities. To capture expert knowledge and make it available to other employees working anywhere in the company, a new technology-based solution was used. Experts can share their knowledge and experience using video lectures that are made available at any time to other employees on the company intranet. To help meet its needs for engineers, Reliance has partnered with educational institutions to create a curriculum that is supported by specific company assignments.

Expand who is trained refers to the recognition that because employees are often the customer's primary point of contact, they need as much if not more training than managers do. University Health System includes an inpatient hospital and seventeen care facilities located throughout Bexar County, Texas.[18] University Health System was challenged to provide opportunities for learning and skills development to its 1,500 remote employees. The learning department expanded opportunities by visiting clinics to develop curriculum and implement training. Education expos bring continuing education providers onsite so employees can see all the opportunities available to them at once. A website provides employees with access to colleges, universities, financial aid, and scholarship. The School at Work program helps employees in entry-level jobs get the skills and knowledge they need to move to new positions. The program covers topics including the math, reading, and communication skills needed to meet certification and degree program requirements. Employees work on the program on their own time using DVDs and online training. The learning department also created the Administrative Professionals Academy, designed to provide high-performing administrative professionals with the knowledge and skills to advance in their careers.

Also, to provide better customer service to suppliers, vendors, and consumers, companies need to distribute information about how to use the products and services they offer. Companies are beginning to train suppliers to ensure that the parts that suppliers provide will meet their customers' quality standards. To be successful, companies have to be able to deal with changes in technology, customer needs, and global markets. Training needs have to be identified quickly and effective training provided. That is, companies have to *accelerate the pace of employee learning.* Also, companies are relying on performance support systems that provide employees with immediate access to information, advice, and guidance (Performance support systems are discussed in more detail in Chapter Five). Performance support systems can be accessed through personal computers, tablets, or mobile phones whenever they are needed. At Qualcomm, employee learning programs have to keep pace with the need for rapid innovation.[19] As a result, Qualcomm provides employees with apps for access anywhere and when they need it. These apps include onboarding tools for new employees, which helps then learn Qualcomm's history and maps showing company locations, nearby restaurants, and shuttle services from airports. Qualcomm also created a website that features user-generated content like video stories that allow employees to share their experiences as well as providing recording and broadcasting capabilities. Because customers now have access to databases and websites and have a greater awareness of high-quality customer service, they are more knowledgeable, are better prepared, and have higher service expectations than ever before. Employees must be prepared to *improve customer service.* Employees have to be knowledgeable about the product or service, they need to have customer service skills, and they need to understand the types of decisions they can make (e.g., are they allowed to make an exception to the policy of no cash refunds?). Umpqua Bank, a small Oregon regional bank, strives to provide a customer experience unlike any other bank.[20] Its concept of concept service is called "slow banking," which is about getting to know customers and building relationships with them. The physical layout of the banks encourages customers to take their time and bank associates to get to know and understand their customers. There are couches, free Wi-Fi, coffee, and interactive video screens showing community activities as well as highlighting the financial products the bank offers. Umpqua want customers to be impressed by the relaxing surroundings, as well as bank associates who are empowered to do whatever it takes to deliver a great customer experience. Training plays an important role in developing employees service skills and reinforcing the company's service culture.

New hires receive extensive training so they can perform every banking function. Associates receive regular training in courses in partnership with Ritz-Carlton Hotel, a model company for customer service. Courses include "Creating a Culture of Service Excellence" and "Radar On, Antenna Up," which focuses on fulfilling customers unexpressed needs. Umpqua also sends employees out to other companies to experience how they are providing customer service and asks them to report back any practices that the bank isn't currently using to satisfy customers.

Providing development opportunities and communicating them to employees is important to ensure that employees believe that they have opportunities to grow and learn new skills. Such opportunities are important for attracting and retaining talented employees. *Capturing and sharing knowledge* ensures that important knowledge about customers, products, or processes is not lost if employees leave the company. Also, giving employees access to knowledge that other employees have may quicken response times to customers and improve product and service quality. For example, rather than "reinventing the wheel," service personnel can tap into a database that allows them to search for problems and identify solutions that other service reps have developed. AT&T uses social networks in three ways. "You Matter" allows employees to share ideas and blogs on a variety of topics, such as money management and wellness.[21] Using "tSpace," an internal company platform for blogs and wikis, employees create their own personal profiles and can join communities of practice organized around specific topics, which give employees the opportunity to learn through sharing ideas and asking questions. With Talent Optimization (TOP), managers can search companywide for employees with the skills they need to match employee talents with open positions. Managers can search companywide for employees who have the skills needed to fill open positions.

Aligning training and development with the company's strategic direction is important to ensure that training contributes to business needs. Companies need to identify what employee capabilities (e.g., knowledge, skills) are needed and whether training programs and services are helping to improve these capabilities. Chief executive officers (CEOs) appreciate the value of learning but want training to be relevant, take less time, and enable employees to quickly use new skills and knowledge on the job. For example, top managers at Modena, a digital design firm, wanted a faster orientation process that helped new employees understand the company's emphasis on team-based project management and quick decision making. They designed a twelve-hour training program that focused on interaction between new employees and current team members as well as executives playing the role of advertising clients. The training ended with new employees making a sales pitch to the "advertising clients."[22] Finally, *a supportive work environment* is necessary for employees to be motivated to participate in training and learning activities, use what they learn on the job, and share their knowledge with others. Tangible support includes time and money for training and learning, as well as work areas that encourage employees to meet and discuss ideas. Psychological support from managers and peers for training and learning is also important. Types of tangible and psychological support for training are discussed in Chapter Five.

How might a company ensure that its training and development initiatives are linked to its business strategy? Table 2.5 shows the questions that a company needs to answer to identify and develop its strategic training and development initiatives. To help answer these questions, trainers need to read the annual reports, strategic plans, earnings releases,

Source: Based on
R. Hughes and
K. Beatty, "Five
Steps to Leading
Strategically," *T+D*
(December 2005):
46–48.

TABLE 2.5
**Questions to
Ask to Develop
Strategic
Training and
Development
Initiatives**

1. What is the vision and mission of the company? Identify the strategic drivers of the business strategy.
2. What capabilities does the company need as a result of the business strategy and business environment challenges?
3. What types of training and development will best attract, retain, and develop the talent needed for success?
4. Which competencies are critical for company success and the business strategy?
5. Does the company have a plan for making the link between training and development and the business strategy understood by executives, managers, and employees or customers?
6. Will the senior management team publicly support and champion training and development?
7. Does the company provide opportunities for training and developing not only individuals but also teams?

and analyst reports for their companies. To understand the business strategy and its implications for training, it may be useful to invite managers to attend training and development staff meetings and present information on the company's business strategy. Also, in companies with multiple divisions, it is important to understand each business, including how it measures effectiveness, how it monitors and reports performance, and what challenges it faces, such as supply chain management, new product development, competitive pressures, or service warranty issues.

Provide Training and Development Activities Linked to Strategic Training and Development Initiatives

After a company chooses its strategic training and development initiatives related to its business strategy, it then identifies specific training and development activities that will enable these initiatives to be achieved. These activities include developing initiatives related to the use of new technology in training, increasing access to training programs for certain groups of employees, reducing development time, and developing new or expanded course offerings. For example, Automatic Data Processing (ADP) provides payroll services, employee benefits administration, and human capital management solutions for businesses of all sizes. Capturing market share in areas where it competes is part of ADP's business strategy. ADP's learning strategy is effective because it is aligned with the business.[23] For example, ADP has realized a 7 percent increase in revenue from sales associates who participated in professional skills courses including development coaching, managing virtual teams, and time management. An onboarding program for new sales associates includes courses in multimedia content, knowledge checks, and online discussions. Based on tracking new employees for ninety days after they completed the program, ADP found they had closed more than $200,000 in new business, 10 percent more than new hires who didn't attend the program. ADP delivered a training program designed to provide its clients with the same success it experienced with its own sales team. It showed 4,500 dealership clients how to use more than three hundred different applications that help profitably sell vehicles, parts, and service. This training resulted in $69 million in revenue for ADP in 2013.

Identify and Collect Metrics to Show Training Success

How does a company determine whether training and development activities actually contribute to the business strategy and goals? This determination involves identifying and collecting **metrics,** business-level outcomes chosen to measure the overall value of training or learning initiatives. Examples of metrics include measures of employee retention, employee engagement, customer service, productivity, and quality. It is important to recognize the difference between training program outcomes and business metrics. Typically, training program evaluation involves measuring trainee satisfaction with the program, assessing improvements in trainee knowledge, skills, and abilities, or identifying if the program influenced business results such as productivity. Accenture, a management consulting, technology services and outsourcing company, collects several different learning delivery metrics.[24] All employees have access to training. In 2012 employees completed more than 3.7 million courses and 1 million course evaluations were submitted. Employees attended more than 208,900 instructor-led training days at Accenture's regional training centers, which are located around the world. Training evaluation, used for determining the effectiveness of training courses or programs, is discussed in more detail in Chapter Six, "Training Evaluation." In comparison to training evaluation outcomes, metrics focus on results rather than on other outcomes. They are strategic business-related measures. That is, they are not linked to one course or program but are chosen to represent the expected value of several programs or learning initiatives. Cognizant evaluates its learning efforts using four outcomes or criteria: business impact, employee satisfaction, business stakeholder satisfaction, and solution effectiveness.[25]

The business-related outcomes should be directly linked to the business strategy and goals. For example, business-related outcomes could evaluate customer service, employee satisfaction or engagement, employee turnover, number of product defects, time spent in product development, number of patents, or time spent filling management positions. Some companies use the balanced scorecard as a process to evaluate all aspects of the business. The **balanced scorecard** is a means of performance measurement that provides managers with a chance to look at the overall company performance or the performance of departments or functions (such as training) from the perspective of internal and external customers, employees, and shareholders.[26] The balanced scorecard considers four different perspectives: customer, internal, innovation and learning, and financial. The emphasis and type of indicators used to measure each of these perspectives are based on the company's business strategy and goals. The four perspectives and examples of metrics used to measure them include:

- Customer (time, quality, performance, service, cost)
- Internal (processes that influence customer satisfaction)
- Innovation and learning (operating efficiency, employee satisfaction, continuous improvement)
- Financial (profitability, growth, shareholder value)

Metrics that might be used to assess training's contribution to the balanced scorecard include employees trained (employees trained divided by total number of employees), training costs (total training costs divided by number of employees trained), and training costs per hour (total training costs divided by total training hours). For example, EMC

Corporation, a technology company, uses a balanced scorecard to track and measure learning.[27] Company performance is tracked quarterly with metrics measuring business alignment, workforce readiness, time-to-market, globalization, and effectiveness. The company has also implemented performance metrics that are directly linked to present and future business needs. Employees are given individual development plans that are based on an analysis of their jobs. Ingersoll Rand requires its business units to make strong business cases for new spending.[28] Following this model, Ingersoll Rand University (IRU) shows that learning makes a difference and contributes to the business strategy by using metrics such as expected benefits, one-time versus ongoing costs, shelf-life of learning products, and employee participation rates in its programs. Each year, IRU provides the company with an annual report communicating accomplishments, challenges, strategic directions, and operational efficiencies. For example, IRU has offered process improvement workshops related to Lean Six Sigma (a quality initiative), which is a business priority. IRU has been able to demonstrate that its workshops have saved the company hundreds of thousands of dollars by reducing vendor delivery costs by 76 percent. The process of identifying and collecting metrics is related to training evaluation, the final step in Figure 1.1 in Chapter One. Chapter Six discusses the different types of outcomes used to evaluate a training program's metrics in more detail. Of course, showing that training directly relates to the company "bottom line" (e.g., increased service, sales, or product quality) is the most convincing evidence of the value of training.

Examples of the Strategic Training and Development Process

Consider the strategic training and development process in two very different companies: Barilla Group and Mike's Carwash. Barilla Group is a leader in the pasta business worldwide, in the pasta sauce business in continental Europe, in the bakery product business in Italy, and in the crisp bread business in Scandinavia.[29] Barilla's mission, vision, and values are shown in Table 2.6. Barilla's business strategy and goals are captured in its "Where to Play" and "How to Win" statements. Barilla wants to be the leading and most reputable company in the global Italian meal experience and bakery product

TABLE 2.6
Barilla's Vision, Mission, and Values

Source: From *www.barilla.com*, the website for Barilla Group, accessed March 16, 2015.

Vision

"We help people live better by bringing well-being and the joy of eating into their everyday lives."

Mission

- Since 1877, Barilla is the Italian Family Company that believes food is a joyful convivial experience, is taste, is a form of sharing and caring.
- Barilla offers delightful and safe products at a great value.
- Barilla believes in the Italian nutritional model that puts together superior-quality ingredients and simple recipes creating unique five-senses experiences.
- Sense of belonging, courage, and intellectual curiosity inspire our behaviors and characterize our people.
- Barilla has always linked its development to people's well-being and to the communities in which it operates.

Values

Passion, trust, intellectual curiosity, integrity, courage.

business by growing volumes and shares in pasta, sauces, and ready meals, developing leadership in its core bakery markets, and customizing products and services to serve shoppers wherever they buy. To do this, Barilla strives to be the brand and product choice for customers, win in the marketplace, drive continuous improvement, do business in an ethical manner, and ensure that employees are proud to work for the company. Barilla's performance-based culture stresses competitiveness, engagement, and leadership. Barilla has 15,000 employees worldwide, including pasta-producing plants in Ames, Iowa, and Avon, New York. In 2015, Barilla will add two new productive lines in Ames, Iowa dedicated to gluten-free pasta.

At Barilla's North American operations, growth leads to expansion and an emphasis on learning. Training and development is necessary to drive continuous improvement. The division's learning organization designs, develops, and facilitates the annual strategic planning session. Corporate strategic goals influence the company's human resource strategic plans, which in turn affect learning priorities. The process includes one-to-one interviews between the director of learning and talent development and executives who work together to determine the objectives of the strategic planning session. The recent agenda of the strategic planning session included a focus on how to grow the business by identifying key business indicators for the business teams, discussing the overall performance of the business teams, and allocating people, processes, and technology to help achieve the business strategy.

There are several strategic training and development initiatives and activities at the company's North American operations. First, to accelerate the pace of employee learning and development, individual development plans are matched to employee strengths and passions, using managers' input to determine if they are aligned. At the directorship level, each member of the leadership team provides input into the development plan. The learning organization plays a key role in change management. The learning organization was responsible for the successful implementation of the company's new resource planning system. Members of a small change management team were responsible for communicating directly with employees, allowing employees to see the conversion process for themselves. They held periodic meetings to solicit input from employees affected by the conversion and explain details of the conversion. A visual timeline gave employees monthly views of the transition to the new system, as well as progress updates and goals achieved. The timeline highlighted connections between the business strategy and daily work, including process change and team performance, from leaders and managers to line employees. To help diversify the learning opportunities and ensure that the necessary training was being conducted to support the business, the learning organization partnered with peers from the company's Italian headquarters to conduct a needs assessment. The needs assessment helped identify performance needs and which skills to develop by department, based on organizational goals, department goals, and skill gaps. Also, the needs assessment data was used to determine the learning methods and priorities of Barilla University.

Mike's Carwash, based in Indianapolis, Indiana, is a privately owned chain of car washes with forty-one locations in Indiana, Ohio, and Kentucky.[30] Opened in 1948, the first Mike's was called "Mike's Minit Man Carwash," named after the type of equipment originally used Mike's reorganized into two different companies Crew Carwash and Mike's Carwash as part of the family's succession plan. Figure 2.3 shows how Mike's Carwash links its business strategy to training and development.

FIGURE 2.3
How Mike's Carwash Links Training and Development to Business Strategy

Business Strategy	Strategic Training and Development Initiatives	Training and Development Activities	Metrics that Show the Value of Training
• Delight the Customer	• Diversify the Learning Portfolio	• Orientation	• Return Customer
• Repeat Business	• Expand Who Is Trained	• Development Plan	• Revenue
• Consistent Service	• Improve Customer Service	• Internal Certification	• Customer Satisfaction
• Growth	• Provide Development Opportunities	• Online Training	• Mystery Shopper Scores
		• Manages Accountable for Employees Training and Provide Coaching to Improve Other Skills	• Ensure work Environments Supports Cleaning & Transfer

Mike's mission is to create lifetime customers by delivering a clean, fast, friendly experience through engaged and valued team members. Mike's business strategy supports its mission: consistent and speedy service, return customers, and growing the business each year. Mike's Carwashes are automated and feature equipment, systems, and technology developed by Mike's employees. Mike's credits some of its success to the Dahm family's business smarts but believes that most of its success comes from its employees and its hiring and training practices. Mike's original founders, Joe and Ed Dahm, were known to tell employees that the company was truly in the people business—it just happened to wash cars. Its mission is to provide friendly and fast service to the boss (i.e., customers) at a good value.

Customer satisfaction is very important to Mike's, with the emphasis placed on repeat business by serving customers so they will come back again. The biggest challenge that Mike's faces is providing a consistently enjoyable customer experience. Mike's is constantly trying to improve the customer experience through innovation and new ideas. If a new idea works, it is implemented in all locations. Mike's believes that the only way to provide a consistent customer experience is not only through finding great employees, but through training and development of those employees. The company website explains that it is "notoriously picky" when it comes to hiring. For every fifty people Mike's considers hiring, just one is hired. Mike's uses training and development to retain and engage its employees. Each employee has a development plan and receives performance appraisals twice each year. New employee training involves familiarizing them with best practices and how to help customers in different situations that they will encounter at the car wash. Before employees wait on their first customer, they receive two days of orientation and participate in workshops that focus on customer service, how to treat customers, how to recover from service errors and mistakes, and how to deal with difficult customers. Mike's also provides training to help employees advance in the company. The career path from hourly associate to supervisor to shift manager to assistant manager is well defined. Movement on the career path is possible through good performance and completing internal certifications that include up to twelve weeks of training and three exams requiring grades of at least 80 percent. Employee engagement and satisfaction are measured by semiannual surveys, as well as by gathering information from employees who are leaving Mike's. Employees play an important role in the choice and design of training and development activities. A fifteen- to twenty-person team consisting of members who have been nominated by their store manager serve a one-year term as subject-matter experts in helping to develop new and modify existing training programs. Team members also are the first trainees in new programs, providing feedback about needed changes and feedback on program effectiveness.

In addition to its regular training programs for new employees and certification programs for advancement, Mike's has developed programs to meet its emerging business needs. The recent economic recession resulted in a decrease in the volume of customers Mike's served, as well as in revenue. As a result, Mike's recognized the need to increase the spending of its customers by making sure that employees made them aware of value-added services such as underbody washes, tire treatments, and clear coat application. To do this, Mike's developed an online training module and taught managers to encourage employees to complete their training and practice using their selling skills at monthly employee meetings.

Mike's recognizes the important role that managers play in helping employees learn. At Mike's, managers need to actively support and help deliver training. They are held accountable for training and developing employees in order to advance and succeed. In this program, managers were taught how to identify weaknesses in employees' service recommendations techniques and use weekly coaching sessions to enhance them. Managers were also encouraged to observe and document employees making service recommendations to customers and to provide them with feedback. The results of this program were positive: overall revenue, revenue per customer, customer satisfaction, and "mystery shopper" scores all increased.

ORGANIZATIONAL CHARACTERISTICS THAT INFLUENCE TRAINING

The amount and type of training, as well as the organization of the training function in a company, are influenced by employee and manager roles; by top management support for training; by the company's degree of integration of business units; by its global presence; by its business conditions; by other HRM practices, including staffing strategies and human resource planning; by the company's extent of unionization; and by the extent of involvement in training and development by managers, employees, and human resource staff.[31]

Roles of Employees and Managers

The roles that employees and managers have in a company influence the focus of training, development, and learning activity. Traditionally, employees' roles were to perform their jobs according to the managers' directions. Employees were not involved in improving the quality of the products or services. However, with the emphasis on the creation of intellectual capital and the movement toward high-performance work systems using teams, employees today are performing many roles once reserved for management (e.g., hiring, scheduling work, and interacting with customers, vendors, and suppliers).[32] If companies are using teams to manufacture goods and provide services, team members need training in interpersonal problem solving and team skills (e.g., how to resolve conflicts and give feedback). If employees are responsible for the quality of products and services, they need to be trained to use data to make decisions, which involves training in statistical process control techniques. As discussed in Chapter One, team members may also receive training in skills needed for all positions on the team (cross training), not just for the specific job they are doing. To encourage cross training, companies may adopt skill-based pay systems, which base employees' pay rates on the number of skills they are competent in rather than what skills they are using for their current jobs.

Research suggests that today's managers are expected to do the following:[33]

- *Manage individual and team performance.* Motivate employees to change performance, provide performance feedback, and monitor training activities. Clarify individual and team goals and ensure alignment with company goals.
- *Develop employees and encourage continuous learning.* Explain work assignments and provide technical expertise. Create environment that encourages learning.
- *Plan and allocate resources.* Translate strategic plans into work assignments and establish target dates for projects.
- *Coordinate activities and interdependent teams.* Persuade other units to provide products or resources needed by the work group, and understand the goals and plans of other units. Ensure that the team is meeting internal and external customer needs.
- *Manage group performance.* Define areas of responsibility, meet with other managers to discuss effects of changes in the work unit on their groups, facilitate change, and implement business strategy.
- *Facilitating decision-making process.* Facilitate team and individual decision making. Encourage the use of effective decision-making processes (dealing with conflict, statistical process control).
- *Creating and maintaining trust.* Ensure that each team member is responsible for his or her workload and customers. Treat all team members with respect. Listen and respond honestly to team ideas.
- *Represent one's work unit.* Develop relationships with other managers, communicate the needs of the work group to other units, and provide information on work group status to other groups.

Regardless of their level in the company (e.g., senior management), all managers are expected to serve as spokespersons to other work units, managers, and vendors (i.e., represent the work unit). Of course, the amount of time that managers devote to some of these roles is affected by their level. Line managers spend more time managing individual performance and developing employees than midlevel managers or executives do. The most important roles for midlevel managers and executives are planning and allocating resources, coordinating interdependent groups, and managing group performance (especially managing change). Executives also spend time monitoring the business environment by analyzing market trends, developing relationships with clients, and overseeing sales and marketing activities.

To manage successfully in a team environment, managers need to be trained in "people skills," including negotiation, sensitivity, coaching, conflict resolution, and communication skills. A lack of people skills has been shown to be related to managers' failure to advance in their careers.[34]

Top Management Support

The CEO, the top manager in the company, plays a key role in determining the importance of training and learning in the company. The CEO is responsible for[35]

- Setting a clear direction for learning (vision)
- Encouragement, resources, and commitment for strategic learning (sponsor)
- Taking an active role in governing learning, including reviewing goals and objectives and providing insight on how to measure training effectiveness (governor)
- Developing new learning programs for the company (subject-matter expert)
- Teaching programs or providing resources online (faculty)
- Serving as a role model for learning for the entire company and demonstrating a willingness to learn constantly (learner)
- Promoting the company's commitment to learning by advocating it in speeches, annual reports, interviews, and other public relations tools (marketing agent)

For example, Bill McDermott, CEO of SAP, a business software company, recognizes that training is critical for the company to stay on the cutting edge of technology and innovation.[36] SAP recently had to move its consultants from implementing software at customer's locations to working for them using cloud computing. He wants to enhance a culture of passion, curiosity, and innovation, which in turn gets employees engaged in learning. Recently, he hired the company's first chief learning officer whose role is to help SAP constantly improve and bring to life SAP's philosophies, which include everyone is a teacher, everyone is a learner, and everyone is a talent. At Ingersoll Rand, to ensure that top managers understand and support the role that training and development can play in the company, a "ladder of engagement" model has been created.[37] Top managers are engaged in training and development in many different ways, including providing input into learning program development, serving as trainers or co-trainers, visiting courses as executive speakers, or serving as advisory council members for Ingersoll Rand's corporate university.

Integration of Business Units

The degree to which a company's units or businesses are integrated affects the kind of training that takes place. In a highly integrated business, employees need to understand other units, services, and products in the company. Training likely includes rotating employees between jobs in different businesses so they can gain an understanding of the whole business.

Global Presence

As noted in Chapter One, the development of global product and service markets is an important challenge for U.S. companies. For companies with global operations, training is used to prepare employees for temporary or long-term overseas assignments. Also, because employees are geographically dispersed outside the United States, companies need to determine whether training will be conducted and coordinated from a central U.S. facility or will be the responsibility of satellite installations located near overseas facilities.

A key challenge is insuring learning is effective for all employees regardless of the language they speak or their cultural background.

Consider how globalization has affected the training practices of Phillips, Accenture, and Etihad Airways.[38] Phillips, the Dutch technology company, focuses on health-care, lighting, and consumer lifestyle products. Phillips learning function has to serve employees in more than one hundred different countries. As a result, the company has developed a standard global learning approach that is locally appropriate. Phillips has global standards in place to ensure learning is high quality, but each business unit is encouraged to tailor learning to match learners' needs at the location. For example, in India and China employees are encouraged to learn using one-on-one coaching, but in Europe employees are more receptive to learning delivered online.

Accenture employs approximately 281,000 employees working in two hundred cities and fifty-six countries around the world. To bring expertise to its multiple worldwide locations, Accenture has created a global network of local classrooms that can connect to each other. This means that experts located in one location can now share their skills with employees in locations around the world who need those skills. Training flight attendants to act as a team in an emergency is one of the biggest challenges facing global airlines.

Etihad Airways, a Persian Gulf airline, operate in English but it is the second language for almost all employees. As a result, Etihad revised its training program to include more visual learning for its employees who come from 113 different countries. Interactive computer programs teach flight attendants how to set a business-class dinner table to the airline's standards by clicking and dragging pictures rather than reading instructions. Also, Etihad has invested millions of dollars into full-motion simulators for flight attendants. The simulators can create turbulence, pour smoke into a cabin, and light fires in storage areas or overhead bins. Trainees have to learn how to evacuate the plane and open cabin doors from simulated bad landings that happen when nose wheels collapse or the plane lands on its side.

Business Conditions

When unemployment is low and/or businesses are growing at a high rate and need more employees, companies often find it difficult to attract new employees, find employees with necessary skills, and retain current employees.[39] Companies may find themselves in the position of hiring employees who might not be qualified for the job. Also, in these types of business conditions, companies need to retain talented employees. In a knowledge-based economy (including the information technology and pharmaceuticals areas), product development depends on employees' specialized skills. Losing a key employee may cause a project to be delayed or hinder a company's taking on new projects. Training plays a key role in preparing employees to be productive, as well as motivating and retaining current employees. Studies of what factors influence employee retention suggest that employees rate working with good colleagues, having challenging job assignments, and getting opportunities for career growth and development as top reasons for staying with a company. Across all industries, from high-tech to retailing, companies are increasingly relying on training and development to attract new employees and retain current ones. For example, companies such as Eli Lilly (a pharmaceutical company) and Microsoft are successful in terms of financial returns. They are typically found on lists of great places to work (for example, they regularly appear on *Fortune* magazine's annual list of "Best Companies to

Work For"). They are quite successful in attracting and retaining employees. Not only do they provide employees with very competitive pay and benefits, but they also are committed to training and development. Retailers such as Macy's and Nordstrom's cannot generate sales unless they have enough skilled employees.[40] For example, Macy's begins its employee retention strategy by starting with executives. Executives are accountable for retaining the employees who report to them. Managers have been trained to run meetings and conduct performance evaluations (skills that influence employees' perceptions of how they are treated, which ultimately affects whether they remain with Macy's). Macy's has also provided training programs and courses for employees.

For companies in an unstable or recessionary business environment—one characterized by mergers, acquisitions, or disinvestment of businesses—training may be abandoned, be left to the discretion of managers, or become more short-term (such as offering training courses only to correct skill deficiencies rather than to prepare staff for new assignments). These programs emphasize the development of skills and characteristics needed (e.g., how to deal with change), regardless of the structure the company takes. Training may not even occur as the result of a planned effort. Employees who remain with a company following a merger, acquisition, or disinvestment usually find that their job now has different responsibilities requiring new skills. For employees in companies experiencing growth—that is, an increased demand for their products and services—there may be many new opportunities for lateral job moves and promotions resulting from the expansion of sales, marketing, and manufacturing operations or from the start-up of new business units. These employees are usually excited about participating in development activities because new positions often offer higher salaries and more challenging tasks.

During periods when companies are trying to revitalize and redirect their business, earnings are often flat. As a result, fewer incentives for participation in training—such as promotions and salary increases—may be available. In many cases, companies downsize their workforces as a way of cutting costs. Training activities under these conditions focus on ensuring that employees are available to fill the positions vacated by retirement or turnover. Training also involves helping employees avoid skill obsolescence. (Strategies to help employees avoid skill obsolescence are discussed in Chapter Ten.)

Other HRM Practices

Human resource management (HRM) practices consist of the management activities related to investments (time, effort, and money) in staffing (determining how many employees are needed, and recruiting and selecting employees), performance management, training, and compensation and benefits. Companies that adopt state-of-the-art HRM practices that contribute to business strategy tend to demonstrate higher level of performance than firms that do not.[41] These HRM practices contribute to the attraction, motivation, and retention of human capital (the knowledge, skills, and abilities embedded in people), which can help a company gain a competitive advantage. Training, along with selection, performance management, and compensation influence attraction motivation and retention of human capital. Training helps develop company-specific skills, which can contribute to productivity and ultimately company performance. Also, training helps provide the skills that employees need to move to new jobs in the company, therefore increasing their satisfaction and engagement. The type of training and the resources devoted to training are influenced by staffing strategy, the strategic value of jobs and employee uniqueness, and human resource planning.

Staffing Strategy

Staffing strategy refers to the company's decisions regarding where to find employees, how to select them, and the desired mix of employee skills and statuses (temporary, full-time, etc.). It is important for you to recognize that training and development and learning opportunities can vary across companies because of differences in companies' evaluation of the labor market, their staffing strategy, or the strategic value and uniqueness of jobs or positions. For example, one staffing decision a company has to make is how much to rely on the internal labor market (within the company) or external labor market (outside the company) to fill vacancies. Two aspects of a company's staffing strategy influence training: the criteria used to make promotion and assignment decisions (assignment flow) and the places where the company prefers to obtain the human resources to fill open positions (supply flow).[42]

Companies vary in terms of the extent to which they make promotion and job assignment decisions based on individual performance or group or business-unit performance. They also vary in terms of the extent to which their staffing needs are met by relying on current employees (internal labor market) or employees from competitors and recent entrants into the labor market, such as college graduates (external labor market). Figure 2.4 displays the two dimensions of staffing strategy. The interaction between assignment flow

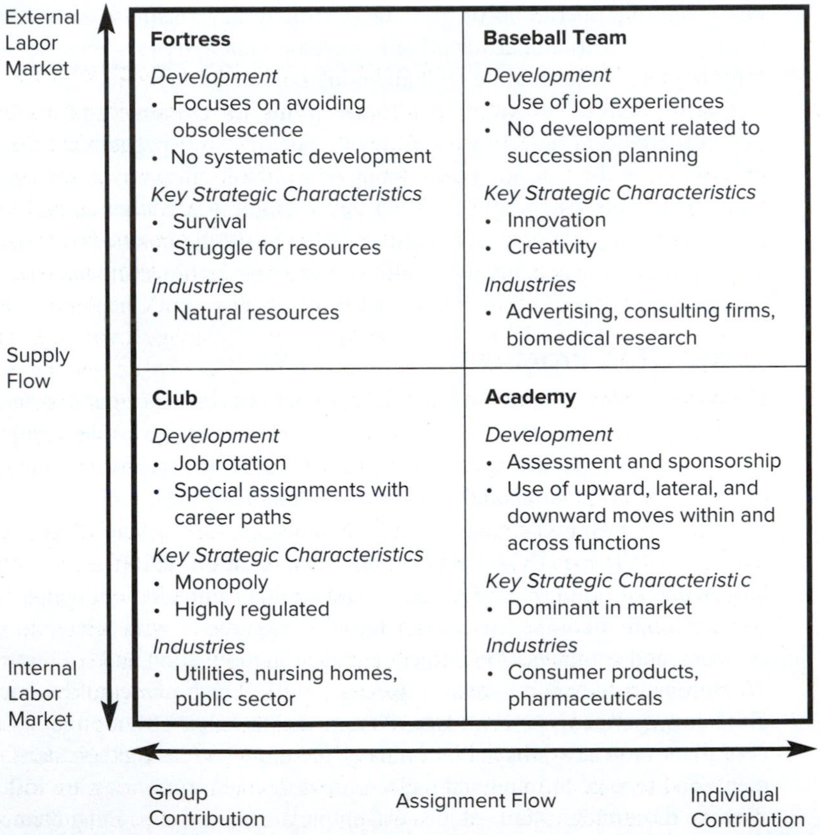

FIGURE 2.4
Implications of Staffing Strategy for Training

Source: Adapted from J. A. Sonnenfeld and M. A. Peiperl, "Staffing policy as a strategic response: A typology of career systems," *Academy of Management Review* 13 (1988): 588–600.

Fortress	**Baseball Team**
Development • Focuses on avoiding obsolescence • No systematic development	*Development* • Use of job experiences • No development related to succession planning
Key Strategic Characteristics • Survival • Struggle for resources	*Key Strategic Characteristics* • Innovation • Creativity
Industries • Natural resources	*Industries* • Advertising, consulting firms, biomedical research
Club	**Academy**
Development • Job rotation • Special assignments with career paths	*Development* • Assessment and sponsorship • Use of upward, lateral, and downward moves within and across functions
Key Strategic Characteristics • Monopoly • Highly regulated	*Key Strategic Characteristic* • Dominant in market
Industries • Utilities, nursing homes, public sector	*Industries* • Consumer products, pharmaceuticals

Vertical axis (top to bottom): External Labor Market — Supply Flow — Internal Labor Market

Horizontal axis (left to right): Group Contribution — Assignment Flow — Individual Contribution

and supply flow results in four distinct types of companies: fortresses, baseball teams, clubs, and academies. Each company type places a different emphasis on training activities. For example, some companies (such as medical research companies) emphasize innovation and creativity. These types of companies are labeled "baseball teams." "Because it may be difficult to train skills related to innovation and creativity, they tend to handle staffing needs by luring employees away from competitors or by hiring graduating students with specialized skills. "Academies" tend to be companies such as Proctor & Gamble (P&G), dominant in their industry or markets, which rely primarily on training and developing their current employees (i.e., the internal labor market) to fill new positions and managerial roles. "Clubs" tend to be companies in highly regulated industries such as energy or health care that also rely on developing talent from their internal labor market but rely on team or department performance to determine promotions or opportunities to obtain important development activities or assignments. "Fortresses" include companies in industries that are undergoing significant change and struggling for survival. In "Fortresses" financial and other resources are not available for development so companies tend to rely on hiring talent from outside, i.e., from the external labor market, on an "as-needed" basis. Figure 2.4 can be used to identify development activities that support a specific staffing strategy. For example, if a company wants to reward individual employee contributions and promote from within (the bottom-right quadrant of Figure 2.4), it needs to use lateral, upward, and downward moves within and across functions to support the staffing strategy.

Strategic Value of Jobs and Employee Uniqueness

Another strategic consideration affecting how companies invest its training and development resources is based on different types of employees. One distinction that some companies make is in training and development activities for managers and individual contributors. Managers may receive development opportunities such as job experiences and international assignments that individual contributors do not because they are being evaluated and prepared for leadership positions in the company. Another way different types of employees can be identified is based on their strategic value and uniqueness to the company.[43] **Uniqueness** refers to the extent to which employees are rare and specialized and not highly available in the labor market. **Strategic value** refers to employee potential to improve company effectiveness and efficiency. This results in four types of employees: knowledge-based workers (high value and uniqueness), job-based employees (high value and low uniqueness), contract employees (low value and low uniqueness), and alliance/partnerships (high uniqueness and low value).

Consider a pharmaceutical company which includes many different employee groups including scientists (knowledge-based workers), lab technicians (job-based workers), secretarial and administrative staff (contract employees), and legal advisers (alliance/partnerships). Because knowledge-based employees posses valuable and unique skills, the company is expected to invest heavily in training and developing them, especially in developing skills specific to the company's needs. Job-based employees are likely to receive less training than knowledge-based employees because although they create value for the firm, they are not unique. If they receive training, it would tend to focus on skills that they need to perform their jobs. Their development opportunities will be limited unless they have been identified as outstanding performers. The training for contractual workers likely would be limited to ensuring that they comply with company policies and legal or industry-based licensure and certification requirements. Because they are not full-time employees of the company but provide valued services, training for alliance/partnership employees tends to focus on encouraging them to share their knowledge and using team training and experiential exercises designed to develop their trust and relationships with job-based and knowledge-based employees.

Human Resource Planning

Human resource planning includes the identification, analysis, forecasting, and planning of changes needed in the human resource area to help the company meet changing business conditions.[44] Human resource planning allows the company to anticipate the movement of human resources in the company because of turnover, transfers, retirements, or promotions. Human resource plans can help identify where employees with certain types of skills are needed in the company. Training can be used to prepare employees for increased responsibilities in their current job, promotions, lateral moves, transfers, and downward moves or demotions that are predicted by the human resource plan.

Extent of Unionization

Unions' interest in training has resulted in joint union-management programs designed to help employees prepare for new jobs. When companies begin retraining and productivity-improvement efforts without involving unions, the efforts are likely to fail. The unions may see the programs as just another attempt to make employees work harder without sharing the productivity gains. Joint union-management programs (detailed in Chapter Ten) ensure that all parties (unions, management, employees) understand the development goals and are committed to making the changes necessary for the company to make profits and for employees to both keep their jobs and share in any increased profits.

Staff Involvement in Training and Development

How often and how well a company's training program is used are affected by the degree to which managers, employees, and specialized development staff are involved in the process. If managers are not involved in the training process (e.g., determining training needs, being used as trainers), training may be unrelated to business needs. Managers also may not be committed to ensuring that training is effective (e.g., giving trainees feedback on the job). As a result, training's potential impact on helping the company reach its goals may be limited because managers may feel that training is a "necessary evil" forced on them by the training department rather than a means of helping them to accomplish business goals.

If line managers are aware of what development activity can achieve, such as reducing the time it takes to fill open positions, they will be more willing to become involved in it. They will also become more involved in the training process if they are rewarded for participating. Constellation Energy, located in Baltimore, Maryland, links employee learning to individual and organizational performance.[45] Each year, the company is involved in a business planning process from the summertime until December, involving monitoring, reviewing, and making changes to its a comprehensive five-year plan detailing organizational and business goals and objectives. The human resources plan, which includes learning, ensures that employee development strategies are aligned with business strategies. Individual development plans and goals jointly established between employees and their managers are established based on the company's business goals and objectives and human resource needs. Managers are held accountable for developing employees. One of the competencies they are evaluated on is human capital management, which includes employee engagement, talent management, and diversity. Part of each manager's bonus is based on the evaluation he or she receives on this competency.

Today, companies expect employees to initiate the training process.[46] Companies with a greater acceptance of a continuous learning philosophy require more development planning. Companies will support training and development activities (such as tuition reimbursement and the offering of courses, seminars, and workshops) but will give employees the responsibility for planning their own development. Training and development planning involve identifying needs, choosing the expected outcome (e.g., behavior change, greater knowledge), identifying the actions that should be taken, deciding how progress toward goal attainment will be measured, and creating a timetable for improvement. To identify strengths and weaknesses and training needs, employees need to analyze what they want to do, what they can do, how others perceive them, and what others expect of them. A need can result from gaps between current capabilities and interests and the type of work or position the employee wants in the future. The needs assessment process is discussed in greater detail in Chapter Three, "Needs Assessment."

TRAINING NEEDS IN DIFFERENT STRATEGIES

Table 2.7 describes four business strategies—concentration, internal growth, external growth, and disinvestment—and highlights the implications of each for training practices.[47] Each strategy differs based on the goal of the business. A **concentration strategy** focuses on increasing market share, reducing costs, or creating and maintaining a market niche for products and services. For many years, Southwest Airlines has had a concentration strategy (although it recently purchased AirTran Airways). It focuses on providing short-haul, low-fare, and high-frequency air transportation. It utilizes one type of aircraft (the Boeing 737), has no reserved seating, and serves no meals. This concentration strategy has enabled Southwest to keep costs low and revenues high. An **internal growth strategy** focuses on new market and product development, innovation, and joint ventures. For example, the merger between Continental and United Airlines created the world's largest airline. An **external growth strategy** emphasizes acquiring vendors and suppliers or buying businesses that allow the company to expand into new markets. For example, General Electric, a manufacturer of lighting products and jet engines, acquired the National Broadcasting Corporation (NBC), a television and communications company. A **disinvestment strategy** emphasizes liquidation and divestiture of businesses. For example, Citigroup, which took over the financially troubled music company EMI, sold it to Universal and Sony.

Research suggests a link between business strategy and amount and type of training.[48] Table 2.7 shows that training issues vary greatly from one strategy to another. Divesting companies need to train employees in job-search skills and to focus on cross-training remaining employees who may find themselves in jobs with expanding responsibilities. Companies focusing on a market niche (a concentration strategy) need to emphasize skill currency and development of their existing workforce. New companies formed from a merger or acquisition need to ensure that employees have the skills needed to help the

TABLE 2.7 Implications of Business Strategy for Training

Strategy	Emphasis	How Achieved	Key Issues	Training Implications
Concentration	• Increased market share • Reduced operating costs • Market niche created or maintained	• Improve product quality • Improve productivity or innovate technical processes • Customize products or services	• Skill currency • Development of existing workforce	• Team building • Cross training • Specialized programs • Interpersonal skill training • On-the-job training
Internal Growth	• Market development • Product development • Innovation • Joint ventures • Mergers • Globalization	• Market existing products/add distribution channels • Expand global market • Modify existing products • Create new or different products • Expand through joint ownership • Identify and develop managers	• Creation of new jobs and tasks • Innovation • Talent Management	• High-quality communication of product value • Cultural training • Development of organizational culture that values creative thinking and analysis • Technical competence in jobs • Manager training in feedback and communication • Conflict negotiation skills
External Growth (Acquisition)	• Horizontal integration • Vertical integration • Concentric diversification	• Acquire firms operating at same stage in product market chain (new market access) • Acquire business that can supply or buy products • Acquire firms that have nothing in common with acquiring firm	• Integration • Redundancy • Restructuring	• Determination of capabilities of employees in acquired firms • Integration of training systems • Methods and procedures of combined firms • Team building • Development of shared culture
Disinvestment	• Retrenchment • Turnaround • Divestiture • Liquidation	• Reduce costs • Reduce assets • Generate revenue • Redefine goals • Sell off all assets	• Efficiency	• Motivation, goal setting, time management, stress management, cross training • Leadership training • Interpersonal communications • Outplacement assistance • Job-search skills training

company reach its new strategic goals. Also, for mergers and acquisitions to be successful, employees need to learn about the new, merged organization and its culture.[49] The organization must provide training in systems, such as instruction on how the e-mail, and company intranet work. Managers need to be educated on how to make the new merger successful (e.g., dealing with resistance to change). Verizon resulted from the merger of four companies with different and distinct cultures.[50] Learning and development at Verizon plays an important role in supporting new products and services. As Verizon has evolved from a telecommunications company to a technology company, it has faced critical business issues including improving the customer experience, growing sales, and developing future company leaders. These issues are seen in the company's 2014 strategic focus: enhancing the customer experience, business growth, profitability, and building the culture. All employees are encouraged to grow within the company by completing and following individual development plans that are tied into training courses and learning opportunities. All employees can access social networking tools, including Yammer, Chatter, internal online discussion forums, and a video-sharing site. Learning & Development at Verizon developed a program to build a customer-focused employee culture. The program includes all of the processes that a customer might interact with, including sales, service, and technical support. To improve both employees' accessibility to training and customer service, Verizon has deployed tablets to retail store employees. Employees can use these tablets to get access to information about devices, service plans, product promotions, processes, and procedures. They can share this information with the customer during their interactions. The tablets are also used to deliver e-learning. Learning and development at Verizon is evaluated based on its contribution to both employee and business performance.

Companies with an internal growth strategy face the challenge of identifying and developing talent. HCL Technologies, an IT consulting firm, grew during the last three years despite the economic recession and competition.[51] To be successful HCL employees must stay current on new tools and mobile and web technologies. To ensure that its employees' skills are up-to-date, HCL developed a technical academy that provides online learning, classroom instruction, on-the-job experiences, and mentoring. To facilitate employees' continuous improvement, employees are encourage to complete technical certifications through taking courses and learning through virtual online labs that simulate real technical environments. Ninety percent of the learning programs are developed internally. HCL invested millions of dollars in learning, but through this investment, the company believes it can stay ahead of the competition and grow the business. HCL has found that employees who finish certification programs generate more billable hours, stay employed with company longer, and are more satisfied.

When facing a downturn in demand for its automobile and trucks, Toyota Motor Corporation is known for retaining employees at its plants and encouraging them to participate in training programs designed to improve their job skills and find more efficient and effective methods of assembling vehicles.[52] Toyota uses downtime to improve employees' quality control and productivity skills, keeping good on its pledge never to lay off any of its full-time non-union employees. The training resulted in continuous improvements (also known as *kaizen*). One example is a Teflon ring that was designed by an assembly line employee that helps prevent paint damage when an electrical switch is installed on the edge of a vehicle's door.

A disinvestment strategy resulted in Edwards Life Sciences Corporation being spun off from another company.[53] The new company's management team developed a new strategic plan that described goals for sales growth, new product development, customer loyalty, and employee commitment and satisfaction. The company realized that it had to prepare leaders who could help the company meet its strategic goals. A review of leadership talent showed that leadership development was needed, and a leadership program was created in response. The program included twenty participants from different functions and company locations. Part of the weeklong program is devoted to a simulation in which teams of managers run their own business and take responsibility for marketing, manufacturing, and financials. The sessions also include classes taught by company executives, who speak about important topics such as the company's business strategy.

MODELS OF ORGANIZING THE TRAINING DEPARTMENT

Most companies want their learning or training function to provide some courses and programs to all employees regardless of their functional area, location, business unit, or division. These courses and programs are developed (or purchased from training vendors or suppliers) and delivered by learning staff working at corporate headquarters or at a corporate university. At the same time, companies want their learning function to provide learning that meets training needs that are unique to a business unit or product line.

One of the important decisions that companies have to consider in choosing how to organize the training department (or learning function) is the extent to which training and learning is centralized. Typically, companies do not choose to entirely centralize or decentralize training and learning completely. Rather, they organize the training department or learning function in a way that best supports the business strategy and helps meet its needs. This typically involves an approach in which some learning is provided by a corporate learning function or corporate university and others learning is customized, developed, and delivered specifically for function, product lines or location needs (business-embedded). **Centralized training** means that training and development programs, resources, and professionals are primarily housed in one location and that decisions about training investment, programs, and delivery methods are made from that department.

One of the advantages of a centralized training function is that it helps drive stronger alignment with business strategy, allows development of a common set of metrics or scorecards to measure and report rates of quality and delivery, helps to streamline processes, and gives the company a cost advantage in purchasing training from vendors and consultants because of the number of trainees who will be involved. Also, a centralized training function helps companies better integrate programs for developing leaders and managing talent with training and learning during times of change. For example, at SAP the funding for learning is centralized for strategic programs that are important across business units.[54] Separate learning groups at SAP will be united under one brand, logo, learning technology, and instructional design philosophy. However, the learning function will continue to be responsive to the learning and development needs of different business areas and types of employees. At STIHL, a producer of outdoor power equipment such as chain saws, blowers, and trimmers, learning has to be tailored to three different stakeholders: employees, wholesale distributors, and retailers.[55] They provide online technical training through ToolingU and support their dealers' businesses and training needs through iCademy, a distance-learning program. The Professional Instruction Program is designed for professional landscaping, tree services, and public utilities to help commercial crews best use their equipment and avoid accidents.

The Corporate University (Corporate Training Universities)

To gain the advantages of centralized training, many companies use a corporate university as shown in Figure 2.5. The **corporate university** includes employees, managers and stakeholders outside the company, including community colleges, universities, high schools, and grade schools. Corporate universities can provide significant advantages for a company's learning efforts by helping to overcome many of the historical problems that have plagued training departments (see the left side of Figure 2.5). A corporate university can help make learning more strategic by providing a clear mission and vision for learning, and ensuring that it is aligned with business needs. It can also help companies who have a strong business culture and values ensure that they are emphasized in the learning curriculum. Also, the corporate university can control costs and maximize the benefits of learning. This occurs through providing consistent training activities, disseminating

FIGURE 2.5
The Corporate University Model

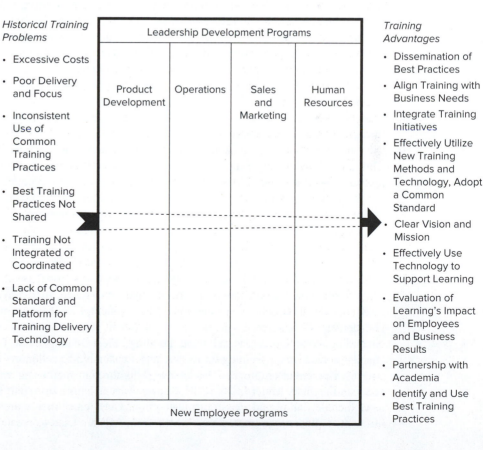

Historical Training Problems	Leadership Development Programs				*Training Advantages*
• Excessive Costs					• Dissemination of Best Practices
• Poor Delivery and Focus	Product Development	Operations	Sales and Marketing	Human Resources	• Align Training with Business Needs
• Inconsistent Use of Common Training Practices					• Integrate Training Initiatives
• Best Training Practices Not Shared					• Effectively Utilize New Training Methods and Technology, Adopt a Common Standard
• Training Not Integrated or Coordinated					• Clear Vision and Mission
• Lack of Common Standard and Platform for Training Delivery Technology					• Effectively Use Technology to Support Learning
					• Evaluation of Learning's Impact on Employees and Business Results
	New Employee Programs				• Partnership with Academia
					• Identify and Use Best Training Practices

best learning practices throughout the company, effectively using technology to support learning, evaluating learning's impact on employees and business results, and establishing partnerships with academia and other company stakeholders (community) to develop custom training and degree programs.[56] Consider the benefits that several different companies have realized from their corporate universities.

Deloitte LLP invested $300 million to build a corporate university in Westlake, Texas.[57] The corporate university includes state-of-the-art learning technology, 800 sleeping rooms, and even a ballroom. Such an investment runs counter to the cost savings and efficiencies resulting from instructional solutions such as mobile learning, virtual reality, and e-learning that require only that learners have access to a personal computer, iPhone, or iPad, eliminating the need to travel to a physical training site. Deloitte conducted extensive research before investing in a physical campus for its corporate university. The results suggested that its partners were supportive and most Generation Y (Gen-Y) employees wanted a physical location where they could meet and learn face to face. Also, the CEO believes that learning is an important investment that can provide a competitive advantage by aiding in the recruiting of talented employees and helping Deloitte LLP cope with the fast rate of change in the business.

The corporate university supports Deloitte's culture of personal and professional development for its employees. Deloitte University provides 1 million hours of the 3 million total training hours the company provides each year. The training will cover technical, professional, industry, and leadership skills. Interactive instructional techniques are used, including case discussions and simulations that require a small instructor-to-student ratio (one instructor to every five students). D Street, Deloitte's social networking system, is used by employees to interact before and after attending courses at the university to discuss what they have learned, explore potential applications, and find expertise across the company.

Corporate universities also can help effectively use new technology. Drug-store chain Walgreens University in Illinois includes technology-enhanced classrooms for face-to-face and virtual instruction, a makeup of an actual drug store, and satellite links with locations throughout the United States.[58] More than four hundred programs are offered to build employees' skills and earn credits in pharmacy-related classes from colleges.

Both large and small companies have started their own universities to train new employees, retain and update the skills and knowledge of current employees, and develop managers. ARI technicians, analysts, and fleet management experts support fleets, including cars and trucks for more than three thousand global companies.[59] These cars and trucks deliver packages and are used by salespeople to call on customers. ARI wanted to create a learning culture that supported its 2,500 employees professional development and taught employees about the company's culture and goals. As a result, ARI University was created. ARI includes three schools: Professional Development, Fleet Management Expertise, and Leadership Excellence. Professional Development focuses on building business skills including communication and team building. Fleet Management Expertise provides hands-on mechanical training for technicians. Leadership Excellence focuses on developing high-potential employees' leadership skills through mentoring with executives and courses taught by leaders across ARI. Courses vary in length from half a day to three days and include online and classroom instruction. Class enrollments are capped at twenty students to encourage interactivity. SMEs from ARI are used to create class content and often co-teach the class with an ARI training expert. In addition to classes, ARI facilitates learning by pairing mentors with new employees and encouraging peer-to-peer training within and across departments. Each department has a "learning champion," who serves as a resource on ARI University courses for other employees. ARI University uses social media including blogs and forums to share best practices. Employees can search the Internet to identify SMEs and ask them questions. ARI University has a virtual library with more than 10,000 books that employees can check out through a website. ARI also partners with more than thirty training vendors, local community colleges, and professional associations to provide courses. ARI University recognizes employees who engage in learning by inducting them into an honor society. Employees who complete 175 hours of training in two years are inducted into the honor society and have their picture taken with the company president. The success of ARI University is evaluated based on employee engagement scores and internal promotions.

Hamburger University, the corporate university for McDonald's, is charged with continuing to teach the core values that founder Ray Kroc believed were the key to success: quality, service, cleanliness, and value.[60] Hamburger University is one of the oldest and most effective corporate universities. Founded in 1961, it is estimated that approximately 5,000 McDonalds employees attend the U.S.-based Hamburger University each year, and more than 90,000 managers and owner-operators have graduated from it. Hamburger University is a global center for operations training and leadership development for McDonalds. It also gives employees the opportunity to get a college degree. McDonalds has a university in Oakbrook, Illinois, six global universities, and twenty-two regional training centers. To promote learning, the facilities and programs offered at Hamburger University are reviewed and revised. As a result, Hamburger University has transitioned away from teaching courses with a lecture format and is moving toward fewer large group sessions and more interactive learning in classes of twenty-five to thirty-five students, which are then further divided into small groups for discussion and exercises. McDonalds changed its learning format to accommodate how most of its students (who would be considered Gen-Y) learn. The typical education level of frontline service workers has influenced curriculum design through the development of more easily understandable coursework. E-learning is used to deliver the basics of restaurant operations or management training, and classroom instruction and simulations are used to help the learner apply the basics on the job. Recently, new audiovisual equipment was installed, a cybercafe was added, and large auditorium classroom spaces were converted into smaller spaces that facilitate collaboration and interaction. Virtual classrooms were also built to connect instructors with McDonalds employees around the world. Learners are provided with headphones that connect them to translators who provide instruction in the learner's native language during class. McDonalds is planning to add connectivity to classrooms that will allow learning using mobile devices and social networking.

Besides classroom instruction, Hamburger University includes a simulated kitchen and drive-through window. Despite having learners at the university who are already familiar with behind-the-counter operations, everyone takes part in the simulation, making real food and filling orders just as they would at a real McDonalds restaurant. Learners have performance goals to meet, and they receive feedback from fellow learners and trainers. Managers can support and track earner development by accessing online course completion reports of their scores on tests of their knowledge and behavior. All of McDonalds restaurant management and middle manager courses are accredited, meaning that participants can receive college credit. The credits for these courses represent half of the credits required to earn an associate's degree at a two-year college and a large number of the credits needed to receive a bachelor's degree in business administration or management at a four-year college or university. The curriculum for department managers now allows them to test content they already know, and training time has been reduced from one-and-a-half years to two years to four to six months.

Are corporate universities effective? Corporate University Xchange surveyed corporate universities at 170 different companies.[61] The top five organizational goals of corporate universities were to improve customer service and retention, improve productivity, reduce costs, retain talented employees, and increase revenue. The survey found that measuring business impact was a high priority; 70 percent of the companies measured business impact through product and service quality and customer service, and more than 50 percent measured reductions in operating costs and increased revenues.

For example, the Ritz-Carlton Hotel Company manages fifty-eight luxury hotels worldwide.[62] The Ritz-Carlton hotels and resorts are renowned for indulgent luxury. Beautiful surroundings and legendary award-winning service are provided to every guest. The Ritz-Carlton Leadership Center is designed to support the growth and expansion of the company's products and services. The Leadership Center includes the School of Performance Excellence, which houses all the training and development for hourly employees; the School of Leadership and Business Excellence, which trains leaders; and the School of Service Excellence, which helps ensure high customer service. Programs at the School of Service Excellence are offered to other companies, which has resulted in yearly revenues for Ritz-Carlton of more than $1 million. These revenues help offset the costs of training and development for employees. For example, a new customized training certification system for housekeeping staff uses CD-ROM and web-based training. The training is linked to the results of room inspections that highlight defects for the day, week, and year. The housekeeper can then identify the correct processes that are needed to remedy the defects. This just-in-time training has helped increase customer satisfaction scores at Ritz-Carlton. One hotel increased its satisfaction score with cleanliness from 82 percent to 92 percent in six months.

Creating a Corporate University

Creating a corporate university from scratch involves several steps.[63] First senior managers and business managers form a governing body with the responsibility of developing a vision for the university. (This group answers questions such as "What are the university's policies, systems, and procedures?" and "What are the key functional areas for which training courses will be developed?") Second, this vision is fleshed out, and the vision statement is linked to the business strategy. For example, Ingersoll Rand has a business goal of obtaining 38 percent of its revenue from new product innovation.[64] As a result, most of the programs and courses offered through Ingersoll Rand University discuss how to get close to the customer, innovation, and strategic marketing. The programs are designed for teams working on real business issues. Subject matter experts and managers teach these programs, which are scheduled based on key product launch dates. Third, the company decides how to fund the university. The university can be funded by charging fees to business units and/or by monies allocated directly from the corporate budget.

Fourth, the company determines the degree to which all training will be centralized. Many universities centralize the development of a learning philosophy, core curriculum design, and policies and procedures related to registration, administration, measurement, marketing, and distance learning. Local and regional on-site delivery and specialized business-unit curriculum are developed by business units. Fifth, it is important to identify the needs of university "customers," including employees, managers, suppliers, and external customers. Sixth, products and services are developed. The Bank of Montreal uses a service team that includes a client-relationship manager, a subject-matter expert, and a learning manager. The client-relationship manager works with the business units to identify their needs. The subject-matter expert identifies the skill requirements for meeting those needs. The learning manager recommends the best mix of learning, including classroom training and training based on, say, the web or CD-ROM. Seventh, the company chooses learning partners, including suppliers, consultants, colleges, and companies specializing in education. Eighth, the company develops a strategy for using technology to train more employees and do so more frequently and more cost-effectively than instructor-led training. Ninth, learning that occurs as a result of a corporate university is linked to performance improvement. This involves identifying how performance improvement will be measured (tests, sales data, etc.). For example, Sprint's corporate university, the University of Excellence, developed the Standard Training Equivalent (STE) unit, an evaluation tool for its customers who are internal business units.[65] The STE unit is equal to one hour of the traditional instructor-led classroom time that would be required to deliver a course to a group of employees at a central location. An STE unit consisting of a one-hour course over the company intranet is worth much more than the same amount of time spent in the classroom. The STE program helps the University of Excellence demonstrate its value to Sprint's business units, who fund the university. Finally, the value of the corporate university is communicated to potential "customers." Questions about the types of programs offered, how learning will occur, and how employees will enroll are addressed.

Business-Embedded Learning Function

Most companies are ensuring that their learning function is centralized to some extent so that they can better control their training costs and ensure that training is aligned with the business strategy, but at the same time respond quickly to client needs and provide high-quality services.[66] A **business-embedded (BE)** learning function is characterized by five competencies: strategic direction, product design, structural versatility, product delivery, and accountability for results. Strategic direction includes a clearly described goal and direction to the department, as well as a customer focus that includes customizing training to meet customer needs and continuously improving programs. A BE learning function not only views trainees as customers, but also views managers as customers who make decisions to send employees to training, and senior-level managers as customers who allocate money for training. Table 2.8 shows the features of a learning function that is business-embedded. BE means the learning function is customer-focused. It takes more responsibility for learning and evaluating training effectiveness, provides customized training solutions based on customer needs, and determines when and how to deliver training based on customer needs. To ensure that EMC's business strategy is supported by training, the company uses learning councils and development frameworks.[67] Every business unit, including the sales, technical, and engineering units, has education and development performance

TABLE 2.8
Features of a BE Learning Function

Source: M, Bolch, "Training Gets Down to Business," training (March/April 2010): 31–33; M. Weinstein, "Look Ahead:Long-Range Learning Plans," training (November/ December 2010): 38–41. S. S. McIntosh, "Envisioning Virtual Training Organization," *Training and Development* (May 1995): 47.

Strategic Direction
Broadly disseminates a clearly articulated mission
Recognizes that its customer base is segmented
Provides customized solutions to its clients' needs
Understands product life cycles
Organizes its offerings by competencies
Competes for internal customers

Product Design
Uses benchmarking and other innovative design
Implements strategies to develop products quickly
Involves suppliers strategically

Structural Versatility
Employs professionals who serve as product and classroom instructors, managers, and internal consultants
Uses resources from many areas
Involves line managers in determining the direction of the department's offerings and content

Product Delivery
Offers a menu of learning options
Delivers training at the work site

Accountability for Results
Believes that individual employees must take responsibility for their personal growth
Provides follow-up on the job to ensure that learning takes place
Considers the manager the key player in supporting learning
Evaluates the strategic effects of training and it's bottom-line results
Guarantees that training will improve performance

consultants who serve on the unit's learning council. The consultant's report to EMC's central training organization, thus ensuring that the needs of the business units are discussed when training delivery or design is discussed. EMC uses a consistent training design framework, which makes it easier for managers and employees in all business units to understand how training leads to skill development and career advancement. At Qualcomm Inc., the maker of cellphone chips, learning is divided into three areas: engineering/technical education, management and leadership development, and business skills development.[68] The learning function operates like an external consulting firm. Account managers are assigned to support business divisions. They assess business needs and build customized learning solutions to meet them.

The most noticeable feature of a BE function is its structure.[69] In BE training functions, all persons who are involved in the training process communicate and share resources. Trainers—who are responsible for developing training materials, delivering instruction, and supporting trainees—work together to ensure that learning occurs. For example, access to project managers and subject-matter experts can be provided by developers to instructors who usually do not have contact with these groups. The number of trainers in BE training functions varies according to the demand for products and services. The trainers not only have specialized competencies (e.g., instructional design) but can also serve as internal consultants and provide a wide range of services (e.g., needs assessment, content improvement, customization of programs, and results measurement).

Current Practice: The BE Model with Centralized Training

Because many companies are recognizing training's critical role in contributing to the business strategy, there is an increasing trend for the training function, especially in companies that have separate business units, to be organized by a blend of the BE model with centralized training that often includes a corporate university. This approach allows the company to gain the benefits of centralized training but at the same time ensure that training can provide programs, content, and delivery methods that meet the needs of specific businesses.

At General Mills, innovation is a core company value.[70] As a result, learning and development is aligned with the business strategy and its internal customers. Each of the company's functional teams develops short- and long-term strategies. For example, the marketing function holds an annual planning process (Plan to Win) to ensure that learning and development activities support the business strategy and help to build the brand. This translates into specific learning programs, such as Brand Champions, which provides brand marketing knowledge to junior marketers. Company leaders also recognize and support the relationship between business success and employee growth and development. Senior leaders sponsor learning activities, ensure that they are aligned with the business, and teach programs. Annual employee surveys include items asking employees about learning and development (such as "I believe I have opportunity for personal growth and development"). Trends in responses to these items are evaluated and considered in designing new learning initiatives, as well as assessing the capabilities and health of the business.

Learning, Training, and Development from a Change Model Perspective

As was discussed in Chapter One, change involves the adoption of a new behavior or idea by a company. There are many reasons why companies are forced to change, including the introduction of new technology, the need to better take advantage of employee skills and capitalize on a diverse workforce, or the desire to enter global markets. For training and development programs and learning initiatives to contribute to the business strategy, they must be successfully implemented, accepted, and used by customers (including managers, executives, and employees).

Four conditions are necessary for change to occur: (1) Employees must understand the reasons for change and agree with those reasons; (2) employees must have the skills needed to implement the change; (3) employees must see that managers and other employees in powerful positions support the change; and (4) organizational structures, such as compensation and performance management systems, must support the change.[71] For managers and employees, change is not easy. Even when employees know that a practice or program could be better, they have learned to adapt to its inadequacies. Therefore, resistance to new training and development practices is likely. Prior to implementing a new training or development practice, trainers should consider how they can increase the likelihood of its acceptance.

Figure 2.6 provides a model of change. The process of change is based on the interaction among four components of the organization: task, employees, formal organizational arrangements (structures, processes, and systems), and informal organization (communication patterns, values, and norms).[72] As shown in the figure, different types of change-related problems occur depending on the organizational component that is influenced by the change. For example, introducing new technology for training into a company (such as

FIGURE 2.6
A Change Model

Sources: David A. Nadler and Michael L. Tushman, "A Congruence Model for Diagnosing Organizational Behavior," in *Organizational Psychology: A Book of Readings,* ed. D. Rabin and J. McIntyre (Englewood Cliffs, NJ: Prentice Hall, 1979), as reprinted in David A. Nadler, "Concepts for the Management of Organizational Change," in *Readings in the Management of Innovation,* 2d ed., eds. M. L. Tushman and N. Moore (Cambridge, MA: Ballinger Publishing Co., 1988): 722.

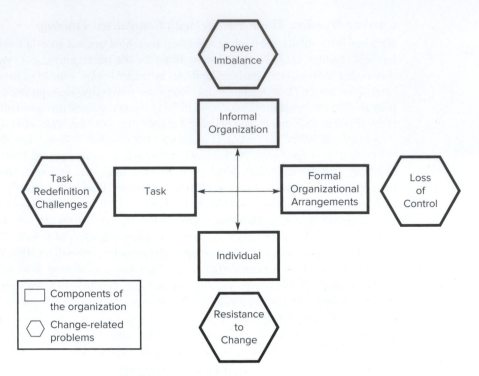

multimedia training using the Internet) might cause changes in the organization's power structure. With the new technology, managers may have less control over access to training programs than they had with traditional methods of training. The result is tension related to the power imbalance created by the new system. If these issues are not dealt with, managers will not accept the new technology or provide support for transfer of training.

The four change-related problems that need to be addressed before implementation of any new training practice are resistance to change, loss of control, power imbalance, and task redefinition. **Resistance to change** refers to managers' and employees' unwillingness to change. Managers and employees may be anxious about change, feel that they will be unable to cope, value the current training practice, or do not understand the value of the new practice. **Control** relates change to managers' and employees' ability to obtain and distribute valuable resources such as data, information, or money. Changes can cause managers and employees to have less control over resources. Change can also give managers and employees control over processes that they have not previously been involved in (e.g., choosing which training programs to attend). **Power** refers to the ability to influence others. Managers may lose the ability to influence employees as employees gain access to databases and other information, thus getting more autonomy to deliver products and services. Employees may be held accountable for learning in self-directed training. Web-based training methods, such as **task redefinition,** create changes in managers' and employees' roles and job responsibilities. Employees may be asked not only to participate in training, but also to consider how to improve its quality. Managers may be asked to become facilitators and coaches.

Senior managers often make three important mistakes in trying to implement change, which can result in failure to produce the desired results.[73] These include telling or issuing communications for employees to "buy in" to the changes, believing that they know enough about the company to understand the impact of change on individuals and how the change should be managed to achieve the desired results, and ignoring or not giving enough consideration to barriers that may slow down or cause change initiatives to fail. Training departments are often in the best position to help senior company leaders implement change, especially if they play a strategic role in the company, because they interact and have the opportunity to hear from business leaders and employees about problems, challenges, and needs they are facing. For example, The Economical Insurance Group (TEIG) restructured its Learning and Development unit into Learning and Education and Organizational Development, consisting of four areas: Leadership, Organizational Culture, Learning Culture, and Learning Transformation.[74] Organizational Development helps in shaping and creating organizational change through assessing the current state of the organization against its future needs, and reduces the gaps between the two through action planning and development. The goal of Learning and Organization Development is to use assessment data, development tools, change interventions, and learning opportunities to promote a culture of excellence and help achieve TEIG's mission, vision, and goals.

Table 2.9 shows seven key steps that training professionals can take to help senior managers effectively manage a change initiative.

MARKETING TRAINING AND CREATING A BRAND

Despite the increased recognition of the importance of training and learning to achieving business goals, many managers and employees may not recognize the value of training. Internal marketing involves making employees and managers excited about training and learning. Internal marketing is especially important for trainers who act as internal consultants to business units. For internal consultants to survive, they must generate fees for their services. Some, if not all, of their operating expenses come from fees paid for their services. Marketing is also important for the successful adoption of new training programs by helping to overcome resistance to change, especially misconceptions about the value of training. Here are some successful internal marketing tactics:[75]

- Involve the target audience in developing the training or learning effort.
- Demonstrate how a training and development program can be used to solve specific business needs.
- Showcase an example of how training has been used within the company to solve specific business needs.
- Identify a "champion" (e.g., a top-level manager) who actively supports training.
- Listen and act on feedback received from clients, managers, and employees.
- Advertise on e-mail, on company websites, and in employee break areas.
- Designate someone in the training function as an account representative who will interact between the training designer or team and the business unit, which is the customer.
- Determine what financial numbers—such as return on assets, cash flow from operations, or net profit or loss—top-level executives are concerned with and show how training and development will help improve those numbers.

- Speak in terms that employees and managers understand. Don't use jargon.
- Win a local or national training industry award or recognition.
- Publicize learner or manager success stories or feature those who have earned certifications or degrees using newsletters or websites.

It is also important to develop and communicate the training brand. A **brand** includes the look and feeling of the training function that is used to create expectations for its customers.[76] The brand is used to acquire and retain customers. To build a training brand, follow the suggestions shown in Table 2.10. The training function also needs to develop its own strategy and communicate it to its customers.[77] The strategy should include what products and services it plans to offer, how training requests will be handled and by whom, how it will demonstrate partnerships with other departments and business units in the company, and the service level that it intends to provide to customers. Service before, during, and after training, development, or other learning initiatives needs to be considered. The training function strategy should be aligned with and contribute to the business strategy.

TABLE 2.9
Steps in a Change Process

Sources: Based on C. McAllaster, "Leading Change by Effectively Utilizing Leverage Points Within an Organization," *Organizational Dynamics* 33 (2004): 318; L. Freifeld, "Changes with Penguins," *training* (June 2008): 24–28, N. Miller, "Brave New World," *T+D* (June 2010): 54–58.

1. **Clarify the request for change.** Is the stated reason for change an important issue? How does the change fit into the company's business strategy? Why are you making the change? How many people does this affect, and how does it affect them? What are the outcomes of the change?
2. **Make the vision clear.** Identify the reason for the change, what will be achieved, and how the change will be achieved.
3. **Design the solution.** What is the best mix of performance measures and feedback, support tools, learning plans, formal training, and job processes? Review the potential risks and benefits of different approaches.
4. **Communicate and market for buy-in.** Connect with other groups that will be involved, including communications, finance, and operations, to consider the impact of the change and develop an internal marketing plan. Employees need to know what is occurring. Use briefings, newsletters, discussion boards, websites, and informational meetings. Senior managers need to be visible and involved in communicating about the change.
5. **Choose and announce the action as soon as possible.** Employees affected by the change must hear about it as soon as possible. Employees need to know why and how the final action was selected, how the process has progressed, and what is going to happen in the next days and months. Communicating logic and reasoning can help overcome resistance to change. Provide short previews to employees so they know what changes are coming.
6. **Execute and create short-term wins.** Success requires management attention and the desire to do it right. Managers and change leaders must model new behavior and become enthusiastic supporters for the process. Leaders should involve employees and provide them with the necessary training and resources. If a pilot test or beta program is used, employees should be kept informed on its progress and asked for their opinions. Learning should occur from any mistakes.
7. **Follow up, reevaluate, and modify.** Be flexible and make changes if they are needed. Share information about mistakes or issues, and work with the employees affected to fix them.

TABLE 2.10
How to Build a Training Brand

Source: Based on A. Hand, "How to enhance your training brand," *T+D* (February 2011): 76–77.

- Ask current "customers" of training, including managers who purchase or ask for training and employees who participate in training what their perceptions are of the brand. For example, what emotions describe how they feel about the training brand? What words summarize their feelings? What conclusions have they made about doing business with you? Answers to these questions provide information regarding the strength of the training brand and if it is being perceived positively or as intended.
- Define how you want to be perceived by current and future customers.
- Identify factors that influence your customer's perceptions of the training function.
- Review each of the factors to determine if it is supporting and communicating the brand to your customers in a way that you intended.
- Make changes so that each factor is supporting the brand.
- Get customers feedback at each step of this process (define the brand, identify factors, suggest changes, etc.).
- When interacting with customers, create an experience that supports and identifies the brand.

For example, ABB, an automation and power technology company whose products include electrical transformers to control systems for power grids, takes several steps to internally market training programs to their software developers.[78] They ensure sure that training is held on days when learners can attend. Employees in every time zone are offered at least one class time during their workday and no classes are scheduled on holidays. They treat employees as customers by providing a learning coordinator to help employees enroll using an online system, to answer questions, and to send a reminder to employees about upcoming classes. A database is used to track the types of classes in which learners enroll so they can be notified of other courses in that area or the next level course. To create a sense of urgency, it is communicated to employees that courses will be offered only during a specific timeframe.

The training department at Booz Allen Hamilton, a consulting firm in McLean, Virginia, develops a marketing plan every year that includes a branding strategy (how the department will be recognized, including logos and slogans); overall marketing objectives; techniques for communications with employees, managers, and all internal customers; and plans for launching all new learning programs.[79] One marketing objective is to increase awareness of the company's Center for Performance Excellence and to make it a tool for employee recruitment and retention. The marketing effort communicates the message that training programs will help workers in their jobs and their careers. Also, Booz Allen's accomplishments, such as appearing on *training* magazine's list of top 100 training companies, are communicated to prospective hires to show them that the company takes training and development seriously.

Training functions are beginning to become profit centers by selling training courses or seats in training courses to other companies.[80] Companies sell training services for a number of reasons. Some businesses are so good at a particular aspect of their operations that other companies are asking for their expertise. Other companies aim training at their own customers or dealers. In some cases, the training department sells unused seats in training programs or e-learning courses. For example, Walt Disney Company sells training on customer service and organizational creativity at the Disney Institute in Florida. The institute gives employees from other companies the opportunity to understand how

Disney developed its business strengths, including leadership development, service, customer loyalty, and team building. Zappos Insights is a department within Zappos that was created to share the Zappos culture with other companies.[81] Zappos is known for its WOW customer service philosophy (see the end of chapter case in Chapter One). Zappos Insights provides programs about building a culture (3 Day Culture Camp), its WOW service philosophy (School of Wow), the power of a coaching-based culture (Coaching Event), how the human resources function protects the culture and how its program's support it (People Academy), and custom programs. The cost to attend these programs ranges from $2,000 to $6,000 for each attendee. Randstad sells online training to its customers, who employ Randstad's workers in customer service call centers.[82] Although Randstad makes revenue by selling the training, its greater benefit is realized from building relationships with its clients. Within a one-year period, Randstad was able to show that $45 million in company business was influenced by providing training to clients who chose the company (or stayed with the company).

OUTSOURCING TRAINING

Outsourcing refers to the use of an outside company (an external services firm) that takes complete responsibility and control of some training or development activities or that takes over all or most of a company's training, including administration, design, delivery, and development.[83] **Business process outsourcing** refers to the outsourcing of any business process, such as HRM, production, or training. Survey results suggest that slightly more than half of all companies outsource instruction.[84] Less than half outsource some or all of the responsibility for developing customized training content and courses. Why would companies outsource training? Some of the reasons are cost savings; time savings that allow a company to focus on business strategy; improvements in compliance and accuracy in training mandated to comply with federal, state, or local rules (e.g., safety training); the lack of capability within the company to meet learning demands; and the desire to access best training practices. Some companies choose a comprehensive approach, outsourcing all training activities. For example, consider the outsource provider Accenture Learning Business Process Outsourcing.[85] Accenture Learning operates Avaya University for Avaya, a global leader in communication systems, applications, and services.[86] Accenture helped Telstra, Australia's leading telecommunications and information services company, develop self-paced e-learning, as well as virtual instructor-led training and podcasting to provide learning opportunities to its geographically diverse workforce. Although some companies are beginning to outsource and the trend appears to be growing, most companies outsource only smaller projects, not the complete training and development function. Two reasons that companies do not outsource their training are (1) the inability of outsourcing providers to meet company needs and (2) companies' desire to maintain control over all aspects of training and development, especially delivery and learning content. Table 2.11 shows some of the questions that should be considered when a company is deciding whether to outsource. Any decision to outsource training is complex. Training functions that do not add any value to the company are likely candidates for outsourcing (see Table 2.11, Questions 1–4 and 9). Many companies have training functions that add value to the business but still may not be capable of meeting all training needs.

TABLE 2.11
**Questions to
Ask When
Considering
Outsourcing**

Sources: Based on
G. Johnson, "To
Outsource or Not to
Outsource . . . That Is
the Question," *Train-
ing* (August 2004):
26–29; K. Tyler,
"Carve Out Training?"
HR Magazine (Febru-
ary 2004): 52–57.
N. Srivastava, "Want
to Stay Competi-
tive and Cut Costs?
Consider Outsourced
Training," *Workforce*
(January 2015): 47.

1. What are the capabilities of your in-house training function? Does the staff know enough that you can grow the training skills you need, or do you need to hire training skills from the outside?
2. Can your in-house training function take on additional training responsibilities?
3. Is training key to your company's strategy? Is it proprietary?
4. Does your company value its training organization?
5. Does the training content change rapidly?
6. Are outsourced trainers viewed as experts, or are they viewed with cynicism?
7. Do you understand the strengths and weaknesses of your current training programs?
8. Do you want to outsource the entire training function?
9. Are executive trying to minimize training's impact on your company? Does your company accept responsibility for building skills and talent?
10. Is a combination of internal and external training the best solution?

For example, a company that has a strong skilled training function, values training, and views it as important to the business strategy probably doesn't need to outsource its entire training function. However, that company may turn to outsourcing providers for special training needs beyond staff capabilities or for certain training content that changes rapidly. Consider the case of Texas Instruments (TI).[87] TI contracted General Physics (now known as 6P strategies), a training outsource provider, to conduct all its open-enrollment courses for professional development and technical training. These courses are offered often by TI in areas in which knowledge changes quickly. As a result, these courses were seen as the best candidates for outsourcing, and TI wanted to achieve cost savings by outsourcing them. TI is still in charge of its customized professional development offerings. In the outsourcing agreement, TI was careful to include contract language that allowed it to raise and lower the amount of training that it was buying as needed. Given the cyclical nature of the semiconductor business, the ability to raise and lower the amount of training, yet still keep customized programs that add significant value to the business, was an important reason that TI decided to outsource some of its training programs. Research suggests that company satisfaction with the outsourcing of training and development depends on company-supplier trust (e.g., managers of both the company and the outsource provider are loyal to each other and look out for each other's interests) and the specificity of the contract (e.g., whether the contract clearly outlines responsibilities).[88]

Summary

For training to help a company gain a competitive advantage, it must help the company reach business goals and objectives. This chapter emphasized how changes in work roles, organizational factors, and the role of training influence the amount and type of training, as well as the organization of the training functions. The process of strategic training and development was discussed. The chapter explained how different strategies (such as concentration, internal growth, external growth, and disinvestment) influence the goals of the business and create different training needs. The chapter included a discussion of different models of the training function. Because training makes a greater contribution to the achievement of business strategies and goals, the business-embedded and corporate university models will become more prevalent. Because learning, training, and development involve change, the chapter discusses the conditions necessary for managers and employees to accept and benefit from new programs. The chapter concluded with information about marketing and outsourcing the training function.

Key Terms

business strategy, *63*

learning organization, *65*

goals, *69*

mission, *69*

vision, *69*

values, *69*

SWOT analysis, *70*

external analysis, *70*

internal analysis, *70*

strategic choice, *71*

strategic training and
  development initiatives, *72*

metrics, *77*

balanced scorecard, *77*

human resource
  management (HRM)
  practices, *85*

staffing strategy, *86*

uniqueness, *87*

strategic value, *87*

human resource
  planning, *88*

concentration strategy, *89*

internal growth strategy, *89*

external growth
  strategy, *89*

disinvestment strategy, *89*

centralized training, *92*

corporate university, *93*

business-embedded
  (BE), *97*

resistance to change, *100*

control, *100*

power, *100*

task redefinition, *100*

brand, *102*

outsourcing, *104*

business process
  outsourcing, *104*

Discussion Questions

1. How would you expect the training activities of a company that is dominant in its product market to differ from those of a company that emphasizes research and development?

2. What do you think is the most important organizational characteristic that influences training? Why?

3. Why could the business-embedded model be considered the best way to organize the training function?

4. Schering-Plough HealthCare Products Inc. decided several years ago to expand its product line by developing pocket-size sticks and sprays of Coppertone sunblock, previously only available as lotions packaged in squeeze bottles. The company placed a strategic emphasis on developing markets for this product. The company knew from market research studies that its Coppertone customers were already using the product in its original squeeze container at the beach. Due to increased awareness of the dangers of excessive skin exposure, consumers who had not previously used sunblock except when at the beach were looking for a daily sunblock product. Company managers reasoned that their market could be expanded significantly if the product were repackaged to fit conveniently in consumers' pockets, purses, and gym bags. Identify the business strategy. What training needs result from this strategy? What are the training implications of this decision for (1) manufacturing and (2) the sales force?

5. Which strategic training and development initiatives do you think all companies should support regardless of economic conditions? Why?

6. Are any of the strategic training and development initiatives more important for small business? Explain.

7. How can a training function support a business strategy?

8. How does the strategic value of jobs and their uniqueness influences how training and learning resources are invested?

9. What is human capital? How is human capital influencing the changing role of training from skill and knowledge acquisition to creating and sharing knowledge?

10. How could SWOT analysis be used to align training activities with business strategies and goals?

11. What are the training implications of the increased use of teams to manufacture products or provide services?

12. How would you design a corporate university? Explain each step you would take.

13. What are the advantages and disadvantages of a centralized training function?

14. What factors should a company consider in deciding whether to outsource its entire training function? Are the considerations different if the company wants to outsource a training program? Explain.

15. What is a training "brand"? Why is it important? How does it relate to marketing the training or learning function in an organization?

16. What does "change" have to do with training and learning? What four change-related problems need to be addressed for a new training program to be accepted by employees?

Application Assignments

1. Go to *www.mcdonalds.com*, the website for McDonalds. Review "Our Story." Next, under "careers," click on "training and education" and "Hamburger University." Watch the video on "college credit connections." Answer the following questions:

   a. Does Hamburger University support the company's business? Explain why or why not.

   b. Identify the learning resources available at Hamburger University and how they contribute to the business strategy.

2. Find a company's annual report by using the Internet or visiting a library. Using the annual report, do the following:

   a. Identify the company's mission, values, and goals.

   b. Find any information provided in the report regarding the company's training practices and how they relate to the goals and strategies. Be prepared to give a brief presentation of your research to the class.

3. Go to *www.orkin.com*, the website for Orkin, a company committed to providing the world's best pest and termite control. Click on "Careers" at the bottom of the page. Investigate the company by clicking on "Who We Are," "Benefits," "Opportunities," and "Community Involvement." Click on "Orkin Training." What type of training does Orkin offer employees? Is training strategic? Why or why not? How does Orkin use training to contribute to the company's competitive advantage?

4. Go to *www.corpu.com*, the website for Corporate University Xchange, a corporate education and research and consulting firm that is an expert on corporate universities. What kind of information about corporate universities is available on this site? Why is it useful?

5. Go to http://*www.9p-strategy.com/*, the website for 6P strategies, an outsourcing company that specializes in training for the automotive industry. What services does 6P strategies provide? What are the advantages and disadvantages of outsourcing training to 6P strategies?

6. Watch the YouTube video on IBM's Learning Administration at *www.youtube .com?watch?v=LefBrIBEYSC*. What is included in learning administration? What are the benefits that a company would gain by having IBM provide learning administration?

Case: *IBM Offers Training (and Pay Cuts) to Employees to Learn New Technologies*

Some employees in IBM's Global Technology Services group received e-mails from the company informing them that a recent evaluation had identified them as an employee who had not kept pace with acquiring the necessary skills and expertise needed to meet changing client needs, technology, and markets. As a result, IBM requires them to dedicate one day a week or up to twenty-three total days between October 2014 and March 2015 to focus on training. During this time, the employee will take a pay cut, receiving only 90 percent of their base salary. Once training is completed, salaries will be restored in full. Employees can either take the training or look for job opportunities within IBM that better match their current skill set.

Employees have reacted negatively toward the program. Some feel the program with its pay cut is unfair because their work has received positive evaluations from their managers. Also, employees noted that all workers in their group were being assigned to the same training program regardless of their individual skill levels. A few employees believe that the training program is a cost-cutting exercise that is being presented as a training program. A spokesperson for IBM emphasized that the salary cut and retraining program was not standard practice across IBM, but affected only a few hundred employees in the U.S. technology services outsourcing business. The purpose of the program is to help employees develop key skills in areas such as cloud and mobile computing and advanced data analytics. Because the program can help employees in the long term to increase their billable hours with clients, IBM believes the salary cut is a co-investment cost shared by both the employees and the company. IBM calculated that it will lose one day of billing clients each week that the employees are in the training program, which matches the 20 percent of the compensation of the employees involved. So the 10 percent salary cut actually splits the difference.

Do you believe this program is strategic? Why or why not? Should employees' salaries be reduced for the time they attend training programs? Provide a rationale for your answer. What other ways might IBM convinced the affected employees to update and gain new skills?

Sources: P. Thibodeau, "IBM Cuts Pay by 10% for Workers Picked for Training," *Computerworld* (September 15, 2014). Accessed from *www.computerworld.com* February 12, 2015; S. Lohr, "IBM Offers Workers Training and Pay Cuts," *New York Times* (September 17, 2014). Accessed from *http://bits .blogs.nytimes.com* February 12, 2015; P. Cappelli, "Back to the Future at IBM," *Human Resource Executive*.

Endnotes

1. J. Meister, "The CEO-Driven Learning Culture," *Training and Development* (June 2000): 52–70. P. Wright, B. Dunford, and S. Snell, "Contributions of the resource-based view of the firm to the field of strategic HRM: Convergence of two fields," *Journal of Management*, 27 (2001): 701–721.

2. S. Rosenbaum and L. Stevens, "At UPS, the algorithm is the driver," *Wall Street Journal* (February 17, 2105): B1, B4; E. Short, "At UPS, strategy is worth 1000 trucks," *Chief Learning Officer* (June 2014): 40–41.

3. R. S. Schuler and S. F. Jackson, "Linking Competitive Strategies with Human Resource Management Practices," *Academy of Management Executive* 1 (1987): 207–219; R. Noe and M. Tews, "Strategic training and development," in *The Routledge Companion to Strategic Human Resource Management, eds.* J. Storey, P. Wright, and D. Ulrich (New York: Routledge, 2009): 262–284.

4. U. Sessa and M. London, *Continuous Learning in Organizations* (Mahwah, NJ: Erlbaum, 2006); J.C. Meister and K. Willyerd, *The 2020 Workplace* (New York: HarperCollins, 2010); D. Garvin, A. Edmondson, and E. Gino, "Is Yours a Learning Organization," *Harvard Business Review* (March 2008): 109–116.

5. K. Andreola, "Groom to move," *HR Magazine* (May 2014): 38–40.

6. F. Gino and G. Pisano, "Why leaders don't learn from success," *Harvard Business Review* (April 2011): 68–74; R. McGrath, "Failing by design," *Harvard Business Review* (April 2011): 77–83.

7. M. Weinstein, "Managing the Magic," *Training* (July/August 2008): 20–22.

8. E. Catmull, "How Pixar Fosters Collective Creativity," *Harvard Business Review* (September 2008): 64–72.

9. J. B. Quinn, P. Andersen, and S. Finkelstein, "Leveraging Intellect," *Academy of Management Executive* 10 (1996): 7–39; B. Campbell, R. Coff, and D. Kryscynski, "Rethinking sustained competitive advantage from human capital," *Academy of Management Review*, 37 (2010): 376–395.

10. K. Ellis, "Share Best Practices Globally," *Training* (July 2001): 32–38.

11. R. Hughes and K. Beatty, "Five Steps to Leading Strategically," *T+D* (December 2005): 46–48; M. Bloch, "Training gets down to business," *training* (March/April 2010): 31–33; M. Weinstein, "Look ahead: Long-range learning plans," *training* (November/December 2010): 38–41; B. O'Connell, "Why CEOs want faster training—No matter the cost," from *http://www.forbes.com/sites/bmoharrisbank/2013/01/08/why-ceos-want-faster-training-no-matter-what-the-cost/*, accessed February 11, 2013.

12. R. Noe, J. Hollenbeck, B. Gerhart, and P. Wright, *Human Resource Management: Gaining a Competitive Advantage* (New York: McGraw-Hill–Irwin, 2013); K. Golden and V. Ramanujam, "Between a dream and a nightmare," *Human Resource Management* 24 (1985): 429–451; C. Hill and G. Jones, *Strategic Management Theory: An Integrated Approach* (Boston: Houghton Mifflin, 1989).

13. M. Weinstein, "Look ahead: Long-range learning plans," *training* (November/December 2010): 38–41.

14. S. Tannenbaum, "A Strategic View of Organizational Training and Learning," in *Creating, Implementing, and Managing Effective Training and Development,* ed. K. Kriger (San Francisco: Jossey-Boss, 2002): 10–52.

15. M. Lippitt, "Fix the Disconnect between Strategy and Execution," *T+D* (August 2007): 54–56.

16. M. Bolch, "Training gets down to business," *training* (March/April 2010): 31–33.

17. Reliance Industries Ltd., Group Manufacturing Services, *T+D* (October 2011): 80.

18. P. Harris, "Instilling competencies from top to bottom," *T+D* (October 2011): 65–66.

19. R. Pyrillis, "Qualcom: Mobile-friendly learning," *Chief Learning Officer* (June 2014): 36–37.

20. A. McIlvaine, "Banking on service," *HR Executive* (April 2014): 14–16.

21. D. Zielinski, "In-house connections," *HR Magazine* (August 2011): 65.

22. B. O'Connell, "Why CEOs want faster training—No matter the cost," from http://www.forbes.com/sites/bmoharrisbank/2013/01/08/why-ceos-want-faster-training-no-matter-what-the-cost/, accessed February 11, 2013.

23. E. Short, "ADP: Help clients, help the company," *Chief Learning Officer* (June 2014): 38–39; *www.adp.com*, website for Automatic Data Processing (ADP), accessed March 16, 2015.

24. F. Kalman, "Accenture: Staying ahead of the curve," *Chief Learning Officer* (June 2014): 24–25.

25. K. Fyfe-Mills, "Committed to talent development excellence," *TD* (October 2014): 38–41.

26. R. Kaplan and D. Norton, "The Balanced Scorecard—Measures That Drive Performance," *Harvard Business Review* (January–February 1992): 71–79; R. Kaplan and D. Norton, "Putting the Balanced Scorecard to Work," *Harvard Business Review* (September–October 1993): 134–147.

27. J. Salopek, "Best 2005: EMC Corporation," *T+D* (October 2005): 42–43.

28. R. Smith, "Aligning Learning with Business Strategy," *T+D* (November 2008): 40–43.

29. "A high-touch, low-tech approach to training," *T+D* (October 2009): 60–62; *www.barilla.com*, website for Barilla. "Barilla Group announces $26.5 million expansion at Ames, Iowa facility," news release from Media Relations (January 16, 2015) at *www.barillagroup.com*, accessed March 16, 2015.

30. J. Salopek, "Learning-assisted service," *T+D*, October 2010, 40–42; website for Mike's Carwash at *www.mikescarwash.com*; T. Jones, "Inner Strength," *Modern Car Magazine,* April 2008, 48–53.

31. R. J. Campbell, "HR Development Strategies," in *Developing Human Resources,* ed. K. N. Wexley (Washington, D.C.: BNA Books, 1991): 5-1–5-34; J. K. Berry, "Linking Management Development to Business Strategy," *Training and Development* (August 1990): 20–22.

32. D. F. Van Eynde, "High-Impact Team Building Made Easy," *HR Horizons* (Spring 1992): 37–41; J. R. Hackman, ed., *Groups That Work and Those That Don't: Creating Conditions for Effective Teamwork* (San Francisco: Jossey-Bass, 1990); D. McCann and C. Margerison, "Managing High-Performance Teams," *Training and Development* (November 1989): 53–60.

33. A. I. Kraut, P. R. Pedigo, D. D. McKenna, and M. D. Dunnette, "The Role of the Manager: What's Really Important in Different Managerial Jobs," *Academy of Management Executive* 4 (1988): 36–48; F. Luthans, "Successful versus Effective Real Managers," *Academy of Management Executive* 2 (1988): 127–32; H. Mintzberg, *The Nature of Managerial Work* (New York: Harper and Row, 1973); S. W. Floyd and B. Wooldridge, "Dinosaurs or Dynamos? Recognizing Middle Management's Strategic Role," *Academy of Management Executive* 8 (1994): 47–57.

34. P. Kizilos, "Fixing Fatal Flaws," *Training* (September 1991): 66–70; F. S. Hall, "Dysfunctional Managers: The Next Human Resource Challenge," *Organizational Dynamics* (August 1991): 48–57; J. Zenger and J. Folkman, "Ten fatal flaws that derail leaders," *Harvard Business Review* (June 2009): 18.

35. J. Meister, "The CEO-Driven Learning Culture," *Training and Development* (June 2000): 52–70.

36. T. Bingham and P. Galagan, "Wanting it more," *TD* (January 2015): 32–36; J. Dearborn, "'Learning at the speed of business,'" SAP leads in the cloud," *TD* (January 2015): 38–41.

37. R. Smith, "Aligning Learning with Business Strategy," *T+D* (November 2008): 40–43.

38. K. Kuehner-Hebert, "Philips: A learning organization transformed," *Chief Learning Officer* (October 2014): 22–25; F. Kalman, "Accenture: Staying ahead of the curve," *Chief Learning Officer* (June 2014): 24–25; S. McCartney, "A future model for flight crews," *Wall Street Journal* (December 4, 2014): D1–D2.

39. K. Dobbs, "Winning the Retention Game," *Training* (September 1999): 50–56. Good to grow: 2014 U.S. CEO survey," PricewaterhouseCoopers LLP, from *www.pwc.com*, accessed February 20, 2015.

40. N. Breuer, "Shelf Life," *Workforce* (August 2000): 28–32.

41. J. Barney, "Firm resources and sustained competitive advantage," *Journal of Management*, 17 (1991): 99–120; P. Wright, B. Dunford, and S. Snell, " Human resources and the resource-based view of the firm," *Journal of Management* 27 (2001): 701–721; R. Ployart, J. Weekley, and K. Baughman, "The structure and function of human capital emergence: A multilevel examination of the attraction-selection-attrition model," *Academy of Management Journal* 49 (2006): 661–677; T. Crook, S. Todd, J. Combs, D. Woehr, and D. Ketchen, "Does human capital matter? A meta-analysis of the relationship between human capital and firm performance," *Journal of Applied Psychology* 96 (2011): 443–456.

42. J. A. Sonnenfeld and M. A. Peiperl, "Staffing policy as a strategic response: A typology of career systems," *Academy of Management Review* 13 (1988): 588–600.

43. D. Lepak and S. Snell, "Examining the human resource architecture: The relationships among human capital, employment, and human resource configurations," *Journal of Management* 28 (2002): 517–543.

44. V. R. Ceriello and C. Freeman, *Human Resource Management Systems: Strategies, Tactics, and Techniques* (Lexington, MA: Lexington Books, 1991).

45. Constellation Energy, "Shining stars," *T+D* (October 2008): 35–36.

46. D. T. Jaffe and C. D. Scott, "Career Development for Empowerment in a Changing Work World," in *New Directions in Career Planning and the Workplace,* ed. J. M. Kummerow (Palo Alto, CA: Consulting Psychologist Press, 1991): 33–60; L. Summers, "A logical approach to development planning," *Training and Development* 48 (1994): 22–31; D. B. Peterson and M. D. Hicks, *Development First* (Minneapolis, MN: Personnel Decisions, 1995).

47. A. P. Carnevale, L. J. Gainer, and J. Villet, *Training in America* (San Francisco: Jossey-Bass, 1990); L. J. Gainer, "Making the competitive connection: Strategic management and training," *Training and Development* (September 1989): s1–s30.

48. S. Raghuram and R. D. Arvey, "Business strategy links with staffing and training practices," *Human Resource Planning* 17 (1994): 55–73.

49. K. Featherly, "Culture shock," *Training* (November 2005): 24–29.

50. J. J. Salopek, "Good Connections," *TD* (October 2014): 48–50.

51. J. Bersin, "Mastering the skills supply chain problem," *Chief Learning Officer* (April 2014): 14.

52. K. Linebaugh, "Idle workers busy at Toyota," *The Wall Street Journal* (October 13, 2008): B1, B3.

53. K. Ellis, "The mindset that matters: Linking learning to the business," *Training* (May 2005): 38–43.

54. J. Dearborn, "'Learning at the speed of business,' SAP leads in the cloud," *TD* (January 2015): 38–41.

55. T. Bingham and Pat Galagan, "Training powers up at STIHL," *T+D* (January 2014): 29–33; C. Gambill, "Creating learning solutions to satisfy customers," *T+D* (January 2014): 35–39.

56. J. Li and A. Abei, "Prioritizing and maximizing the impact of corporate universities," *T+D* (May 2011): 54–57.

57. P. Galagan, "Back to bricks and mortar," *T+D* (March 2011): 30–31.

58. P. Harris, "The value-add of learning," *TD* (October 2014): 53–55.

59. K. Andreola, "Groom to move," *HR Magazine* (May 2014): 38–40.

60. M. Weinstein, "Getting McSmart," *Training* (May 2008): 44–47.

61. "Training Today: Update on corporate universities," *Training* (April 2005): 8.

62. "Ritz-Carlton: #9," *Training* (March 2005): 45–46.

63. J. Meister, "Ten steps to creating a corporate university," *Training and Development* (November 1998): 38–43.

64. L. Freifeld, "CU there," *Training* (May 2008): 48–49.

65. G. Johnson, "Nine tactics to take your corporate university from good to great," *Training* (July/August 2003) 38–42. "Professional and career development," from Sprint website. *http://careers.sprint.com/work.html,* accessed December 21, 2001.

66. S. S. McIntosh, "Envisioning virtual training organization," *Training and Development* (May 1995): 46–49.

67. H. Dolezalek, "EMC's competitive advantage," *Training* (February 2009): 42–46.

68. R. Pyrillis, "Qualcom: Mobile-friendly Learning," *Chief Learning Officer* (June 2014): 36–37.

69. B. Mosher, "How 'siloed' is your training organization?" *Chief Learning Officer* (July 2003): 13.

70. N. Morera, "A 'brand' new way of learning," *Chief Learning Officer* (May 30, 2011) at http://clomedia.com, accessed September 28, 2011.

71. E. Lowsen and C. Prive, "The psychology of change management," *The McKinsey Quarterly 2* (2003).

72. D. A. Nadler, "Concepts for the Management of Organizational Change," in *Readings in the Management of Innovation,* 2d ed, M. L. Tushman and N. L.Moore (Cambridge, MA: Ballenger): 722.

73. N. Miller, "Brave new role," *T+D* (June 2010): 54–58.

74. L. Freifeld, "TEIG locks in on leadership," *training* (January/February 2012): 34–39.

75. W. Webb, "Who moved my training?" *Training* (January 2003): 22–26; T. Seagraves, "The inside pitch," *T+D* (February 2005): 40–45; K. Oakes, "Over the top or on the money," *T+D* (November 2005): 20–22; H. Dolezalek, "Building buzz," *training* (March/April 2010): 36–38; J. Burandt, "Be the talk of the office," *T+D* (February 2014): 24–26.

76. A. Hand, "How to enhance your training brand," *T+D* (February 2011): 76–77.

77. R. Cooperman, "Value over profit," *T+D* (May 2010): 58–62.

78. J. Hudepohl, "Consistency brings results," *T+D* (June 2014): 64–69.

79. S. Boehle, "Get your message out," *Training* (February 2005): 36–41.

80. J. Gordon, "Selling it on the side," *Training* (December 2005): 34–39.

81. "Zappos insights" from *www.zapposinsights.com*, accessed March 16, 2015.

82. D. Sussman, "What HPLOs know," *T+D* (August 2005); 35–39.

83. N. DeViney and B. Sugrue, "Learning outsourcing: A reality check," *T+D* (December 2004): 40–45; G. Johnson, "To outsource or not to outsource . . . That is the question," *Training* (August 2004): 26–29.

84. "2014 training industry report," *training* (November/December 2014): 16–29.

85. P. Harris, "Outsourced training begins to find its niche," *T+D* (November 2004); DeViney and Sugrue, "Learning outsourcing."

86. Harris, "Outsourced training begins." "Learning BPO Client Successes," from *www.accenture.com*, website for Accenture, accessed December 21, 2011.

87. C. Cornell, "Changing the supply chain," *Human Resource Executive* (March 2, 2005): 32–35.

88. T. Gainey and B. Klass, "The outsourcing of training and development: Factors affecting client satisfaction," *Journal of Management* 29(2): 207–229 (2003).

Case 1 — Learning in Practice

Dow Chemical Develops Leaders by Sending Them to Work in Unfamiliar Surroundings

Dow Chemical's mission is "To passionately create innovation for our stakeholders at the intersection of chemistry, biology, and physics." It intends to do so by maximizing long-term value per share by being the most valuable and respected science company in the world. Its strategy is to invest in a market-driven portfolio of advantaged and technology-enabled businesses that create value for our shareholders and customers.

As Dow Chemical expands its global presence, it needs employees who have the ability to network and develop relationships with local commercial and government leaders. To develop global leaders, Dow had been sending high-potential employees to a week of leadership development classes at its Midland, Michigan, headquarters. After completing the classes, employees spent the next week in one of Dow's international location such as Shanghai, China; Sao Paulo, Brazil; or Dubai, United Arab Emirates. These locations had Dow regional headquarters with work environments similar to what employees experience at corporate headquarters.

Dow's global manager for leadership development and its vice president for human resources both recognized that the program had a major weakness. The program was missing a hands-on experience that taught participants how to understand culture context. Exposing participants to problems within different cultural contexts helps get learners to self-reflect and consider how they deal with uncertainty and change. It would also help develop leaders that understood what needed to be done to do business in new cultures. Dow wanted to change the program to create a learning experience that developed leadership skills, as well as developed humility and integrity needed for doing business in new markets.

Dow developed a new leadership development program, Leadership in Action, with its first location in Accra, Ghana, where the company had recently opened its first office. The program is part of Dow's approach to meeting the world's basic needs by matching its employees with organizations that need support for sustainable development projects, especially in business growth areas for Dow. Accra, the western African country's capital, was chosen because it provided a way to get potential leaders to understand a new business territory, develop a new market, and establish relationships in the local community. Thirty-six high-potential employees were organized into seven teams. Each team was assigned to work with a nongovernment organization to help with a project that the community needed. Projects included determining where to grow plants that could provide medicine for malaria and working with a trade school to develop education science, technology, engineering, and math curriculum. Program participants spend five months virtually planning and collaborating from their home offices. This helped them develop their consulting skills and adapt to the unexpected such as the sudden loss of electricity or telephone service. After working virtually for five months, the group traveled to Africa to examine their finished projects. Participants in the second class worked in Addis Ababa, Ethiopia, where Dow was considering opening an office. One of the teams worked with a team of IBM employees to develop marketing to promote hygiene and sanitation practices. These participants gained valuable skills in collaborating with both humanitarian groups and corporate partners. The teams working in Ghana and Ethiopia both had to learn how to solve problems in a culture and community that was extremely different from the one they were accustomed to experiencing. They had to focus on understanding social structures and values of the people in the communities to create meaningful, accepted, and useful solutions. Both groups also represented Dow Chemical in news interviews, which enhanced their media relations skills and understanding of how to best represent the company.

Surveys completed after the program was completed showed that participants feel they have a new view of the world. Almost all participants wanted to continue to be involved in some way working on Dow's growth in Africa.

Questions

1. What competitive challenges motivated Dow Chemical to develop the Leadership in Action?

2. Do you think the Leadership in Action contributes to Dow Chemicals business strategy and goals? Explain.

3. How would you determine if the Leadership in Action program was effective? What metrics or outcomes would you collect? Why?

4. What are the advantages and disadvantages of the Leadership in Action program, compared to more traditional ways of training leaders such as formal courses (e.g., an MBA program) or giving them more increased job responsibility?

Source: Based on K. Everson, "Dow Chemical's New Formula for Global Leaders," *Chief Learning Officer* (April 2015): 42–43, 49; "Mission & Vision," from *www.dow.com*, accessed April 14, 2015; "Leadership in Action: Ethiopia," from *www.dow.com/en-us/careers/working-at-dow /learning-and-development*, accessed April 14, 2015.

Designing Training

Part Two focuses on how to systematically design effective training. Chapter Three, "Needs Assessment," discusses the process used to determine whether training is necessary. Needs assessment includes analyzing the organization, people, and tasks involved. Chapter Four, "Learning and Transfer of Training," discusses learning and transfer of training theories and their implications for creating an environment that will help trainees learn the desired outcomes from training and use them on their jobs. Chapter Five, "Program Design," reviews practical issues in training program design, including developing training courses and programs, how to choose and prepare a training site, choosing a consultant or vendor, and how to create a work environment that maximizes learning and transfer of training, including manager and peer support. The role of knowledge management in transfer of training is also discussed. Chapter Six, "Training Evaluation," provides an overview of how to evaluate training programs, including the types of outcomes that need to be measured and the types of evaluation designs available.

Part Two concludes with a case on the use of on-the-job video gaming for the purpose of training.

Chapter **Three**

Needs Assessment

Objectives

After reading this chapter, you should be able to

1. Discuss the role of organization analysis, person analysis, and task analysis in needs assessment.
2. Identify different methods used in needs assessment and identify the advantages and disadvantages of each method.
3. Discuss the concerns of upper- and mid-level managers and trainers in needs assessment.
4. Explain how personal characteristics, input, output, consequences, and feedback influence performance and learning.
5. Create conditions to ensure that employees are receptive to training.
6. Discuss the steps involved in conducting a task analysis.
7. Analyze task analysis data to determine the tasks for which people need to be trained.
8. Explain competency models and the process used to develop them.

Needs Assessment at B&W Pantex and MasTec

Needs assessment is a critical first step in designing new and revising current training courses. Consider how needs assessment was used at B&W Pantex and MasTec.

The B&W Pantex plant, located near Amarillo, Texas, is charged with maintaining the safety, security, and reliability of the nation's nuclear weapons stockpile. The facility is managed and operated by B&W Pantex for the U.S. Department of Energy/National Nuclear Security Administration. The nuclear weapons industry is highly regulated, and most training is focused on mandatory safety and compliance. However, B&W Pantex also offers technical training and management development courses, and every employee has an individual development plan. Training and development at B&W Pantex is of high quality and delivers business results: the company was recognized by the American Society for Training and Development (ASTD, now the Association for Talent Development [ATD]) as a 2010 Best Award winner. The mission of the technical training department is to provide quality training that is necessary, precise, timely, and behavior- or ability-changing. Recently, the technical training program was reviewed to help improve its efficiency and effectiveness. The review found that training required a great time commitment by employees to be away from their jobs, and 20 percent of the courses accounted for 8 percent of the training hours. As a result, the technical training department reexamined its course offerings by considering if the training was still necessary, if the training objectives were still relevant, if the course provided redundant information, and if the target audience for the course had changed. This analysis led the technical training department to consolidate or remove more than seven hundred courses, and many courses were redesigned to reduce the time of completion by more than half. Many classroom sessions were replaced with computer-based training or informal meetings between employees and their manager. As a result, training efficiency has improved by 49 percent, and employees now participate in 5.5 hours of training each month. MasTec, a construction company that engineers, procures, constructs, and maintains the infrastructures for electric transmission and distribution, oil and natural gas pipeline, and communications companies, wanted to develop an online learning management system through which employees could access training and development courses. MasTec conducted a needs assessment to determine the technology and functionality that was needed to support new training programs, and to identify unique employee needs. As a result, the development team started by conducting a stakeholder analysis. This involved considering who would be involved in the process, understanding how to partner with them, and determining what type of information they could offer. It included meeting with safety team leaders, trainers, and construction crew members, observing employees performing their jobs, and attending existing training classes. The development team recorded every need and request made throughout this process. As a result of this analysis, they identified four goals for the learning management system. These goals include increasing accessibility of training content, increasing flexibility and variety in how training was delivered and completed, improving the training registering process for employees, and creating reporting tools that make training requirements, participation, and completion visible to employees, their managers, and the employee development group.

Sources: Based on J. Salopek, "Keeping Knowledge Safe and Sound," *T + D* (October 2010): 64 –66; *www.pantex.com*, the website for B&W Pantex.; J. Congemi, "MasTec Tackles the LMS," *training* (July/August 2014): 52–54.

INTRODUCTION

As discussed in Chapter One, "Introduction to Employee Training and Development," effective training practices involve the use of a training design process. The design process begins with a needs assessment. Subsequent steps in the process include ensuring that employees have the motivation and basic skills necessary to learn, creating a positive learning environment, making sure that trainees use learned skills on the job, choosing the training method, and evaluating whether training has achieved the desired outcomes. As the NetApp example highlights, before you choose a training method, it is important to determine what type of training is necessary and how it should be delivered. **Needs assessment** refers to the process used to determine whether training is necessary.

Needs assessment typically involves organizational analysis, person analysis, and task analysis.[1] An organizational analysis considers the context in which training will occur. That is, **organizational analysis** involves determining the appropriateness of training, given the company's business strategy, its resources available for training, and support by managers and peers for training activities. You are already familiar with one aspect of organizational analysis. Chapter Two, "Strategic Training," discussed the role of the company's business strategy in determining the frequency and type of training.

Person analysis helps identify who needs training. **Person analysis** involves (1) determining whether performance deficiencies result from a lack of knowledge, skill, or ability (a training issue) or from a motivational or work-design problem; (2) identifying who needs training; and (3) determining employee readiness for training. **Task analysis** identifies the important tasks and knowledge, skills, and behaviors that need to be emphasized in training for employees to complete their tasks.

WHY IS NEEDS ASSESSMENT NECESSARY?

Needs assessment is important because a manager or other client asking for training (which focuses on closing skill gaps resulting from a lack of knowledge or skill) could really be asking for or need something else, such as employee motivation, changing perspectives or attitudes, or redesigning workflow.[2] If a manager requests training for a performance problem, what he or she is looking for is a solution to a problem that may (or may not) involve training. In conducting a needs assessment, your role is to determine if training is the appropriate solution.

Needs assessment is the first step in the instructional design process, and if it is not properly conducted, any one or more of the following situations could occur:

- Training may be incorrectly used as a solution to a performance problem (when the solution should deal with employee motivation, job design, or a better communication of performance expectations).
- Training programs may have the wrong content, objectives, or methods.
- Trainees may be sent to training programs for which they do not have the basic skills, prerequisite skills, or confidence needed to learn.
- Training will not deliver the expected learning, behavior change, or financial results that the company expects.
- Money will be spent on training programs that are unnecessary because they are unrelated to the company's business strategy.

Figure 3.1 shows the three types of analysis involved in needs assessment and the causes and outcomes that result. There are many different causes or "pressure points" that suggest that training is necessary. These pressure points include performance problems, new technology, internal or external customer requests for training, job redesign, new legislation, changes in customer preferences, new products, or employees' lack of basic skills. WakeMed, a North Carolina–based health-care system, spends more than $2

FIGURE 3.1   **Causes and Outcomes of Needs Assessment**

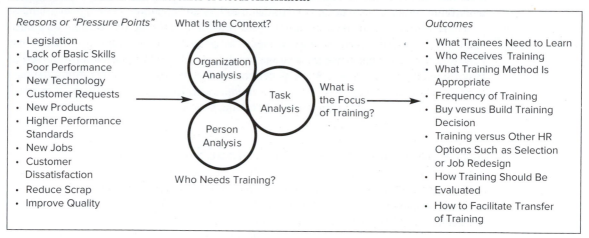

Reasons or "Pressure Points"

- Legislation
- Lack of Basic Skills
- Poor Performance
- New Technology
- Customer Requests
- New Products
- Higher Performance
  Standards
- New Jobs
- Customer
  Dissatisfaction
- Reduce Scrap
- Improve Quality

What Is the Context?

Organization Analysis

Task Analysis

Person Analysis

What is the Focus of Training?

Who Needs Training?

Outcomes

- What Trainees Need to Learn
- Who Receives Training
- What Training Method Is
  Appropriate
- Frequency of Training
- Buy versus Build Training
  Decision
- Training versus Other HR
  Options Such as Selection
  or Job Redesign
- How Training Should Be
  Evaluated
- How to Facilitate Transfer
  of Training

million on clinical, compliance, safety, and interpersonal skills training each year.[3] The "pressure point" facing WakeMed has been transitioning all patient information from paper records to an electronic format. To give you an idea of the scope, more than 230,000 patients visit its emergency departments each year! Because the electronic health records were the single source of patient information, it was important that all employees having access to the system received training and demonstrated that they were competent in using it. To prepare for the transition, multiple departments worked together to design training plans to meet the needs of both clinical and nonclinical employees. Training was made available using a variety of methods, including instructor-led classes and online modules.

Note that these pressure points do not automatically mean that training is the correct solution. For example, consider a delivery truck driver whose job is to deliver anesthetic gases to medical facilities. The driver mistakenly hooks up the supply line of a mild anesthetic to the supply line of a hospital's oxygen system, contaminating the hospital's oxygen supply. Why did the driver make this mistake, which is clearly a performance problem? The driver may have made this mistake because of a lack of knowledge about the appropriate line hookup for the anesthetic, because of anger over a requested salary increase that his manager recently denied, or because of mislabeled valves for connecting the gas supply. Only the lack of knowledge can be addressed by training. The other pressure points require reviewing and making decisions related to the driver's anger-motivated behavior (fire the driver) or the design of the work environment (remind supervisor and drivers to check to that valves and hookup lines are properly labeled at all work sites).

What outcomes result from a needs assessment? Needs assessment provides important input into most of the remaining steps in the training design. As shown in Figure 3.1, the needs assessment process results in information related to who needs training and what trainees need to learn, including the tasks in which they need to be trained, plus knowledge, skill, behavior, or other job requirements. Needs assessment helps determine whether the company will outsource its training (i.e. purchase training from a vendor or consultant, or develop training through internal resources). Determining exactly what trainees need to learn is critical for the next step in the instructional design process: identifying learning outcomes and objectives. Chapter Four, "Learning and Transfer of Training," explores identifying learning outcomes and learning objectives and creating a training environment so that learning occurs and is used on the job. Through identifying the learning outcomes and resources available for training, the needs assessment also provides information that helps the company choose the appropriate training or development method (discussed in Part Three of this book). Needs assessment also provides information regarding the outcomes that should be collected to evaluate training effectiveness. The process of evaluating training is discussed in Chapter Six, "Training Evaluation."

WHO SHOULD PARTICIPATE IN NEEDS ASSESSMENT?

Because the goal of needs assessment is to determine whether a training need exists, who it exists for, and for what tasks training is needed, it is important that all stakeholders are included in the needs assessment. **Stakeholders** include persons in the organization who have an interest in training and development and their support is important for determining its success (or failure). Stakeholders include company leaders and top-level managers, mid-level managers, trainers, and employees who are end users of learning. There are several ways to ensure that stakeholders are involved in needs assessment. One way is through establishing formal advisory groups that meet on a regular basis to discuss learning issues. Another way is to ensure that relevant stakeholders are included in interviews, focus groups, crowdsourcing, and surveys used for needs assessment. Traditionally, only trainers were concerned with the needs assessment process. But, as Chapter Two showed, as training increasingly becomes used to help the company achieve its strategic goals, both upper- and mid-level managers are involved in the needs assessment process.

Table 3.1 shows the questions that company leaders, mid-level managers, trainers, and employees are interested in answering for organizational analysis, person analysis, and task analysis. Company leaders include directors, CEOs, and vice presidents. Company leaders view the needs assessment process from the broader company perspective rather than focusing on specific jobs. Company leaders are involved in the needs assessment process to identify the role of training in relation to other human resource practices in the company (e.g., selection and compensation of employees). Company leaders want training to anticipate needs, aligned with where the business is going. Training and development needs to improve employee performance in such a way that it supports the business strategy. Learning efforts (training, development, knowledge management) need to be an integrated and holistic approach (rather than a series of fragmented courses and programs) that adds value to the company. Company leaders are also involved in identifying what business functions or units need training (person analysis) and in determining if the company has the knowledge, skills, and abilities in the workforce that are necessary to meet its strategy and be competitive in the marketplace. Mid-level managers are more concerned with how training may affect the attainment of financial goals for the particular units they supervise. As a result, for mid-level managers, organizational analysis focuses on identifying (1) how much of their budgets they want to devote to training; (2) the types of employees who should receive training (e.g., engineers, or core employees who are directly involved in producing goods or providing services); and (3) for what jobs training can make a difference in terms of improving products or customer service.

TABLE 3.1   **Key Concerns of Company Leaders, Mid-Level Managers, Trainers, and Employees in Needs Assessment**

	Company Leaders	Mid-Level Managers	Trainers	Employees
Organizational Analysis	Is training important to achieve our business objectives? How does training support our business strategy? What are the threats to our talent base?	Do I want to spend money on training? How much? How will training and development help meet my business goals? Are we retaining top talent?	Do I have the budget to buy training services? Will managers support training?	Is learning rewarded? Can I advance my career? Does my manager encourage and allow me to attend training? Can I access learning?
Person Analysis	Do employees in specific functions or business units need training? What do employees need to do to accomplish our business objectives?	Who should be trained? Managers? Professionals? Core employees?	How will I identify which employees need training?	Do I want to learn? Can I learn the training content? Will the content be valuable to me?
Task Analysis	Does the company have people with the knowledge, skills, and abilities or competencies needed to compete in the marketplace?	For what jobs can training make the biggest difference in product quality or customer service?	For what tasks should employees be trained? What knowledge, skills, ability, or other characteristics are necessary?	What knowledge, skills, tasks, or competencies do I need for my current job? Future jobs? My career?

Hilton Worldwide has executive sponsors for each of its five different learning universities. The executive sponsors meet quarterly to review learning initiatives and discuss business needs. This helps the learning function stay in touch with the company's strategic goals and identify short- and long-term learning needs that are important for the business.[4] IMG College is a collegiate sports marketing company, offering national, regional, and local marketing targeting college sports fans. IMG has a salesforce of more than four hundred employees who interact with schools, sponsors, and licensees to provide coaches' shows and endorsements; manage digital assets such as websites, mobile applications, and social media campaigns; and coordinate game-day events and hospitality.[5] IMG determined that its salesforce had numerous training needs. The needs assessment included phone calls and meetings with senior leaders and middle managers. After reviewing their feedback, sixty-one different topics were identified as skill gaps and areas for improvement. To identify the most important and strategic gaps, IMG held a one-day retreat involving professionals from its training and development and human resources departments. Based on the retreat, twelve topics were chosen for training that aligned with the company's strategic plan and culture. Examples of the topics included effective communication skills, public safety, and financial skills.

As discussed in Chapter Two, trainers (including training managers and instructional designers) need to consider whether training is aligned with the business strategy. However, trainers are primarily interested in needs assessment to provide them with information that they need to administer, develop, and support training programs. This information includes determining if training should be purchased or developed in-house, identifying the tasks for which employees need to be trained, and determining upper- and mid-level managers' interest in and support for training.

Employees have several interests in needs assessment. From an organizational perspective they are concerned with how the company values learning: Is learning rewarded? Does learning help them improve their job performance or meet their career goals? Is it easy to get access to formal and informal learning opportunities? They also want to know if their manager can be expected to encourage them to take courses and programs, or informally learn, and if they will provide support to apply what they have learned. Employees have to determine if they are motivated to learn as well as what tasks, knowledge, skills, or competencies they need for their current job or career.

Company leaders are usually involved in determining whether training meets the company's strategy and then providing the appropriate financial resources. Upper-level managers are not usually involved in identifying which employees need training, the tasks for which training is needed, or the knowledge, skills, abilities, and other characteristics needed to complete those tasks. This is the role of subject-matter experts (SMEs). **Subject-matter experts (SMEs)** are employees, academics, managers, technical experts, trainers, and even customers or suppliers who are knowledgeable with regard to (1) training issues, including tasks to be performed; (2) the knowledge, skills, and abilities required for successful task performance; (3) the necessary equipment; and (4) the conditions under which the tasks have to be performed. A key issue with SMEs is making sure that they are knowledgeable about the content that training must cover, as well as realistic enough to be able to prioritize what content is critical to cover in the time allotted for the subject in the training curriculum. SMEs must also have information that is relevant to the company's business and have an understanding of the company's language, tools, and products. There is no rule regarding how many types of employees should be represented in the group conducting the needs assessment. Still, it is important to get a sample of **job incumbents** (employees who are currently performing the job) involved in the process because they tend to be most knowledgeable about the job and can be a great hindrance to the training process if they do not feel they have had input into the needs assessment.

Philips, the Dutch technology company, reinvented itself by limiting its focus to three business sectors: health care, lighting, and consumer lifestyle products.[6] Philips also recognized the need to change its culture to react faster to the marketplace. It had to encourage employees to quickly develop new products to beat competitors, and, if the products were not successful, to abandon them and come up with new ideas. The cultural shift required a change in the company's learning and development structure to more closely align with the business. To understand the company's learning needs, the leader of the learning function and his team met with Philips's employees across all businesses to find out how they wanted to learn. For example, sales representatives expressed a preference for learning using short videos and podcasts that provide tips on sales skills such as closing a sale. This fit with their need to learn while traveling or meeting with customers. Also, they found that most employees would take online learning courses at home in the evening rather than at work, but they were often interrupted.

To conduct needs assessment at Saudi Aramco, a oil company headquartered in Dhahran, Saudi Arabia, they relied on an team consisting of a professional development advisor who reports to the management team, a supporting advisory committee, and a group of subject matter experts.[7] This team determines the knowledge, skills, and behaviors required to be a successful performer in a specific job family such as engineering production and drilling. The team also determines the training required to support more experienced professionals.

METHODS USED IN NEEDS ASSESSMENT

Several methods are used to conduct needs assessment, including observing employees performing the job, using online technology, reading technical manuals and other documentation, interviewing SMEs, conducting focus groups with SMEs, and asking SMEs to complete surveys designed to identify the tasks and knowledge, skills, abilities, and other characteristics required for a job. Table 3.2 presents the advantages and disadvantages of each method. Nuance Communications, a global company with headquarters in Massachusetts, focuses on voice communications that can help people use new technologies to interact and communicate with machines.[8] Nuance's CEO wanted its learning and development team to help improve the retention and career progression of its technologists. The learning and development team talked with the company's leaders to understand their concerns and expectations. Based on their input, they provided some initial training ideas and asked them for feedback. Also, they interviewed technologists to get their impressions of the strategic direction of the company and identify the characteristics and behaviors of average and outstanding performers. The interviews with the leaders and technologists were critical for designing three training programs that met their needs. These training programs included one in which internal experts shared their knowledge and experiences, another that helped technologists develop a better understanding of the company, and a third that helped technologists acquire knowledge specific to the industry or technology in which they worked.

For newly created jobs, trainers often do not have job incumbents to rely on for this information. Rather, technical diagrams, simulations, and equipment designers can provide information regarding the training requirements, tasks, and conditions under which the job is performed. Historical data review involves collecting performance data from electronic or paper records. It provides information regarding current performance levels, which is useful for identifying gaps between actual and desired performance. For example, a needs assessment conducted at a hospital to determine the causes of a high number of errors in radiology orders (e.g., x-rays) from physicians collected historical data on errors, including incorrect exams, examination of the wrong side of the patient's body, use of incorrect diagnosis codes, and duplicate orders.[9] The historical data was used along with semistructured interviews and observations to identify the causes for the errors and interventions to reduce them. Another source of information for companies that have introduced a new technology is the help desk that companies often set up to deal with calls regarding problems,

TABLE 3.2   Advantages and Disadvantages of Needs Assessment Techniques

Technique	Advantages	Disadvantages
Observation	• Generates data relevant to work environment • Minimizes interruption of work	• Needs skilled observers • Employees' behavior may be affected by being observed
Surveys	• Inexpensive • Can collect data from a large number of persons • Data easily summarized	• Requires time • Possible low return rates, inappropriate responses • Lacks detail • Only provides information directly related to questions asked
Interviews	• Good at uncovering details of training needs, as well as causes of and solutions to problems • Can explore unanticipated issues that come up • Questions can be modified	• Time-consuming • Difficult to analyze • Needs skilled interviewers • Can be threatening to SMEs • Difficult to schedule • SMEs provide only such information they think you want to hear
Focus groups Crowdsourcing	• Useful with complex or controversial issues that one person may be unable or unwilling to explore • Questions can be modified to explore unanticipated issues • Reduces risk that training based on needs assessment will be rejected by stakeholders	• Time-consuming to organize • Group members provide only information they think you want to hear
Documentation (technical manuals, records)	• Good source of information on procedure • Objective • Good source of task information for new jobs and jobs in the process of being created	• You may be unable to understand technical language • Materials may be obsolete
Online technology (software)	• Objective • Minimizes interruption of work • Requires limited human involvement	• May threaten employees • Manager may use information to punish rather than train • Limited to jobs requiring interaction with customers via computer or phone
Historical data reviews	• Provides data related to performance and practices	• Available data may be inaccurate, incomplete, or not fully represent performance

Sources: Based on S. V. Steadham, "Learning to Select a Needs Assessment Strategy," *Training and Development Journal* (January 1980): 56–61; R. J. Mirabile, "Everything You Wanted to Know About Competency Modeling," *Training and Development* (August 1997): 74; K. Gupta, *A Practical Guide to Needs Assessment* (San Francisco: Jossey-Bass, 1999); M. Casey and D. Doverspike, "Training Needs Analysis and Evaluation for New Technologies Through the Use of Problem-Based Inquiry," *Performance Improvement Quarterly* 18(1) (2005): 110–124.

deficiencies in training, or deficiencies in documentation, software, or systems.[10] Help-desk management software can categorize and track calls and questions by application, by caller, or by vendor. Report creation capability built into the software makes it easy to generate documents on user problems and identify themes among calls. Analyzing these calls is practical for identifying gaps in training. For example, common types of call problems can be analyzed to determine if they are due to inadequate coverage in the training program and/or inadequate written documentation and job aids used by trainees.

Online technology is available to monitor and track employee performance. This information is useful for identifying training needs and providing employees with feedback regarding their skill strengths and weaknesses. In call centers, for example, technology provides an ongoing assessment of performance.[11] An employee who triggers the online system by failing to meet a defined standard, such as receiving more than five callbacks on an unresolved issue, is automatically referred to the appropriate job aid or training event. As shown in Table 3.2, online technology has several advantages: it provides an objective report of behaviors, the data can be quickly summarized into reports, it does not require a trainer or SME to observe or interview employees, and it minimizes work interruptions. However, the use of online technology in needs assessment is best suited for only a small number of jobs requiring interactions with customers through the use of a computer or telephone.[12] Also, for online technology to be effective, managers need to ensure that the information is used to train employees, not to punish them. Otherwise, employees will feel threatened, which will contribute to employee dissatisfaction and turnover.

Because no single method of conducting needs assessment is superior to the others, multiple methods are usually used. The methods vary in the type of information, as well as the level of detail provided. The advantage of surveys is that information can be collected from a large number of persons. Also, surveys allow many employees to participate in the needs assessment process. However, when using surveys, it is difficult to collect detailed information regarding training needs. Face-to-face and telephone interviews are time consuming, but more detailed information regarding training needs can be collected. **Focus groups** are a type of SME interview that involves a face-to-face meeting with groups of SMEs in which the questions that are asked relate to specific training needs. Crowdsourcing can also be used for needs assessment. In this context, **crowdsourcing** refers to asking stakeholders to provide information for needs assessment. Computer Services Corporation uses "Ideation," a web-based tool for collaboration and crowdsourcing, to help identify training needs.[13] The process requires a review team to filter, sort, and build on the best ideas. The process allows the learning department to get a larger number of employees involved in the needs assessment process rather than relying only on interviews with SMEs. It is important to verify the results of interviews and observations because what employees and managers say they do and what they really do may differ. At Brown-Forman Corporation, producer and marketer of beverages and alcohol brands such as Jack Daniel's Tennessee Whiskey, training needs are identified in a number of different ways, including monitoring employee development and performance management data, trends in the beverage alcohol industry, and issues raised by the company's operating groups who pay for training services.[14] Yapi Kredi Academy was established to provide learning and development for Yapi ve Kredi Bank's headquarters in Istanbul, Turkey.[15] The bank's executive committee (including the CEO, executive vice presidents, and an advisory committee with senior managers and individuals from outside the bank who identify trends, challenges, and opportunities in the industry) provides the strategic direction and vision for the academy.

The bank's needs assessment process includes branch visits, surveys, and focus groups, as well as meetings with business units. The academy surveyed more than 3,000 branch employees about their satisfaction with the training they received, and their experiences with individual development plans and training offerings. The results are used to determine how to meet learning and development needs.

With the increasing emphasis on Total Quality Management (TQM), many companies are also using information about other companies' training practices (a process known as **benchmarking**) to help determine the appropriate type, level, and frequency of training.[16] For example, Chevron, Federal Express, GTE, Xerox, and several other companies are members of the ATD benchmarking forum. A common survey instrument is completed by each company. The survey includes questions on training costs, staff size, administration, design, program development, and delivery. The information is summarized and shared with the participating companies.

THE NEEDS ASSESSMENT PROCESS

This section examines the three elements of needs assessment: organizational analysis, person analysis, and task analysis. Figure 3.2 illustrates the needs assessment process. In practice, organizational analysis, person analysis, and task analysis are not conducted

FIGURE 3.2 **The Needs Assessment Process**

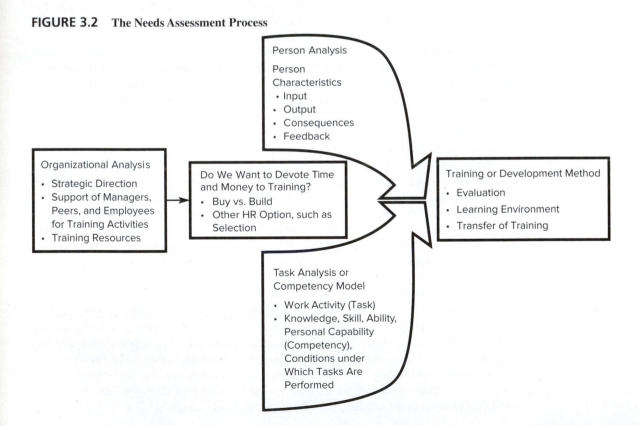

in any order. The question of whether time and money are devoted to training is contingent on the results of organizational, person, and task analyses. While any one analysis can indicate the need for training, companies need to consider the information from all three types of analysis before the decision is made to devote time and money to training. Because organizational analysis is concerned with identifying whether training suits the company's strategic objectives and whether the company has the budget, time, and expertise for training (the context for training), it is usually conducted first. Person analysis and task analysis are often conducted at the same time because it is difficult to determine whether performance deficiencies are a training problem without understanding the tasks and the work environment. An initial organizational analysis may suggest that a company does not want to spend financial resources on training. However, if person analysis reveals that a large number of employees lack a skill in an important area that is related to the company's business objectives (such as customer service), upper-level managers may decide to reallocate financial resources for training.

Organizational Analysis

Organizational analysis involves identifying whether training supports the company's strategic direction; whether managers, peers, and employees support training activity; and what training resources are available. Table 3.3 provides questions that trainers should address in an organizational analysis. Some combination of documentation, interviews, focus groups, or surveys of managers, individuals in the training function, and employees should be used to answer these questions.

The Company's Strategic Direction

How the company's business strategy influences training was discussed in Chapter Two. The strategic role of training influences the frequency and type of training and how the training function is organized in the company. In companies in which training is expected

TABLE 3.3   Questions to Ask in an Organizational Analysis

How might the training content affect our employees' relationship with our customers?
What might suppliers, customers, or partners need to know about the training program?
How does this program align with the strategic needs of the business?
Should organizational resources be devoted to this program?
What do we need from managers and peers for this training to succeed?
What features of the work environment might interfere with training (e.g., lack of equipment, no time to use new skills)?
Do we have experts who can help us develop the program content and ensure that we understand the needs of the business as we develop the program?
Will employees perceive the training program as an opportunity? Reward? Punishment? Waste of time?
Which persons or groups (e.g., employees, managers, vendors, suppliers, and program developers) have an interest in seeing training succeed? Whose support do we need?

Sources: Based on F. Nickols, "Why a Stakeholder Approach to Evaluating Training?" *Advances in Developing Human Resources* (February 2005): 121–134; S. Tannenbaum, "A Strategic View of Organizational Training and Learning." In *Creating, Implementing, and Managing Effective Training and Development*, ed. K. Kraiger (San Francisco: Jossey-Bass, 2002): 10–52.

to contribute to the achievement of business strategies and goals, the amount of money allocated to training and the frequency of training will likely be higher than in companies in which training is done haphazardly or with no strategic intent. For example, companies that believe that learning contributes to their competitive advantage or that have adopted high-performance work systems (e.g., teams) are likely to have greater training budgets and conduct more training. The business strategy also influences the type of training. For example, as noted in Chapter Two, companies that have adopted a disinvestment strategy are more likely to focus on outplacement assistance and job search skills training than are companies with other strategic initiatives. Last, the greater the strategic role of training, the more likely that the company will organize the training function using the business-embedded or corporate university models. Both these models emphasize that training is used to help solve business problems.

For example, to stay competitive, IBM has to stay up-to-date on the newest technology and business trends.[17] IBM has to constantly reinvent itself to ensure that it can meet the needs of its customers. This means that employees also have to continue to develop new knowledge and skills. From a learning perspective, IBM has to ensure that the learning content it offers, including both face-to-face and online courses, provide employees with the latest knowledge and skills. To accomplish this, IBM keeps track both of how often employees use the learning content it offers as well as of the usefulness of employees' evaluations. At the end of 2013 IBM eliminated 39 percent of the learning content that few employees found useful or used. This included 7,600 courses!

Support of Managers, Peers, and Employees for Training Activities

A number of studies have found that peer and manager support for training is critical, along with employee enthusiasm and motivation to attend training. The key factors for success are a positive attitude among peers, managers, and employees about participation in training activities; managers' and peers' willingness to provide information to trainees about how they can use the knowledge, skills, or behaviors learned in training to perform their jobs more effectively; and opportunities for trainees to use training content in their jobs.[18] If peers' and managers' attitudes and behaviors are not supportive, employees are not likely to apply training content to their jobs.

Training Resources

It is necessary to identify whether the company has the budget, time, and expertise for training. One of the questions that the company must answer is whether it has the resources (i.e., time, money, and expertise) to build or develop training programs itself or whether it should buy them from a vendor or consulting firm. This is known as the "buy versus build" decision. For example, if the company is installing computer-based manufacturing equipment in one of its plants, it has three possible strategies for dealing with the need to have computer-literate employees. First, the company can decide that, given its staff expertise and budget, it can use internal consultants to train all affected employees. Second, the company may decide that it is more cost effective to identify employees who are computer literate by using tests and work samples. Employees who fail the test or perform below standards on the work sample can be reassigned to other jobs. Choosing this strategy suggests that the company has decided to devote resources to selection and placement rather than training. Third, because it lacks time or expertise, the company may decide to buy training from a consultant. We will discuss how to identify and choose a high-quality vendor or consultant to provide training services in Chapter Five, "Program Design."

One way to identify training resources is for companies that have similar operations or departments located across the country or the world to share ideas and practices. Kaiser Permanente is organized by regional business units.[19] In each region the company integrates health-care delivery, including hospitals, outpatient services, and insurance providers. One of the concerns was how to provide consistent and high-quality learning and development opportunities for employees in all of the regions. To do so, the vice president of learning and development created a group, The National Learning Leaders, which included leaders from account management, sales, compliance, quality improvement, and patient safety. The National Learning Leaders meet three times every year and in smaller working groups in the months when the full membership is not scheduled to meet. They discuss how to develop learning solutions that can be implemented across the business and what kinds of services should be provided by the learning organizations within each region. This has resulted in learning initiatives that are consistent across the regions and are delivered in a way that enhances employee participation. For example, based on input from The National Learning Leaders, online and hybrid training courses on patient safety were developed. Nineteen thousand employees so far have completed these modules compared to only fifty who attended classroom-based training.

Person Analysis

Person analysis helps identify employees who need training; lack of training or poor training is one possible explanation. This is often referred to as a gap analysis. A **gap analysis** includes determining what is responsible for the difference between employees' current and expected performance. The need for training may result from the pressure points in Figure 3.1, including performance problems, changes in the job, or use of new technology. Person analysis also helps determining employees' readiness for training. **Readiness for training** refers to whether (1) employees have the personal characteristics (ability, attitudes, beliefs, and motivation) necessary to learn program content and apply it on the job, and (2) the work environment will facilitate learning and not interfere with performance. This process includes evaluating person characteristics, input, output, consequences, and feedback.[20]

A major pressure point for training is poor or substandard performance. Poor performance is indicated by customer complaints, low performance ratings, or on-the-job incidents such as accidents and unsafe behavior. Another potential indicator of the need for training is if the job changes such that current levels of performance need to be improved or employees must be able to complete new tasks.

The Process for Person Analysis

Figure 3.3 shows a process for analyzing the factors that influence performance and learning. **Person characteristics** refer to employee knowledge, skill, ability, and attitudes. **Input** relates to the instructions that tell employees what, how, and when to perform. Input also refers to the resources that the employees are given to help them perform. These resources may include equipment, time, or budget. **Output** refers to the job's performance standards. **Consequences** refer to the type of incentives that employees receive

FIGURE 3.3

The Process for Analyzing the Factors That Influence Employee Performance and Learning

Sources: R. Jaenke, "Identify the Real Reasons Behind Performance Gaps", *T+D* (August 2013): 76–77.; C. Reinhart, "How to Leap over Barriers to Performance," *Training and Development* (January 2000): 20–24; G. Rummler and K. Morrill, "The Results Chain," *T+D* (February 2005): 27–35.

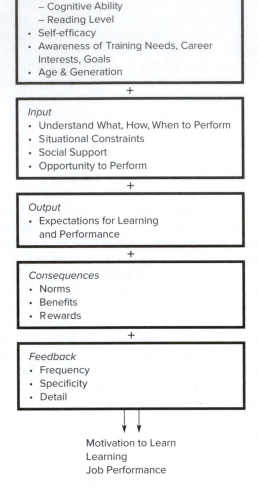

Person Characteristics
- Basic Skills
  – Cognitive Ability
  – Reading Level
- Self-efficacy
- Awareness of Training Needs, Career Interests, Goals
- Age & Generation

+

Input
- Understand What, How, When to Perform
- Situational Constraints
- Social Support
- Opportunity to Perform

+

Output
- Expectations for Learning and Performance

+

Consequences
- Norms
- Benefits
- Rewards

+

Feedback
- Frequency
- Specificity
- Detail

Motivation to Learn
Learning
Job Performance

for performing well. **Feedback** refers to the information that employees receive while they are performing.

Interviews or questionnaires can be used to measure personal characteristics, input, output, consequences, and feedback. For example, a package delivery company believed that lead drivers were valuable for providing on-the-job training for new employees.[21] The company employed 110 lead drivers, and the job involved driving, delivery, and book-keeping duties. The lead drivers benefited from training because coaching and training made their jobs more interesting, and the company benefited because on-the-job training was relatively inexpensive and effective. Lead drivers often quickly spotted and corrected performance problems with new trainees, and they knew the technical aspects of the delivery job quite well. Although many of the lead drivers were good trainers and coaches, the company believed that they needed to learn how to coach and train the new drivers.

The company used interviews to identify what type of coaching and training skills the lead drivers needed. Interviews were conducted with fourteen lead drivers, six supervisors, and two regional vice presidents. The interview for the lead drivers consisted of questions such as the following:

- What types of situations call for coaching on your part?
- What keeps you from being a good coach on the job?
- How do you encourage or motivate other lead drivers? Do you use incentives or rewards? Do you try other things (compliments, personal attention)?
- What common types of performance problems do new hires have?
- What were the biggest problems you encountered as a new coach and trainer? What mistakes did you make? What lessons have you learned over time?
- Tell me about a successful coaching experience and an unsuccessful coaching experience.

Recurring trends in the interview data were noted and categorized. For example, interview questions on obstacles to coaching related to three themes: lack of time to coach, the physical environment (no privacy), and reluctance to coach peers. These three topics were covered in the coaching course.

Person characteristics, input, output, consequences, and feedback influence the motivation to learn. **Motivation to learn** is trainees' desire to learn the content of training programs.[22] Consider how your motivation to learn may be influenced by personal characteristics and the environment. You may have no problem understanding and comprehending the contents of this textbook. But your learning may be inhibited because of your attitude toward the course. That is, perhaps you do not believe that the course will be important for your career. Maybe you are taking the course only because it fits your schedule or is required in your degree program. Learning may also be inhibited by the environment. For example, maybe you want to learn, but your study environment prevents you from doing so. Every time you are prepared to read and review your notes and the textbook, your roommates could be having a party. Even if you do not join them, the music may be so loud that you cannot concentrate.

Marriott International, the hotel and restaurant chain, found that personal characteristics were having a significant influence on the success rate of the company's welfare-to-work program.[23] This program involved training welfare recipients for jobs in the company's hotels and restaurants. (These types of programs are discussed in greater detail in Chapter Ten, "Social Responsibility: Legal Issues, Managing Diversity, and Career Challenges.") Many trainees were unable to complete the training program because of poor attendance due to unreliable child care, drug problems, or abusive partners As a result, Marriott has instituted strict standards for selecting welfare recipients for the training program. These standards include requiring trainees to have child care, transportation, and housing arrangements. Also, Marriott added an additional drug test during training.

A number of research studies have shown that motivation to learn is related to knowledge gained, behavior changes, or skill acquisition resulting from training.[24] Besides considering the factors of personal characteristics, input, output, consequences, and feedback in determining whether training is the best solution to a performance problem, managers should also take them into account when selecting which employees will attend a training program. These factors relate to the employees' motivation to learn. The following sections describe each of these factors and its relationship to performance and learning.

Personal Characteristics

Personal characteristics include basic skills, cognitive ability, language skills, and other traits that employees need to perform their jobs or learn in training and development programs effectively. Personal characteristics also include employees' age or generation, which might affect how they prefer to learn. As mentioned in Chapter One, recent forecasts of workforce skill levels and survey results suggest that companies are experiencing a skills gap. That is, companies are having difficulty finding employees who have the right knowledge, skills, or abilities to fill open positions or succeed in training to prepare them for today's jobs.

Basic Skills

Basic skills refer to skills that are necessary for employees to perform on the job and learn the content of training programs successfully. Basic skills include cognitive ability and reading and writing skills. For example, one assumption that your professor is making in this course is that you have the necessary reading level to comprehend this textbook and the other course materials such as Powerpoint slides, videos, or readings. If you lacked the necessary reading level, you likely would not learn much about training in this course. As Chapter One discussed, recent forecasts of skill levels of the U.S. workforce indicate that managers will likely have to work with employees who lack basic skills. A literacy audit can be used to determine employees' basic skill levels. Table 3.4 shows the activities involved in conducting a literacy audit.

TABLE 3.4
Steps in Performing a Literacy Audit

Sources: U.S. Department of Education, U.S. Department of Labor, *The Bottom Line: Basic Skills in the Workplace* (Washington, DC: 1988): 14–15.

Step 1:	Observe employees to determine the basic skills that they need to be successful in their job. Note the materials the employee uses on the job, the tasks performed, and the reading, writing, and computations completed.
Step 2:	Collect all materials that are written and read on the job and identify the computations that must be performed to determine the necessary level of basic skill proficiency. Materials include bills, memos, and forms such as inventory lists and requisition sheets.
Step 3:	Interview employees to determine the basic skills that they believe are needed to do the job. Consider the basic skill requirements of the job yourself.
Step 4:	Determine whether employees have the basic skills needed to perform the job successfully. Combine the information gathered by observing and interviewing employees and evaluating materials they use on their job. Write a description of each job in terms of the reading, writing, and computation skills needed to perform the job successfully.
Step 5:	Develop or buy tests that ask questions relating specifically to the employees' job. Ask employees to complete the tests.
Step 6:	Compare test results (from step 5) with the description of the basic skills required for the job (from step 4). If the level of the employees' reading, writing, and computation skills does not match the basic skills required by the job, then a basic skills problem exists.

It is important to note that possession of a high school diploma or a college degree is no guarantee that an employee has basic skills. If participants do not have the fundamental reading, writing, and math skills to understand the training, they will not be able to learn, they will not apply their training to the job (a process known as transfer, which is discussed in Chapter Four), and the company will have wasted money on training that does not work. Trainers need to evaluate the strengths and weaknesses of trainees before designing a training program. The skill weaknesses that are identified can be used to determine prerequisites that trainees need or must acquire before entering a training program. How do trainers identify skills gaps?[25] First, trainers collect general information through position-specific training materials and job descriptions. They also observe the job to become familiar with the necessary skills. Next, trainers meet with SMEs, including employees, managers, engineers, or others who are familiar with the job. With the help of these SMEs, trainers identify a list of regularly performed activities and prioritize the list according to importance. Finally, trainers identify the skills and skill levels that are needed to perform the activities or job tasks. For example, nurses must watch for changes in patient conditions, reactions, and comfort levels; they need to identify and recall details when observing patients. These activities require good observation skills, and the trainer needs to find or create a test to measure those skills. Once the skills analysis is complete, trainers conduct a basic (or pretraining) skills evaluation to identify skills gaps that need to be addressed prior to enrolling employees in a training session.

Cognitive Ability

Research shows that cognitive ability influences learning and job performance. **Cognitive ability** includes three dimensions: verbal comprehension, quantitative ability, and reasoning ability.[26] *Verbal comprehension* refers to the person's capacity to understand and use written and spoken language. *Quantitative ability* refers to how fast and accurately a person can solve math problems. *Reasoning ability* refers to the person's capacity to invent solutions to problems. Research shows that cognitive ability is related to successful performance in all jobs.[27] The importance of cognitive ability for job success increases as the job becomes more complex.

For example, a supermarket cashier needs low to moderate levels of all three dimensions of cognitive ability to perform that job successfully. An emergency room physician needs higher levels of verbal comprehension, quantitative ability, and reasoning ability than the cashier. The supermarket cashier needs to understand the different denominations of bills and coins to give customers the correct amount of change. The cashier also needs to invent solutions to problems. (For example, how does the cashier deal with items that are not priced that the customer wants to purchase?) The cashier also needs to be able to understand and communicate with customers (verbal comprehension). The physician also needs quantitative ability, but at a higher level. For example, when dealing with an infant experiencing seizures in an emergency situation, the physician needs to be able to calculate the correct dosage of medicine (based on an adult dosage) to stop the seizures after considering the child's weight. The physician has to be able to diagnose the situation quickly and determine what actions (blood tests, x-rays, respiratory therapy, etc.) are necessary. In this case, the physician also needs to communicate clearly to the patient's parents the treatment and recovery process.

Trainees' level of cognitive ability also can influence how well they can learn in training programs.[28] Trainees with low levels of cognitive ability are more likely to fail to complete training or (at the end of training) receive lower grades on tests that measure how much they have learned.

To identify employees without the cognitive ability to succeed on the job or in training programs, companies use cognitive ability tests. For example, consider the actions taken by the Federal Aviation Administration (FAA) to identify potential air traffic controllers who will complete training successfully.[29] Air traffic control work requires quick analytical thinking and strong communications skills. These skills are emphasized and further developed in air traffic controller training. In addition to classroom training, air traffic controllers receive training through computer-based simulations of airport towers and en route centers, which direct planes between airports. The FAA estimates that in the past, it spent $10 million per year on unsuccessful trainees, which resulted in a doubling of training costs. To reduce its training costs and increase the number of new controllers who will be successful, the FAA uses an eight-hour test of cognitive skills that identifies whether applicants can think spatially, have good short- and long-term memory, and can work well under pressure—skills that are needed by successful air traffic controllers. Determining a job's cognitive ability requirement is part of the task analysis process, discussed later in this chapter.

Reading Ability

Readability refers to the difficulty level of written materials.[30] Lack of the appropriate reading level can impede performance and learning in training programs. Material used in training should be evaluated to ensure that its reading level does not exceed that required by the job. A readability assessment usually involves analysis of sentence length and word difficulty.

If trainees' reading level does not match the level needed for the training materials, four options are available. First, trainers can determine whether it is feasible to lower the reading level of training materials or use video or on-the-job training, which involves learning by watching and practicing rather than by reading. Second, employees without the necessary reading level could be identified through reading tests and reassigned to other positions more congruent with their skill levels. Third, again using reading tests, trainers can identify employees who lack the necessary reading skills and provide them with remedial training. Fourth, trainers can consider whether the job can be redesigned to accommodate employees' reading levels. The fourth option is certainly the most costly and least practical. Therefore, alternative training methods need to be considered, or managers can elect a nontraining option. Nontraining options include selecting employees for jobs and training opportunities on the basis of reading, computation, writing, and other basic skill requirements.

To develop basic skills or close the skills gap, many companies are engaging in skills assessment, training, or a combination of the two. They are working to identify and close skill gaps, either alone or in partnerships with state government agencies.[31] For example, to help ensure that employees have the necessary basic skills needed to succeed in training, Georgia-Pacific, a paper manufacturer, used skills assessment in combination with a training program. For employees to be eligible to attend training programs, they had to take reading and math skills tests and score at or above a ninth-grade level. Those who scored below ninth-grade level were advised to attend basic skills training. Test results were communicated confidentially and were not part of employees' personnel files. This was done to alleviate employees' fears that their lack of literacy would cost them their jobs and to establish trust needed to motivate them to attend the basic skills training. A local community college provided the basic training at sites close to Georgia-Pacific plants to make it easy for employees to attend classes before or after work. As a result of the assessment and training, the current workforce has reached the basic skills standard established by the company. To ensure that new employees met the basic skill standards, Georgia-Pacific changed its hiring qualifications. New job applicants are required to have completed (or met the requirements for) a specific eighteen-month schedule of courses at the local community college. Delta Wire, a small manufacturing company in Mississippi, developed a basic skills training program to help employees understand how to record, interpret, and communicate information on a statistical control chart. That helped reduce product defects from 7 percent to 2 percent.

Like many U.S. companies, Southwire Company, a cable manufacturer with 7,500 employees, has experienced difficulties finding employees who had the appropriate skill set and would reliably show up for work. Southwire realized that part of the problem finding employees was the high dropout rate for economically disadvantaged high school students in the areas where the company's plants were located. As a result, Southwire partnered with local school districts to help high school teens stay engaged in school, gain valuable work experience, and develop a more positive attitude toward work. Southwire works with local school districts to help redesign courses that focus on abstract concepts that easily frustrate students but are necessary to learn and apply on the factory floor. For example, physics and chemistry classes include lessons on electricity and the properties of electric cables, which include students learning to conduct quality control tests on cables. In addition to learning in the classroom, students gain valuable work experience by working in Southwire's factories. One group of teenagers earns up to $9 an hour packaging electricity cables for sale at big-box retail stores like Home Depot and Lowe's. The effort has benefited Southwire, the students, and local communities. Since 2007, when the program started, the graduation rate of students considered economically disadvantaged increased from 56 to 77 percent. Forty percent of the students have continued their education at two- or four-year colleges or universities, while 18 percent have taken full-time jobs at Southwire. For local communities where Southwire's plants are located, the program has provided a skilled workforce of high school graduates.

Self-Efficacy

Self-efficacy is employees' belief that they can perform their job or learn the content of the training program successfully. The job environment can be threatening to too many employees who may not have been successful performers in the past. For example, as you will see in Chapter Ten, people who are hired through a welfare-to-work program—a program designed to help find jobs for welfare recipients—may lack self-efficacy. The training environment can also be threatening to people who have not received training or formal education for some length of time, lack education, or are not experienced in the training program's subject matter. For example, training employees to use equipment for computer-based manufacturing may represent a potential threat, especially if they are intimidated by new technology and lack confidence in their ability to master the skills needed to use a computer. Research has demonstrated that self-efficacy is related to performance in training programs.[32] Employees' self-efficacy level can be increased by

1. Letting employees know that the purpose of training is to try to improve performance rather than to identify areas in which employees are incompetent.
2. Providing as much information as possible about the training program and the purpose of training prior to the actual training.
3. Showing employees the training success of their peers who are now in similar jobs.
4. Providing employees with feedback that learning is under their control and they have the ability and the responsibility to overcome any learning difficulties they experience in the program.

Awareness of Training Needs, Career Interests, and Goals

To be motivated to learn in training programs, employees must be aware of their skill strengths and weaknesses and of the link between the training program and improvement of their weaknesses.[33] Managers should make sure that employees understand why they have been asked to attend training programs, and they should communicate the link between training and improvement of skill weaknesses or knowledge deficiencies. This can be accomplished by sharing performance feedback with employees, holding career development discussions, or having employees complete a self-evaluation of their skill strengths and weaknesses as well as career interests and goals. For example, Reynolds and Reynolds, an Ohio-based information services company, uses surveys to obtain sales employees' opinions about what kinds of training they want.[34] The survey asks questions about what additional training the company could provide to improve sales effectiveness and productivity and how employees want to receive training. In response, 60 percent of the employees felt that they needed more training on how to create and present credible estimates of return on investments for each solution they offer customers. Time management training, working in a virtual environment, problem-solving decision making, and listening skills were personal development areas identified by the employees as needing improvement. Most employees preferred classroom training, but they also mentioned webcasts, on-the-job training, or DVDs. The internal training director shares the results with the sales leadership teams, including vice presidents and service directors. The results are being used as part of the process for setting goals for the training department.

If possible, employees need to be given a choice of what programs to attend and must understand how actual training assignments are made to maximize motivation to learn. Several studies have suggested that giving trainees a choice regarding which programs to attend and then honoring those choices maximizes motivation to learn. Giving employees choices but not necessarily honoring them can undermine motivation to learn.[35]

Age and Generation

There is biological evidence that certain mental capacities decrease from age twenty to age seventy.[36] Short-term memory and the speed at which people process information decline as we age. However, with age comes experience, which can compensate for the loss of memory and mental quickness. Although mental quickness and memory losses diminish at a steady pace, at older ages, memory loss is much greater because mental resources are more depleted than at earlier ages.

Chapter One discussed some of the differences (and similarities) of employees from different generations. The terms *millenniums* and *Generation Y* refer to people born after 1980. They are optimistic, willing to work and learn, and technology-literate; they appreciate diversity. The term *Gen Xers* refers to people born from 1965 to 1980. Gen Xers need feedback and flexibility; they dislike close supervision. They have experienced change all their lives (in terms of parents, homes, and cities). Gen Xers value a balance between their work and nonwork lives. *Baby boomers* are people born between 1946 and 1964. They are competitive, hardworking, and concerned that all employees be fairly treated. *Traditionalists* are people born between 1925 and 1945. They are patriotic and loyal, and they have a great deal of knowledge of the history of organizations and work life. Each generation may have specific preferences for the arrangement of the learning environment, type of instruction, and learning activities.[37] For example, traditionalists prefer a stable, orderly training environment and expect the instructor to provide expertise. But Gen Xers prefer more of a self-directed training environment in which they can experiment and receive feedback. As a result, it is important to consider the learners' ages and generations as part of the person analysis. We will discuss these preferences and their implications for training design in Chapter Five.

Input

Employees' perceptions of two characteristics of the work environment—situational constraints and social support—are determinants of performance and motivation to learn. **Situational constraints** include lack of proper tools and equipment, materials and supplies, budgetary support, and time. **Social support** refers to managers' and peers' willingness to provide feedback and reinforcement.[38] If employees have the knowledge, skills, attitudes, and behavior needed to perform but do not have the proper tools and equipment needed, their performance will be inadequate.

To ensure that the work environment enhances trainees' motivation to learn, managers should take the following steps:

1. Provide materials, time, job-related information, and other work aids necessary for employees to use new skills or behavior before participating in training programs.
2. Speak positively about the company's training programs to employees.
3. Let employees know they are doing a good job when they are using training content in their work.
4. Encourage work-group members to involve each other in trying to use new skills on the job by soliciting feedback and sharing training experiences and situations in which training content has been helpful.
5. Provide employees with time and opportunities to practice and apply new skills or behaviors to their work.

Output

Poor or substandard performance can occur on the job because employees do not know at what level they are expected to perform. For example, they may not be aware of quality standards related to speed or the degree of personalization of service that is expected. Employees may have the knowledge, skill, and attitudes necessary to perform and yet fail to perform because they are not aware of the performance standards. Lack of awareness of the performance standards is a communications problem, but it is not a problem that training can "fix."

Understanding the need to perform is important for learning. Trainees need to understand what specifically they are expected to learn in the training program. To ensure that trainees master training content at the appropriate level, trainees in training programs also need to understand the level of proficiency that is expected of them. For example, for tasks, level of proficiency relates to how well employees are to perform a task. For knowledge, level of proficiency may relate to a score on a written test. The standards or the level of performance is part of the learning objectives (discussed in Chapter Four).

Consequences

If employees do not believe that rewards or incentives for performance are adequate, they will be unlikely to meet performance standards even if they have the necessary knowledge, behavior, skill, or attitudes. Also, work-group norms may encourage employees not to meet performance standards. **Norms** refer to accepted standards of behavior for work-group members. For example, during labor contract negotiations, baggage handlers for Northwest Airlines worked slowly loading and unloading baggage from airplanes. As a result, many passenger departures and arrivals were delayed. The baggage handlers had the knowledge, skills, and behaviors necessary to unload the planes more quickly, but they worked slowly because they were trying to send a message to management that the airlines could not perform effectively if their contract demands were not met.

Consequences also affect learning in training programs. Incentive systems, such as providing gift cards redeemable for food, clothes, or movies or accumulating points that can be used toward paying for enrollment in future courses, may be useful for motivating some employees to attend and complete training courses (discussed in Chapter Five).[39] However, one of the most powerful ways to motivate employees to attend and learn from training is to communicate the personal value of the training. For example, how will it help them improve their skills, career, or deal with problems they encounter on the job? It is important that the communication from the manager about potential benefits be realistic. Unmet expectations about training programs can hinder the motivation to learn.[40]

Feedback

Performance problems can result when employees do not receive feedback regarding the extent to which they are meeting performance standards. Training may not be the best solution to this type of problem if employees know what they are supposed to do (output) but do not understand how close their performance is to the standard. Employees need to be given specific, detailed feedback of effective and ineffective performance. For employees to perform to standard, feedback needs to be given frequently, not just during a yearly performance evaluation.

In Chapter Four, the role of feedback in learning is discussed in detail. Keep in mind that feedback is critical for shaping trainees' behaviors and skills.

Determining Whether Training Is the Best Solution

To determine whether training is needed to solve a performance problem, managers need to analyze characteristics of the performer, input, output, consequences, and feedback. How might this be done?[41] Managers should assess the following:

1. Is the performance problem important? Does it have the potential to cost the company a significant amount of money from lost productivity or customers?

2. Do employees know how to perform effectively? Perhaps they received little or no previous training, or the training was ineffective. (This problem is a characteristic of the person.)

3. Can employees demonstrate the correct knowledge or behavior? Perhaps employees were trained but they infrequently or never used the training content (knowledge, skills, etc.) on the job. (This is an input problem.)

4. Were performance expectations clear (input)? Were there any obstacles to performance, such as faulty tools or equipment?

5. Were positive consequences offered for good performance? Was good performance not rewarded? For example, if employees are dissatisfied with their compensation, their peers or a union may encourage them to slow down their pace of work. (This involves consequences.)

6. Did employees receive timely, relevant, accurate, constructive, and specific feedback about their performance (a feedback issue)?

7. Were other solutions—such as job redesign or transferring employees to other jobs—too expensive or unrealistic?

If employees lack the knowledge and skill to perform a job and the other factors are satisfactory, training is needed. If employees have the knowledge and skill to perform but input, output, consequences, or feedback is inadequate, training may not be the best solution. For example, if poor performance results from faulty equipment, training cannot solve this problem, but repairing the equipment will. If poor performance results from lack of feedback, then employees may not need training, but their managers may need training on how to give performance feedback.

It is also important to consider the relationships among a critical job issue (a problem or opportunity that is critical to the success of a job within the company), a critical process issue (a problem or opportunity that is critical to the success of a business process), and a critical business issue (a problem or opportunity that is critical to the success of the company).[42] If the critical job issue, critical process issue, and critical business issue are related, training should be a top priority because it will have a greater effect on business outcomes and results and will likely receive greater management support. Table 3.5 shows the relationships among the critical job, process, and business issues for a sales representative. This analysis resulted from a request from a top manager who suggested that sales representatives needed more training because incomplete sales orders were being submitted to production.

TABLE 3.5   **Example of the Relationships Among a Critical Job Issue, a Critical Process Issue, and a Critical Business Issue**

Critical Job Issue	Critical Process Issue	Critical Business Issue
Desired Results No incomplete order forms 100% accurate orders	*Desired Results* Order cycle time of three days	*Desired Results* Market share of 60%
Current Results 10% incomplete order forms 83% accurate orders	*Current Results* Order cycle time of thirty days	*Current Results* Market Share of 48%

Source: Based on G. A. Rummler and K. Morrill, "The Results Chain," *T + D* (February 2005): 27–35.

FIGURE 3.4
Identifying
How to Solve
Performance
Issues

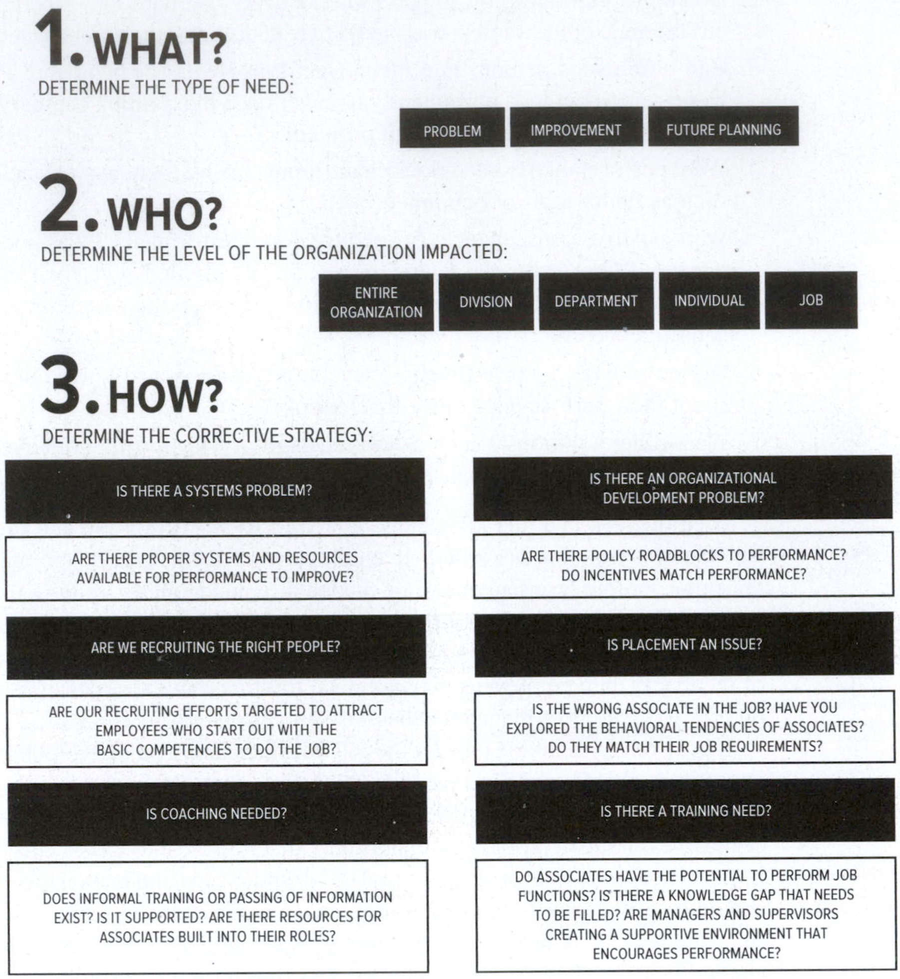

1.WHAT?
DETERMINE THE TYPE OF NEED:

| PROBLEM | IMPROVEMENT | FUTURE PLANNING |

2.WHO?
DETERMINE THE LEVEL OF THE ORGANIZATION IMPACTED:

| ENTIRE ORGANIZATION | DIVISION | DEPARTMENT | INDIVIDUAL | JOB |

3.HOW?
DETERMINE THE CORRECTIVE STRATEGY:

IS THERE A SYSTEMS PROBLEM?

ARE THERE PROPER SYSTEMS AND RESOURCES AVAILABLE FOR PERFORMANCE TO IMPROVE?

ARE WE RECRUITING THE RIGHT PEOPLE?

ARE OUR RECRUITING EFFORTS TARGETED TO ATTRACT EMPLOYEES WHO START OUT WITH THE BASIC COMPETENCIES TO DO THE JOB?

IS COACHING NEEDED?

DOES INFORMAL TRAINING OR PASSING OF INFORMATION EXIST? IS IT SUPPORTED? ARE THERE RESOURCES FOR ASSOCIATES BUILT INTO THEIR ROLES?

IS THERE AN ORGANIZATIONAL DEVELOPMENT PROBLEM?

ARE THERE POLICY ROADBLOCKS TO PERFORMANCE? DO INCENTIVES MATCH PERFORMANCE?

IS PLACEMENT AN ISSUE?

IS THE WRONG ASSOCIATE IN THE JOB? HAVE YOU EXPLORED THE BEHAVIORAL TENDENCIES OF ASSOCIATES? DO THEY MATCH THEIR JOB REQUIREMENTS?

IS THERE A TRAINING NEED?

DO ASSOCIATES HAVE THE POTENTIAL TO PERFORM JOB FUNCTIONS? IS THERE A KNOWLEDGE GAP THAT NEEDS TO BE FILLED? ARE MANAGERS AND SUPERVISORS CREATING A SUPPORTIVE ENVIRONMENT THAT ENCOURAGES PERFORMANCE?

Consider how a global retailer of rugged, athletic, casual, and stylish clothes for kids and young adults identifies whether a performance need should be addressed by training or other solutions. Figure 3.4 shows how this retailer determines the type of need, who is affected, and the corrective strategy. As you can see from Figure 3.4, training and development is only one of several possible solutions and addresses issues related specifically to knowledge gaps, sharing knowledge and skills, informal learning, and manager and supervisor support.

Task Analysis

Task analysis results in a description of work activities, including tasks performed by the employee and the knowledge, skills, and abilities required to complete the tasks. A **job** is a specific position requiring the completion of certain tasks. (The job exemplified in Table 3.6 is that of an electrical maintenance worker.) A **task** is the employee's work

TABLE 3.6   **Sample Items from Task Analysis Questionnaires for the Electrical Maintenance Job**

Job: Electrical Maintenance Worker				
		Task Performance Ratings		
Task #	**Task Description**	**Frequency of Performance**	**Importance**	**Difficulty**
199–264	Replace a light bulb	0 1 2 3 4 5	0 1 2 3 4 5	0 1 2 3 4 5
199–265	Replace an electrical outlet	0 1 2 3 4 5	0 1 2 3 4 5	0 1 2 3 4 5
199–266	Install a light fixture	0 1 2 3 4 5	0 1 2 3 4 5	0 1 2 3 4 5
199–267	Replace a light switch	0 1 2 3 4 5	0 1 2 3 4 5	0 1 2 3 4 5
199–268	Install a new circuit breaker	0 1 2 3 4 5	0 1 2 3 4 5	0 1 2 3 4 5
		Frequency of Performance	**Importance**	**Difficulty**
		0 = Never 5 = Often	1 = Negligible 5 = Extremely high	1 = Easiest 5 = Most difficult

Source: E. F. Holton III and C. Bailey, "Top to Bottom Curriculum Redesign," *Training and Development* (March 1995): 40–44.

activity in a specific job. Table 3.6 shows several tasks for the electrical maintenance worker job. These tasks include replacing lightbulbs, electrical outlets, and light switches. To complete tasks, employees must have specific levels of knowledge, skill, ability, and other considerations (KSAOs). **Knowledge** includes facts or procedures (e.g., the chemical properties of gold). **Skill** indicates competency in performing a task (e.g., negotiation skill, a skill in getting another person to agree to take a certain course of action). **Ability** includes the physical and mental capacities to perform a task (e.g., spatial ability, the ability to see the relationship between objects in physical space). **Other** refers to the conditions under which tasks are performed. These conditions include identifying the equipment and environment that the employee works in (e.g., the need to wear an oxygen mask, work in extremely hot conditions), time constraints for a task (e.g., deadlines), safety considerations, or performance standards.

Task analysis should be undertaken only after the organizational analysis has determined that the company wants to devote time and money for training. Why? Task analysis is a time-consuming, tedious process that involves a large time commitment to gather and summarize data from many different persons in the company, including managers, job incumbents, and trainers.

Steps in a Task Analysis

A task analysis involves four steps:[43]

1. Select the job or jobs to be analyzed.
2. Develop a preliminary list of tasks performed on the job by (1) interviewing and observing expert employees and their managers and (2) talking with others who have performed a task analysis.
3. Validate or confirm the preliminary list of tasks. This step involves having a group of SMEs (job incumbents, managers, etc.) answer in a meeting or on a written survey

several questions regarding the tasks. The types of questions that may be asked include the following: How frequently is the task performed? How much time is spent performing each task? How important or critical is the task for successful performance of the job? How difficult is the task to learn? Is performance of the task expected of entry-level employees?

Table 3.7 presents a sample task analysis questionnaire. This information is used to determine which tasks will be focused on in the training program. The person or committee conducting the needs assessment must decide the level of ratings across dimensions that will determine that a task should be included in the training program. Tasks that are important, frequently performed, and of moderate-to-high level of difficulty are tasks for which training should be provided. Tasks that are not important and are infrequently performed should not involve training. It is difficult for managers and trainers to decide if tasks that are important but are performed infrequently and require minimal difficulty should be included in training. Managers and trainers must determine

TABLE 3.7   **Sample Task Statement Questionnaire**

Name   Date

Position

Please rate each of the task statements according to three factors: (1) the *importance* of the task for effective performance, (2) how *frequently* the task is performed, and (3) the degree of *difficulty* required to become effective in the task. Use the following scales in making your ratings.

Importance	*Frequency*
4 = Task is critical for effective performance.	4 = Task is performed once a day.
3 = Task is important but not critical for effective performance.	3 = Task is performed once a week.
2 = Task is of some importance for effective performance.	2 = Task is performed once every few months.
1 = Task is of no importance for effective performance.	1 = Task is performed once or twice a year.
0 = Task is not performed.	0 = Task is not performed.

Difficulty

4 = Effective performance of the task requires extensive prior experience and/or training (12–18 months or longer).
3 = Effective performance of the task requires minimal prior experience and training (6–12 months).
2 = Effective performance of the task requires a brief period of prior training and experience (1–6 months).
1 = Effective performance of the task does not require specific prior training and/or experience.
0 = This task is not performed.

Task	Importance	Frequency	Difficulty
1. Ensuring maintenance on equipment, tools, and safety controls			
2. Monitoring employee performance			
3. Scheduling employees			
4. Using statistical software on the computer			
5. Monitoring changes made in processes using statistical methods			

whether or not important tasks—regardless of how frequently they are performed or their level of difficulty—will be included in training.

4. Once the tasks have been identified, it is important to identify the knowledge, skills, or tasks that are difficult to learn or prone to errors such as decision-making or problem-solving tasks. For these tasks it is necessary to determine how the thought processes of experts differ from those of novices. This information is useful for designing training that includes the right amount of practice and feedback for novices to learn. This information can be collected through interviews and questionnaires. Recall this chapter's discussion of how ability influences learning. Information concerning basic skill and cognitive ability requirements is critical for determining if certain levels of knowledge, skills, and abilities will be prerequisites for entrance to the training program (or job) or if supplementary training in underlying skills is needed. For training purposes, information concerning how difficult it is to learn the knowledge, skill, or ability is important—as is whether the knowledge, skill, or ability is expected to be acquired by the employee before taking the job.[44]

Table 3.8 summarizes key points to remember regarding task analysis.

Example of a Task Analysis

Each of the four steps of a task analysis can be seen in this example from a utility company. Trainers were given the job of developing a training system in six months.[45] The purpose of the program was to identify tasks and KSAOs that would serve as the basis for training program objectives and lesson plans.

The first phase of the project involved identifying potential tasks for each job in the utility's electrical maintenance area. Procedures, equipment lists, and information provided by SMEs were used to generate the tasks. SMEs included managers, instructors, and senior technicians. The tasks were incorporated into a questionnaire administered to all technicians in the electrical maintenance department. The questionnaire included 550 tasks. Table 3.6 shows sample items from the questionnaire for the electrical maintenance job. Technicians were asked to rate each task on importance, difficulty, and frequency of performance. The rating scale for frequency included zero. A zero rating indicated that the technician rating the task had never performed the task. Technicians who rated a task zero were asked not to evaluate the task's difficulty and importance.

TABLE 3.8 Key Points to Remember When Conducting a Task Analysis

A task analysis should identify both what employees are actually doing and what they should be doing on the job.

Task analysis begins by breaking the job into duties and tasks.

Use more than two methods for collecting task information to increase the validity of the analysis.

For task analysis to be useful, information needs to be collected from SMEs, including job incumbents, managers, and employees familiar with the job.

In deciding how to evaluate tasks, the focus should be on tasks necessary to accomplish the company's goals and objectives. These may not be the tasks that are the most difficult or take the most time.

Source: Based on A. P. Carnevale, L. J. Gainer, and A. S. Meltzer, *Workplace Basics Training Manual* (San Francisco: Jossey-Bass, 1990); Surface, E. A. (2012). Training need assessment: aligning learning and capability with performance requirements and organizational objectives. In M. A. Wilson, W. Bennett, S. G. Gibson, & G. M. Alliger (Eds.), *The Handbook of Work Analysis: Methods, Systems, Applications and Science of Work Measurement in Organizations* (1st ed.) (pp. 437-462). Routledge Academic.

Customized software was used to analyze the ratings collected via the questionnaire. The primary requirement used to determine whether a task required training was its importance rating. A task rated "very important" was identified as one requiring training regardless of its frequency or difficulty. If a task was rated moderately important but difficult, it also was designated for training. Tasks rated as unimportant, not difficult, or done infrequently were not designated for training.

The list of tasks designated for training was reviewed by the SMEs to determine if it accurately described job tasks. The result was a list of 487 tasks. For each of the 487 tasks, two SMEs identified the necessary KSAOs required for performance. This included information on working conditions, cues that initiate the task's start and end, performance standards, safety considerations, and necessary tools and equipment. All data were reviewed by plant technicians and members of the training department. More than 14,000 KSAOs were grouped into common areas and assigned an identification code. These groups were then combined into clusters that represented qualification areas. That is, the task clusters were related to linked tasks that the employees must be certified in to perform the job. The clusters were used to identify training lesson plans and course objectives. Trainers also reviewed the clusters to identify prerequisite skills for each cluster.

COMPETENCY MODELS

In today's global and competitive business environment, many companies are finding that it is difficult to determine whether employees have the capabilities needed for success. The necessary capabilities may vary from one business unit to another, and even across roles, within a business unit. As a result, many companies are using competency models to help them identify the knowledge, skills, and personal characteristics (attitudes, personality) needed for successful performance in a job. Competency models are also useful for ensuring that training and development systems are contributing to the development of such knowledge, skills, and personal characteristics.

Traditionally, needs assessment has involved identifying knowledge, skills, abilities, and tasks. However, a current trend in training is for needs assessment to focus on competencies, especially for managerial positions. **Competencies** are sets of skills, knowledge, abilities, and personal characteristics that enable employees to perform their jobs successfully.[46]

A **competency model** identifies the competencies necessary for each job. Competency models provide descriptions of competencies that are common for an entire occupation, organization, job family, or specific job. Competency models can be used for performance management. However, one of the strengths of competency models is that they are useful for a variety of human resource (HR) practices, including recruiting, selection, training, and development. Competency models can be used to help identify the best employees to fill open positions and to serve as the foundation for development plans that allow employees and their manager to target specific strengths and development areas. The competencies included in competency models vary according to the company's business strategy and goals. They can include sales, leadership, interpersonal, technical, and other types of competencies. Competency models typically included the name of each competency, the behaviors that represent proficiency in the competency, and levels that include descriptions

TABLE 3.9 **Competencies from a Competency Model**

Technical Cluster	Proficiency Ratings
Systems Architecture Ability to design complex software applications, establish protocols, and create prototypes.	**0**—Is not able to perform basic tasks. **1**—Understands basic principles; can perform tasks with assistance or direction. **2**—Performs routine tasks with reliable results; works with minimal supervision. **3**—Performs complex and multiple tasks; can coach or teach others. **4**—Considered an expert in this task; can describe, teach, and lead others.
Data Migration Ability to establish the necessary platform requirements to efficiently and completely coordinate data transfer.	**0**—Is not able to perform basic tasks. **1**—Understands basic principles; can perform tasks with assistance or direction. **2**—Performs routine tasks with reliable results; works with minimal supervision. **3**—Performs complex and multiple tasks; can coach or teach others. **4**—Considered an expert in this task; can describe, teach, and lead others.
Documentation Ability to prepare comprehensive and complete documentation, including specifications, flow diagrams, process control, and budgets.	**0**—Is not able to perform basic tasks. **1**—Understands basic principles; can perform tasks with assistance or direction. **2**—Performs routine tasks with reliable results; works with minimal supervision. **3**—Performs complex and multiple tasks; can coach or teach others. **4**—Considered an expert in this task; can describe, teach, and lead others.

Source: R. J. Mirabile, "Everything You Wanted to Know About Competency Modeling," *Training and Development* (August 1997): 73–77.

representing demonstrated levels of mastery or proficiency. Table 3.9 shows the technical cluster of competencies from a competency model for a systems engineer. The left side of the table lists technical competencies within the technical cluster (such as systems architecture, data migration, and documentation). The right side shows behaviors that might be used to determine a systems engineer's level of proficiency for each competency.

One way to understand competency models is to compare them to job analysis. As you may recall from other classes or experiences, **job analysis** refers to the process of developing a description of the job (tasks, duties, and responsibilities) and the specifications (knowledge, skills, and abilities) that an employee must have to perform it. How does job analysis compare to competency models? Job analysis is more work- and task-focused (what is accomplished), whereas competency modeling is worker-focused (how objectives are met or how work is accomplished). Focusing on "how" versus "what" provides valuable information for training and development. A recent study asked competency modeling experts (consultants, HR practitioners, academics, and industrial psychologists) to compare and contrast competency modeling and job analysis.[47] The study found several differences between job analysis and competency models. Competency models are more likely to link competencies and the company's business goals. Competency models provide descriptions of competencies that are common for an entire occupational group, level of jobs, or an entire organization. Job analysis describes what is different across jobs, occupational groups, or organization levels. Finally, job analysis generates specific knowledge, skills, and abilities for particular jobs. It is used to generate specific requirements to be used for employee selection. The competencies generated by competency modeling are more general and believed to have greater application to a wider variety of purposes, including selection, training, employee development, and performance management.

Another way to think about competency models is by considering performance management.[48] Unfortunately, many performance management systems suffer from a lack of agreement on what outcomes should be used to evaluate performance. Manager–employee discussions about performance deficiencies tend to lack specificity. By identifying the areas of personal capability that enable employees to perform their jobs successfully, competency models ensure an evaluation of what gets done and how it gets done. Performance feedback can be directed toward specific concrete examples of behavior, and knowledge, skills, ability, and other characteristics that are necessary for success are clearly described.

How are competencies identified and competency models developed? Figure 3.5 shows the process used to develop a competency model. First, the business strategy is identified. The implications of business strategy for training were discussed in Chapter Two. The business strategy helps identify what types of competencies are needed to ensure that business goals are met and the company's strategy is supported. Changes in the business strategy might cause new competencies to be needed or old competencies to be altered. Second, the job or position to be analyzed is identified. Third, effective and ineffective performers are identified. Fourth, the competencies responsible for effective and ineffective performance are identified. There are several approaches for identifying competencies. These include analyzing one or several "star" performers, surveying persons who are familiar with the job (SMEs), and investigating benchmark data of good performers in other companies.[49] Fifth, the model is validated. That is, a determination is made as to whether the competencies included in the model truly are related to effective performance. In the example of the technical competencies for the systems engineer shown in Table 3.9, it is important to verify that (1) these three competencies are necessary for job success, and (2) the level of proficiency of the competency is appropriate.

Following the development process outlined in Figure 3.5 will ensure that competencies and competency models are valid. However, trainers, employees, managers, and other experts should be trained (especially inexperienced raters) in how to determine accurate competency ratings. Training should ensure that raters understand each competency and the differences between them and can distinguish between low, medium, and high levels of proficiency.[50]

FIGURE 3.5   **The Process Used in Developing a Competency Model**

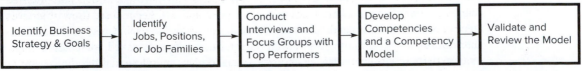

Competency models are useful for training and development in several ways:[52]

- They identify behaviors needed for effective job performance. These models ensure that feedback given to employees as part of a development program (such as 360-degree feedback) relate specifically to individual and organizational success.
- They provide a tool for determining what skills are necessary to meet today's needs, as well as the company's future skill needs. They can be used to evaluate the relationship between the company's current training programs and present needs. That is, they help align training and development activities with the company's business goals. They can be used to evaluate how well the offerings relate to anticipated future skill needs.
- They help determine what skills are needed at different career points.
- They provide a framework for ongoing coaching and feedback to develop employees for current and future roles. By comparing their current personal competencies to those required for a job, employees can identify competencies that need development and choose actions to develop those competencies. These actions may include courses, job experiences, and other types of development. (Development methods are detailed in Chapter Nine, "Employee Development and Career Management.")
- They create a "road map" for identifying and developing employees who may be candidates for managerial positions (succession planning).
- They provide a common set of criteria that are used for identifying appropriate development training and learning activities for employees, as well as for evaluating and rewarding them. This helps integrate and align the company's HR systems and practices.

For example, at American Express, competency models are used to help managers lead their own teams by providing a framework that their employees can use to capitalize on strengths and improve weaknesses.[53] At the company level, competencies are used to determine the talent level of the entire company, including capabilities, strengths, and opportunities. This information is provided to managers who use the data to identify key needs and plan actions to ensure that current and future competencies are developed in employees.

Table 3.10 shows the competency model that Luxottica Retail, known for premium, luxury, and sports eyewear sold through LensCrafters, Sunglass Hut, and Pearle Vision, developed for its associates in field and store positions.[54] The competency model includes leadership and managerial, functional, and foundational competencies. The goal was to define and identify competencies that managers could use for hiring, performance management, and training. Also, competencies would help associates identify and develop the skills they needed to apply for different jobs. To use competency models effectively for performance evaluation, they must be up to date, drive business performance, job-related (valid), relevant (or customized) for all of the company's business units, and provide sufficient detail to make an accurate assessment of employees performance. At Luxottica Retail, developing competencies started with meeting with business leaders to understand their current and future business strategies. Business drivers were identified and questionnaires, focus groups, and meetings with managers and associates were used to identify important competencies and examples of behaviors related to each. Competencies across business units and brands are reviewed every four or five years, or whenever a major change in jobs or business strategy occurs to ensure they are relevant. Also, the weighting

TABLE 3.10
Luxottica
Retail's
Competency
Model

Leadership and Managerial
Leadership
Coach and Develop Others
Motivate Others
Foster Teamwork
Think Strategically

Functional
Global Perspective
Financial Acumen
Business Key Performance Indicators

Foundational
Critical Thinking
Foster Open Communications
Build Relationships and Interpersonal Skills
Develop and Manage Oneself
Adaptability and Flexibility
Customer Focus
Act with Integrity
Diversity and Multiculturalism
Drive and Commitment

Source: From C. Spicer, "Building a Competency Model," *HR Magazine*, April 2009, 34–36.

given to each set of competencies in the performance evaluation is reviewed to ensure that they are appropriate (e.g., what weights should be given to the functional skills?). Depending on their relevance for a specific job, various combinations of these competencies are used for evaluating associates' performance. Associates are rated on a 1–5 scale for each competency, with 5 meaning "far exceeds expectations" HR, training and development and operations teams worked together to define the levels of each competency. That is, what does it mean and what does the competency look like when an employee is rated "meets expectations" versus "below expectations"? This was necessary to ensure that managers are using a similar frame of reference when they evaluate associates using the competencies.

SCOPE OF NEEDS ASSESSMENT

Up to this point, the chapter has discussed the various aspects of needs assessment, including organizational, person, and task analyses. This involves interviews, observations, and potentially even surveying employees. You might be saying to yourself, "This sounds good, but it appears to be a very elaborate process that takes time. What happens if I don't have time to conduct a thorough needs assessment? Should I abandon the process?"

Needs assessment is often skipped for several reasons based on assumptions such as training is always the issue or is mandated; it's too costly, takes too long, and is too complex; and managers will not cooperate. Despite the constraints to conducting a needs assessment, it is necessary to determine if a problem or pressure point exists and to identify the best solution, which could be training.

However, even if managers demand a training course right now, needs assessment should still be conducted. There are several ways to conduct a rapid needs assessment. A **rapid needs assessment** refers to a needs assessment that is done quickly and accurately, but without sacrificing the quality of the process or the outcomes.[55] The key to conducting a rapid needs assessment is choosing the needs assessment methods that will provide the results you can have the greatest confidences in while using the fewest resources (time, money, SMEs). There are several ways to conduct a rapid needs assessment. First, the scope of needs assessment depends on the size of the potential pressure point. If the pressure point seems to be local and has a potentially small impact on the business, then the information-gathering part of needs assessment could consist of only a few interviews with managers or job incumbents. If the pressure point will have a large impact on the business, then more information gathering should be conducted. If, after interviewing SMEs and job incumbents, you can tell that you are not learning anything new about the job, then interviewing could be stopped. Second, consider using already available data collected for other purposes. Error data, sales data, customer complaints, and exit interviews might provide valuable clues as to the source of performance and survey problems. JetBlue uses on-the-job performance data and business results data to identify training needs.[56] For example, using data collected when aircraft are regularly serviced, JetBlue found that there was an increase in cosmetic damage to airplanes. This triggered the learning team to conduct more in-depth assessment to identify potential learning needs that may have resulted in an increase in the damage rate over time. Customer complaints tracked by the U.S. Transportation Department revealed an increase in problems experienced by JetBlue's disabled passengers before boarding. Based on this data, training was revised and expanded, resulting in fewer complaints. The web may be a useful source for quickly conducting interviews and surveys with SMEs in different locations. Finally, if you are attuned to the business problems, technological developments, and other issues facing the organization, you will be able to anticipate training needs. For example, if the company is opening sales offices in an international location and introducing new technology in the manufacturing plants, cross-cultural training and training designed to help employees use the new technology undoubtedly will be needed. Be prepared by understanding the business.

Needs Assessment in Practice

KLA-Tencor supplies process controls and equipment to the semiconductor industry.[57] KLA-Tencor service engineers need to diagnose and repair its customers' complex machines that use advanced laser, optical, and robotic technologies. The engineers need to main proficiency in their current skills as well as add new skills to keep pace with new technology used in the company's equipment. This is critical for KLA-Tencor to quickly solve equipment problems, which, if unresolved, can result in millions of dollars of lost revenue for its customers. Providing effective service is critical for the company to keep current customers and develop new business. In fact, one of the company's values is "Indispensable" (the other values are "Perseverance," "Drive to Be Better," "High Performance Teams," and "Honest, Forthright and Consistent").

KLA-Tencor uses a skill management process (the Right People, Right Knowledge process) to monitor its workforce skills and uses this information to change its training programs. The process involves developing a task list, training on the task, practicing on-the-job training to gain certification, and conducting an annual skills assessment. To conduct the skills assessment, a survey was sent to all of KLA-Tencor's more than one thousand service engineers. For each task the engineers were asked to rate their capability of doing the task on a scale from "I don't know how" to "I can teach it to others." Also, they were asked to evaluate how frequently they performed the task from "Never" to "More than two times per year." Based on their responses, they were assigned a training task. More than two hundred courses were created to train the engineers. To ensure that the training was completed, both engineers and their managers were accountable. This helped achieve a 95 percent completion rate within one year after training was assigned. The skills assessment data was also used to identify gaps in current training, resulting in more than two thousand changes in courses and certification programs. The skills assessment is done annually to ensure that service engineers keep up to date with new technology and products.

This example illustrates several aspects of the needs assessment process. First, training was viewed as critical for helping the company meet its strategic objectives. As a result, resources and time were allocated for needs assessment and training. Second, the needs assessment included a task or skill assessment that helped determine who needed training and what tasks they needed to learn. Third, based on the needs assessment, training programs were developed or changed to improve the identified skill deficiencies.

Summary

The first step in a successful training effort is to determine that a training need exists through a process known as needs assessment. Needs assessment involves three steps: organizational analysis, person analysis, and task analysis. Various methods—including observation, interviews, and surveys or questionnaires—are used to conduct a needs assessment. Each has advantages and disadvantages. Organizational analysis involves determining (1) the extent to which training is congruent with the company's business strategy and resources and (2) if peers and managers are likely to provide the support needed for trainees to use training content in the work setting.

Person analysis focuses on identifying whether there is evidence that training is the solution, who needs training, and whether employees have the prerequisite skills, attitudes, and beliefs needed to ensure that they master the content of training programs. Because performance problems are one of the major reasons that companies consider training for employees, it is important to investigate how personal characteristics, input, output, consequences, and feedback relate to performance and learning. Managers and trainers need to be concerned about employees' basic skill levels, attitudes, age and generation, and the work environment in determining if performance problems can be solved using training and how training should be designed.

Training is likely the best solution to a performance problem if employees don't know how to perform. If employees have not received feedback about their performance, if they lack the equipment needed to perform the job, if the consequences for good performance are negative, or if they are unaware of an expected standard for performance, then training is not likely to be the best solution.

To maximize employees' motivation to learn in training programs, managers and trainers need to understand these factors prior to sending employees to training. For example, lack of basic skills or reading skills can inhibit both job performance and learning.

A task analysis involves identifying the task and the training that employees will require in terms of knowledge, skills, and abilities. Competency modeling is a new approach to needs assessment that focuses on identifying personal capabilities, including knowledge, skills, attitudes, values, and personal characteristics.

Key Terms

needs assessment, *118*
organizational analysis, *118*
person analysis, *118*
task analysis, *118*
stakeholders, *120*
subject-matter experts
(SMEs), *122*
job incumbent, *122*
focus groups, *125*
crowdsourcing, *125*
benchmarking, *126*
gap analysis *129*

readiness for training, *129*
person characteristics, *129*
input, *129*
output, *129*
consequences, *129*
feedback, *130*
motivation to learn, *131*
basic skills, *132*
cognitive ability, *133*
readability, *134*
self-efficacy, *135*
situational constraints, *137*

social support, *137*
norms, *138*
job, *140*
task, *140*
knowledge, *141*
skill, *141*
ability, *141*
other, *141*
competencies, *144*
competency model, *144*
job analysis, *145*
rapid needs assessment, *149*

Discussion Questions

1. Which of the factors that influence performance and learning do you think is most important? Which is least important?

2. If you had to conduct a needs assessment for a new job at a new plant, describe the method you would use.

3. If you were going to use online technology to identify training needs for customer service representatives for a web-based clothing company, what steps would you take to ensure that the technology was not threatening to employees?

4. Needs assessment involves organization, person, and task analyses. Which one of these analyses do you believe is most important? Which is least important? Why?

5. Why should upper-level managers be included in the needs assessment process?

6. Explain how you would determine if employees had the reading level necessary to succeed in a training program. How would you determine if employees had the necessary computer skills needed to use a web-based training program?

7. What conditions would suggest that a company should buy a training program from an outside vendor? Which would suggest that the firm should develop the program itself?

8. Assume that you have to prepare older employees with little computer experience to attend a training course on how to use the Internet. How will you ensure that they have high levels of readiness for training? How will you determine their readiness for training?

9. Review the accompanying sample tasks and task ratings for the electronic technician's job. What tasks do you believe should be emphasized in the training program? Why?

10. Explain the process you would use to determine the cause of a performance problem. Draw a picture showing the process.

Task	Importance	Frequency	Learning Difficulty
1. Replaces components	1	2	1
2. Repairs equipment	2	5	5
3. Interprets instrument readings	1	4	5
4. Uses small tools	2	5	1

Explanation of ratings:
Frequency: 1 = very infrequently to 5 = very frequently
Importance: 1 = very important to 5 = very unimportant
Learning difficulty: 1 = easy to 5 = very difficult

11. Why would we consider age and generational differences as part of needs assessment? Is this important? Explain. Discuss the types of evidence that you would look for to determine whether a needs analysis has been conducted improperly.

12. How is competency modeling similar to traditional needs assessment? How does it differ?

13. What is a rapid needs assessment? How would you conduct a rapid needs assessment so that it is valuable and accurately identifies training needs?

Application Assignments

1. Develop a competency model for a job held by a friend, spouse, or roommate (someone other than yourself). Use the process discussed in this chapter to develop your model. Note the most difficult part of developing the model. How could the model be used?

2. The Department of Social Services represents a large portion of your county's budget and total number of employees. The job of eligibility technician is responsible for all client contact, policy interpretation, and financial decisions related to several forms of public aid (e.g., food stamps, aid to families with dependent children). Eligibility technicians must read a large number of memos and announcements of new and revised policies and procedures. Eligibility technicians were complaining that they had difficulty reading and responding to this correspondence. The county decided to send the employees to a speed reading program costing $250 per person. The county has 200 eligibility technicians.

    Preliminary evaluation of the speed reading program was that trainees liked it. Two months after the training was conducted, the technicians told their managers that they were not using the speed reading course in their jobs, but were using it in leisure reading at home. When their managers asked why they weren't using it on the job, the typical response was, "I never read those memos and policy announcements anyway."

    a. Evaluate the needs assessment process used to determine that speed reading was necessary. What was good about it? Where was it faulty?

    b. How would you have conducted the needs assessment? Be realistic.

3. Consider the interview questions for the lead drivers that are shown on page 131. Write questions that could be used to interview the six lead driver supervisors and the two

regional vice presidents. How do these questions differ from those for the lead drivers? How are they similar?

4. Several companies are known for linking their mission, values, and HR practices in ways that have led to business success as well as employee satisfaction. These companies include Southwest Airlines (*www.iflyswa.com*), Cisco Systems (*www.cisco.com*), SAS Institute (*www.sas.com*), Men's Wearhouse (*www.menswearhouse.com*), Container Store (*www.containerstore.com*), Google (*www.google.com*), Steelcase (*www.steelcase.com*), Whole Foods (*www.wholefoods.com*), and TELUS (http://abouttelus.com). Choose one of these companies' websites and reviews of the companies at *www.glassdoor.com* and perform an organizational needs analysis. Read about the company's values and vision; look for statements about the importance of training and personal development. Is training important in the company? Why or why not? Provide supporting evidence.

5. Go to *www.careeronestop.org/CompetencyModel*, the website for CareerOneStop, sponsored by the U.S. Department of Labor, Employment and Training Administration to help job seekers, students, businesses, and career professionals. Choose and review one of the industry competency models. How might these competency models be useful for training and development for companies within the industry you selected? For their employees? For individuals such as students or the unemployed interested in working in the industry?

6. ConocoPhillips finds and produces oil and natural gas. Go to *www.conocophillips.com*. Choose "Careers" and click on "Career Development." Next, click on "Leadership Competencies." Review the competencies. How could they be used for learning and development of new and aspiring company leaders and managers?

Case:

Determining Training Needs at Summit Credit Union

Summit Credit Union, located in Madison and Milwaukee, Wisconsin, is a small company with 366 employees. A merger in 2015 doubled the size of the company and made it necessary to build a new corporate culture. Summit's mission is to improve credit members' financial lives to help them achieve their dreams. For example, in 2013 Summit members saved over $13 million based on higher savings rates, lower loan rates, and lowerfees compared to for-profit banking institutions in Wisconsin. Summit has invested in creating a world-class learning function, which includes a team of seven professionals who are able to design and deliver instructor-led training as well as e-learning. Summit has shifted away from generic off-the-shelf training to develop online and face-to-face programs customized to

employee needs and the company's goals and initiatives. For example, the learning function is expected to play a key role in dealing with business issues such as efficiency, loan growth, and increased sales. All learning staff members are expected to contribute to new company initiatives, such as new products and services, systems, or regulations. Summit has recently identified a problem with its new lenders. They were starting to perform their jobs without the necessary skills, information, and knowledge that they needed. One potential reason for this is how the lending training curriculum is organized. New lenders attend a course on different types of loans and the lending system, start their jobs, and then later return for a course on lending guidelines, underwriting, and sales skills.

How would you conduct a needs assessment to determine if new lenders are starting their jobs without the necessary knowledge and skills to perform well, and if the organization of the training curriculum (or another training issue) is responsible for this problem? Who would be involved in the needs assessment?

Source: Based on J. Salopek, "Investing in learning," *T+D* (October 2011): 56–58; "Connect, Inspire, Impact" 2013 Annual Report from *www.summitcreditunion.com*.

Endnotes

1. I. L. Goldstein, E. P. Braverman, and H. Goldstein, "Needs assessment," In *Developing Human Resources*, ed. K. N. Wexley (Washington, DC: Bureau of National Affairs, 1991): 5-35 to 5-75; E. Surface, "Training need assessment: Aligning learning and capability with performance requirements and organizational objectives." In *The Handbook of Work Analysis: Methods, Systems, Applications and Science of Work Measurement in Organizations*, eds. M. A. Wilson, W. Bennett, S. G. Gibson, and G. M. Alliger (Routledge Academic, 2012): 437–462.

2. K. Tyler, "The strongest link," *HR Magazine* (January 2011): 51–53; S. Villachica, D. Stepich, and S. Rist, "Surviving troubled times: Five best practices for training solutions," *Performance Improvement*, 50 (March 2011): 9–15.

3. J. J. Salopek, "Tackling business-critical issues through training," *TD* (October 2014): 64–67.

4. S. Lindenberg, "Advisory groups can help L&D initiatives," *TD* (September 2014): 28–31.

5. L. Freifeld, "Solving today's skill gaps," *training* (November/December 2013): 52–57.

6. K. Kuehner-Herbert, "Philips: A learning organization transformed," *Chief Learning Officer* (October 2014): 22–25.

7. G. Mcardle and S. Salamy, "Drilling to the core of training and education," *T+D* (September 2013): 52.

8. C. Crain, "Collect input to increase output," *T+D* (June 2014): 26–29.

9. B. Durman, S. Chyung, S. Villachica and D. Winiecki, "Root causes of errant ordered radiology exams: Results of a needs assessment," *Performance Improvement*, 50 (January 2011): 17–24.

10. M. Casey and D. Doverspike, "Training needs analysis and evaluation for new technologies through the use of problem-based inquiry," *Performance Improvement Quarterly* 18(1) (2005): 110–124.

11. K. Ellis, "The right track," *training* (September 2004): 40–45.

12. K. Mahler, "Big Employer is watching," *The Wall Street Journal* (November 4, 2003): B1 and B6.

13. G. Siekierka, H. Huntley, and M. Johnson, "Learning is center stage at CSC," *T+D* (October 2009): 48–50.

14. P. Schamore, "Spirited learning," *T+D* (October 2009): 56–58.

15. J. Salopek, "From learning department to learning partner," *T+D* (October 2010): 48–50.

16. L. E. Day, "Benchmarking training," *Training and Development* (November 1995): 27–30.

17. M. Mihelich, "Change is a way of life, learning at IBM," *Chief Learning Officer* (June 2014): 28–29.

18. J. Rouiller and I. Goldstein, "The relationship between organizational transfer climate and positive transfer of training," *Human Resource Development Quarterly* 4 (1993): 377–90; R. Noe and J. Colquitt, "Planning for Training Impact." In *Creating, Implementing, and Managing Effective Training and Development*, ed. K. Kraiger (San Francisco: Jossey-Bass, 2002): 53–79.

19. S. Sipek, "Learning developed with surgical precision," *Chief Learning Officer* (January 2015): 22–25.

20. G. Rummler, "In search of the Holy Performance Grail," *Training and Development* (April 1996): 26–31; D. G. Langdon, "Selecting interventions," *Performance Improvement* 36 (1997): 11–15.

21. K. Gupta, *A Practical Guide to Needs Assessment* (San Francisco: Jossey-Bass/Pfeiffer, 1999).

22. R. A. Noe, "Trainee attributes and attitudes: Neglected influences on training effectiveness," *Academy of Management Review* 11 (1986): 736–49; R. Noe and J. Colquitt, "Planning for Training Impact." In *Creating, Implementing, and Managing Effective Training and Development*, ed. K. Kraiger (San Francisco: Jossey-Bass, 2002): 53–79.

23. D. Milibank, "Marriott tightens job program screening," *The Wall Street Journal* (July 15, 1997): A1, A12.

24. T. T. Baldwin, R. T. Magjuka, and B. T. Loher, "The perils of participation: Effects of choice on trainee motivation and learning," *Personnel Psychology* 44 (1991): 51–66; S. I. Tannenbaum, J. E. Mathieu, E. Salas, and J. A. Cannon-Bowers, "Meeting trainees' expectations: The influence of training fulfillment on the development of commitment, self-efficacy, and motivation," *Journal of Applied Psychology* 76 (1991): 759–769; J. Colquitt, J. LePine, and R. Noe, "Toward an integrative theory of training motivation: A meta-analytic path analysis of 20 years of research," *Journal of Applied Psychology* 85 (2000): 678–707.

25. M. Eisenstein, "Test, then train," *T+D* (May 2005): 26–27.

26. J. Nunally, *Psychometric Theory* (New York: McGraw-Hill, 1978).

27. L. Gottsfredson, "The G factor in employment," *Journal of Vocational Behavior* 19 (1986): 293–296.

28. M. J. Ree and J. A. Earles, "Predicting training success: Not much more than G," *Personnel Psychology* 44 (1991): 321–332.

29. S. McCartney, "The air-traffic cops go to school," *The Wall Street Journal* (March 29, 2005): D1, D7.

30. D. R. Torrence and J. A. Torrence, "Training in the face of illiteracy," *Training and Development Journal* (August 1987): 44–49.

31. American Society for Training and Development, *Bridging the Skills Gap* (Alexandria, VA: American Society for Training and Development, 2009); R. Davenport, "Eliminate the skills gap," *T+D* (February 2006): 26–31; R. Zamora, "Developing your team members' basic skills," *Wenatchee Business Journal* (August 2005): C8; M. Davis, "Getting workers back to basics," *Training and Development* (October 1997): 14–15; J. House, "Factory helps teens get diplomas," *Wall Street Journal* (August 8, 2014): B1, B6.

32. M. E. Gist, C. Schwoerer, and B. Rosen, "Effects of alternative training methods on self-efficacy and performance in computer software training," *Journal of Applied Psychology* 74 (1990): 884–891; J. Martocchio and J. Dulebohn, "Performance feedback effects in training: The role of perceived controllability," *Personnel Psychology* 47 (1994): 357–373; J. Martocchio, "Ability conceptions and learning," *Journal of Applied Psychology* 79 (1994): 819–825.

33. R. A. Noe and N. Schmitt, "The influence of trainee attitudes on training effectiveness: Test of a model," *Personnel Psychology* 39 (1986): 497–523.

34. H. Johnson, "The Whole Picture," *training* (July 2004): 30–34.

35. M. A. Quinones, "Pretraining context effects: Training assignments as feedback," *Journal of Applied Psychology* 80 (1995): 226–38; T. T. Baldwin, R. J. Magjuka, and B. T. Loher, "The perils of participation," *Personnel Psychology* 44 (1991): 51–66.

36. R. Boyd, "Steady drop in brain process starts in 20s," *Columbus Dispatch*, November 17, 2000: A5.

37. C. Houck, "Multigenerational and virtual: How do we build a mentoring program for today's workforce?" *Performance Improvement*, 50 (February 2011): 25–30; K. Ball and G. Gotsill, *Surviving the Baby Boom Exodus* (Boston: Cengage Learning, 2011); R. Zemke, C. Raines, and B. Filipezak, "Generation gaps in the classroom," *Training* (November 2000): 48–54; J. Salopek, "The young and the rest of us," *Training and Development* (February 2000): 26–30; A. Ort, "Embrace differences when training intergenerational groups," *T+D* (April 2014): 60–65.

38. L. H. Peters, E. J. O'Connor, and J. R. Eulberg, "Situational Constraints: Sources, Consequences, and Future Considerations." In *Research in Personnel and Human Resource Management,* eds. K. M. Rowland and G. R. Ferris (Greenwich, CT: JAI Press, 1985), 79–114; E. J. O'Connor, L. H. Peters, A. Pooyan, J. Weekley, B. Frank, and B. Erenkranz, "Situational constraints effects on performance, affective reactions, and turnover: A field replication and extension," *Journal of Applied Psychology* 69 (1984): 663–672; D. J. Cohen, "What motivates trainees?" *Training and Development Journal* (November 1990): 91–93; J. S. Russell, J. R. Terborg, and M. L. Power, "Organizational performance and organizational level training and support," *Personnel Psychology* 38 (1985): 849–863.

39. L. Freifeld, "Why cash doesn't motivate …," *training* (July/August 2011): 16–20.

40. W. D. Hicks and R. J. Klimoski, "Entry into training programs and its effects on training outcomes: A field experiment," *Academy of Management Journal* 30 (1987): 542–552.

41. R. F. Mager and P. Pipe, *Analyzing Performance Problems: Or You Really Oughta Wanna,* 2d ed. (Belmont, CA: Pittman Learning, 1984); A. P. Carnevale, L. J. Gainer, and A. S. Meltzer, *Workplace Basics Training Manual* (San Francisco: Jossey-Bass, 1990); G. Rummler, "In search of the holy performance

grail," *Training and Development* (April 1996): 26–31; C. Reinhart, "How to leap over barriers to per-formance," *Training Development* (January 2000): 46–49; R. Jaenke, "Identify the real reasons behind performance gaps," *T+D* (August 2013): 76–77; E. Holton, R. Bates, and S. S. Naquin, "Large-scale per-formance-driven training needs assessment," *Public Personnel Management*, 29 (2000): 249–267.

42. G. A. Rummler and K. Morrill, "The results chain," *T+D* (February 2005): 27–35; D. LaFleur, K. Smalley, and J. Austin, "Improving performance in a nuclear cardiology department," *Performance Improvement Quarterly* 18(1) (2005): 83–109.

43. C. E. Schneier, J. P. Guthrie, and J. D. Olian, "A practical approach to conducting and using training needs assessment," *Public Personnel Management* (Summer 1988): 191–205; J. Annett and N. Stanton, "Task Analysis." In *International Review of Industrial and Organizational Psychology*, eds. G. Hodgkinson and J. Ford, 21 (John Wiley and Sons, 2006): 45–74.

44. I. Goldstein, "Training in Organizations." In *Handbook of Industrial/Organizational Psychology,* 2d ed., eds. M. D. Dunnette and L. M. Hough (Palo Alto, CA: Consulting Psychologists Press, 1991): 507–619.

45. E. F. Holton III and C. Bailey, "Top-to-bottom curriculum redesign," *Training and Development* (March 1995): 40–44.

46. M. Campion et al., "Doing competencies well: Best practices in competency modeling," *Personnel Psychology*, 64 (2011): 225–262; J. Shippmann et al., "The practice of competency modeling," *Personnel Psychology* 53 (2000): 703–740; A. Lucia and R. Lepsinger, *The Art and Science of Competency Models* (San Francisco: Jossey-Bass, 1999).

47. J. S. Shippmann et al., "The practice of competency modeling," *Personnel Psychology* 53 (2000): 703–740.

48. A. Lucia and R. Lepsinger, *The Art and Science of Competency Models* (San Francisco: Jossey-Bass, 1999).

49. J. Kochanski, "Competency-based management," *Training and Development* (October 1997): 41–44; D. Dubois and W. Rothwell, "Competency-based or a traditional approach to training," *T+D* (April 2004): 46–57; E. Kahane, "Competency management: Cracking the code," *T+D* (May 2008): 71–76.

50. F. Morgeson, K. Delaney-Klinger, M. Mayfield, P. Ferrara, and M. Campion, "Self-presentation processes in job analysis: A field experiment investigating inflation in abilities, tasks, and competencies," *Journal of Applied Psychology* 89 (2004): 674–686; F. Lievens and J. Sanchez, "Can training improve the quality of inferences made by raters in competency modeling? A quasi-experiment," *Journal of Applied Psychology* 92 (2007): 812–819; F. Lievens, J. Sanchez, and W. DeCorte, "Easing the inferential leap in competency modeling: The effects of task-related information and subject matter expertise," *Personnel Psychology* 57 (2004): 881–904; R. Tartell, "Use focus groups for rapid needs assessment," *training* (March/April 2014): 14.

51. A. Lucia and R. Lepsinger, *The Art and Science of Competency Models* (San Francisco: Jossey-Bass, 1999); M. Derven, "Lessons Learned," *T+D* (December 2008) 68–73; M. Campion, A. Fink, B. Ruggerberg, L. Carr, G. Phillips, and R. Odman, "Doing competencies well: best practices in competency modeling," *Personnel Psychology*, 64 (2011): 225–262.

52. M. Derven, "Lessons learned," *T+D* (December 2008): 68–73.

53. C. Spicer, "Building a competency model," *HR Magazine* (April 2009): 34–36.

54. K. Gupta, *A Practical Guide to Needs Assessment* (San Francisco: Jossey-Bass, 1999)*;* R. Zemke, "How to do a needs assessment when you don't have the time," *Training* (March 1998): 38–44; G. Piskurich, *Rapid Instructional Design* (San Francisco, CA: Pfeiffer, 2006).

55. B. Hall, "Learning analytics at JetBlue," *Chief Learning Officer* (November 2014): 16.

56. "KLA-Tencor Corporation: Right people, right knowledge," *training* (January/February 2015): 56–57; "About US," from http://kla-tencor.com/careers/usa-about-us.html, accessed February 25, 2015.

Chapter **Four**

Learning and Transfer of Training

Objectives

After reading this chapter, you should be able to

1. Discuss the five types of learner outcomes.
2. Explain the implications of learning theory for instructional design.
3. Incorporate adult learning theory into the design of a training program.
4. Describe how learners receive, process, store, retrieve, and act upon information.
5. Discuss the internal conditions (within the learner) and external conditions (learning environment) necessary for the trainee to learn each type of capability.
6. Discuss the implications of open and closed skills and near and far transfer for designing training programs.
7. Explain the features of instruction and the work environment that are necessary for learning and transfer of training.

Energizing Training Means Better Learning and Transfer of Training

Boring lectures, lack of meaningful content in e-learning, training that doesn't give employees the opportunity to practice and receive feedback—all demotivate trainees and make it difficult for them to learn and use what they learned on the job. However, many companies are using innovative instructional methods to make training more interesting and to help trainees learn and apply it to their work.

At PNC Financial Services Group, PNC University provided web-based training to all its employees to aid in the conversion to a new HR system. The training was customized to the employee role and organization within the company to ensure that it was relevant and meaningful. An online help feature allowed employees to use their preferred method of learning through one of four approaches: "See it!" "Try it!" "Do it!" or "Print it!" "See it!" provided a short instructional video showing how a task is completed. "Try it!" let employees practice entering transactions with coaching, in a simulated version of the system. "Do it!" allowed employees to enter transactions in the live system with a Help coaching tool, going through the task step by step. "Print it!" allowed employees to print step-by-step procedures for completing transactions.

Feedback about a learning program at Mindtree Limited, a global information technology solutions company, suggested that trainees were not transferring learning to the job. The program was redesigned to ensure that employees would learn skills such as analyzing the impact of change and how to successfully integrate, review, and resolve coding problems. The new program includes four phases, each with clear objectives and expected outcomes. Trainees are actively involved in learning through the use of project simulations in which they work in teams, under the supervision of a more experienced technical employee, to fix defects, address change requests, and implement new features. Trainees are evaluated and provided feedback throughout the program on their analysis, design, coding, and documentation skills, turnaround time, and collaboration skills.

Nemours Foundation, a children's health system, emphasizes family-centered care. Nemours partners with parents and children to help deliver care in both inpatient and outpatient settings, design facilities, educate staff, and develop and evaluate policies and programs. Nemours provides high-quality educational opportunities for associates: continuing medical education for physicians, nurses, and other allied health professionals through internships, residency programs, fellowship training, and graduate medical education. Its pediatric emergency medical skills course for first-year fellows involves role-playing. The role-playing scenarios often involve patient and family interactions. These can be difficult because they can be emotionally complex such as when difficult news must be provided to patients' families. Experienced clinicians observe and mentor the fellows and provide feedback on their communications and interpersonal skills.

Sources: Based on M. Weinstein, "PNC invests in excellence," *training,* January/February 2011: 48–50; "Mindtree Limited," *T+D* (October 2014): 46; "Nemours," *T+D* (October 2013): 41.

INTRODUCTION

Although they use different methods, the purpose of the training at the four companies just described is to help employees learn so they can perform their jobs successfully. Regardless of the training method, certain conditions must be present for learning to occur and employees to use what they learned on their jobs. These include (1) providing opportunities for trainees to practice and receive feedback, i.e., information about how well people are meeting the training objectives, (2) offering meaningful training content, (3) identifying any prerequisites that trainees need to complete the program successfully, (4) allowing trainees to learn through observation and experience, and (5) ensuring that the work environment, including managers and peers, support learning and use of skills on the job. For example, feedback from trainers and mentors is provided at Mindtree Limited and Nemours. The meaningfulness of what is being learned is enhanced at both Mindtree Limited and Nemours by having learners work in situations (role plays and projects) that are identical to those they may encounter on the job. Recognizing that employees may have preferences regarding how they want to learn, PNC allowed employees to choose how they wanted to learn about the new HR system.

As you may have recognized by now, this chapter emphasizes not only what has to occur during training sessions for learning to occur, but also how to ensure that trainees use what they have learned in their jobs. That is, this chapter discusses both learning and transfer of training. **Learning** refers to a relatively permanent change in human capabilities that can include knowledge, skills, attitudes, behaviors, and competencies that are not the result of growth processes.[1] A key part of learning is that trainees commit to memory (i.e., remember) what they have learned and can recall it. **Transfer of training** refers to trainees effectively and continually applying what they have learned in training to their jobs.[2] As the organizations in the chapter opener illustrate, trainee characteristics, the design of the training program (or what occurs during training), and the work environment influence whether trainees learn and use or apply what they have learned to their jobs. Figure 4.1 presents a model of learning and transfer of training. As the model shows, transfer of training includes both the generalization of training to the job and maintenance of learned material. **Generalization** refers to a trainee's ability to apply what they learned to on-the-job work problems and situations that are similar but not necessarily identical to those problems and situations encountered in the learning environment, i.e., the training program. **Maintenance** refers to the process of trainees continuing to use what they learned over time.

It is important to realize that for training to be effective, both learning and transfer of training are needed. Trainees can fail or incorrectly apply training content (what was emphasized in training) to their jobs, either because the training was not conducive to learning, the work environment provides them with the opportunity to use training content or supports its correct use, or both. Also, it is a mistake to consider transfer of training as something to be concerned about after training because it deals with the use of training content on the job. Instead, transfer of training should be considered during the design or purchase of training. If you wait until after training to consider transfer of training, it is likely too late. Trainees' perceptions of the work environment and its support for training have likely influenced their motivation to learn and what, if anything, they have learned (recall the discussion of motivation to learn in Chapter Three, "Needs Assessment").

FIGURE 4.1
A Model of Learning and Transfer of Training

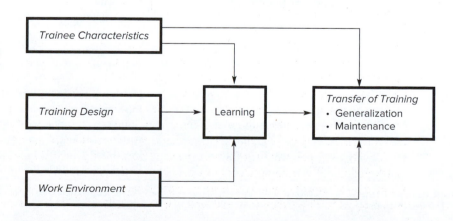

This chapter coverage is based on the model shown in Figure 4.1. First, we discuss learning. We begin by identifying what is to be learned—that is, to identify learning outcomes. Learning outcomes should be related to what is required to perform the job successfully. As the chapter opener illustrates, this may include selling products, providing services, working with operating systems, or developing and fixing software. As a student, you are familiar with one type of learning outcome: intellectual skills. We also discuss how trainees' learning style may influence the way they prefer to learn. The influence of other trainee characteristics, such as basic skills, cognitive ability, self-efficacy, age and generation, and interests on motivation to learn and learning, was discussed in Chapter Three.

Next, we consider training design. Training design includes consideration of how to create a learning environment to help the trainee acquire the learning outcomes. We discuss various learning and transfer of training theories. Last, we look at how these theories are used to create a learning environment and supportive work environment designed to help the trainee learn the desired outcomes and apply them on the job.

WHAT IS LEARNING? WHAT IS LEARNED?

Understanding learning outcomes is crucial because they influence the characteristics of the training environment that are necessary for learning to occur. For example, if trainees are to master motor skills such as climbing a pole, they must have opportunities to practice climbing and receive feedback about their climbing skills. Learning outcomes are presented in Table 4.1.

Verbal information includes names or labels, facts, and bodies of knowledge. Verbal information includes specialized knowledge that employees need in their jobs. For example, a manager must know the names of different types of equipment as well as the body of knowledge related to Total Quality Management (TQM).

TABLE 4.1 **Learning Outcomes**

Type of Learning Outcome	Description of Capability	Example
Verbal information	State, tell, or describe previously stored information.	State three reasons for following company safety procedures.
Intellectual skills	Apply generalizable concepts and rules to solve problems and generate novel products.	Design and code a computer program that meets customer requirements.
Motor skills	Execute a physical action with precision and timing.	Shoot a gun and consistently hit a small moving target.
Attitudes	Choose a personal course of action.	Choose to respond to all incoming mail within 24 hours.
Cognitive strategies	Manage one's own thinking and learning processes.	Use three different strategies selectively to diagnose engine malfunctions.

Source: Based on R. Gagne and K. Medsker, *The Conditions of Learning* (New York: Harcourt-Brace, 1996) ; K. Kapp, "Matching the Right Design Strategy to the Right Content", *T+D* (July 2011): 48–52.

Intellectual skills include concepts and rules, which are critical to solve problems, serve customers, and create products. For example, a manager must know the steps in the performance appraisal process (e.g., gather data, summarize data, or prepare for an appraisal interview with an employee) in order to conduct an employee appraisal.

Motor skills include coordination of physical movements. For example, a telephone repair person must have the coordination and dexterity required to climb ladders and telephone poles.

Attitudes are a combination of beliefs and feelings that predispose a person to behave a certain way. Attitudes include a cognitive component (beliefs), an affective component (feeling), and an intentional component (the way a person intends to behave with regard to the focus of the attitude). Important work-related attitudes include job satisfaction, commitment to the organization, and job involvement. Suppose you say that an employee has a "positive attitude" toward her work. This means the person likes her job (the affective component). She may like her job because it is challenging and provides an opportunity to meet people (the cognitive component). Because she likes her job, she intends to stay with the company and do her best at work (the intentional component). Training programs may be used to develop or change attitudes because attitudes have been shown to be related to physical and mental withdrawal from work, turnover, and behaviors that affect the well-being of the company (e.g., helping new employees).

Cognitive strategies regulate the processes of learning. They relate to the learner's decision regarding what information to attend to (i.e., pay attention to), how to remember, and how to solve problems. For example, a physicist recalls the colors of the light spectrum through remembering the name "Roy G. Biv" (red, orange, yellow, green, blue, indigo, violet).

As this chapter points out, each learning outcome requires a different set of conditions for learning to occur. Before this chapter investigates the learning process in detail, it looks at the theories that help explain how people learn.

LEARNING THEORIES

Each theory about how people learn relates to different aspects of the learning process. Many of the theories also relate to trainees' motivation to learn, which was discussed in Chapter Three. The application of these theories for instruction and program design are discussed later in this chapter and in Chapter Five, "Program Design."

Reinforcement Theory

Reinforcement theory emphasizes that people are motivated to perform or avoid certain behaviors because of past outcomes that have resulted from those behaviors.[3] There are several processes in reinforcement theory. *Positive reinforcement* is a pleasurable outcome resulting from a behavior. *Negative reinforcement* is the removal of an unpleasant outcome. For example, consider a machine that makes screeching and grinding noises unless the operator holds levers in a certain position. The operator will learn to hold the levers in that position to avoid the noises. The process of withdrawing positive or negative reinforcers to eliminate a behavior is known as *extinction*. Punishment is presenting an unpleasant outcome after a behavior, leading to a decrease in that behavior. For example, if a manager yells at employees when they are late, they may avoid the yelling by being on time (but they may also call in sick, quit, or fool the boss into not noticing when they arrive late).

From a training perspective, reinforcement theory suggests that for learners to acquire knowledge, change behavior, or modify skills, the trainer needs to identify what outcomes the learner finds most positive (and negative). Trainers then need to link these outcomes to learners' acquiring knowledge or skills or changing behaviors. As was mentioned in Chapter Three, learners can obtain several types of benefits from participating in training programs. The benefits may include learning an easier or more interesting way to perform their job (job-related), meeting other employees who can serve as resources when problems occur (personal), or increasing opportunities to consider new positions in the company (career-related). According to reinforcement theory, trainers can withhold or provide these benefits to learners who master program content. The effectiveness of learning depends on the pattern or schedule for providing these reinforcers or benefits. Similarly, managers can provide these benefits to help ensure transfer of training.

Behavior modification is a training method that is primarily based on reinforcement theory. For example, a training program in a bakery focused on eliminating unsafe behaviors such as climbing over conveyor belts (rather than walking around them) and sticking hands into equipment to dislodge jammed materials without turning off the equipment.[4] Employees were shown slides depicting safe and unsafe work behaviors. After viewing the slides, employees were shown a graph of the number of times that safe behaviors were observed during past weeks. Employees were encouraged to increase the number of safe behaviors they demonstrated on the job. They were given several reasons for doing so: for their own protection, to decrease costs for the company, and to help their plant get out of last place in the safety rankings of the company's plants. Immediately after the training, safety reminders were posted in employees' work areas. Data about the number of safe behaviors performed by employees continued to be collected and displayed on the graph in the work area following the training. Employees' supervisors were also instructed to recognize workers whenever they saw them performing a safe work behavior. In this example, the data of safe behavior posted in the work areas and supervisors' recognition of safe work behavior represent positive reinforcers.

Social Learning Theory

Social learning theory emphasizes that people learn by observing other persons (models) whom they believe are credible and knowledgeable.[5] Social learning theory also recognizes that behavior that is reinforced or rewarded tends to be repeated. The models' behavior or skill that is rewarded is adopted by the observer. According to social learning theory, learning new skills or behaviors comes from (1) directly experiencing the consequences of using that behavior or skill, or (2) the process of observing others and seeing the consequences of their behavior.[6]

According to social learning theory, learning also is influenced by a person's self-efficacy. **Self-efficacy** is a person's judgment about whether he or she can successfully learn knowledge and skills. Chapter Three emphasizes self-efficacy as an important factor to consider in the person analysis phase of needs assessment. Why? Self-efficacy is one determinant of readiness to learn. A trainee with high self-efficacy will make efforts to learn in a training program and will be most likely to persist in learning even if an environment is not conducive to learning (e.g., a noisy training room). In contrast, a person with low self-efficacy will have self-doubts about mastering the content of a training program and is more likely to withdraw psychologically and/or physically (e.g., daydream or fail to attend the program). These persons believe that they are unable to learn, and regardless of their effort level, they will be unable to learn.

A person's self-efficacy can be increased using several methods: verbal persuasion, logical verification, observation of others (modeling), and past accomplishments.[7] **Verbal persuasion** means offering words of encouragement to convince others they can learn. **Logical verification** involves perceiving a relationship between a new task and a task already mastered. Trainers and managers can remind employees when they encounter learning difficulties that they have been successful at learning similar tasks. **Modeling** involves having employees who already have mastered the learning outcomes demonstrate them for trainees. As a result, employees are likely to be motivated by the confidence and success of their peers. **Past accomplishments** refers to allowing employees to build a history of successful accomplishments. Managers can place employees in situations where they are likely to succeed and provide training so that employees know what to do and how to do it.

Social learning theory suggests that four processes are involved in learning: attention, retention, motor reproduction, and motivational processes (see Figure 4.2).

Attention suggests that persons cannot learn by observation unless they are aware of the important aspects of a model's performance. Attention is influenced by characteristics of the model and the learner. Learners must be aware of the skills or behavior they are supposed to observe. The model must be clearly identified and credible. The learner must have the physical capability (sensory capability) to observe the model. Also, a learner who has successfully learned other skills or behavior by observing the model is more likely to attend to the model.

Learners must remember the behaviors or skills that they observe. This is the role of *retention*. Learners have to code the observed behavior and skills in memory in an organized manner so they can recall them for the appropriate situation. Behaviors or skills can be coded as visual images (symbols) or verbal statements.

Motor reproduction involves trying out the observed behaviors to see if they result in the same reinforcement that the model received. The ability to reproduce the behaviors

FIGURE 4.2   **Processes of Social Learning Theory**

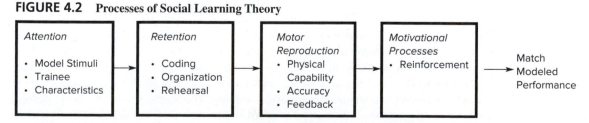

Sources: Based on A. Bandura, *Social Foundations of Thoughts and Actions* (Englewood Cliffs, NJ: Prentice Hall, 1986); P. Taylor, D. Russ-Eft, and D. Chan, "A meta-analytic review of behavior modeling training," *Journal of Applied Psychology,* 90 (2005): 692–709.

or skills depends on the extent to which the learner can recall the skills or behavior. The learner must also have the physical capability to perform the behavior or exhibit the skill. For example, a firefighter can learn the behaviors necessary to carry a person away from a dangerous situation, but he may be unable to demonstrate the behavior because he lacks upper body strength. Note that performance of behavior is usually not perfect on the first attempt. Learners must have the opportunity to practice and receive feedback to modify their behavior to be similar to the model behavior.

Learners are more likely to adopt a modeled behavior if it results in positive outcomes. Social learning theory emphasizes that behaviors that are reinforced (a *motivational process*) will be repeated in the future. For example, a major source of conflict and stress for managers often relates to the performance appraisal interview. A manager may, through observing successful managers, learn behaviors that allow employees to be more participative in a performance appraisal interview (e.g., give employees the opportunity to voice their concerns). If the manager uses this behavior in the performance appraisal interview and the behavior is rewarded by employees (e.g., they make comments such as, "I really felt the feedback meeting was the best we have ever had") or the new behavior leads to reduced conflicts with employees (e.g., negative reinforcement), the manager will more likely use this behavior in subsequent appraisal interviews.

As you will see in the discussion of training methods in Chapters Seven, "Traditional Training Methods," and Eight, "Technology-Based Training Methods," social learning theory is the primary basis for behavior modeling training and has influenced how models are used in videos, which can be part of face-to-face, online, or mobile training programs. For example, in the training program developed by Zenger Miller called "Getting Your Ideas Across," trainees are first presented with five key behaviors for getting their ideas across: (1) state the point and purpose of the message, (2) present points to aid understanding, (3) check the audience for reactions and understanding, (4) handle reactions from the audience to what was presented, and (5) summarize the main point. The trainer provides a rationale for each key behavior. Next, trainees view a video of a business meeting in which a manager is having difficulty getting subordinates to accept his ideas regarding how to manage an impending office move. The manager, who is the model, is ineffective in getting his ideas across to his subordinates. As a result, the video shows that the subordinates are dissatisfied with the manager and his ideas. The video is turned off and the trainer leads the trainees in a discussion of what the manager did wrong in trying to get his ideas across. Trainees again view the video. But this time the manager, in the same situation, is shown using the key behaviors. As a result, subordinates react quite positively to their boss (the model). Following this video segment, the trainer leads a discussion of how the model used the key behaviors to get his ideas across.

After observing the model and discussing the key behaviors, each trainee is paired with another trainee for practice. Each group is given a situation and a message to communicate. The trainees take turns trying to get their ideas across to each other using the key behaviors. Each trainee is expected to provide feedback regarding the partner's use of the key behaviors. The trainer also observes and provides feedback to each group. Before leaving training, the trainees are given a pocket-size card with the key behaviors, which they take back with them to their jobs. Also, they complete a planning guide in which they describe a situation where they want to use the key behaviors and how they plan to use them.

Goal Theories
Goal Setting Theory

Goal setting theory assumes that behavior results from a person's conscious goals and intentions.[8] Goals influence a person's behavior by directing energy and attention, sustaining effort over time, and motivating the person to develop strategies for goal attainment.[9] Research suggests that specific, challenging goals result in better performance than vague, unchallenging goals.[10] Goals have been shown to lead to high performance only if people are committed to the goal. Employees are less likely to be committed to a goal if they believe that it is too difficult.

An example of how goal setting theory influences training methods is seen in a program designed to improve pizza deliverers' driving practices.[11] The majority of pizza deliverers are young (ages 18–24) and inexperienced drivers, who are compensated based on the number of pizzas they can deliver. This creates a situation in which deliverers are rewarded for fast but unsafe driving practices—for example, not wearing a safety belt, failing to use turn signals, and not coming to complete stops at intersections. These unsafe practices have resulted in a high driving accident rate.

Prior to goal setting, pizza deliverers were observed by their managers leaving the store and then returning from deliveries. The managers observed the number of complete stops at intersections over a one-week period. In the training session, managers and trainers presented the deliverers with a series of questions for discussion. Here are examples: In what situations should you come to a complete stop? What are the reasons for coming to a complete stop? What are the reasons for not coming to a complete stop?

After the discussion, pizza deliverers were asked to agree on the need to come to a complete stop at intersections. Following the deliverers' agreement, the managers shared the data they collected regarding the number of complete stops at intersections they had observed the previous week. (Complete stops were made 55 percent of the time.) The trainer asked the pizza deliverers to set a goal for complete stopping over the next month. They decided on a goal of 75 percent complete stops.

After the goal setting session, managers at each store continued observing their drivers' intersection stops. The following month in the work area, a poster showed the percentages of complete stops for every four-day period. The current percentage of total complete stops was also displayed.

Goal setting theory also is used in training program design. Goal setting theory suggests that learning can be facilitated by providing trainees with specific challenging goals and objectives. Specifically, the influence of goal setting theory can be seen in the development of training lesson plans. Lesson plans begin with specific goals providing information regarding the expected action that the learner will demonstrate, conditions under which learning will occur, and the level of performance that will be judged acceptable. Goals can also be part of action plans or application assignments that are used to motivate trainees to transfer training.

Goal Orientation

Goal orientation refers to the goals held by a trainee in a learning situation. Goal orientation can include a learning orientation or a performance orientation. **Learning orientation** relates to trying to increase ability or competence in a task. People with a learning orientation believe that training success is defined as showing improvement and making progress, prefer trainers who are more interested in how trainees are learning than in how they are performing, and view errors and mistakes as part of the learning process. **Performance orientation** refers to learners who focus on task performance and how they compare to others. Persons with a performance orientation define success as high performance relative to others, value high ability more than learning, and find that errors and mistakes cause anxiety and want to avoid them.

Goal orientation is believed to affect the amount of effort that a trainee will expend in learning (motivation to learn). Learners with a high learning orientation will direct greater attention to the task and learn for the sake of learning, as opposed to learners with a performance orientation. Learners with a performance orientation will direct more attention to performing well and less effort to learning. Research has shown that trainees with a learning orientation exert greater effort to learn and use more complex learning strategies than do trainees with a performance orientation.[12] There are several ways to create a learning orientation in trainees.[13] These include setting goals around learning and experimenting with new ways of having trainees perform trained tasks rather than emphasizing trained-task performance, deemphasizing competition among trainees, creating a community of learning (discussed later in the chapter), and allowing trainees to make errors and to experiment with new knowledge, skills, and behaviors during training.

Need Theories

Need theories help explain the value that a person places on certain outcomes. A **need** is a deficiency that a person is experiencing at any point in time. A need motivates a person to behave in a manner that satisfies the deficiency. Abraham Maslow's and Clayton Alderfer's need theories focused on physiological needs, relatedness needs (needs to interact with other persons), and growth needs (self-esteem and self-actualization).[14] Both Maslow and Alderfer believed that persons start by trying to satisfy needs at the lowest level, then progress up the hierarchy as lower-level needs are satisfied. That is, if physiological needs are not met, a person's behavior will focus on satisfying these needs before relatedness or growth needs receive attention. The major difference between Alderfer's and Maslow's hierarchies of needs is that Alderfer allows the possibility that if higher-level needs are not satisfied, employees will refocus on lower-level needs.

David McClelland's need theory focused primarily on needs for achievement, affiliation, and power.[15] According to McClelland, these needs can be learned. The need for achievement relates to a concern for attaining and maintaining self-set standards of excellence. The need for affiliation involves concern for building and maintaining relationships with other people and for being accepted by others. The need for power is a concern for obtaining responsibility, influence, and reputation.

Need theories suggest that to motivate learning, trainers should identify trainees' needs and communicate how training program content relates to fulfilling these needs. Also, if certain basic needs of trainees (e.g., physiological and safety needs) are not met, they are unlikely to be motivated to learn. For example, consider a word processing training class for secretaries in a downsizing company. It is doubtful that even the best-designed training class will result in learning if employees believe that their job security is threatened (unmet need for security) by the company's downsizing strategy. Also, it is unlikely the secretaries will be motivated to learn if they believe that word processing skills emphasized in the program will not help them keep their current employment or increase their chances of finding another job inside (or even outside) the company.

Another implication of need theory relates to providing employees with a choice of training programs to attend. As Chapter Three mentioned, giving employees a choice of which training course to attend can increase their motivation to learn. This occurs because trainees are able to choose programs that best match their needs.

Expectancy Theory

Expectancy theory suggests that a person's behavior is based on three factors: expectancy, instrumentality, and valence.[16] Beliefs about the link between trying to perform a behavior and actually performing well are called **expectancies.** Expectancy is similar to self-efficacy. In expectancy theory, a belief that performing a given behavior (e.g., attending a training program) is associated with a particular outcome (e.g., being able to better perform your job) is called **instrumentality. Valence** is the value that a person places on an outcome (e.g., how important it is to perform better on the job).

According to expectancy theory, various choices of behavior are evaluated according to their expectancy, instrumentality, and valence. Figure 4.3 shows how behavior is determined based on finding the mathematical product of expectancy, instrumentality, and valence. People choose the behavior with the highest value.

From a training perspective, expectancy theory suggests that learning is most likely to occur when employees believe that they can learn the content of the program (expectancy). Also, learning and transfer of training are enhanced when they are linked to outcomes such as better job performance, a salary increase, or peer recognition (instrumentality), and when employees value these outcomes (valence).

Adult Learning Theory

Adult learning theory was developed out of a need for a specific theory of how adults learn. Most educational theories, as well as formal educational institutions, have been developed exclusively to educate children and youths. Pedagogy, the art and science of teaching children, has dominated educational theory. Pedagogy gives the instructor the major responsibility for making decisions about learning content, method, and evaluation. Students are generally seen as (1) being passive recipients of directions and content and (2) bringing few experiences that may serve as resources to the learning environment.[17]

FIGURE 4.3 **Expectancy Theory of Motivation**

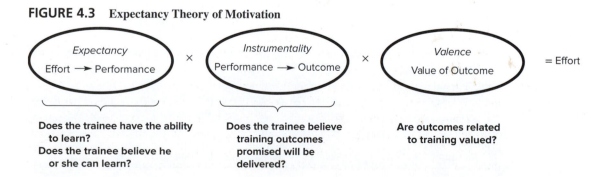

Educational psychologists, recognizing the limitations of formal education theories, developed **andragogy,** the theory of adult learning. Malcolm Knowles is most frequently associated with adult learning theory. Knowles's model is based on several assumptions:[18]

1. Adults have the need to know why they are learning something.
2. Adults have a need to be self-directed.
3. Adults bring more work-related experiences into the learning situation.
4. Adults enter a learning experience with a problem-centered approach to learning.
5. Adults are motivated to learn by both extrinsic and intrinsic motivators.

Adult learning theory is especially important to consider in developing training programs because the audience for many such programs tends to be adults, most of whom have not spent a majority of their time in a formal education setting. Table 4.2 shows implications of adult learning theory for learning. Consider how adult learning theory is incorporated into training programs.[19] Yapi ve Kredi Bank's program to help managers improve their skills in motivating and coaching their employees includes classroom sessions in which trainers reviewed common case studies of common situations in coaching and provided students with online readings and videos. Senior managers reviewed coaching and development techniques, and program participants were given coaching assignments with their peers to complete. The first-line manager course at B&W Pantex focuses on soft skills as well as human resource (HR) policies, discipline, and supervision using instructor-led training with video presentations and role-playing. The course includes real-life scenarios based on actual situations that have occurred in its facilities. The program also includes on-the-job training in which trained and qualified subject matter experts (SMEs) teach tasks and procedures. Brown-Forman, one of the largest companies in the global wine and spirits industry (its brands include Jack Daniel's Tennessee Whiskey, Southern Comfort, Findlandia vodka, and Herradura tequila) created a two-and-a-half-day training program focused on helping the company's marketing professionals build the brand. The company's chief marketing officer visits the class to explain the importance of its content and why the course was developed. In the course, participants work in teams to develop a brand campaign for a sample brand. This includes making presentations and completing exercises. Representatives from Brown-Forman's creative agencies attend the program, part of which involves interacting with consumers to identify their drinking patterns and preferences. At the end of the program, participant teams present their final project to a panel of senior marketing executives who serve as judges.

TABLE 4.2
Implications of Adult Learning Theory for Training

Design Issue	Implications
Self-concept	Mutual planning and collaboration in instruction
Experience	Use learner experience as basis for examples and applications
Readiness	Develop instruction based on the learner's interests and competencies
Time perspective	Immediate application of content
Orientation to learning	Problem-centered instead of subject-centered

Information Processing Theory

Compared to other learning theories, information processing theories give more emphasis to the internal processes that occur when training content is learned and retained. Figure 4.4 shows a model of information processing. Information processing theories propose that information or messages taken in by the learner undergo several transformations in the human brain.[20] Information processing begins when a message or stimulus (which could be a sound, smell, touch, or picture) from the environment is received by receptors (i.e., ears, nose, skin, and eyes). The message is registered in the senses and stored in short-term memory, and then it is transformed or coded for storage in long-term memory. A search process occurs in memory, during which time a response to the message or stimulus is organized. The response generator organizes the learner's response and tells the effectors (muscles) what to do. The "what to do" instruction relates to one of the five learning outcomes: verbal information, cognitive skills, motor skills, intellectual skills, or attitudes. The final link in the model is feedback from the environment. This feedback provides the learner with an evaluation of the response given. This information can come from another person or the learner's observation of the results of his or her own action. A positive evaluation of the response provides reinforcement that the behavior is desirable and should be stored in long-term memory for use in similar situations.

Besides emphasizing the internal processes needed to capture, store, retrieve, and respond to messages, the information processing model highlights how external events influence learning. These events include:[21]

1. Changes in the intensity or frequency of the stimulus that affect attention.
2. Informing the learner of the objectives to establish an expectation.
3. Enhancing perceptual features of the material (stimulus), drawing the attention of the learner to certain features.
4. Verbal instructions, pictures, diagrams, and maps suggesting ways to code the training content so that it can be stored in memory.
5. Meaningful learning context (examples, problems) creating cues that facilitate coding.
6. Demonstration or verbal instructions helping to organize the learner's response, as well as facilitating the selection of the correct response.

FIGURE 4.4
A Model of Human Information Processing

Source: Based on R. Gagne, "Learning processes and instruction," *Training Research Journal,* 1 (1995/96): 17–28 ; D. Rock, "Your Brain on Learning", Chief Learning Officer (May 2015): 30–48.

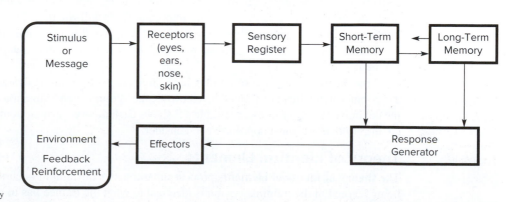

TRANSFER OF TRAINING THEORY

Transfer of training is more likely to occur when the trainee works on tasks during training (e.g., knowledge, equipment, or processes) that are very similar, if not identical, to the work environment (near transfer). Transfer of training is more difficult when tasks during training are different from the work environment, i.e., far transfer, such as applying customer service principles to interaction with an angry customer in front of a long line of customers at a cash register. The tasks that are used during training relate to the training objectives.

Closed skills refer to training objectives that are linked to learning specific skills that are to be identically produced by the trainee on their job. There is only one correct way to complete a task if it requires closed skills. In contrast, **open skills** are linked to more general learning principles. For example, customer service skills are examples of open skills. There is not a single correct way to perform and the learner is given some general principles to follow. For example a sales clerk is likely trained on general principles or process for how to interact with an angry customer but has the freedom to choose how to interact with them because their intentions and responses are not entirely predictable.[22] Open skills are more difficult to train than closed skills because they require the trainee to not only acquire and recall general principles, but also to consider how they can be adapted and used to fit a wide range of circumstances, many of which cannot be practiced during training. Also, manager and peer support on the job is important for giving the trainee the opportunity to learn by seeing how experienced employees use the skills and to get feedback when they have the chance to apply them. Later in this chapter, we discuss the implications of transfer of training theories for designing training. In Chapter Five, we will discuss how specific training program design features can facilitate learning and transfer of both open and closed skills.

Consider the transfer of training issues that Continental Airlines currently faces in preparing its pilots to fly the new 787 Dreamliner airplane.[23] First, Continental will fly the airplane on its U.S. routes to familiarize flight and ground crew staff with it. Continental plans to train approximately twenty-four pilots for each plane that is delivered. The 787 flight deck is similar but not identical to the 777 airplane that Continental's pilots are currently flying. Training includes use of a flight simulator of the 787 and computer-based courses. One of the most difficult tasks for pilots is to become familiar with a display that drops down in front of them, providing important flight information. The purpose of the display is to improve visibility during difficult flying conditions. Pilots like the display but find that it takes time to get used to it because it requires them to adjust their depth perception.

Three theories of transfer of training have implications for training design (the learning environment): the theory of identical elements, the stimulus generalization approach, and the cognitive theory of transfer.[24] Table 4.3 shows each theory's primary emphasis and the conditions that it is most appropriate to consider.

Theory of Identical Elements

The **theory of identical elements** proposes that transfer of training occurs when what is being learned in the training session is identical to what the trainee has to perform on the

TABLE 4.3
Transfer of Training Theories

Theory	Emphasis	Appropriate Conditions	Type of Transfer
Identical elements	Training environment is identical to work environment.	Training focuses on closed skills. Work environment features are predictable and stable. *Example*: Training to use equipment.	Near
Stimulus generalization	General principles are applicable to many different work situations.	Training focuses on open skills. Work environment is unpredictable and highly variable. *Example*: Training in interpersonal skills.	Far
Cognitive theory	Meaningful material and coding schemes enhance storage and recall of training content.	All types of training and environments.	Near and far

job.[25] Transfer will be maximized to the degree that the tasks, materials, equipment, and other characteristics of the learning environment are similar to those encountered in the work environment.

The use of identical elements theory is shown in the hostage training simulation used by the Baltimore Police Department. The Baltimore Police Department needed to teach police sergeants the skills to handle hostage-barricade situations in which lives are at stake—skills such as negotiating with a troubled husband holding his wife and/or children hostage. The first hour of a hostage situation is critical. The sergeant must organize resources quickly to achieve a successful end to the situation, with minimal or no injuries. A simulation was chosen because it provides a model of reality, a mock-up of a real situation without the danger. Multiple scenarios can be incorporated into the simulation, allowing the sergeants to practice the exact skills that they will need when facing a hostage crisis.

The simulation begins by having the trainees briefed on the hostage situation. Then they are directed to take charge of resolving the incident in the presence of an instructor who has personally been involved in similar real-life incidents. Each trainee supervises one difficult and one easy scenario. The simulation is designed to emphasize the importance of clear thinking and decision making in a situation in which time is critical. It is essential that the trainees take actions according to a set of priorities that place the greatest value on minimizing the risks to the hostages and isolating the suspects before communicating with them. The simulation scenarios include elements of many actual hostage incidents, such as forced entry, taking persons against their will, the presence of a weapon, and threats. As trainees work in the simulation, their actions are evaluated by the instructor. The instructor provides feedback to the trainees in writing after they complete the simulation, or the instructor can correct mistakes as they happen.

The training simulation mirrors the exact circumstances of actual hostage situations encountered by police officers. Also, the checklist of activities and behaviors that the sergeants are provided in training is the exact checklist used in hostage situations that occur on the street. Evidence of generalization is provided by police sergeants who have successfully dealt with a bank-hostage situation by using the skills emphasized in the simulation. The Baltimore Police Department is also concerned with maintenance. At the conclusion of the simulation, officers may be able to demonstrate how to free hostages successfully. However, the incidence of hostage situations is fairly low compared to other tasks that police officers perform (e.g., issuing traffic citations or investigating burglaries). As a result, the police department is concerned that officers may forget what they learned in training and therefore have difficulties in hostage situations. To ensure that officers have opportunities to practice these infrequently used but important skills, the training department occasionally schedules mock hostage situations.[26]

Another application of the theory of identical elements is found in the use of simulators for training airline pilots. Pilots are trained in a simulator that looks exactly like the cockpit of a commercial aircraft. All aspects of the cockpit in the simulator (e.g., gauges, dials, and lights) are the same as in a real aircraft. In psychological terms, the learning environment has complete fidelity with the work environment. **Fidelity** refers to the extent to which the training environment is similar to the work environment. If skills in flying, taking off, landing, and dealing with emergency situations are learned in the simulator, they will be transferred to the work setting (commercial aircraft).

The identical elements approach has also been used to develop instruments that are designed to measure the similarity of jobs.[27] Job similarity can be used as one measure of the extent to which training in the knowledge and skills required for one job prepares an employee to perform a different job.

The theory of identical elements has been applied to many training programs, particularly those that deal with the use of equipment or that involve specific procedures that must be learned. Identical elements theory is particularly relevant in making sure that near transfer occurs. **Near transfer** refers to trainees' ability to apply learned capabilities exactly to the work situation.

Identical elements theory does not encourage transfer where the learning environment and the training environment are not necessarily identical. This situation arises particularly in interpersonal skills training. For example, a person's behavior in a conflict situation is not easily predictable. Therefore, trainees must learn general principles of conflict resolution that they can apply to a wide variety of situations as circumstances dictate (e.g., an irate customer versus a customer who lacks product knowledge).

Stimulus Generalization Approach

The **stimulus generalization approach** suggests that the way to understand the transfer of training issue is to construct training so that the most important features or general principles are emphasized. It is also important to identify the range of work situations in which these general principles can be applied. The stimulus generalization approach emphasizes far transfer. **Far transfer** refers to the trainee's ability to apply learned capabilities to the work environment, even though the work environment (equipment, problems, and tasks) is not identical to that of the training session.

The stimulus generalization approach can be seen in the design of some skill training programs, which are based on social learning theory. Recall from the discussion of social learning theory that modeling, practice, feedback, and reinforcement play key roles in learning. One step in developing effective interpersonal skill training programs is to identify key behaviors that are needed to be successful in a situation. **Key behaviors** refer to behaviors that can be used successfully in a wide variety of situations. The model demonstrates these key behaviors in a video, and trainees have opportunities to practice them. The key behaviors are believed to be applicable to a wide variety of situations. In fact, the practice sessions in this type of training requires the trainee to use the behaviors in a variety of situations that are not identical.

Cognitive Theory of Transfer

The cognitive theory of transfer is based on the information processing theory of learning discussed earlier in the chapter. Recall that the storage and retrieval of information are key aspects of this model of learning. According to the **cognitive theory of transfer,** the likelihood of transfer depends on the trainees' ability to retrieve learned capabilities. This theory suggests that the likelihood of transfer is increased by providing trainees with meaningful material that enhances the chances that they will link what they encounter in the work environment to the learned capability. Also important is providing the trainee with cognitive strategies for coding the learned capabilities in memory so that they are easily retrievable.

The influence of cognitive theory is seen in training design that encourages trainees, as part of the program, to consider potential applications of the training content to their jobs. Many training programs include having trainees identify a work problem or situation and discuss the potential application of training content.

THE LEARNING PROCESS

Now that you have reviewed the learning and transfer of training theories, you are ready to address three questions: What are the physical and mental processes involved in learning? How does learning and transfer occur? Do trainees have different learning styles?

Mental and Physical Processes

Table 4.4 shows the learning processes, which include expectancy, perception, working storage, semantic encoding, long-term storage, retrieval, generalizing, and gratification.[28] Table 4.4 emphasizes that learning depends on the learner's cognitive processes, including attending to what is to be learned (learning content), organizing the learning content into a mental representation, and relating the learning content to existing knowledge from long-term memory.[29] **Expectancy** refers to the mental state that the learner brings to the instructional process. This includes factors such as readiness for training (motivation to learn, basic skills) as well as an understanding of the purpose of the instruction and the likely benefits that may result from learning and using the learned capabilities on the job. **Perception** refers to the ability to organize the message from the environment so that it can be processed and acted upon. Both working storage and semantic encoding relate to short-term memory. In **working storage,** rehearsal and repetition of information occur, allowing material to be coded for memory.

TABLE 4.4   The Relationship Among Learning Processes, Instructional Events, and Forms of Instruction

Processes of Learning	External Instructional Events	Forms of Instruction
1. Expectancy	1. Informing the learner of the lesson objective	1a. Demonstrate the expected performance. 1b. Indicate the kind of verbal question to be answered.
2. Perception	2. Presenting stimuli with distinctive features	2a. Emphasize the features of the subject to be perceived. 2b. Use formatting and figures in text to emphasize features.
3. Working storage	3. Limiting the amount to be learned	3a. Arrange lengthier material in chunks. 3b. Provide a visual image of material to be learned. 3c. Provide practice and overlearning to aid the attainment of automaticity.
4. Semantic encoding	4. Providing learning guidance	4a. Provide verbal cues to the proper combining sequence. 4b. Provide verbal links to a larger meaningful context. 4c. Use diagrams and models to show relationships among concepts.
5. Long-term storage	5. Elaborating the amount to be learned	5a. Vary the context and setting for presentation and recall of material. 5b. Relate newly learned material to previously learned information. 5c. Provide a variety of contexts and situations during practice.
6. Retrieval	6. Providing cues that are used in recall	6a. Suggest cues that elicit the recall of material. 6b. Use familiar sounds or rhymes as cues.
7. Generalizing	7. Enhancing retention and learning transfer	7a. Design the learning situation to share elements with the situation to which learning applies. 7b. Provide verbal links to additional complexes of information.
8. Gratifying	8. Providing feedback about performance correctness	8a. Provide feedback on degree of accuracy and timing of performance. 8b. Confirm whether original expectancies were met.

Source: Based on R. Gagne, "Learning processes and instruction," *Training Research Journal*, 1 (1995/96): 17–28; D. Rock, "Your Brain on Learning", Chief Learning Officer (May 2015): 30–48; A. Beninghof, "Pathways to Retention", T+D (June 2015): 21–22; M. Torrance, "Nine Moments of Learning", *T+D* (September 2014): 76–77.

Working storage is limited by the amount of material that can be processed at any one time. Research suggests that not more than five messages can be prepared for storage at the same time. **Semantic encoding** refers to the actual coding process of incoming messages.

Different learning strategies influence how training content is coded. Learning strategies include rehearsal, organizing, and elaboration.[30] **Rehearsal,** the simplest learning strategy, focuses on learning through repetition (memorization). **Organizing** requires the learner to find similarities and themes in the training material. **Elaboration** requires the trainee to relate the training material to other, more familiar knowledge, skills, or behaviors. Trainees use a combination of these strategies to learn. The "best" strategy depends on the learning outcome. For knowledge outcomes, rehearsal and organization are most appropriate. For skill application, elaboration is necessary. After messages have been attended to, rehearsed, and coded, they are ready for storage in long-term memory.

To use learned material (e.g., cognitive skills or verbal information), it must be retrieved. **Retrieval** involves identifying learned material in long-term memory and using it to influence performance. An important part of the learning process is not only being able to reproduce exactly what was learned, but also being able to adapt the learning for use in similar but not identical situations. This is known as **generalizing.** Finally, **gratifying** refers to the feedback that the learner receives as a result of using learning content. Feedback is necessary to allow the learner to adapt responses so they are more appropriate. Feedback also provides information about the incentives or reinforcers that may result from performance.

The Learning Cycle

Learning can be considered a dynamic cycle that involves four stages: concrete experience, reflective observation, abstract conceptualization, and active experimentation.[31] First, a trainee encounters a concrete experience (e.g., a work problem). This is followed by thinking (reflective observation) about the problem, which leads to generation of ideas of how to solve the problem (abstract conceptualization) and finally to implementation of the ideas directly to the problem (active experimentation). Implementing the ideas provides feedback as to their effectiveness, so the learner can see the results and start the learning process over again. Trainees continually develop concepts, translate them into ideas, implement them, and adapt them as a result of their personal observations about their experiences.

Researchers have developed questionnaires to measure trainees' weak and strong points in the learning cycle. Some people have a tendency to overemphasize or underemphasize one stage of the learning cycle, or to avoid certain stages altogether. The key to effective learning is to be competent in each of the four stages. Four fundamental learning styles are believed to exist. These learning styles combine elements of each of the four stages of the learning cycle.

Table 4.5 shows the characteristics and dominant learning stage of individuals in each style, called Divergers, Assimilators, Convergers, and Accommodators.[32] Keep in mind that researchers disagree about whether we have learning styles and preferences and they can be measured several different ways.[33]

In trying to match instruction to learning preferences, it is important that instructional or training strategies should be determined first by *what* is being taught or the learning outcomes. Then, learning styles should be considered to adjust the training or instructional strategy.[34]

For example, AmeriCredit, an auto finance company located in Fort Worth, Texas, is trying to modify training to better match its employees' learning styles.[35] The company has created a database to identify and track each employee's learning style. Also, employees' learning styles are being considered in course design. In a new e-learning class, employees who prefer learning by action will receive information in bullet points and will complete activities that help them learn. Employees who prefer thought and reasoning will receive more conceptual material during the course and be involved in fewer experiences. The company plans to compare the new e-learning class that takes into account learning styles with one that does not, so it can determine whether the adaptation to learning styles makes a difference in trainee satisfaction and learning.

TABLE 4.5 Learning Styles

Learning Style Type	Dominant Learning Abilities	Learning Characteristics
Diverger	• Concrete experience • Reflective observation	• Is good at generating ideas, seeing a situation from multiple perspectives, and being aware of meaning and value • Tends to be interested in people, culture, and the arts
Assimilator	• Abstract conceptualization • Reflective observation	• Is good at inductive reasoning, creating theoretical models, and combining disparate observations into an integrated explanation • Tends to be less concerned with people than with ideas and abstract concepts
Converger	• Abstract conceptualization • Active experimentation	• Is good at decisiveness, practical application of ideas, and hypothetical deductive reasoning • Prefers dealing with technical tasks rather than interpersonal issues
Accommodator	• Concrete experience • Active experimentation	• Is good at implementing decisions, carrying out plans, and getting involved in new experiences • Tends to be at ease with people but may be seen as impatient or pushy

Source: Based on D. Kolb, *Learning Style Inventory, Version 3.1* (Boston, MA: Hay/McBer Training Resources Group, 2005).

TABLE 4.6
Features of Instruction and the Work Environment That Facilitate Learning and Transfer of Training

• Objectives
• Meaningful content
• Opportunities to practice
• Methods for committing training content to memory
• Feedback
• Observation, experience, and social interaction
• Proper coordination and arrangement of the training program
• Encourage trainee responsibility and self-management
• Ensure that the work environment supports learning and transfer

Implications of the Learning Process and Transfer of Training for Instruction

Instruction refers to the trainer's manipulation of the environment in order to help train-ees learn.[36] The right side of Table 4.4 shows the forms of instruction that support learning. To provide trainees with the best chance to learn, it is important to ensure that these forms of instruction are included in training. Table 4.6 summarizes the features of good instruc-tion that facilitate the learning process. The features of a positive learning environment and transfer of training need to be designed into training courses, programs, or specific training methods that might be used, whether in the form of lectures, e-learning, or on-the-job training. Here, as well as later in the chapter, we discuss these features.

Employees Need to Know the Objectives

Employees learn best when they understand the objective of the training program. The **objective** refers to the purpose and expected outcome of training activities. There may be objectives for each training session, as well as overall objectives for the program. Recall the discussion of goal setting theory earlier in the chapter. Because objectives can serve as goals, trainees need to understand, accept, and be committed to achieving the training objectives for learning to occur. Training objectives based on the training needs analysis help employees understand why they need training and what they need to learn. Objectives are also useful for identifying the types of training outcomes that should be measured to evaluate a training program's effectiveness.

A training objective has three components:[37]

1. A statement of what the employee is expected to do (performance or outcome)
2. A statement of the quality or level of performance that is acceptable (criterion)
3. A statement of the conditions under which the trainee is expected to perform the desired outcome (conditions)

The objective should not describe performance that cannot be observed, such as "understand" or "know." Table 4.7 shows verbs that can be used for cognitive, affective, and psychomotor (physical abilities and skills) outcomes. For example, a training objective for a customer-service training program for retail salespeople might be "After training, the employee will be able to express concern [performance] to all irate customers by offering a brief, sincere (fewer than 10-word) apology, in a professional manner, [criteria] no matter how upset the customer is [conditions]." Table 4.8 shows the characteristics of good training objectives.

TABLE 4.7 **Examples of Performance or Outcomes for Objectives**

Domain	Performance
Knowledge (recall of information)	Arrange, define, label, list, recall, repeat
Comprehension (interpret in own words)	Classify, discuss, explain, review, translate
Application (apply to new situation)	Apply, choose, demonstrate, illustrate, prepare
Analysis (break down into parts and show relationships)	Analyze, categorize, compare, diagram, test
Synthesis (bring together to form a whole)	Arrange, collect, assemble, propose, set up
Evaluation (judgments based on criteria)	Appraise, attack, argue, choose, compare
Receiving (pay attention)	Listen to, perceive, be alert to
Responding (minimal participation)	Reply, answer, approve, obey
Valuing (preferences)	Attain, assume, support, participate
Organization (development of values)	Judge, decide, identify with, select
Characterization (total philosophy of life)	Believe, practice, carry out
Reflexes (involuntary movement)	Stiffen, extend, flex
Fundamental movements (simple movements)	Crawl, walk, run, reach
Perception (response to stimuli)	Turn, bend, balance, crawl
Physical abilities (psychomotor movements)	Move heavy objects; make quick motions
Skilled movements (advanced learned movements)	Play an instrument; use a hand tool

Sources: Based on H. Sredl and W. Rothwell, "Setting Instructional Objectives," Chapter 16 in *The ASTD Reference Guide to Professional Training Roles and Competencies, Vol. II* (New York: Random House, 1987); R. Mager, *Preparing Instructional Objectives*, 3d ed. (Atlanta: Center for Effective Performance, 1997).

TABLE 4.8
Characteristics of Good Training Objectives

- Provide a clear idea of what the trainee is expected to be able to do at the end of training.
- Include standards of performance that can be measured or evaluated.
- State the specific resources (e.g., tools and equipment) that the trainee needs to perform the action or behavior specified.
- Describe the conditions under which performance of the objective is expected to occur (e.g., the physical work environment, such as at night or in high temperatures; mental stresses, such as angry customers; or equipment failure, such as malfunctioning computer equipment).

TABLE 4.9
Examples of Learning Objectives

- Develop a diverse multifunctional team that can compete in a challenging environment to produce outcomes that will enhance results.
- Use conflict management skills when faced with a conflict.
- Smile at all customers, even when exhausted, unless the customer is irate.
- Reduce product defects from 10% to 7%.
- List all of the nodes of a DC-3 multi-switch correctly, without using a reference manual.
- Use the software 100% accurately, given access to the quick reference guide.

Some of the most common problems with objectives include that they are unclear, incomplete, or unspecific.[38] Table 4.9 provides some example of learning objectives. As you review each objective, identify if it includes each of the three components (performance, criteria, condition). Are these good objectives? How can they be improved?

Employees Need Meaningful Training Content

Employees are most likely to learn when the training is linked to their current job experiences and tasks—that is, when it is meaningful to them.[39] To enhance the meaningfulness of training content, the message should be presented using concepts, terms, and examples familiar to trainees. Also, the training context should mirror the work environment. The **training context** refers to the physical, intellectual, and emotional environment in which training occurs. For example, in a retail salesperson customer-service program, the meaningfulness of the material will be increased by using scenarios of unhappy customers actually encountered by salespersons in stores. Some useful techniques for convincing trainees that the training program content is meaningful include:[40]

- Telling stories about others' success in applying training content, especially former trainees
- Relating training content to what trainees already know about their jobs
- Showing how training relates to company goals and strategy
- Showing how trainees can use training content ideas at work
- Discussing examples or cases that remind trainees of the good and poor work they have seen
- Repeating the application of ideas in different contexts
- Presenting evidence that what they will learn during training is what high-performing employees use in their jobs

- Showing how the conditions that trainees face in training are similar to those on the job
- Providing practice or application activities that can be used on the job
- Providing hard copies or electronic access to well-organized materials so trainees can refer to them on the job or use them to teach others
- Allowing trainees to choose their practice strategy and how they want training content presented (e.g., verbally, visually, problem-based, or a combination of approaches)

Employees Need Opportunities to Practice

Practice refers to the physical or mental rehearsal of a task, knowledge, or skill to achieve proficiency in performing the task or skill or demonstrating the knowledge. Practice involves having the employee demonstrate the learned capability (e.g., cognitive strategy, verbal information) emphasized in the training objectives under conditions and performance standards specified by the objectives. For practice to be effective, it needs to involve the trainee actively, include overlearning (repeated practice), take the appropriate amount of time, and include the appropriate unit of learning (amount of material). Practice also needs to be relevant to the training objectives. It is best to include a combination of examples and practice, rather than all practice.[41] This helps avoid overloading trainees' memory so they can engage in the cognitive processes needed for learning to occur (selecting, organizing, and integrating content). Viewing examples helps learners develop a new mental model of skills, which they can then use in practice. Some examples of ways to practice include case studies, simulations, role-plays, games, and oral and written questions.

Pre-practice Conditions

Trainers need to focus not just on training content, but also on how to enable trainees to process information in a way that will facilitate learning and the use of training on the job. There are several steps that trainers can take within the training course prior to practice to enhance trainees' motivation to learn and facilitate retention of training content. Before practice, trainers can[42]

1. Provide information about the process or strategy that will result in the greatest learning. For example, let trainees in a customer service class know about the types of calls they will receive (irate customer, request for information on a product, challenge of a bill), how to recognize such calls, and how to complete the calls.
2. Encourage trainees to develop a strategy (metacognition) to reflect on their own learning process. **Metacognition** refers to individual control over one's thinking. Two ways that individuals engage in metacognition are monitoring and control.[43] Research shows that metacognition, including self-regulation, promotes learning.[44] **Self-regulation** refers to the learner's involvement with the training material and assessing their progress toward learning. Learners who engage in self-regulation likely learn more effectively because they are able to monitor their progress, identify areas needing improvement, and adjust their learning. Self-regulation may be especially important for online training courses, in which learners have control over the learning experience such that they can decide to drop out of courses and decide how much effort, if any, they want to exert to learn the training content. Table 4.10 shows how trainers can encourage self-regulation.

TABLE 4.10
Examples of Questions That Encourage Self-Regulation

Source: From T. Sitzmann, "Self-regulating online course engagement," *T+D* (March 2010): 26.

- Am I concentrating on the training material?
- Do I understand the key points?
- Am I setting goals to help me remember the material after I finish the course?
- Are the study tactics I have been using effective for learning the training material?
- Would I do better on the test if I studied more?
- Have I spent enough time reviewing to remember the information after I finish the course?

3. Provide **advance organizers**—outlines, texts, diagrams, and graphs that help trainees organize the information that will be presented and practiced.

4. Help trainees set challenging mastery or learning goals.

5. Create realistic expectations for trainees by communicating what will occur in training.

6. When training employees in teams, communicate performance expectations and clarify the roles and responsibilities of team members.

Practice Involves Experience

Learning will not occur if employees practice only by talking about what they are expected to do. For example, using the objective for the customer service course previously discussed, practice would involve having trainees participate in role-playing with unhappy customers (customers upset with poor service, poor merchandise, or unsatisfactory exchange policies). Training should involve an active learning approach in which trainees must explore and experiment to determine the rules, principles, and strategies for effective performance.[45] Trainees need to continue to practice even if they have been able to perform the objective several times (known as **overlearning**). Overlearning helps the trainee become more comfortable using new knowledge and skills and increases the length of time the trainee will retain the knowledge, skill, or behavior.

Conventional wisdom is that we all learn the most from our errors. However, most people feel that errors are frustrating and lead to anger and despair. Research suggests that from a training perspective, errors can be useful.[46] **Error management training** refers to giving trainees opportunities to make errors during training. In error management training, trainees are instructed that errors can help learning, and they are encouraged to make errors and learn from them. Trainees may actually commit more errors and may take longer to complete training that incorporates error management training. However, error management training helps improve employee use of learned skills on the job, i.e., transfer of training.

Error management training is effective because it provides the opportunity for trainees to engage in metacognition (i.e., to plan how to use training content, to monitor use of training content, and to evaluate how training content was used). This results in a deeper level of cognitive processing, leading to better memory and recall of training. Trainers should consider using error management training in the training program along with traditional approaches by giving trainees the opportunity to make errors when they work alone on difficult problems and tasks while encouraging them to use errors as a way to learn.

It is important to note that allowing trainees simply to make errors does not help learning. For errors to have a positive influence on learning, trainees need to be taught to use errors as a chance to learn. Error management training may be particularly useful whenever the training content to be learned cannot be completely covered during a training session. As a result, trainees have to discover on their own what to do when confronted with new tasks or problems.

Massed versus Spaced Practice

The frequency of practice has been shown to influence learning, depending on the type of task being trained.[47] **Massed practice** conditions are those in which individuals practice a task continuously, without resting. Massed practice also involves having trainees complete practice exercises at one time within a lesson or class rather than distributing the exercises within the lesson. In **spaced practice** conditions, individuals are given rest intervals within practice sessions. Spaced practice is superior to massed practice in general. However, the difference in effectiveness of massed versus spaced practice varies by the characteristics of the task. Task characteristics include overall task complexity, mental requirements, and physical requirements. **Overall task complexity** refers to the degree to which a task requires a number of distinct behaviors, the number of choices involved in performing the task, and the degree of uncertainty in performing the task. **Mental requirements** refers to the degree to which the task requires the subject to use or demonstrate mental skills or cognitive skills or abilities to perform the task. **Physical requirements** refers to the degree to which the task requires the person to use or demonstrate physical skills and abilities to perform and complete the task. Table 4.11 shows how tasks can differ.

For more complex tasks (including those that are representative of training settings, such as web-based instruction, lecture, and distance learning), relatively long rest periods appear to be beneficial for task learning.

After practice, trainees need specific feedback to enhance learning. This includes feedback from the task or job itself, trainers, managers, and peers.

TABLE 4.11 **Mental and Physical Requirements and Overall Complexity for Tasks**

Mental Requirements	Overall Complexity	Physical Requirements	Tasks
Low	Low	High	Rotary pursuit, typing, ball toss, ladder climb, peg reversal, bilateral transfer, crank turning
High	Average	Low	Free recall task, video games, foreign language, slide-bar task, voice recognition, classroom lecture, sound localization, word processing, stoop task, verbal discrimination, maze learning, connecting numbers, upside-down alphabet printing, distance learning, web training
Low	High	High	Gymnastic skills, balancing task
High	High	High	Air traffic controller simulation, milk pasteurization simulation, airplane control simulation, hand movement memorization, puzzle box task, music memorization and performance

Source: J. Donovan and D. Radosevich, "A meta-analytic review of the distribution of practice effect: Now you see it, now you don't," *Journal of Applied Psychology*, 84 (1999): 795–805.

Whole versus Part Practice

A final issue related to practice is how much of the training should be practiced at one time. One option is that all tasks or objectives should be practiced at the same time (**whole practice**). Another option is that an objective or task should be practiced individually as soon as each is introduced in the training program (**part practice**). It is probably best to employ both whole and part practice in a training session. Trainees should have the opportunity to practice individual skills or behaviors. If the skills or behaviors introduced in training are related to one another, the trainee should demonstrate all of them in a practice session after they have been practiced individually.

For example, one objective of the customer service training for retail salespeople is learning how to deal with an unhappy customer. Salespeople are likely to have to learn three key behaviors: (1) greeting disgruntled customers, (2) understanding their complaints, and then (3) identifying and taking appropriate action. Practice sessions should be held for each of the three behaviors (part practice). Then another practice session should be held so that trainees can practice all three skills together (whole practice). If trainees are only given the opportunity to practice the behaviors individually, it is unlikely that they will be able to deal with an unhappy customer.

Effective Practice Conditions

For practice to be relevant to the training objectives, several conditions must be met.[48] Practice must involve the actions emphasized in the training objectives, be completed under the conditions specified in the training objectives, help trainees perform to meet the criteria or standard that was set, provide some means to evaluate the extent to which trainees' performance meets the standards, and allow trainees to correct their mistakes.

Practice must be related to the training objectives. The trainer should identify what trainees will be doing when practicing the objectives (performance), the criteria for attainment of the objective, and the conditions under which they may perform. These conditions should be present in the practice session. Next, the trainer needs to consider the adequacy of the trainees' performance. That is, how will trainees know whether their performance meets performance standards? Will they see a model of desired performance? Will they be provided with a checklist or description of desired performance? Can the trainees decide if their performance meets standards, or will the trainer or a piece of equipment compare their performance with standards?

The trainer must also decide—if trainees' performance does not meet standards—whether trainees will be able to understand what is wrong and how to fix it. That is, trainers need to consider whether trainees will be able to diagnose their performance and take corrective action, or if they will need help from the trainer or a fellow trainee.

Employees Need to Commit Training Content to Memory

Memory works by processing stimuli we perceive through our senses into short-term memory. If the information is determined to be "important," it moves to long-term memory, where new interconnections are made between neurons or electrical connections in the brain. There are several ways that trainers can help employees store knowledge, skills, behavior, and other training in long-term memory.[49] One way is to make trainees aware of how they are creating, processing, and accessing memory. It is important for trainees to understand how they learn. A presentation of learning styles (discussed earlier in this chapter) can be a useful way to determine how trainees prefer to learn.

To create long-term memory, training programs must be explicit on content and elaborate on details. There are several ways to create long-term memory. One approach that trainers use is to create a concept map to show relationships among ideas. Another is to use multiple forms of review including writing, drawings, and role-playing to access memory through multiple methods. Teaching key words, a procedure, or a sequence, or providing a visual image gives trainees another way to retrieve information. Reminding trainees of knowledge, behavior, and skills that they already know that are relevant to the current training content creates a link to long-term memory that provides a framework for recalling the new training content. External retrieval cues can also be useful. Consider a time when you misplaced your keys or wallet. In trying to remember, we often review all the information we can recall that was close in time to the event or preceded the loss. We often go to the place where we were when we last saw the item because the environment can provide cues that aid in recall. Like other teams in the National Football League, the Cleveland Browns players have notebook computers to learn plays, schemes, and prepare for opponents by watching videos and taking notes.[50] However, the Browns coaches also believe that players can't just watch videos, they need to actively learn. So coaches are encouraging players not just to type on their notebooks but to write things down using pencil and paper. The idea is to get the players to mentally process what they are supposed to be learning, which helps commit them to memory. Taking notes by writing rather than typing causes the learner to re-phrase ideas in their own words, which means they must process the information at a deeper level in the brain. Another way to help employees commit to memory what they learned is through reflection. **Reflection** involves having trainees spend a short amount of time such as fifteen minutes, reviewing and writing about what they learned and how they performed.[51]

Research suggests that no more than four or five items can be attended to at one time. If a lengthy process or procedure is to be taught, instruction needs to be delivered in relatively small chunks or short sessions in order to not exceed memory limits.[52] Rather than requiring employees to take the time to go through an entire course that may include information that is not helpful or needed, courses are being modularized or broken down into small chunks of learning.[53] Learners can skip content they are not interested in or can demonstrate mastery in by completing tests. Chunking courses allows employees to save time and money by focusing on topics that they need for their job or want to learn. Long-term memory is also enhanced by going beyond one-trial learning. That is, once trainees correctly demonstrate a behavior or skill or correctly recall knowledge, it is often assumed that they have learned it, but this is not always true. Making trainees review and practice over multiple days (overlearning) can help them retain information in long-term memory. Overlearning also helps automize a task.

Automatization refers to making performance of a task, recall of knowledge, or demonstration of a skill so automatic that it requires little thought or attention. Automatization also helps reduce memory demands. The more that automatization occurs, the more that memory is freed up to concentrate on other learning and thinking. The more active a trainee is in rehearsal and practice, the greater the amount of information retained in long-term memory and the less memory decay occurs over time. For example, opportunities for learners to retrieve what they have learned can also increase retention.[54] **Boosters** refer to retrieval opportunities that can help the learner's brain consider training information as important and help retain it. Boosters can include short multiple choice, short-answer quizzes, or other activities that require learners to retrieve what they have learned from long-term memory.

Another way to avoid overwhelming trainees with complex material is to give them pretraining work that can be completed online or using workbooks.[55] For example, trainees can become familiar with the "basics" such as names, definitions, principles, and characteristics of components before they are trained in how the principles are applied (e.g., dealing with angry customers) or how a process works (e.g., testing for pathogens in a blood sample, changing a car's water pump).

Employees Need Feedback

Feedback is information about how well people are meeting the training objectives. To be effective, feedback should focus on specific behaviors and be provided as soon as possible after the trainees' behavior.[56] Also, positive trainee behavior should be verbally praised or reinforced. Videotape is a powerful tool for giving feedback. Trainers should view the videotape with trainees, provide specific information about how behaviors need to be modified, and praise trainee behaviors that meet objectives. Feedback can also come from tests and quizzes, on-the-job observation, performance data, a mentor or coach, written communications, or interpersonal interactions.

The specificity of the level of feedback provided to trainees needs to vary if trainees are expected to understand what leads to poor performance as well as good performance.[57] For example, employees may need to learn how to respond when equipment is malfunctioning as well as when it is working properly; therefore, feedback provided during training should not be so specific that it leads only to employee knowledge about equipment that is working properly. Less specific feedback can cause trainees to make errors that lead to equipment problems, providing trainees with opportunities to learn which behaviors lead to equipment problems and how to fix those problems. Difficulties encountered during practice as a result of errors or reduced frequency of feedback can help trainees engage more in exploration and information processing to identify correct responses.

Employees Learn Through Observation, Experience, and Interaction

As mentioned earlier in the chapter, one way employees learn is through observing and imitating the actions of models. For the model to be effective, the desired behaviors or skills need to be clearly specified and the model should have characteristics (e.g., age or position) similar to the target audience.[58] After observing the model, trainees should have the opportunity in practice sessions to reproduce the skills or behavior shown by the model. According to adult learning theory, employees also learn best if they learn by doing,[59] which involves giving employees hands-on experiences or putting them with more experienced employees and providing them with the tools and materials needed to manage their knowledge gaps. One way to model behavior or skills is to show learners what to do using YouTube videos. For example, the Cheesecake Factory has videos of outstanding servers at work available at its Video Café.[60]

Employees also learn best through interaction interacting with training content, with other learners, and with the trainer or instructor.[61] Table 4.12 shows the three ways that employees learn through interaction and when to use them. **Learner-content interaction** means that the learner interacts with the training content. Learner-content interaction includes reading text on the web or in books, listening to multimedia modules, performing activities that require the manipulation of tools or objects (such as writing), completing case studies and worksheets, or creating new content based on learned information.

TABLE 4.12
Three Types of Instructional Interaction

Type	When to Use
Learner-content	Requires mastering a task that is completed alone. Learn process of studying information and acting on it in a team context.
Learner-learner	Requires mastering a task that is completed in a group. Learners will gain new knowledge or validate their understanding by discussing content with peers.
Learner-instructor	Best for in-depth topic exploration and to develop strengths in critical analysis and thinking. Discussion may be limited when large amounts of material need to be presented in a short timespan.

Sources: Based on H. Nuriddin, "Building the right interaction," *T+D* (March 2010): 32–35; D. Leonard and W. Swap, "Deep smarts," *Harvard Business Review* (September 2004): 88–97.

Learner-instructor interaction refers to interaction between the learner and the expert (trainer). Trainers can facilitate learning by presenting, demonstrating, and reinforcing content. Also, trainers provide support, encouragement, and feedback that are valued by most learners. Learner-instructor discussions can be useful for helping learners understand content, enhance learners' self-awareness and self-assessment, gain an appreciation for different opinions, and implement ideas on the job. To maximize learners' critical thinking and analysis skills, discussion should go beyond instructors asking questions and learners providing answers.

Learner-learner interaction refers to interaction between learners, with or without an instructor. Learner-learner interaction, including observing and sharing experience with peers, may be especially useful for training interpersonal skills (such as communications), acquiring personal knowledge based on experience (such as tacit knowledge about how to close a sale or resolve a conflict), context-specific knowledge (such as managing in an international location), and learning to cope with uncertainty or new situations (such as marketing a new product or service).[62]

Consider how Urban Meyer, the Ohio State University head football coach (National College Football Champions in 2014!), built more learner-learner and learner-content interaction to teach players offensive plays and defensive schemes.[63] Traditionally, learning consisted of coach-led or learner-instructor interaction. In this type of learning environment players passively learned by listening, taking notes, asking a few questions, and then spending most of the time memorizing plays and their assignments. Now, Meyer uses a "flipped classroom." Prior to face-to-face meetings coaches send plays and game plans to players using videos and graphics that can be accessed on smartphones and iPads. Players are expected to understand the plays, formations, and schemes prior to coming to team meetings. Players are now actively involved in learning during team meetings. Team meetings include a mix of hands-on exercises, walk-throughs of schemes, and quizzes. Most of team meetings are devoted to reviewing specific situations that may occur during a game. Players know to come to the meetings prepared and ready to participate because the coaches will call on them to see if they know what they should have learned prior to coming to the meetings.

Communities of practice (COPs) refers to groups of employees who work together, learn from each other, and develop a common understanding of how to get work accomplished.[64] COPs can involve face-to-face or electronic interaction. The idea of COPs suggests that learning occurs on the job as a result of social interaction. Every company has naturally occurring COPs that arise as a result of relationships that employees develop to accomplish work, and as a result of the design of the work environment. For example, at Siemens Power Transmission in Wendell, North Carolina, managers were wondering how to stop employees from gathering in the employee cafeteria for informal discussions.[65] But that was before the managers discovered that the informal discussions actually encouraged learning. In the discussions, employees were developing problem-solving strategies, sharing product and procedural information, and providing career counseling to each other. Now Siemens is placing pads of paper and overhead projectors in the lunchroom as aids for these informal meetings. Managers who were previously focused on keeping workers on the job are now encouraging employees by providing essential tools and information and giving employees the freedom to meet.

COPs also take the form of social networks, discussion boards, list servers, or other forms of computer-mediated communication in which employees communicate electronically. In doing so, each employee's knowledge can be accessed in a relatively quick manner. It is as if employees are having a conversation with a group of experts. Wyeth Pharmaceuticals has 11 COPs that focus on maintaining shop floor excellence.[66] The COPs make it easy for employees to share best practices, learn from one another, and improve business processes. The maintenance function used its COP to deliver more than 600 hours of training on new technology and maintenance processes. This has resulted in more reliable equipment and higher productivity, such as increasing equipment use in one manufacturing plant from 72 to 92 percent.

COPs are most effective for learning and improving work performance when managers and employees believe they contribute to the core operating processes of the company, such as engineering or quality.[67] Despite the benefits of improved communication, a drawback to these communities is that participation is often voluntary, so some employees may not share their knowledge unless the organizational culture supports participation. That is, employees may be reluctant to participate without an incentive or may be fearful that if they share their knowledge with others, they will give away their personal advantage in salary and promotion decisions.[68] Another potential drawback is information overload. Employees may receive so much information that they fail to process it, which may cause them to withdraw from the COP.

Employees Need the Training Program To Be Properly Coordinated and Arranged

Training coordination is one of several aspects of training administration. **Training administration** refers to coordinating activities before, during, and after the program.[69] Training administration involves:

1. Communicating courses and programs to employees
2. Enrolling employees in courses and programs
3. Preparing and processing any pretraining materials, such as readings or tests
4. Preparing materials that will be used in instruction (e.g., copies of overheads, cases)
5. Arranging for the training facility and room
6. Testing equipment that will be used in instruction

7. Having backup equipment (e.g., paper copy of slides or an extra overhead projector bulb) should equipment fail
8. Providing support during instruction
9. Distributing evaluation materials (e.g., tests, reaction measures, surveys)
10. Facilitating communications between trainer and trainees during and after training (e.g., coordinating exchange of e-mail addresses)
11. Recording course completion in the trainees' training records or personnel files

Good coordination ensures that trainees are not distracted by events (such as an uncomfortable room or poorly organized materials) that could interfere with learning. Activities before the program include communicating to trainees the purpose of the program, the place it will be held, the name of a person to contact if they have questions, and any preprogram work they are supposed to complete. Books, speakers, handouts, and videotapes need to be prepared. Any necessary arrangements to secure rooms and equipment (such as DVD players) should be made. The physical arrangement of the training room should complement the training technique. For example, it would be difficult for a team-building session to be effective if the seats could not be moved for group activities. If visual aids will be used, all trainees should be able to see them. Make sure that the room is physically comfortable with adequate lighting and ventilation. Trainees should be informed of starting and finishing times, break times, and location of bathrooms. Minimize distractions such as phone messages; request that trainees turn off cell phones and pagers. If trainees will be asked to evaluate the program or take tests to determine what they have learned, allot time for this activity at the end of the program. Following the program, any credits or recording of the names of trainees who completed the program should be done. Handouts and other training materials should be stored or returned to the consultant. The end of the program is also a good time to consider how the program could be improved if it will be offered again. Practical issues in selecting and preparing a training site and designing a program are discussed in more detail in Chapter Five.

Encourage Trainee Responsibility and Self-Management

Trainees need to take responsibility for learning and transfer,[70] which includes preparing for training, being involved and engaged during training, and using training content back on the job. Before training, trainees need to consider why they are attending training and set specific learning goals (either alone or, preferably, in a discussion with their manager) as part of completing an action plan (action plans are discussed in more detail later in this chapter). Also, trainees need to complete any assigned pretraining assignments. During training, trainees need to be involved. That is, they need to participate and share experiences in discussions, to practice, and to ask questions if they are confused. After training, trainees need to review and work toward reaching the goals established in their action plan. They need to be willing to change (e.g., try new behaviors or apply new knowledge) and ask peers and managers for help if they need it.

Self-management refers to a person's attempt to control certain aspects of decision making and behavior. Training programs should prepare employees to self-manage their use of new skills and behaviors on the job. Self-management involves:

1. Determining the degree of support and negative consequences in the work setting for using newly acquired capabilities

2. Setting goals for using learned capabilities
3. Applying learned capabilities to the job
4. Monitoring use of learned capabilities on the job
5. Engaging in self-reinforcement[71]

Research suggests that trainees exposed to self-management strategies exhibit higher levels of transfer of behavior and skills than do trainees who are not provided with self-management strategies.[72]

Ensure That the Work Environment Supports Learning and Transfer

There is no magic "formula" for ensuring that transfer of training occurs. Effective strategies for transfer of training include ensuring that trainees are motivated and managers and coworkers support learning and transfer.[73] These strategies are especially important when training open skills; that is, trainees have more choice about what and how to apply trained principles. Closed skills include prescribed behaviors that likely are less influenced by managers, peers, and the work environment. Also, designing training to increase knowledge and self-efficacy has a positive relationship with transfer of training.

Table 4.13 shows a list of obstacles in the work environment that can inhibit learning and transfer of training. They include (1) lack of support from peers and managers and (2) factors related to the work itself (e.g., time pressure).

For example, new technologies allow employees to gain access to resources and product demonstrations using the Internet or notebook computers. But while employees are being trained to use these resources with state-of-the-art technology, they often become

TABLE 4.13   Examples of Obstacles in the Work Environment That Inhibit Transfer of Training

Obstacle Work Conditions	Description of Influence
Time pressures Inadequate equipment Few opportunities to use skills Inadequate budget	Trainee has difficulty using new knowledge, skills, or behavior.
Lack of Peer Support Peers discourage use of new knowledge and skills on the job. Peers are unwilling to provide feedback. Peers see training as waste of time.	Peers do not support use of new knowledge, skills, or behavior.
Lack of Management Support Management does not accept ideas or suggestions that are learned in training. Management does not discuss training opportunities. Management opposes use of skills learned in training. Management communicates that training is a waste of time. Management is unwilling to provide reinforcement, feedback, and encouragement needed for trainees to use training content.	Managers do not reinforce training or provide opportunities to use new knowledge, skills, or behavior.

Sources: Based on J. Tracey and M. Tews, "Construct validity of a general training climate scale," *Organizational Research Methods*, 8 (2005): 353–374; R. D. Marx, "Self-managed skill retention," *Training and Development Journal* (January 1986): 54–57.

frustrated because comparable technology is not available to them at their work site. Employees' computers may lack sufficient memory or links to the Internet for them to use what they have learned.

These obstacles inhibit transfer because they cause lapses. **Lapses** take place when the trainee uses previously learned, less effective capabilities instead of trying to apply the capability emphasized in the training program. Lapses into old behavior and skill patterns are common. Trainees should try to avoid a consistent pattern of slipping back or using old, ineffective learned capabilities (e.g., knowledge, skills, behaviors, and strategies). Also, trainees should understand that lapses are common and be prepared to cope with them. Trainees who are unprepared for lapses may give up trying to use new capabilities—especially trainees with low self-efficacy and/or self-confidence.

One way to ensure that learning and transfer of training occurs is to ensure that the climate for transfer is positive. **Climate for transfer** refers to trainees' perceptions about a wide variety of characteristics of the work environment that facilitate or inhibit the use of trained skills or behavior. These characteristics include manager and peer support, the opportunity to use skills, and the consequences of using learned capabilities.[74] Table 4.14 shows characteristics of a positive climate for transfer of training. Research has shown that transfer of training climate is significantly related to positive changes in managers' administrative and interpersonal behaviors following training. To support the transfer of financial training emphasizing Southwest Airlines's key business metrics, cost

TABLE 4.14   Characteristics of a Positive Climate for Learning Transfer of Training

Characteristic	Example
Supervisors and coworkers encourage and set goals for trainees to use new skills and behaviors acquired in training.	Newly trained managers discuss how to apply their training on the job with their supervisors and other managers.
Task cues: Characteristics of a trainee's job prompt or remind him or her to use new skills and behaviors acquired in training.	The job of a newly trained manager is designed in such a way as to allow him or her to use the skills taught in training.
Feedback consequences: Supervisors support the application of new skills and behaviors acquired in training.	Supervisors notice newly trained managers who use their training.
Lack of punishment: Trainees are not openly discouraged from using new skills and behaviors acquired in training.	When newly trained managers fail to use their training, they are not reprimanded.
Extrinsic reinforcement consequences: Trainees receive extrinsic rewards for using new skills and behaviors acquired in training.	Newly trained managers who successfully use their training will receive a salary increase.
Intrinsic reinforcement consequences: Trainees receive intrinsic rewards for using new skills and behaviors acquired in training.	Supervisors and other managers appreciate newly trained managers who perform their job as taught in training.

Source: Adapted from J. B. Tracey, S. I. Tannenbaum, and M. J. Kavanagh, "Applying trained skills on the job: The importance of the work environment," *Journal of Applied Psychology*, 80 (1995): 235–252; E. Holton, "What's *Really* Wrong: Diagnosis for Learning Transfer System Change." In *Improving Learning Transfer in Organizations*, ed. E. Holton and T. Baldwin (San Fransisco: Jossey-Bass, 2003): 59–79.

checklists explaining how employees can contribute to the company's bottom line are distributed companywide following training.[75] Flip charts showing highlights from manager-employee question-and-answer sessions are posted in work areas. All managers receive large posters displaying the company's four "magic numbers" (net income, unit cost measure, net margin, and invested capital). The posters include blank columns that managers are expected to complete and regularly update to show the past year's performance, the current year's goals, year-to-date numbers, and quarterly results.

Consider what Vanguard and ESL Federal Credit Union are doing to create a positive climate for learning and overcoming obstacles to transfer of training.[76] At Vanguard, the mutual fund company, one of the competencies used to evaluate its top managers' performance is a commitment to developing employees' professional skills. As a result, managers are expected to share their knowledge with employees in the classroom. Senior leaders, company officers, and executive staff members serve as adjunct faculty members who teach workshops. In addition to serving as workshop instructors, they conduct small-group or individual coaching sessions, participate in client interaction simulations, and make themselves available to help employees apply what they have learned. Vanguard's managers spend an average of 120 hours per year in the classroom. ESL Federal Credit Union uses performance contracts for some of its training classes. Before training, employees meet with their managers to discuss and agree on expectations and goals for learning. Employees meet with their managers thirty, sixty, and ninety days after training to discuss progress toward the goals and expectations. Managers send the results of the post-training meetings to the learning and development team. The learning and development team follows up after the course with learners and trainers to find out if the course provided useful knowledge that could be applied to the job.

Incentives help create a positive climate for learning and transfer. Hudson Trail Outfitters has three hundred employees who work in its stores selling outdoor equipment.[77] Managers found that employee are motivated to learn and value free jackets and merchandise discounts more than bonus checks for completing training programs. The benefits for Hudson Trail Outfitters outweigh the costs of providing the jackets and other gear. Employees who complete training stay longer with the company and they make more sales per day and sell more items in each transaction. Dunkin' Brands (you might know them for their donuts and coffee) awards stores with certificates and trophies, and provides employees with cash rewards, "money" employees can use to cash in for gifts, and field trips to meet with executive chefs.

Some companies are using digital badges for awarding employees who have completed courses, earned a certification, or mastered a skill.[78] The badges can be placed in the employee's personal profile, shared on social networks, and even put in a virtual backpack to take them to job interviews! Deloitte found that the company's leaders were not visiting its online learning site. The site included content from business schools, videos, tests, and quizzes. Deloitte found that adding missions, badges, and leaderboards to the site increased traffic. The badges are given for completing orientation to the site and personalizing a home page as well as based on the number of videos watched and the amount of information contributed to the site. The number of learners returning to the site has increased and course completion is up 50 percent.

INSTRUCTIONAL EMPHASIS FOR LEARNING OUTCOMES

The discussion of the implications of the learning process for instruction provide general principles regarding how to facilitate learning. However, you should understand the relationship between these general principles and the learning process. Different internal and external conditions are necessary for learning each outcome. **Internal conditions** refer to processes within the learner that must be present for learning to occur. These processes include how information is registered, stored in memory, and recalled. **External conditions** refer to processes in the learning environment that facilitate learning. These conditions include the physical learning environment, as well as opportunities to practice and receive feedback and reinforcement. The external conditions should directly influence the design or form of instruction. Table 4.15 shows what is needed during instruction at each step of the learning process. For example, during the process of committing training content to memory, verbal cues, verbal links to a meaningful context, and diagrams and models are necessary. If training content is not coded (or is incorrectly coded), learning will be inhibited. An example that illustrates many of the internal and external conditions necessary to achieve learning outcomes are shown in the training programs of The Culinary Institute of America (CIA) with campuses in New York, California, Texas, and Singapore.

The CIA, the world's finest training facility for chefs, has approximately 2,000 full-time students in its degree programs. CIA graduates are chefs in some of the best restaurants in the world and in prestigious private dining rooms (such as the White House), and they direct food service operations for large hotel chains such as the Marriott, Hyatt, Radisson, and Hilton. For example, you might have heard of Cat Cora, the Iron Chef on the television show *Iron Chef America*. Besides offering degree programs, the CIA also hosts more than 6,000 trainees from a wide variety of companies that have food service operations.

Whether an instructor is teaching meat-cutting or sautéing techniques, the programs' learning environments are basically the same. A lecture is followed by demonstration and several hours of guided hands-on practice. The trainee then receives feedback from the instructor. The trainer moves from a show-and-tell approach to become a coach over the course of the training session. Videos are produced for every class that a student will take. They can be viewed from residence halls or can be seen at the video learning center where students can review the tapes at their own pace; the students control what they see.

CIA programs deal not only with cognitive learning, but also with physical and emotional learning. In addition to cooking and baking courses, students are required to study psychology, total quality management practices, languages, marketing, communications, restaurant management, and team supervision. Food ethics, sustainability, physical fitness and stress management are required parts of the curriculum. Why? Running a commercial kitchen involves long hours and high levels of stress—it is very physically demanding. Thanks to the learning environment created at CIA, the institute is recognized as the world leader in gastronomic training, providing a foundation of basic knowledge for chefs from around the world.[79]

TABLE 4.15   Internal and External Conditions Necessary for Learning Outcomes

Learning Outcome	Internal Conditions	External Conditions
Verbal Information		
Labels, facts, and propositions	Previously learned knowledge and verbal information Strategies for coding information into memory	Repeated practice Meaningful chunks Advance organizers Recall cues
Intellectual Skills		
Knowing how		Link between new and previously learned knowledge
Cognitive Strategies		
Process of thinking and learning	Recall of prerequisites, similar tasks, and strategies	Verbal description of strategy Strategy demonstration Practice with feedback Variety of tasks that provide opportunity to apply strategy
Attitudes		
Choice of personal action	Mastery of prerequisites Identification with model Cognitive dissonance	Demonstration by a model Positive learning environment Strong message from credible source Reinforcement
Motor Skills		
Muscular actions	Recall of part skills Coordination program	Practice Demonstration Gradual decrease of external feedback

Source: Based on R. M. Gagne and K. L. Medsker, *The Conditions of Learning* (Fort Worth, TX: Harcourt-Brace College Publishers, 1996).

Summary

Learning and transfer of learning must occur for training to be effective. This chapter began by defining learning and transfer of learning and identifying the capabilities that can be learned: verbal information, intellectual skills, motor skills, attitudes, and cognitive strategies. To explain how these capabilities can be learned, the chapter discussed several theories of learning: reinforcement theory, social learning theory, goal setting theory, need theories, expectancy theory, adult learning theory, and information processing theory. To understand how to ensure that what is learned is applied to the job, three transfer of training theories were discussed: identical elements, stimulus generalization, and cognitive theory. Next, the chapter investigated the learning process and its implications about how people learn. The section on learning process emphasized that internal processes (expectancy, storage, and retrieval), as well as external processes (gratifying), influence learning. The potential influence of learning styles in learning was examined. The chapter then discussed the relationship between the implications of the learning process, transfer of training, and the design of instruction. Important design elements include providing learners with an understanding of why they should learn, meaningful content, practice opportunities, feedback, opportunities for interaction and a coordinated program. Also, the training design should encourage learners to self-manage and ensure that the learners' work environment supports learning and transfer.

Key Terms

learning, *159*
transfer of training, *159*
generalization, *159*
maintenance, *159*
verbal information, *160*
intellectual skills, *161*
motor skills, *161*
attitudes, *161*
cognitive strategies, *161*
reinforcement theory, *161*
social learning theory, *162*
self-efficacy, *162*
verbal persuasion, *163*
logical verification, *163*
modeling, *163*
past accomplishments, *163*
goal setting theory, *165*
goal orientation, *165*
learning orientation, *165*
performance orientation, *166*
need, *166*
expectancies, *167*
instrumentality, *167*
valence, *167*
andragogy, *168*
closed skills, *170*
open skills, *170*

theory of identical elements, *170*
fidelity, *172*
near transfer, *172*
stimulus generalization approach, *172*
far transfer, 172
key behaviors, *173*
cognitive theory of transfer, *173*
expectancy, *173*
perception, *173*
working storage, *173*
semantic encoding, *174*
rehearsal, *174*
organizing, *174*
elaboration, *174*
retrieval, *175*
generalizing, *175*
gratifying, *175*
instruction, *176*
objective, *177*
training context, *178*
practice, *179*
metacognition, *179*
self-regulation, *179*
advance organizers, *180*
overlearning, *180*

error management training, *180*
massed practice, *181*
spaced practice, *181*
overall task complexity, *181*
mental requirements, *181*
physical requirements, *181*
whole practice, *182*
part practice, *182*
reflection, *183*
automatization, *183*
boosters *183*
feedback, *184*
learner-content interaction, *184*
learner-instructor interaction, *185*
learner-learner interaction, *185*
communities of practice (COP), *186*
training administration, *186*
self-management, *187*
lapses, *189*
climate for transfer, *189*
internal conditions, *191*
external conditions, *191*

Discussion Questions

1. Compare and contrast any two of the following learning theories: expectancy theory, social learning theory, reinforcement theory, information processing theory.
2. What learning condition do you think is most necessary for learning to occur? Which is least critical? Why?
3. Are learning and transfer of training related? Explain why or why not.
4. How do instructional objectives help learning to occur?

5. Assume that you are training an employee to diagnose and repair a loose wire in an electrical socket. After demonstrating the procedure to follow, you let the trainee show you how to do it. The trainee correctly demonstrates the process and repairs the connection on the first attempt. Has learning occurred? Justify your answer.

6. Your boss says, "Why do I need to tell you what type of learning capability I'm interested in? I just want a training program to teach employees how to give good customer service!" Explain to the boss how "good customer service" can be translated into different learning outcomes.

7. How does practice help learning? What could a trainer do in a training session to ensure that trainees engage in self-regulation?

8. Can allowing trainees to make errors in training be useful? Explain.

9. What learning conditions are necessary for short- and long-term retention of training content to occur?

10. What is near transfer? Far transfer? What are their implications for training design?

11. How can employees learn through interaction? Are some types of interaction best for learning in some situations but not others? Explain.

12. How can the work environment inhibit learning and transfer of training? Explain. What work environment characteristics do you believe have the largest influence on transfer of training? Justify your answer.

13. You have a one-day classroom experience in which you need to help a group of engineers and software programmers learn to become project managers. After training, they will have to manage some significant projects. Discuss the instructional characteristics and activities you will use to ensure that the engineers and software programmers learn project management.

Application Assignments

1. Using any source possible (magazines, journals, personal conversation with a trainer, etc.), find a description of a training program. Consider the learning process and the implications of the learning process for instruction discussed in the chapter. Evaluate the degree to which the program facilitates learning. Provide suggestions for improving the program.

2. You are the training director of a hotel chain, Noe Suites. Each Noe Suites hotel has 100 to 150 rooms, a small indoor pool, and a restaurant. Hotels are strategically located near exit ramps of major highways in college towns such as East Lansing, Michigan, and Columbus, Ohio. You receive the following e-mail message from the vice president of operations. Prepare an answer.

To: You, Training Director

From: Vice President of Operations, Noe Suites

   As you are probably aware, one of the most important aspects of quality service is known as "recovery"—that is, the employee's ability to respond effectively to customer complaints. There are three possible outcomes to a customer complaint: The customer complains and is satisfied by the response; the customer complains and is dissatisfied with the response; and the customer does not complain but remains dissatisfied. Many dissatisfied customers do not complain because they want to avoid confrontation, there is no convenient way to complain, or they do not believe that complaining will do much good.

I have decided that to improve our level of customer service, we need to train our hotel staff in the "recovery" aspect of customer service. My decision is based on the results of recent focus groups we held with customers. One theme that emerged from these focus groups was that we had some weaknesses in the recovery area. For example, last month in one of the restaurants, a waiter dropped the last available piece of blueberry pie on a customer as he was serving her. The waiter did not know how to correct the problem other than offer an apology.

I have decided to hire two well-known consultants in the service industry to discuss recovery, as well as to provide an overview of different aspects of quality customer service. These consultants have worked in service industries and manufacturing industries.

I have scheduled the consultants to deliver a presentation in three training sessions. Each session will last three hours. There will be one session for each shift of employees (day, afternoon, and midnight shift).

The sessions will consist of a presentation and question-and-answer session. The presentation will last one and a half hours, and the question-and-answer session approximately 45 minutes. There will be a half-hour break.

My expectations are that following this training, the service staff will be able to recover successfully from service problems.

Because you are an expert on training, I want your feedback on the training session. Specifically, I am interested in your opinion regarding whether our employees will learn about service recovery from attending this program. Will they be able to recover from service problems in their interactions with customers? What recommendations do you have for improving the program?

3. Identify what is wrong with each of the following training objectives. Then rewrite it.

   a. To be aware of the safety rules for operating the ribbon-cutting machine in three minutes.

   b. Given a personal computer, a table, and a chair, enter the data into a Microsoft Excel spreadsheet.

   c. Use the Internet to learn about training practices.

   d. Given a street address in the city of Dublin, Ohio, be able to drive the ambulance from the station to the address in less than 10 minutes.

4. Go to *www.nwlink.com/~donclark/hrd/sat.html*, Big Dog's Instructional System Design (ISD) page. This website is an excellent resource that describes all aspects of the ISD model. Click on "Learning" and scroll to the concept map or list of terms under the map. Click on "Learning Styles" and take the Visual, Auditory, and Kinesthetic (VAK) survey. What are the implications of your learning style for how you best learn? What type of learning environment is best suited for your style? Be as specific as possible.

5. Go to *cs.gmu.edu/cne/modules/dau/algebra/algebra_frm.html*, the website for an interactive tutorial that provides a refresher on algebra. Choose a topic (such as Fractions), and review the module for the topic. What does the module include that can help make the learning process effective? Why?

6. Go to *http://agelesslearner.com/intros/adultlearning.html*, a site created by Marcia L. Conner about how adults learn. Click on "Learning Style Assessment" and complete it. What are the assessment's implications for the way that you learn best?

7. Go to *www.schneider.com*, the website for Schneider National, a transportation management company that provides logistics and trucking services. Click on "Jobs." Under "Orientation" click on "New CDL Holders," Under "Company Drivers," click on "Orientation." Watch the videos "The best in the industry" and "Your Training Engineer." What types of learning outcomes are emphasized in training? Considering the features of good instruction discussed in the chapter, identify the features of Schneider's training program that contribute to learning and transfer of training. Explain how each feature you identify contributes to learning.

Case:

Safety First

BNSF Railway is a North American freight transportation company with over 32,000 miles of routes. BNSF hauls agricultural, consumer, industrial products, and coal. BNSF puts safety above everything else it does, including productivity. BNSF recognizes that safety is based on having well-trained employees who share BNSF's vision for an injury- and accident-free workplace and who are willing to look out for one another. Thanks to our employees' commitment, a carefully maintained network and equipment, and well-prepared communities, BNSF is a safety leader in the rail industry. Approaching Others About Safety (AOAS) is a training program for all BNSF Railway employees. The goal of the program is for BNSF employees to be confident about giving feedback to each other about safe behavior and avoiding unsafe situations. Employees need to learn the value of providing feedback when they see unsafe behavior or situations, including positively recognizing when someone is working safely or correcting them when they perceive another employee is at risk. Training should focus on the types of exposures that tend to result in most injuries, including walking/path of travel around trains, rails, and equipment, pinch points between the railway cars, and climbing or descending locomotives and railway cars.

Describe the different types of instructional characteristics that this program should have for learning and transfer to occur resulting in a decrease in injuries and accident. Would these characteristics vary depending on who was attending the program (e.g., managers, train crew, employees who maintain track, structures, or signals)? If so, how would they vary?

Source: Based on "BNSF Railway: Approaching Others About Safety," *training* (January/February 2014): 108–109; *www.bnsf.com*, website for BNSF Railways, accessed March 11, 2015.

Endnotes

1. R. M. Gagne and K. L. Medsker, *The Conditions of Learning* (Fort Worth, TX: Harcourt-Brace, 1996).

2. M. L. Broad and J. W. Newstrom, *Transfer of Training* (Reading, MA: Addison-Wesley, 1992).

3. B. F. Skinner, *Science and Human Behavior* (New York: Macmillan, 1953).

4. J. Komaki, K. D. Barwick, and L. R. Scott, "A behavioral approach to occupational safety: Pinpointing and reinforcing safe performance in a food manufacturing plant," *Journal of Applied Psychology,* 63 (1978): 434–445.

5. A. Bandura, *Social Foundations of Thought and Action* (Englewood Cliffs, NJ: Prentice Hall, 1986); A. Bandura, "Self-efficacy mechanisms in human behavior," *American Psychologist* 37 (1982): 122–147.

6. A. Bandura, *Social Foundations of Thought and Action.*

7. M. E. Gist and T. R. Mitchell, "Self-efficacy: A theoretical analysis of its determinants and malleability," *Academy of Management Review,*17 (1992): 183–221.

8. E. A. Locke and G. D. Latham, *A Theory of Goal Setting and Task Performance* (Englewood Cliffs, NJ: Prentice Hall, 1990).

9. Ibid.

10. E. A. Locke et al., "Goal setting and task performance," *Psychological Bulletin,* 90 (1981): 125–152.

11. T. D. Ludwig and E. S. Geller, "Assigned versus participative goal setting and response generalization: Managing injury control among professional pizza drivers," *Journal of Applied Psychology,* 82 (1997): 253–261.

12. S. Fisher and J. Ford, "Differential effects of learner effort and goal orientation on two learning outcomes," *Personnel Psychology,* 51 (1998): 397–420; S. Payne, S. Youngcourt, and J. M. Beaubien, "A meta-analytic examination of the goal orientation nomological net," *Journal of Applied Psychology,* 92 (2007): 128–150.

13. D. VandeWalle, D. W. Cron, and J. Slocum, "The role of goal orientation following performance feedback," *Journal of Applied Psychology,* 86 (2001): 629–640; R. Noe and J. Colquitt, "Planning for Impact Training: Principles of Training Effectiveness," in *Creating, Implementing, and Managing Effective Training and Development,* ed. K. Kraiger (San Francisco: Jossey-Bass, 2002): 53–79; A. Schmidt and J. Ford, "Learning within a learner control training environment: The interactive effects of goal orientation and metacognitive instruction on learning outcomes," *Personnel Psychology,* 56 (2003): 405–429.

14. A. H. Maslow, "A theory of human motivation," *Psychological Reports,* 50 (1943): 370–396; C. P. Alderfer, "An empirical test of a new theory of human needs," *Organizational Behavior and Human Performance,* 4 (1969): 142–175.

15. D. McClelland, "Managing motivation to expand human freedom," *American Psychologist,* 33 (1978): 201–210.

16. V. H. Vroom, *Work and Motivation* (New York: John Wiley, 1964).

17. M. S. Knowles, "Adult Learning." In *The ASTD Training and Development Handbook,* ed. R. L. Craig (New York: McGraw-Hill): 253–265.

18. M. Knowles, *The Adult Learner,* 4th ed. (Houston: Gulf Publishing, 1990).

19. "Spirited learning," *T+D,* October 2009, 56–58; J. Salopek, "From learning department to learning partner," *T+D,* October 2010, 48–50; J. Salopek, "Keeping knowledge safe and sound," *T+D,* October 2010, 64–66.

20. R. M. Gagne and K. L. Medsker, *The Conditions of Learning* (Fort Worth, TX: Harcourt-Brace, 1996); W. C. Howell and N. J. Cooke, "Training the Human Information Processor: A Review of Cognitive Models," in *Training and Development in Organizations,* ed. I. L. Goldstein and Associates (San Francisco: Jossey-Bass, 1991): 121–182.

21. R. M. Gagne, "Learning processes and instruction," *Training Research Journal,* 1 (1995/96): 17–28.

22. S. L. Yelonand, and J. K. Ford, "Pursuing a multidimensional view of transfer," *Performance Improvement Quarterly,* *12,* 58–78 (1999); K. Kapp, "Matching the right design strategy to the right content," *T+D* (July 2011): 48–52. S. Yelon, J. Ford, and S. Bhatia, "How trainees transfer what they have learned," *Performance Improvement Quarterly,* 27 (2014): 27–52.

23. D. Cameron, "Dreamliner's here: Now learn to fly it," *Wall Street Journal* (November 1, 2011): B3.

24. J. M. Royer, "Theories of the transfer of learning," *Educational Psychologist,* 14 (1979): 53–69.

25. E. L. Thorndike and R. S. Woodworth, "The influence of improvement of one mental function upon the efficiency of other functions," *Psychological Review,* 8 (1901): 247–261.

26. J. F. Reintzell, "When training saves lives," *Training and Development,* 51 (1997): 41–42.

27. J. A. Sparrow, "The measurement of job profile similarity for the prediction of transfer of learning," *Journal of Occupational Psychology,* 62 (1989): 337–341.

28. R. M. Gagne, "Learning processes and instruction," *Training Research Journal,* 1 (1995/96): 17–28.

29. R. Mayer, "Applying the science of learning: Evidence-based principles for the design of multimedia instruction," *American Psychologist* (November 2008): 760–769; R. Clark and R. Mayer, "Learning by

viewing versus learning by doing: Evidence-based guidelines for principled learning environments," *Performance Improvement* 47 (2008): 5–13.

30. "Cognitive Strategies," Chapter 6 in Gagne and Medsker, *The Conditions of Learning* (Fort Worth, TX: Harcourt-Brace, 1996); M. Gist, "Training Design and Pedagogy: Implications for Skill Acquisition, Maintenance, and Generalization." In *Training for a Rapidly Changing Workplace,* eds. R. Quinches and A. Ehrenstein (Washington, D.C.: American Psychological Association, 1997): 201–222.

31. D. Kolb, "Management and the learning process," *California Management Review,* 18 (1996): 21–31.

32. D. Kolb, I. Rubin, and J. McIntyre, *Organizational Psychology: An Experimental Approach,* 3d ed. (Englewood Cliffs, NJ: Prentice Hall, 1984): 27–54; M. Delahousaye, "The perfect learner: An expert debate on learning styles," *Training* (March 2002): 28–36.

33. P. Galagan, "Learning styles: Going, going, almost gone," *T+D* (January 2104): 22–23.

34. D. Merrill, "Instructional Strategies and Learning Styles: Which takes Precedence?" In *Trends and Issues in Instructional Technology,* eds. R. Reiser and J. Dempsey (Englewood Cliffs, NJ: Prentice Hall, 2000).

35. H. Dolezalek, "AmeriCredit," *Training* (March 2003): 46–47.

36. R. M. Gagne, "Learning processes and instruction," *Training Research Journal,* 1 (1995/96): 17–28; R. Brinkerhoff and A. Apking, *High Impact Learning Strategies for Leveraging Performance and Business Results from Training Investments* (Cambridge, MA: Perseus, 2001); M. Torrance, "Nine moments of learning," *T+D* (September 2014): 76–77.

37. B. Mager, *Preparing Instructional Objectives,* 5th ed. (Belmont, CA: Lake Publishing, 1997); B. J. Smith and B. L. Delahaye, *How to Be an Effective Trainer,* 2d ed. (New York: John Wiley and Sons, 1987); S. Moore, J. Ellsworth, and R. Kaufman, "Objectives—are they useful? A quick assessment," *Performance Improvement Quarterly,* 47 (2008): 41–47.

38. J. Phillips and P. Phillips, "The power of objectives: Moving beyond learning objectives,"*Performance Improvement* (July 2010): 17–24.

39. K. A. Smith-Jentsch et al., "Can pre-training experiences explain individual differences in learning?" *Journal of Applied Psychology,* 81 (1996): 110–116; S. Caudron, "Learners speak out. What actual learners think about actual training," *Training and Development* (April 2000): 52–27.

40. J. K. Ford et al., "Relationship of goal orientation, metacognitive activity, and practice strategies with learning outcomes and transfer," *Journal of Applied Psychology,* 83 (1998): 218–233; A. Schmidt and J. Ford, "Learning within a learner control training environment: The interactive effects of goal orientation and metacognitive instruction on learning outcomes," *Personnel Psychology,* 56 (2003): 405–429; S. Yelon, L. Sheppard, and J. Ford, "Intention to transfer: How do autonomous professionals become motivated to use new ideas?" *Performance Improvement Quarterly,* 17(2) (2004): 82–103; M. Hequet, "Training no one wants," *Training* (January 2004): 22–28.

41. R. Clark and R. Mayer, "Learning by viewing versus learning by doing: Evidence-based guidelines for principled learning environments," *Performance Improvement,* 47 (2008): 5–13; T. Katz-Navon, E. Naveh, and Z. Stren, "Active learning: When is more better? The case of resident physicians' medical errors" *Journal of Applied Psychology,* 94 (2009): 1200–1209.

42. J. Cannon-Bowers et al., "A framework for understanding pre-practice conditions and their impact on learning," *Personnel Psychology,* 51 (1998): 291–320.

43. A. Schmidt and J. Ford, "Learning within a learner control training environment: The interactive effects of goal orientation and metacognitive instruction on learning outcomes," *Personnel Psychology,* 56 (2003): 405–429.

44. T. Sitzmann et al., "A multilevel analysis of the effect of prompting self-regulation in technology driven instruction," *Personnel Psychology,* 62 (2009): 697–734; T. Sitzmann and K. Ely, "Sometimes you need a reminder: The effects of prompting self-regulation on regulatory processes, learning, and attrition," *Journal of Applied Psychology,* 95 (2010): 132–144; T. Sitzmann and K. Ely, "A meta-analysis of self-regulated learning in work-related training and educational attainment: what we know and where we need to go," *Psychological Bulletin,* 137 (2011): 421–422.

45. B. S. Bell and S. W. J. Kozlowski, "Active learning: Effects of core training design elements on self-regulatory processes, learning, and adaptability," *Journal of Applied Psychology,* 93 (2008): 296–316; K. Pagano, "The missing piece," *T+D* (June 2014): 40–45.

46. D. Heimbeck et al., "Integrating errors into the training process: The function of error management instructions and the role of goal orientation," *Personnel Psychology,* 56 (2003): 333–61; N. Keith and M. Frese, "Self-regulation in error management training: Emotion control and metacognition as mediators of performance effects," *Journal of Applied Psychology,* 90 (2005): 677–91; N. Keith and M. Frese, "Effectiveness of error management training: A meta-analysis," *Journal of Applied Psychology,* 93 (2008): 59–69.

47. J. Donovan and D. Radosevich, "A meta-analytic review of the distribution of practice effect: Now you see it, now you don't," *Journal of Applied Psychology,* 84 (1999): 795–805.

48. R. M. Mager, *Making Instruction Work* (Belmont, CA: David Lake, 1988).

49. R. Weiss, "Memory and learning," *Training and Development* (October 2000): 46–50; R. Zemke, "Toward a science of training," *Training* (July 1999): 32–36.

50. K. Clark, "The Browns' strategy: Write this down," *Wall Street Journal* (August 12, 2014): D6.

51. R. Feloni, "The simple daily exercise boost employee performance," from *www.businessinsider.in,* accessed July 29, 2014; G. Di Stefano, F. Gino, G. Pisano, and B. Staats, "Learning by thinking: How reflection aids performance," Harvard Business School Working Paper, 14-093 (March 25, 2014).

52. J. C. Naylor and G. D. Briggs, "The effects of task complexity and task organization on the relative efficiency of part and whole training methods," *Journal of Experimental Psychology,* 65 (1963): 217–224.

53. M. Plater, "Three trends shaping learning," *Chief Learning Officer* (June 2014): 44–47.

54. A. Kohn, "Use it or lose it." *T+D* (February 2015): 56–61; J. Karpicke and Henry Roediger III, "The critical importance of retrieval for learning," *Science* (February 15, 2008): 966–968.

55. R. Mayer, "Applying the science of learning: Evidence-based principles for the design of multimedia instruction," *American Psychologist* (November 2008): 760–769.

56. R. M. Gagne and K. L. Medsker, *The Conditions of Learning* (Fort Worth, TX: Harcourt-Brace, 1996).

57. J. Goodman and R. Wood, "Feedback specificity, learning opportunities, and learning," *Journal of Applied Psychology,* 89 (2004): 809–821.

58. P. J. Decker and B. R. Nathan, *Behavior Modeling Training: Principles and Applications* (New York: Praeger, 1985); M. Merril, "First principles of instruction," *Educational Technology Research and Development,* 50 (2002): 43–59; K. Kapp, "Matching the right design strategy to the right content," *T+D* (July 2011): 48–52.

59. S. Caudron, "Learners Speak Out. What actual learners think about actual training."

60. J. Bozarth, "Show your work," *T+D* (May 2013): 46–51.

61. B. Bell and S. W. J. Kozlowski, "Active learning: Effects of core training design elements on self-regulatory processes, learning, and adaptability," *Journal of Applied Psychology,* 93 (2008): 296–316; H. Nuriddin, "Building the right interaction," *T+D* (March 2010): 32–35.

62. D. Leonard and W. Swap, "Deep smarts," *Harvard Business Review* (September 2004): 88–97.

63. J. Clegg, "Taking the Buckeyes to school," *Wall Street Journal* (Saturday/Sunday, December 6–7, accessed from wsj.com, December 7, 2014).

64. D. Stamps, "Communities of practice," *Training* (February 1997): 35–42. S. Gilbert and A. Silvers, "Learning communities with purpose," *T+D* (January 2015): 48–51.

65. D. Goldwasser, "Me, a trainer," *Training* (April 2001): 61–66.

66. M. Weinstein, "Rx for excellence," *Training* (February 2009): 48–52.

67. B. Kirkman et al., "Managing a new collaborative entity in business organizations: Understanding organizational communities of practice effectiveness." *Journal of Applied Psychology,* 96 (2011): 1234–1245.

68. R. Williams and J. Cothrel, "Four smart ways to run on-line communities," *Sloan Management Review* (Summer, 2000): 81–91.

69. B. J. Smith and B. L. Delahaye, *How to Be an Effective Trainer,* 2d ed. (New York: John Wiley and Sons, 1987)*;* M. Van Wa, N. J Cayer, and S. Cook, *Handbook of Training and Development for the Public Sector* (San Francisco: Jossey-Bass, 1993).

70. J. Barbazette, *Managing the Training Function for Bottom-Line Results* (San Francisco: Pfeiffer, 2008).

71. C. A. Frayne and J. M. Geringer, "Self-management training for joint venture general managers," *Human Resource Planning* 15 (1993): 69–85; L. Burke and T. Baldwin, "Workforce training transfer: A study of

the effect of relapse prevention training and transfer climate." *Human Resource Management* (Fall 1999): 227–242; C. Frayne and J. Geringer, "Self-management training for improving job performance: A field experiment involving salespeople," *Journal of Applied Psychology* (2000): 361–372.

72. A. Tziner, R. R. Haccoun, and A. Kadish, "Personal and situational characteristics influencing the ef-fectiveness of transfer of training strategies," *Journal of Occupational Pyschology* 64 (1991): 167–177; R. A. Noe, J. A. Sears, and A. M. Fullenkamp, "'Release training: Does it influence trainees' post-training behavior and cognitive strategies?" *Journal of Business and Psychology* 4 (1990): 317–328; M. E. Gist, C. K. Stevens, and A. G. Bavetta, "Effects of self-efficacy and post-training intervention on the acquisition and maintenance of complete interpersonal skills," *Personal Psychology* 44 (1991): 837–861; M. J. Tews and J. B. Tracey, "An empirical examination of post training on-the-job supplements for enhancing the effectiveness of interpersonal skills training," *Personnel Psychology*, 61 (2008): 375–401.

73. B. Bell and S. W. J. Kozlowski, "Active learning: Effects of core training design elements on self–regulatory processes, learning, and adaptability," *Journal of Applied Psychology*, 93 (2008): 296–316; H. Nuriddin, "Building the right interaction," *T+D* (March 2010): 32–35; B. Blume, J. Ford, T. Baldwin, and J. Huang, "Transfer of training: A meta-analytic review," *Journal of Management*, 36 (2010): 1065–1105.

74. J. B. Tracey, S. I. Tannenbaum, and M. J. Kavanaugh, "Applying trained skills on the job: The impor-tance of the work environment," *Journal of Applied Psychology,* 80 (1995): 239–252; P. E. Tesluk et al., "Generalization of employee involvement training to the job setting: Individual and situations effects," *Personnel Psychology,* 48 (1995): 607–632; J. K. Ford, et al., "Factors affecting the opportunity to perform trained tasks on the job," *Personnel Psychology,* 45 (1992): 511–527; E. Holton, R. Bates, and W. Ruona, "Development of a generalized learning transfer system inventory," *Human Resource Development Quar-terly,* 11 (2001): 333–360; K. Bunch, "Training failure as a consequence of organizational culture," *Human Resource Development Review,* 6 (2007): 142–163.

75. S. Boehle, "Dollars and sense," *Training* (June 2007): 42–45.

76. M. Weinstein, "Taking training's measure," *training* (November/December 2014): 42–43; M. Mihelich, "Vanguard: A top- and bottom-line learning imperative," *Chief Learning Officer* (June 2014): 32–33.

77. M. Plater, "Three trends shaping learning," *Chief Learning Officer* (June 2014): 44–47; P. Galagan, "Playing nice," *T+D* (September 2014): 24–27.

78. E. Krell, "Get sold on training incentives," *HR Magazine* (February 2013): 57–58.

79. R. Zemke, "Cooking up world-class training," *Training* 34 (1997): 52–58; *www.ciachef.edu*, website for The Culinary Institute of America, accessed March 18, 2015.

Chapter **Five**

Program Design

Objectives

After reading this chapter, you should be able to:

1. Choose and prepare a training site based on how trainees will be involved and interact with the content and each other in the course.

2. Prepare for instruction using a curriculum road map, lesson plan, design document, and concept map.

3. Explain how trainees' age, generational differences, and personality might influence how programs are designed.

4. Prepare a request for proposal (RFP) and a list of questions to evaluate training consultants and suppliers.

5. Explain the program design elements that should be included to ensure near and far transfer of training.

6. Develop a self-management module for a training program.

7. Design application assignments and action plans to enhance learning and transfer of training.

8. Make recommendations about what managers can do before, during, and after training to facilitate learning and transfer.

9. Identify different ways to manage knowledge and the conditions necessary for employees to share knowledge.

Designing Learning with the Learners in Mind

Gables Residential is a real estate company that builds and manages multifamily communities throughout the United States. Gables manages approximately 35,000 apartment homes and 400,000 square feet of retail space and has received national recognition for excellence in developing communities and training its employees. Gables has been honored as an ATD BEST Award winner and recognized as a *training* magazine's Top 125 Company. Gables's Learning and Development department is dedicated to creating an active, vibrant culture of learning. Gables strives to provide its associates with comprehensive and dynamic training. For example, associates can earn certifications as they complete learning opportunities. Learning opportunities include a mix of instructor-led courses, e-learning, videos, learning projects, one-on-one coaching, and webinars. Associates can complete comprehensive training plans online using Foundations Online, Gables's learning management system.

One of the characteristics of companies with award-winning training practices is that they periodically review them and make improvements. Recently, Gables revamped its sales training program because they felt that learners were too passive. The program included learner guides and worksheets but few opportunities for active learning. They developed a new program called Engage, Connect, and Inspire. The program includes a series of workshops presented over a one-week time period. The workshops focus on improving customer service interactions during the sales process. They include opportunities for active learning through job shadowing and self-assessments. Nine months after the new program was introduced, customer satisfaction scores increased by 19 percent.

Gables also recognizes that associates often need to learn or review what they previously learned while on the job. To address this need, the learning and development team created a series of short videos that cover sales, customer service, and team building. Also, videos have been developed for apartment maintenance employees. Maintenance employees can use notebooks or smartphones to access these videos. Employees find the videos especially helpful because they are often created by other employees. This makes the video content meaningful and relevant. Also, making the videos provides employees with the opportunity to review what they know and learn how to best present skills and knowledge to teach other.

Incentives help motivate learning at Gables. Employees compete for cash prizes for the best videos and associates can receive up to $300 if they receive a perfect score from a "mystery shopper." Associates who earn perfect scores from mystery shoppers are eligible to be a guest speaker or trainer and can be selected into the Circle of Excellence advisory group.

Source: Based on "Gables Residential," *T+D* (October 2014): 79; Gables Residential website http://gables.com, accessed March 11, 2015.

INTRODUCTION

As emphasized in Chapter Four, "Learning and Transfer of Training," for learning and transfer of training to occur, training programs need to include meaningful material, clear objectives, opportunities for practice and feedback, learner interaction, and a supportive work environment. However, these features are not enough to create an effective training program. An effective training program also needs a high-quality program design to maximize trainee learning and transfer of training. **Program design** refers to the organization and coordination of the training program. For example, the chapter opener showed how Gales Residential training ensures that trainees are actively involved in learning, meaningful content is provided, and incentives are provided to reinforce and motivate learning.

It is important to take a broad perspective when designing training, regardless of whether it is an online or a face-to-face training program, class, or course. Employees have to be motivated to attend training events, use what they learned on their job, share their knowledge and skills with others, and continue to shape and modify the knowledge and skills acquired to meet changing business and job demands. This means that program

FIGURE 5.1

The Program Design Process

Sources: Based on J. Zenger, J. Folkman, and K. Sherwin, "The promise of phase 3," *T+D* (January 2005): 31–34; R. Hewes, "Step by Step", *T+D* (February 2014): 56–61; J. Halsey, "How to ENGAGE and bring out the brilliance in everyone," From *www .trainingmag.com*, the website for *training* magazine, accessed August 3, 2011.

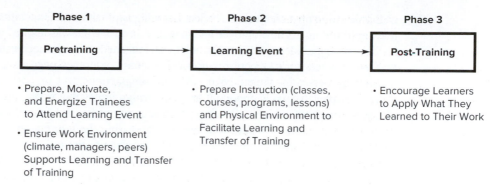

design should include not only what goes on during training based on course and lesson plans, but also creating conditions before the training event to ensure that trainees are willing, ready, and motivated to learn knowledge and skills. In addition, program design should include taking steps to ensure that after training, the acquired knowledge and skills are used on the job and shared with other employees.

Figure 5.1 shows the three phases of the program design process: pretraining, the learning event, and post-training. As discussed in Chapter Three, "Needs Assessment," information collected during the needs assessment is important in identifying appropriate pretraining activities, designing the learning event, and helping to ensure that transfer of training occurs after training ends. Phase 1, pretraining, involves preparing, motivating, and energizing trainees to attend the learning event. Phase 1 also involves ensuring that the work environment (i.e., climate, managers, and peers) supports learning and transfer. Phase 2, the learning event, involves preparing instruction (classes, the overall program) and the physical environment to facilitate learning. Phase 2 focuses on creating a positive learning environment, including planning the activities that occur during training, selecting a high-quality instructor or trainer, choosing a training room and creating positive interaction with learners, and having a proper program design. Phase 3, post-training, refers to transfer of training, or getting learners to apply what they have learned to their work. Typically, most effort, attention, and financial resources tend to be devoted to designing and choosing the learning event itself.[1] However, what happens before the learning event (pretraining) and after the learning event (post-training) may be equally, if not more, important in determining if learners are motivated to learn, acquire new knowledge and skills, and apply, share, and use what they have learned.

For example, the learning team for customer service development, a sales function within Procter & Gamble (P&G) Co. relies on three phases known as "Li-La-La" to ensure that learning and transfer of training occurs.[2] Learning intent (Li) includes the employee and manager agreeing to a contract. Employees agree that they will take responsibility for achieving learning objectives. Managers confirm that the objectives will help the employees improve their performance and relate to business outcomes and agree to help employees achieve them. Learning action (La) focuses on how the employee will learn. P&G uses a blended learning model, which includes web-based, classroom, and experiential learning that allows employees to access courses they have planned to take as well as learning opportunities as needed. Learning application (La) specifically focuses on transfer of training. The employee and manager discuss what was learned in the "learning action" phase and identify the on-the-job behaviors needed to enhance business outcomes. The learning team tracks performance and business outcomes over a six-month period, which helps determine the effectiveness of learning actions.

This chapter discusses important program design issues that relate to the three phases of the instructional process. It begins by discussing important considerations in effective program design, including selecting and preparing the training site, identifying and choosing the best trainers, and how trainers can arrange the training site and create an instructional environment that is conducive to learning. Next, the chapter introduces you to curricula, courses, and lessons and shows how to manage learning projects and use design documents and lesson plans. Because many companies do not have the staff, resources, or expertise needed to design training programs, this section of the chapter ends with a discussion of how to identify and choose a vendor or consultant for training services. The chapter concludes by discussing important post-training issues related to transfer of training, including how to create a supportive work environment, provide trainees with self-management skills, and gain manager and peer support. The important role of knowledge management in facilitating learning and transfer of training is also discussed.

CONSIDERATIONS IN DESIGNING EFFECTIVE PROGRAMS

Selecting and Preparing the Training Site

The **training site** refers to the room where training will be conducted. A good training site offers the following features:[3]

1. It is comfortable and accessible.
2. It is quiet, private, and free from interruptions.
3. It has sufficient space for trainees to move around easily, offers enough room for trainees to have adequate work space, and has good visibility for trainees to see each other, the trainer, and any visual displays or examples that will be used (e.g., videos, product samples, charts, and slides).

Training sites can be on-site in a training room located at company offices or off-site at a hotel, resort, conference center, or college campus. There is no right answer as to whether training should be held on-site or off-site. Both on-site and off-site training have potential benefits that need to be considered.[4] The benefits of off-site training include actual and perceived savings of transportation, food and beverage costs, space and equipment rental costs, and ease of using local employees to serve as instructors for some or part of the training. The benefits of off-site training include less chance of business-related disruptions resulting in improved trainee focus, a more memorable training setting and experience, providing a message that the company values training by investing in it, and better opportunities for networking. For example, leaving the office for off-site training provides a mental and physical break from work that can help trainees focus on learning rather than being distracted by interruptions from staff and customers. Regardless of the location, to improve their focus on training content, trainers need to ask learners to turn off their cell phones (unless they are being used for learning purposes).

TABLE 5.1
Details to Consider When Evaluating a Training Room

Source: Based on M. Weinstein, "Training spaces", training (September/October 2010): 34–37. C. L. Finkel, "Meeting Facilities," in the *ASTD Training and Development Handbook*, 3d ed., ed. R. L. Craig (New York: McGraw-Hill, 1996): 978–989.

Noise. Check for noise from heating and air conditioning systems, adjacent rooms and corridors, and outside the building.

Colors. Pastel hues such as oranges, greens, blues, and yellows are warm colors. Variations of white are cold and sterile. Blacks and brown shades will close the room in psychologically and become fatiguing.

Room structure. Use rooms that are somewhat square in shape. Are the rooms and seating tiered? Long, narrow rooms make it difficult for trainees to see, hear, and participate in the discussion. Check for availability and proximity of breakout or case rooms if needed.

Lighting. The main source of lighting should be fluorescent lights. Incandescent lighting should be spread throughout the room and used with dimmers when projection is required.

Wall and floor covering. Carpeting should be placed in the meeting area. Solid colors are preferable because they are not distracting. Only meeting-related materials should be on the walls.

Meeting room chairs. Chairs should have wheels, swivels, and backs that provide support for the lower lumbar region.

Glare. Check and eliminate glare from metal surfaces, TV monitors, and mirrors.

Ceiling. Ten-foot-high ceilings are preferable.

Electrical outlets. Outlets should be available every six feet around the room. A telephone jack should be next to the outlets. Outlets for the trainer should be available as well. Make sure that outlets are available for trainees to plug in their laptops, if necessary.

Acoustics. Check the bounce or absorption of sound from the walls, ceiling, floor, and furniture. Try voice checks with three or four different people, monitoring voice clarity and level.

Technology. Check that the room has permanent screens and a computer with Internet access for the trainer (and for trainees if needed).

Details to Be Considered in the Training Room

Table 5.1 presents characteristics of the meeting room that a trainer, program designer, or manager should use to evaluate a training site. Keep in mind that many times, trainers do not have the luxury of choosing the "perfect" training site. Rather, they use their evaluation of the training site to familiarize themselves with the site's strengths and weaknesses in order to adjust the training program and/or physical arrangements of the site (e.g., rearrange the trainer's position so it is closer to electrical outlets needed to run equipment).

Recognizing that trainee learning can be facilitated though both mental and physical involvement, it is important to consider this when choosing, designing, or deciding how to use a training space. For example, Blue Cross Blue Shield of Michigan has transitioned to classrooms with spaces that can be configured as needed.[5] Because training classes might involve online learning, teamwork, physical movement, and quiet contemplation, spaces need flexible furniture and equipment that can be moved within the class (or moved out altogether to make more space). The key is to have a classroom that is able to accommodate a wide variety of activities and instructor-learner, learner-learner, and learner-content interactions. For example, in a sales course, learners work with a partner. They physically walk through the sales process using a map on the floor outlining the steps in the process. The physical movement through the steps has helped learners better recall the sales process. When choosing training spaces, whether on-site or off-site at a conference site or hotel, trainers at The Economical Insurance Group (TEIG) consider the size of the room needed for the number of trainees attending, and ensure that the physical space is engaging to the learner and promotes a sense of community between the facilitator and the instructor. They make certain that the training space can incorporate a blend of technology-based (such as graphics, multimedia, flash technology, and immediate feedback tools) with face-to-face training methods (such as roundtable discussions among small groups of trainees). Also, for courses such as leadership training, the environment outside the classroom needs to be comfortable (e.g., quiet areas, gardens, and lounge chairs) to encourage networking, creativity, and innovation. Sometimes, trainers may find themselves having to work in a training space that is not ideal. At Century 21 Real Estate LLC, trainers make sure that they get a look at the space before the training course to consider its strengths and limitations and how to use it to best maximize learning. For example, at one training session held at a local hotel, trainers had to work around banquet tables. As a result, they decided to get trainees energized and involved by using a team exercise that trainees seated at each table could work on. Steelcase modified its classrooms so that content is projected from different sides of the room, not just the front, so learners look over one another.[6] Instructors can be anywhere in the room because they can use a switcher to project content from any student's or instructor's laptop to any or all screens in the room. Also, in addition to classrooms, Steelcase also has cafes, booths, and small rooms to encourage collaboration and knowledge sharing, as well as areas for quiet, individual work.

Seating Arrangements   Seating arrangements at the training site should be based on an understanding of the desired type of trainee interaction and trainee-trainer interaction.[7] Figure 5.2 shows several types of seating arrangements.

Fan-type seating is conducive to allowing trainees to see from any point in the room. Trainees can easily switch from listening to a presentation to practicing in groups, and trainees can communicate easily with everyone in the room. Fan-type seating is also effective for training that includes trainees working in groups and teams to analyze problems and synthesize information.

If the training primarily involves knowledge acquisition, with lecture and audiovisual presentation being the primary training method, traditional classroom–type seating is appropriate. Traditional classroom instruction allows trainee interaction with the trainer, but it also makes it difficult for trainees to work in teams (particularly if the seats are not movable to other locations in the room).

If training emphasizes total-group discussion with limited presentation and no small-group interaction, a conference-type arrangement may be most effective. If the training requires both presentation and total-group instruction, the horseshoe arrangement is useful.

Choosing Trainers

Selecting professional trainers or consultants is one obvious possibility for companies. Trainers, whether from inside or outside the company, should have expertise in the topic and experience in training.[8] Train-the-trainer programs are necessary for managers, employees, and "experts" who may have content knowledge but need to improve presentation

**FIGURE 5.2
Examples
of Seating
Arrangements**

Source: Based on
F. H. Margolis and
C. R. Bell, *Managing
the Learning Process*
(Minneapolis,
MN: Lakewood
Publications, 1984).

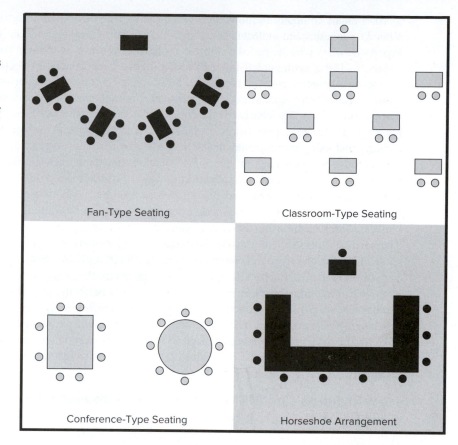

Fan-Type Seating

Classroom-Type Seating

Conference-Type Seating

Horseshoe Arrangement

and communications skills, gain an understanding of the key components of the learning process (e.g., feedback, practice), or learn to develop lesson plans. This may involve having employees and managers earn a certificate verifying that they have the skills needed to be effective trainers. To increase their chances of success in their first courses, new trainers should be observed and should receive coaching and feedback from more experienced trainers. When companies use in-house experts for training, it is important to emphasize that these experts convey training content in as concrete a manner as possible (e.g., use examples), especially if the audience is unfamiliar with the content. Experts may have a tendency to use more abstract and advanced concepts that may confuse trainees.[9]

Using managers and employees as trainers may help increase the perceived meaningfulness of the training content. Because they understand the company's business, employee and manager trainers tend to make the training content more directly applicable to the trainees' work. Also, having managers and employees lead training sessions can help increase their support for learning and reduce the company's dependency on expensive outside consultants. Serving as trainers can be rewarding for employees and managers if they are recognized by the company, or if the training experience is linked to their personal development plans.

As a small company introducing a new product line of clinical information systems related to genetics and molecular diagnostics, SCC Soft Computer needed subject-matter experts (SMEs) who helped develop the tools to also serve as trainers for its staff and clients.[10] Hiring professional trainers with genetics backgrounds in needed disciplines such as cytogenetics was too expensive. SCC created a train-the-trainer course for non-trainers who already conducted some informal training, such as product demonstrations during client visits. The content of the course included applying adult learning principles, identifying and developing learning objectives, creating content for learning objectives, creating and using training aids, developing a lesson plan and structuring a lesson, planning evaluation using reaction, learning, behavior, and outcomes (discussed in Chapter Six, "Training Evaluation"), and identifying ways to transfer the skills.

Consider how and Merck and Boeing choose trainers.[11] Merck often uses an instructor from academic faculty paired with an internal leader in its training and development classes. Merck ensures that they meet before they teach to share models and frameworks. The academic perspective provides best practice and models and the internal leader discusses how the practices and models are used in Merck and how they can be used to deal with business issues. Each of Boeing's vice presidents teach at least two leadership classes each year. Teaching classes is included in their annual performance evaluation. Boeing's leaders-teaching-leaders method involves preparing leaders to engage in dialogue, ask challenging questions, and tell compelling stories. Program participants are encouraged to question and challenge leaders, listen to the leader's experiences, and take what they learned and teach it to others. This helps create a continuous learning environment where all employees are both learners and teachers.

How Trainers Can Make the Training Site and Instruction Conducive to Learning

As a trainer, you can take several steps before and during training to make the room and instruction conducive to learning.[12]

Creating a Learning Setting

Before choosing a training room, consider how the trainees are expected to learn. That is, determine the extent to which trainees decide when, where, and how they will learn (self-direction), and whether learning will occur by interaction with others (collaboration).[13] Table 5.2 describes the types of training rooms that are appropriate for the amount of self-direction and collaboration necessary for learning. For example, a classroom with easy-to-move furniture supports high collaboration but low self-direction; this classroom can be used for lectures, presentations, discussions, and small groups. A distance learning room that includes computers, cameras, and data equipment supports learning that requires low collaboration but high self-direction. Self-directed learning that requires little collaboration is best suited for labs equipped with computers and software that support online learning, computer-based training, or software instruction. Of course, a dedicated training space may not be necessary for these learning requirements because trainees can work from their own personal computers, at home or at work. The advantages and disadvantages of online learning are discussed in Chapter Eight, "Technology-Based Training Methods," but be aware that employees may not like the lack of face-to-face collaboration that occurs in online learning programs.

TABLE 5.2
Matching Training Rooms with Learning Requirements

Sources: Based on "Workplace Issues: One in a Series. Learning Environments for the Information Age," available from the *www.steelcase.com* (accessed March 1, 2006), and "Rethinking Higher Education Spaces," available at *www.steelcase.com* (accessed June 12, 2012).

For Learning That Requires	Suggested Training Rooms
High collaboration, low self-direction	Classroom with breakout rooms Lecture hall with breakout rooms
High collaboration, high self-direction	Breakout rooms Project room Conference room
Low collaboration, low self-direction	Classroom Computer classroom Lecture hall
Low collaboration, high self-direction	Distance learning room Media lab Computer lab

Think about the physical requirements of the training room. Do trainees need to be able to concentrate and write? Do they need to be able to see detailed visuals? Choose a room that is large enough to meet your purpose, not just to accommodate a certain number of trainees. Avoid putting 25 people in a room that can seat 250. A small number of trainees in a large room makes it impersonal and leaves people feeling insignificant. Consider the room design well in advance of the session, and work with the training site coordinator to design a setting that meets your learning needs.

Preparation of Materials

You need to know your content very well. Use mental and physical rehearsals to help build your confidence and to evaluate the pace and timing of material. Observe master trainers to get new ideas. Design the training from the audience's perspective—ask "So what?" about everything you plan to do. If you are using computers, videos, the Internet, distance learning, or other technologies, make sure you know how to work the equipment and have backup materials in case the technology fails. Make sure that your visuals are available in at least two formats (e.g., PowerPoint slides and overheads). Arrive at the training room at least 15 minutes early to make sure the room is set up correctly, materials are available, and technology is functioning. Greet the trainees as they enter the room.

Know the Audience: Age, Generation, and Personality Differences

To be an effective trainer, you need to stay in touch with pop culture and world events, be familiar with relevant studies and surveys, and know your audience.[14] Trainers need to be aware of the shared values of the learners that may be based around age, personality, or other characteristics such as geography or profession. This will help you use language, examples, stories, illustrations, and references in training that the learners can relate to based on their experiences.

Age and Generational Differences   Traditionalists prefer a standard training room with a stable, orderly learning environment. They do not like to be put on the spot in front of other trainees. They value direct presentation of information and training materials that are organized logically. They like trainers to ask them to share their experiences or anecdotes; but they also look to the trainer to provide expertise.

Baby boomers prefer classroom learning. Baby boomers respond well to interactive training activities—they like group activities and well-organized training materials with an overview of the information and an easy way to access more detailed information. Compared to the other groups, they are especially motivated to learn if they believe that training content will benefit them personally. Baby boomers need to work on translating the knowledge they have into skills. This means trainers should ensure that within courses and programs there are opportunities for boomers to put knowledge gained into practice.

Members of Generation X (Gen Xers) prefer a self-directed learning environment that includes technology-delivered methods. They respond best to training methods that allow them to work at their own pace: CD-ROMs and web-based training, for instance. Gen Xers are highly motivated learners who view training as a way to increase their employability. They like to learn by doing, through experimentation and feedback. They respond best to training materials that provide visual stimulation with relatively few words. Question and answer sessions help meet Gen Xers' need for giving and receiving feedback.

Although they are techno-savvy, millenniums like to learn by working alone and helping others to learn. They prefer a blended learning approach that involves self-paced online learning for acquiring basic concepts, ideas, and knowledge, followed by group activities and hands-on practice in which they work with others on questions, cases, and role-playing.[15] They are motivated to learn skills and acquire knowledge that will help make their working lives less stressful and increase their employability. They place a high value on money so linking training to monetary incentives may facilitate learning. Millennials value experiences that can help them grow, want meaning from their work, access to great technology, space for socialization and collaboration, and honest feedback. Nexters (like Gen Xers) prefer interactive training activities that are visually stimulating with more images than text. Training should be interactive, use multimedia presentation (visuals, voice, and music), and incorporate gaming, if possible. Milliennials have adopted the social media platforms and technology for not just networking but for learning. UPS was experiencing much higher than normal failure rates among its millennium drivers. The initial idea was to train millenniums using video games and simulations. However, needs assessment found that while these employees wanted to use technology in their training, they also wanted hands-on training in the skills needed to be successful drivers. As a result, UPS's new learning facility for driver trainees in Maryland includes online learning, podcasts, and videos, along with classroom training and simulations involving driving delivery trucks and delivering packages on the streets of a fictitious town named Clarksville.[16]

The potential for generational differences to affect learning suggests that an awareness of the learners' ages and generations is important because it can help trainers try to create a learning environment and develop materials that meet learner preferences. Recent research summarizing the findings of studies on the influence of age on performance in training found that self-paced training had the largest influence on the training performance of trainees over 40 years of age.[17] Self-pacing gives older trainees time to assume responsibility for their learning, to focus on what is required to learn, and to understand the training and its importance. Also, training that occurred in small groups was advantageous for older trainees. Because most training groups include a mix of generations, it is important to provide a learning environment that can benefit all learners.[18] Employees can learn from cross-generation interaction if it is managed well. Regardless of their generation, all trainees need to understand how learning is relevant to their jobs. That is, they need to know "what's in it for them." All trainees desire to be included and respond positively to social interaction. To develop and deliver effective training, trainers need to minimize conflict and leverage the strengths of each generation. Trainers should try to find common ground to enhance the learning of all employees. Trainers should consider face-to-face as well as with technology-based learning methods such as e-learning modules and webcasts to help engage all learners (this is known as blended learning, which we will discuss in Chapter Eight). Also, using music, games, and group activities will help keep all learners interested. To keep all learners' attention, information should be presented in shorter modules no longer than twenty minutes. This should be followed by activities and discussion to help learners store the information in memory and understand how it can be applied to their work and benefit them.

Personality   In addition to understanding trainees' learning styles, which was discussed in Chapter Four, some companies are using other assessment tools to help instructors better understand the preferences and characteristics of learners who will be in their courses and programs. The Learning and Development Group within PricewaterhouseCoopers (PwC) is using the Myers-Briggs Type Indicator (MBTI) as a tool for instructors to understand learner needs and styles.[19] The MBTI focuses on how we gather information and how we make decisions. It is an assessment tool designed to help individuals understand their personality and how to use their personality preferences at work and in their lives. MBTI theory suggests that personalities differ on four dimensions. We gather information with an emphasis on either facts and details (Sensing or S) or on abstract patterns and possibilities (Intuition). We make decisions based on logical analysis (Thinking or T) or on personal values (Feeling). Also, we differ in our orientation toward and how we deal with the environment. Individuals with an Extroversion (E) gain energy from interpersonal interactions, while those with an Introversion (I) preference draw energy from within themselves. Individuals with a preference for Judging (J) desire structure and closure, while those with a Perceiving (P) preference prefer to have many decision options. The MBTI assessment provides a four-letter personality type that is related to each of the four personality dimensions. The dimensions combine to form sixteen personality types (e.g., an individual can be an ISTJ, an ENFP, or an INFP).

Instructors can have learners complete the assessment prior to attending training courses. Then, instructors can use this information about learners' personality types to help design training that the learners will find interesting, increasing their motivation to learn. For example, if an instructor has a course with trainees who are high on Sensing, this means they tend to receive and process information through a linear approach involving the five senses. As a result, the instructor would want to be sure that they included training methods that involved multiple senses. Logic and analysis appeal to Thinking learners, while Feeling learners needs a personal reason for learning. For Thinking learners, instructors can emphasize the logic of an approach, while for Feeling learners, personal needs, beliefs, values, and experiences should be emphasized. The extent to which learners are extraverts or introverts can help an instructor decide whether to use a structured or flexible learning environment.

If you can't assess trainees' learning styles or personality type in advance, you can still ensure that at least some parts of training appeal to most learners. At American Fidelity Assurance Company, training emphasizes a learner-centered approach to reach employees with different learning styles. This means that in each course, company trainers are encouraged to include multiple activities and create a learning environment that includes toys, music, vivid figures, charts, and graphs, and exercises that require working in pairs to stimulate interaction.

Pretraining: Enhance Motivation to Learn Through Communications, Prework, and Manager Involvement

The important role of motivation in learning was discussed in Chapter Four. To enhance trainee motivation to learn, it is important to communicate to trainees before they attend training the purpose of the course, learning objectives, course prerequisites, and who else will be attending. It is important to also communicate how the course will be meaningful and useful. One way to do this is by sharing testimonials or examples of how other trainees have benefited from the course. Prework or pretraining assignments such as readings, cases, or asking trainees to e-mail trainers or bring to class work-related problems or issues that will be used as examples or discussed during class also increase the meaningfulness of the course and motivation to learn, and help trainees come to the course or program with a sense of purpose and focus. For example, Shapiro Negotiations Institute asks participants in its training courses to bring real deals they are working on so they can apply what they are learning in the course.[20] Prior to attending a course on how Johnsonville Sausage's products are sold, employees are asked to go on a scavenger hunt during which they go to a grocery store, use the store's ads, and observe store promotions.[21] This helps prepare employees to share ideas when they attend the course and highlights the importance of the course.

Trainee motivation to learn and use training content on the job can also be enhanced by getting their managers to communicate and reinforce the importance of training, provide trainees with the opportunity to attend, and discussing with them their expectations for using training content in their work (or even teaching others to use what they learned). Later in the chapter, it is discussed in detail how to get a manager's support for training.

Provide an Overview of the Course

When beginning a course or workshop, it is important to give learners an idea of the "big picture" (i.e., what will be covered), including the objectives, timeline, activities, assignments, and other relevant information.[22] The overall concept, usefulness of the course, the objective, and its relevance to the job should be presented first, followed by an explanation of how the course is structured to achieve its objectives. This is important to get learners into the appropriate mental state for learning and helps them understand the personal and work-related meaningfulness and relevance of course content (recall the discussion of meaningfulness in Chapter Four). Using a flowchart or course outline, you should present the general topics first, followed by more specific subtopics. A concept map can also be used for organizing and presenting knowledge or skills. A **concept map** includes concepts shown in boxes, with the relationships between the concepts indicated by connecting lines. At the start of each part, you can present the appropriate part of the concept map, outline or flowchart. This helps the learner organize the content in memory. Also, you can return to the entire concept map, flowchart or outline during the course to show how the content covered fits into the course and its relationship to the next topic. Figure 5.3 shows a concept map for a course on conducting an effective performance review. The concept map shows that the course includes three main topics and the knowledge and skills that will be emphasized. For example, one of the course concepts is helping trainees understand

FIGURE 5.3
A Concept Map for a Course on Conducting an Effective Performance Review

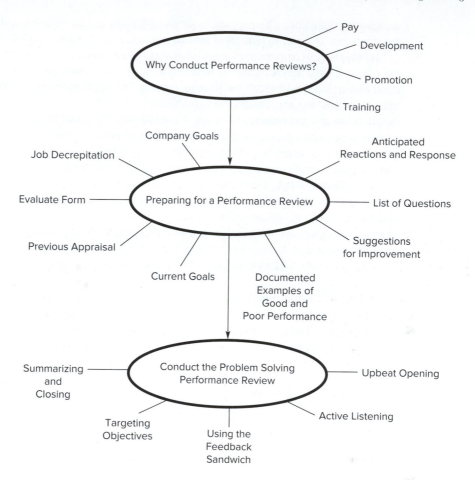

why to conduct performance reviews. Pay, development, promotion, and training will be emphasized as the four reasons for conducting performance reviews.

Help Trainees Retain and Recall Training Content   You need to carefully consider if you can chunk learning topics into short sessions of no longer than twenty minutes in length.[23] After twenty minutes you need to either take a break or use different learning techniques (such as exercises, a question-and-answer session, work in break out rooms on a case or problem). This helps refresh and maintain the learners' attention to commit learning content to memory. Mnemonics and metaphors can be useful for recalling important ideas. They help relate concepts, behaviors, and knowledge to be learned to concepts that the learner already knows. This makes it easier to retrieve the information from memory. *Mnemonics* are acronyms in which the first letter of the word represents a term or step in the process. For example, in a course emphasizing a method for presenting new ideas in meetings, the acronym PIN is used to help learners remember to identify the positive aspects of the idea (P), present interesting or important implications of the ideas (I), and only after they have considered the value of the idea do they criticize it (N).[24] The instructor may give each learner a small safety pin as a souvenir and symbol to help them recall how to present ideas in meetings, or demonstrate idea killing by popping balloons with a pin and then introduce the metaphor of the safety pin as a way to remember how easy it is to suppress and squelch new ideas.

Another way to help trainees recall what they have learned is to have them consider how they can use what they are learning in training. Application assignments increase the likelihood that trainees will recall the training content and apply it to their work setting when they encounter the appropriate cues (problems and work situations) in the environment. **Application assignments** refer to assignments in which trainees are asked to identify work problems or situations and to apply training content to solve them. The use of application assignments in training helps trainees understand the link between the learned capabilities and real-world application, which makes it easier to recall the capability when needed.

Sandy Spring Bank, a community bank headquartered in Maryland, uses application assignments in its management skills training classes.[25] The application assignments include topics such as building effective teams, change leadership, and delegation. To complete the assignments, they had to research the topic they selected, prepare a summary, and apply what they learned to the teams they supervised. This was then shared with their manager who met with them to discuss what they learned and applied.

Classroom Management

Monitor the room for extra chairs, overflowing trash cans, and piles of materials left over from previous training sessions. A messy, disorganized, uninviting training room creates learning distractions. Give trainees frequent breaks so they can leave the room and return ready to start learning again.

Interacting with Trainees

As a trainer, you carry the responsibility for the trainees' learning experience. You need to communicate the topics that will be covered, the learning approach that will be used, and the expectations for trainees. You need to be dramatic to draw attention to important points. Research suggests that trainees have the best recall of training content when the trainer is enthusiastic and avoids vocal distractions (e.g., use of "er" and "um").[26] Also, you should use a relaxed style and make learners comfortable.[27] As a trainer, you should recognize that your expectations for trainees' learning and your stereotypes can result in learners confirming those expectations (i.e., a self-fulfilling prophecy).[28] Negative expectations held by instructors can lead to learners' negative evaluation of the training and the trainer.[29]

How you should engage trainees is based on both the size of the room and the number of trainees. The larger the room, the more your gestures and movements must be exaggerated to get the audience's attention. To create intimacy with the training group, you must move close to them. Standing in the front of the room is a way to establish authority. One of the best ways to gain trainees' attention is to facilitate discussion from different places in the room. Strive to lead the instruction, but focus on the trainees. Help trainees develop their own answers, apply tools and techniques, and use reference materials to reach solutions that are effective in training and on the job. Use questions that lead trainees to answers or points that you want to make. Strive continually for interaction with trainees—trainees may have more real-life experiences with, exposure to, or applications related to training topics than you do. Create a training environment where trainees can learn from each other. Listen to trainees, summarize learning points, and provide feedback. Consider how Edward Jones, a financial services company based in St. Louis, Missouri, encourages learning by combining a training course with ongoing coaching and feedback.

TABLE 5.3
**Examples
of How to
Get Trainees
Involved**

Source: Based on M.
Torrance, "Nine Mo-
ments of Learning",
T+D (September 2014):
76–77; J. Curtis,
"Engage Me, Please!"
T+D (November
2008): 68–73.

- Prepare and distribute content-related, open-ended questions to be discussed in break-out groups.
- Use creative activities or games that relate to the training content.
- Use assessment or measures that allow the trainees to learn about themselves and each other.
- Incorporate role-playing.
- Conclude the training session by asking trainees, either individually or in teams from the same company or work group, to consider the following questions: "As a result of this session, what do you plan to start, stop, or continue doing? On what topic would you like to have more information?"

Also, typical class sizes are no more than twelve learners, often including SMEs and an instructor. The training sessions are based on an interactive question-and-answer format, which engages learners. Edward Jones also distributes surveys during the course that asks learners how difficult they found the lessons and whether they think they are learning. This allows instructors to change lesson plans during the session to better facilitate learning. Table 5.3 provides examples of how to get trainees involved in a training session.

Leading a Discussion

As we mentioned in Chapter Four, learner-learner and learner-instructor interactions are useful. They help learners understand the meaningfulness of training content and help commit it to memory. Effective discussions are based on clearly defined goals, topic focus, and time frame, planned questions, and clear rules for participation.[30] Discussions can have a number of goals including brainstorming sessions to identify solutions to problems or issues (before or after training), debriefing or reflection on learning activities (end of a learning event), application of knowledge and skills resulting in a learner action plan (during or at the end of a learning event), and evaluating the learning experience by focusing on impressions and key lessons about the learning event (at the end of training). After you choose the goals, it is important to consider what topics will be discussed, time expectations, the type of seating best suited for the discussion, and materials needed such as pictures, PowerPoint slides, or handouts. Questions for starting the discussion are needed. These should be open-ended questions that require more than a yes or no response. It is also important have different opening questions as well as follow-up questions and discussion prompts. For example, "What are the benefits of performance feedback?" could be followed up with prompts like "Share an instance when you received what you considered as effective feedback? Why did you consider it effective feedback?" You also need to consider how you will invite learners to participate in the discussion (raise hands or just jump into the discussion). Also, you need to decide the rules for interrupting others, cell phone use, respecting others opinions, and when leaving to take a break is appropriate. Finally, you need to consider your role. Are you an observer, facilitator, or leader of the discussion? The goals, topics, time frame and expectations, and structure for the discussion should be communicated to the learners before the discussion begins.

Dealing with Disruptive Trainees

How can you deal with employees who don't want to be trained despite being informed in advance of the course and how it relates to the business?[31] First, take charge of the session immediately, communicate your credentials, and in a friendly but assertive way tell employees why the training is important and how it will help them. Then let them vent their frustrations. Useful methods for this activity are to have trainees describe what they would be doing if they were not in the program, have trainees draw pictures of how the person next to them feels about attending the training, or have trainees break into groups and then ask some groups to make a list of the top 10 reasons not to be in the class and the other groups to list 10 reasons to be in the class. Reassemble the class and discuss first the reasons not to be in the class, and then end with the reasons to be in the class. For trainees who disrupt, sleep through, or constantly interrupt the training sessions, consider using activities that get them moving, engaged, and energized. Ask disruptive trainees to leave the session only as a last resort when all other options discussed here have failed.

Managing Group Dynamics

To ensure an even distribution of knowledge or expertise in groups, ask trainees to indicate whether they consider themselves novice, experienced, or expert in terms of knowledge about a topic. Arrange the groups so that they contain a mix of novice, experienced, and expert trainees. Group dynamics can be altered by changing learners' positions in the room. Pay attention to group dynamics by wandering through the room and noticing which groups are frustrated or stalled, who is withdrawn, and who is dominating the group. Your role is to make sure that everyone in a group has an opportunity to contribute. Seating arrangements such as rectangular tables often give trainees authority based on where they are seated. For example, the end of a rectangular table is the position of authority. Putting a quiet person in the "power seat" creates an opportunity for that person to assume a leadership role within the group.

At India-based pharmaceutical company Lupin Ltd., training and development is critical for the company to keep up with its growth, which has been two to three times the industry rate each year.[32] One of the barriers that Lupin faced for effective learning was a cultural tradition within Indian society to respect hierarchy. This meant that in the classroom, employees sit according to their place in the hierarchy, and junior employees don't question the opinions of more senior employees. However, Lupin requires that all learners participate without regard to their status. This has resulted in greater levels of participation in training classes and enhanced learning.

Curriculum, Course, and Lesson Design

Keep in mind that although the responsibility for designing the training program may belong to the instructional designer, human resource professional, or manager, the "clients" of the program should also be involved in program design. As already discussed in Chapter Three, managers and employees should be involved in the needs assessment process. In addition, their role may include reviewing prototypes of the program, providing examples and program content, and participating in the program as instructors.[33]

A **curriculum** refers to an organized program of study designed to meet a complex learning objective, such as preparing a learner to become a salesperson, certified computer network technician, licensed nurse, or manager.[34] A curriculum usually includes several courses, and it usually focuses on developing a set of competencies needed to perform a job. Because these competencies are often expected to be developed over time, curricula and the courses within the curricula are completed over an extended time period.

In comparison to a curriculum, a **course** or **program** usually covers more specific learning objectives and addresses a more limited number of competencies or skills. For example, courses can address topics such as negotiations, talent management, customer service, and (as you are learning) even training and development. A course typically includes units or lessons that are smaller sections or modules covering different topics. The time frame for courses can range from one to several hours, a half-day, a full day, or even weeks.

Although curricula, courses, and lessons all use learning objectives, they tend to vary in specificity. Learning objectives for curricula tend to be broader and less measurable than objectives for courses or lessons.[35] For example, for a project management course within a curriculum, an objective might be "Describe the four stages of the project life cycle using text and graphs." However, one of the objectives for a project management curriculum might include "Apply decision-aiding models when selecting a project." This objective is much broader than the course objectives because it describes the general knowledge, skills, and abilities developed throughout the curriculum and is likely emphasized in several courses.

Program design should be considered a special case of project management. In this case, **project management** refers to the skills needed to manage a team of people and resources to create a learning solution.[36] SPADES (start, plan, administer, develop, engage, and stop) includes project management concepts that incorporate principles of ISD (recall our discussion of ISD in Chapter One). "Start" involves understanding the stakeholders for the learning solution (employees, managers, subject-matter experts). It also involves conducting a needs analysis or revisiting the results to understand who needs training, the context, the focus, and the expected outcomes. The "Plan" phase involves identifying what you need to do as well as any resources that may be needed. This includes identifying tasks, how long it will take to complete them, and any expertise that is needed to execute your plan such as web designers or subject-matter experts. "Administer" involves overseeing the tasks and communicating with the project team, stakeholders, and subject-matter experts. It also involves ensuring that tasks are completed and deadlines and budgets are met. "Develop" involves many of the steps in the ISD process including identifying the training objectives and methods, how the program will be evaluated, and ensuring transfer of training. It also involves designing the actual training including any materials or online modules. "Engage" is where the training "goes live" or is implemented. It also includes conducting an evaluation of training (evaluation is discussed in Chapter Six). The "Stop" phase includes finishing the project, paying vendor and suppliers, and meeting with stakeholders to see if they feel that the project met its objectives and their expectations.

Curriculum Road Map

A **curriculum road map** refers to a figure showing all of the courses in a curriculum, the paths that learners can take through it, and the sequences in which courses have to be completed (e.g., identify prerequisite courses). Figure 5.4 shows an example of a curriculum road map for a security management training program. For each course, information that can be used to help develop and design detailed courses is provided. This includes[37]:

1. A brief statement of the course purpose, including why the course is important.
2. Prerequisite skills needed for the course.

FIGURE 5.4
An Example of a Curriculum Road Map for a Security Management Training Curriculum

Source: Based on SANS Security Management Training Curriculum, from http://www .suns.org/security- training/curriculums/ management.

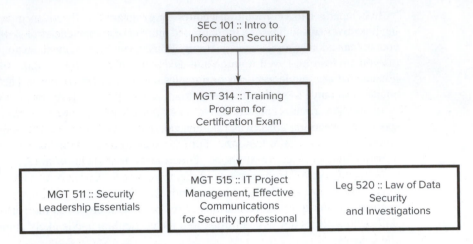

TABLE 5.4
Design Document Template

Source: Based on G. Piskurich, *Rapid Instructional Design* (San Francisco: Pfeiffer, 2006).

Scope of Project
- Goal
- Audience
- Design time and checkpoints
- Length of the course

Delivery
- Content
- Method
- Training time
- Problems and opportunities

Objectives
- Resources
- Who is involved
- Topical outline
- Administration and evaluation
- Links to other programs

3. Learning objectives or competencies covered by the course and a supporting or enabling objective(i.e., an objective that has to be reached in order for the learning objective to be accomplished).

4. The format of the content and course expectations. Expectations might relate to the type of content to be covered, how the content will be presented, and the structure of the content.

5. Delivery method for the content (e.g., online, classroom, blended learning).

Design Document

A design document can be used to guide the development of training and to explain the training to managers, SMEs, reviewers, or other trainers. Table 5.4 shows a design document template.[38] Information for the design document is based on the information obtained from the needs assessment discussed in Chapter Three.

The level of detail in the design document can vary. *Scope of project* includes the goals, outcomes, or achievement expectations for trainees; a description of the trainees; a description of how long it will take to develop the course and the checkpoints or tasks that need to be completed as the course is developed; and the length of the course. The length of a course is determined by considering trainees' abilities and their availability for training, the resources needed for training, whether the course is part of a larger curriculum or is a stand-alone course, and the need to develop modules in order to provide an opportunity for trainees to practice concepts and skills to avoid being overwhelmed.

Delivery includes what the course will cover, how it will be delivered (e.g., face-to-face or online), an estimate of the training time, and the identification of any special conditions or issues that may affect the course (e.g., problems getting equipment for video role-plays and providing feedback).

Objectives refers to the course or program objectives. Those are broader summary statements of the purpose of the program.

Resources refers to the materials—cases, DVDs, videos, models, process maps, podcasts, lesson plans, or guides for use by the facilitator or participants—that need to be purchased or developed for the course. *Who is involved* includes trainers, program designers, and individuals who will be involved in the design, delivery, and evaluation of the program. The *topical outline* includes a brief outline of the topics that will be covered in the program. *Administration and evaluation* refers to who will be in charge of course scheduling, how trainees will enroll, how the course will be evaluated, and who will review and update the course. *Links to other programs* refers to any other needs, such as a train-the-trainer program or manager introduction or kickoff for the program. Table 5.5 shows a simple design document for the performance appraisal review course designed to increase managers' effectiveness in conducting performance appraisal reviews. Performance appraisal review sessions are meetings between a manager and employee, during which the strengths and weaknesses of the employee's performance are discussed and improvement goals agreed upon.

TABLE 5.5
Design
Document

Purpose: To prepare managers to conduct effective performance review sessions with their direct reports

Goals: Managers will be able to conduct a performance review session using the problem-solving approach

Target audience: Managers

Training time: 1 day

Method: Lecture, video, role-plays

Number of participants per session: 20–25

Locations: Various

Prerequisites: None

Problems and opportunities: New performance appraisal system introduced; manager dislikes conducting feedback sessions

Instructor: Caroline O'Connell and facilitators

Course or Lesson Plan

Lesson plans are typically more detailed than the design document. They include the specific steps involved in the lesson, instructor and trainee activities, and the time allocated to each topic included in the lesson.

Lesson plans can be designed for programs lasting a day, a week, or several hours. If training takes place over several days, a separate lesson plan is prepared for each day.

The **detailed lesson plan** translated the content and sequence of training activities into a guide that is used by the trainer to help deliver the training. That is, lesson plans include the sequence of activities that will be conducted in the training session and identify the administrative details. Table 5.6 shows a lesson plan. The lesson plan provides a table of contents for the training activity, which helps ensure that training activities are consistent regardless of the trainer. Lesson plans also help ensure that both the trainee and the trainer are aware of the course and program objectives. Most training departments have written lesson plans that are stored in notebooks or in an electronic database. Because lesson plans are documented, they can be shared with customers of the training department (i.e., managers who pay for training services) to provide them with detailed information regarding program activities and objectives.

Table 5.7 shows the features of an effective lesson plan. The lesson plan includes the learning objectives, topics to be covered, target audience, time of session, lesson outline, the activity involved, any required preparation or prerequisites, how learning will be evaluated, and steps to ensure transfer of training.[39]

In developing the lesson outline, trainers need to consider the proper sequencing of topics. Trainers must answer questions such as, "What knowledge and skills need to be learned first?" "In what order should the knowledge, skills, and behavior be taught?" "What order will make sense to the trainees?" There are different options for sequencing.[40] For example, *job task* or *functioning sequencing* starts with an overview of the job and lists the steps of completing a task or job in the order in which they are completed. *Familiar to unfamiliar sequencing* starts with an idea or content that is familiar to the learner and builds to newer information. Make sure that you communicate the sequencing of the topics to the trainee because it makes it easier for them to follow the flow of the lesson, which helps organize it in memory, aiding in retention of learning.

A storyboard is useful for course and lesson design and determining sequencing. A **storyboard** is a group of pictures that tell a story. You can story board using pencil-and-paper or markers on notebooks, erasable marker boards, flip charts, or using Powerpoint slides. A storyboard is useful for showing the correct process or procedure as well as the order of activities or presentation of ideas in a training module, course, or program.[41]

It is also important to consider the target audience. Any information about their training and experience, their motivation for taking the course, and their interests, learning styles, and background (e.g., education and work experience) will be useful for choosing meaningful examples, determining program content, deciding on support materials, and building the credibility of the training. Information about the target audience should be available from the person analysis of the needs assessment (see Chapter Three). Additional information can be collected by talking to the "clients" (e.g., managers) who requested the training program and to past program participants, if available. Support materials include any equipment needed for delivery of instruction, such as computers, overhead projectors, or tablet computers. Trainers should arrange for the purchase of any whiteboards, flip

TABLE 5.6
Sample of
a Detailed
Lesson Plan

Course title: Conducting an Effective Performance Review Session

Lesson title: Using the problem-solving style in the performance review

Lesson length: Full day

Learning objectives:

1. Explain the purpose of performance reviews.

2. Describe steps in preparing for a performance review.

3. Describe the behaviors used in the problem-solving style of giving appraisal feedback without error.

4. Demonstrate the behaviors in an appraisal feedback role-play without error.

Target audience: Managers

Prerequisites:

Trainee: None

Instructor: Familiarity with the tell-and-sell, tell-and-listen, and problem-solving approaches used in performance appraisal feedback interviews

Room arrangement: Fan-type

Materials and equipment needed: VCR, overhead projector, pens, transparencies, VCR tape titled "Performance Appraisal Interviews," role-play exercises

Evaluation and assignments: Role-playing; read article titled, "Conducting Effective Appraisal Interviews"

Comment: Article needs to be distributed two weeks prior to session.

Lesson Outline	Instructor Activity	Trainee Activity	Time
Introduction and why conduct reviews	Presentation	Listening	8–8:50 A.M.
Discussion of how to prepare and steps in conducting the review	Questioning	Participation	8:50–10 A.M.
Break			10–10:20 A.M.
View videos of three styles	Discussion of strengths and weaknesses of each	Watching	10:20–11:20 A.M.
Lunch			11:30 A.M.–1 P.M.
Presentation and video of eight key behaviors of problem-solving style	Presentation	Listening	1–2 P.M.
Role-plays	Watch exercise	Practice using key behaviors	2–3 P.M.
Wrap-up	Answer questions	Ask questions	3–3:15 P.M.

charts, or markers that may be used in instruction. Any exercises needed for trainees' practice or preparation, such as readings, role-play exercises, assessments, or pretests, need to be ordered or reproduced (after copyright permission is obtained). In considering instructor and trainee activity, the focus should be on ensuring that the lesson has as many features of a positive learning process as possible, including communication of objectives,

TABLE 5.7   Features of an Effective Lesson Plan

Feature	
Learning objectives or outcomes	What is the lesson designed to accomplish?
	What is the standard for successful learning?
Target audience	Who is attending the lesson? What are the characteristics of the audience?
Prerequisites (trainees and instructor)	What will trainees need to be able to do before they can benefit from the course? Who is qualified to be in the program? Who is qualified to be an instructor?
Time	How much time is devoted to each part of the lesson?
Lesson outline	What topics will be covered? In what sequence?
Activity	What will trainees' and instructor's role be during each topic covered?
Support materials	What materials and/or equipment is needed for delivery of instruction or to facilitate instruction?
Physical environment	Is a certain size or arrangement of room necessary?
Preparation	Do the trainees have homework that needs to be completed before the lesson?
	What does the instructor need to do?
Lesson topic	What topic is the lesson going to cover?
Evaluation	How will learning be evaluated (e.g., tests, role plays)?
Transfer and retention	What will be done to ensure that training content is used on the job?

Sources: Based on R. Vaughn, *The Professional Trainer* (Euclid, OH: Williams Custom Publishing, 2000); R. F. Mager, *Making Instruction Work,* 2d ed. (Atlanta, GA: Center for Effective Performance, 1997); L. Nadler and Z. Nadler, *Designing Training Programs,* 2d ed. (Houston, TX: Gulf Publishing, 1992); Big Dog's Human Resource Development website, *www.nwlink.com/donclark/hrd.html;* A. Barron, "Design Workshops for Maximum Engagement", *T+D* (June 2015): 68–69.

feedback, opportunities for practice, opportunities for trainees to share experiences and ask questions, and modeling or demonstration. Transfer and retention strategies might include chat rooms, follow-up meetings with the manager, and action planning. Transfer and retention strategies are discussed later in this chapter.

The four learning objectives for the course, "Conducting an Effective Performance Review Session," are shown in Table 5.6. The eight key behaviors referred to in the "Learning Objectives" section are as follows: (1) explain the purpose of the meeting; (2) ask the employee to describe what he or she has done to deserve recognition; (3) ask the employee to describe what to stop doing, start doing, or do differently; (4) ask the employee for areas in which you can provide assistance; (5) give the employee your opinion of his or her performance; (6) ask for and listen to the employee's concerns about your evaluation; (7) agree on steps/actions to be taken by each of you; and (8) agree to a follow-up date.[42]

The prerequisites include (1) arrangement of the training site, equipment, and materials needed; (2) instructor preparation; and (3) trainee prerequisites. In the example, the trainer needs a computer with a DVD player to show a video of performance appraisal feedback styles. The trainer also needs an overhead projector to record points made by the trainees during the planned discussion of the strengths and weaknesses of the appraisal styles presented on the video. The room needs to be fan-shaped, so trainees can see the trainer and each other. Also, the fan arrangement is good for role-play exercises that involve trainees working in groups of two or three.

Trainee prerequisites refer to any preparation, basic skills, or knowledge that the trainee needs prior to participating in the program. Recall our discussion of basic skills in Chapter Three. Trainee prerequisites may include basic math and reading skills, completion of prior training sessions, or successful completion of tests or certificate or degree programs.

Instructor prerequisites indicate what the instructor needs to do to prepare for the session (e.g., rent equipment or review the previous day's training session) and any educational qualifications the instructor needs. Lesson plans also may cover how the lesson will be evaluated and any assignments that the trainees need to complete. In the example, trainees are required to read an article on effective performance appraisal feedback interviews. The instructor needs to be familiar with the purpose for performance review, how to prepare for a performance review, and the behaviors for conducting problem-solving appraisal feedback interviews.

Lesson Plan Overview

The **lesson plan overview** matches major activities of the training program and specific times or time intervals.[43] Table 5.8 provides an example of a lesson plan overview for the performance appraisal feedback training.

Completing a lesson plan overview helps the trainer determine the amount of time that needs to be allocated for each topic covered in the program. The lesson plan overview is also useful in determining when trainers are needed during a program; time demands on trainees; program breaks for snacks, lunch, and dinner; and opportunities for practice and feedback. For the performance appraisal feedback training, the lesson plan shows that approximately half the training time is devoted to active learning by the trainees (discussion, role-plays, question-and-answer session).

The experience of Health Partners, which administers Medicaid and Medicare coverage for patients in and around Philadelphia, Pennsylvania, illustrates the importance of lesson planning and program design.[44] The company installed a major upgrade to its data processing system, but the upgrade was unfamiliar to most employees. To conduct the training, Health Partners identified employees who were familiar with the program and asked them to be part-time instructors. Instead of providing daylong classes that would likely be boring and overwhelming, the company's training staff broke the training into a series of 45-minute sessions that employees could fit easily into their work schedules. The curriculum was organized by department rather than by tasks, and staff from other departments were invited to attend the program so they could understand how the entire company used the system. Portions of the training time were devoted to discussing with

TABLE 5.8
Sample Lesson Overview

Time	Activity
8–8:50 A.M.	Introduction, and why conduct performance reviews?
8–8:50 A.M.	Introduction: Why conduct performance reviews?
10–10:00 A.M.	Discussion of how to prepare, and steps in the problem-solving review
10:00–10:20 A.M.	Break
10:20–11:30 A.M.	Watch videos of three styles of appraisal feedback. Discussion of strengths and weaknesses of each style
11:30 A.M.–1 P.M.	Lunch
1–2 P.M.	Presentation and video of eight key behaviors of the problem-solving approach
2–3 P.M.	Role-plays
3–3:15 P.M.	Wrap-up (questions and answers)

employees the stress of change in the workplace and the benefits of the new system. The management teams also met periodically with the instructors to keep them up to date on the types of problems that employees faced in working with the new system so that those issues could be incorporated into the training.

An Example of Program Design

Consider the steps that Saudi Aramco, an oil company headquartered in Dhahran, Saudi Arabia, took to develop a program to train geoscientists and petroleum engineers to encourage critical thinking and exploration of options.[45] To develop the program, they relied on a development team, including an instructional designer, a technical writer, a graphics professional, a professional development advisor, and a subject-matter expert. The program included courses, modules within the courses, and activities within the modules. The program design included the following steps:

1. They worked with key job performers to determine what work processes and tasks were considered critical for effective performance and to identify if they could be improved through training.
2. Structured interviews were conducted and they observed jobs to collect data about job functions, tasks within those functions, key performance elements included in the tasks, important job outcomes, and the knowledge required to perform the tasks.
3. Work processes and tasks that needed training were identified. The team analyzed the tasks and identified ways to achieve important performance outcomes. This resulted in a framework to show how work gets done.
4. The tasks were analyzed to design the content and sequence the course activities. This involved identifying how to combine concepts and tasks into modules.
5. Program topics were identified as well as how they would be delivered, and the order in which they would be trained was identified. Also, program prerequisites and evaluation outcomes were discussed.
6. Module objectives, outcomes, sequence, instructional methods, and practice activities were developed. Learners were required to demonstrate the desired performance level before returning to their jobs.
7. Media, tools, and equipment needed for each activity included in the modules were chosen. These choices were based on the actions expected from learners.

How to Choose a Vendor or Consultant for Training Services

If a company decides to purchase a training program from a consultant or vendor rather than build the program in-house, it is important to choose a high-quality provider. Training providers may include individual consultants, consulting firms, companies that specialize in designing and selling training programs or academic institutions. How could you identify a vendor for training services? Personal networks, professional associations, conferences, and trade shows are frequently used by persons in charge of company training, i.e., Chief Learning Officers.[46]

The most important qualities for vendors include providing a high-quality product with positive results, providing good value for the cost, and easy to work with. It is important for the vendor to try to understand the business issues and deliver high-quality products and services to resolve them. Good vendors have to ask the right questions and listen to your answers, customize and deliver learning as expected, on time, and within the budget. A common criticism of vendors is that they try to provide an existing learning solution rather than provide a customized product to fit the company needs.

Many companies identify vendors and consultants who can provide training services by using requests for proposals.[47] A **request for proposal (RFP)** is a document that outlines for potential vendors and consultants the type of service the company is seeking, the type and number of references needed, the number of employees who need to be trained, funding for the project, the follow-up process used to determined level of satisfaction and service, the expected date of completion of the project, and the date when proposals must be received by the company. It also describes scoring criteria that will be used to evaluate the proposal. The RFP may be mailed to potential consultants and vendors or posted on the company's website. The RFP is valuable because it provides a standard set of criteria against which all consultants will be evaluated. The RFP also helps eliminate the need to evaluate outside vendors that cannot provide the needed services.

Usually, the RFP helps identify several vendors who meet the criteria. The next step is to choose the preferred provider. Table 5.9 provides examples of questions to ask vendors. Managers and trainers should check every vendor's reputation by contacting prior clients and professional organizations such as the Association for Talent Development (ATD). The consultant's experience should be evaluated. (For example, in what industry has the vendor worked?) Managers should carefully consider the services, materials, and fees outlined in the consulting contract. For example, it is not uncommon for training materials such as manuals and handouts to remain the property of the consultant. If the company wants to use the consultant's materials for training at a later date, it would have to pay additional fees to the consultant.

When using a consultant or other outside vendor to provide training services, it is also important to consider the extent to which the training program will be customized based on the company's needs or whether the consultant is going to provide training services based on a generic framework that it applies to many different organizations. For example, Towers Perrin, a well-known, successful New York consulting firm, told several clients that it would study their companies in detail and provide a customized diversity training program to fit their needs. However, six companies (including Nissan North America, Thompson

TABLE 5.9
Questions to Ask Vendors and Consultants

How much and what type of experience does your company have in designing and delivering training?
What are the qualifications and experiences of your staff?
Can you provide demonstrations or examples of training programs you have developed?
Can you provide references of clients for whom you have worked?
What evidence do you have that your programs work?
What instructional design methods do you use?
How do your products or services fit our needs?
What about recurring costs, such as costs related to administering, updating, and maintaining the training program? Do you provide technical support?

Sources: Based on C. Anderson, "Do You Have the Right Business Partners?", *Chief Learning Officer*, (March 2014): 48–50; B. Chapman, "How to Create the Ideal RFP," *Training* (January 2004): 40–43; M. Weinstein, "What Vendors Wished You Knew," *Training* (February 2010): 122–125.

Consumer Electronics, and Harris Bank) were given the exact same 18 recommendations (e.g., separate the concept of affirmative action from that of managing diversity).[48]

How long should it take a vendor or consultant to develop a training program? The answer is, "It depends."[49] Some consultants estimate that development time ranges from 10 to 20 hours for each hour of instruction. Highly technical content, which may require more frequent meetings with SMEs, can add up to 50 percent more time. For online, mobile, or virtual reality training programs, development time can range from 300 to 1,000 hours per hour of program time, depending on how much animation, graphics, video, and audio are included; how much new content needs to be developed; the number of practice exercises and the type of feedback to be provided to trainees; and the amount of "branches" to different instructional sequences.

Program Design Implications for Transfer of Training

Recall the discussion of identical elements and near transfer and stimulus generalization and far transfer in Chapter Four. One of the important decisions that trainers have to make is to determine whether the learning environment and learning conditions should perfectly match the job environment, or if it should emphasize general principles that can be applied to many different work situations. Also, to facilitate transfer of training, instructors need to consider encouraging trainees to self-manage the use of learned skills, how to ensure that managers and peers provide trainees with opportunities to use training content, support training, and provide electronic performance support.

Determine if Focus Is on Near or Far Transfer

The degree of flexibility and variability in the skills and knowledge that the learner needs for successful performance is important to consider in determining the extent to which the learning environment and learning conditions should match the job and working conditions.[50] For example, if the tasks emphasized in training involves responding to predictable situations with standardized responses, then training should be designed with an emphasis on identical elements and near transfer. This is often the case when the focus is on procedural knowledge, or when a series of steps must be followed in a specific way to complete a task successfully. Examples of procedures that company employees often must follow to that level of exactness include answering the phone, securing offices and buildings, handling client questions, logging into computers, and using software. In these cases, instruction should emphasize near transfer. Near transfer means the need to apply learned capabilities exactly in a work situation. Programs that emphasizes near transfer should include the following:[51]

- Trainees need to follow standardized procedures, processes, and checklists.
- Trainees should be given an explanation as to any differences between training and work tasks.
- Trainees should be encouraged to focus only on important differences between training tasks and work tasks (e.g., speed of completion) rather than unimportant differences (e.g., equipment with the same features but a different model).
- Trainees should be provided with an explanation of why as well as how the procedure should be performed to help them understand the concepts behind the procedure.
- Behaviors or skills that trainees learn in the program should contribute to effective performance.

For example, consider the importance of carefully following these principles in designing training for police officers. In police officer training, new hires (cadets) practice shooting targets. During practice sessions, cadets fire a round of shells, empty the cartridges into their hands, and dispose of the empty cartridges into the nearest garbage can. This process is repeated several times. After graduation from the police academy, one new officer was involved in a shooting. He fired his gun, emptied the cartridges into his hand, and proceeded to look for a garbage can for the empty cartridges. As a result, he was seen by the gunman, shot, and killed!

In contrast, if the tasks emphasized in training involve more variable interactions with people or equipment and unpredictable responses, then instruction should emphasize learning more general principles and knowing when and why to pursue a course of action. That is, instruction should emphasize far transfer. This is the case when teaching learners how to deal with novel situations involving original thinking to develop a solution, create a new product, or solve a difficult problem. Programs that emphasize far transfer should include the following:[52]

- Teach General concepts, broad principles, or key behaviors.
- General principles that might apply to a greater set of contexts than those presented in the training session.
- Provide A list of prompts or questions to help trigger thoughts and question sets, such as "How is this similar to problems I have encountered before?" and "Have I identified the real problem?" This helps trainees see connections among strategies that have been effective in different situations.

Encourage Self-Management

One way to prepare trainees to deal with the obstacles that they may face in work environments (such as lack of opportunity to use skills or an unsupportive manager) is to provide instruction in self-management techniques at the end of the training program. Table 5.10

TABLE 5.10 **Content of a Sample Self-Management Module**

1. Discuss lapses.
- Note evidence of inadequacy
- Provide direction for improvement

2. Identify skills targeted for transfer.
- Specify the skills
- Make them measurable and countable

3. Identify personal or environment factors contributing to lapses.
- Low self-efficacy
- Time pressure
- Lack of manager or peer support

4. Discuss coping skills and strategies.
- Time management
- Setting priorities
- Self-monitoring
- Self-rewards
- Creating a personal support network

5. Identify when lapses are likely.
- Situations
- Actions to deal with lapses

6. Discuss resources to ensure transfer of skills.
- Manager
- Trainer
- Other trainees

Sources: Adapted from R. D. Marx, "Improving management development through relapse prevention strategies," *Journal of Management Development* 5 (1986): 27–40; M. L. Broad and J. W. Newstrom, *Transfer of Training* (Reading, MA: Addison-Wesley, 1992); R. D. Marx and L. A. Burke, "Transfer Is Personal." In *Improving Learning Transfer in Organizations,* eds. E. Holton and T. Baldwin (San Francisco: Jossey-Bass, 2003): 227–242.

shows an example of self-management instruction. The module begins with a discussion of lapses, emphasizing that lapses are not evidence of personal inadequacy; rather, they result from habits of usage of knowledge and skill that have developed over time. Lapses provide information necessary for improvement. They help identify the circumstances that will have the most negative influence on transfer of training. Next, a specific behavior, skill, or strategy is targeted for transfer. The skill should be measurable and countable. Then, obstacles that inhibit transfer of training are identified; these can include both work environment characteristics and personal characteristics (such as low self-efficacy). Trainees are then provided with an overview of coping skills or strategies that they can use to deal with these obstacles. These skills and strategies include time management, creating a personal support network (persons to talk with about how to transfer skills to the work setting), and self-monitoring to identify successes in transferring skills to the job. Next, to deal with lapses, trainees are instructed to be aware of where the situations are most likely to occur. The final part of the module deals with the use of resources to aid transfer of training. These resources may include communications with the trainer or fellow trainees via e-mail and discussions with their boss.

For example, a manager may have attended a training program designed to increase her leadership skills. After a discussion of lapses, the manager identifies a target skill (say, participative decision making—that is, discussing problems and potential solutions with subordinates before making decisions that will affect the work group). The manager defines the skill and how to measure it: "Discussing problems and solutions with my subordinates at least two times each week." Next, the manager identifies factors that may contribute to a lapse. One factor may be the manager's lack of confidence in being able to deal with subordinates who disagree with her view. Potential coping strategies that the manager identifies may include (1) scheduling time on the calendar to meet with subordinates (time management), (2) communicating to the boss the transfer goal and asking for help (create a support group), and (3) taking an assertiveness training course. In what situation may the manager be especially likely to experience a lapse? The manager identifies that she may be most likely to lapse back into an autocratic style when faced with a short time frame for making a decision (time pressure being an obstacle). The manager recognizes that it may be inappropriate to try to gain consensus for a decision when time constraints are severe and subordinates lack expertise. In the last step of the module, the manager suggests that she will (1) meet with her mentor to review her progress, (2) talk with other managers about how they use participative decision making effectively, and (3) resolve to communicate with other managers who attended the training session with her. The manager also commits to monitoring her use of participative decision making, noting successes and failures in a diary.

Encourage Manager Support for Training

Manager support refers to the degree to which trainees' managers (1) emphasize the importance of attending training programs, (2) stress the application of training content to the job, and (3) provide opportunities for trainees to use what they have learned on the job. Managers can communicate expectations to trainees, as well as provide the encouragement and resources needed to apply training on the job. One company asked trainees and their bosses to prepare and send memos to each other. The memos described what the other person should "start to do," "continue to do," "do less," or "stop doing" to improve learning transfer.[53]

Managers can provide different levels of support for training activities, as illustrated in Figure 5.5.[54] The greater the level of support, the more likely that transfer of training will occur. Managers should be actively involved in the design and delivery of training programs. The basic level of support that a manager can provide is acceptance (allowing trainees to attend training). The greatest level of support is to participate in training as an instructor (teaching in the program). Managers who serve as instructors are more likely to provide many of the lower-level support functions, such as reinforcing use of newly learned capabilities, discussing progress with trainees, and providing opportunities to practice. To maximize transfer of training, trainers need to achieve the highest level of support possible. Managers can also facilitate transfer through reinforcement (use of action plans). An **action plan** is a written document that includes the steps that the trainee and manager will take to ensure that training transfers to the job (see the sample action plan shown in Figure 5.6). The action plan includes (1) a goal identifying what training content will be used and how it will be used (project, problem); (2) strategies for reaching the goal (including what the trainee will do differently, resources needed, and type of support from managers and peers); (3) strategies for receiving feedback; and (4) expected results. The action plan also provides a progress check schedule, with specific dates and times when the manager and trainee agree to meet to discuss the progress being made in using learned capabilities on the job. The action planning process should start by identifying a goal and the strategies for reaching that goal. Once those are determined, strategies for obtaining feedback and identifying what the accomplishment of the goal will look like are completed. To complete their action plans, trainees may need additional technical support, such as access to experts who can answer questions or reference materials. Trainers or project managers can help trainees get the resources that they need to complete their action plans through either face-to-face or electronic meetings.

FIGURE 5.5
Levels of Management Support for Training

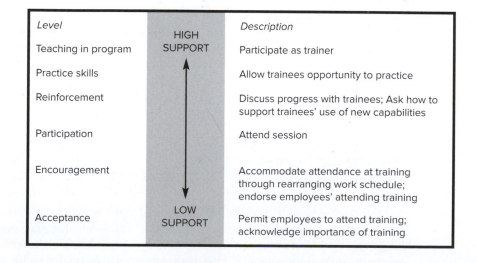

Level		Description
	HIGH SUPPORT	
Teaching in program		Participate as trainer
Practice skills		Allow trainees opportunity to practice
Reinforcement		Discuss progress with trainees; Ask how to support trainees' use of new capabilities
Participation		Attend session
Encouragement		Accommodate attendance at training through rearranging work schedule; endorse employees' attending training
Acceptance	LOW SUPPORT	Permit employees to attend training; acknowledge importance of training

FIGURE 5.6
A Sample
Action Plan

Training Topic_____
Goal *Include training content (knowledge, skill, behavior, competency, etc.) and application (project, problem, etc.)*
_____
_____
_____
_____

Strategies for Reaching Goal
Modifying behavior (What will I do differently?)
_____
_____
_____
_____

Resources needed (Equipment, financial)
_____
_____
_____
_____

Support from peers and manager (Be as specific as possible.)
_____
_____
_____
_____

Strategies for Receiving Feedback About My Progress *(Include meetings with peers and managers, self-monitoring of progress, customer reactions, etc.)*
_____
_____
_____
_____

Expected Results *(When I reach the goal, what will be different? Who will notice the difference? What will they notice?)*

What will be different?
_____
_____
_____

Who will notice?
_____
_____
_____

What will they notice?
_____
_____
_____

Progress Date Checks _____   _____   _____

Table 5.11 presents a checklist that can be used to determine the level of manager support before, during, and after training. The more statements that managers agree with, the greater their level of support for the training program. There are several ways to gain managers' support for training.[55] First, managers need to be briefed on the purpose of the

TABLE 5.11   **Checklist for Determining a Manager's Level of Support for Training**

Please read each statement and check all that apply to you:

_____ I have discussed the course and set learning objectives for employees.
_____ I understand the purpose of training.
_____ I know how training matches what the employee needs to learn.
_____ I know enough about the training to support employees use of what they learn when they return.
_____ The employee has completed action plans or other types of learning contracts designed to help apply learning on the job.
_____ I have communicated my expectations regarding training.
_____ I encourage employees to share what they have learning after the course or program.
_____ I encourage employees attending training to prevent distractions using phone forwarding and Out of Office e-mail notices.
_____ I allow employees to attend training.
_____ After training, I will debrief employees on the learning objectives and discuss how to apply them.
_____ After training, I will meet with employees to hear their ideas of how to apply what they learned.
_____ I will provide opportunities to share what they learned with other employees.
_____ I recognize and reward learning that is demonstrated on the job.

Source: Based on R. Saunderson, "ROI for recognition," *training* (November/December 2010): 52–54; A. Rossett, "That was a great class, but . . ." *Training & Development* (July 1997): 21.

program and its relationship to business objectives and the business strategy. Managers should be given the schedule of topics and a checklist of what they should do after the training to ensure that transfer occurs. Second, trainees should be encouraged to bring to the training session work problems and situations they face on the job. These can be used as practice exercises or put into action plans. Trainees should jointly identify the problems and situations with their managers. Third, information regarding the benefits of the course collected from past participants should be shared with managers. Fourth, trainers can assign trainees to complete action plans with their managers. Fifth, if possible, use managers as trainers. That is, train the managers first, and then give them the responsibility of training their subordinates.

To help ensure learning and transfer of training, Spectrum Health, a non-profit health system in Michigan creates shared accountability between manager and employees.[56] Every skill that is taught must be reinforced by a manager. To ensure that this occurs, when an employee plans to attend training, their manager is sent a coaching guide describing the training objectives. Also the guide provides questions that managers are supposed to ask employees, such as "What are you suppose to get out of the training?" After employees attend training, managers are asked to have another conversation with the employee to reinforce and apply what was learned. To support on-the-job training, InterContinental Hotels Group PLC is training managers to put together lists of learning objectives that can be discussed during pre-shift meetings with hotel employees. This helps managers and employees think about what they planned to learn, what was learned, and discuss strategies for practicing skills and applying them on the job.

At a minimum, meetings should be scheduled with managers to explain the purpose of the training and to set expectations that they will encourage attendance at the training session, provide practice opportunities, reinforce use of training, and follow up with trainees to determine the progress in using newly acquired capabilities.

Alltel Wireless uses managers as trainers.[57] When changes in systems, products, or policies occur, managers are the primary trainers for employees. Alltel uses a series of monthly teleconferences to educate managers in the field about new marketing strategies, new rate plans, new wireless or data services, and new offerings in products such as telephone headsets. The emphasis in the sessions is not only on communicating changes, but also on teaching managers to use learning principles effectively to train employees. For example, the teleconferences might have managers participate in a role-play designed to teach salespeople how to talk to customers about an equipment upgrade.

KLA-Tencor, a supplier of process control solutions for the semiconductor industry, values training and development, invests in training and development, and ties it to the company's business strategy. Because of its high level of investment in training, KLA-Tencor takes several steps with employees and managers to ensure that training is taken seriously and is used on the job.[58]

One of the company's concerns was that too many employees viewed training as a vacation from their job. To deal with this concern, KLA-Tencor has incorporated a pass/fail policy into its training curriculum. If an employee fails any section within a training course, management action is immediately taken. The employee is removed from the course, and a performance improvement plan is developed that requires the employee to retake the course. The pass/fail policy has resulted in improved employee competency levels, a reduction in marginally performing employees, and savings of $1.4 million. But the most important result has been that the policy has changed employees' view of training. Instead of leaving quickly when a training session has ended, trainees are staying late and forming study groups to complete homework and assignments. The class tardiness rate has dropped from 20 percent to zero. The pass/fail policy has also boosted the morale of the technical instructors because they can see that students are actually learning from and are interested in the courses.

Managers pay attention to the development of their staff because part of their incentive plan is based on training and development. The incentive plan comprises fiscal, productivity, and strategic goals. Training and development is considered a strategic goal. Typically, 10 percent to 30 percent of a manager's bonus pay is based on development. For some managers, as much as 75 percent of their bonus pay can be based on staff development, as measured by employee training and certification levels. The percentage varies depending on how critical the training is for business operations. The incentive plans also help employees receive bonuses, which are tied to productivity goals. Only employees who maintain training and certification levels are eligible for productivity bonuses. For some jobs, such as service engineer, bonuses can range from 10 percent to 15 percent. This incentive plan makes training the responsibility of not only managers, but each employee as well.

Peer Support

Transfer of training can also be enhanced by a support network among the trainees.[59] A **support network** is a group of two or more trainees who agree to meet and discuss their progress in using learned capabilities on the job. This may involve face-to-face meetings, communications via e-mail, or interactions on an electronic social network similar to Facebook. Trainees may share successful experiences in using training content on the job. They also might discuss how they obtained resources needed to use training content or how they coped with a work environment that interfered with the use of training content.

Trainers also might use a newsletter to show how trainees are dealing with transfer of training issues. Distributed to all trainees, the newsletter might feature interviews with trainees who have been successful in using new skills. Trainers may also provide trainees with a mentor—a more experienced employee, or even a peer who previously attended the same training program. The mentor can provide advice and support related to transfer of training issues (e.g., how to find opportunities to use the learned capabilities).

VSP Global, a company in the eyecare, eyeware, and eye technology business, uses Socialcast to support learning following training.[60] Socialcast, which has a Facebook-like interface, gives learners the opportunity to post and respond to questions, conduct discussions, and communicate with others about how they have applied learning. This allows employees to share their insights and gather new ones for any training course. Since Socialcast was introduced employees hve exchanged more than 7,000 messages, posted 12,000 comments in response to questions, and confirmed or clarified the accuracy of responses with more than 19,000 likes.

Opportunity to Use Learned Capabilities

Opportunity to use learned capabilities (**opportunity to perform**) refers to the extent to which the trainee is provided with or actively seeks experiences that allow application of the newly learned knowledge, skill, and behaviors from the training program. Opportunity to perform is influenced by both the work environment and trainee motivation. One way that trainees have the opportunity to use learned capabilities is through assigned work experiences (e.g., problems or tasks) that require their use. The trainees' manager usually plays a key role in determining work assignments. Opportunity to perform is also influenced by the degree to which trainees take personal responsibility to seek out assignments actively that allow them to use newly acquired capabilities.

Opportunity to perform is determined by breadth, activity level, and task type.[61] *Breadth* includes the number of trained tasks performed on the job. *Activity level* is the number of times or the frequency with which trained tasks are performed on the job. *Task type* refers to the difficulty or critical nature of the trained tasks that are actually performed on the job. Trainees who are given opportunities to use training content on the job are more likely to maintain learned capabilities than trainees given few opportunities.[62]

Opportunity to perform can be measured by asking former trainees to indicate (1) whether they perform a task, (2) how many times they perform the task, and (3) the extent to which they perform difficult and challenging tasks. Individuals who report low levels of opportunity to perform may be prime candidates for "refresher courses" (courses designed to let trainees practice and review training content). Refresher courses are necessary because these persons have likely experienced a decay in learned capabilities because they have not had opportunities to perform. Low levels of opportunity to perform may also indicate that the work environment is interfering with using new skills. For example, the manager may not support training activities or give the employee the opportunity to perform tasks using skills emphasized in training. Finally, low levels of opportunity to perform may indicate that training content is not important for the employee's job.

Technological Support

A **performance support system** is a computer application that can provide skills training, information access, and expert advice, as requested.[63] A performance support system may be used to enhance transfer of training by providing trainees with an electronic information source that they can refer to on an as-needed basis while they attempt to apply learned capabilities on the job. The use of performance support training is discussed in detail in Chapter Eight.

Northwestern Mutual uses several apps to provide performance support to its employees available on any device that can connect to the Internet.[64] The Learning Path Web app allows employees to access training courses and best practices related to products, planning, technology, and marketing. Its Technology in Your Practice app is a job aid that shows employees what tasks are performed for sales and what technology to use to perform the tasks. The app also provides links to the training page on Northwestern's intranet that can teach employees how to use the technology.

Using Knowledge Management for Learning and Transfer of Training

Recall from Chapter Two, "Strategic Training," that the term *knowledge* refers to what individuals or teams of employees know or know how to do (human and social knowledge), as well as a company's rules, processes, tools, and routines (structured knowledge). Knowledge is either tacit knowledge or explicit knowledge. Tacit knowledge is personal knowledge based on individual experience and influenced by perceptions and values. The communication of tacit knowledge requires personal communications through discussion and demonstrations. Explicit knowledge refers to manuals, formulas, and specifications that are described in formal language. Explicit knowledge can be managed by placing it in a knowledge database, or it can be managed by a knowledge management system. For example, Fluor Corporation has a web-based knowledge system that gives employees access to all procedures, guidelines, standards, and best practices needed for their specific job function.[65]

Knowledge management refers to the process of enhancing company performance by designing and implementing tools, processes, systems, structures, and cultures to create, capture, share, and use knowledge.[66] Knowledge management can help companies get products to market quicker, better serve customers, develop innovative products and services, and attract new employees and retain current ones by giving people the opportunity to learn and develop.

How might knowledge management occur? There are several ways to help create, share, and use knowledge:[67]

1. Use technology, e-mail, and social networking sites (such as Facebook or MySpace) or portals on the company intranet that allow people to store information and share it with others.
2. Publish directories that list what employees do, how they can be contacted, and the type of knowledge they have.
3. Develop informational maps that identify where specific knowledge is stored in the company.

4. Create chief information officer (CIO) and chief learning officer (CLO) positions for cataloging and facilitating the exchange of information in the company.

5. Require employees to give presentations to other employees about what they have learned from training programs that they have attended.

6. Allow employees to take time off from work to acquire knowledge, study problems, attend training, and use technology.

7. Create an online library of learning resources, such as journals, technical manuals, training opportunities, and video seminars.

8. Design office space to facilitate interaction between employees.

9. Create communities of practice (COPs) using face-to-face meetings, wikis, or blogs for employees who share a common interest in a subject (e.g., product, service, customer, or type of problem), where they can collaborate and share ideas, solutions, and innovations.

10. Use "after-action reviews" at the end of each project to review what happened and what can be learned from it.

11. Storytelling can be used to pass on knowledge. A story provides a description of what happened in a situation (e.g., problem, challenge), the actions taken (e.g., use of knowledge, skill, competency), and the resulting outcomes (e.g., happy customer, leak repaired, sales made).

12. Discuss and record top performers' passion for their jobs, what people need to know, and what they need to learn.

Consider the following examples of how companies share and create knowledge.

Knowledge sharing can involve reviews or audits of projects after they are completed, followed by sharing insights gained from the review with other employees. For example, the U.S. Army's "After-Action Review" process, adopted by many companies, involves a review of every mission, project, or critical activity.[68] The review involves considering four questions: (1) What did we set out to do? (2) What actually happened? (3) Why did it happen? and (4) What do we do (stop doing, continue to do, consider doing) next? Lessons learned are made available through websites and debriefings up and down the army leadership. Research has shown that After-Action Reviews are effective for facilitating team performance and are useful ways to increase leadership behavior following a development program.[69]

McAfee, a security company, uses a software program (Jive) that gives employees and customers the ability to access discussions, videos, and blogs.[70] The software recommends relevant content and identifies individuals who can help with specific issues. As a result, knowledge sharing has improved between customer support, sales, and research and development functions. Customer satisfaction ratings have improved 25 percent and call volume has decreased even as the company has added customers.

IBM provides its employees with an app that they can use on their smartphones to find fellow IBMers who have expertise and skills.[71] The app checks internal blogs, message boards, presentations, and employee profile databases. The app is used for identifying IBMers who have the skills that are needed on work teams or just answer questions.

NASA needs to manage knowledge to ensure that its space missions are successful.[72] At NASA knowledge management means sharing solutions and expertise across employees, teams, projects, programs, centers, and missions. This includes scientific, engineering, and technical knowledge, and business processes as well as know-how including tech-niques and procedures. To manage knowledge, NASA uses online tools including col-laboration sites, video and document libraries, search and tagging tools, case studies and publications, processes to identify and retain lessons learned, knowledge networks, and social exchanges such as forums and workshops.

As we mentioned in Chapter One, "Introduction to Employee Training and Develop-ment," many companies are interested in knowledge management because they are expe-riencing the loss of explicit and tacit knowledge resulting from older employees retiring. The electric power industry is facing the loss of many talented skilled workers, including engineers and managers.[73] (One estimate is that 30 to 40 percent of employees in the elec-tric power industry are eligible to retire.) They also are facing a shortage of high school graduates who have the science, technology, and math skills needed to immediately fill or even train for the jobs. This means that utility companies need to find ways to capture and share knowledge between experienced and less experienced employees. PacificCorp in Portland, Oregon, has a document that it asks employees to use to record the procedures they use. Puget Sound Energy, in Washington State, hired technical writers to interview employees and write reports. DTE Energy Corporation, in Ann Arbor, Michigan, encour-ages experienced engineers to mentor less experienced engineers. For example, the lead instrumentation and controls engineer at the Fermi II nuclear power plant, with forty-two years of experience, is mentoring a new engineer hired in 2007. They are working together on replacing instruments with new digital equipment, which is helping the less experienced engineer learn about the equipment and control room, as well as pick up the interpersonal skills needed for dealing with maintenance workers.

Keys for Effective Knowledge Management

There are several key considerations for effective knowledge management. They include collaborating between training and the information technology department, creating lead-ership positions in charge of knowledge management, providing easy-to-use technology, and ensuring employee trust and willingness to share knowledge.[74]

Training and Information Technology Collaboration   For knowledge management to be effective, the training department and information technology department must col-laborate.[75] Training can help develop the culture, as well as the content and learning strat-egies. Information technology develops the systems for accessing, sharing, and storing knowledge and delivering training. For example, the intranet at the Royal Bank of Canada serves as the central depository for information about initiatives completed, planned, or under way in the company. It also contains templates and other tools for training project managers. A separate website features summaries posted by employees who have attended conferences and courses. Technologists developed the infrastructure, and trainers recom-mended what features should be included.[76] After every U.S. Army mission, project, or critical activity, the lessons learned are identified, codified, and made accessible through websites.[77] The lessons learned include an evaluation of the four simple but critical ques-tions described previously (What did we set out to do? What happened? Why did it hap-pen? and What will we do again the next time and what will we try to improve?). The Center for Army Lessons Learned (CALL) has created a network that has disseminated more than 265,000 products, briefed more than 54,000 soldiers and leaders, and trans-ferred more than 24,000 lessons from military and civilian analysts to forces both in com-bat and stationed in the United States.

Create Knowledge Management Leadership Positions   Some companies, such as IBM, General Mills, and Randstad of North America, have created leadership positions to foster continuous learning and knowledge management. **Chief learning officers (CLOs)**, also known as **knowledge officers**, are the leaders of a company's knowledge management efforts. The CLO's job is to develop, implement, and link a knowledge/learning culture with the company's technology infrastructure, including databases and intranets. CLOs locate knowledge and find ways to create, capture, and distribute it. The CLO has to ensure that trainers, information technologists, and business units support and contribute to the development of knowledge management practices. The CLO also is responsible for actively supporting strategic business objectives by providing management direction and support for learning and development activities and by ensuring that knowledge management translates into visible benefits for the business.[78] For example, the CLO at Computer Sciences Corporation (CSC) sponsors a Learning Officer Council, which includes learning officers from the business units who help her understand the training and development needs of the company.[79] Her Department of Global Learning and Development recently created a development program designed to meet the learning needs of 1,800 senior executives and managers with high potential. The program is sponsored by the company's board of directors, chief operating officer, and chief executive officer. At Whirlpool, an appliance company, knowledge management has led to the development of "innovation mentors" around the world who encourage employees to try new ideas.[80]

Easy-to-Use Technology   Knowledge management systems fail for two reasons: the technology is too complicated or companies don't give enough consideration to how to motivate employees to share knowledge.[81] Knowledge management systems can make it harder, not easier, for employees to perform their jobs. If the system asks employees to use multiple search engines, collaboration tools, and document management software all on different computer systems, the knowledge management system won't be used. It is important to build the correct technology infrastructure and make it easy for employees to access and share information within the context of their jobs. A new approach to knowledge management imbeds knowledge into the workflow of the job. For example, to help physicians keep up with the many new articles on diseases, medication, and research that are added to the medical literature each year, Partners HealthCare imbeds knowledge though an online patient order management system.[82] The system links the most current clinical knowledge and the patient's history to the management system. The system may question physicians' actions, and they have to respond with a reason. Of course, the physicians still have the ability to override the system.

The sales support staff at Exact Target Inc., a software company, was having difficulty answering all the questions about products and clients from its 75 sales representatives.[83] Some of the technical questions took many hours to answer, and many of the same questions were asked by different sales representatives. To answer the questions, Exact Target started getting sales representatives to answer each other's questions using a website where all posted questions and answers are stored. The website is accessible from a computer, handheld device, or mobile phone. Sales representatives can subscribe to e-mail alerts every time a new question is posted. The sales representatives currently using the system are accessing it an average of three times a week. Twelve sales reps who have found the system to be effective in their work are encouraging and showing others how to use it. Sales representatives can rank each other's questions and answers using a five-star scale to identify the most useful posts or to identify inaccurate or incorrect postings. The search function on the site shows the postings with the highest rankings. Besides posting questions and answers, the sales reps can post useful information or documents they find in their work. Exact Target is combining the informal information exchange between sales representatives with formal training. The company has posted twenty-five training videos and case studies and plans to post more sales training information, client case studies, and videos with online quizzes that the sales reps will be required to pass in order to become certified as competent to sell certain software products or services.

Employee Trust and Willingness to Share Information   Trust and a willingness to share information are key personal factors that relate to knowledge sharing. Employees may not know or trust other employees, may hoard knowledge to have power over others, may fear that their ideas will be ridiculed or challenged, or may see knowledge sharing as involving too much work and additional responsibility.[84] To encourage knowledge sharing, companies must recognize and promote employees who learn, teach, and share. For example, the incentive for Xerox field technicians around the world to contribute to the company's maintenance tips database is that they become known as a thought leader or expert.[85] When the system was first available, technicians did not find it natural to submit what they knew. To overcome the engineers' anxiety, managers submitted suggestions from the mat company headquarters and offered rewards such as cash and T-shirts for submitting tips. Managers also featured the names of people who did contribute, resulting in contributors receiving notes from individuals who found their submissions to be helpful. Today, the system holds 70,000 suggestions and saves the company millions of dollars a year in repair costs. Other ways to encourage knowledge sharing are to show that ideas that are shared are used by the company and to show successes. AT&T used knowledge sharing to help global sales force teams share competitive information, which was useful in closing sales.

Because knowledge management has the potential to improve a company's competitive position, companies that are managing knowledge use several measures to evaluate the effectiveness of their knowledge management practices. (Evaluation is discussed in detail in Chapter Six.) These measures are related to company and customer benefits. They include the ability to attract and retain key employees; employee commitment to the company, the encouragement and facilitation of effective teamwork, the use of best practices and the review and updating of these practices, new product introductions, customer satisfaction, and repeat relationships with customers.[86]

Summary   Learning is an important aspect of any training program. But equally important is encouraging trainees to use learned capabilities on the job (transfer of training). This chapter discussed important program design issues that relate to the three phases of the instructional process: pretraining, during the learning event, and post-training. The chapter discussed effective program design, including selecting and preparing the training site, identifying and choosing the best trainers, communicating with trainees, and deciding how trainers can arrange the training site and create an instructional environment that is conducive to learning. Trainees' age and generation and personality differences should be considered in training design. The chapter introduced and discussed the importance of curriculum, curriculum maps, courses, and lessons, and showed how to use project management, design documents, and lesson plans in program design. Because many companies do not have the staff, resources, or expertise needed to design training programs, the chapter also discussed how to identify and choose a vendor or consultant for training services. The chapter concluded by discussing important post-training issues related to transfer of training, including how to create a supportive work environment, provide trainees with self-management skills, and gain manager and peer support. The important role that knowledge management in facilitating learning and transfer of training was discussed. For employees to use a knowledge management system, it needs to be easy to find and use knowledge, and they need to trust and a willingness to share knowledge.

Key Terms

program design, *202*
training site, *204*
concept map, *212*
application assignments, *214*
curriculum, *216*
course, *217*
program, *217*
project management, *217*
curriculum road map, *217*

detailed lesson plan, *220*
storyboard, *220*
trainee prerequisites, *222*
lesson plan overview, *223*
request for proposal (RFP), *225*
manager support, *228*
action plan, *229*
support network, *232*

opportunity to perform, *233*
performance support system, *234*
knowledge management, *234*
chief learning officers (CLOs), *237*
knowledge officers, *237*

Discussion Questions

1. What is a design document? What is included in a design document? How is it useful for training?
2. How might course design differ for baby boomers compared to Gen Xers?
3. How does a concept map help learners?
4. Explain the three phases of the instructional process, which phase do you think is most important? Why?
5. What could be done to increase the likelihood of transfer of training if the work environment conditions are unfavorable and cannot be changed?
6. Customer service training involves far transfer. What design features would you include in a customer service training program to ensure that transfer of training occurred? What is a curriculum road map? Why is it important?
7. What is an application assignment? Why should it be considered in designing a training program or course?
8. How might you motivate managers to play a more active role in ensuring transfer of training?
9. If you were asked to implement a knowledge management system, what would you recommend to ensure that employees shared and accessed knowledge? Explain your recommendations.

10. What type of seating arrangements would you choose for a training course that involved small-group case discussions? For a lecture including Powerpoint and use of YouTube videos? Explain your choices.

11. List the steps in project management. Discuss how each step helps in effective design.

Application Assignments

1. Develop a questionnaire to measure the degree to which the work environment supports transfer of training. Include the questions and the rating scales that you would use. Use the checklist in Table 5.10 as an example. Provide a rationale for your choice of rating scales and questions, i. e., why did you include them on your questionnaire?

2. Listed here are questions designed to measure trainees' motivation to transfer training. Ask several working friends, colleagues, or fellow employees these questions. Also, ask them to discuss why they responded the way they did.

    For each of the following statements, indicate whether you strongly agree, somewhat agree, somewhat disagree, or strongly disagree.

    a. The skills and knowledge that I have obtained by attending training programs have been helpful in solving work-related problems.

    b. Before I attend training programs, I usually consider how I will use the content of the program.

    c. I believe my job performance will likely improve if I use the knowledge and skills acquired in training programs.

    d. It is unrealistic to believe that mastering the content of training programs can improve my work productivity.

    e. I am usually able to use skills or knowledge acquired in training programs in my work.

    f. There are usually more problems than the trainers realize in applying training program content in my daily work activities.

    g. Before I attend training programs, I usually identify particular problems or projects that I would like the training to help me with.

    Prepare a written summary of what you learned about motivation to transfer training.

3. Design an action planning sheet that a manager and employee could use to facilitate transfer of training. Justify each category included in the action plan.

4. Draw a curriculum map for your major. How does this help you as the learner? How do you think this helps the faculty? Your academic adviser?

5. This assignment relates to Application Assignment 2 in Chapter Four. You now receive the following e-mail from the vice president of operations. Prepare an answer.

    Thanks for your recommendations regarding how to make the "Improving Service Quality Program" a success. To improve hotel staff ability to respond effectively to customer complaints (that is, "recovery"), we have incorporated many of your ideas into the program, including the following:

    a. Having trainees bring an example of a customer problem to class.

    b. Giving trainees the opportunity to practice dealing with irate customers.

    c. Providing trainees with feedback during role-plays.

    d. Having trainers identify and communicate objectives of the program to trainees.

    e. Having trainers communicate to the trainees specific key behaviors related to customer service.

    I am now concerned about how to make sure that our training investments pay off. That is, I am really interested in seeing that employees effectively and continuously apply in their jobs the skills and knowledge they have gained in training. What recommendations do you have?

6. Go to http://sans.org, the website for the SANS Institute, which provides information security training. Under "Find Training," move down to "Training Curricula" and click on one of the topics listed. What information is provided? How is it useful for learners? For instructors?

7. One way to diagnose transfer of training problems or to ensure that transfer of training occurs is to complete the matrix shown below. This matrix considers the responsibilities of the manager, the trainer, and the trainee for transfer of training before, during, and after training. Complete each cell of the matrix showing manager, trainer, and trainee responsibilities.

	Before Training	During Training	After Training
Manager			
Trainer			
Trainee			

8. Go to *https://www.youtube.com/watch?v=RuiSExp2s7M*, and watch the training video for new servers at Country Cookin restaurants. What features does this video include that would help new servers learn about the job and their role at Country Cookin? Assume you were an instructional designer or trainer at Country Cookin. Provide your recommendations for designing a training program that includes this video.

9. Go to *www.weavethepeople.com*, the website for a company that makes "weaves." Review the sample weaves on the website. How are weaves useful for knowledge management and knowledge sharing?

10. Watch the YouTube video about knowledge sharing at Accenture at *http://www.youtube.com/watch?v=ssZPn1r5O6c*. In what ways does Accenture expect employees will contribute through learning by sharing knowledge? Which do you believe is most beneficial? Why?

Case:

Program Redesign Reduces Costs and Satisfies Learners

Autodesk, Inc., is a leader in three-dimensional design, engineering, and entertainment software for customers in manufacturing, architecture, building, construction, and the entertainment industries. (In fact, most Academy Award winners for Best Visual Effects used Autodesk software.)

Traditionally, Autodesk used to hold two annual training events for its partners in the United States and Canada. These events were attended by more than 300 salespeople, who learned about new product features and the customer base, and more than 700 engineers, who learned how to support the products. The high cost, planning demands, and logistical support needed for the annual training events motivated Autodesk to redesign the training.

Autodesk decided to convert the face-to-face, instructor-led training event to a virtual, instructor-led training event. To develop the virtual classroom, the program's core content (which included Microsoft PowerPoint presentations and product demonstrations) was reviewed. Quality content was kept and other materials were either revised or eliminated from the program. To make the content more engaging, interactive, and to keep participants motivated, polls, questions and answers, and quizzes were developed. Questions, exercises, and polls kept learners' attention and provided insight into whether learning was occurring. The instructional designers created "rooms" in which each class was held. They also developed pods that delivered a specific learning activity, such as conducting an exercise. Session maps were created for instructors to use as outlines for their presentations. This helped the instructors organize content, plan interactions, and identify necessary technical support. All roles and responsibilities for the virtual learning event were carefully defined. To help facilitate the instruction and aid the instructor, each event had a producer, host, and moderator. The producer facilitated the learning event, loaded files for sharing, was responsible for rehearsing, and kept the session running on time. The host presented an overview of the session, reviewed tools, and providing closing comments. The moderator was responsible for answering learner questions and solving technical issues. The entire crew held practice sessions to help the instructor become comfortable with giving the class and keep the pace fast to maintain the learners' interest.

Identify the design elements which help ensure that participants learned and put it into practice. Explain how these design elements encourage learning and transfer.

Source: S. Hall, "Virtual instructor-led training: Powerful, not PowerPoint," *T+D* (July 2010): 72–73; *www.autodesk.com* website for Autodesk.

Endnotes

1. S. Bailey, "The answer to transfer," *Chief Learning Office* (November 2014): 33–41.

2. L. Nikravan, "Learning is the business at Procter & Gamble," *Chief Learning Officer* (June 2014): 30–31.

3. B. Smith and B. Delahaye, *How to Be an Effective Trainer* (New York: Wiley, 1987); M. Van Wart, N. Cayer, and S. Cook, *Handbook of Training and Development for the Public Sector* (San Francisco: Jossey-Bass, 1993).

4. G. Seli, "On-site vs. off-site training," *training* (March/April 2014): 20–22.

5. M. Weinstein, "Training spaces," *training* (September/October 2010): 34–37.

6. J. Meister and K. Willyerd, *The 2020 Workplace* (New York: HarperCollins, 2010).

7. L. Nadler and Z. Nadler, *Designing Training Programs,* 2d ed. (Houston: Gulf Publishing Company, 1994); T. W. Goad, "Building Presentations: A Top-Down Approach," in *Effective Training Delivery* (Minneapolis: Lakewood Publishing, 1989): 21–24; F. H. Margolis and C. R. Bell, *Managing the Learning Process* (Minneapolis: Lakewood, 1984).

8. M. Welber, "Save by growing your own trainers," *Workforce* (September 2002): 44–48; T. Adams, A. Kennedy, and M. Marquart, "The reluctant trainer," *T+D* (March 2008): 24–27.

9. P. Hinds, M. Patterson, and J. Pfeffer, "Bothered by abstraction: The effects of expertise on knowledge transfer and subsequent novice performance," *Journal of Applied Psychology,* 86 (2001): 1232–1243; S. Merrill, "Training the Trainer 101," *T+D* (June 2008): 28–31.

10. M. Weinstein, "Training is in SCC's genes," *training* (January/February 2011): 44–46.

11. E. Betof, L. Owens, and S. Todd, "The key to success in a VUCA world," *T+D* (July 2014): 38–43.

12. D. Booher, "Make the room work for you," *Training and Development,* S5–S7; D. Abernathy, "Presentation tips from the pros," *Training and Development* (October 1999): 19–25; N. Germond, "Off to a good start: Tips for new trainers," *T+D* (February 2015): 29–31.

13. Steelcase, "Workplace Issues: One in a Series. Learning Environments for the Information Age," available from the Steelcase website, *www.steelcase.com*, accessed March 1, 2006.
14. G. Dutton, "Are you tuned in to your trainees?" *training* (January/February 2011): 104–105.
15. K. Tyler, "Generation gaps," *HR Magazine* (January 2008): 69–72.
16. P. Ketter, "What can training do for Brown?" *T+D* (May 2008): 30–36.
17. J. Callahan, D. Kiker, and T. Cross, "Does method matter? A meta-analysis of the effects of training method on older learner training performance," *Journal of Management,* 29 (2003): 663–680; S. Milligan, "Wisdom of the ages," *HR Magazine* (November 2014): 22–27.
18. A. Ort, "Embrace differences when training intergenerational groups," *T+D* (April 2014): 60–65.
19. R. Daisley, "Considering personality type in adult learning: Using the Myers-Briggs Type Indicator in instructor preparation at PricewaterhouseCoopers," *Performance Improvement* (February 2011): 15–23.
20. M. Weinstein, "Taking training's measure," *training* (November/December 2014): 42–43.
21. M. Torrance, "Nine moments of learning," *T+D* (September 2014): 76–77.
22. E. Albu, "Presenting course outlines in a flow chart format," *T+D* (February 2010): 76–77.
23. J. Davis, M. Balda, and D. Rock, "Keep an eye on time," *T+D* (January 2014): 50–53.
24. K. Albrecht, "Take time for effective learning," *training,* (July 2004): 38–42; K. Kapp, "Matching the right design strategy to the right content," *T+D* (July 2011): 48–52.
25. S. Maxey, "Putting the focus on coaching," *T+D* (April 2014): 42–46.
26. A. Towler and R. Dipboye, "Effects of trainer expressiveness, organizations, and trainee goal orientation on training outcomes," *Journal of Applied Psychology,* 86 (2001): 664–673.
27. A. Towler and R. Dipboye, "Effects of Trainer Expressiveness, Organization, and Trainee Goal Orientation on Training Outcomes"; T. Sitzmann et al., "A review and meta-analysis of the nomological network of trainee reactions," *Journal of Applied Psychology,* 93 (2008): 280–295.
28. D. Eden and A. Shani, "Pygmalion goes to boot camp: Expectancy, leadership, and trainee performance," *Journal of Applied Psychology,* 67 (1982): 194–199.
29. J. Shapiro, E. King, and M. Quinones, "Expectation of obese trainees: How stigmatized trainee characteristics influence training effectiveness," *Journal of Applied Psychology,* 92 (2007): 239–249.
30. A. Barron, "Discussion prompts," *T+D* (January 2014): 24–26.
31. M. Hequet. "Training No One Wants," *training* (January 2004): 22–28.
32. P. Harris, "Encouraging talent to rise and shine," *T+D* (October 2014): 68–70.
33. P. Kirschner, C. Carr, and P. Sloep, "How expert designers design," *Performance Improvement Quarterly,* 15 (2002): 86–104.
34. J. Phillips, "Seven issues to consider when designing training curricula," *Performance Improvement* (August 2010): 9–15.
35. Ibid.
36. A. Harris, "Training in spades," *T+D* (June 2013): 58–62.
37. M. Driscoll and S. Carliner, *Advanced Web-based Training Strategies: Unlocking Instructionally Sound Online Learning* (Hoboken, NJ: Wiley, 2005).
38. G. Piskurich, *Rapid Instructional Design* (San Francisco: Pfeiffer, 2006).
39. M. Van Wart, N. J. Cayer, and S. Cook, *Handbook of Training and Development for the Public Sector.*
40. J. Barbazette, "Take the pain out of writing training materials," *T+D* (April 2013): 108–109.
41. From "Knowledge Transfer Strategies," from *http://www.ohr.sc.gov,* accessed March 1, 2015.
42. G. P. Latham and K. N. Wexley, *Increasing Productivity Through Performance Appraisal,* 2d ed. (Reading, MA: Addison-Wesley, 1994).
43. Ibid.
44. P. Kiger, "Health Partners delivers training that works," *Workforce* (November 2002): 60–64.
45. G. Mcardle and S. Salamy, "Drilling to the core of training and education," *T+D* (September 2013: 52.
46. C. Anderson, "Do you have the right business partners?" *Chief Learning Officer* (March 2014): 48–50.

47. B. Gerber, "How to buy training programs," *Training* (June 1989): 59–68. J. McMillan, "Develop RFPs That Produce the Best Outcomes", *T+D* (July 2013): 78–79.

48. D. Blackmen, "Consultants' advice on diversity was anything but diverse," *The Wall Street Journal* (March 11, 1997): A1, A16.

49. R. Zemke and J. Armstrong, "How long does it take? (The sequel)," *Training* (May 1997): 11–15.

50. S. L. Yelon, and J. K. Ford, "Pursuing a multidimensional view of transfer," *Performance Improvement Quarterly,* 12 (1999), 58–78; K. Kapp, "Matching the right design strategy to the right content," *T+D* (July 2011): 48–52; M. Merrill, "First principles of instruction," *Educational Technology Research and Development*, 50 (2002): 43–59.

51. M. Machin, "Planning, Managing, and Optimizing Transfer of Training," in *Creating Implementing, and Managing Effective Training and Development,* ed. K. Kraiger (San Francisco: Jossey-Bass, 2002): 263–301; J. Kim and C. Lee, "Implications of near and far transfer of training on structured on-the-job training," *Advances in Developing Human Resources* (November 2001): 442–451; S. Yelon and J. Ford, "Pursuing a multidimensional view of transfer," *Performance Improvement Quarterly,* 12 (1999): 58–78.

52. S. Yelon and J. Ford, "Pursuing a multidimensional view of transfer," *Performance Improvement Quarterly* 12 (1999): 55–78.

53. H. Martin, "Lessons learned," *The Wall Street Journal* (December 15, 2008): R11.

54. J. M. Cusimano, "Managers as facilitators," *Training and Development,* 50 (1996): 31–33; R. Bates, "Managers as Transfer Agents," in *Improving Learning Transfer in Organizations,* ed. E. Holton and T. Baldwin (San Francisco: Jossey-Bass, 2003): 243–270.

55. S. B. Parry. "Ten ways to get management buy-in," *Training and Development* (September 1997): 21–22; M. L. Broad and J. W. Newstrom, *Transfer of Training* (Reading, MA: Addison-Wesley, 1992); S. Bailey, "The answer to transfer," *Chief Learning Office* (November 2014): 33–41; R. Hewes, "Step by step," *T+D* (February 2014): 56–61.

56. F. Kalman, "Taking control of on-the-job learning," *Chief Learning Office* (August 2014): 49–54.

57. J. Gordon. "Getting serious about supervisory training," *Training* (February 2006): 27–29.

58. K. Ellis, "Developing for dollars," *Training* (May 2003): 34–39; G. Johnson, "KLA-Tencor," *Training* (Match 2003): 48–49.

59. C. M. Petrini, "Bringing it back to work," *Training and Development Journal* (December 1990): 15–21.

60. Global Training and Development Team, VSP, "Social earning," (September/October 2013): 46–47.

61. J. Ford, M. Quinones, D. Sego, and J. Sorra. "Factors Affecting the Opportunity to Perform Trained Tasks on the Job," *Personnel Psychology* 45 (1992): 511–527.

62. M. Quinones, J. Ford, D. Sego, and E. Smith, "The effects of individual and transfer environment characteristics on the opportunity to perform trained tasks," *Training Research Journal,* 1 (1995/96): 29–48.

63. G. Stevens and E. Stevens, "The truth about EPSS," *Training and Development*, 50 (1996): 59–61.

64. M. Weinstein, "Taking training's measure," *training* (November/December 2014): 42–43.

65. T. Davenport, L. Prusak, and B. Strong, "Putting ideas to work," *The Wall Street Journal* (March 10, 2008): R11.

66. D. DeLong and L. Fahey, "Diagnosing cultural barriers to knowledge management," *Academy of Management Executive,* 14 (2000): 113–127; A. Rossett, "Knowledge management meets analysis," *Training and Development* (May 1999): 63–68; M. Van Buren, "A yardstick for knowledge management," *Training and Development* (May 1999): 71–78.

67. Gephart, Marsick, Van Buren, and Spiro, "Learning Organizations Come Alive"; T. Davenport, L. Prusak, and B. Strong, "Putting ideas to work", The Wall Street Journal (March 10, 2008): R11. From "Knowledge Transfer Strategies," from *http://www.ohr.sc.gov*, accessed March 1, 2015; R. Grbavac and W. Seidman, "Capturing the wisdom and knowledge of top performers," *T+D* (December 2014): 76–77.

68. "Center for Army Lessons Learned Named in Info World 100 for 2008 Top IT Solutions," at http://usacac .army.mil/cacz/call/index.asp, website for the Center for Army Lessons Learned, accessed March 30, 2009.

69. A. Villado and J. Arthur, "The comparative effect of subjective and objective after-action reviews on team performance on a complex task," *Journal of Applied Psychology*, 98 (2013): 514–528 ; S. DeRue,

J. Nahrgang , J. Hollenbeck , and K. Workman, "A quasi-experimental study of after-event reviews and leadership development," *Journal of Applied Psychology*, 97(2012): 997–1015.

70. S. Ante, "Identifying experts in the company," *Wall Street Journal* (September 16, 2013): R6.

71. L. Gentile, "Information station," *T+D* (January 2015): 88.

72. E. Hoffman and J. Boyle, "Managing mission knowledge at NASA," *T+D* (July 2014): 50–55.

73. B. Roberts, "Can they keep the lights on?" *HR Magazine* (June 2010): 62–68.

74. J. Collins, "It's all in here! How do we get it out?" *T+D* (January 2011): 59–61.

75. J. Gordon, "Intellectual capital and you," *Training* (September 1999): 30–38; D. Zielinski, "Have you shared a bright idea today?" *Training* (July 2000): 65–68.

76. K. Ellis, "Share best practices globally," *Training* (July 2001): 32–38.

77. D. Garvin, A. Edmondson, and F. Gino, "Is yours a learning organization?" *Harvard Business Review* (March 2008): 109–116; "Center for Army Lessons Learned Named in Info World 100 for 2008 Top IT Solutions."

78. T. O'Driscoll, B. Sugrue, and M. Vona, "The C-level and the value of learning," *T+D* (October 2005): 70–77.

79. J. Salopek. "Computer Sciences Corporation," *T+D* (October 2005): 58.

80. D. Pringle, "Learning gurus adapt to escape corporate axes," *The Wall Street Journal* (January 7, 2003): B1, B4.

81. P. Babcock, "Shedding light on knowledge management," *HR Magazine* (May 2004): 46–50; R. Davenport, "Does knowledge management still matter?" *T+D* (February 2005): 19–25.

82. Babcock, "Shedding Light on Knowledge Management."

83. K. Spors, "Getting Workers to Share Their Know-how with Their Peers," *The Wall Street Journal* (April 3, 2008): B6.

84. T. Aeppel, "On factory floor, top workers hide secrets to success," *The Wall Street Journal* (July 1, 2002): A1, A15. S. Wang, R. Noe, and Z. Wang, "Motivating knowledge sharing in knowledge management systems: A quasi-field experiment," *Journal of Management*, 40 (2014): 978–1009; S. Wang and R. Noe, "Knowledge sharing from a human resource perspective: A review and directions for future research," *Human Resource Management Review*, 20 (2010): 115–131; S. Kim and S. Yun, "The effects of coworker knowledge sharing on performance and its boundary conditions: An interactional perspective," *Journal of Applied Psychology*, 100 (2015): 575–582.

85. S. Thurm, "Companies Struggle to Pass on Knowledge That Workers Acquire," *The Wall Street Journal*, (January 23, 2006): B1.

86. M. Van Buren, "A yardstick for knowledge management," *Training and Development* (May 1999): 71–78; L. Bassi and D. McMumer, "Developing measurement systems for managing in the knowledge era," *Organizational Dynamics*, 34 (2005): 185–196.

Chapter **Six**

Training Evaluation

Objectives

After reading this chapter, you should be able to

1. Explain why evaluation is important.
2. Identify and choose outcomes to evaluate a training program.
3. Discuss the process used to plan and implement a good training evaluation.
4. Discuss the strengths and weaknesses of different evaluation designs.
5. Choose the appropriate evaluation design based on the characteristics of the company and the importance and purpose of the training.
6. Conduct a cost-benefit analysis for a training program.
7. Explain the role of Big Data workforce analytics and dashboards in determining the value of training practices.

Evaluation Helps Ensure Guests Find Paradise on Hawaii's North Coast

Turtle Bay Resort is located on the stunning coastline of Oahu, Hawaii. Guests can choose many activities while enjoying the beautiful surroundings at the at the resort including dining on farm-to-table meals, enjoying the ocean while surfing and paddling, relaxing with a massage, or taking an invigorating horseback ride. New management made a $40 million investment and renovations to revitalize the resort and inspire its guests to make them part of the local community. They recognized that the physical changes to the resort were necessary and important. But they also believe that investing in training leads to happier and more engaged employees, and, in turn, leads to satisfied guests. Training at Turtle Bay includes classroom learning, role-plays, and social learning. All training incorporates Turtle Bay's 6 Values that provide the standard by which employees work and serve guests. The values relate to time (Manawa), goodness (Pono), caring for others (Malama), support of family (Hanai), Aloha (kindness), and local engagement and culture (Kama'aina). The values include underlying behaviors and practices such as greeting guests promptly (Manawa), hold others accountable (Malama), demonstrating interest in peers (Hanai), engage guests and peers (Aloha), and treat locals as guests and guests as locals (Kama'aina). Every employee is required to attend a training program that focuses on the values. Managers are asked to complete an individual development plan based on their self-rating as well as ratings from employees, peers, and their manager on how well they applied these values at work. Employees also complete a self-assessment and personal improvement plan based on the values.

Laulima (many hands working together), a service quality training program, is an extension of the values. The program includes modules on greeting guests, service delivery, service recovery, and knowledge of service, food and beverages, history, and culture. The program was developed using input from employees who were chosen as the best service providers at Turtle Bay. Each module has a workbook that guides employees through a series of exercises. New employees attend a scavenger hunt to help them understand the property and its plants and animals. Managers are expected to help teach employees and reinforce what they learn. Employees also have to learn how to use Guidepost, a lobby experience center that provides concierge and guest services in an interactive space. Guidepost includes iPads and touchscreen panels for viewing activities and reviewing, learning about, and booking local activities.

To reinforce delightful customer service and emphasize the importance of training, Turtle Bay has several rewards programs. The Ho'ohana Awards recognize employees for exceptional service for guest and employees. Ali'i and Ilima Awards for exceptional service are given each quarter to a manager and two other employees. The Best of the Best Award is given to outstanding employees who continuously demonstrate exceptional service.

Turtle Bay collects several different types of data to determine the success of training. The most important measure is guest satisfaction, which includes using social media tools like TripAdvisor, Revinate, and Market Metrix. A values feedback system is used to determine how well employees are applying the Value practices. This data is evaluated for employees, managers, department, and functional areas. Occupancy rates, market share, sales performance, internal promotions, and turnover are used as financial measures. To assess employee engagement, two surveys are conducted each year.

Source: L. Freifeld, "Turtle Bay turnaround," *training* (January/February 2015): 120–123.

INTRODUCTION

As the opening vignette illustrates, Turtle Bay Resort wants to show that the time, money, and effort devoted to training makes a difference. That is, the training function was interested in assessing the effectiveness of training programs. **Training effectiveness** refers to the benefits that the company and the trainees receive from training. Benefits for trainees may include learning new skills or behaviors. Benefits for the company may include increased sales and more satisfied customers. A training evaluation measures specific outcomes or criteria to determine the benefits of the program. **Training outcomes** or **criteria** refer to measures that the trainer and the company use to evaluate training programs. To determine the effectiveness of training, an evaluation needs to occur. **Training evaluation** refs to the process of collecting the outcomes needed to determine whether training is effective. For Turtle Bay, the outcomes included engagement, guest satisfaction, and financial measures such as occupancy rates. Although not discussed in the vignette, Turtle Bay also has to be confident that the data its information-gathering process is providing accurate data for making conclusions about the effectiveness of its training programs. The **evaluation design** refers to the collection of information—including what, when, how, and from whom—that will be used to determine the effectiveness of the training program. Any organization that evaluates training has to be confident that training—rather than same other factor—is responsible for changes in the outcomes of interest (e.g., turnover, productivity). The degree of confidence that any changes in the outcomes of interest is due to training depends on the type of evaluation design that is used.

Recall the Instructional Systems Design model shown in Figure 1.1 and the topics covered in Chapters Two through Five. The information from the needs assessment, the characteristics of the learning environment, and the steps taken to ensure transfer of training should all be used to develop an evaluation plan. In order to identify appropriate training outcomes, a company needs to look at its business strategy, its organizational analysis (Why are we conducting training? How is it related to the business?), its person analysis (Who needs training?), its task analysis (What is the training content?), the learning objectives of the training, and its plan for training transfer.

This chapter will help you understand why and how to evaluate training programs. The chapter begins by discussing the types of outcomes used in training program evaluation. The next section of the chapter discusses the practical factors to consider when choosing an evaluation design. An overview of the types of designs is presented. The chapter reviews the process involved in conducting a program evaluation. The chapter concludes with a discussion of metrics that can be used to evaluate the strategic value of the training function.

REASONS FOR EVALUATING TRAINING

Companies are investing millions of dollars in training programs to help gain a competitive advantage. Companies invest in training because learning creates knowledge; often, it is this knowledge that distinguishes successful companies and employees from those who are not. Research summarizing the results of studies that have examined the linkage between training and human resource outcomes (such as attitudes and motivation, behaviors, and human capital), organizational performance outcomes (performance and productivity), or financial outcomes (profits and financial indicators) has found that companies that conduct training are likely to have more positive human resource outcomes and greater performance outcomes.[1] The influence of training is largest for organizational performance outcomes and human resource outcomes and weakest for financial outcomes. This result is not surprising, given that training can least affect an organization's financial performance and may do so through its influence on human resource practices. As emphasized in Chapter Two, "Strategic Training," training is more strongly related to organizational outcomes when it is matched with the organization's business strategy and capital intensity. Because companies have made large dollar investments in training and education and view training as a strategy to be successful, they expect the outcomes or benefits related to training to be measurable.

Asurion developed a leadership development program for high-potential employees.[2] The program includes on-the-job rotations, mentoring and coaching from senior leaders, and classroom and on-the-job training. Asurion conducted an evaluation to determine the program's influence on both high-potential employees and business results. Evaluation showed that since it was developed, 71 percent of program participants have received promotions. Also, program participants have rated professional development as one of the top three strengths on the company's engagement surveys. Departments have found that projects completed during the job rotations have led to positive business results, including reducing product handling time and improved quality scores. At Jiffy Lube, training evaluation involves more than just counting the number of programs employees attend each year.[3] Jiffy Lube's business depends on properly servicing customers' cars so they are satisfied and will be repeat customers. As a result, Jiffy Lube employees must be certified to perform a service. Jiffy Lube tracks both certifications and their relationship to business results. They track both employee and store-level certifications. Entry-level certifications must be completed within thirty days after an employee is hired. Seventy-six percent of Jiffy Lube's stores are at 80 to 100 percent certification. One-third of the stores with 100 percent certification have average customer sales 9 percent higher than all stores.

Training evaluation provides a way to understand the investments that training produces and provides information needed to improve training.[4] If the company receives an inadequate return on its investment in training, the company will likely reduce its investment in training or look for training providers outside the company who can provide training experiences that improve performance, productivity, customer satisfaction, or whatever other outcomes the company is interested in achieving. Training evaluation provides the data needed to demonstrate that training does offer benefits to the company. Training evaluation involves both formative and summative evaluation.[5]

Formative Evaluation

Formative evaluation refers to the evaluation of training that takes place during program design and development. That is, formative evaluation helps ensure that (1) the training program is well organized and runs smoothly, and (2) trainees learn and are satisfied with the program. Formative evaluation provides information about how to make the program better; it usually involves collecting qualitative data about the program. Qualitative data include opinions, beliefs, and feelings about the program. Formative evaluations ask customers, employees, managers, and subject-matter experts (SMEs) their opinions on the description of the training content and objectives and the program design. These people are also asked to evaluate the clarity and ease of use of a part of the training program that is demonstrated to them in the way that it will be delivered (e.g., online, face-to-face, or video).[6] The formative evaluation is conducted either individually or in groups before the program is made available to the rest of the company. Trainers may also be involved to measure the time requirements of the program. As a result of the formative evaluation, training content may be changed to be more accurate, easier to understand, or more appealing. The training method can be adjusted to improve learning (e.g., provide trainees with more opportunities to practice or give feedback). Also, introducing the training program as early as possible to managers and customers helps in getting them to buy into the program, which is critical for their role in helping employees learn and transfer skills. It also allows their concerns to be addressed before the program is implemented.

Formative evaluation involves pilot testing. **Pilot testing** refers to the process of previewing the training program with potential trainees and managers or with other customers (persons who are paying for the development of the program). Pilot testing can be used as a "dress rehearsal" to show the program to managers, trainees, and customers. It should also be used for formative evaluation. For example, a group of potential trainees and their managers may be asked to preview or pilot test a web-based training program. As they complete the program, trainees and managers may be asked to provide their opinions about whether graphics, videos, or music used in the program contributed to (or interfered with) learning. They may also be asked how easy it was to move through the program and complete the exercises, and they may be asked to evaluate the quality of feedback the training program provided after they completed the exercises. The information gained from this preview would be used by program developers to improve the program before it is made available to all employees. St. George Bank developed a new web-based training system for bank tellers.[7] Before the program was provided to all bank tellers, it was reviewed by a small group of them who were considered to be typical users of the program. The tellers provided suggestions for improvement, and the instructional designers incorporated their suggestions into the final version of the program.

Summative Evaluation

Summative evaluation refers to an evaluation conducted to determine the extent to which trainees have changed as a result of participating in the training program. That is, have trainees acquired knowledge, skills, attitudes, behavior, or other outcomes identified in the training objectives? Summative evaluation may also include measuring the monetary benefits (also known as *return on investment* or *ROI*) that the company receives from the program. Summative evaluation usually involves collecting quantitative (numerical) data through tests, ratings of behavior, or objective measures of performance such as volume of sales, accidents, or patents.

From the discussion of summative and formative evaluation, it is probably apparent to you why a training program should be evaluated:

1. To identify the program's strengths and weaknesses. This includes determining if the program is meeting the learning objectives, if the quality of the learning environment is satisfactory, and if transfer of training to the job is occurring.

2. To assess whether the content, organization, and administration of the program—including the schedule, accommodations, trainers, and materials—contribute to learning and the use of training content on the job.

3. To identify which trainees benefit most or least from the program.

4. To assist in marketing programs through the collection of information from participants about whether they would recommend the program to others, why they attended the program, and their level of satisfaction with the program.

5. To determine the financial benefits and costs of the program.

6. To compare the costs and benefits of training versus nontraining investments (such as work redesign or a better employee selection system).

7. To compare the costs and benefits of different training programs to choose the best program.

OVERVIEW OF THE EVALUATION PROCESS

Before the chapter explains each aspect of training evaluation in detail, you need to understand the evaluation process, which is summarized in Figure 6.1. The previous discussion of formative and summative evaluation suggests that training evaluation involves scrutinizing the program both before and after the program is completed. Figure 6.1 emphasizes that training evaluation must be considered by managers and trainers before training has actually occurred. As was suggested earlier in this chapter, information gained from the training design process shown in Figure 6.1 is valuable for training evaluation.

The evaluation process should begin with determining training needs (as discussed in Chapter Three, "Needs Assessment"). Needs assessment helps identify what knowledge, skills, behavior, or other learned capabilities are needed. Needs assessment also helps identify where the training is expected to have an impact. Needs assessment helps focus the evaluation by identifying the purpose of the program, the resources needed (human, financial, and company), and the outcomes that will provide evidence that the program has been effective.[8] The next step in the process is to identify specific, measurable training objectives to guide the program. The characteristics of good objectives are discussed in Chapter Four, "Learning and Transfer of Training." The more specific and measurable these objectives are, the easier it is to identify relevant outcomes for the evaluation. Besides considering the learning and program objectives in developing learning outcomes, it is also important to consider the expectations of those individuals who support the program and have an interest in it (stakeholders such as trainees, managers, and trainers).[9] If the needs assessment was done well, the stakeholders' interests likely overlap considerably with the learning and program objectives. Analysis of the work environment to determine transfer of training (discussed in Chapter Five, "Program Design") can be useful for determining how training content will be used on the job. Based on the learning objectives and analysis of transfer of training, outcome measures are designed to assess the extent to which learning and transfer have occurred.

FIGURE 6.1
The Evaluation Process

Sources: Based on D. A. Grove and C. Ostroff, "Program Evaluation," in *Developing Human Resources,* ed. K. N. Wexley (Washington, D. C.: Bureau of National Affairs, 1991): 5-185–5-220; K. Kraiger, D. McLinden, and W. Casper, "Collaborative Planning for Training Impact," *Human Resource Management* (Winter 2004): 337–351.

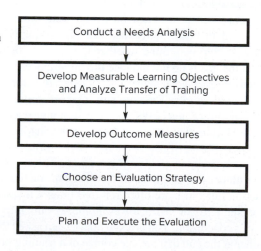

Once the outcomes have been identified, the next step is to determine an evaluation strategy. Factors such as expertise, how quickly the information is needed, change potential, and the organizational culture should be considered in choosing a design. Planning and executing the evaluation involves previewing the program (formative evaluation), as well as collecting training outcomes based on the evaluation design. The results of the evaluation are used to modify, market, or gain additional support for the program. The results of the evaluation should also be used to encourage all stakeholders in the training process—including managers, employees, and trainers—to design or choose training that helps the company meet its business strategy and helps managers and employees meet their goals.[10]

OUTCOMES USED IN THE EVALUATION OF TRAINING PROGRAMS

To evaluate its training program, a company must decide *how* it will determine the program's effectiveness; that is, it must identify what training outcomes or criteria it will measure.

Table 6.1 shows the six categories of training outcomes: reaction outcomes, learning or cognitive outcomes, behavior and skill-based outcomes, affective outcomes, results, and return on investment.[11]

Table 6.1 shows training outcomes, the level they correspond to in Kirkpatrick's evaluation model, a description of each of the outcomes and how they are measured, and the question that each outcome can help answer. Kirkpatrick's original evaluation model included only four levels (reaction, learning, behavior, and results) but recent thinking suggests a fifth level, return on investment (ROI), is necessary to demonstrate the financial value of training. Both level 1 and level 2 outcomes (reactions and learning) are collected at the completion of training, before trainees return to the job. Level 3 outcomes (behavior/skills) can also be collected at the completion of training to determine trainees' behavior or skill level at that point. To determine whether trainees are using training content back on the job (i.e., whether transfer of training has occurred), level 3, level 4, and/or level 5 outcomes can be collected. Level 3 criteria can be collected to determine whether behavior/skills are being used on the job. Level 4 and level 5 criteria (results and return on investment) can also be used to determine whether training has resulted in an improvement in business results, such as productivity or customer satisfaction. These criteria also help determine whether the benefits of training exceed their costs. Keep in mind that the levels do not indicate the importance of the outcomes or that lower-level outcomes cause higher-level outcomes.[12] That is, reactions cause learning, which in turn influences skills and results. The outcomes that are collected in evaluation are based on training needs, program objectives, and the strategic reasons for training. We discuss this in the section "Evaluation Practices," later in the chapter.

Reaction Outcomes

Reaction outcomes refer to trainees' perceptions of the program, including the facilities, trainers, and content. (Reaction outcomes are often referred to as a measure of "creature comfort.") They are often called *class* or *instructor evaluations*. This information is typically collected at the program's conclusion. You probably have been asked to complete class or instructor evaluations either at the end of a college course or a training program at work. Reactions are useful for identifying what trainees thought was successful or what inhibited learning. Reaction outcomes are level 1 (reaction) criteria in Kirkpatrick's framework.

TABLE 6.1 **Evaluation Outcomes**

Outcome or Criterion	Level	What Is Measured	Examples	Measurement Methods	Question
Reactions	1	Learners' satisfaction	Comfortable training room Useful materials and program content	Surveys Interviews	Did they like it?
Learning or cognitive	2	Principles, facts, techniques, procedures, or processes that the learners have acquired	Electrical principles Safety rules Steps in interviewing	Tests Work samples	What did they learn?
Behavior and skill-based	2 or 3	Interpersonal Technical or motor skills or behaviors acquired by learners	Preparing a dessert Sawing wood Landing an airplane Listening	Tests Observations Self, peer, customer, and/or managers' ratings Work samples	Do they use it?
Affective	2, 3, or 4	Learners' attitudes and motivation	Tolerance for diversity Safety attitudes Customer service orientation Engagement	Attitude surveys Interviews Focus groups	Did it change their attitudes?
Results	4	Payoffs for the company	Productivity Quality Costs Repeat customers Customer satisfaction Accidents	Observation Performance data from records or company databases	Did it impact the bottom line?
Return on investment	5	Identification and comparison of learning benefits with costs	Dollar value of productivity divided by training costs	Economic value	What is the return from investing in learning?

Sources: Based on K. Kraiger, J. K. Ford, and E. Salas, "Application of cognitive, skill-based, and affective theories of learning outcomes to new methods of training evaluation," *Journal of Applied Psychology,* 78 (2) (1993): 311–328; K. Kraiger, "Decision-Based Evaluation," in *Creating, Implementing, and Managing Effective Training and Development,* ed. K. Kraiger (San Francisco: Jossey-Bass, 2002): 331–375; D. Kirkpatrick, "Evaluation," in *The ASTD Training and Development Handbook,* 2nd ed., ed. R. L. Craig (New York: McGraw-Hill, 1996): 294–312.

Reaction outcomes are typically collected via a questionnaire completed by trainees. A reaction measure should include questions related to the trainee's satisfaction with the instructor, training materials, and training administration (e.g., ease of registration and accuracy of course description), as well as the clarity of course objectives and usefulness of the training content.[13] Table 6.2 shows a reaction measure that contains questions about

TABLE 6.2 Sample Reaction Measure

Read each statement below. Indicate the extent to which you agree or disagree with each statement using the scale below.

Strongly Disagree	Disagree	Neither	Agree	Strongly Agree
1	2	3	4	5

1. I had the knowledge and skills needed to learn in this course.
2. The facilities and equipment made it easy to learn.
3. The course met all of the stated objectives.
4. I clearly understood the course objectives.
5. The way the course was delivered was an effective way to learn.
6. The materials I received during the course were useful.
7. The course content was logically organized.
8. There was enough time to learn the course content.
9. I felt that the instructor wanted us to learn.
10. I was comfortable asking the instructor questions.
11. The instructor was prepared.
12. The instructor was knowledgeable about the course content.
13. I learned a lot from this course.
14. What I learned in this course is useful for my job.
15. The information I received about the course was accurate.
16. Overall, I was satisfied with the instructor.
17. Overall, I was satisfied with the course.

these areas. Reaction measures can also include open-ended questions that ask learners about the experience.[14] Example of open-ended questions include "What did you learn that you are most likely to try on the job?" and "What topics covered in the class still seem confusing?" These types of questions will take longer to review than analyzing items such as are shown in Table 6.2, but they can potentially provide more detailed suggestions about how to improve program design and delivery.

An accurate evaluation needs to include all the factors related to a successful learning environment.[15] Most instructor or class evaluations include items related to the trainer's preparation, delivery, ability to lead a discussion, organization of the training materials and content, use of visual aids, presentation style, ability and willingness to answer questions, and ability to stimulate trainees' interest in the course. These items come from trainer's manuals, trainer certification programs, and observation of successful trainers. Conventional wisdom suggests that trainees who like a training program (who have positive reactions) learn more and are more likely to change behaviors and improve their performance (transfer of training). Is this really the case? Recent studies suggest that reactions have the largest relationship to changes in affective learning outcomes.[16] Also, research has found that reactions are significantly related to changes in declarative and procedural knowledge, which challenges previous research suggesting that reactions are unrelated to learning. For courses such as diversity training or ethics training, trainee reactions are especially important because they affect learners' receptivity to attitude change. Reactions have been found to have the strongest relationship with post-training motivation, trainee self-efficacy, and declarative knowledge when technology is used for instructional delivery. This suggests that for online or e-learning training methods, it is important to ensure that it is easy for trainees to access them and the training content is meaningful (i.e., linked to their current job experiences, tasks, or work issues).

Learning or Cognitive Outcomes

Cognitive outcomes are used to determine the degree to which trainees are familiar with the principles, facts, techniques, procedures, and processes emphasized in the training program. Cognitive outcomes measure what knowledge trainees learned in the program. Cognitive outcomes are level 2 (learning) criteria in Kirkpatrick's framework. Typically, pencil-and-paper tests or self-assessments are used to assess cognitive outcomes. **Self-assessments** refer to learners' estimates of how much they know or have learned from training. Tests and quizzes rather than self-assessments are the preferred measures of learning. This is because self-assessments are only moderately related to learning and influenced by how much learners liked the course or were motivated to learn rather than what they actually learned.[17] Table 6.3 provides an example of items from a pencil-and-paper test used to measure trainees' knowledge of decision-making skills. These items help measure whether a trainee knows how to make a decision (the process that he or she would use). They do not help to determine if the trainee will actually use decision-making skills on the job.

Consider how Grant Thornton, the public accounting and consulting firm, used tests to evaluate one of its training programs. The company introduced a new tax services methodology and tools to approximately 1,400 tax professionals in more than fifty offices.[18] The training solution, known as Tax Symphony, involved blended learning, which included a three-day national- and local-office classroom programs, web-based performance support, and webcasts. The new methodology was introduced during a tax conference. After the conference, the content was taught at local offices using avatars presenting prerecorded audio clips combined with group application activities. Evaluation results showed that 86 percent of the program participants completing the post-test passed it with an average passing score of 85 percent. Average post-test scores improved by 11 percentage points over national classroom post-test scores. Using avatars instead of real instructors in local offices saved $72,000 in costs.

TABLE 6.3
Sample Test Items Used to Measure Learning

Source: Based on A. P. Carnevale, L. J. Gainer, and A. S. Meltzer, *Workplace Basics Training Manual* (San Francisco: Jossey-Bass, 1990): 8–12.

For each question, check all that apply.

1. If my boss returned a piece of work to me and asked me to make changes on it, I would:
   __ Prove to my boss that the work didn't need to be changed.
   __ Do what the boss said, but ask where the boss thought changes were needed
   __ Make the changes without talking to my boss.
   __ Request a transfer from the department.
2. If I were setting up a new process in my office, I would:
   __ Do it on my own, without asking for help.
   __ Ask my boss for suggestions.
   __ Ask the people who work for me for suggestions.
   __ Discuss it with friends outside the company.

Behavior and Skill-Based Outcomes

Skill-based outcomes are used to assess the level of technical or motor skills and behaviors. Skill-based outcomes include acquisition or learning of skills (skill learning) and use of skills on the job (skill transfer). Skill-based outcomes relate to Kirkpatrick's level 2 (learning) and level 3 (behavior). The extent to which trainees have learned skills can be evaluated by observing their performance in work samples such as simulators. Skill transfer is usually determined by observation. For example, a resident medical student may perform surgery while the surgeon carefully observes, giving advice and assistance as needed. Trainees may be asked to provide ratings of their own behavior or skills (self-ratings). Peers, managers, and subordinates may also be asked to rate trainees' behavior or skills based on their observations. Because research suggests that the use of only self-ratings likely results in an inaccurately positive assessment of skill or behavior transfer of training, it is recommended that skill or behavior ratings be collected from multiple perspectives (e.g., managers and subordinates or peers).[19] Table 6.4 shows a sample rating form. This form was used as part of an evaluation of a training program developed to improve school principals' management skills. To evaluate several of its training programs, Orkin, a pest control company, requires managers to observe each employee's

TABLE 6.4   Sample Rating Form Used to Measure Behavior

Rating task: Consider your opportunities over the past three months to observe and interact with the principal/assistant principal you are rating. Read the definition and behaviors associated with the skill. Then complete your ratings using the following scale:

Always	Usually	Sometimes	Seldom	Never
1	2	3	4	5

I. *Sensitivity:* Ability to perceive the needs, concerns, and personal problems of others; tact in dealing with persons from different backgrounds; skill in resolving conflict; ability to deal effectively with people concerning emotional needs; knowing what information to communicate to whom.

To what extent in the past three months has the principal or assistant principal:

__ 1. Elicited the perceptions, feelings, and concerns of others?
__ 2. Expressed verbal and nonverbal recognition of the feelings, needs, and concerns of others?
__ 3. Taken actions that anticipated the emotional effects of specific behaviors?
__ 4. Accurately reflected the point of view of others by restating it, applying it, or encouraging feedback?
__ 5. Communicated all information to others that they needed to perform their job?
__ 6. Diverted unnecessary conflict with others in problem situations?

II. *Decisiveness:* Ability to recognize when a decision is required and act quickly. (Disregard the quality of the decision.)

To what extent in the past three months has this individual:

__ 7. Recognized when a decision was required by determining the results if the decision was made or not made?
__ 8. Determined whether a short- or long-term solution was most appropriate to various situations encountered in the school?
__ 9. Considered decision alternatives?
__10. Made a timely decision based on available data?
__11. Stuck to decisions once they were made, resisting pressures from others?

performance on the job and complete a detailed checklist.[20] The checklist helps determine that behaviors introduced in training are being used at work.

Affective Outcomes

Affective outcomes include attitudes and motivation. Affective outcomes that might be collected in an evaluation include tolerance for diversity, employee engagement, motivation to learn, safety attitudes, and customer service orientation. Affective outcomes can be measured using surveys. Table 6.5 shows an example of questions on a survey used to measure career goals, plans, and interests. The specific attitude of interest depends on the program objectives. Affective outcomes relate to Kirkpatrick's level 2 (learning), level 3 (behavior), or level 4 (results), depending on how they are evaluated. If trainees were asked about their attitudes on a survey, that would be considered a learning measure. For example, attitudes toward career goals and interests might be an appropriate outcome to use to evaluate training focusing on employees self-managing their careers. Walgreens included engagement survey scores as one of the outcomes in its new Assistant Store Manager training program.[21] The program included action learning projects (work in a small team with other trainees to solve a business problem), videos, on-the-job projects, and online learning. Trainees' engagement scores improved 15 percent a year after attending the program.

Results

Results are used to determine the training program's payoff for the company. Examples of results outcomes include increased production and reduced costs related to employee turnover rates of top talent (managers or other employees), accidents, and equipment downtime, as well as improvements in product quality or customer service.[22] Results outcomes are level 4 (results) criteria in Kirkpatrick's framework. For example, Aetna, Inc. determines the effectiveness of performance support tools based on how it impacts the client experience (Kirpatrick's Level 4 criteria).[23] Customer service at Aetna depends on the successful training of employees on fourteen different products that are provided to customers. Aetna developed a wiki so that each of its product areas would be responsible for uploading content. The wiki provided performance support to employees who might need access to information about each of the fourteen products. Feedback from customers indicated that they felt the tool was useful and effective. USAA, a company who provides insurance, banking, investments, and retirement products to current and former members of the U.S. military and their families, designed a new e-learning program to help its new sales team members learn about its products and systems.[24] Sales data was used to evaluate effectiveness of the program. Program graduates exceeded sales goals by

TABLE 6.5
Example of Affective Outcomes: Career Goals, Plans, and Interests

1. At this time, I have a definite career goal in mind.
2. I have a strategy for achieving my career goals.
3. My manager is aware of my career goals.
4. I have sought information regarding my specific areas of career interest from friends, colleagues, or company career sources.
5. I have initiated conversations concerning my career plans with my manager.

over 22 percent three to six months after completing the program. WakeMed Health and Hospitals, a health-care system located in North Carolina, uses a human patient simulator, known as Stan, for training.[25] Stan can blink, breathe, and be given oxygen, CPR, and medications. Stan was used in simulations attending by nurses and other patient care and emergency staff involved in transporting critically ill heart patients to WakeMed's Heart Center to help them understand how to improve the efficiency and care administered during the transportation process and mortality rates. Results of the simulation found that the simulation helped decrease mortality rates, prevent delays in catheter placement, and improve efficiency.

Return on Investment

Return on investment (ROI) refers to comparing the training's monetary benefits with the cost of the training. ROI is often referred to as level 5 evaluation (see Table 6.1). ROI can be measured and communicated based on a percentage or a ratio. For example, assume that a new safety training program results in a decline of 5 percent in a company's accident rate. This provides a total annual savings (the benefit) of $150,000 in terms of lost workdays, material and equipment damage, and workers' compensation costs. The training program costs $50,000 to implement (including both direct and indirect costs). To calculate the ROI, you need to subtract the training costs from the benefits, divide by the costs, and multiply by 100. That is, ROI = ((150,000 − 50,000) ÷ 50,000) × 100% = 200%. The ROI for this program is 200 percent. Another way to think about ROI is to consider it as ratio based on the return for every dollar spent. In this example, the company gained a net benefit of $2 for every dollar spent. This means the ROI is 2:1. Training costs can be direct and indirect.[26] **Direct costs** include salaries and benefits for all employees involved in training, including trainees, instructors, consultants, and employees who design the program; program material and supplies; equipment or classroom rentals or purchases; and travel costs. **Indirect costs** are not related directly to the design, development, or delivery of the training program. They include general office supplies, facilities, equipment, and related expenses; travel and expenses not directly billed to one program; training department management and staff salaries not related to any one program; and administrative and staff support salaries. **Benefits** are the value that the company gains from the training program.

Tata Consultancy Services LTD, a global information technology service company headquartered in India, measures ROI for its technology training programs.[27] To calculate the ROI, revenues earned as a result of training are calculated based on the billing rates of participants who attend the training and use the new skills. Then, training costs are subtracted from the revenues. ROI for the technical programs is 483 percent.

DETERMINING WHETHER OUTCOMES ARE APPROPRIATE

An important issue in choosing outcomes is to determine whether they are appropriate. That is, are these outcomes the best ones to measure to determine whether the training program is effective? Appropriate training outcomes need to be relevant, reliable, discriminative, and practical.[28]

Relevance

Criteria relevance refers to the extent to which training outcomes are related to the learned capabilities emphasized in the training program. The learned capabilities required to succeed in the training program should be the same as those required to be successful on the job. The outcomes collected in training should be as similar as possible to what trainees learned in the program. That is, the outcomes need to be valid measures of learning. One way to ensure the relevancy of the outcomes is to choose outcomes based on the learning objectives for the program. Recall from Chapter Four that learning objectives show the expected action, the conditions under which the trainee is to perform, and the level or standard of performance.

Figure 6.2 shows two ways that training outcomes may lack relevance. **Criterion contamination** refers to the extent that training outcomes measure inappropriate capabilities or are affected by extraneous conditions. For example, if managers' evaluations of job performance are used as a training outcome, trainees may receive higher ratings of job performance simply because the managers know they attended the training program, believe the program is valuable, and therefore give high ratings to ensure that the training looks like it positively affects performance. Criteria may also be contaminated if the conditions under which the outcomes are measured vary from the learning environment. That is, trainees may be asked to perform their learned capabilities using equipment, time constraints, or physical working conditions that are not similar to those in the learning environment.

For example, trainees may be asked to demonstrate spreadsheet skills using a newer version of spreadsheet software than they used in the training program. This demonstration likely will result in no changes in their spreadsheet skills from pretraining levels. In this case, poor-quality training is not the cause for the lack of change in their spreadsheet skills. Trainees may have learned the necessary spreadsheet skills, but the environment for the evaluation differs substantially from the learning environment, so no change in skill level is observed.

FIGURE 6.2
Criterion Deficiency, Relevance, and Contamination.

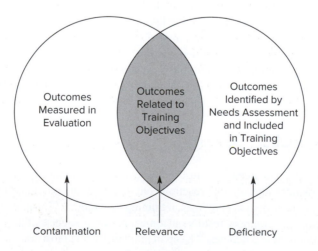

| Outcomes Measured in Evaluation | Outcomes Related to Training Objectives | Outcomes Identified by Needs Assessment and Included in Training Objectives |

Contamination   Relevance   Deficiency

Criteria may also be deficient. **Criterion deficiency** refers to the failure to measure training outcomes that were emphasized in the training objectives. For example, the objectives of a spreadsheet skills training program emphasize that trainees both understand the commands available on the spreadsheet (e.g., compute) and use the spreadsheet to calculate statistics using a data set. An evaluation design that uses only learning outcomes such as a test of knowledge of the purpose of keystrokes is deficient because the evaluation does not measure outcomes that were included in the training objectives (e.g., use a spreadsheet to compute the mean and standard deviation of a set of data).

Reliability

Reliability refers to the degree to which outcomes can be measured consistently over time. For example, a trainer gives restaurant employees a written test measuring knowledge of safety standards to evaluate a safety training program that they attended. The test is given before (pretraining) and after (post-training) employees attend the program. A reliable test includes items for which the meaning or interpretation does not change over time. A reliable test allows the trainer to have confidence that any improvements in post-training test scores from pretraining levels are the result of learning that occurred in the training program, not test characteristics (e.g., items are more understandable the second time) or the test environment (e.g., trainees performed better on the post-training test because the classroom was more comfortable and quieter).

Discrimination

Discrimination refers to the degree to which trainees' performance on the outcome actually reflects true differences in performance. For example, a paper-and-pencil test that measures electricians' knowledge of electrical principles must detect true differences in trainees' knowledge of electrical principles. That is, the test should discriminate on the basis of trainees' knowledge of electrical principles. (People who score high on the test have a better understanding of the principles of electricity than do those who score low.)

Practicality

Practicality refers to the ease with which the outcome measures can be collected. One reason companies give for not including learning, performance, and behavior outcomes in their evaluation of training programs is that collecting them is too burdensome. (It takes too much time and energy, which detracts from the business.) For example, in evaluating a sales training program, it may be impractical to ask customers to rate the salesperson's behavior because this would place too much of a time commitment on the customer (and probably damage future sales relationships).

EVALUATION PRACTICES

Figure 6.3 shows outcomes used in training evaluation practices. Surveys of companies' evaluation practices indicate that reactions (an affective outcome) and cognitive outcomes are the most frequently used outcomes in training evaluation.[29] Despite the less frequent use of cognitive, behavioral, and results outcomes, research suggests that training can have a positive effect on these outcomes.[30] Keep in mind that while most companies are conducting training evaluations, some surveys indicate that 20 percent of all companies are not!

FIGURE 6.3
**Training
Evaluation
Practices**

Note: Respondents
were 704 high-level
business, HR and
learning professionals
participating in the
ASTD/i4cp study,
"The Value of
Evaluation: Making
Training Evaluations
More Effective."
Source: Based on
L. Patel, *2010 State
of the Industry Report*
(Alexandria, VA:
American Society
for Training and
Development, 2010).

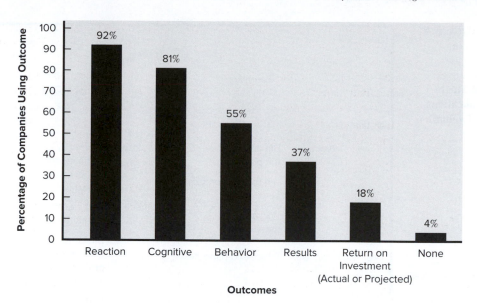

There are a number of reasons why companies don't evaluate training. Learning professional reports with access to results and tools needed to obtain them are the most significant barriers.[31] Access to results is often determined by the extent to which managers and leaders understand the need for evaluation and support it. Getting key stakeholders (managers, executives) to understand the importance of training and its link to business goals and their involvement in designing training (recall our discussion in Chapters Two and Three) can help you get access to the type of data needed to conduct an evaluation. But to gain managers' support for evaluation and conduct an effective evaluation, you need to identify and assess relevant and important outcomes and choose and implement the appropriate evaluation design.

Which Training Outcomes Should be Collected?

From our discussion of evaluation outcomes and evaluation practices, you may have the mistaken impression that it is necessary to collect all five levels of outcomes to evaluate a training program. While collecting all five levels of outcomes is ideal, the training program objectives determine which ones should be linked to the broader business strategy, as discussed in Chapter Two. To ensure adequate training evaluation, companies should collect outcome measures related to both learning (levels 1 and 2) and transfer of training (levels 3, 4, and 5).

It is important to recognize the limitations of choosing to measure only reaction and cognitive outcomes. Consider the previous discussions of learning and transfer of training in Chapters Four and Five. Remember that for training to be successful, learning *and* transfer of training must occur. Figure 6.4 shows the multiple objectives of training programs and their implication for choosing evaluation outcomes. Training programs usually have objectives related to both learning and transfer. That is, they want trainees to acquire knowledge and cognitive skills and also to demonstrate the use of the knowledge or strategies they learned in their on-the-job behavior. As a result, to ensure an adequate training evaluation, companies must collect outcome measures related to both learning and transfer.

FIGURE 6.4
Training Program Objectives and Their Implications for Evaluation

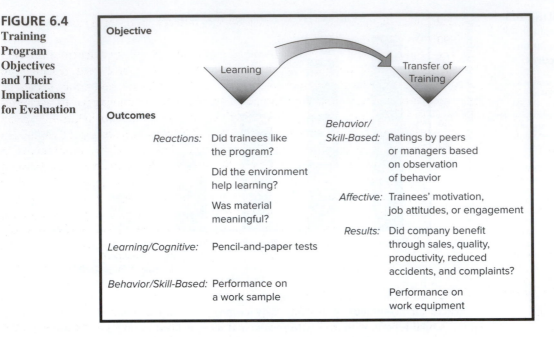

Objective

Learning → Transfer of Training

Outcomes

Reactions: Did trainees like the program?

Did the environment help learning?

Was material meaningful?

Learning/Cognitive: Pencil-and-paper tests

Behavior/Skill-Based: Performance on a work sample

Behavior/Skill-Based: Ratings by peers or managers based on observation of behavior

Affective: Trainees' motivation, job attitudes, or engagement

Results: Did company benefit through sales, quality, productivity, reduced accidents, and complaints?

Performance on work equipment

Verizon Wireless developed Tech U to prepare its technological service representatives to support both current and future technologies.[32] Verizon created Tech U to provide courses in deductive reasoning, device trouble shooting, and network provisioning. An activity called "Prove It" was developed to determine representatives' skill and behavior on their jobs after training. Their managers observe the demonstration, score it, and provide feedback to the service representative. Verizon evaluated the program using Level 2, 3, 4, and 5 outcomes. The outcomes included course pass rates (Level 2), completion and evaluation of "Prove Its" (Level 3), repair ticket volume and repeat calls (Level 4), and ROI (Level 5).

Note that outcome measures are not perfectly related to each other. That is, it is tempting to assume that satisfied trainees learn more and will apply their knowledge and skills to the job, resulting in behavior change and positive results for the company. However, research indicates that the relationships among reaction, cognitive, behavior, and results outcomes are small.[33]

Which training outcomes measure is best? The answer depends on the training objectives. For example, if the instructional objectives identified business-related outcomes such as increased customer service or product quality, then results outcomes should be included in the evaluation. As Figure 6.4 shows, both reaction and cognitive outcomes may affect learning. Reaction outcomes provide information regarding the extent to which the trainer, facilities, or learning environment may have hindered learning. Learning or cognitive outcomes directly measure the extent to which trainees have mastered training content. However, reaction and cognitive outcomes do not help determine how much trainees actually use the training content in their jobs. As much as possible, evaluation should include behavior or skill-based, affective, or results outcomes to determine the extent to which transfer of training has occurred—that is, whether training has influenced a change in behavior, skill, or attitude or has directly influenced objective measures related to company effectiveness (e.g., sales).

How long after training should outcomes be collected? There is no accepted standard for when the different training outcomes should be collected. In most cases, reactions are usually measured immediately after training.[34] Learning, behavior, and results should be measured after sufficient time has elapsed to determine whether training has had an influence on these outcomes. Positive transfer of training is demonstrated when learning occurs and positive changes in skill-based, affective, or results outcomes are also observed. No transfer of training is demonstrated if learning occurs but no changes are observed in skill-based, affective, or learning outcomes. Negative transfer is evident when learning occurs but skills, affective outcomes, or results are less than at pretraining levels. Results of evaluation studies that find no transfer or negative transfer suggest that the trainer and the manager need to investigate whether a good learning environment (e.g., opportunities for feedback and practice) was provided in the training program, trainees were motivated and able to learn, and the needs assessment correctly identified training needs.

EVALUATION DESIGNS

The design of the training evaluation determines the confidence that can be placed in the results, that is, how sure a company can be that training is either responsible for changes in evaluation outcomes or has failed to influence the outcomes. No evaluation design can ensure that the results of the evaluation are completely due to training. What the evaluator strives for is to use the most rigorous design possible (given the circumstances under which the evaluation occurs) to rule out alternative explanations for the results of the evaluation.

This discussion of evaluation designs begins by identifying these "alternative explanations" that the evaluator should attempt to control for. Next, various evaluation designs are compared. Finally, this section discusses practical circumstances that the trainer needs to consider in selecting an evaluation design.

Threats to Validity: Alternative Explanations for Evaluation Results

Table 6.6 presents threats to validity of an evaluation. **Threats to validity** refer to factors that will lead an evaluator to question either (1) the believability of the study results or (2) the extent to which the evaluation results are generalizable to other groups of trainees and situations.[35] The believability of study results refers to **internal validity.** The internal threats to validity relate to characteristics of the company (history), the outcome measures (instrumentation, testing), and the persons in the evaluation study (maturation, regression toward the mean, mortality, initial group differences). These characteristics can cause the evaluator to reach the wrong conclusions about training effectiveness. An evaluation study needs internal validity to provide confidence that the results of the evaluation (particularly if they are positive) are due to the training program and not to another factor. For example, consider a group of managers who have attended a communication skills training program. At the same time that they attend the program, it is announced that the company will be restructured. After the program, the managers may become better

TABLE 6.6   **Threats to Validity**

Threats to Internal Validity	Description
Company	
History	Event occurs, producing changes in training outcomes.
Persons	
Maturation	Changes in training outcomes result from trainees' physical growth or emotional state.
Mortality	Study participants drop out of study (e.g., leave company).
Initial group differences	Training group differs from comparison group on individual differences that influence outcomes (knowledge, skills, ability, and behavior).
Outcome Measures	
Testing	Trainees are sensitized to perform well on post-test measures.
Instrumentation	Trainee interpretation of outcomes changes over course of evaluation.
Regression toward the mean	High-and low-scoring trainees move toward the middle or average on post-training measure.
Threats to External Validity	**Description**
Reaction to pretest	Use of a test before training causes trainees to pay attention to material on the test.
Reaction to evaluation	Being evaluated causes trainees to try harder in training program.
Interaction of selection and training	Characteristics of trainees influence program effectiveness.
Interaction of methods	Results of trainees who received different methods can be generalized only to trainees who receive same training in the same order.

Source: Based on T. D. Cook, D. T. Campbell, and L. Peracchio, "Quasi-Experimentation," in *Handbook of Industrial and Organizational Psychology,* 2d ed., Vol. 1, eds. M. D. Dunnette and L. M. Hough (Palo Alto, CA: Consulting Psychologists Press, 1990): 491–576.

communicators simply because they are scared that if they don't they will lose their jobs. Perhaps no learning actually occurred in the training program at all.

Trainers are also interested in the generalizability of the study results to other groups and situations (i.e., they are interested in the **external validity** of the study). As shown in Table 6.6, threats to external validity relate to how study participants react to being included in the study and the effects of multiple types of training. Because evaluation usually does not involve all employees who have completed a program (or who may take training in the future), trainers want to be able to say that the training program will be effective in the future with similar groups.

Methods to Control for Threats to Validity

Because trainers often want to use evaluation study results as a basis for changing training programs or demonstrating that training does work (as a means to gain additional funding for training from those who control the training budget), it is important to minimize the threats to validity. There are three ways to minimize threats to validity: the use of pretests and post-tests in evaluation designs, comparison groups, and random assignment.

Pretests and Post-tests   One way to improve the internal validity of the study results is to first establish a baseline or **pretraining measure** of the outcome. Another measure of the outcomes can be taken after training. This is referred to as a **post-training measure.** A comparison of the post-training and pretraining measures can indicate the degree to which trainees have changed as a result of training.

Use of Comparison Groups   Internal validity can be improved by using a control or comparison group. A **comparison group** refers to a group of employees who participate in the evaluation study but do not attend the training program. The comparison employees have personal characteristics (e.g., gender, education, age, tenure, and skill level) as similar to the trainees as possible. Use of a comparison group in training evaluation helps rule out the possibility that changes found in the outcome measures are due to factors other than training. The **Hawthorne effect** refers to employees in an evaluation study performing at a high level simply because of the attention they are receiving. Use of a comparison group helps show that any effects observed are due specifically to the training rather than the attention the trainees are receiving. Use of a comparison group helps control the effects of history, testing, instrumentation, and maturation because both the comparison group and the training group are treated similarly, receive the same measures, and have the same amount of time to develop.

For example, consider an evaluation of a safety training program. Safe behaviors are measured before and after safety training for both trainees and a comparison group. If the level of safe behavior improves for the training group from pretraining levels but remains relatively the same for the comparison group at both pretraining and post-training, the reasonable conclusion is that the observed differences in safe behaviors are due to the training and not some other factor, such as the attention given to both the trainees and the comparison group by asking them to participate in the study.

Keep in mind that a comparison group can be naturally available for training evaluation because all employees may not receive training at the same time or training may be attended by employees at one or several company locations but not at all locations. Employees who do not initially receive training can serve as a comparison group. These employees can be scheduled to receive training at a later time after the evaluation is completed.

Random Assignment   **Random assignment** refers to assigning employees to the training or comparison group on the basis of chance alone. That is, employees are assigned to the training program without consideration of individual differences (ability or motivation) or prior experiences. Random assignment helps ensure that trainees are similar in individual characteristics such as age, gender, ability, and motivation. Because it is often impossible to identify and measure all the individual characteristics that might influence the outcome measures, random assignment ensures that these characteristics are equally distributed in the comparison group and the training group. Random assignment helps reduce the effects of employees dropping out of the study (mortality) and differences between the training group and comparison group in ability, knowledge, skill, or other personal characteristics.

Keep in mind that random assignment is often impractical. Companies want to train employees who need training. Also, companies may be unwilling to provide a comparison group. One solution to this problem is to identify the factors in which the training and comparison groups differ and control for these factors in the analysis of the data (a statistical procedure known as *analysis of covariance*). Another method is to determine trainees' characteristics after they are assigned and ensure that the comparison group includes employees with similar characteristics.

Types of Evaluation Designs

A number of different designs can be used to evaluate training programs.[36] Table 6.8 compares each design on the basis of who is involved (trainees or comparison group), when measures are collected (pretraining, post-training), the costs, the time it takes to conduct the evaluation, and the strength of the design for ruling out alternative explanations for the results. As shown in Table 6.7, research designs vary based on whether they include pretraining and post-training measurement of outcomes and a comparison group. In general, designs that use pretraining and post-training measures of outcomes and include a comparison group reduce the risk that alternative factors (other than the training itself) are responsible for the results of the evaluation. This increases the trainer's confidence in using the results to make decisions. Of course, the trade-off is that evaluations using these designs are more costly and take more time to conduct than do evaluations not using pretraining and post-training measures or comparison groups.

Post-test Only

The **post-test-only** design refers to an evaluation design in which only post-training outcomes are collected. This design can be strengthened by adding a comparison group (which helps rule out alternative explanations for changes). The post-test-only design is appropriate when trainees (and the comparison group, if one is used) can be expected to have similar levels of knowledge, behavior, or results outcomes (e.g., same number of sales or equal awareness of how to close a sale) prior to training.

TABLE 6.7   **Comparison of Evaluation Designs**

Design	Groups	Measures Pretraining	Post-training	Cost	Time	Strength
Post-test only	Trainees	No	Yes	Low	Low	Low
Pretest/post-test	Trainees	Yes	Yes	Low	Low	Med.
Post-test only with comparison group	Trainees and comparison	No	Yes	Med.	Med.	Med.
Pretest/post-test with comparison group	Trainees and comparison	Yes	Yes	Med.	Med.	High
Time series	Trainees	Yes	Yes, several	Med.	Med.	Med.
Time series with comparison group and reversal	Trainees and comparison	Yes	Yes, several	High	Med.	High
Solomon Four-Group	Trainees A	Yes	Yes	High	High	High
	Trainees B	No	Yes			
	Comparison A	Yes	Yes			
	Comparison B	No	Yes			

Consider the evaluation design that the Mayo Clinic used to compare two methods for delivering new manager training.[37] The Mayo Clinic is one of the world's leading centers of medical education and research. Recently, Mayo has undergone considerable growth because a new hospital and clinic have been added in the Phoenix area (the Mayo Clinic is also located in Rochester, Minnesota). In the process, employees who were not fully prepared were moved into management positions, which resulted in increased employee dissatisfaction and employee turnover rates. After a needs assessment indicated that employees were leaving because of dissatisfaction with management, Mayo decided to initiate a new training program designed to help the new managers improve their skills. There was some debate whether the training would be best administered in a classroom or one-on-one with a coach. Because using coaching would be more expensive than classroom training, Mayo decided to conduct an evaluation using a post-test comparison group design. Before training all managers, Mayo held three training sessions with no more than 75 managers included in each. Within each session, managers were divided into three groups: a group that received four days of classroom training, a group that received one-on-one training from a coach, and a group that received no training (a comparison group). Mayo collected reaction (did the trainees like the program?), learning, transfer, and results outcomes. The evaluation found no statistically significant differences in the effects of coaching compared to classroom training and no training. As a result, Mayo decided to rely on classroom courses for new managers and to consider coaching only for managers with critical and immediate job issues.

Pretest/Post-test

The **pretest/post-test** refers to an evaluation design in which both pretraining and post-training outcome measures are collected. There is no comparison group. The lack of a comparison group makes it difficult to rule out the effects of business conditions or other factors as explanations for changes. This design is often used by companies that want to evaluate a training program but are uncomfortable with excluding certain employees or that intend to train only a small group of employees.

Pretest/Post-test with Comparison Group

The **pretest/post-test with comparison group** refers to an evaluation design that includes trainees and a comparison group. Pretraining and post-training outcome measures are collected from both groups. If improvement is greater for the training group than the comparison group, this finding provides evidence that training is responsible for the change. This type of design controls for most threats to validity.

Table 6.8 presents an example of a pretest/post-test comparison group design. This evaluation involved determining the relationship between three conditions or treatments and learning, satisfaction, and use of computer skills.[38] The three conditions or treatments (types of computer training) were behavior modeling, self-paced study, and lecture. A comparison group was also included in the study. Behavior modeling involved watching a video showing a model performing key behaviors necessary to complete a task. In this case the task was procedures on the computer. (Behavior modeling is discussed in detail in Chapter Seven, "Traditional Training Methods.")

Forty trainees were included in each condition. Measures of learning included a test consisting of eleven items designed to measure information that trainees needed to know

TABLE 6.8 **Example of a Pretest/Post-test Comparison Group Design**

	Pretraining	Training	Post-training Time 1	Post-training Time 2
Lecture	Yes	Yes	Yes	Yes
Self-paced study	Yes	Yes	Yes	Yes
Behavior modeling	Yes	Yes	Yes	Yes
No training (Comparison)	Yes	No	Yes	Yes

Source: Based on S. J. Simon and J. M. Werner, "Computer training through behavior modeling, self-paced, and instructional approaches: A field experiment," *Journal of Applied Psychology*, 81 (1996): 648–659.

to operate the computer system (e.g., "Does formatting destroy all data on the disk?"). Also, trainees' comprehension of computer procedures (procedural comprehension) was measured by presenting trainees with scenarios on the computer screens and asking them what would appear next on the screen. Use of computer skills (skill-based learning outcome) was measured by asking trainees to complete six computer tasks (e.g., changing directories). Satisfaction with the program (reaction) was measured by six items (e.g., "I would recommend this program to others").

As shown in Table 6.8, measures of learning and skills were collected from the trainees prior to attending the program (pretraining). Measures of learning and skills were also collected immediately after training (post-training time 1) and four weeks after training (post-training time 2). The satisfaction measure was collected immediately following training.

The post-training time 2 measures collected in this study help determine the occurrence of training transfer and retention of the information and skills. That is, immediately following training, trainees may have appeared to learn and acquire skills related to computer training. Collection of the post-training measures four weeks after training provides information about trainees' level of retention of the skills and knowledge.

Statistical procedures known as analysis of variance and analysis of covariance were used to test for differences between pretraining measures and post-training measures for each condition. Also, differences between each of the training conditions and the comparison group were analyzed. These procedures determine whether differences between the groups are large enough to conclude with a high degree of confidence that the differences were caused by training rather than by chance fluctuations in trainees' scores on the measures.

Time Series

Time series refers to an evaluation design in which training outcomes are collected at periodic intervals both before and after training. (In the other evaluation designs discussed here, training outcomes are collected only once after and maybe once before training.) The strength of this design can be improved by using **reversal,** which refers to a time period in which participants no longer receive the training intervention. A comparison group can also be used with a time series design. One advantage of the time series design is that it allows an analysis of the stability of training outcomes over time. Another advantage is that using both the reversal and comparison group helps rule out alternative explanations for the evaluation results. The time series design is frequently used to evaluate training programs that focus on improving readily observable outcomes (such as accident rates, productivity, and absenteeism) that vary over time. CHG Healthcare Services evaluates the effects of new hire training by first establishing a performance baseline that includes measures of total billing, applications received, and interviews.[39] As new training courses are introduced, CHG can track their influence on new hires performance on these measures.

Figure 6.5 shows a time series design that was used to evaluate how much a training program improved the number of safe work behaviors in a food manufacturing plant.[40] This plant was experiencing an accident rate similar to that of the mining industry, the most dangerous area of work. Employees were engaging in unsafe behaviors, such as putting their hands into conveyors to unjam them (resulting in crushed limbs).

To improve safety, the company developed a training program that taught employees safe behaviors, provided them with incentives for safe behaviors, and encouraged them to monitor their own behavior. To evaluate the program, the design included a comparison group (the Makeup department) and a trained group (the Wrapping department). The Makeup department is responsible for measuring and mixing ingredients, preparing the dough, placing the dough in the oven and removing it when it is cooked, and packaging the finished product. The Wrapping department is responsible for bagging, sealing, and labeling the packages and stacking them on skids for shipping. Outcomes included observations of safe work behaviors. These observations were taken over a twenty-five-week period.

The baseline shows the percentage of safe acts prior to introduction of the safety training program. Training directed at increasing the number of safe behaviors was introduced after approximately five weeks (twenty observation sessions) in the Wrapping department and ten weeks (fifty observation sessions) in the Makeup department. Training was withdrawn from the Wrapping and Makeup departments after approximately sixty-two observation sessions. The withdrawal of training resulted in a reduction of the work incidents

FIGURE 6.5
Example of a Time Series Design

Source: J. Komaki, K. D. Badwick, and L. R. Scott, "A behavioral approach to occupational safety: Pinpointing safe performance in a food manufacturing plant," *Journal of Applied Psychology,* 63 (1978). Copyright 1978 by the American Psychological Association. Adapted by permission.

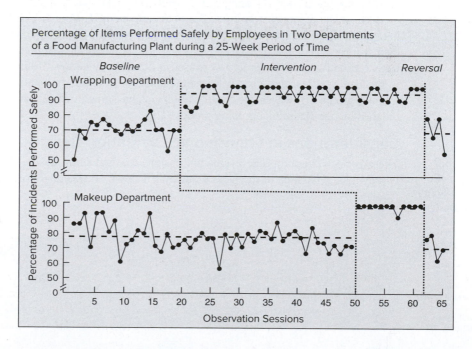

performed safely (to pretraining levels). As shown, the number of safe acts observed varied across the observation period for both groups. However, the number of safe behaviors increased after the training program was conducted for the trained group (Wrapping department). The level of safe acts remained stable across the observation period. (See the intervention period.) When the Makeup department received training (at ten weeks, or after fifty observations), a similar increase in the percentage of safe behaviors was observed.

Solomon Four-Group

The **Solomon four-group** design combines the pretest/post-test comparison group and the post-test-only control group design. In the Solomon four-group design, a training group and a comparison group are measured on the outcomes both before and after training. Another training group and control group are measured only after training. This design controls for most threats to internal and external validity. However, it is not frequently used in training evaluation because of its complexity and the number of groups required.

An application of the Solomon four-group design is shown in Table 6.9. This design was used to compare the effects of training based on integrative learning (IL) with traditional (lecture-based) training of manufacturing resource planning. Manufacturing resource planning is a method for effectively planning, coordinating, and integrating the use of all resources of a manufacturing company.[41] The IL-based training differed from traditional training in several ways. IL-based training sessions began with a series of activities intended to create a relaxed, positive environment for learning. The students were asked what manufacturing resource planning meant to them, and attempts were made to reaffirm their beliefs and unite the trainees around a common understanding of manufacturing resource planning. Students presented training material and participated in group discussions, games, stories, and poetry related to the manufacturing processes.

Because the company was interested in the effects of IL compared to traditional training, groups that received traditional training were used as the comparison groups (rather than groups who received no training). A test of manufacturing resource planning (knowledge test) and a reaction measure were used as outcomes. The study found that participants in the IL-based learning groups learned slightly less than participants in the traditional training groups. However, IL-group participants had much more positive reactions than did those in the traditional training groups.

Considerations in Choosing an Evaluation Design

There is no one appropriate evaluation design. An evaluation design should be chosen based on an evaluation of the factors shown in Table 6.10. There are several reasons why

TABLE 6.9
Example of a Solomon Four-Group Design

Source: Based on R. D. Bretz and R. E. Thompsett, "Comparing traditional and integrative learning methods in organizational training programs," *Journal of Applied Psychology,* 77 (1992): 941–951.

	Pretest	Training	Post-test
Group 1	Yes	IL-based	Yes
Group 2	Yes	Traditional	Yes
Group 3	No	IL-based	Yes
Group 4	No	Traditional	Yes

TABLE 6.10
Factors That
Influence
the Type of
Evaluation
Design

Source: Based on
S. I. Tannenbaum
and S. B. Woods,
"Determining a
strategy for evaluating
training: Operating
within organizational
constraints," *Human
Resource Planning*, 15
(1992): 63–81.

Factor	How the Factor Influences the Type of Evaluation Design
Change potential	Can the program be modified?
Importance	Does ineffective training affect customer service, safety, product development, or relationships among employees?
Scale	How many trainees are involved?
Purpose of training	Is training conducted for learning, results, or both?
Organization culture	Is demonstrating results part of company norms and expectations?
Expertise	Can a complex study be analyzed?
Cost	Is evaluation too expensive?
Time frame	When is the information needed?

no evaluation or a less rigorous evaluation design may be more appropriate than a more rigorous design that includes a comparison group, random assignment, or pretraining and post-training measures. First, managers and trainers may be unwilling to devote the time and effort necessary to collect training outcomes. Second, managers or trainers may lack the expertise to conduct an evaluation study. Third, a company may view training as an investment from which it expects to receive little or no return. A more rigorous evaluation design (pretest/post-test with comparison group) should be considered if any of the following conditions is true:[42]

1. The evaluation results can be used to change the program.

2. The training program is ongoing and has the potential to have an important influence on employees or customers.

3. The training program involves multiple classes and a large number of trainees.

4. Cost justification for training is based on numerical indicators. (Here, the company has a strong orientation toward evaluation.)

5. Trainers or others in the company have the expertise (or the budget to purchase expertise from outside the company) to design and evaluate the data collected from an evaluation study.

6. The cost of the training creates a need to show that it works.

7. There is sufficient time for conducting an evaluation. Here, information regarding training effectiveness is not needed immediately.

8. There is interest in measuring change (in knowledge, behavior, skill, etc.) from pre-training levels or in comparing two or more different programs.

For example, if the company is interested in determining how much employees' communications skills have changed as a result of a training program, a pretest/post-test comparison group design is necessary. Trainees should be randomly assigned to training and no-training conditions. These evaluation design features offer a high degree of confidence that any communication skill change is the result of participation in the training program.[43] This type of evaluation design is also necessary if the company wants to compare the effectiveness of two training programs.

Evaluation designs without pretest or comparison groups are most appropriate in situations in which the company is interested in identifying whether a specific level of performance has been achieved. (For example, are employees who participated in training able to communicate their ideas adequately?) In these situations, companies are not interested in determining how much change has occurred, but rather whether the trainees have achieved a certain proficiency level.

Sometimes naturally occurring comparison groups are available, which provides the opportunity to use the pretest and the post-test with comparison group or the post-test with comparison group evaluation designs. This can occur because of the realities of scheduling employees to attend training (all employees cannot attend training at the same time) or when new training is implemented. For example, some employees may be scheduled to receive training later than others. The employees who do not initially receive training can be considered the comparison group. Outcomes can be measured and comparisons made between the employee group who received training and the employees who are waiting to receive the training. Consider how Mountain America Credit Union evaluated the effectiveness of a revised sales training program.[44] Mountain American tracked of the average monthly sales of thirty new employees during their first two months of employment. Ten of the thirty employees attended training before it was revised (they called this the Traditional Group). Twenty employees attended the program after it was revised (the Express Group). The revised program included more interactions with a variety of customers with different needs. Monthly sales were compared between the Express Group and the Traditional Group. Sales in the Express Group exceeded sales in the Traditional Group in both the first (11.4 versus 3.5 average sales) and second month (34.83 versus 5.5) of employment.

One company's evaluation strategy for a training course delivered to the company's tax professionals shows how company norms regarding evaluation and the purpose of training influence the type of evaluation design chosen.[45] This accounting firm views training as an effective method for developing human resources. Training is expected to provide a good return on investment. The company used a combination of affective, cognitive, behavior, and results criteria to evaluate a five-week course designed to prepare tax professionals to understand state and local tax law. The course involved two weeks of self-study and three weeks of classroom work. A pretest/post-test comparison design was used. Before they took the course, trainees were tested to determine their knowledge of state and local tax laws, and they completed a survey designed to assess their self-confidence in preparing accurate tax returns. The evaluators also identified the trainees' (accountants') billable hours related to calculating state and local tax returns and the revenue generated by the activity. After the course, evaluators again identified billable hours and surveyed trainees' self-confidence. The results of the evaluation indicated that the accountants were spending more time doing state and local tax work than before training. Also, the trained accountants produced more revenue doing state and local tax work than did accountants who had not yet received the training (comparison group). There was also a significant improvement in the accountants' confidence following training, and they were more willing to promote their expertise in state and local tax preparation. Finally, after fifteen months, the revenue gained by the company more than offset the cost of training. On average, the increase in revenue for the trained tax accountants was more than 10 percent.

DETERMINING RETURN ON INVESTMENT

Return on investment (ROI) is an important training outcome. This section discusses how to calculate ROI through a cost-benefit analysis. **Cost-benefit analysis** in this situation is the process of determining the economic benefits of a training program using accounting methods that look at training costs and benefits. Training cost information is important for several reasons:[46]

1. To understand total expenditures for training, including direct and indirect costs
2. To compare the costs of alternative training programs
3. To evaluate the proportion of money spent on training development, administration, and evaluation, as well as to compare monies spent on training for different groups of employees (exempt versus nonexempt, for example)
4. To control costs

There is an increased interest in measuring the ROI of training and development programs because of the need to show the results of these programs to justify funding and to increase the status of the training and development function.[47] Most trainers and managers believe that there is a value provided by training and development activities, such as productivity or customer service improvements, cost reductions, time savings, and decreased employee turnover. ROI provides evidence of the economic value provided by training and development programs. However, it is important to keep in mind that ROI is not a substitute for other program outcomes that provide data regarding the success of a program based on trainees' reactions and whether learning and transfer of training have occurred.

Typically, ROI is used to show a training program's cost effectiveness after it has been delivered. However, ROI is also useful for forecasting the potential value of a new training program, choosing the most cost-effective training method by estimating and comparing the costs and benefits of each approach, and making decisions about whether to fund and offer training programs in the future.[48]

Consider the use of ROI at LensCrafters. LensCrafters brings the eye doctor, a wide selection of frames and lenses, and the lens-making laboratory together in one location.[49] LensCrafters has convenient locations and hours of operations, and it has the ability to make eyewear on-site. Emphasizing customer service, the company offers a one-stop location and promises to make eyewear in one hour. Dave Palm, a training professional at LensCrafters, received a call from a concerned regional manager. He told Palm that although company executives knew that LensCrafters employees had to be well trained to design eyewear and that employees were satisfied with the training, the executives wanted to know whether the money that they were investing in training was providing any return. Palm decided to partner with the operations people to identify how to link training to measurable outcomes such as profitability, quality, and sales. After conversations with the operations employees, he decided to link training to waste from mistakes in quality and remakes, store performance and sales, and customer satisfaction. He chose two geographic regions for the evaluation study and compared the results from these two regions with results from one that had not yet received the training. Palm found that all stores in the two regions that received training reduced waste, increased sales, and improved customer satisfaction. As a result, LensCrafters allotted its training department more financial resources—$10 million a year for training program development and administration—than any other optical retail competitor. Because the training department demonstrated that it does contribute to business operations, it also received money to develop a multimedia-based training system.

The process of determining ROI begins with an understanding of the objectives of the training program.[50] Plans are developed for collecting data related to measuring these objectives. The next step is to isolate, if possible, the effects of training from other factors that might influence the data. Last, the data are converted to a monetary value and ROI is calculated. Choosing evaluation outcomes and designing an evaluation that helps isolate the effects of training were explained earlier in this chapter. The following sections discuss how to determine costs and benefits and provide examples of cost-benefit analysis and ROI calculations.

Because ROI analysis can be costly, it should be limited only to certain training programs. ROI analysis is best for training programs that are focused on an operational issue (measurable identifiable outcomes are available), are linked to a companywide strategy (e.g., better customer service), are expensive, are highly visible, have management interest, are attended by many employees, and are permanent.[51] At Deloitte, the tax and auditing firm, managers don't require analysis of ROI for many training programs.[52] Because knowledge is the product at Deloitte, investment in training is seen as an important part of the business. Deloitte makes money through the billable hours that its consultants provide to clients. Training helps prepare the consultants to serve clients' needs. ROI is primarily calculated for courses or programs that are new or expensive. For example, ROI analysis was conducted for a simulation designed to help new employees learn more quickly how to service clients. At Deloitte, use of the simulation has resulted in new hires being 30 to 40 percent faster in serving clients—resulting in an ROI of over $66 billion after subtracting program costs.

Determining Costs

One method for comparing costs of alternative training programs is the resource requirements model.[53] The resource requirements model compares equipment, facilities, personnel, and materials costs across different stages of the training process (needs assessment, development, training design, implementation, and evaluation). Use of the resource requirements model can help determine overall differences in costs among training programs. Also, costs incurred at different stages of the training process can be compared across programs.

Accounting can also be used to calculate costs.[54] Seven categories of cost sources are costs related to program development or purchase, instructional materials for trainers and trainees, equipment and hardware, facilities, travel and lodging, salary of trainer and support staff, and the cost of lost productivity while trainees attend the program (or the cost of temporary employees who replace the trainees while they are away from their jobs). This method also identifies when the costs are incurred. Onetime costs include those related to needs assessment and program development. Costs per offering relate to training site rental fees, trainer salaries, and other costs that are realized every time the program is offered. Costs per trainee include meals, materials, and lost productivity or expenses incurred to replace the trainees while they attend training. For example, consider the costs for virtual training compared to instructor-led training. Aetna has moved from face-to-face instructor-led classroom training to virtual training for its sixteen-week program for new customer service representatives.[55] The cost to bring a trainer to locations without one onsite was more than $27,000. The comparable costs for the same training program conducted virtually are approximately $3,000.

Determining Benefits

To identify the potential benefits of training, the company must review the original reasons that the training was conducted. For example, training may have been conducted to reduce production costs or overtime costs or to increase the amount of repeat business. A number of methods may be helpful in identifying the benefits of training:

1. Technical, academic, and practitioner literature summarizes the benefits that have been shown to relate to a specific training program.
2. Pilot training programs assess the benefits from a small group of trainees before a company commits more resources.
3. Observance of successful job performers helps a company determine what successful job performers do differently than unsuccessful job performers.[56]
4. Trainees and their managers provide estimates of training benefits.

For example, a training and development consultant at Apple Computer was concerned with the quality and consistency of the training program used in assembly operations.[57] She wanted to show that training was not only effective but also resulted in financial benefits. To do this, the consultant chose an evaluation design that involved two separately trained groups—each consisting of twenty-seven employees—and two untrained groups (comparison groups). The consultant collected a pretraining history of what was happening on the production line in each outcome that she was measuring (i.e., productivity, quality, and labor efficiency). She determined the effectiveness of training by comparing performance between the comparison and training groups for two months after training. The consultant was able to show that the untrained comparison group had 2,000 more minutes of downtime than the trained group did. This finding meant that the trained employees built and shipped more products to customers—showing definitively that training was contributing to Apple's business objectives.

To conduct a cost-benefit analysis, the consultant had each employee in the training group estimate the effect of a behavior change on a specific business measure (e.g., breaking down tasks will improve productivity or efficiency). The trainees assigned a confidence percentage to the estimates. To get a cost-benefit estimate for each group of trainees, the consultant multiplied the monthly cost-benefit by the confidence level and divided by the number of trainees. For example, one group of 20 trainees estimated a total overall monthly cost benefit of $336,000 related to business improvements and showed an average 70 percent confidence level with that estimate. The calculation is as follows: 70 percent multiplied by $336,000 gave a cost-benefit of $235,200. This number was divided by 20 ($235,200/20 trainees) to give an average estimated cost benefit for each of the trainees ($11,760). To calculate ROI, follow these steps:[58]

1. Identify outcomes (e.g., quality, accidents).
2. Place a value on the outcomes.

3. Determine the change in performance after eliminating other potential influences on training results.
4. Obtain an annual amount of benefits (operational results) from training by comparing results after training to results before training (in dollars).
5. Determine the training costs (direct costs + indirect costs + development costs + overhead costs + compensation for trainees).
6. Calculate the total benefits by subtracting the training costs from benefits (operational results).
7. Calculate the ROI by dividing operational results by costs. The ROI gives an estimate of the dollar return expected from each dollar invested in training.

Example of a Cost-Benefit Analysis

A cost-benefit analysis is best explained by an example.[59] A wood plant produced panels that contractors used as building materials. The plant employed 300 workers, 48 supervisors, 7 shift superintendents, and a plant manager. The business had three problems. First, 2 percent of the wood panels produced each day were rejected because of poor quality. Second, the production area was experiencing poor housekeeping, such as improperly stacked finished panels that would fall on employees. Third, the number of preventable accidents was higher than the industry average. To correct these problems, the supervisors, shift superintendents, and plant manager attended training in (1) performance management and interpersonal skills related to quality problems and poor work habits of employees, and (2) rewarding employees for performance improvement. Training was conducted in a hotel close to the plant. The training program was a purchased videotape, and the instructor for the program was a consultant. Table 6.11 shows each type of cost and how it was determined.

The benefits of the training were identified by considering the objectives of the training program and the type of outcomes the program was to influence. These outcomes included the quality of panels, housekeeping in the production area, and the accident rate. Table 6.12 shows how the benefits of the program were calculated.

Once the costs and benefits of the program are determined, ROI is calculated by dividing return or benefits by costs. In this example, ROI was 5.72. That is, every dollar invested in the program returned almost $6 in benefits. How can the company determine if the ROI is acceptable? One way is for managers and trainers to agree on what level of ROI is acceptable. Another method is to use the ROI that other companies obtain from similar types of training. Table 6.13 provides examples of ROIs obtained from several types of training programs.

Recall the discussion of the new manager training program at the Mayo Clinic.[60] To determine Mayo's ROI, the human resource department calculated that one-third of the eighty-four employees retained (twenty-nine employees) would have left Mayo as a result of dissatisfaction. The department believed that this retention was due to the impact of the training. Mayo's cost of a single employee turnover was calculated to be 75 percent of average total compensation, or $42,000 per employee. Multiplying $42,000 by the twenty-nine employees retained equals a savings of $609,000. However, the cost of the training program needs to be considered. If the annual cost of the training program ($125,000) is subtracted from the savings, the new savings amount is $484,000. These numbers are

TABLE 6.11   **Determining Costs for a Cost-Benefit Analysis**

Direct Costs	
Instructor	$ 0
In-house instructor (12 days @ $125 per day)	1,500
Fringe benefits (25% of salary)	375
Travel expenses	0
Materials ($60 × 56 trainees)	3,360
Classroom space and audiovisual equipment (12 days @ $50 per day)	600
Refreshments ($4 per day × 3 days × 56 trainees)	672
Total direct costs	**$ 6,507**
Indirect Costs	
Training management	$ 0
Clerical and administrative salaries	750
Fringe benefits (25% of salary)	187
Postage, shipping, and telephone	0
Pre- and post-training learning materials ($4 × 56 trainees)	224
Total indirect costs	**$ 1,161**
Development Costs	
Fee for program purchase	$ 3,600
Instructor training	
Registration fee	1,400
Travel and lodging	975
Salary	625
Benefits (25% of salary)	156
Total development costs	**$ 6,756**
Overhead Costs	
General organizational support, top management time (10% of direct, indirect, and development costs)	$ 1,443
Total overhead costs	**$ 1,443**
Compensation for Trainees	
Trainees' salaries and benefits (based on time away from job)	$16,969
Total training costs	$32,836
Cost per trainee	**$ 587**

based on estimates, but even if the net savings figure were cut in half, the ROI is still over 100 percent. By being able to quantify the benefits delivered by the program, Mayo's human resource department achieved greater credibility within the company.

Other Methods for Cost-Benefit Analysis

Other more sophisticated methods are available for determining the dollar value of training. For example, **utility analysis** is a cost-benefit analysis method that involves assessing the dollar value of training based on estimates of the difference in job performance between trained and untrained employees, the number of individuals trained, the length of time a training program is expected to influence performance, and the variability in job performance in the untrained group of employees.[61] Utility analysis requires the use of

TABLE 6.12   **Determining Benefits for a Cost-Benefit Analysis**

Operational Results Area	How Measured	Results Before Training	Results After Training	Differences (+ or −)	Costs
Quality of panels	Percentage rejected	2% rejected—1,440 panels per day	1.5% rejected—1,080 panels per day	0.5%— 360 panels	$720 per day; $172,800 per year
Housekeeping	Visual inspection using twenty-item checklist	Ten defects (average)	Two defects (average)	Eight defects	Not measurable in dollars
Preventable accidents	Number of accidents	Twenty-four per year	Sixteen per year	Eight per year	$48,000 per year
	Direct cost of accidents	$144,000 per year	$96,000 per year	$48,000 per year	

$$ROI = \frac{Return}{Investment} = \frac{Benefits - Costs}{Costs} = \frac{220,800 - 32,836}{32,836} = 5.72$$

Total benefits = $187,964

Source: Adapted from D. G. Robinson and J. Robinson, "Training for impact," *Training and Development Journal* (August 1989): 30–42.

TABLE 6.13 Examples of ROIs

Source: Based on Top 125 Rankings 2015, training (January/February 2015): 62–101. J. J. Philips, "ROI: The search for best practices," *Training and Development* (February 1996): 45.

Industry	Training Program	ROI
Bottling company	Workshops on managers' roles	15:1
Large commercial bank	Sales training	21:1
Electric and gas utility	Behavior modification	5:1
Oil company	Customer service	4.8:1
Health maintenance organization	Team training	13.7:1
Health medical services	Coaching for Leaders	2:1

a pretest/post-test design with a comparison group to obtain an estimate of the difference in job performance for trained versus untrained employees. Other types of economic analyses evaluate training as it benefits the firm or the government using direct and indirect training costs, government incentives paid for training, wage increases received by trainees as a result of completion of training, tax rates, and discount rates.[62]

Practical Considerations in Determining ROI

As mentioned earlier in the chapter, ROI analysis may not be appropriate for all training programs. Training programs best suited for ROI analysis have clearly identified outcomes, are not onetime events, are highly visible in the company, are strategically focused, and have effects that can be isolated. In the examples of ROI analysis in this chapter, the outcomes were very measurable. That is, in the wood plant example, it was easy to see changes in quality, to count accident rates, and to observe housekeeping behavior. For training programs that focus on soft outcomes (e.g., attitudes or interpersonal skills), it may be more difficult to estimate the value.

Showing the link between training and market share gain or other higher-level strategic business outcomes can be very problematic. These outcomes can be influenced by too many other factors not directly related to training (or even under the control of the business), such as competitors' performance and economic upswings and downturns. Business units may not be collecting the data needed to identify the ROI of training programs on individual performance. Also, the measurement of training can often be very expensive. Verizon Communications employs over 200,000 people.[63] The company estimates that it spends approximately $5,000 for an ROI study. Given the large number of training programs that the company offers, it is too expensive to conduct an ROI for each program.

Companies are finding that, despite these difficulties, the demand for measuring ROI is still high. As a result, companies are using creative ways to measure the costs and benefits of training.[64] For example, to calculate ROI for a training program designed to cut absenteeism, trainees and their supervisors were asked to estimate the cost of an absence. The values were averaged to obtain an estimate. Cisco Systems tracks how often its partners return to its website for additional instruction. A. T. Kearney, a management consulting firm, tracks the success of its training by how much business is generated from past clients.

Success Cases and Return on Expectations

One way to establish the value of training and overcome the difficulty of evaluating training using a design that can rule out and isolate its effects on results is to rely on return on expectations or success cases. **Return on expectations (ROE)** refers to the process through which evaluation demonstrates to key business stakeholders, such as top-level managers, that their expectations about training have been satisfied.[65] ROE depends on establishing a business partnership with business stakeholders from the start of a training program through its evaluation.

Rather than relying on ROI, Verizon Communications uses training ROE. Prior to training, the senior managers who are financially accountable for the training program are asked to identify their expectations regarding what the training program should accomplish, as well as a cost estimate of the current issue or problem. After training, the senior managers are asked whether their expectations have been met, and they are encouraged to attach a monetary value to those met expectations. The ROE is used as an estimate in an ROI analysis. Verizon Communications continues to conduct ROI analysis for training programs and courses in which objective numbers are available (e.g., sales training) and in which the influence of training can be better isolated (evaluation designs that have comparison groups and that collect pretraining and post-training outcomes).

Success cases or stories refer to concrete examples of the impact of training that show how learning has led to results that the company finds worthwhile and the managers find credible.[66] Success cases do not attempt to isolate the influence of training, but rather to provide evidence that it was useful. Both Agilent Technologies, a high-tech measurement equipment company, and Standard Chartered Bank, an international bank, use success stories.[67] Agilent provides senior managers with the use of specific example, written by trainees, of what they are doing better and differently as they apply what they learned to their work. For example, a manufacturing engineer realized that, as a result of attending a training program, they could expand their area of influence outside of their own team to solve a financial reporting problem. Through expanding the area of influence, the engineer is now more aware and in control of expenses, which has improved the bottom line of the business unit. At Standard, one hundred days after training the trainees connect on a conference call to share stories about changes that have occurred. Trainees are asked to prepare for the call by considering four question: What learning did you apply? What achievement or result are you most proud of? What have been the personal and business benefits? What advice do you have for how others can use what they learned?

MEASURING HUMAN CAPITAL AND TRAINING ACTIVITY

So far, this chapter has focused on how to evaluate training programs. It is important to remember that evaluation can also involve determining the extent to which learning and training activities and the training function contribute to the company strategy and help achieve business goals. Chapter One emphasized that there is increased recognition that training, development, and learning can and should contribute to employee performance and business goals (see Figure 1.1). We discussed the role of metrics in the strategic training and development process in Chapter Two. Metrics are used to determine the value that learning activities or the training function provide to the company.

One way to understand the value that learning activities or the training function provides is through comparisons to other companies. Each year, the American Society of Training and Development (ASTD, now the Association for Talent Development [ATD]) prepares a report that summarizes company-provided training in the United States. This report provides information about training hours and delivery methods that companies can use to benchmark, or compare themselves to other companies in similar industries or size.

Table 6.14 provides examples of different measurements, or metrics. These metrics are valuable for benchmarking purposes, for understanding the current amount of training activity in a company, and for tracking historical trends in training activity. However, collecting these metrics does not address such issues as whether training is effective, or whether the company is using the data to make strategic training decisions.[68]

Big Data and Workforce Analytics

Big data refers to complex data sets developed by compiling data across different organizational systems including marketing and sales, human resources, finance, accounting, customer service, and operations. Three dimensions characterize big data: volume, variety,

TABLE 6.14
Training Metrics

Sources: L. Miller, *2014 State of the Industry* (Alexandria, VA: Association for Talent Development, 2014); T. Wilk, "How to Run Learning Like a Business," *Chief Learning Officer* (June 2014): 48–60.

Expenditure per employee
Learning hours received per employee
Expenditure as a percentage of payroll
Expenditure as a percentage of revenue
Cost per learning hour received
Percentage of expenditures for external services
Learning hours received per training and development staff member
Average percentage of learning activities outsourced
Average percentage of learning content by content area (e.g., basic skills, customer service, executive development)
Average percentage of learning hours provided via different delivery methods (instructor-led, technology-based, etc.)

and velocity.[69] Volume refers to the large amount of available data. Variety includes the large number of sources and types of data that are available come from. Velocity refers to the huge amount of data that is being generated and the speed with which it must be evaluated, captured, and made useful. Big data can come from many different sources including transactions, business applications, e-mails, social media, smartphones, and even sensors embedded in employees' identification badges or company products.

The goal of big data is to make decisions about human capital based on data rather than intuition or conventional wisdom, which likely lead to incorrect conclusions and recommendations. Big data can be used for many purposes, including to evaluate the effectiveness of learning and development programs, determine their impact on business results, and develop predictive models that can be used for forecasting training needs, course enrollments, costs, and outcomes. For example, big data can help predict when employees will take training in their careers and how that relates to their retention and promotion. Including learning-related data as part of big data can help show the strategic value of learning for a company. Using big data requires the use of workforce analytics. **Workforce analytics** refers to the practice of using quantitative methods and scientific methods to analyze data from human resource databases, corporate financial statements, employee surveys and other data sources to make evidence-based decisions and show that human resource practices (including training, development, and learning) influence important company metrics.[70]

Several examples show how companies are using big data and workforce analytics.[71] To analyze data about how learning contributed to the success of their salesforce, SuccessFactors used data from three systems: customer relationship management, learning and performance management, and employee records. Customer relations data included number and size of sales. Learning data included courses taken and **self-evaluation** of training effectiveness. Performance data included managers' performance ratings and learning plans. Employee records included sales experience and hire date. They analyzed the performance and number and value of sales made by employees who completed training compared to those who did not. Defense Acquisition University (DAU) used big data to determine the effectiveness of its learning programs. DAU provides training for active and reserve information technology employees in the U.S. military. DAU integrated data from human resources, budgeting, and accounting systems with learning data and trainee information. For example, some of the training data includes post-training surveys of course quality and instructor evaluations completed by trainees immediately after they complete a course. Also, two months later trainees are asked to assess how the course affected their job performance and business outcomes. This data sets allows DAU to determine the trends in courses, quality, preferred course location, business unit participation rates in training, and how the number of employees enrolling in a course relates to business performance. For example, one of the analyses showed that guest speakers in courses were highly related to individual learning, which subsequently influenced job performance and business results. Another analysis of room cost, instructor salary and travel costs, expected attendance, and travel costs for students helped DAU determine the least expensive places to conduct classroom training. Juniper Networks uses LinkedIn to track and analyze the skills, knowledge, experience, and career paths of potential, current, and former employees. Juniper was interested in determining how long it took new salespersons to generate expected revenue and what types of training might shorten that time period. TELUS, a telecommunications company that uses online, face-to-face, and informal learning, created a measurement system that assesses accessing training (clicking, opening, attending), usage (viewing, staying, reading, participating), grade (knowledge acquisition), evaluation (learner assessment), and return (performance impact). TELUS's learning team collects data from different tracking systems (individual, corporate, department, business). All employees can access a learning dashboard that displays learning investments, assessment results, and analytics by work team, region, or division. To determine return every quarter, TELUS randomly surveys employees to ask about their learning activities from the past ninety days. Return on learning (ROL) is determined by the percentage of employees who respond that learning had a positive impact on their knowledge and skills. In 2013 the average ROL was 75 percent.

Some companies are using dashboards to help measure the effectiveness, financial benefits, and relationship of learning activities to business strategy and goals. A **dashboard** refers to a computer interface designed to receive and analyze the data from departments within the company to provide information to managers and other decision-makers.[72] Dashboards can draw their data from different sources, such as the company's human resource information system or learning management or course enrollment system. Dashboards are useful because they can provide a visual display using charts of the relationship between learning activities and business performance data, including measures related to intangible assets such as human capital (recall the discussion of human capital in Chapter One). The dashboard allows the user to access and use the data in different ways, including isolating problem areas and creating categories based on precalculated formulas (such as cost per learning hour received). Jiffy Lube provides store managers, company leaders, franchisees, and learning professionals with access to an online report that shows completion of certifications by employee, store, franchisee, and region.[73] Color-coding is provided to make it easy to understand. Completions at or above target are shown in green, 50 to 99 percent in yellow, and less than 50 percent in red.

Key Bank, headquartered in Cleveland, Ohio, is one of the largest bank-based financial services companies in the United States.[74] Its business strategy is to build client relationships through client-focused solutions and extraordinary service. Key Bank provides a wide variety of training and development programs to help employees grow personally and professionally. To help ensure the efficiency and effectiveness of its training and development activity, Key Bank uses a dashboard that allows access to real-time data providing access to information about the strategic alignment, effectiveness, and investment in training programs across the company. The training activity dashboard provides historical information on learning and training (a "rear-view" perspective). The user identifies the time period that he or she is interested in and then can select companywide or business-specific information. The dashboard offers information on total training activities, the distribution of training activities across the company or business, identifies which training areas are receiving the most funding, and can identify employee progress in completing training and acquiring skills. The dashboard also can be used to provide a perspective of future learning (a "windshield" perspective). Users can look at completion rates for training courses and programs and identify the progress rates at Key Bank locations across the United States. This information is useful for training managers to understand whether local training goals are met, in progress, or behind completion dates, helping them better plan future training and adjust training goals with local managers.

Summary

Evaluation provides information used to determine training effectiveness. Evaluation involves identifying the appropriate outcomes to measure. The chapter notes that a good evaluation requires thinking about evaluation before conducting training. Information from the needs assessment and specific and measurable learning objectives help identify outcomes that should be included in the evaluation design. The outcomes used in evaluating training programs include trainees' satisfaction with the training program, learning of knowledge or skills, use of knowledge and skills on the job, and results such as sales, productivity, or accident prevention. Evaluation may also involve comparing the costs of training to the benefits received (ROI). Outcomes used in training evaluation help determine the degree to which the program has resulted in both learning and transfer of training. Evaluation also involves choosing the appropriate design to maximize the confidence that can be placed in the results. The design is based on a careful analysis of how to minimize threats to internal and external validity, as well as the purpose, expertise, and other company and training characteristics. The types of designs used for evaluation vary on the basis of whether they include pretraining and post-training measures of outcomes and use of a training group and a comparison group. The chapter concludes with a discussion of how to use big data, workforce analytics, and dashboards to measure, analyze, and display the contribution of training to a company's human capital assets.

Key Terms

training effectiveness, 247
training outcomes, 247
criteria, 247
training evaluation, 247
evaluation design, 248
formative evaluation, 249
pilot testing, 250
summative evaluation, 250
reaction outcomes, 252
cognitive outcomes, 255
self-assessments, 255
skill-based outcomes, 256
affective outcomes, 257
results, 257
return on investment (ROI), 258
direct costs, 258

indirect costs, 258
benefits, 258
criteria relevance, 259
criterion contamination, 259
criterion deficiency, 260
reliability, 260
discrimination, 260
practicality, 260
threats to validity, 263
internal validity, 263
external validity, 264
pretraining measure, 265
post-training measure, 265
comparison group, 265
Hawthorne effect, 265
random assignment, 265
post-test-only, 266

pretest/post-test, 267
pretest/post-test with comparison group, 267
time series, 268
reversal, 268
Solomon four-group, 270
cost-benefit analysis, 273
utility analysis, 277
return on expectations (ROE), 279
success cases or success stories, 279
big data, 280
workforce analytics, 281
self-evaluation, 281
dashboard, 282

Discussion Questions

1. What can be done to motivate companies to evaluate training programs?
2. What do threats to validity have to do with training evaluation? Identify internal and external threats to validity. Are internal and external threats similar? Explain.

3. What are the strengths and weaknesses of each of the following designs: post-test-only, pretest/post-test with comparison group, and pretest/post-test only?

4. What are results outcomes? Why do you think most organizations don't use results outcomes to evaluate their training programs?

5. This chapter discussed several factors that influence the choice of evaluation design. Which of these factors would have the greatest influence on your choice of an evaluation design? Which would have the least influence? Explain your choices.

6. How might you estimate the benefits of a training program designed to teach employees how to use the Internet to monitor stock prices?

7. A group of managers ($N = 25$) participated in the problem-solving module of a leadership development program two weeks ago. The module consisted of two days in which the group focused on the correct process to use in problem solving. Each manager supervises fifteen to twenty employees. The company is willing to change the program, and there is an increasing emphasis in the company to show that training expenses are justifiable. You are asked to evaluate this program. Your boss would like the results of the evaluation no later than six weeks from now. Discuss the outcomes you would collect and the design you would use. How might your answer change if the managers had not yet attended the program?

8. What practical considerations need to be taken into account when calculating a training program's ROI?

9. What is return on expectations (ROE)? How can it be used to show the costs and benefits of training without collecting statistics and conducting analyses? Explain its strengths and weaknesses compared to a cost-benefit analysis.

10. What are the characteristics of big data? Explain how big data could be used to show that learning influences business outcomes.

Application Assignments

1. Consider this course as a training program. In teams of up to five students, identify (a) the types of outcomes you would recommend to use in evaluating this course and (b) the evaluation design you would use. Justify your choice of a design based on minimizing threats to validity and practical considerations.

2. Domino's Pizza was interested in determining whether a new employee could learn how to make a pizza using a computer-based training method (CD-ROM). The CD-ROM application addresses the proper procedure for "massaging" a dough ball and stretching it to fit a 12-inch pizza pan. Domino's quality standards emphasize the roundness of the pizza, an even border, and uniform thickness of the dough. Traditionally, on-the-job training is used to teach new employees how to stretch pizza dough to fit the pizza pan.

   a. What outcomes or criteria should Domino's Pizza measure to determine if CD-ROM training is an effective method for teaching new employees how to stretch pizza dough to fit a 12-inch pan? Who would be involved in the evaluation?

   b. Describe the evaluation design that you would recommend using to determine if CD-ROM training is more effective than on-the-job training.

3. Ask your instructor for a copy of the evaluation form, survey, or rating sheet that is used by your college, university, or business to evaluate the course or program in which you are using this text. As you look over the evaluation, answer the following questions:

   a. What are the strengths and weaknesses of the evaluation form?

   b. What changes would you suggest to improve the evaluation form (e.g., different questions, additional questions)?

   c. How should the evaluation be used to actually improve the instruction that you receive?

4. Sears designed a training program to improve tool and hardware sales. The two-hour program involved distance learning and was broadcast from the Sears training facility to fifty salespersons at ten store locations in the United States. The salespersons are paid $15 per hour. The program involved training salespeople in how to set up merchandise displays so they attract buyers' attention. Sales of tools and merchandise at the ten stores included in the program averaged $5,000 per week before the program and $6,500 per week after the program. Program costs included:

Instructor	$10,000
Distance learning (satellite space rental)	5,000
Materials ($100 per trainee @ 50 trainees)	5,000
Trainees' salaries and benefits (50 trainees with wages of $15 per hour in a 2-hour training program)	1,500

   What is the ROI from this program?

5. Cablevision developed an e-learning course that taught salespersons how to increase the number of cable television subscribers, thereby increasing revenue. The company wants to know if salespersons will increase upselling of cable television services (e.g., premium channels) and will try to sell other products (e.g., e-mail and web access). The company also wants to know the ROI of this training program.

   a. What training outcomes should the company collect? From whom should the outcomes be collected?

   b. What evaluation design would you recommend? Defend your recommendation.

   c. Show how Cablevision can conduct an ROI analysis. Describe the information that the company should collect and how it should be collected.

6. The 100-employee information technology department of a financial services company had a high turnover rate. A survey of employees revealed that the reason that most of them left was dissatisfaction with the level of training. The average turnover rate was 23 percent per year. The cost to recruit and train one new employee was $56,625. To address the turnover problem, the company developed a skills training program that averaged 80 hours per year per employee. The average employee wage was $35 per hour. Instructor, classroom, and other costs were $170,000.

   a. What is the total cost of training? The total cost of turnover?

   b. If the turnover rate dropped 8 percent (from 23 percent to 15 percent), what was the financial benefit of the training program?

   c. What was the ROI of the training program?

   d. How much would the turnover rate have to be reduced (from 23 percent) for the
      training program to show a benefit?

7. Go to *www.roiinstitute.net*, the website for ROI Institute, Inc., the leading resource
   on research, training, and networking for practitioners of the Phillips ROI Method-
   ology™. Click on "Free Tools," Review the "Nations Hotels—Measuring the ROI
   in Business Coaching." What are the strengths of this approach for determining ROI?
   What are the weaknesses?

8. Watch the video about how Skillsoft and IBM are using big data at *http://www
   .youtube.com/watch?v=Texn4xpaZ0w*. How is using big data to analyze employees
   learning usage patterns useful for companies? For employees?

Case:

Developing Financial Planners at AMP

AMP, an Australian-based financial services company, recognized that the greatest challenge to company growth was attracting and developing the best financial planners. As a result, AMP developed the Career Changer Program, a twelve-month learning program for individuals who desire to be financial advisors but lack financial experience. Aspiring financial planners participate in both online and face-to-face learning during the first ten weeks of the program. In the classroom, instructors provide knowledge about finance, financial products, and selling. Also, to enhance selling skills and customer service, learners engage in role-plays. The next nine months of the program include mentoring and on-the-job experiences. Learners work with financial planners in their practices, providing real advice to clients. During this nine months learners are provided with on-the-job coaching, professional development, and complete compliance training. After successfully completing the program, learners achieve the status allowing them to start their own join one of AMP's personal financial practices.

What outcomes should AMP collect to determine the effectiveness of the Career Changer Program? What evaluation design should it use? Explain your choice of outcomes and design.

Source: "Training Broadens Career Horizons," *T+D* (July 2014): 80.

Endnotes

1. P. Tharenou, A. Saks, and C. Moore, "A review and critique of research on training and organizational-level outcomes," *Human Resource Management Review,* 17 (2007): 251–273; S. Sung and J. Choi, "Do organizations spend wisely on employees? Effects of training and development investments on learning and innovation in organizations," *Journal of Organizational Behavior*, 35 (2014): 393–412; H. Aguinis and K. Kraiger, "Benefits of training and development for individuals, teams, organizations, and society," *Annual Review of Psychology*, 60 (2009): 451–474; Y. Kim and R. E. Ployhart, "The effects of staffing and training on firm productivity and profit growth before, during, and after the Great Recession," *Journal of Applied Psychology*, 99 (2014): 361–389.

2. "Leaders take flight," *T+D* (February 2014): 72.

3. J. Dearborn, "Big data: A quick start guide for learning practitioners," *T+D* (May 2014): 52–57.

4. A. Purcell, "20/20 ROI," *Training and Development* (July 2000): 28–33.

5. M. Van Wart, N. J. Cayer, and S. Cook, *Handbook of Training and Development for the Public Sector* (San Francisco: Jossey-Bass, 1993).

6. K. Brown and M. Gerhardt, "Formative evaluation: An integrative practice model and case study," *Personnel Psychology,* 55 (2002): 951–983.

7. J. Salopek, "BEST 2005: St. George Bank," *T + D* (October 2005): 68.

8. D. Russ-Eft and H. Preskill, "In search of the Holy Grail: Return on investment evaluation in human resource development," *Advances in Developing Human Resources,* 7 (February 2005): 71–85.

9. K. Kraiger, D. McLinden, and W. Casper, "Collaborative planning for training impact," *Human Resource Management,* 43 (4) (2004): 337–351; F. Nickols, "Why a stakeholder approach to evaluating training," *Advances in Developing Human Resources,* 7 (February 2005): 121–134.

10. K. Kraiger, D. McLinden, and W. Casper, "Collaborative planning for training impact," *Human Resource Management* (Winter 2004): 337–351; R. Brinkerhoff, "The success case method: A strategic evaluation approach to increasing the value and effect of training," *Advances in Developing Human Resources,* 7 (February 2005): 86–101.

11. K. Kraiger, J. K. Ford, and E. Salas, "Application of cognitive, skill-based, and affective theories of learning outcomes to new methods of training evaluation," Journal of Applied Psychology, 78 (1993): 311–328; J. J. Phillips, "ROI: The search for best practices," Training and Development (February 1996): 42–47; D. L. Kirkpatrick, "Evaluation of Training," in *Training and Development Handbook,* 2d ed., ed. R. L. Craig (New York: McGraw-Hill, 1976): 18-1–18-27; J. Kirkpatrick and W. Kirkpatrick, "Creating a post-training evaluation plan," *T+D* (January 2013): 26–28.

12. K. Kraiger, J. K. Ford, and E. Salas, "Application of cognitive, skill-based, and affective theories of learning outcomes to new methods of training evaluation," *Journal of Applied Psychology,* 78 (1993): 311–328; J. J. Phillips, "ROI: The search for best practices," *Training and Development* (February 1996): 42–47; G. M. Alliger et al., "A meta-analysis of the relations among training criteria," *Personnel Psychology,* 50 (1997): 341–355; K. Kraiger, "Decision-Based Evaluation," in *Creating, Implementing, and Managing Effective Training and Development,* ed. K. Kraiger (San Francisco: Jossey-Bass, 2002): 331–375; G. Alliger and E. Janek, "Kirkpatrick's levels of training criteria: Thirty years later," *Personnel Psychology,* 42 (1989): 331–342.

13. R. Morgan and W. Casper, "Examining the factor structure of participant reactions to training: A multidimensional approach," *Human Resource Development Quarterly,* 11 (2000): 301–317; K. Brown, "An examination of the structure and nomological network of trainee reactions: A closer look at 'smile sheets,'" *Journal of Applied Psychology,* 90 (2005): 991–1001; G. Vellios, "On the level," *T+D* (December 2008): 26–29.

14. A. Beninghof, "How's My Training", *TD* (January 2015): 28–31.

15. G. Hopkins, "How to design an instructor evaluation," *Training and Development* (March 2000): 51–53.

16. T. Sitzmann et al., "A review and meta-analysis of the nomological network of trainee reactions," *Journal of Applied Psychology,* 93 (2008): 280–295.

17. T. Sitzmann, K. Ely, K. Brown, and K. Bauer, "Self-assessment of knowledge: A cognitive learning or affective measure," *Academy of Management Learning & Education,* 9 (2010): 169–191.

18. "Grant Thornton," *T+D* (October 2010): 75.

19. P. Taylor, D. Russ-Eft, and H. Taylor, "Transfer of management training from alternative perspectives," *Journal of Applied Psychology,* 94 (2009): 104–121.

20. M. Weinstein, "Taking training's measure," *training* (November/December 2014): 42–43.

21. "Walgreens: Leadership leap," *training* (January/February 2014): 113.

22. J. J. Phillips, "Was it the training?" *Training and Development* (March 1996): 28–32.

23. G. Dutton, "Training at your fingertips," *training* (March/April 2014): 26–30.

24. "USAA," *TD* (October 2014): 98.

25. J. Salopek, "Tackling business-critical issues through training," *TD* (October 2014): 65–68.

26. J. J. Phillips, "ROI: The search for best practices," *Training and Development* (February 1996): 42–47.

27. P. Harris, "Short can be oh, so sweet," *T+D* (October 2013): 66–69.

28. D. A. Grove and C. Ostroff, "Program Evaluation." In *Developing Human Resources,* ed. K. N. Wexley (Washington, D.C.: Bureau of National Affairs, 1991): 5-185–5-220.

29. H. J. Frazis, D. E. Herz, and M. W. Horrigan, "Employer-provided training: Results from a new survey," *Monthly Labor Review,* 118 (1995): 3–17.

30. W. Arthur, Jr. et al., "Effectiveness of training in organizations: A meta-analysis of design and evaluation features," *Journal of Applied Psychology,* 88 (2003): 234–245.

31. C. Anderson, "Bad measurement affects training impact," *Chief Learning* Officer (May 2014): 44–46; J. Marshall and A. Rossett, "Perceptions of barriers to the evaluation of workplace learning programs," *Performance Improvement Quarterly,* 27 (2014): 7–26.

32. "Verizon: Tech University (Tech U) – Deductive reasoning," *training* (January/February 2015): 57.

33. G. Alliger and E. Janek, "Kirkpatrick's levels of training criteria: Thirty years later," *Personnel Psychology,* 42 (1989): 331–342.

34. W. Arthur, Jr., W. Bennett, P. Edens, and S. Bell, "Effectiveness of training in organizations: A meta-analysis of design and evaluation features," *Journal of Applied Psychology,* 88 (2003): 234–245.

35. T. D. Cook, D. T. Campbell, and L. Peracchio, "Quasi-experimentation." In *Handbook of Industrial and Organizational Psychology,* 2d ed., Vol. 1, eds. M. D. Dunnette and L. M. Hough (Palo Alto, CA: Consulting Psychologists Press, 1990): 491–576.

36. Ibid.; J. J. Phillips, *Handbook of Training Evaluation and Measurement Methods,* 2d ed. (Houston, TX: Gulf Publishing, 1991).

37. D. Sussman, "Strong medicine required," *T+D* (November 2005): 34–38.

38. S. J. Simon and J. M. Werner, "Computer training through behavior modeling, self-paced, and instructional approaches: A field experiment," *Journal of Applied Psychology,* 81 (1996): 648–659.

39. CHG Healthcare Services, "2011 Training Top 125," *Training* (January/February 2011): 87.

40. J. Komaki, K. D. Bardwick, and L. R. Scott, "A behavioral approach to occupational safety: Pinpointing and reinforcing safe performance in a food manufacturing plant," *Journal of Applied Psychology,* 63 (1978): 434–445.

41. R. D. Bretz and R. E. Thompsett, "Comparing traditional and integrative learning methods in organizational training programs," *Journal of Applied Psychology,* 77 (1992): 941–951.

42. S. I. Tannenbaum and S. B. Woods, "Determining a strategy for evaluating training: Operating within organizational constraints," *Human Resource Planning,* 15 (1992): 63–81; R. D. Arvey, S. E. Maxwell, and E. Salas, "The relative power of training evaluation designs under different cost configurations," *Journal of Applied Psychology,* 77 (1992): 155–160.

43. P. R. Sackett and E. J. Mullen, "Beyond formal experimental design: Toward an expanded view of the training evaluation process," *Personnel Psychology,* 46 (1993): 613–627.

44. "Mountain American Credit Union: Flow philosophy training," *training* (January/February 2015): 103.

45. B. Gerber, "Does your training make a difference? Prove it!" *Training* (March 1995): 27–34.

46. A. P. Carnevale and E. R. Schulz, "Return on investment: Accounting for training," *Training and Development Journal* (July 1990): S1–S32.

47. J. Phillips and P. Phillips, "Distinguishing ROI myths from reality," *Performance Improvement* (July 2008): 12–17.

48. J. Mattox, "ROI: The report of my death is an exaggeration," *T+D* (August 2011): 30–33.

49. A. Purcell, "20/20 ROI," *Training and Development* (July 2000): 28–33.

50. J. Phillips and P. Phillips, "Using action plans to measure ROI," *Performance Improvement,* 42 (2003): 22–31.

51. K. Ellis, "What's the ROI of ROI?" *Training* (January 2005): 16–21; B. Worthen, "Measuring the ROI of training," *CIO* (February 15, 2001): 128–136; D. Russ-Eft and H. Preskill, "In search of the Holy Grail: Return on investment evaluation in human resource development," *Advances in Developing Human Resources* (February 2005): 71–85.

52. J. Gordon, "Eye on ROI," *Training* (May 2007): 43–45.

53. A. P. Carnevale and E. R. Schulz, "Return on investment: Accounting for training," *Training and Development Journal* (July 1990): S1–S32; G. Kearsley, *Costs, Benefits, and Productivity in Training Systems* (Boston: Addison-Wesley, 1982).

54. S. D. Parry, "Measuring training's ROI," *Training and Development* (May 1996): 72–77.

55. Aetna Inc., "*Training* Top 125 Rankings," *training* (January/February 2013): 81.

56. D. G. Robinson and J. Robinson, "Training for impact," *Training and Development Journal* (August 1989): 30–42; J. J. Phillips, "How much is the training worth?" *Training and Development* (April 1996): 20–24.

57. A. Purcell, "20/20 ROI," *Training and Development* (July 2000): 28–33.

58. J. J. Phillips, *Handbook of Training Evaluation and Measurement Methods,* 2d ed. (Houston, TX: Gulf Publishing, 1991); J. J. Phillips, "ROI: The search for best practices," *Training and Development* (February 1996): 42–47; J. Phillips and P. Phillips, "Moving from evidence to proof," *T+D* (August 2011): 34–39.

59. D. G. Robinson and J. Robinson, "Training for impact," *Training and Development Journal* (August 1989): 30–42.

60. D. Sussman, "Strong medicine required," *T+D* (November 2005): 34–38.

61. J. E. Matheiu and R. L. Leonard, "Applying utility analysis to a training program in supervisory skills: A time-based approach," *Academy of Management Journal,* 30 (1987): 316–335; F. L. Schmidt, J. E. Hunter, and K. Pearlman, "Assessing the economic impact of personnel programs on workforce productivity," *Personnel Psychology,* 35 (1982): 333–347; J. W. Boudreau, "Economic considerations in estimating the utility of human resource productivity programs," *Personnel Psychology,* 36 (1983): 551–576.

62. U. E. Gattiker, "Firm and taxpayer returns from training of semiskilled employees," *Academy of Management Journal,* 38 (1995): 1151–1173.

63. B. Worthen, "Measuring the ROI of training," *CIO* (February 15, 2001): 128–136.

64. D. Abernathy, "Thinking outside the evaluation box," *Training and Development* (February 1999): 19–23; E. Krell, "Calculating success," *Training* (December 2002): 47–52; D. Goldwater, "Beyond ROI," *Training* (January 2001): 82–90.

65. J. Kirpatrick and W. Kirkpatrick, "Creating ROE: The end is the beginning," *T+D* (November 2011): 60–64; J. Kirkpatrick and W. Kirkpatrick, "ROE's rising star: Why return on expectations is getting so much attention," *T+D* (August 2010): 34–38.

66. R. Brinkerhoff, "The success case method: A strategic evaluation approach to increasing the value and effect of training," *Advances in Developing Human Resources,* 7 (February 2005): 86–101; J. Kirkpatrick and W. Kirkpatrick, "ROE's rising star: Why return on expectations is getting so much attention," *T+D* (August 2010): 34–38.

67. C. Wick and M. Papay, "Feasting on achievement," *T+D* (January 2013): 56–60.

68. E. Holton and S. Naquin, "New metrics for employee development," *Performance Improvement Quarterly,* 17 (2004): 56–80.

69. E. Massie, "Big learning data," (Alexandria, VA: American Society for Training & Development, 2013); L. Miller, *Big Data, Better Learning? How Big Data is Affecting Organizational Learning* (Alexandria, VA; American Society for Training & Development, 2014).

70. E. Frauenheim, "Numbers game," *Workforce Management* (March 2011): 20–21; P. Gallagher, "Rethinking HR," *Human Resource Executive* (September 2, 2009): 1, 18–23; B. Roberts, "How to put analytics 'on your side,'" *HR Magazine* (October 2009): 43–46; A. Rossett, "Metrics matter," *T+D* (March 2010): 64–69.

71. G. Dutton, "What's the big deal about big data?" *training* (March/April 2014): 16–19; B. Roberts, "The benefits of big data," *HR Magazine* (October 2013): 20–24; J. Dearborn, "Big data: A quick start guide for learning practitioners," *T+D* (May 2014): 52–57.

72. D. Galloway, "Achieving accurate metrics using balanced scorecards and dashboards," *Performance Improvement* (August 2010): 38–45.

73. J. Dearborn, "Big Data: A Quick Start Guide for Learning Practitioners," *T+D* (May 2014): 52–57.

74. D. Mallon, "At a glance," *T+D* (December 2009): 66–68; *www.key.com*, webpage for Key Bank, accessed September 15, 2011.

Case 2   Learning in Practice

Business Goals Drive Learning at Verizon

Verizon's three business goals for 2011 were to build a business and a workforce that were as good as its networks, to lead in shareholder value creation, and to be recognized as an iconic technology company. The company's strategic business units align their priorities with the overall company business goals. The Learning and Development section of Verizon establishes training priorities and initiatives that support the business unit and overall company goals. To help create shareholder value, a customized executive education development program sponsored by the company president and CEO was developed to help senior managers understand how to drive long-term value creation. The program provides them with tools, processes, and metrics to help them understand how to positively influence shareholder value. As part of the program, senior managers work in cross-functional teams and are given an assignment to identify barriers to creating more shareholder value. At the end of the session, each team presents its recommendations to top executives. Many of these recommendations have been implemented, resulting in such changes as new budgeting processes and new process improvement programs. Also, as part of the program, each manager chooses one or two actions that they will commit to for positively influencing shareholder value. These actions are part of the senior manager's performance review. Because innovation and new technology drives Verizon's success, the company is using social media for training and on-demand learning. Videos distributed through the company's YouTube site are one of the employees' favorite ways to learn. For example, videos are used to demonstrating system processes for sales teams. Many videos go "viral," with employees recommending to their peers a video they may have just watched. Verizon also expanded its internal social network for peer-to-peer collaboration. Also, Yammer.com was recently launched. It has more than 8,000 members and over 400 groups using it. Sales teams use the site to post questions and share best practices. In 2013 Verizon implemented tablet computers for performance support and training of retail store employees. An app puts all the data that retail store employees need to learn about devices, service plans, promotions, and policies on the easy to use and readily accessible tablet computer. The app called SIMON (Simplified Information for the Moment of Need) runs on both Apple and Android devices and is designed to be used when interacting with a customer. Also, Verizon provided its field technicians with tablets to access product knowledge and fixes to service problems. Previously, each day local managers gave them handouts with this information. Verizon envisions that by 2022, its learning organization will have a greater emphasis on facilitating and moderating user-generated content rather than generating or providing content itself. The company expects that its workforce will use mobile online performance support on an as-needed basis into the future.

Questions

1. Do you think it is easier for a company like Verizon, which emphasizes technology and innovation, to adopt and use new technologies such as social media for training? Why?

2. What metrics should Verizon use to show the effectiveness of its internal YouTube video site?

3. Should all training that Verizon offers be available to employees on an "as-needed" basis? Explain your answer. Is performance support the same as learning?

Sources: Based on L. Freifeld, "Verizon's new # is 1," *training* (January/February 2012): 28–30; M. Weinstein, "Verizon Connects to Success," *training* (January/February 2011): 40–42; J. Salopek, "Good Connections," *T+D* (October 2014): 48–50.

Training and Development Methods

Part Three of this book covers the different types of training and development methods. Chapter Seven, "Traditional Training Methods," introduces you to presentational, hands-on, and group training methods, which include on-the-job training (OJT), simulations and games, lectures, and various group building methods such as action learning and team training. Chapter Eight, "Technology-Based Training Methods," covers topics such as Twitter and Facebook and focuses on some of the newest technology-based methods that are being used for training and development. E-learning, online learning, distance learning, Massive Open Online Courses, virtual reality, virtual worlds such as Second Life, collaboration tools such as blogs and wikis, and mobile learning using social media smartphones and tablet computers such as i-Pads are examples of some of the methods discussed. Blended learning is also covered. Chapters Seven and Eight both show how each method is used and help you understand the potential strengths and weaknesses of each method, as well as important research results. Many companies are moving toward a blended learning approach to take advantage of the strengths of both face-to-face and technology-aided instruction.

Chapter Nine, "Employee Development and Career Management," details development planning and different types of development activities, including assessment, formal courses and programs, experiences, and interpersonal relationships involving mentoring and coaching. Chapter Nine also provides you with examples of companies' development systems.

The Part Three case, "Development Is Served 24/7 in InterContinental Hotel Group's Leaders Lounge," illustrates how companies can use technology to develop leadership talent.

Chapter **Seven**

Traditional Training Methods

Objectives

After reading this chapter, you should be able to

1. Discuss the strengths and weaknesses of presentational, hands-on, and group building training methods.
2. Provide recommendations for effective on-the-job training (OJT).
3. Develop a case study.
4. Develop a self-directed learning module.
5. Discuss the key components of behavior modeling training.
6. Explain the conditions necessary for adventure learning to be effective.
7. Discuss what team training should focus on to improve team performance.

Learning Develops Skills of Staff Dedicated to Battling Cancer

The American Cancer Society (ACS) is a nonprofit nationwide, community-based, voluntary health organization dedicated to creating a world without cancer. ACS strives to save lives by helping people stay well and get well, by finding cures for cancer, and by helping those who have cancer to fight the disease. ACS is headquartered in Atlanta, Georgia, and has regional and local offices throughout the United States that support eleven geographical divisions to ensure a presence in every community. The corporate office in Atlanta is responsible for overall strategic planning, corporate support services including training, development and implementation of research programs, health program, a 24-hour call center, and providing technical support and materials to regional and local offices. Regional and local offices deliver patient programs and services and engage in fund-raising activities.

The philosophy of the talent development department is to provide "the right learning solution at the right time for the right person." One guiding principle is to support and drive the business through employee development and training. Another is that ACS wants employees to grow and develop, which is captured by the slogan "save lives, fulfill *yours*." Staff are encouraged to participate in leadership development, mentoring, coaching, and job-specific training classes. For staff interested in pursuing formal education, ACS has partnerships with online universities. Also, staff are encouraged to work with their manager to establish clear professional and development goals that map a path to career success.

At ACS it is important for training and development programs to be realistic in terms of taking into account budgetary constraints and job responsibilities. The programs need to be both efficient and effective and minimize the time that staff members are taken away from their primary responsibilities such as helping patients, working with the community, and planning and carrying out fund-raising events. All delivered content is evaluated on the extent to which it is related to the job, staff member performance, and the organization's mission. For example, the Nationwide Manager Development Program is designed to help build management strength for ACS. The program is marketed as an "adventure in management" and its design is intended to make training engaging, enjoyable, and enriching for the participants. The eighteen-month program helps participants learn management concepts using virtual discussion forums and e-learning. Also, participants are put into learning teams designed to represent a diversity of thought, tenure, and experience. These teams engage in action learning, which focuses on developing management skills, while developing solutions to business issues and problems facing ACS.

Source: Based on P. Harris, "Training as a change agent," *TD* (October 2014): 84–86; *www.cancer.org*, website for the American Cancer Society.

INTRODUCTION

The American Cancer Society uses a combination of training methods to develop the skills of its staff members. For most companies, including the American Cancer Society, training methods have to be developed or purchased within a budget, there usually is a sense of urgency for the training, and training must be made available to those employees who need it.

Several studies have shown that most workplace learning doesn't occur through formal courses or programs but rather on the job, informally, and through social interactions with others.[1] For example, one study of executives found that 70 percent of learning occurred on the job in the workplace, 20 percent occurred socially through coaching and mentoring, and only 10 percent occurred through formal classroom instruction. This is known as the **70-20-10 model** of learning. Many trainers rely on this model for designing or choosing training methods that will be included in courses and programs. Similar to the emphasis on conditions for learning and transfer discussed in Chapter Four, "Learning and Transfer of Training," this model suggests that to increase the likelihood that learning will occur in training, the content needs to be meaningful and practical, the learner has to be actively involved in the learning process, and learning involves feedback and reinforcement from others.

Before we discuss specific training methods, it is important for you to consider more broadly the training methods that companies are using to help employees learn and how the emphasis placed on these different methods is changing. Figure 7.1 shows a learning system with four quadrants. This learning system shows that how and what employees learn

FIGURE 7.1
A Learning System

Source: From
J. Meister and
K. Willyerd, *The
2020 Workplace. How
Innovative Companies
Attract, Develop, and
Keep Tomorrow's
Employees Today*
(New York: Harper
Business 2010).

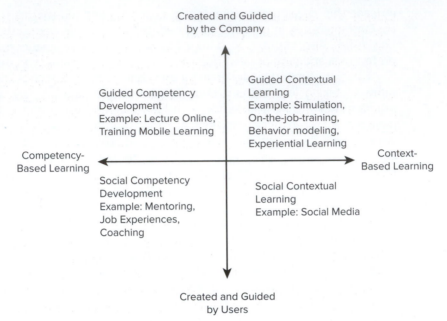

varies and influences the type of training methods used.[2] Guided competency development means that the company has defined a broad set of competencies or skills for positions or for the entire company. Training and development methods such as lectures or online training are directed at the most common needs in the company. Context-based learning, learning that occurs on the job and during the everyday performance of work, tends to be more unique to the employee's needs and includes training methods such as OJT, simulations, and mobile learning. Both guided competence development and guided contextual learning are usually formal training activities designed and developed by the company to achieve specific learning goals. Employees are expected to participate in these learning activities. The bottom quadrants include social learning, that is, learning activities that involve employees collaborating with each other either one-to-one or in groups or teams. Social competency development enhances specific job-related competencies through interaction with others such as a mentor or coach, or through encountering challenging job experiences. The competencies that are developed are typically not necessary for successful performance of one's job but help prepare employees for future roles or positions. As a result, mentoring, coaching, and job experiences are considered development activities. We discuss development activities in Chapter Nine, "Employee Development and Career Management." Social contextual learning is informal and peer-to-peer, and it occurs spontaneously on an as-needed basis. It usually involves employees sharing knowledge on issues, problems, and topics related to their current job. Employees have always learned from face-to-face meetings and phone conversations with peers. What is new is that the increased availability and access to smartphones and tablet computers provide a multimedia, low-cost, easy-to-use, and familiar way to interact with others using social media such as blogs, wikis, social networks (such as Facebook), and microblogs (such as Twitter). This provides many possibilities for technology-aided social contextual learning. We will discuss blogs, wikis, social networks, and microblogs in Chapter Eight, "Technology-Based Training Methods." Keep in mind that training methods can cut across the quadrant shown in Figure 7.1 if they include multiple types of learning, such as a virtual classroom that includes simulations and use of social networks.

Today, most companies' training methods would be found in Quadrants 1, 2, and 3, but some are beginning to explore how to facilitate learning from peers either face to face or through the use of social media. This is because traditionally training and development activities have been largely "instructor focused." This means that the instructor or trainer, along with the company, has the primary responsibility for ensuring that employees learn.[3] The learner plays a passive role as the receiver of information, and learning occurs to the extent that the appropriate conditions are provided by the learning "experts" or are inherent in the learning method. For example, the instructor bears the responsibility for identifying what should be learned, determining the most appropriate methods, and evaluating the extent to which knowledge and skill acquisition resulted from the learning activity. Increased recognition of the 70-20-10 model has resulted in training emphasizing a more active role for the learner and informal learning.[4] Also, the greater availability and use of online and mobile technology (e.g., iPads) to deliver instruction and facilitate social collaboration gives the employee the opportunity to choose when, how, from whom, and even what content to learn.[5] Figure 7.1 provides an overview of how much companies are using different training methods. Instructor-led classroom training remains the most frequently used method, but the use of online learning, virtual classroom, or a combination of methods continues to grow.

Regardless of whether the training method is traditional or technology-based, for training to be effective, it needs to be based on the training design model shown in Figure 1.2 in Chapter One, "Introduction to Employee Training and Development." Needs assessment, a positive learning environment, and transfer of training are critical for training program effectiveness. Recall the discussions of needs assessment, learning, and transfer of training in Chapters Three to Five.

This chapter and Chapter Eight present various training methods. This chapter focuses on **traditional training methods,** which require an instructor or facilitator and involve face-to-face interaction between trainees. However, most methods discussed here can be adapted for online, virtual reality, mobile learning, or other new training technologies used for training delivery or instruction. For example, a classroom lecture can occur face to face with trainees (traditional training) or can be delivered through a virtual classroom, in which the instructor is not in the same room as the trainees. Also, instruction can be real-time (synchronous) or time-delayed (asynchronous). Through technology, a lecture can be attended live (although the trainees are not in the same classroom as the trainer), or the lecture can be videotaped or burned onto a DVD. The lecture can be viewed by the trainees at their convenience on a notebook computer that gives them access to the appropriate medium for viewing the lecture (e.g., DVD player or Internet connection).

Chapter Eight discusses web-based training, e-learning, virtual reality, and social media. The increased use of technology-based training for delivery of instruction is occurring because of the potential increases in learning effectiveness, as well as the reductions in training costs.

Keep in mind that many companies' training programs use a combination of methods to capitalize on each method's strengths for learning and transfer. For example, LQ Management, LLC is an owner operator of limited service hotels in the United States.

It operates more than eight hundred hotels in forty-six states, Canada, and Mexico, under La Quinta Inns and Suites brands.[6] La Quinta wants its employees to provide the best rooms, atmosphere, and courteous service at every hotel. La Quinta's culture emphasizes continuous improvement and its operating philosophy stresses taking care of employees and guests, and keeping the hotels spotlessly cleaned and well maintained.

This means that training plays an important role in the success of every employee. La Quinta uses different training methods to help employees learn, including web-based training, small-group training involving games where they are challenged with real-world scenarios that have occurred at hotel properties, and DVDs. The goal of the small-group training is to make learning fun and at the same time promote learning through conversation and idea sharing. Additionally, employees have multiple training resources available, including LQUniversity (LQU), LQ Connect, and LQ Video Portal. LQU provides access to formal training courses, LQ Connect is a web-based portal that provides learning resources, and LQ Video Portal provides training videos that employees can access at any time. The videos cover La Quinta's service philosophy, values, and housekeeping and maintenance topics.

The traditional training methods discussed in this chapter are organized into three broad categories: presentation methods, hands-on methods, and group building methods.[7] The following sections provide a description of each method, a discussion of its advantages and disadvantages, and tips for the trainer who is designing or choosing the method. The chapter concludes by comparing methods based on several characteristics, including the learning outcomes influenced, the extent to which the method facilitates learning transfer, cost, and effectiveness.

PRESENTATION METHODS

Presentation methods are methods in which trainees are passive recipients of information. This information may include facts, processes, and problem-solving methods. Lectures and audiovisual techniques are presentation methods. It is important to note that instructor-led classroom presentation methods may include lectures, video, workbooks and manuals, DVDs, and games. That is, a mix of methods can actively engage trainees in learning and can help with transfer of training.

Lecture

In a **lecture,** trainers communicate through spoken words what they want the trainees to learn. The communication of learned capabilities is primarily one-way—from the trainer to the audience. As Figure 7.2 shows, instructor-led classroom presentation remains a popular training method despite new technologies such as interactive video and computer-assisted instruction.

Lectures have several uses and advantages.[8] A lecture is one of the least expensive, least time-consuming ways to present a large amount of information efficiently and in an organized manner to groups of trainees. Lectures are useful when the instructor is the main knowledge holder and it is the most efficient and direct way to provide learners with that knowledge. Lectures that are scripted can be used to deliver a consistent message. A lecture can also demonstrate a subject-matter expert's passion and enthusiasm for a topic.

For example, an AT&T executive who is in charge of emerging enterprises and partnerships at AT&T shares stories with general managers about how the company created its partnership with Apple to provide service for the iPhone.[9] The purpose of the lecture is to convey the message that managers should not be afraid of failure. At the annual meeting of Skanska, a construction company, two former fighter pilots lectured senior executives about the steps needed to successfully execute a mission, including how to define a project, analyze progress, debrief, and celebrate success.[10] This was an especially relevant topic because the company was implementing a new business strategy. Also, TED talks (see *www.ted.com*) are a good example of how lectures can be motivational, interesting, and provide a simple message to learners in less than twenty minutes. Lectures are also used to support other training methods such as behavior modeling and technology-based techniques. For example, a lecture may be used to communicate information regarding the purpose of the training program, conceptual models, or key behaviors to trainees prior to their receiving training that is more interactive and customized to their specific needs.

Table 7.1 describes several variations of the standard lecture method. All have advantages and disadvantages.[11] Team teaching brings more expertise and alternative perspectives to

FIGURE 7.2
Use of training methods

Source: Based on "2014 Training Industry report," *Training* (November/December 2014): 24.

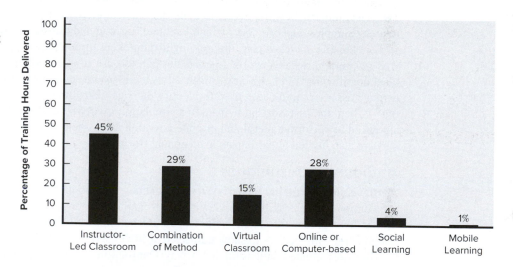

TABLE 7.1
Variations of the Lecture Method

Method	Description
Standard lecture	Trainer talks and may use visual aids provided on the blackboard, whiteboard, or Microsoft PowerPoint slides, while trainees listen and absorb information.
Team teaching	Two or more trainers present different topics or alternative views of the same topic.
Guest speakers	A speaker or speakers visit the session for a predetermined time period. Primary instruction is conducted by the instructor.
Panels	Two or more speakers present information and ask questions.
Student presentations	Groups of trainees present topics to the class.

the training session. Team teaching does require more time on the part of trainers to not only prepare their particular session but also coordinate with other trainers, especially when there is a great deal of integration between topics. Panels are good for showing trainees different viewpoints in a debate. A potential disadvantage of a panel, however, is that trainees who are relatively naive about a topic may have difficulty understanding the important points. Guest speakers can motivate learning by bringing to the trainees relevant examples and applications. For guest speakers to be effective, trainers need to set expectations with speakers regarding how their presentation should relate to the course content. Student presentations may increase the material's meaningfulness and trainees' attentiveness, but they can inhibit learning if the trainees do not have presentation skills.

The lecture method has several disadvantages. Lectures tend to lack participant involvement, feedback, and meaningful connection to the work environment—all of which inhibit learning and transfer of training. Lectures appeal to few of the trainees' senses because trainees focus primarily on hearing information or seeing facts, principles, or processes. Lectures also make it difficult for the trainer to judge quickly and efficiently the learners' level of understanding. To overcome these problems, the lecture is often supplemented with question-and-answer periods, discussion, video, games, case studies, or simulations. These techniques allow the trainer to build into the lecture more active participation, job-related examples, and exercises, which facilitate learning and transfer of training.

For example, Paychex provides training to employees through lectures provided on the web (webinars), which involve learners through the use of chat, polling, and electronic blackboard work.[12] PPL Electric Utilities uses a classroom session to introduce its storm damage assessors to devices used to identify damage, patrolling techniques, and reporting.[13] Then, the assessors participate in a simulation involving a downed power line and are asked to perform a patrol and provide a written assessment of the power line. Assessors are also invited to participate in an annual storm drill.

Audiovisual Techniques

Audiovisual instruction includes overheads, slides, and video. Video is used for improving communications skills, interviewing skills, and customer-service skills and for illustrating how procedures (e.g., welding) should be followed. Video is usually used in conjunction with lectures to show trainees real-life experiences and examples.

Microsoft created videos in its AlwaysOnprogram for sales, marketing, and services employees.[14] The purpose of the program is to help these employees learn about devices and services that Microsoft offers so they can promote and sell the products. The ten-minute videos are released to employees the same day as new or updated products and services. The videos include product demos, breaking news and announcements, and the latest Windows hardware. The videos can be tagged by product, series, or business group. Links to the videos are provided on the Microsoft web home page and in a weekly newsletter.

Video is also a major component of behavior modeling and, naturally, interactive video instruction. The use of video in training has a number of advantages.[15] First, trainers can review, slow down, or speed up the lesson, which gives them flexibility in customizing the session depending on trainees' expertise. Second, trainees can watch the video multiple times if they have access to it during and after the training session. This gives them control over their learning. Third, trainees can be exposed to equipment, problems, and events that cannot be easily demonstrated, such as equipment malfunctions, angry customers, or emergencies. Fourth, trainees are provided with consistent instruction. Program content is not affected by the interests and goals of a particular trainer. Fifth, videotaping trainees allows them to see and hear their own performance without the interpretation of the trainer. That is, video provides immediate objective feedback. As a result, trainees cannot attribute poor performance to the bias of external evaluators such as the trainer or peers. Sixth, video requires minimal knowledge of technology and equipment. Most trainers and trainees can easily use a VCR or DVD player.

Most problems in video result from the creative approach used.[16] These problems include too much content for the trainee to learn, poor dialogue between the actors (which hinders the credibility and clarity of the message), overuse of humor or music, and drama that makes it confusing for the trainee to understand the important learning points emphasized in the video.

HANDS-ON METHODS

Hands-on methods are training methods that require the trainee to be actively involved in learning. These methods include OJT, simulations, case studies, business games, role-playing, and behavior modeling. These methods are ideal for developing specific skills, understanding how skills and behaviors can be transferred to the job, experiencing all aspects of completing a task, or dealing with interpersonal issues that arise on the job.

On-the-job training (OJT)

On-the-job training (OJT) refers to new or inexperienced employees learning in the work setting and during work by observing peers or managers performing the job and then trying to imitate their behavior. OJT is one of the oldest and most used types of informal training.[17] It is considered informal because it does not necessarily occur as part of a training program, and because managers, peers, or mentors serve as trainers. If OJT is too informal, learning is less likely to occur. OJT can be useful for training newly hired employees, upgrading experienced employees' skills when new technology is introduced, cross-training employees within a department or work unit, and orienting transferred or promoted employees to their new jobs.

OJT takes various forms, including apprenticeships and self-directed learning programs. (Both of these are discussed later in this section.) OJT has several advantages over other training methods.[18] It can be customized to the experiences and abilities of trainees. Training is immediately applicable to the job because OJT occurs on the job using actual tools and equipment. As a result, trainees are highly motivated to learn. Both trainees and trainers are at the job site and continue to work while training occurs. This means that companies save the costs related to bringing trainees to a central location, hiring trainers, and renting training facilities. OJT can be offered at any time, and trainers will be available because they are peers or managers. Finally, OJT uses actual job tasks and occurs at work. As a result, skills learned in OJT more easily transfer to the job.

Reliance Industries, one of India's largest businesses, uses OJT in its Nagothane Manufacturing Division (a refinery that makes polymers and chemicals).[19] Because of rapid company growth and the demand for experienced employees, the company needed to decrease the length of time required for new engineers to contribute. In response to this need, the training staff identified mentors who would help accelerate learning for the new engineers. The mentors and new hires are carefully matched based on an assessment of the mentor's training style and the new employee's learning style. Mentors are paired with up to three new employees, each for nine months. The mentors and new employees work together on four learning modules, each of which takes two months to complete. Each module includes predetermined lesson plans, and progress is tracked using an online portal. As a result, the length of time that it takes new engineers to contribute at work has decreased from twelve to six months.

At Sweets Candy, a candy maker based in Salt Lake City, Utah, new employees receive training in basic safety and emergency evacuation procedures in an orientation session and then are assigned a mentor.[20] The mentor works with the new employee for two weeks, providing hands-on, one-on-one training. Teams hold weekly meetings, and managers provide training on safety issues throughout the year. Employees also receive a weekly safety contact card on which they note safety hazards that they have encountered on their job and how they have fixed the problem. The safety contact cards are turned in, and each month the company has a safety celebration where the cards are put into a drawing. Employees win prizes such as a day off or a $10 gift card. All of the safety contact cards are reviewed to identify safety issues and hazards, which are then communicated to the employees.

OJT is an attractive training method because compared to other methods, it needs less investment in time or money for materials, the trainer's salary, or instructional design. Managers or peers who are job-knowledge experts are used as instructors. As a result, it may be tempting to let them conduct the training as they believe it should be done.

There are several disadvantages to this unstructured approach to OJT. Managers and peers may not use the same process to complete a task. They may pass on bad habits as well as useful skills. Also, they may not understand that demonstration, practice, and feedback are important conditions for effective OJT. Unstructured OJT can result in poorly trained employees, employees who use ineffective or dangerous methods to produce a product or provide a service, and products or services that vary in quality.

OJT must be structured to be effective. Table 7.2 shows the principles of structured OJT. Because OJT involves learning by observing others, successful OJT is based on the principles emphasized by social learning theory. These include the use of a credible trainer, a manager or peer who models the behavior or skill, communication of specific key behaviors, practice, feedback, and reinforcement. For example, at Rochester Gas and Electric in Rochester, New York, radiation and chemistry instructors teach experienced employees how to conduct OJT.[21] While teaching these employees how to demonstrate software to new employees, the trainer may ask the employees to watch other OJT instructors as they train new recruits so that they can learn new teaching techniques. Regardless of the specific type, effective OJT programs include:

1. A policy statement that describes the purpose of OJT and emphasizes the company's support for it.
2. A clear specification of who is accountable for conducting OJT. If managers conduct OJT, this is mentioned in their job descriptions and is part of their performance evaluations.

3. A thorough review of OJT practices (program content, types of jobs, length of program, cost savings) at other companies in similar industries.

4. Training of managers and peers in the principles of structured OJT (see Table 7.2).

5. Availability of lesson plans, checklists, procedure manuals, training manuals, learning contracts, and progress reports for use by employees who conduct OJT.

6. Evaluation of employees' levels of basic skills (reading, computation, and writing) before OJT.[22]

Self-Directed Learning

Self-directed learning has employees take responsibility for all aspects of learning, including when it is conducted and who will be involved.[23] Trainees master predetermined training content at their own pace without an instructor. Trainers may serve as facilitators. That is, trainers are available to evaluate learning or answer questions for the trainee. The trainer does not control or disseminate instruction. The learning process is controlled by the trainee. Hilton Worldwide uses self-guided tutorials for its revenue management professionals.[24] The Revenue Management at Work course is designed to help learners acquire knowledge, skills, and use tools to help them improve revenue management. Learners identify their own objectives and complete exercises that help them determine what they need to know as well as a learning action plan. Also, self-directed learning could

TABLE 7.2 Principles of OJT

Preparing for Instruction

1. Break down the job into important steps.
2. Prepare the necessary equipment, materials, and supplies.
3. Decide how much time you will devote to OJT and when you expect the employees to be competent in skill areas.

Actual Instruction

1. Tell the trainees the objective of the task and ask them to watch you demonstrate it.
2. Show the trainees how to do the task without saying anything.
3. Explain the key points or behaviors. (Write out the key points for the trainees, if possible.)
4. Show the trainees how to do it again.
5. Have the trainees do one or more single parts of the task and praise them for correct reproduction (optional).
6. Have the trainees do the entire task and praise them for correct reproduction.
7. If mistakes are made, have the trainees practice until accurate reproduction is achieved.
8. Praise the trainees for their success in learning the task.

Transfer of Training

Provide support materials and job aids such as flowcharts, checklists, or procedures. Arrange for manager or trainer support and observation on the job, especially for difficult or complex tasks.

Evaluation

Prepare and allow time for final tests and exercises and surveys of trainee reactions.

Sources: Based on R. Buckley and J. Caple, "Developing one-to-one training programs," *T+D* (April 2010): 108–109; W. J. Rothwell and H. C. Kazanas, "Planned OJT is productive OJT," *Training and Development Journal* (October 1990): 53–55; P. J. Decker and B. R. Nathan, *Behavior Modeling Training* (New York: Praeger Scientific, 1985).

involve the company providing employees with information such as databases, training courses, and seminars while still holding them responsible for taking the initiative to learn. Because the effectiveness of self-directed learning is based on an employee's motivation to learn, companies may want to provide seminars on the self-directed learning process, self-management, and incentives for completing learning. Best Buy rewards employees with virtual "badges" when they complete training that is appropriate and necessary for their current career stage.[25] For example, employees receive bronze status when they have prepared for a new role by completing foundational training courses. Gold status can be reached when employees become leaders and complete courses relating to managing other employees. In addition to badges for completing training, employees earn pins they can wear on their uniforms and points they can exchange for products and services.

Self-directed learning has several advantages.[26] It allows trainees to learn at their own pace and receive feedback about the learning performance. For the company, self-directed learning requires fewer trainers, reduces costs associated with travel and meeting rooms, and makes multiple-site training more realistic. Self-directed learning provides consistent training content that captures the knowledge of experts. Self-directed learning also makes it easier for shift employees to gain access to training materials.

A major disadvantage of self-directed learning, however, is that trainees must be willing to learn on their own and feel comfortable doing so. That is, trainees must be motivated to learn. From the company perspective, self-directed learning results in higher development costs, and development time is longer than with other types of training programs.

Several steps are necessary to develop effective self-directed learning:[27]

1. Conduct a job analysis to identify the tasks that must be covered.
2. Write trainee-centered learning objectives directly related to the tasks. Because the objectives take the place of the instructor, they must indicate what information is important, what actions the trainee should take, and what the trainee should master.
3. Develop the content for the learning package. This involves developing scripts (for video) or text screens (for computer-based training). The content should be based on the trainee-centered learning objectives. Another consideration in developing the content is the medium (e.g., paper, video, computer, or website) that will be used to communicate the content.
4. Break the content into smaller pieces ("chunks"). The chunks should always begin with the objectives that will be covered and include a method for trainees to evaluate their learning. Practice exercises should also appear in each chunk.
5. Develop an evaluation package that includes evaluation of the trainee and evaluation of the self-directed learning package. Trainee evaluation should be based on the objectives (a process known as *criterion referencing*). That is, questions should be developed that are written directly from the objectives and can be answered directly from the materials. Evaluation of the self-directed learning package should involve determining ease of use, how up-to-date the material is, whether the package is being used as intended, and whether trainees are mastering the objectives.

Self-directed learning is likely to become more common in the future, as companies seek to train staff flexibly, take advantage of technology, and encourage employees to be proactive in their learning rather than driven by the employer.

Apprenticeship

Apprenticeship is a work-study training method with both on-the-job and classroom training.[28] The typical length of an apprenticeship is four years but this can range from two to six years. To qualify as a registered apprentice under state or federal guidelines, apprentices in most cases must complete at least 144 hours of classroom instruction and, depending on state rules, must obtain a certain number of hours of on-the-job experience.[29] For example, learners in the Ohio State Apprenticeship Program are required to complete 144 hours of instruction and a minimum of 2,000 hours of paid, on-the-job training.[30] Once their training is complete, apprentices are called *journey workers,* and they earn certification from the U.S. Department of Labor or a state apprenticeship agency. Table 7.3 shows the top occupations for apprentices. In 2013, there were over 375,000 active apprentices in over 19,000 registered apprenticeship programs. Apprenticeships can be sponsored by individual companies or by groups of companies cooperating with a union. The typical costs of apprenticeships for employers ranges from $170,000 to $250,000, including four years of classroom training, medical benefits, and salary on the job while the apprentices learn. Apprentices are not required to work for the company after they graduate. Unions' collective bargaining agreements designate what proportion of union dues or hours worked by its members are used to fund apprenticeship programs. As Table 7.3 shows, most apprenticeship programs are in the skilled trades such as plumbing, carpentry, electrical work, and pipe fitting. Table 7.4 is an example of an apprenticeship program for a machinist.

In an apprenticeship program, the hours and weeks that must be devoted to completing specific skill units are clearly defined. The OJT involves assisting a certified tradesperson (a journey worker) at the work site. The OJT portion of the apprenticeship follows the guidelines for effective OJT by including modeling, practice, feedback, and evaluation.[31] First, the employer verifies that the trainee has the required knowledge of the operation or process. Next, the trainer (who is usually a more experienced, licensed employee) demonstrates each step of the process, emphasizing safety issues and key steps. The senior employee provides the apprentice with the opportunity to perform the process until all are satisfied that the apprentice can perform it properly and safely.

Apprenticeships have benefits for both the learner and the company.[32] Learners earn pay while they learn and their wages increase automatically as their skills improve. Learners

TABLE 7.3
Top 10 Occupations for Active Apprentices

Source: Based on "Top 10 Occupations for Fiscal year 2013," from U.S. Department of Labor, Employment and Training Administration. Available at *www.doleta.gov/OA/data_statistics2013.cfm.*

Rank	Occupation	Active Apprentices
1	Electrician	36,237
2	Carpenter	13,685
3	Plumber	12,116
4	Pipe fitter (construction)	8,665
5	Construction craft laborers	7,901
6	Sheet metal worker	7,101
7	Roofer	5,285
8	Structural-steel worker	4,651
9	Painter (construction)	3,254
10	Sprinkler fitter	3,052

TABLE 7.4
Example of a Machinist Apprenticeship

Source: A. H. Howard III, "Apprenticeship." In *The ASTD Training and Development Handbook*, 4th ed., ed. R. L. Craig (New York: McGraw-Hill, 1996): 808.

Hours	Weeks	Unit
240	6.0	Bench Work
360	9.0	Drill Press
240	6.0	Heat Treat
200	5.0	Elementary Layout
680	17.0	Turret Lathe (Conventional and Numerical Control)
800	20.0	Engine Lathe
320	8.0	Tool Grind
640	16.0	Advanced Layout
960	24.0	Milling Machine
280	7.0	Profile Milling
160	4.0	Surface Grinding
240	6.0	External Grinding
280	7.0	Internal Grinding
200	5.0	Thread Grinding
520	13.0	Horizontal Boring Mills
240	6.0	Jig Bore/Jig Grinder
160	4.0	Vertical Boring
600	15.0	Numerical Control Milling
240	6.0	Computer Numerical Control
640	16.0	Related Training
8,000	200.0	TOTAL

Probationary: **The following hours are included in the totals above, but must be completed in the first 1,000 hours of apprenticeship:**

Hours	Weeks	Unit
80	2.0	Drill Press (probation)
280	7.0	Lathe Work (probation)
360	9.0	Milling Machine (probation)
40	1.0	Elementary Layout (probation)
80	2.0	Related Training (probation)
840	**21.0**	**TOTAL**

often receive a job offer and good wages from the company that sponsors their training. Apprentices gain a wide range of skills and knowledge based on their classroom and on-the-job experience. They tend to be cross-trained, which means they can move to different tasks and jobs. For example, an individual who completes a machinist apprenticeship can begin working as a machinist, move to other areas of production, sales, and eventually to management. The costs for the learner are usually limited to textbooks unlike the expense of a college education. Employers benefit from high employee retention and loyalty rates among apprentices, improved morale and emphasis on continuous learning, a talent pool, improved safety, and training customized to their needs. For example, graduates of apprenticeship programs make up 13 percent of Newport News Shipbuilding's workforce. Their program includes eight hundred apprentices in twenty-five occupations. Eighty percent of graduates are still employed by Newport News ten years later. Because apprentices want to learn, it helps create an environment where more experienced employees want to share their knowledge and help apprentices learn new skills. This helps develop a skilled internal labor force, which is likely unavailable outside the company (recall the discussion in Chapter One of how companies are having difficulty finding employees with the skills they need). At its manufacturing facility in Toledo, Ohio, Libbey Glass has apprenticeship programs in mold making, machine repair, millwrighting, and maintenance repair.[33] These programs are viewed as the best jobs within the company because the wage rates are high and because most apprentices are scheduled to work day shifts instead of afternoon or midnight shifts. The apprenticeship program has been costly for the company but has paid dividends. Each apprentice requires the support of a journey worker for each work assignment. This means that work is being performed by two employees when only one worker is normally required. The program also requires apprentices to be evaluated every 1,000 hours to meet U.S. Department of Labor standards. The reviews are conducted by a committee that includes management and department journey workers. The committee also develops tests and other evaluation materials. The committee members cannot perform their normal duties during the time they are reviewing apprentices, so their workload has to be distributed among other employees or rescheduled for some other time. The program offers many benefits to Libbey: The company is developing employees who are more receptive to changes in the work environment; work can be performed at Libbey, so the company does not have to outsource jobs to contract labor; and Libbey is given an edge in attracting talented employees who like the idea that after completing an apprenticeship, they are eligible for promotions to other positions in the company, including management positions. Also, the apprenticeship program helps Libbey tailor training and work experiences to meet specific needs in maintenance repair, which is necessary to create and repair production mold equipment used in making glass products.

Apprentice-like programs are also used to prepare new managers. The president and chief executive officer of Goldcorp, a company in the mining industry, offers the chance for MBAs to apply for a nine-month apprenticeship.[34] The apprentice shadows Goldcorp's CEO and observes board meetings, negotiations, mine acquisitions, and other important aspects of the mining industry. Goldcorp hopes the apprenticeships will attract more MBAs to the mining industry, which is viewed by many graduates as an unsafe and dirty business. Hyatt Hotels offers several programs in which management trainees complete training in the areas of facilities, culinary arts, sales, hotel operations, accounting, and catering.[35] Trainees rotate through all parts of the hotel and perform all aspects of each job, ranging from washing dishes to catering, and then spend the rest of the training time in their specialty area. Employees who complete the training are placed in entry-level management positions.

Besides the development costs and time commitment that management and journey workers have to make to apprenticeship programs, another disadvantage of many of these programs is that despite efforts to be inclusive, there still may be limited access for minorities and women.[36] Also, there is no guarantee that jobs will be available when the program is completed. This is especially a problem in poor economic times such as the 2009 recession.

Simulations

A **simulation** is a training method that represents a real-life situation, with trainees' decisions resulting in outcomes that mirror what would happen if they were on the job. A common example of the use of simulators for training is flight simulators for pilots. Simulations, which allow trainees to see the impact of their decisions in an artificial, risk-free environment, are used to teach production and process skills as well as management and interpersonal skills. As you will see in Chapter Eight, new technology has helped in the development of virtual reality, a type of simulation that even more closely mimics the work environment.

Simulators replicate the physical equipment, patients, and conditions that employees encounter on the job. For example, the Fire Division of the City of Columbus trains its paramedics and firefighters using mannequins that can present a variety of medical conditions, including strokes and drug overdoses.[37] The mannequins can vomit, sweat, breathe, give birth, and be programmed with different mental states. Drugs can be injected and IVs run into the mannequins. For example, at training, paramedics recently encountered a child mannequin that was choking on a piece of candy. After the paramedics ran an IV, applied chest compressions, and gave medications, the mannequin had a pulse. The trainer was controlling the mannequin through a wireless tablet. He observed the paramedics to make sure they were giving the right amount of fluids at the correct time. A debrief including trainers and paramedics is held immediately after training. The debrief focuses on what the paramedics did correctly, what they did wrong, and the knowledge and skills they need to improve.

Thirty high-potential global managers at Automatic Data Processing, Inc., in teams of six, participate in a computer-based business simulation that replicates the company's business model.[38] The team, acting as the company's executive board, must operate a financially sound and profitable business through five rounds by creating growth opportunities in a competitive global market.

A key aspect of simulators is the degree to which they are similar to the equipment and situations that the trainee will encounter on the job. Recall the discussion of near transfer in Chapter Five, "Program Design." Simulators need to have elements identical to those found in the work environment. The simulator needs to respond exactly like the equipment would under the conditions and response given by the trainee. For example, flight simulators include distractions that pilots have to deal with, such as hearing chimes in the cockpit from traffic alerts generated by an onboard computer warning system while listening to directions from an air traffic controller.[39] For this reason, simulators are expensive to develop and need constant updating as new information about the work environment is obtained.

Case Studies

A **case study** is a description about how employees or an organization dealt with a difficult situation. Trainees are required to analyze and critique the actions taken, indicating the appropriate actions and suggesting what might have been done differently.[40] A major assumption of the case study approach is that employees are most likely to recall and use knowledge and skills if they learn through a process of discovery.[41] Cases may be especially appropriate for developing higher-order intellectual skills such as analysis, synthesis, and evaluation. These skills are often required by managers, physicians, and other professional employees. Cases also help trainees develop the willingness to take risks given uncertain outcomes, based on their analysis of the situation. To use cases effectively, the learning environment must give trainees the opportunity to prepare and discuss their case analyses. Also, face-to-face or electronic communication among trainees must be arranged. Because trainee involvement is critical for the effectiveness of the case method, learners must be willing and able to analyze the case and then communicate and defend their positions.

Table 7.5 presents the process used for case development. The first step in the process is to identify a problem or situation. It is important to consider if the story is related to the instructional objectives, will provoke a discussion, forces decision making, can be told in a reasonable time period, and is applicable to the situations that trainees may face. Information on the problem or situation must also be readily accessible. The next step is to research documents, interview participants, and obtain data that provide the details of the case. The third step is to outline the story and link the details and exhibits to relevant points in the story. Fourth, the media used to present the case should be determined. Also, at this point in case development, the trainer should consider how the case exercise will be conducted. This may involve determining if trainees will work individually or in teams, and how the students will report results of their analyses. Finally, the actual case materials need to be prepared. This includes assembling exhibits (figures, tables, articles, job descriptions, etc.), writing the story, preparing questions to guide trainees' analysis, and writing an interesting, attention-getting case opening that will attract trainees' attention and provide a quick orientation to the case.

There are a number of available sources of preexisting cases. A major advantage of preexisting cases is that they are already developed, but a disadvantage is that the case may not actually relate to the work situation or problem that the trainee will encounter. It is especially important to review preexisting cases to determine how meaningful they will be to the trainee. Preexisting cases on a wide variety of problems in business management (e.g., in human resource management, operations, marketing, advertising) are available from Harvard Business School, the Darden Business School at the University of Virginia, Ivey Business School at the University of Western Ontario, and various other sources.

KLA-Tencor uses cases studies as part of a program known as "The Situation Room" to help managers learn how to deal with common leadership problems.[42] A group of between eight and twenty managers get together face to face or virtually each month for one year and read one of twelve 350–400 word case studies. The case is based on a real situation or problem that occurred at KLA-Tencor. IT has to be broad enough for most managers to have experienced the situation, issue, or problem, but specific enough to be useful. After they read the case, the managers are given three minutes to write their response to the situation. Participants share their responses and their peers provide feedback. If a peer doesn't like the response, he or she can provide an alternative. After all participants have shared their responses, four teams are formed and they are given "homework." Between the first and next session participants are expected to meet for an hour in their teams and review content, models, methodology, and or tools that they have been exposed to in prior courses. Based on this review, they are asked to provide a response to the situation. During the second session each of the participants share their prepared responses and discuss

TABLE 7.5
Process for Case Development

Source: Based on J. Alden and J. K. Kirkhorn, "Case Studies." In *The ASTD Training and Development Handbook,* 4th ed., ed. R. L. Craig (New York: McGraw-Hill, 1996): 497–516.

1. Identify a story.
2. Gather information.
3. Prepare a story outline.
4. Decide on administrative issues.
5. Prepare case materials.

them. Based on what they learned from both the first and second session, participants are asked to prepare a personal response focusing on how they will handle this situation if they encounter it on their job. The outcomes of the sessions are documented on the company's knowledge management system so practices can be shared with other managers facing similar challenges. Managers who completed the program felt that it was valuable and the company is currently analyzing employee engagement survey scores to see if managers who participated in The Situation Room have improved in the leadership and management categories assessed on the survey.

Business Games

Business games require trainees to gather information, analyze it, and make decisions. Business games are primarily used for management skill development. Games stimulate learning because participants are actively involved and because games mimic the competitive nature of business. The types of decisions that participants make in games include all aspects of management practice: labor relations (agreement in contract negotiations), ethics, marketing (the price to charge for a new product), and finance (financing the purchase of new technology). Games are also used for developing job-specific skills such as patient triage or aircraft repair. They are similar to simulations in that they can be used for training that otherwise would involve risk of injury, accidents, or would be too costly.[43]

Typical games have several characteristics.[44] The game involves a contest among trainees or teams of trainees or against an established criterion such as time or quantity. The game is designed to demonstrate an understanding of or application of a knowledge, skill, or behavior. Several alternative courses of action are available to trainees, and trainees can estimate the consequences of each alternative, but only with some uncertainty. Trainees do not know for certain what the consequences of their actions will be because the consequences are partially based on the decisions of other game participants. Finally, rules limit participant behavior.

To ensure learning and transfer of training, games used in training should be simple enough that trainees can play them in a short period of time. The best games generate excitement among the participants and interest in the game. Meaningfulness of the game is enhanced if it is realistic. Trainees need to feel that they are participating in a business and acquiring knowledge, skills, and behaviors that are useful on the job.[45] Debriefing from a trainer can help trainees understand the game experience and facilitate learning and transfer. Debriefing can include feedback, discussions of the concepts presented during the game, and instructions in how to use at work the knowledge, skills, or behavior emphasized in the game. Table 7.6 contains some questions that can be used for debriefing.

At ConAgra Foods, new vice-presidents participate in a game on the last of eight days of leadership training.[46] Teams run a simulated business based on ConAgra, rotating

TABLE 7.6
Questions to Use When Debriefing a Game

Source: Based on S. Sugar, "Using Games to Energize Dry Material." In *The ASTD Handbook of Training Design and Delivery*, eds. G. Piskurich, P. Beckschi, and B. Hall (New York: McGraw-Hill, 2000): 107–120.

How did the score of the game affect your behavior and the behavior of the team?
What did you learn from the game?
What aspects of the game remind you of situations at work?
How does the game relate to your work?
What did you learn from the game that you plan to use at work?

through roles including sales and marketing, research and development, and finance. The teams compete for business and market share while developing their teamwork and other interpersonal skills. At the end of the game, ConAgra executives determine the winning teams based on financial measures, as well as team work skills. CMS Energy uses an online game (The Resolver) to teach employees about conflicts of interest.[47] For example, employees understand that accepting bribes is illegal, but they might not understand all of the different types of bribes. The Resolver begins with clinking champagne glasses and receiving tickets for a sporting event. In the game players interact with different characters and make decisions. Each decision they make affects different people, including colleagues, friends, and family members. Those affected by each decision discuss how the player's decision affects them. Teams of five employees were formed to compete against each other. During game play, the team format facilitated conversations and questions among team members about ethics and conflicts of interest. When the competition ended, team members could see how they ranked against others on an electronic online leaderboard. This stimulated further employee conversations about how they responded to the scenarios and what they should have done differently to earn more points.

A review of research on computer games shows that trainees learn more when they are actively involved in learning the content (rather than reading text or listening), they have unlimited access to the game, and the game is used as a supplement to other training methods such as lecturing.[48] Games may give team members a quick start at developing a framework for information and may help develop cohesive groups. For some groups (such as senior executives), games may be more meaningful training activities (because the game is realistic) than are presentation techniques such as classroom instruction.

Role-Plays

Role-plays refer to experiences in which trainees take on a role such as a manager, client, or disgruntled employee, and explore what is involved in the role.[49] Role-plays are usually included in training programs involving interpersonal skills such as communications, sales, providing performance feedback, coaching, leadership, and team building. Role-plays can be completed in small groups of two to three persons in which all trainees complete the role-play. Or several trainees can volunteer to role-play while the remaining trainees observe them. In a role-play, outcomes depend on the emotional (and subjective) reactions of the other trainees.

At Wequassett Resort and Golf Club in Chatham, Massachusetts, the training schedule considers both the need to make guests happy and the need to help both new and returning employees learn to do that.[50] From April to October, the resort is closed, but 340 employees start work in the spring before the resort opens. Half of the employees are receiving training for the first time, while the returning employees need refresher training. Wequassett Academy offers seventy courses in four schools (customer intimacy, technical training, information and technology, and management). The goal of training is to provide the kind of service that will encourage guests to come back again, as well as recommend the resort to their friends. The resort's training is in step with its business, which requires a personal touch. Training involves classroom instruction with role-plays, as well as the use of DVDs. Employees have to successfully complete competency checklists before they are able to work. For example, food servers may have to take courses in menu knowledge, food service, and wine knowledge.

TABLE 7.7
Activities for Effective Role-Plays

Sources: Based on S. Karve, "Setting the stage for effective role plays," *T+D* (November 2011): 76–77; S. Thiagarajan, "Instructional Games, Simulations, and Role Plays." In *The ASTD Training and Development Handbook*: 517–533.

Provide background information on the purpose of and context for the role-play.
Make sure that a script is provided with enough detail for trainees to understand their role.
The room is arranged so trainees can see and hear the role-players.
Observations sheets and checklists that emphasize the issues in the role-play are developed and used.
Debriefing occurs on the experience of the role-players and observers, the relationship of the role play to the company context, and important learning points.

For role-plays to be effective, trainers need to engage in several activities before, during, and after the role-play. Table 7.7 shows the activities that comprise effective role-plays.

Behavior Modeling

Behavior modeling presents trainees with a model who demonstrates key behaviors to replicate and provides trainees with the opportunity to practice the key behaviors. Behavior modeling is based on the principles of social learning theory (discussed in Chapter Four), which emphasize that learning occurs by (1) observation of behaviors demonstrated by a model and (2) vicarious reinforcement. **Vicarious reinforcement** occurs when a trainee sees a model receiving reinforcement for using certain behaviors.

Behavior modeling is more appropriate for teaching skills and behaviors than for teaching factual information or knowledge. Research suggests that behavior modeling is one of the most effective techniques for teaching interpersonal and computer skills.[51]

Table 7.8 presents the activities in a behavior modeling training session. These activities include an introduction, skill preparation and development, and application planning.[52] Each training session, which typically lasts four hours, focuses on one interpersonal skill such as coaching or communicating ideas. Each session includes a presentation of the rationale behind the key behaviors, a video of a model performing the key behaviors, practice opportunities using role-playing, evaluation of a model's performance in the videotape, and a planning session devoted to understanding how the key behaviors can be used on the job. In the practice sessions, trainees are provided with feedback regarding

TABLE 7.8
Activities in a Behavior Modeling Training Program

Introduction (45 mins.)
- Watch video that presents key behaviors.
- Listen to rationale for skill module.
- Discuss experiences in using skill.

Skill Preparation and Development (2 hrs., 30 mins.)
- View model.
- Participate in role-plays and practice.
- Receive oral and video feedback on performance of key behaviors.

Application Planning (1 hr.)
- Set improvement goals.
- Identify situations in which to use key behaviors.
- Identify on-the-job applications of the key behaviors.

how closely their behavior matches the key behaviors demonstrated by the model. The role-playing and modeled performance are based on actual incidents in the employment setting in which the trainee needs to demonstrate success.

Well-prepared behavior modeling training programs identify the key behaviors, create the modeling display, provide opportunities for practice, and facilitate transfer of training.[53] The first step in developing behavior modeling training programs is to determine (1) the tasks that are not being adequately performed due to lack of skill or behavior and (2) the key behaviors that are required to perform the task. A **key behavior** is one of a set of behaviors that are necessary to complete a task. In behavior modeling, key behaviors are typically performed in a specific order for the task to be completed. Key behaviors are identified through a study of the skills and behaviors necessary to complete the task and the skills or behaviors used by employees who are effective in completing the task.

Table 7.9 presents key behaviors for a behavior modeling training program on problem analysis. The table specifies behaviors that the trainee needs to engage in to be effective in problem analysis skills. Note that the key behaviors do not specify the exact behaviors needed at every step of solving a problem. Rather, the key behaviors in this skill module specify more general behaviors that are appropriate across a wide range of situations. If a task involves a clearly defined series of specific steps that must be accomplished in a specific order, then the key behaviors that are provided are usually more specific and explained in greater detail. For example, tennis players learning how to serve must follow a detailed sequence of activities (e.g., align feet with the baseline, take the racquet back over the head, toss the ball, bring the racquet forward over the head again, pronate the wrist, and strike the ball). People learning interpersonal skills must develop more general key behaviors because there is always more than one way to complete the task. The development of general key behaviors promotes far transfer (discussed in Chapter Five). That is, trainees are prepared to use the key behaviors in a variety of situations.

Another important consideration in developing behavior modeling programs is the modeling display. The **modeling display** provides the key behaviors that the trainees will practice to develop the same set of behaviors. DVDs and online video are the predominant methods used to present modeling displays. In online behavior modeling training the learner can practice the key behaviors by watching scenarios that mimic an interpersonal interaction. At certain points during the scenario, for example, when asked a question, the learner is asked to choose one of several choices of how they would respond. Just like in a real interpersonal interaction, they then see how the other person would react to their

TABLE 7.9
Example of Key Behaviors in Problem Analysis

Get all relevant information by:
• Rephrasing the question or problem to see if new issues emerge
• Listing the key problem issues
• Considering other possible sources of information
Identify possible causes.
If necessary, obtain additional information.
Evaluate the information to ensure that all essential criteria are met.
Restate the problem considering new information.
Determine what criteria indicate that the problem or issue has been resolved.

response. (The use of new technology in training is discussed in Chapter Eight.) Effective modeling displays have six characteristics:[54]

1. The display clearly presents the key behaviors. The music and the characteristics of the situation shown in the display do not interfere with the trainee seeing and understanding the key behaviors.
2. The model is credible to the trainees.
3. An overview of the key behaviors is presented.
4. Each key behavior is repeated. The trainee is shown the relationship between the behavior of the model and each key behavior.
5. A review of the key behaviors is included.
6. The display presents models engaging in both positive use of key behaviors and negative use (i.e., ineffective models not using the key behaviors).

Providing opportunities for practice involves (1) having trainees cognitively rehearse and think about the key behaviors and (2) placing trainees in situations (such as role-plays) in which they have to use the key behaviors. Trainees may interact with one other person in the role-play or in groups of three or more in which each trainee can practice the key behaviors. The most effective practice session allows trainees to practice the behaviors multiple times, in a small group of trainees where anxiety or evaluation apprehension is reduced, with other trainees who understand the company and the job.

Practice sessions should include a method for providing trainees with feedback that should provide reinforcement to the trainee for behaviors performed correctly, as well as information needed to improve behaviors. For example, if role-plays are used, trainees can receive feedback from the other participants who serve as observers when not playing the role. Practice sessions may also be videotaped and played back to the trainees. The use of video objectively captures the trainees' behavior and provides useful, detailed feedback. Having the trainees view the video shows them specifically how they need to improve their behaviors and identifies behaviors that they are successfully replicating.

Behavior modeling helps ensure that transfer of training occurs by using application planning. **Application planning** prepares trainees to use the key behaviors on the job (i.e., enhances transfer of training). Application planning involves having all participants prepare a written document identifying specific situations in which they should use the key behaviors. Some training programs actually have trainees complete a "contract" outlining the key behaviors that they agree to use on the job. The trainer may follow up with the trainees to see if they are performing according to the contract. Application planning may also involve preparing trainees to deal with situational factors that may inhibit their use of the key behaviors (similar to relapse prevention, discussed in Chapter Four). As part of the application planning process, a trainee may be paired with another participant, with the stated expectation that the two should periodically communicate with each other to discuss successes and failures in the use of key behaviors.

GROUP BUILDING METHODS

Group building methods are training methods designed to improve team or group effectiveness. A **team** refers to two or more people with specific roles or functions who work together with shared responsibility to achieve a common goal or mission or complete tasks in a company.[55] In group building methods, trainees share ideas and experiences, build group identity, understand the dynamics of interpersonal relationships, and get to know their own strengths and weaknesses and those of their co-workers. Group techniques focus on helping teams increase their skills for effective teamwork. A number of training techniques are available to improve work group or team performance, to establish a new team, or to improve interactions among different teams. All involve examination of feelings, perceptions, and beliefs about the functioning of the team; discussion; and development of plans to apply what was learned in training to the team's performance in the work setting. Group building methods include adventure learning, team training, and action learning.

Group building methods often involve experiential learning. **Experiential learning** training programs have four stages: (1) gain conceptual knowledge and theory; (2) take part in a behavioral simulation; (3) analyze the activity; and (4) connect the theory and activity with on-the-job or real-life situations.[56]

For experiential training programs to be successful, several guidelines should be followed. The program needs to tie in to a specific business problem. The trainees need to be moved outside their personal comfort zones, but within limits so as not to reduce trainee motivation or ability to understand the purpose of the program. Multiple learning modes should be used, including audio, visual, and kinesthetic. When preparing activities for an experiential training program, trainers should ask trainees for input on the program goals. Clear expectations about the purpose, expected outcomes, and trainees' role in the program are important. Finally, the training program needs to be evaluated. Training programs that include experiential learning should be linked to changes in employee attitudes, behaviors, and other business results. If training programs that involve experiential learning do not follow these guidelines, they may be questioned. For example, the U.S. Postal Inspector resigned after criticisms surfaced about postal team training activities. Current and former postal employees complained to several U.S. senators about training activities that included having employees wrap each other in toilet paper, dress as cats, and hold signs that spelled "teamwork."[57]

Adventure Learning

Adventure learning is an experiential learning method that focuses on the development of teamwork and leadership skills through structured activities.[58] Adventure learning includes wilderness training, outdoor training, improvisational activities, drum circles, and even cooking classes. Adventure learning appears to be best suited for developing skills related to group effectiveness, such as self-awareness, problem solving, conflict management, and risk taking. Adventure learning may involve strenuous, challenging physical activities such as dogsledding or mountain climbing. Adventure learning can also use structured individual and group activities, such as wall climbing, rope courses, trust falls, ladder climbing, and traveling from one tower to another using a device attached to a wire that connects the two towers.

For example, "The Beam" requires team members to cross a six-foot-high beam placed between two trees, using only help from the team. Trainees can help by shouting advice and encouragement.[59] Rope-based activities may be held three to four feet or twenty-five to thirty feet above the ground. The high-ropes course is an individual-based exercise whose purpose is to help the trainee overcome fear. The low-ropes course requires the entire team of trainees to complete the course successfully. The purpose is to develop team identity, cohesiveness, and communication skills.

To improve their leadership skills and teamwork, lawyers at Weil, Gotshal & Manges in New York worked with New York City firefighters to learn how to hook up a fire hose, set the water pressure, and extinguish fires.[60] At the fire academy, four-person teams rushed into burning buildings and rescued passengers in simulated subway accidents or other emergency drills. The Fire Department of New York (FDNY) program, Firefighter for a Day Team Challenge, was created to help teams develop decision-making and problem-solving skills. These skills are especially necessary for work teams made up of employees from different specialties or areas of expertise who work on large projects or deal with complex problems requiring coordination and delegation. Companies pay up to $2,500 for each four-person team.

Adventure learning can also include demanding activities that require coordination but place less of a physical strain on team members. In drum circles, each team member is given a drum, and facilitators work with the team to create a drumming orchestra. Toyota spent $20,000 for drums to accommodate forty people at its training center in Torrance, California.[61] Drum circles are held twice a week. Toyota believes that the drum circles are metaphors for how high-performance teams should operate: cooperatively and smoothly. Cookin' Up Change is one of many team-building courses offered around the United States by chefs, caterers, hotels, and cooking schools.[62] These courses have been used by companies such as Honda and Microsoft. The idea is that cooking classes help strengthen communications and networking skills by requiring team members to work together to create a full-course meal. Each team has to decide who does what kitchen tasks (e.g., cooking, cutting, cleaning) and who prepares the main course, salads, and dessert. Often, team members are required to switch assignments in mid-preparation to see how the team reacts to change.

For adventure learning programs to be successful, exercises should relate to the types of skills that participants are expected to develop. Also, after the exercises, a skilled facilitator should lead a discussion about what happened in the exercise, what was learned, how events in the exercise relate to the job situation, and how to set goals and apply what was learned on the job.[63] DaVita Healthcare Partners provides kidney-related health care services such as dialysis.[64] DaVita contracted with a training provider to develop a three-hour experiential learning activity that would be collaborative, have a sense of purpose, and reinforce the company's values of teamwork, fulfillment, and fun. The goals of the program were to understand the importance or why of work, understand how team members relate to patients and to each other, and how to address challenges. The activity started with a discussion of the importance of communicating and collaborating for successful teamwork on the job. Employees were divided into three-member teams and given the task of building prosthetic hands, which would be donated to organizations serving amputees. Building the prostheses provided an opportunity for the achievement of the program goals. The employees built more than fourteen thousand prostheses during the three-hour activity! The activity concluded with a discussion of ways to apply what they learned to their jobs at DaVita.

This approach does have disadvantages, however. The physical demands of some types of adventure learning and the requirement that trainees often touch each other in the exercises may increase a company's risk for negligence claims due to personal injury, intentional infliction of emotional distress, and invasion of privacy. Also, the Americans with Disabilities Act (ADA) raises questions about requiring disabled employees to participate in physically demanding training experiences.[65]

Given the physically demanding nature of adventure learning, it is important to consider when to use it instead of another training method. Adventure learning allows trainees to interact interpersonally in a situation not governed by formal business rules. This type of environment may be important for employees to mold themselves into a cohesive work team. Also, adventure learning exercises allow trainees to share a strong emotional experience. Significant emotional experiences can help trainees break difficult behavior patterns and open trainees to change their behaviors. One of the most important characteristics of adventure learning is that the exercises can serve as metaphors for organizational behavior. That is, trainees will behave in the same way in the exercises that they would when working as a team (e.g., developing a product launch plan). As a result, by analyzing behaviors that occur during the exercise, trainees gain insight into ineffective behaviors.

Does adventure learning work? Rigorous evaluations of its impact on productivity or performance have not been conducted. However, former participants often report that they gained a greater understanding of themselves and how they interact with co-workers.[66] One key to an adventure learning program's success may be the insistence that whole work groups participate together so that group dynamics that inhibit effectiveness can emerge and be discussed.

Team Training

Team training refers to training that is designed to improve team effectiveness. There are many different types of teams in companies, including production teams, service teams, committees, project teams, and management teams. Teamwork tends to be episodic.[67] That is, teams engage in a cycle of identifying their goals, engage in interpersonal interactions, and take actions to achieve their goals. They repeat this cycle as goals are reached and tasks are completed and they move on to new tasks or goals. Regardless of the type of team, successful team performance depends on the knowledge, attitudes, and behaviors of its members. Figure 7.3 shows the three components of team performance: knowledge, attitudes, and behavior.[68] The behavioral requirement means that team members must perform actions that allow them to communicate, coordinate, adapt, and complete complex tasks to accomplish their objective. The knowledge component requires team members to have mental models or memory structures that allow them to function effectively in unanticipated or new situations. Team members' beliefs about the task and feelings toward each other relate to the attitude component. Team morale, cohesion, and identity are related to team performance. For example, in the military, as well as many areas of the private sector (e.g., nuclear power plants and commercial airlines), much work is

FIGURE 7.3
Components of Team Performance

Source: Based on E. Salas and J. A. Cannon-Bowers, "Strategies for Team Training." In *Training for 21st-Century Technology: Applications of Psychological Research,* eds. M. A. Quinones and A. Dutta (Washington, D.C.: American Psychological Association, 1997): 249–281.

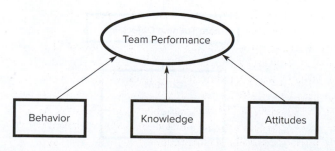

performed by crews, groups, or teams. Successful performance depends on coordination of individual activities to make decisions, on team performance, and on readiness to deal with potentially dangerous situations (e.g., an overheating nuclear reactor). Research suggests that teams that are effectively trained develop procedures to identify and resolve errors, coordinate information gathering, and reinforce each other.[69]

Figure 7.4 illustrates the four main elements of the structure of team training (tools, methods, strategies, and team training objectives). Several tools help define and organize the delivery of team training.[70] These tools also provide the environment (e.g., feedback) needed for learning to occur. These tools work in combination with different training methods to help create instructional strategies. These strategies are a combination of the methods, tools, and content required to perform effectively.

The strategies include cross training, coordination training, and team leader training. **Cross training** has team members understand and practice each other's skills so that members are prepared to step in and take the place of a member who may temporarily or permanently leave the team. Research suggests that most work teams would benefit from providing members with at least enough understanding of teammates' roles to discuss trade-offs of various strategies and behaviors that affect team performance.[71] **Coordination training** instructs the team in how to share information and decision- making responsibilities to maximize team performance. Coordination training is especially important for

FIGURE 7.4
Main Elements of the Structure of Team Training

Sources: Based on E. Salas and J. A. Cannon-Bowers, "Strategies for Team Training." In *Training for 21st-Century Technology: Applications of Psychological Research*, eds. M. A. Quinones and A. Dutta (Washington, D.C.: American Psychological Association, 1997): 249–281; J. Cannon-Bowers and C. Bowers, "Team Development and Functioning." In S. Zedeck (eds.). *APA Handbook of Industrial and Organizational Psychology*, eds. S. Zedeck (Washington, D.C.: American Psychological Association, 2011): 597–650.

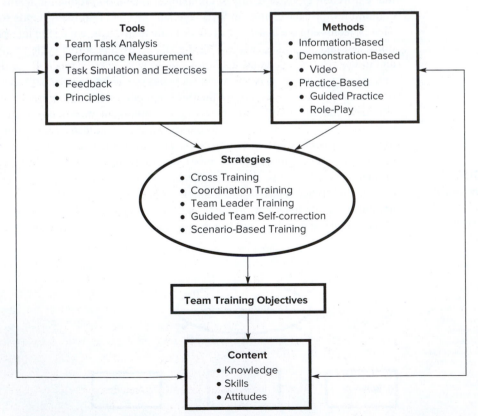

commercial aviation or surgical teams who are in charge of monitoring different aspects of equipment and the environment but who must share information to make the most effective decisions regarding patient care or aircraft safety and performance. **Team leader training** refers to training that the team manager or facilitator receives. This may involve training the manager on how to resolve conflict within the team or helping the team coordinate activities or other team skills. **Scenario-based training** refers to training that places team members in a realistic context while learning. This type of team training helps trainees experience the consequences of their actions, make adjustments, accomplish their tasks, and build team self-efficacy (feeling that the team can successfully perform tasks). **Guided team self-correction** refers to training that emphasizes continuous learning and knowledge sharing in teams. In this type of training, team members observe each other's behavior and give and receive performance feedback.

Employees obviously need technical skills that can help the team accomplish its task. But team members also need skills in communication, adaptability, conflict resolution, and other teamwork issues.[72] Team training usually involves multiple methods. For example, a lecture or video may be used to disseminate knowledge regarding communication skills to trainees. Role-plays or simulations may be used to give trainees the opportunity to put into practice the communication skills emphasized in the lecture. Regardless of the method chosen, opportunities for practice and feedback need to be included.

For example, Aquarius is an undersea laboratory used during the NASA Extreme Environment Mission Operations (NEEMO). The base, located several miles off the coast of Key Largo, Florida, is owned by the National Oceanic and Atmospheric Administration (NOAA) and managed by the University of North Carolina.[73] The NEEMO experience places astronauts in an environment with challenges that parallels the hostile physical and stressful psychological environment experienced in long-duration missions. These challenges can include allowing the crew to experience the effects of gravity in space, on the moon, and Mars, providing a compressed timeline for completing tasks, practicing procedures such as spacewalks to repair or replace equipment and emergency procedures used to rescue crew members, and performing tasks with delayed and limited communications with the mission control crew. The NEEMO experience helps crew members develop important team processes, such as communication, coordination, performance monitoring and back up behaviors, to successfully meet the challenges and perform the task they encounter, both in Aquarius and on their space missions.

United Airlines sent its supervisor, or lead, ramp employees to Pit Instruction and Training (Pit Crew U), which focuses on the preparation, practices, and teamwork of NASCAR pit crews. United is using the training to develop standardized methods to safely and more efficiently unload, load, and send off its airplanes.[74] Pit Instruction and Training, located outside Charlotte, North Carolina, has a quarter-mile race track and a pit road with pit stops for six cars. The school offers programs to train new racing pit crews, but most of its business comes from companies interested in teaching their teams to work as safely, efficiently, and effectively as NASCAR pit crews do. NASCAR pit crews work safely, quickly, and efficiently because each crew member knows what tasks to do (change tires, use an air gun, add gasoline, or clean up spills), and after the crew members have finished servicing the race car, they move new equipment into position in anticipation of the next pit stop. At Pit Crew U, trainees actually work as pit crews. They learn how to handle jacks, change tires, and fill fuel tanks on race cars. They are videotaped and timed just like real pit crews, and they receive feedback from trainers and from professional pit crew members who work on NASCAR teams. Also, the program requires trainees to deal with unforeseen circumstances similar to what they may encounter on the job. For example, at one pit stop, lug nuts had been sprinkled intentionally in the area where the race car stops, and the United employees were observed to see whether they noticed the lug nuts and cleaned them up. On their jobs, ramp employees are responsible for removing debris from the tarmac so that it is not sucked into jet engines or does not harm equipment. At another pit stop, United teams had to work with fewer members, which sometimes occurs when ramp crews are understaffed due to absences.

United's training is part of a multimillion-dollar investment that includes updating equipment and providing bag scanners. The purpose of the training is to standardize the tasks of ramp team members, to reinforce the need for ramp teams to be orderly and communicative, and to increase morale. Training has been optional for ramp employees, and they have survived layoffs and have been asked to make wage concessions to help pull the company out of bankruptcy. United has already started scheduling shorter ground times at some airports in anticipation of the positive results of the program. With shorter ground times, United can offer more daily flights without having to buy more airplanes. United hopes to make the airline more competitive by cutting the average airplane ground time by eight minutes.

Action Learning

Action learning gives teams or work groups an actual problem, has them work on solving it and committing to an action plan, and then holds them accountable for carrying out the plan.[75] Companies use action learning to solve important problems, develop leaders, quickly build high-performance teams, and transform the organizational culture. Table 7.10 shows the steps involved in action learning. Several types of problems are addressed in action learning, including how to change the business, better use technology, remove barriers between the customer and company, and develop global leaders.

TABLE 7.10
Steps in Action Learning

Sources: Based on P. Malone, "The untapped power of action learning," *T+D* (August 2013): 54–59; M. Pedler and C. Abbott, *Facilitating Action Learning* (New York: McGraw-Hill, 2013).

- Identification of the sponsors of action learning, including CEOs and top managers
- Identification of the problem or issue
- Identification and selection of the group who can address the problem
- Identification of coaches who can help the group reframe the problem and improve its problem solving by listening, giving feedback, offering assumptions, and so on
- Presentation of the problem to the group
- Group discussion that includes reframing the problem and agreement on what the problem is, what the group should do to solve the problem, and how the group should proceed
- Data gathering and analysis relevant to solving the problem, done by the group as a whole as well as by individual members
- Group presentation on how to solve the problem, with the goal of securing a commitment from the sponsors to act on the group's recommendations
- Self-reflection and debriefing (e.g., What have the group and group members learned? What might they have done differently?)

Typically, action learning involves between six and thirty employees. It may also include customers and vendors. There are several variations in the composition of the group. One variation is that the group includes a single customer for the problem being dealt with. Sometimes the groups include cross-functional representatives who all have a stake in the problem. Or the group may involve employees from multiple functions who all focus on their own functional problems, each contributing to solving the problems identified. Employees are asked to develop novel ideas and solutions in a short period of time. The teams usually need to gather data for problem solving by visiting customers, employees, academics, and/or industry leaders. Once the teams have gathered data and developed their recommendations they are required to present them to top-level executives.

Consider how Sony Music and Kirin Brewery used action learning teams to provide solutions to urgent and complex business problems.[76] Sony Music was losing income because of sales losses due to consumers' increased use of downloaded music such as iTunes. An action learning team of seven managers, all from different countries, met for a week in London, England, to identify ways to increase revenue. The solution they developed was a services contract in which Sony Music would distribute music and arrange artists tours, market their merchandise, and help get their music placed in movies and television shows. This solution led to millions of dollars in revenue and helped Sony sign contracts with music artists from other record labels. Leaking beer cans and stale beer were examples of the types of quality problems that Kirin Brewery was experiencing, resulting in decreased sales and undermining customer relationships. An action learning team with representatives from customer service, sales, manufacturing, and quality control was given the problem to develop a strategy for producing a higher quality can. The action learning team developed a redesigned beer can, resulting in reduced manufacturing time, costs, and customer complaints. The process action learning maximizes learning and transfer of training because it involves real-time problems that employees are facing. Also, action learning can be useful for identifying dysfunctional team dynamics that can get in the way of effective problem solving. Action learning at General Electric has required employees to use and apply skills to team building, problem solving, change management, conflict resolution, communications, coaching, and facilitation. General Electric believes that action learning has resulted in such benefits as greater speed in decision making and implementation, employees who work more easily across borders and business units, management that is willing to take more risks, and an increase in open dialogue and trust among employees.[77]

Six Sigma, Black Belt Training, and Kaizen

Six Sigma and Kaizen, black belt training programs, involve principles of action learning. Six Sigma and Kaizen provide employees with measurement and statistical tools to help reduce defects and to cut costs.[78] Six Sigma is a quality standard with a goal of no more than 3.4 defects per million processes. There are several levels of Six Sigma training, resulting in employees becoming certified as green belts, champions, or black belts.[79] To become black belts, trainees must participate in workshops and written assignments coached by expert instructors. The training involves four 4-day sessions over about sixteen weeks. Between training sessions, candidates apply what they learn to assigned projects and then use them in the next training session. Trainees are also required to complete not only oral and written exams but also two or more projects that have a significant impact on the company's bottom line. After completing black belt training, employees are able to develop, coach, and lead Six Sigma teams; mentor and give advice to management on useful Six Sigma projects; and provide Six Sigma tools and statistical methods to team members. After black belts lead several project teams, they can take additional training and be certified as master black belts. Master black belts can teach other black belts and help senior managers integrate Six Sigma into the company's business goals.

First Data Corporation used Six Sigma to train green belts and yellow belts with the goal of improving the execution of projects, alignment with customers, and creating a continuous improvement culture.[80] The green belts and yellow belt programs include e-learning, instructor-led courses, coaching, and support transfer of training through an online community of practice, Six Sigma fair days, assignments, and projects linked to business goals. The Six Sigma training has resulted in beneficial projects, resulting in outcomes such as reducing the time it takes to hire a new employee from seventy-five to forty-five days and reducing waste, defects, and rework.

Just Born, the company that makes Mike and Ike and Peeps candies, uses the Wow . . . Now Improvement Process, a customized Kaizen process to improve business processes and results.[81] The Wow . . . Now Improvement Process includes training employees how to identify improvement opportunities, collect data, make improvements, measure results, and refine practices based on the results. *Kaizen,* the Japanese word for improvement, is one of the underlying principles of lean manufacturing and total quality management (we discussed lean thinking in Chapter One). **Kaizen** refers to practices participated in by employees from all levels of the company that focus on continuous improvement of business processes.[82] As the Wow … Now Improvement Process illustrates, Kaizen involves considering a continuous cycle of activities, including planning, doing, checking, and acting (PDCA). Statistical process control techniques are used by employees to identify causes of problems and potential solutions. They include process flow analysis, cause-and-effect diagrams, control charts, histograms, and scattergrams.

CHOOSING A TRAINING METHOD

As a trainer or manager, you will likely be asked to choose a training method. Given the large number of training methods available to you, this task may seem difficult. One way to choose a training method is to compare methods. Table 7.11 evaluates each training method discussed in this chapter according to a number of characteristics. The types of learning outcomes related to each method are identified. Also, for each method, a high, medium, or low rating is provided for each characteristic of the learning environment, for transfer of training, for cost, and for effectiveness.

How might you use this table to choose a training method? The first step in choosing a method is to identify the type of learning outcome that you want training to influence. As discussed in Chapter Four, these outcomes include verbal information, intellectual skills, cognitive strategies, attitudes, and motor skills. Training methods may influence one or several learning outcomes. Research on specific learning methods has shown that for learning to be effective, the instructional method needs to match the desired learning outcome. For example, research on behavior modeling and role-playing shows that these

TABLE 7.11 Comparison of Training Methods

	Presentation			Hands-On							Group Building		
	Lecture	Video	OJT	Self-Directed Learning	Apprenticeship	Simulation	Case Study	Business Games	Role-Playing	Behavior Modeling	Adventure Learning	Team Training	Action Learning
Learning Outcome													
Verbal information	Yes	Yes	Yes	Yes	Yes	No	Yes	Yes	No	No	No	No	No
Intellectual skills	Yes	No	No	Yes	Yes	Yes	Yes	Yes	No	No	No	Yes	No
Cognitive strategies	Yes	No	Yes	Yes	No	Yes	Yes	Yes	Yes	Yes	Yes	Yes	Yes
Attitudes	Yes	Yes	No	No	No	No	No	No	Yes	No	Yes	Yes	Yes
Motor skills	No	Yes	Yes	No	Yes	Yes	No	No	No	Yes	No	No	No
Learning Environment													
Clear objective	Medium	Low	High	High	High	High	Medium	High	Medium	High	Medium	High	High
Practice	Low	Low	High	High	High	High	Medium	Medium	Medium	High	Medium	High	Medium
Meaningfulness	Medium	Medium	High	Medium	High	High	Medium	Medium	Medium	Medium	Low	High	High
Feedback	Low	Low	High	Medium	High	High	Medium	High	Medium	High	Medium	Medium	High
Observation and interaction with others	Low	Medium	High	Medium	High	High	High	High	High	High	High	High	High
Transfer of Training	Low	Low	High	Medium	High	High	Medium	Medium	Medium	High	Low	High	High
Cost													
Development	Medium	Medium	Medium	High	High	High	Medium	High	Medium	Medium	Medium	Medium	Low
Administrative	Low	Low	Low	Medium	High	Low	Low	Medium	Medium	Medium	Medium	Medium	Medium
Effectiveness	High for verbal information	Medium	High for structured OJT	Medium	High	High	Medium	Medium	Medium	High	Low	Medium	High

methods lead to positive results, but their effectiveness varies according to the evaluation criteria used.[83] This emphasizes that the particular learning *method* used to deliver learning is not what is most important. Rather, the choice of the learning method should be based on the desired learning outcomes and the features that facilitate learning and transfer of training. Once you have identified a learning method, the next step is to consider the extent to which the method facilitates learning and transfer of training, the costs related to the development and use of the method, and its effectiveness.

As was discussed in Chapter Four, for learning to occur, trainees must understand the objectives of the training program, training content should be meaningful, and trainees should have the opportunity to practice and receive feedback. Also, a powerful way to learn is through observing and interacting with others. As you may recall from Chapter Five, transfer of training refers to the extent to which training will be used on the job. In general, the more the training content and environment prepare trainees for use of learning outcomes on the job, the greater the likelihood that transfer will occur. As discussed in Chapter Six, "Training Evaluation," two types of costs are important: development costs and administrative costs. Development costs relate to design of the training program, including costs to buy or create the program. Administrative costs are incurred each time that the training method is used. These include costs related to consultants, instructors, materials, and trainers. The effectiveness rating is based on both academic research and practitioner recommendations.

Several trends in Table 7.11 are worth noting. First, there is considerable overlap between learning outcomes across the training methods. Group building methods are unique because they focus on individual as well as team learning (e.g., improving group processes). If you are interested in improving the effectiveness of groups or teams, you should choose one of the group building methods (e.g., adventure learning, team training, or action learning). Second, comparing the presentation methods to the hands-on methods illustrates that most hands-on methods provide a better learning environment and transfer of training than do the presentation methods. The presentation methods are also less effective than the hands-on methods. If you are not limited by the amount of money that can be used for development or administration, choose a hands-on method over a presentation method. The training budget for developing training methods can influence the method chosen. If you have a limited budget for developing new training methods, use structured OJT—a relatively inexpensive, yet effective, hands-on method. If you have a larger budget, you might want to consider hands-on methods that facilitate transfer of training, such as simulators. Keep in mind that many of the methods discussed in this chapter can be adapted for use in online learning, e-learning, and distance learning. These training methods are discussed in Chapter Eight.

If possible, you may want to use several different methods within a single training program to capitalize on the different strengths of each method for facilitating learning and transfer. For example, Nationwide Mutual Insurance uses several different methods to train new agents.[84] An interactive game is used to help agents understand the life cycle of an insurance policy. It includes an animated simulation using different customer profiles. New agents watch and listen to experienced agents interacting and communicating with customers both face to face and over the phone. They also engage in self-directed learning, including calling competitors to get an insurance quote and evaluating their experience.

Summary

Companies are using a variety of training methods to guide competency development and contextual learning. Although new technology such as social networks are being used by some companies for training delivery and instruction, most training is still conducted face to face with an instructor. This chapter discussed traditional face-to-face training methods, including presentation, hands-on, and group building training methods. Presentation methods (such as lecturing) are effective for efficiently communicating information (knowledge) to a large number of trainees. Presentation methods need to be supplemented with opportunities for trainees to practice, discuss, and receive feedback to facilitate learning. Hands-on methods get trainees directly involved in learning. Hands-on methods are ideal for developing skills and behaviors. Hands-on methods include OJT, simulations, self-directed learning, business games, case studies, role-playing, and behavior modeling. These methods can be expensive to develop but incorporate the conditions needed for learning and transfer of training to occur. Group building methods such as team training, action learning, and adventure learning focus on helping teams increase the skills needed for effective teamwork (e.g., self-awareness, conflict resolution, and coordination) and help build team cohesion and identity. Group building techniques may include the use of presentation methods, as well as exercises during which team members interact and communicate with each other. Team training has a long history of success in preparing flight crews and surgical teams, but its effectiveness for developing management teams has not been clearly established.

Key Terms

70-20-10 model, *293*
traditional training methods, *295*
presentation methods, *296*
lecture, *296*
audiovisual instruction, *298*
hands-on methods, *299*
on-the-job training (OJT), *299*
self-directed learning, *301*
apprenticeship, *303*

simulation, *305*
case study, *306*
business games, *308*
role-plays, *309*
behavior modeling, *310*
vicarious reinforcement, *310*
key behavior, *311*
modeling display, *311*
application planning, *312*
group building methods, *312*
team, *312*

experiential learning, *313*
adventure learning, *313*
team training, *315*
cross training, *316*
coordination training, *316*
team leader training, *317*
scenario-based training, *317*
guided team self-correction, *317*
action learning, *318*
kaizen, *320*

Discussion Questions

1. What are the implications of the 70-20-10 model for choosing a training method?
2. What are the differences between social contextual learning and guided competency development? Are both types of learning (and associated training methods) necessary? Explain.
3. What are the strengths and weaknesses of the lecture, the case study, and behavior modeling?
4. If you had to choose between adventure learning and action learning for developing an effective team, which would you choose? Defend your choice.
5. Discuss the process of behavior modeling training.

6. How can the characteristics of the trainee affect self-directed learning?

7. What are the components of effective team performance? How might training strengthen these components?

8. Table 7.11 compares training methods on a number of characteristics. Explain why simulation and behavior modeling receive high ratings for transfer of training.

9. What are some reasons why on-the-job training (OJT) can prove ineffective? What can be done to ensure its effectiveness?

10. Why are apprenticeship programs attractive to employees? Why are they attractive to companies?

11. Discuss the steps of an action learning program. Which aspect of action learning do you think is most beneficial for learning? Which aspect is most beneficial for transfer of training? Explain why. Defend your choices.

Application Assignments

1. Choose a job with which you are familiar. Develop a self-directed learning module for a skill that is important for that job.

2. Go to *www.sabrehq.com*, the website for Sabre Corporate Development. Click on Team Building Events. Choose one of the activities and events found on this page, and review it. Discuss what you would do to ensure that the team building event you selected is successful.

3. Divide into teams of two students. One student should be designated as a "trainer," the other as a "trainee." The trainee should briefly leave the room while the trainer reads the instructions for folding a paper cup. After the trainers have read the instructions, the trainees should return to the room. The trainers should then train the trainees in how to fold a paper cup (which should take about 15 minutes). When the instructor calls time, the trainers should note the steps they followed to conduct the training. The trainees should record their evaluations of the strengths and weaknesses of the training session (5–10 minutes). If time allows, switch roles.

SUPPLEMENT TO APPLICATION ASSIGNMENT 3
Steps and Key Points in Folding a Paper Cup:

	Steps in the Operation	Key Points
	Step: A logical segment of the operation in which something is done to advance the task.	Key point: Any directions or bits of information that help perform the step correctly, safely, and easily.
8 1/2" 11"	Place 8 1/2" × 11" sheet of paper in front of you on a flat surface.	1. Be sure that the surface is flat—free of interfering objects.
	Fold the lower-left corner up.	2a. Line up the right edges. b. Make a sharp crease.

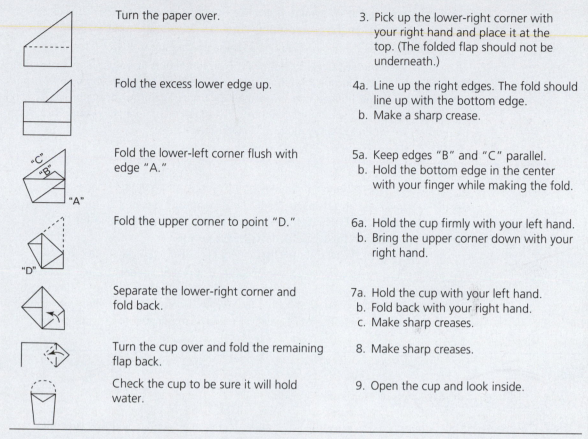

Turn the paper over.	3. Pick up the lower-right corner with your right hand and place it at the top. (The folded flap should not be underneath.)
Fold the excess lower edge up.	4a. Line up the right edges. The fold should line up with the bottom edge. b. Make a sharp crease.
Fold the lower-left corner flush with edge "A."	5a. Keep edges "B" and "C" parallel. b. Hold the bottom edge in the center with your finger while making the fold.
Fold the upper corner to point "D."	6a. Hold the cup firmly with your left hand. b. Bring the upper corner down with your right hand.
Separate the lower-right corner and fold back.	7a. Hold the cup with your left hand. b. Fold back with your right hand. c. Make sharp creases.
Turn the cup over and fold the remaining flap back.	8. Make sharp creases.
Check the cup to be sure it will hold water.	9. Open the cup and look inside.

Source: Adapted from P. Decker and B. Nathan, *Behavior Modeling Training* (New York: Praeger Scientific, 1985).

Be prepared to discuss the training process and your reactions as a trainer or trainee. Also, be prepared to discuss the extent to which the training followed the steps for effective OJT.

4. Review one of the following websites, which feature simulations: www.incomeoutcome.com or www.celemi.com.

   Describe the situation that the simulation is designed to represent. What elements in the simulation replicate the work environment? How could the simulation be improved to ensure that learning and transfer of training occur?

5. Watch the Wendy's training video "Wendy's Training Video Chili Can Be Served With Cheese" on YouTube at https://www.youtube.com/watch?v=eOvHZDGK-kY.

   How is this video effective for helping staff learn how to serve Wendy's food to customers? What would you add to the video to increase its effectiveness?

6. Go to *www.drumcafe.com*, the website for Drum Cafe, a company that specializes in corporate team building through the use of drum circles. Review the website and answer the following questions:

   a. What are drum circles? What skills can participants develop?

   b. What recommendations would you make to a company that uses drum circles to train teams regarding how to ensure that transfer of training occurs?

   c. Do you think that drum circles are good for team training? Why or why not?

7. Go to *www.5off5on.com*, the website for Pit Instruction and Training, a company that provides training for auto racing pit crews as well as team training. Click on "Corporate Training." Read about Lean Performance U and Team Performance U. Watch the YouTube video of the training at http://www.youtube.com/watch?v=u6akX9THcrg and http://www.youtube.com/watch?v=VVQefr0bMNo.

   a. What skills can this type of training improve?

   b. What could be done to ensure transfer of training occurs?

   c. How would you recommend evaluating the effectiveness of this program?

8. Go to *www.ted.com*, the website for TED, a nonprofit devoted to spreading ideas through short talks. TED stands for "Technology, Entertainment, & Design." Choose a TED talk and watch it. First, briefly describe the purpose and content of the talk. Next, consider the speaker. What did they do that held (or distracted) your attention?

9. Go to http://www.wtb.wa.gov/Documents/OJTBestPracticesManual_emailversion.pdf, which describes on-the-job training best practices for the Aerospace Joint Apprenticeship Committee. What steps should be taken to develop an on-the-job training program for apprentices? List and briefly describe each step and its importance to the training process.

Case

Training Methods for Bank Tellers

BB&T Corporation, headquartered in Winston-Salem, North Carolina, is among the nation's top financial holding companies, with $186 billion in assets. Its bank subsidiaries operate approximately 1,800 financial centers in twelve states and Washington, D.C. BB&T's operating strategy distinguishes it from other financial holding companies. BB&T's banking subsidiaries are organized as a group of community banks, each with a regional president, which allows decisions to be made locally, close to the client. This also makes BB&T's client service more responsive, reliable, and empathetic. Typical the bank tellers' tasks include:

- Balancing currency, coin, and checks in cash drawers at the end of each shift, and calculating daily transactions using computers, calculators, or adding machines
- Cashing checks and paying out money after verifying that signatures are correct, that written and numerical amounts agree, and that accounts have sufficient funds
- Receiving checks and cash for deposit, verifying amounts, and checking the accuracy of deposit slips
- Examining checks for endorsements and to verify other information such as dates, bank names, identification of the persons receiving payments, and the legality of the documents
- Entering customers' transactions into computers to record transactions and issue computer-generated receipts
- Counting currency, coins, and checks received, either by hand or using a currency-counting machine, to prepare them for deposit or shipment to branch banks or the Federal Reserve Bank
- Preparing and verifying cashier's checks
- Sorting and filing deposit slips and checks
- Ordering a supply of cash to meet daily needs
- Receiving and counting daily inventories of cash drafts and travelers' checks

Recently, Apple introduced Apple Pay, which allows customers to make credit card purchases or pay bills using contactless payment technology and unique security features. Customers can use their iPhones, Apple Watches, or iPads to make payments and purchases in a simple, secure, and private way. You can learn more about Apple Pay at *www.apple. com/apple-pay*.

Describe the methods or combination of methods you would recommend to train BB&T's tellers on Apple Pay. Justify your choice of methods.

Sources: Based on "BB&T Winston-Salem, North Carolina, Channeling Aristotle," *T+D* (October 2008): 50–52; *www. bbt.com*, website for BB&T. Tasks and work responsibilities are taken from http://onlinecenter.onet.org, O*Net online summary report for bank tellers (Job Code 43-3071.00), accessed March 25, 2015, www.apple.com/apple-pay.

Endnotes

1. M. Lombardo and R. Eichinger, *The Career Architect Development Planner*, 3rd ed. (Minneapolis, MN: Lominger Limited); D. Pontefract, *Flat Army: Creating a Connected and Engaged Organization* (Boston: Jossey-Bass, 2013); E. Sinar, R. Wellins, and R. Ray, "Seeking Answers on the Lackluster State of Leadership," *TD* (December 2014): 37–41.

2. J. Meister and K. Willyerd, *The 2020 Workplace* (New York: HarperCollins, 2010).

3. K. Kraiger, "Transforming our models of learning and development: Web-based instruction as enabler of third-generation instruction," *Industrial and Organizational Psychology: Perspectives on Science and Practice*, 1 (2008): 454–457.

4. B, Bell, and S. Kozlowski, "Goal orientation and ability: Interactive effects on self-efficacy, performance, and knowledge," *Journal of Applied Psychology*, 87 (2002): 495–505; J. Colquitt, J. LePine, and R. Noe, "Toward an integrative theory of training motivation: A meta-analytic path analysis of 20 years of research," *Journal of Applied Psychology*, 85 (2000): 678–707.

5. L. Miller, *2014 State of the Industry* (Alexandria, VA: American Society for Training & Development, 2014).

6. "Who is La Quinta?" "Culture," and "Training" from *www.lq.com*, website for La Quinta Inns and Suites, accessed March 24, 2015; "LQ Management, LLC," *training* (January/February 2013): 94.

7. L. Miller, *2014 State of the Industry* (Alexandria, VA: American Society for Training & Development, 2013); "2014 Training Industry Report," *training* (November/December 2014): 24.

8. M. Van Wart, N. J. Cayer, and S. Cook, *Handbook of Training and Development for the Public Sector* (San Francisco: Jossey-Bass, 1993); R. S. House, "Classroom Instruction." In *The ASTD Training and Development Handbook,* 4th ed., ed. R. L. Craig (New York: McGraw-Hill, 1996): 437–452; J. J. Goldsmith, "Revisiting the Lecture," *T+D* (June 2014): 30–32.

9. R. Feintzeig, "Managing in the Middle: Building Middle-Manager Morale", Wall Street Journal (August 8, 2013): B1.

10. M. Korn, "Wanted: Gurus with actual experience," *Wall Street Journal* (July 3, 2013): B6.

11. M. Van Wart, N. J. Cayer, and S. Cook, *Handbook of Training and Development for the Public Sector* (San Francisco: Jossey-Bass, 1993).

12. "Paychex, Inc.," *training* (January/February 2015): 65.

13. "PPL Electric Utilities," *training* (January/February 2015): 101.

14. " Microsoft: The readiness edge always on program," *training* (January/February 2015): 58–59.

15. L. Ford, "Caught on Tape," *T+D* (December 2005): 63–64.

16. R. B. Cohn, "How to Choose a Video Producer," *training* (July 1996): 58–61.

17. R. DeRouin, T. Parrish, and E. Salas, "On-the-job training: Tips for ensuring success," *Ergonomics in Design* 13 (Spring 2005): 23–26; D. Gallup and K. Beauchemin, "On-the-job training." In *The ASTD Handbook of Training Design and Delivery,* eds. G. Piskurich, P. Beckschi, and B. Hall (New York: McGraw-Hill, 2000): 121–132.

18. R. DeRouin, T. Parrish, and E. Salas, "On-the-job training: Tips for ensuring success," *Ergonomics in Design* 13 (Spring 2005): 23–26; C. Aik, "The synergies of the learning organization, visual factory management, and on-the-job training," *Performance Improvement* 44 (2005): 15–20.

19. "Reliance Industries Limited, Nagothane Manufacturing Division," *T+D* (October) 2008: 78.

20. N. Woodward, "Making safety job no. 1," *HR Magazine* (January 2007): 60–65.

21. B. Filipczak, "Who owns your OJT?" *training* (December 1996). 44–49; R. DeRouin, T. Parrish, and E. Salas, "On-the-job training: Tips for ensuring success," *Ergonomics in Design* 13 (Spring 2005): 23–26; D. Gallup and K. Beauchemin, "On-the-Job Training." In *The ASTD Handbook of Training Design and Delivery,* eds. G. Piskurich, P. Beckschi, and B. Hall (New York: McGraw-Hill, 2000): 121–132.

22. W. J. Rothwell and H. C. Kazanas, "Planned OJT is productive OJT," *Training and Development Journal* (October 1996): 53–56; R. Buckley and J. Caple, "Developing one-to-one training programs," *T+D* (April 2010): 108–109.

23. G. M. Piskurich, *Self-Directed Learning* (San Francisco: Jossey-Bass, 1993).

24. S. Boyer and B. Lambert, "Take the handcuffs off sales team development with self-directed learning," *T+D* (November 2008): 62–66; "Hilton Worldwide," *T+D* (October 2014): 72.

25. "'Best Buy' path to excellence," *training* (January/February 2013): 106.

26. G. M. Piskurich, "Self-Directed Learning." In *The ASTD Training and Development Handbook,* 4th ed., ed. R. L. Craig (New York: McGraw-Hill, 1996), 453–72; G. M. Piskurich, "Developing Self-Directed Learning," *Training and Development* (March 1994): 31–36.

27. P. Warr and D. Bunce, "Trainee characteristics and the outcomes of open learning," *Personnel Psychology* 48 (1995): 347–375; T. G. Hatcher, "The ins and outs of self-directed learning," *Training and Development* (February 1997): 35–39.

28. R. W. Glover, *Apprenticeship Lessons from Abroad* (Columbus, OH: National Center for Research in Vocational Education, 1986).

29. Commerce Clearing House, *Orientation-Training* (Chicago: Personnel Practices Communications, Commerce Clearing House, 1981): 501–505; K. Tyler, "The American apprentice," *HR Magazine* (November 2013): 33–36.

30. "S. Wartenberg, "No snow days," *The Columbus Dispatch* (February 22, 2015): D1, D3.

31. A. H. Howard III, "Apprenticeships." In *The ASTD Training and Development Handbook:* 803–813.

32. K. Tyler, "The American apprentice," *HR Magazine* (November 2013): 33–36; S. Wartenberg, "No snow days," *The Columbus Dispatch* (February 22, 2015): D1, D3; L. Weber, "Here's one way to solve the skills gap," *Wall Street Journal* (April 28, 2014): R3.

33. M. Rowh, "The rise of the apprentice," *Human Resource Executive* (February 2006): 38–43.

34. A. Ciaccio, "'You're hired': Goldcorp stint touts opportunities in mining," *The Wall Street Journal,* September 25, 2005: B6.

35. M. Rowh, "The rise of the apprentice."

36. *Eldredge v. Carpenters JATC* (1981), 27 Fair Employment Practices (Bureau of National Affairs): 479.

37. L. Sullivan, "Programmed for success," *The Columbus Dispatch* (November 3, 2013): B1, B3.

38. "Best practices and outstanding initiatives: Automatic Data Processing, Inc.: Leaders in action," *training* (January/February 2011): 94–95.

39. S. McCartney, "Addressing small errors in the cockpit," *The Wall Street Journal* (September 13, 2005): D5.

40. J. Alden and J. Kirkhorn, "Case Studies." In *The ASTD Training and Development Handbook:* 497–516.

41. H. Kelly, "Case Method Training: What It Is and How It Works." In *Effective Training Delivery,* ed. D. Zielinski (Minneapolis: Lakewood Books, 1989): 95–96.

42. "KLA-Tencor: The Situation Room," *training* (September/October 2014): 60–61.

43. J. Martin, "Serious games," *training* (September/October 2014): 43.

44. S. Wiebenga, "Guidelines for selecting, using, and evaluating games in corporate training," *Performance Improvement Quarterly* 18 (2004): 19–36; S. Sugar, "Using Games to Energize Dry Material," In *The ASTD Handbook of Training Design and Delivery:* 107–120.

45. D. Schwartz, J. Bransford, and D. Sears, "Efficiency and Innovation in Transfer" In *Transfer of Learning: Research and Perspectives,* ed. J. Mestre (Greenwich, CT: Information Age Publishing, 2004); B. Roberts, "Gamification: Win, lose, or draw," *HR Magazine* (May 2014): 28–35.

46. D. Zielinski, "Training games," *HR Magazine* (March 2010): 64–66.

47. "CMS Energy: Tackling conflicts with 'The Resolver,'" *training* (September/October 2014): 46.

48. T. Sitzmann, "A meta-analytic examination of the instructional effectiveness of computer-based simulation games," *Personnel Psychology,* 64 (2011): 489–528.

49. S. Thiagarajan, "Instructional Games, Simulations, and Role Plays." In *The ASTD Training and Development Handbook:* 517–533; S. Karre, "Setting the stage for effective role plays," *T+D* (November 2011): 76–77.

50. "Wequassett Resort and Golf Club: Heroic customer service," *Training* (March/April 2008): 36–37.

51. S. J. Simon and J. M. Werner, "Computer training through behavior modeling, self-paced, and instructional approaches: A field experiment," *Journal of Applied Psychology* 81 (1996): 648–659; P. Taylor, D. Russ-Eft, and D. Chan, "A meta-analytic review of behavior modeling training," *Journal of Applied Psychology* 90 (2005): 692–709.

52. W. C. Byham and A. Pescuric, "Behavior modeling at the teachable moment," *Training* (December 1996): 51–56.

53. P. Decker and B. Nathan, *Behavior Modeling Training* (New York: Praeger Scientific, 1985).

54. Ibid.; T. T. Baldwin, "Effects of alternative modeling strategies on outcomes of interpersonal/skills training," *Journal of Applied Psychology,* 77 (1992): 147–154.

55. J. Cannon-Bowers and C. Bowers, "Team development and functioning." In S. Zedeck (ed.) *APA Handbook of Industrial and Organizational Psychology* (Washington, D.C.: American Psychological Association, 2010): 597–650; J. Mathieu et al., "Team effectiveness 1997–2007: A review of recent advancements and a glimpse into the future," *Journal of Management* 34 (2008): 410–476; S. Kozlowski and D. Ilgen, "Enhancing the effectiveness of work groups and teams," *Psychological Science in the Public Interest* 7 (2006): 77–124.

56. D. Brown and D. Harvey, *An Experiential Approach to Organizational Development* (Englewood Cliffs, NJ: Prentice Hall, 2000); J. Schettler, "Learning by doing," *Training* (April 2002): 38–43; P. Mirvis, "Executive development through consciousness-raising experiences," *Academy of Management Learning and Education* (June 2008): 173–188.

57. S. Lueck, "Postal Service's top inspector should be fired, senators say," *The Wall Street Journal,* (May 2, 2003): A2.

58. R. J. Wagner, T. T. Baldwin, and C. C. Rowland, "Outdoor training: Revolution or fad?" *Training and Development Journal* (March 1991): 51–57; C. J. Cantoni, "Learning the ropes of teamwork," *The Wall Street Journal,* (October 2, 1995): A14.

59. C. Steinfeld, "Challenge courses can build strong teams," *Training and Development* (April 1997): 12–13.

60. G. Kranz, "From fire drills to funny skills," *Workforce Management* (May 2011): 28–32.

61. M. Regan, "Execs scale new heights in the name of teamwork," *Columbus Dispatch* (February 15, 2004): F2.

62. D. Mishev, "Cooking for the company," *Cooking Light* (August 2004): 142–147.

63. G. M. Tarullo, "Making outdoor experiential training work," *training* (August 1992): 47–52.

64. "Lending a hand," *T+D* (December 2013): 72.

65. C. Clements, R. J. Wagner, and C. C. Roland, "The ins and outs of experiential training," *Training and Development* (February 1995): 52–56.

66. G. M. McEvoy, "Organizational change and outdoor management education," *Human Resource Management* 36 (1997): 235–250.

67. M. Marks, J. Mathieu, and S. Zaccaro, "A temporally based framework and taxonomy of team processes," *Academy of Management Review* 26 (2001): 356–376.

68. E. Salas and J. A. Cannon-Bowers, "Strategies for Team Training." In *Training for 21st-Century Technology: Applications for Psychological Research,* eds. M. A. Quinones and A. Dutta (Washington, D.C.: American Psychological Association, 1997): 249–281.

69. R. L. Oser et al., *Toward a Definition of Teamwork: An Analysis of Critical Team Behaviors,* Technical Report 89-004 (Orlando, FL: Naval Training Research Center, 1989).

70. E. Salas and J. A. Cannon-Bowers, "Strategies for Team Training." In *Training for 21st-Century Technology: Applications of Psychological Research,* eds. M. A. Quinones and A. Dutta (Washington, D.C.: American Psychological Association, 1997): 249–281.

71. M. Marks et al., "The impact of cross-training on team effectiveness," *Journal of Applied Psychology,* 87 (2002): 3–13.

72. E. Salas, C. Burke, and J. Cannon-Bowers, "What We Know about Designing and Delivering Team Training: Tips and Guidelines." In *Creating, Implementing, and Managing Effective Training and Development,* ed. K. Kraiger (San Francisco: Jossey-Bass, 2002): 234–262.

73. R. Noe, A. Dachner, B. Saxton, and K. Keeton, *Team Training for Long-Duration Missions in Isolated and Confined Environments: A Literature Review, Operational Assessment, and Recommendations for Practice and Research.* National Aeronautics and Space Administration (NASA) Technical Report NASM/TM- 2011-216162, available from http://ston.jsc.nasa.giv/collections/TRS.

74. S. Carey, "Racing to improve," *The Wall Street Journal* (March 24, 2006): B1, B6.

75. M. Pedler and C. Abbott, *Facilitating Action Learning* (New York: McGraw-Hill, 2013); D. Dotlich and J. Noel, *Active Learning: How the World's Top Companies Are Recreating Their Leaders and Themselves* (San Francisco: Jossey-Bass, 1998).

76. M. Marquardt, "Action learning around the world," *T+D* (February 2015): 44–49.

77. M. Marquardt, "Harnessing the power of action learning," *T+D* (June 2004): 26–32

78. H. Lancaster, "This kind of black belt can help you score some points at work," *The Wall Street Journal,* (September 14, 1999): B1; S. Gale, "Building frameworks for six sigma success," *Workforce* (May 2003): 64–66.

79. J. DeFeo, "An ROI story," *Training and Development* (July 2000): 25–27.

80. "First Data Corporation: Six Sigma accreditation program," *training* (January/February 2014): 110–111.

81. M. Sallie-Dosunmu, "Born to grow," *TD* (May 2006): 33–37.

82. A. Brunet and S. New, "Kaizen in Japan: An empirical study," *International Journal of Production and Operations Management* 23 (2003): 1426–1446.

83. M. Burke and R. Day, "A cumulative study of the effectiveness of managerial training," *Journal of Applied Psychology* 71 (1986): 232–245.

84. "Nationwide Mutual Insurance Company: Fast-start for agents," *training* (January/February 2015): 107.

Chapter **Eight**

Technology-Based Training Methods

Objectives

After reading this chapter, you should be able to:

1. Explain how new technologies are influencing training.

2. Evaluate a web-based training site.

3. Explain how learning and transfer of training are enhanced by new training technologies.

4. Explain the strengths and limitations of e-learning, mobile learning training methods (such as iPads), and simulations.

5. Explain the different types of social media and the conditions conducive to their use for training.

6. Describe to a manager the different types of distance learning.

7. Recommend what should be included in an electronic performance support system.

8. Compare and contrast the strengths and weaknesses of traditional training methods versus those of technology-based training methods.

9. Identify and explain the benefits of learning management systems.

Time and Location Don't Stall Learning at Nissan

Nissan has more than 150,000 people working around the world, including automobile production locations in twenty countries and product markets in more than 160 countries. To ensure that the company could meet its global plans for growth and expansion, Nissan identified sixty high-potential employees who needed to develop the skills and competencies that would prepare them to be successful in their careers. The high-potential employees worked in different functional areas, levels, and locations, including Latin America, Europe, Africa, the Middle East, Asia, and Australia. For these employees, face-to-face interaction in a classroom would be invaluable because it would help them develop and expand their professional network and work together on group projects. Also, classroom instruction would ensure that the employees would receive a consistent message and approach to developing leadership skills and competencies based on Nissan's core business principles and their questions could be immediately answered by the instructor or facilitator. But face-to-face classroom instruction was unrealistic because these employees could not be away from their work for an extended period of time and traveling to one location for training from sites around the world was too expensive.

To gain the benefits of face-to-face instruction and overcome time and travel challenges, Nissan created an e-learning program, which included a virtual classroom. This allowed Nissan to combine the strengths of a classroom experience, including relationship building, immediate feedback, and the ability to practice skills with those of an online learning environment (easily accessible resources at any time or place). The first step in the program was that program participants assessed their own competencies. Their boss and peers completed a similar assessment. Next, the participants attended a virtual feedback session where the assessment results were explained. Courses designed to improve their current skills or develop new skills were offered in a virtual classroom. The courses included a virtual learning lab for skill practice. Course content in the virtual classroom was delivered by a live instructor. Learners could connect to the course online. They could ask questions, role-play, interact using virtual white boards and polling tools, and work in small groups. To help the participants build working relationships, they could view photos of each other and the virtual class size was limited to twenty learners.

The first twenty learners were from ten different countries! Yet, the participants reported that they felt they were interacting in a real classroom. They liked the ability to interact in real time, work with small groups of other learners, and learn about other participants' roles. Evaluation results suggested that the program was successful: Boss and peer assessments after the program indicated that participants improved their leadership behavior.

Source: Based on A. Lang, "Accelerate the leadership engine," *Chief Learning Officer* (April 2013): 42–47.

INTRODUCTION

As the opening vignette illustrates, technology is having a major influence on how training is delivered. Nissan is using technology-based training methods that provide a learning environment that has similar benefits as well-designed face-to-face instruction (practice, feedback, learner involvement) but overcome the cost and time challenges related to trying to bring employees together in one physical location for training. Online learning provides trainees with access to training at any time and place. The effective development and use of technology for delivering training such as online learning requires collaboration among the areas of training, information technology, and top management. In addition, needs assessment, design, transfer, and evaluation (training design) are critical components of the effective use of training technology. Although technologies such as social media, tablet computers, and virtual reality provide exciting capabilities and possibilities, it is critical that companies use training technologies that support both business and learner needs.

Nissan is not alone in its use of new training technologies. Technology is changing learning and training in corporate settings, as well as in grade schools, high schools, colleges, and universities.

In high school and elementary school classes, students are playing games that are fun, engage them in the learning content, and allow them to explore without fear of failure.[1] For example, Los Angeles, California, teachers are using "Minecraft" in architecture classes to help students learn how to work in a community to get things accomplished. A middle school physics teacher in Houston, Texas, is using "Angry Birds," which involves using slingshots to send birds to knock out pigs hiding in wood, rock, or glass towers. To knock out the pigs requires correct estimates of the birds' trajectories. The teacher is using "Angry Birds" to help students understand arcs, and Newton's law of force, motion, mass, speed, and velocity by examining how the birds fall and collide with the pigs. Medical students at Columbia University are using digital technology to help them identify the muscles and bones on cadavers.[2] Medical students use iPads to provide images of the types of muscles and tissues that they are looking to identify on the cadaver. Students use the iPad to magnify what they are looking for and to zoom out to see supporting bones, veins, and other anatomical structures.

As we discussed in Chapter Seven, "Traditional Training Methods," instructor-led classroom training is still the most popular training method. However, the use of technology for training delivery and instruction is increasing and anticipated to grow in the future. Table 8.1 provides a snapshot of the use of new technology in training. The use of training technologies is expected to increase dramatically in the next decade as technology improves; the cost of technology decreases; companies recognize the potential cost savings of training via tablets, mobile phones, and social media; and the need for customized training increases.[3] As you will see later in this chapter, new training technologies are unlikely to totally replace face-to-face instruction. Rather, face-to-face instruction will be combined with new training technologies (a combination known as *blended learning*) to maximize learning.

The development, availability, and use of social media such as Twitter and Facebook have the potential to have a significant influence on training and learning. These tools are used by many people in their daily lives, especially the millennial generation. Many companies are using these tools for recruiting new employees and marketing and developing products and services. These tools are also increasingly being used for learning. Figure 8.1 shows the use of social media tools for work-related learning. Social media tools are reshaping learning by giving employees access to and control of their own learning through relationships and collaborations with others. Social media tools, including

TABLE 8.1
Use of New Technology in Training

Sources: L. Miller, *2014 State of the Industry* (Alexandria, VA: American Society for Training and Development, 2013); "2014 Industry Report," *training* (November/December 2014):16–29.

- 15 percent of training hours are delivered in a virtual classroom and 29 percent is delivered online.
- 39 percent of learning hours involve technology-based training methods.
- 74 percent of companies use learning management systems. Broken down by size, 88 percent of large (10,000 or more employees), 75 percent of midsize (1,000–9,999 employees), and 65 percent of small companies (100–999 employees) use learning management systems.
- 36 percent of large companies (10,000 or more employees) deliver training online, compared to 26 percent of midsize (1,000–9,999 employees) and 28 percent of small (100 or less employees) companies.

FIGURE 8.1
Use of Social Media Tools for Work-Related Learning

Source: Based on L. Patel, "The rise of social media," *T+D* (July 2010): 60–61.

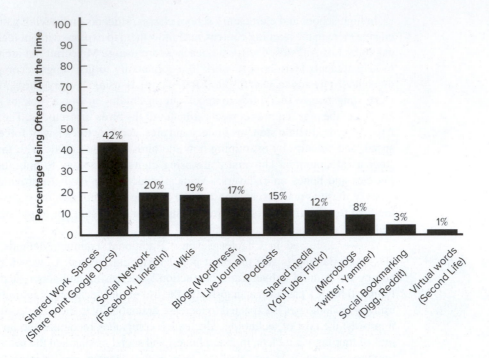

shared workspaces, social networks, wikis, blogs, podcasts, and microblogs, are being used for learning. As shown in Figure 8.1, shared workspaces, social networks, and wikis are the most commonly used social media for learning.[4] There appear to be generational differences in using and realizing the potential benefits of social media tools. Millennials believe that social media tools are helpful for learning and getting work done, and do so to a greater extent than baby boomers or Generation Xers. This may be because millennials are more likely to use social media tools in their personal lives, resulting in their being more comfortable using them at work.

The development of tablet computers such as the iPad also has the potential to influence training and learning. One estimate is that nearly 40 percent of executives plan to incorporate tablets such as the iPad into their new training and development initiatives.[5] These devices are expected to be used for learning and performance support, but also for coaching and mentoring employees, mobile gaming, and microblogging (e.g., Twitter).

This chapter begins by discussing the influence of new technology on training delivery, support, and administration. How technology has changed the learning environment also is addressed. Next, the chapter explores computer-based training, online learning, and e-learning. E-learning emphasizes learning through interaction with training content, sharing with other trainees, and using Internet resources. Technologies that are familiar to us in our nonwork life, such as social media, tablets such as iPads, and mobile smartphones, which are just beginning to be used for training purposes, are introduced. Next, the use of expert systems and intelligent tutoring systems as an instructional method and for on-the-job performance support is discussed. The chapter also shows how learning management systems aid in the delivery and administration of training programs. The last section of the chapter compares the various training methods that are based on new technology. A blended learning approach combining traditional face-to-face and technology-based training methods may be the best way to capitalize on the strengths of available training methods.

TECHNOLOGY'S INFLUENCE ON TRAINING AND LEARNING

Chapters One and Two discussed the role that training and development should play in helping companies to execute their business strategy and deal with forces influencing the workplace. For training to help a company gain a competitive advantage, it needs to support business goals and be delivered as needed to geographically dispersed employees who may be working at home or in another country. Training costs (such as travel costs) should be minimized and maximum benefits gained, including learning and transfer of training. For learning and transfer to occur (i.e., for the benefits of training to be realized), the training environment must include learning principles such as practice, feedback, meaningful material, and the ability to learn by interacting with others.

New technologies have made it possible to reduce the costs associated with delivering training to employees, to increase the effectiveness of the learning environment, and to help training contribute to business goals. Table 8.2 lists, describes, and provides examples of some of the new technology training methods that we will discuss in this chapter. New technologies have influenced the delivery of training, training administration, and training support. Technology has made several benefits possible:[6]

- Employees can gain control over when and where they receive training.
- Employees can access knowledge and expert systems on an as-needed basis.
- Through the use of avatars, virtual reality, and simulations, the learning environment can look, feel, and sound just like the work environment.
- Employees can choose the type of media (print, sound, video, etc.) that they want to use in a training program.
- Course enrollment, testing, and training records can be handled electronically, reducing the paperwork and time needed for administrative activities.
- Employees' accomplishments during training can be monitored.
- Traditional training methods, such as classroom instruction and behavior modeling, can be delivered to trainees rather than requiring them to come to a central training location.

Three of the most important ways that technology has influenced training and learning is that it has provided for greater collaboration, learner control, and a more dynamic learning environment.[7]

Technology Facilitates Collaboration

Technology allows digital collaboration to occur. **Digital collaboration** is the use of technology to enhance and extend employees' abilities to work together regardless of their geographic proximity.[8] Digital collaboration includes electronic messaging systems, electronic meeting systems, online communities of learning organized by subject where employees can access interactive discussion areas and share training content and web links, social networks, and document-handling systems with collaboration technologies that allow interpersonal interaction. Digital collaboration requires a computer,

TABLE 8.2
New Technologies Used for Training

Sources: Based on R. Johnson and H. Gueutal, *Transforming HR Through Technology* (Alexandria, VA: SHRM Foundation, 2010); American Society for Training and Development, *Transforming Learning with Web 2.0 Technologies*, 2010 survey report; T. Bingham and M. Conner, *The New Social Learning* (Alexandria, VA: American Society for Training and Development Press, 2010); A. Kaplan and M. Haenlein, "Users of the world unite! The challenges and opportunities of social media," *Business Horizons*, 53 (2010): 59–68. T. Poeppelman, E. Lobene, and N. Blacksmith, "Personalizing the learning experience through adaptive training," *The Industrial-Organizational Psychologist* (April 2015), from *www.siop.org.*; R. Grossman, "Are massive open online courses in your future," *HR* Magazine (August 2013): 30–36.

E-learning, Online Learning, Computer-Based Training (CBT), Web-Based Training (WBT)
Training delivered using a computer or the web. Can include CDs or DVDs of text and/or video.

Webcasts/Webinars
Live web-based delivery of instruction to trainees in dispersed locations.

Podcasts
Web-based delivery of audio and video files.

Mobile Learning
Delivery of training through handheld mobile devices such as smartphones or tablet computers.

Blended Learning
Training is delivered using a combined technology and face-to-face instructional delivery approach, such as classroom and WBT.

Wikis
Websites that allow many users to create, edit, and update content and share knowledge.

Distance Learning
Training delivered to trainees in other locations online, or through webcasts or virtual classroom often supported with communications tools such as chat, e-mail, and online discussions.

Social Media
Online and mobile technology used to create interactive communications allowing the creation and exchange of user-generated content. They include wikis, blogs, networks such as Facebook, MySpace, and LinkedIn, microsharing sites such as Twitter, and shared media such as YouTube.

Shared Workspaces (Example: Google Docs)
A space hosted on a web server where people can share information and documents.

RSS Feeds
Updated content sent to subscribers automatically instead of by e-mail.

Blogs (Example: WorldPress)
A webpage where an author posts entries and readers can comment.

Chat Rooms and Discussion Boards
An electronic room or message board on which learners communicate. Communications between learners can occur at the same or different times. A facilitator or instructor can moderate the conversations, which may be grouped by topic.

Microblogs or Microsharing (Example: Twitter)
Software tools that enable communications in short bursts of text, links, and multimedia, either through stand-alone applications or through online communities or social networks.

Massive Open Online Courses (MOOC)
Learning that is designed to enroll large number of learners (massive), it is free and accessible to anyone with an Internet connection (open), it takes place online using videos of lectures, interactive coursework including discussion groups, and wikis (online), and it has specific start and completion dates, quizzes and assessment, and exams (courses).

Adaptive Training
Training that customizes the content presented to the trainee based on their needs.

tablet, or phone with a web browser or app, but collaborative. Digital collaboration can be synchronous or asynchronous.[9] In **synchronous communication,** trainers, experts, and learners interact with each other live and in real time, the same way they would in face-to-face classroom instruction. Technologies such as video teleconferencing and live online courses (virtual classrooms) make synchronous communication possible. **Asynchronous communication** refers to non-real-time interactions. That is, persons are not online and cannot communicate with each other without a time delay, but learners can still access information resources when they desire them. E-mail, self-paced courses on the web or on CD-ROM, discussion groups, and virtual libraries allow asynchronous communication.

Technology Creates a Dynamic Learning Environment

As discussed in Chapter Seven, learning can be an instructor-driven primary process. That is, instructors present information to the learners, and practice and applications occurred after instruction was completed (see the classroom learning environment shown in Figure 8.1). Many learning environments include only the instructor or trainer and the learners. The trainer is responsible for delivering content, answering questions, and testing learning. Trainees play a passive role in learning. Communication on course content is one-way: from the instructor to the learner. Experts and resource materials are separate from the learning environment. Contact with resource materials and experts beyond the instructor and course materials assigned for the course requires learners to go outside the formal learning environment. Also, learners often have to wait to access resource materials and experts until instruction is completed. Interaction among learners occurs primarily outside the training room and tended to be limited to those who worked in the same geographic area.

Technology has allowed learning to become a more dynamic process. As shown on the right side of Figure 8.2, the learning environment can be expanded to include greater interaction between learners and the training content, as well as between learners and the instructor. The trainer may help design the instruction, but the instruction is delivered to the learners primarily through technology such as online learning, simulations, iPods, or iPads. The instructor becomes more of a coach and resource person to answer students' questions and is less involved in the delivery of content. Learning occurs primarily through exchanges with other learners, using blogs, wikis, or other types of social media training, working on virtual team projects, participating in games, listening, exchanging ideas, interacting with experts (engineers, managers, etc.), and discovering ideas and applications using hyperlinks that take the learner to other websites. Experts and resource materials may be part of the learning environment. While learners interact with the training content through exercises, applications, and simulations, they can discuss what they are learning with other learners or access experts or resource materials available on the Internet. Training delivery and administration (e.g., tracking learner progress) is all done through a learning management system (discussed later in the chapter). In the blended learning environment, shown at the bottom of Figure 8.2, trainees have access to a blended training curriculum that consists of both online and classroom instruction. Collaboration can occur between learners, between learners and training content (e.g., simulation or game), between learners and instructors, and between learners and experts. It is important that new technologies create a dynamic learning environment, including collaboration, active learner involvement, and access to other resources. A dynamic learning environment

FIGURE 8.2 Types of Learning Environments

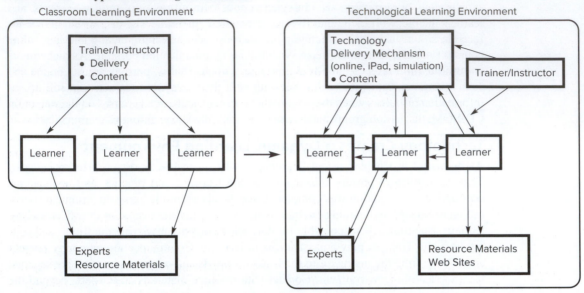

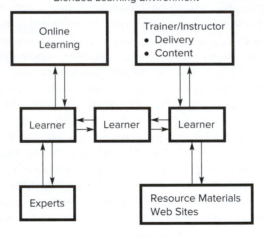

likely includes the use of **Web 2.0** technologies, including social networking, blogs, wikis, and microblogs such as Twitter.[10]

Technology Gives Learner's Control

Learner control refers to giving trainees the option to learn through self-pacing exercises, exploring links to other material, and conversations with trainees and experts. It includes the ability to select how content is presented (e.g., text, pictures, videos, etc.) to pause, skip, and review content, and to link to additional resources. That is, online learning allows activities typically led by the instructor (presentation, slides, videos, visuals) or trainees (discussions, questions), as well as group interaction (discussion of application of training content) to be incorporated into training without trainees having to be physically present in the training room. Recent technologies enable training to be delivered and accessed by trainees anytime and anywhere, including home, work, or even on the beach! Training content can be delivered in a consistent manner to trainees, who can decide when and where to participate.

Many of the training methods discussed in this chapter have these features. For example, online learning, or e-learning, includes instruction and delivery of training using the Internet or web. Distance learning typically involves videoconferencing and/or computers for delivery of instruction from a trainer to trainees who are not in the same location as the trainer. Mobile technologies allow training to be delivered through iPods, iPhones, personal data assistants (PDAs), iPads, and notebook computers that allow trainees to tune in to training programs at any time or place. New training technologies allow for the use of multiple media, including text, graphics, video, and audio. This allows for learning content to be presented in multiple ways, appealing to trainee preferences and learning styles.

Consider how technology has influenced how training is delivered and instruction occurs at Farmers Insurance Group.[11] Farmers uses a blended learning approach to deliver effective learning to its multigenerational employees and insurance agents who are located across the United States. Farmers Insurance training programs integrate face-to-face instruction, print, online, video, audio, virtual simulations, and coaching. Technology is used for delivering knowledge, and instructor-led training is used for skill development. In the past five years the amount of learning delivered through instructor-led classroom-based training has dropped from 90 to 50 percent. The other 50 percent is online or informal learning. For example, Farmers Insurance is using various training methods to help its employees cope with the changes made in claims processing, ratings, billing, and product systems in support of the company's business strategy (Farmers Future 2020), which emphasizes customer experience, distribution, and product management excellence. Field managers were required to complete online training and webinars designed to provide the new knowledge they needed. Then the managers received instructor-led training, videos, and coaching guides.

Farmers Insurance is also using virtual classrooms, mobile learning, social networks, electronic tablets such as iPads, and learning simulations. While taking courses at the University of Farmers, learners can use electronic tablets to take notes, access websites and articles, and view videos. The video capabilities of the tablets allow instructors to use them to record the learners practicing skills and then provide feedback and coaching. Also, the instructors can create learning materials such as iBooks with embedded videos. To encourage learning outside of a formal classroom environment, Farmers developed iFarmers apps for customers, sales agents, and employees. The iFarmers customer app helps customers learn about different insurance products. An iClaims app gives customers access to input and manage their insurance claims. The iAgent app provides business-focused learning for sales agents. Farmers Insurance has also been experimenting with social networking for employees to collaborate, create, and share knowledge, and to provide performance support. Some training programs are using the social network for collaborative exercises. Farmers' "Agency Insider" program allows learners to specify whether they want to use Twitter, Facebook, e-mail, or an RSS feed.

The next section of the chapter discusses training technologies, how they are used, and their potential advantages and disadvantages.

COMPUTER-BASED TRAINING, ONLINE LEARNING, WEB-BASED TRAINING, E-LEARNING

Computer-based training (CBT), online learning, e-learning, and **web-based training** refer to instruction and delivery of training by computer through the Internet or the web.[12] All of these training methods can include and integrate into instruction text, interaction using simulations and games, and video, and collaboration using blogs, wikis, and social networks, and hyperlinks to additional resources. In some types of CBT, content is provided stand-alone using software or DVDs with no connection to the Internet. Trainees can still interact with the training content, answer questions, and choose responses regarding how they would behave in certain situations, but they cannot collaborate with other learners. For example, Wipro Technologies developed a tool they call a Unified Learning Kit (ULK), a portable laptop programmable computer that enables new employees to experiment in engineering subjects.[13] One ULK can teach more than ten different technical subjects related to hardware and software engineering.

Online learning, e-learning, and web-based training all include delivery of instruction using the Internet or web. The training program can be accessed using a password through the public Internet or the company's private intranet. There are many potential features that can be included in online learning to help trainees learn and transfer training to their jobs. For example, online programs that use video may make it an interactive experience for trainees. That is, trainees watch the video and have the opportunity to use the keyboard or touch the screen to answer questions, provide responses to how they would act in certain situations, or identify the steps they would take to solve a problem. Interactive video is especially valuable for helping trainees learn technical or interpersonal skills. Online learning can also include opportunities to collaborate with other learners through discussion boards, wikis, and blogs. We discuss more of the potential features and advantages of online learning next.

For example, during training needs assessment, Bayer Pharmaceuticals discovered that its technical experts needed new skills to manage large projects.[14] These skills related to keeping project managers focused on the task, managing competing priorities, managing large cross-functional teams, and supervising employees who did not report to them. These skills are important to reduce the time needed to bring research discoveries to the marketplace. To train in these skills, Bayer used a computer-based simulation that requires teams of trainees to manage a large-scale project. The management decisions they make affect their odds of being successful. A computer calculates each team's probability of succeeding. The simulation includes obstacles that can affect a project negatively, such as unmotivated employees, absenteeism, and projects being completed late. The simulation also includes online work that trainees complete prior to training. The prework provides trainees with an overview of the steps involved in project management. All trainees complete a self-assessment of their team-related behavior (e.g., conflict resolution). The assessments are used for discussing leader/team-member relationships. After completing the simulation, trainees can access a program website that includes a newsletter and tips for project management. Employees who have completed the simulation are demonstrating increased confidence in their ability to manage a project and to handle changing priorities, and they are addressing team issues more quickly.

Discover Financial Services uses online training to teach new customer service representatives self-reliance, self-direction, creative problem solving, and how to satisfy the customer.[15] An online syllabus provides trainees with expectations, goals, and links to access coursework. Trainees can ask questions and share experiences using online discussions. Each trainee has an advisor whose job is to help them set learning goals, evaluate their performance, and provide coaching. Also, trainees participate in an online game daily, monthly, and between customer calls.

Potential Features of Online Learning

In online learning, it is possible to enable learners to interact with the training content and other learners and to decide how they want to learn.[16] Figure 8.3 shows the possible features that can be built into online learning. These features include content, collaboration

FIGURE 8.3   Potential Features of E-learning

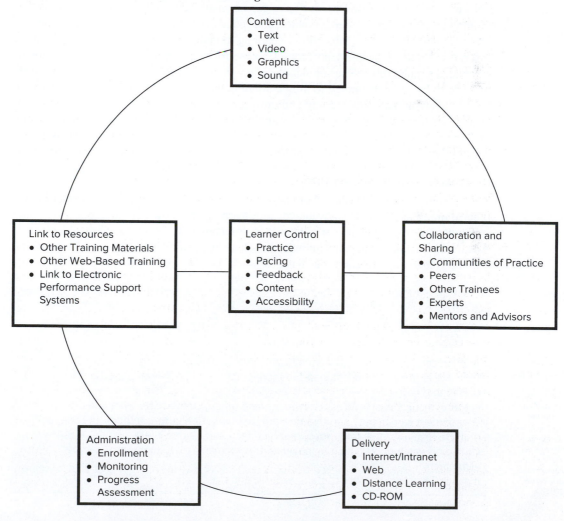

and sharing, links to resources, learner control, delivery, and administration. It is important to note that not all these features are incorporated into online learning methods. One reason is that certain methods make it difficult to incorporate some of these features. For example, as you will see later in the chapter, distance learning that involves teleconferencing may limit the amount of collaboration between trainees and the instructor. Also, in distance learning, trainees do not have control over the content, practice, and speed of learning. Another reason why a feature may not be incorporated is that the designers may have chosen not to include it. Although e-learning *can* include all the features to facilitate learning that are shown in Figure 8.3, it may fall short of its potential because, for example, program developers do not include opportunities for trainees to collaborate. As Figure 8.3 shows, not only can online learning provide the trainee with content, but it also can give learners the ability to control what they learn, the speed at which they progress through the program, how much they practice, and even when they learn. In addition, online learning can allow learners to collaborate or interact with other trainees and experts and can provide links to other learning resources such as reference materials, company websites, and other training programs. Text, video, graphics, and sound can be used to present course content. Also, simulations can be included in e-learning modules to engage learners. Economical Insurance developed a safety procedures course for risk control inspectors that includes embedded simulations.[17] The simulations allow the learner to practice each step in safety procedures by using the mouse to mimic different had movements. All learners received a perfect score on mandatory testing and most reported that the simulations were effective in understanding the safety procedures and helped them engage in more safe behaviors. Online learning may also include various aspects of training administration such as course enrollment, testing and evaluating trainees, and monitoring of trainees' learning progress.

Advantages of Online Learning

The possible features that can be built into online learning give it potential advantages over other training methods. The advantages of e-learning are shown in Table 8.3. E-learning initiatives are designed to contribute to a company's strategic business objectives.[18] E-learning supports company initiatives such as expanding the number of customers, initiating new ways to carry out business such as e-business (providing products and

TABLE 8.3 Advantages of E-learning

Sources: Based on D. Hartley, "All aboard the e-learning train," *Training and Development* (July 2000): 37–42; V. Beer, *The Web Learning Field Book: Using the World Wide Web to Build Workplace Learning Environments* (San Francisco: Jossey-Bass, 2000).

It supports the company's business strategy and objectives.
It is accessible at any time and any place.
The audience can include employees and managers, as well as vendors, customers, and clients.
Training can be delivered to geographically dispersed employees.
Training can be delivered faster and to more employees in a shorter period of time.
Updating is easy.
Practice, feedback, objectives, assessment, and other positive features of a learning environment can be built into the program. Learning is enhanced through the use of multiple media (sound, text, video, graphics, etc.) and trainee interaction.
Paperwork related to training management (enrollment, assessment, etc.) can be eliminated.
It can link learners to other content, experts, and peers.

services through the internet), and speeding the development of new products or services. E-learning may involve a larger audience than traditional training programs that focus on employees. E-learning may involve partners, suppliers, vendors, and potential customers.

E-learning allows faster and more efficient delivery of training and reduces geographic and time constraints for employees' learning. Consider the advantages of e-learning for Jiffy Lube, Greyhound Lines, and the San Diego Zoo.[19] Jiffy Lube determined that its instructor-led leadership training class needed to be updated to include new information but not to expand the class beyond its current three days. As a result, content on time management, goal setting, and financials was moved to e-learning, which freed up more than eight hours in the class. Also, Jiffy Lube realized a 75 percent increase in the number of employees who completed the new e-learning courses. Greyhound Lines, the transportation company, has geographically dispersed employees including supervisors, field representatives, counter and customer service staff, and bus drivers who work around the clock every day of the year. Greyhound uses e-learning to give employees access to leadership, business, and customer service skills courses when they need them. Employees access the courses on the company's learning management system. The learning management system allows Greyhound to track assignments, course participation, and monitor employees' progress in a course. Course assignments are made available on the learning management system with automatic reminders sent to the trainees. Greyhound plans to provide iPhones to its bus drivers to make it easier for them to access e-learning. Historically, the San Diego Zoo used formal classroom training to provide its animal care staff with knowledge and skills in care and feeding of animal, regulatory requirements, safety procedures, conservation, education, animal enrichment, and customer service. However, they realized that they needed more cost-effective training and a strategy on how to teach animal care staff who have varied work schedules, are impossible to get together in one place for training, and prefer hands-on learning. Thirteen courses that would serve as basic courses were identified. They covered transmission of diseases such as swine flu, avian flu, and West Nile viruses, compliance with government regulations, working safely with dangerous animals, and the fundamentals of animal behavior, care, and management. Subject-matter experts were identified and provided course content. Instructional designers worked with the content and developed it into an interactive online format. The online training included video case studies, used rich visuals, illustrated facts and concepts, and used module organization to ensure the training was the right length and did not overload the learner's memory. Also, following the presentation of material, the online training included interactive assessment, which provided the learner with feedback and positive reinforcement and learning guidance in the form of advanced organizers about topics to be covered and how mastery of one topic could help improve mastery of the next topic.

Some companies have training requirements that all employees have to complete for the company to meet quality or legal requirements. Online learning allows more employees to gain access to these types of programs in a quicker time period than if face-to-face instruction is used. A grocery store chain had to train its pharmacy staff about the privacy rules that were part of the Health Insurance Portability and Accountability Act (HIPAA). To quickly train the staff, a training course was posted online, making it easier for employees to access it through a laptop computer, cash register, smartphone, or iPad.[20] Online training allows retailers such as Luxottica, the eyewear and optical company, the ability to track who enrolls and complete online courses that are required for certification to some positions (such as licensed opticians).

E-learning is also easy to update, thanks to user-friendly authoring languages such as HTML. Changes can be made on the server that stores the e-learning program. Employees worldwide can access the updated program. The administrative features of e-learning make training management a more efficient, paperless process. For example, CCH developed Shared Learning, an online administration module that allows companies to monitor employees' completion of e-learning. It tracks how many times employees complete the same class and how much time employees spend per class, and it bookmarks the point at which trainees leave an online class so they can enter the program at the place they left it when they again begin training.[21]

Effectiveness of Online Learning

Is e-learning effective for all types of learning outcomes and trainees? Both research and company experiences suggest that e-learning is effective for a wide range of outcomes, including knowledge, skills, and behaviors.[22] Table 8.4 shows some of the research results regarding the effectiveness of online learning compared to other training methods. Online learning may be most effective for training that emphasizes cognitive outcomes, such as declarative and procedural knowledge (recall the discussion of learning outcomes in Chapters Four, "Learning and Transfer of Training," and Six, "Training Evaluation"). Courses need to comply with laws and regulations (such as sexual harassment or fraud) or software/technical skill-building courses such as Windows or Java may be best suited for online learning especially if these courses are video based and allow employees to apply the lesson on their own computer. For example, Allied Bank, based in Pakistan, used e-learning to meet federal law requiring bank employees to identify and report money laundering and funding for terrorism.[23] Designers created a learning portal in both English and Urdu

TABLE 8.4 **Research Results Regarding the Effectiveness of Online Learning**

- Online instruction is more effective than face-to-face classroom instruction for teaching declarative knowledge (cognitive knowledge assessed using written tests designed to measure whether trainees remember concepts presented in training).
- Web-based instruction and classroom instruction are equally effective in teaching procedural knowledge (the ability of learners to perform the skills taught in training).
- Learners are equally satisfied with web-based and classroom instruction.
- Web-based instruction appears to be more effective than classroom instruction (1) when learners are provided with control over content, sequence, and pace; (2) in long courses; and (3) when learners are able to practice the content and receive feedback.
- Web-based instruction and classroom instruction are equally effective when similar instructional methods are used (e.g., both approaches use video, practice assignments, and learning tests).
- The employees who get the most from online learning are those who complete more of the available practice opportunities and take more time to complete the training.
- E-learning is not effective for all learners, especially those with low computer self-efficacy.

Sources: Based on K. Kraiger, "Transforming our models of learning and development: Web-based instruction as enabler of third-generation instruction," *Industrial Organizational Psychology* 1 (2008): 454–467; T. Sitzmann et al., "The comparative effectiveness of web-based and classroom instruction: A meta-analysis," *Personnel Psychology* 59 (2006): 623–634; E. Welsh et al., "E-learning: Emerging uses, empirical results and future directions," *International Journal of Training and Development* 7 (2003): 245–258.

for employees so they could take training based on the language they understood. This reduced travel expenses related to attending training from $420,000 to $218,000, lowered training costs per employee from $250 to $150, and increased the number of employees who received training from 6,500 to 9,200 in one year. Jiffy Lube offers thirteen e-learning courses as part of its management certification program. These courses could be taught using face-to-face instruction but Jiffy Lube believes that the content is easily communicated and understood in an interactive e-learning course.[24] However, at Jiffy Lube learners encounter other topics that benefit from discussion, collaboration, role-play, and problem solving such as change management, performance management, and building a team, so they are trained using a combination of online learning and face-to-face instruction.

Online learning may facilitate greater social interaction between trainees than face-to-face learning methods because other trainees are equally accessible or more accessible than the instructor and there are more methods available that allow learners to interact, such as e-mail, blogs, wikis, and chat rooms.[25] Also, trainees may be more motivated to participate because they avoid feelings of inadequacy and low self-confidence, which can hinder participation in face-to-face learning. Delaware North Companies (DNC), a hospitality and food services company based in Buffalo, New York, provides hospitality and food services to national parks, stadiums, and airports. DNC delivers self-paced interactive training via the web, followed by virtual classes.[26] At DNC, soft skills, such as managing a team, effective communication techniques, delegation, empowerment, and conflict resolution, have been identified as best for online training. Functional and technical skills have been found to be best suited for OJT.

In considering whether to move some or all training online, there are several things you have to consider.[27] First, is whether online training relates to business goals or employees learning needs. Online training can save costs without compromising quality and provide access to employees who have difficulties attending face-to-face training because of their schedules or locations. Moving training online likely will result in development costs related to designing or purchasing training and providing access. One estimate is that it takes eight hours of development time for one hour of face-to-face instruction but that number can be much higher depending on the sophistication and complexity of the online course. It is also important to consider if employees will be resistant to using online training because of personal preferences or lack of familiarity with training technology. If online training is developed, employees need to know why it is being used, how they can use it to meet their learning needs, how to find courses, and how to gain the most benefits from them.

Despite the increasing popularity of online learning, many companies such as Home Depot, Inc., Recreational Equipment, Inc., and Qwest Communications International still prefer face-to-face training methods for teaching skills for complex jobs involving selling and repairing equipment.[28] Online learning is used to train employees when their job requires them to use a standard set of facts or procedures. For example, Recreational Equipment, Inc., uses role-playing between new employees and trainers who simulate a wide range of customer behaviors, helping them understand the difference between customers who want a specific product and customers who want to discuss different product choices. Qwest Communications estimates that 80 percent of training in its network department is completed face to face, compared to 20 percent online. To learn how to fix and install equipment, the company believes that employees must have hands-on experience that is similar to what they will encounter working in homes and commercial locations. Online learning may be valuable, but it is insufficient for teaching complex analytical, conceptual, and interpersonal skills.[29] This may be because online learning lacks communication richness, some online learners may be reluctant to interact with other learners, and, although online learning increases accessibility to training, employees with busy work schedules have a greater opportunity to more easily delay, fail to complete, or poorly perform learning activities. Later in the chapter, we discuss how online learning can be combined with face-to-face instruction, known as blended learning, to take advantage of the strengths of both methods. Learning can be enhanced by combining face-to-face instruction and e-learning because learners are more engaged; the use of video, graphics, sound, and text is combined with active learning experiences such as cases, role-playing, and simulations. Also, blended learning provides opportunities for learners to practice, ask questions, and interact with other learners and peers both face to face and online.

DEVELOPING EFFECTIVE ONLINE LEARNING

Table 8.5 provides tips for developing effective online learning.[30] The training design or ADDIE model discussed in Chapter One, "Introduction to Employee Training and Development," should still be used in designing e-learning. However, the emphasis at each stage should be slightly different.[31] Needs assessment, creating a positive online learning experience, learner control, and providing time and space for online learning are three central issues that need to be addressed for effective online learning, including web-based training.

Needs Assessment

Needs assessment includes getting management to support online learning. Also, the information technology department needs to be involved in the design of any web-based program to ensure that the technology capabilities of the company network are understood, to guarantee that trainees can get access to the browsers and connections that they need to participate in e-learning and use all of the tools (e.g., e-mail, chat rooms, hyperlinks) that may accompany it, and to get technical support when needed. Online tutorials may be needed to acquaint trainees with the capabilities of the e-learning system and how to navigate the web. Recall from Chapter Three, "Needs Assessment," that a needs assessment determines the company's resources for training and the tasks to be trained for, and it analyzes the employees who may need training. The needs assessment process for web-based training or any other type of online learning should include a technology assessment (as part of the organizational analysis) and an assessment of the skills that users need for online training (person analysis). This should include a technical analysis focused on identifying minimum computing requirements (bandwidth, memory, hard drive space, software, processing speed).

Bandwidth refers to the number of bytes and bits (information) that can travel between computers per second. Graphics, photos, animation, and video in courses can be slow to download and can "crash" the system. Online learning courses should be designed for the available bandwidth on the company's system. Bandwidth can be increased by upgrading access speed on the users' computers, buying and installing faster servers and switches

TABLE 8.5 Tips for Developing Effective Online Learning

Needs assessment	Identify the connection between online learning and the needs of the business. Get management to buy in. Make sure that employees have access to technology and technology support. Consult with information technology experts about system requirements. Identify specific training needs (knowledge, skills, competencies, behaviors). If needed, train learners on computer and Internet basics.
Creating a positive learning experience	Incorporate learning principles (practice, feedback, meaningful material, an appeal to active learner involvement, and an appeal to multiple senses). Design the course for the available bandwidth (or increase the available bandwidth to suit the course needs). Use games and simulations, which are attractive to learners. Structure materials properly. Allow trainees the opportunity to communicate and collaborate with each other and with the trainer, experts, or facilitators. Make the program user-friendly: Learning modules should be kept short, the content should not overload trainees, and webpages should not be confusing. Provide incentives for completing training. Keep each instructional segment self-contained. "Chunk" training modules. Create smooth transitions between instructional segments. Any audio, video, or animation should be useful to the learner; otherwise, it is a waste of time and bandwidth. Provide the developer/producer with clear specifications regarding required file formats, maximum file sizes, window and image dimensions, navigation, screen fonts, and available bandwidth. Provide writers and instructional designers with clear guidelines for the maximum number of words per screen, how many interactive exercises to include, and which exercises are best suited to the content. Conduct a formative evaluation (pilot test) before large scale use of online learning.
Provide time and space under learner control	Provide learners with control, including the opportunity to skip sections or modules and the ability to pause, bookmark, review, and return to where they left off. Give learners dedicated training time to participate in online learning.

Sources: Based on K. Dobbs, "What the online world needs now: Quality," *Training* (September 2000): 84–94; P. Galagan, "Getting started with e-learning." *Training and Development* (May 2000): 62–64; D. Zielinski, "Can you keep learners online?" *training* (March 2000): 65–75; V. Beer, *The Web Learning Field Book: Using the World Wide Web to Build Workplace Learning Environments* (San Francisco Jossey-Bass, 2000); E. Zimmerman, "Better training is just a click away," *Workforce* (January 2001): 36–42; R. Clark and R. Mayer, *E-Learning and the Science of Instruction* (San Francisco: John Wiley, 2003); E. Salas, R. DeRouin, and L. Littrell, "Research-Based Guidelines for Designing Distance Learning: What We Know So Far." In *The Brave New World of eHR*, ed. H. Gueutal and D. Stone (San Francisco: Jossey-Bass, 2005): 104–137; S. Boehle, "Putting the learning back into e-learning," *training* (January 2006): 29–35; A Rossett and L. Schafer, "What to do about e-dropouts," *T+D* (June 2003): 40–46; M. Morrison, "Leaner e-learning," *training* (January 2008): 16–18; M. Allen, "The return of serious design," *Chief Learning Officer* (July 2014): 31–33.

(computer hardware) on the company's network, or encouraging trainees to access the web when demand is not high.[32] Soon bandwidth may not be an issue because computer servers will be able to transfer more data faster, personal computers will have greater processing speed, and cables and wireless communications systems that carry data will have greater capacity. Online learning should also try to build in interactivity without requiring the use of plug-ins. A **plug-in** refers to additional software that needs to be loaded on the computer to listen to sound, watch video, or perform other functions. Plug-ins can be expensive because they may require the company to pay licensing fees. Plug-ins also can affect how the computer processes tasks. If trainees experience repeated technology problems (such as slow download times, network downtimes, or plug-in difficulties), they are likely to lose patience and be reluctant to participate in online learning.

Grant Thornton LLP, a global accounting, tax, and business advisory firm, created Grant Thornton University (GTU), one place for all of its employees' training needs.[33] Through GTU, employees can register for any course, whether it is classroom-based or online, and have access to more than 1,000 hours of self-paced, live webcasts and virtual classroom courses. To ensure that GTU was successful, the company investigated its business learning needs and the best delivery method for each topic (a needs assessment). Learning paths are broken down by competencies and skill requirements and are related to job performance. For example, if employees receive performance feedback suggesting that they need to improve their teamwork skills, managers can identify an appropriate course by position and required competencies. A combination of self-paced lessons and live virtual classroom is the optimal instructional method. The self-paced lessons deliver content, and the live training is used for question-and-answer sessions and case studies. Live training also provides trainees with the opportunity to interact with peers and course experts. To obtain support for GTU, the company's chief learning officer invited managers to participate in a virtual kickoff from their desktop personal computers. The kickoff covered the strategic goals of the initiative, showed managers how the technology worked, and let them sample various content.

Creating a Positive Online Learning Experience

In the design and development phase, the characteristics of a positive learning environment discussed in Chapters Four and Five (e.g., objectives, practice, interaction) should be included to help aid retention of learning content and create a meaningful experience that motivates learners. Flowcharts or storyboards should be created that include all of the course components such as a main menu, modules, webpages for each lesson, assessments, discussion forums, images, color specifications, and help menus. Rapid prototyping should be used for designing the program.[34] **Rapid prototyping** refers to an iterative process in which initial design ideas are proposed and provided in rough form in an online working prototype that is reviewed and refined by design team members and key learning stakeholders. Watching how the users interact with the prototype provides feedback about how easy (or difficult) it is to navigate through the course and understand its contents, elements, and instructions. Also, multiple types of media should be chosen in order to appeal to different learning styles to the greatest possible extent. This includes text, animation, pictures, video, audio, games, simulations, or even e-books. E-learning should be designed to minimize content or work that is unrelated to the learning objectives. Extraneous content may take up trainees' limited cognitive processing resources, resulting in less learning. Table 8.6 provides several design principles that should be considered to create a positive online learning experience.

Remember that just putting text online isn't necessarily an effective way to learn. **Repurposing** refers to directly translating an instructor-led, face-to-face training program to an online format. Online learning that merely repurposes an ineffective training

**TABLE 8.6
Principles
for Creating
a Positive
Learning
Experience**

Sources: Based
on R. Clark and
R. Mayer, "Learning
by doing: Evidence-
based guidelines for
principled learning
environments,"
*Performance
Improvement* 47
(2008): 5–13;
R. Mayer, "Applying
the science of
learning: Evidence-
based principles
for the design
of multimedia
instruction," *American
Psychologist*
(November 2008):
760–769; R. Clark and
R. Mayer, *E-Learning
and the Science of
Instruction*, 2d ed.
(San Francisco:
Jossey-Bass/Pfeiffer,
2008); T. Sitz
Mann and K. Ely.
"Sometimes you
need a reminder: The
effects of prompting
self- regulation on
regulatory processes,
learning, and attrition."
Personnel Psychology
95 (2010): 132–144.

Instruction includes relevant visuals and words.
Text is aligned close to visuals.
Complex visuals are explained by audio or text, rather than by both text and audio that narrates the text.
Extraneous visuals, words, and sounds are omitted.
Learners are socially engaged through conversational language agents.
Key concepts are explained prior to the full process or task associated with the concepts.
Prompts are provided that encourage self-regulation.
Content is presented in short sequences over which learners have control.
Activities and exercises that mimic the context of the job are provided.
Explanations are provided for learner responses to quizzes and exercises.
Exercises are distributed within and among the module(s) rather than in a single place.

program will still result in ineffective training. Unfortunately, in their haste to develop online learning, many companies are repurposing bad training. The best e-learning uses the advantages of the Internet in combination with the principles of a good learning environment. Effective online learning takes advantage of the web's dynamic nature and ability to use many positive learning features, including linking to other training sites and content through the use of hyperlinks, providing learner control, and allowing the trainee to collaborate with other learners. Effective online learning uses video, sound, text, and graphics to hold learners' attention. Effective online learning provides trainees with meaningful content related to realistic on-the-job activities, relevant examples, and the ability to apply content to work problems and issues. Also, trainees have opportunities to practice and receive feedback through the use of problems, exercises, assignments, and tests.

To ensure that materials are not confusing or overwhelming to the learner, online learning content needs to be properly arranged.[35] An orientation to the new program should be provided to learners to explain how to learn online, how to get help, and how to interact with peers, trainers, and facilitators.[36] Participants should be provided with an overview of the course or program and success factors for completion. After an e-learning program is implemented, the focus should shift to on how to best distribute, maintain, update, and improve it. Evaluation still involves collecting some combination of reaction, learning, behavior, and results outcomes, including an emphasis on questions related to the number and quality of the interactive exercises and multimedia and the ease of use of the navigation tools. Materials in online learning need to be organized in small, meaningful modules of information. Each module should relate to one idea or concept. The modules should be connected in a way that encourages the learner to be actively involved in learning. Active involvement may include asking trainees to find resources on the Internet, try quizzes or games, choose between alternative actions, or compare what they know to the knowledge of an expert or model. Objectives, videos, practice exercises, links to material that elaborates on the module content, and tests should be accessible within each module. The modules should be linked in an arrangement that makes sense, such as by importance or by the order in which content has to be learned (prerequisites). Trainees can choose to skip over material that they are familiar with or that they are competent in, based on a test of the content, or they can return to modules they need more practice in.

Learner Control

As mentioned earlier in the chapter learner control refers to giving trainees the option to learn actively though self-pacing, exercises, exploring links to other material, and conversations with other trainees and experts. Simply providing learner control does not ensure that trainees will use all the features provided by online learning (e.g., practice exercises).[37] Trainees should have access to instructions on how to use learner control tools, or else difficulty using them will take away from time and attention that they can devote to learning. Companies must communicate the importance and meaningfulness of the training content for employees' jobs and must hold employees accountable for completing the training.

Research provides several recommendations for maximizing the benefits of learner control.[38] Training programs should not allow trainees to control the amount of feedback they receive because they may rely too much on the feedback, reducing their long-term retention of the training material. The program should offer practice on each topic repeatedly throughout the program so that trainees will not forget topics they have already completed. The program should provide practice to trainees using different examples to help the transfer of training content (skills or knowledge), not only to the full range of situations that trainees may encounter on the job, but also to unexpected situations. Trainees should be allowed to control the sequence in which they receive instruction but not be able to skip practice. Prompting self-regulation improves performance in online training. As was discussed in Chapter Four, **self-regulation** refers to the learner's involvement with the training material and assessing their progress toward learning. Online prompts asking trainees to recall key points or to set goals to help them use and remember the content after the course will help trainees remember the key principles/objectives presented in training and how to apply their knowledge and skills.

Provide Time and Space for Online Learning

Using formative evaluation of prototypes of web training can be helpful in identifying the appropriate length and time of modules (formative evaluations were discussed in Chapter Six). End users (managers, potential trainees) should be involved in a formative evaluation to ensure that music, graphics, icons, animation, video, and other features facilitate rather than interfere with learning. Also, end users need to test the content, the navigator, and the site map to guarantee that they can easily move through the learning module and access resources and links to other websites as needed. Online learning blurs the distinction between training and work. Expectations that trainees will be motivated and able to complete web-based training during breaks in their normal workday or on their personal time are unrealistic.[39] Companies need to ensure that employees are given time and space for e-learning to occur.[40] That is, employees need dedicated time, protected from work tasks, for learning to occur. As with other training programs, employees need to understand why they should attend e-learning and the benefits they will receive so as to enhance their motivation to learn. Accurate communications about the content and types of learning activities in e-learning courses need to be provided to employees.[41] Managers need to give employees time in their schedules, and employees need to schedule "training time" to complete training and avoid interruptions that can interfere with learning. Some companies are moving away from their initial expectation that online learning can be completed at the employee's desktop without time away from the job; instead, they are setting up learning labs for online learning to occur without the distractions of the workplace. "Chunking," or using one- to two-hour training modules, helps trainees learn and retain more than they might in a standard full-day or half-day training class. Training can also be more easily integrated into the typical workday. Trainees can devote one to two hours to a learning session from their office and then return to their work responsibilities.

Technology for Collaboration and Linking

Chapter Four emphasized that learning often occurs as a result of interaction or sharing between employees. Employees learn by informal, unstructured contact with experts and peers. Collaboration can involve an exchange among two or more trainees or among the trainer or other experts. Linking includes the use of hyperlinks.

Hyperlinks are links that allow a trainee to access other websites that include printed materials, as well as communications links to experts, trainers, and other learners. Owens Corning's learning resource home page has hyperlinks to all available forms of training information, including CD-ROM, web-based, and trainer-led programs. The site supports online course registration and allows tests to be sent to trainees, scored, and used to register trainees in appropriate courses.[42]

Research suggests that the reason some employees fail to complete online learning and prefer instructor-led face-to-face instruction over online learning is that they want to be able to learn and network with their peers.[43] Effective online learning connects trainees and facilitates interaction and sharing through the use of collaborative learning tools such as chat rooms, discussion boards, or social media. Other methods for learner interaction and sharing include having trainees participate in collaborative online projects and receive tutoring, coaching, and mentoring by experts. Online learning also should provide a link between the trainees and the "instructor," who can answer questions, provide additional learning resources, and stimulate discussion between trainees on topics such as potential applications of the training content and common learning problems.

Massive Open Online Courses (MOOCs)

Massive open online courses (MOOCs) refers to learning that is designed to enroll large number of learners (massive), it is free and accessible to anyone with an Internet connection (open), it takes place online using videos of lectures, interactive coursework including discussion groups, and wikis (online), and it has specific start and completion dates, quizzes and assessment, and exams (courses).[44] MOOCs cover a wide variety of subject matter, including chemistry, math, physics, computer science, philosophy, mythology, health policy, cardiac arrest and resuscitation, and even poetry! Popular providers of MOOCs include Coursera, edX (nonprofit founded by Harvard and MIT), and Udacity (a for-profit company founded by a Stanford University research professor and founder of Google X Labs). The courses are often developed in partnership with colleges and universities, and, recently, private companies.

The interest in MOOCs likely originated in a free 2011 Stanford University class, Introduction to Artificial Intelligence, that had 160,000 students.[45] Since then, colleges and universities have partnered with MOOC providers to offer free or low-cost online courses, which learners can complete and earn certificates or even college credit if they pass a credential exam. Typically, there is a registration fee to take the exam. The fees range from tens to hundreds of dollars depending on the course length and content. What are the characteristics of learners who participate in MOOCs? Typically, the learners have already graduated from college and are taking the course to explore an interest or develop their skills, although the numbers of undergrads taking courses has increased. MOOCs have been able to attract huge numbers of learners. For example, Coursera estimates that it has attracted over 5 million learners based in the United States and around the world.

Companies are starting to work with the MOOC providers to design custom courses or to create their own MOOCs that can help them meet their skill needs.[46] Also edX is working with UPS, Procter & Gamble, and Walmart to design computer science and supply-chain management courses. Learners can take the course and complete a test that will earn them a certificate. BloomNet partnered with Udemy (an online course provider) to offer management and finance courses to floral shop owners located across the United States.[47] BloomNet also created custom courses focused on skills related to the floral industry. For some courses, employees take prerequisite courses on Udemy before they take instructor-led courses offered by BloomNet. Aquent, a staffing firm, was having difficulty meeting client needs for HTML5 developers.[48] To try to find a way to meet this need, Aquent created a MOOC on HTML5. More than ten thousand people registered for the class. Of the 367 who took the final exam, Aquent was able to place almost two-thirds of them in jobs with clients. Udacity is offering an online master's degree program with the Georgia Institute of Technology.[49] The program fees are less than one-third of in-state fees and one-seventh of out-of-state fees. It is the first accredited degree to be offered by a MOOC provider. The Georgia Tech professor will admit students and teach the courses, students will get the Georgia State diploma, and Udacity hosts the course material. AT&T is paying for the program expenses because it will give the company access to a talent pool of trained engineers. AT&T also plans to send some of its employees to the program.

MOOCs have several advantages and disadvantages.[50] Their low cost, accessibility, and wide range of topics make them attractive to learners. They include many features that facilitate learning and transfer: Learning is interactive and learner-controlled; it involves social interaction and emphasizes application. Learning happens through engaging short lectures combined with interaction with the course materials, interaction with other students and the instructor. It emphasizes applying knowledge and skills using role-plays, cases, and projects. It is semi-synchronous, meaning that learners receive the same assignments, video lectures, readings, quizzes, and discussions, but they can complete the coursework on their own time. Also, many MOOCs offer college credit or certificates of completion, which provide incentives for learning and formal acknowledgment. However, despite claims that MOOCs will revolutionize training and education, they have significant disadvantages. Among those who enroll in MOOCs, their interaction with the course tends to drop off after the first two weeks of the course; course completion rates are low (10 to 20 percent); and most students who complete the courses don't take the credential exam. MOOCs may also be inappropriate for courses where synchronous or real-time collaboration or interaction is needed.

To enhance their chances of being effective, MOOCs need to provide an interesting and engaging lecture that is broken up into quizzes and problem sets that learners must complete before they can progress. Learners who complete course topics should be provided with incentives such as badges. Visual meters should be used to provide feedback on progress toward completing the course. The course also needs to include interaction through discussion boards, and interactive videos. Also, learners need to have the technological skills and technology capability needed to access the MOOC, view videos, and participate in online discussions.

SOCIAL MEDIA: WIKIS, BLOGS, MICROBLOGS, AND SOCIAL NETWORKS

Social media are online and mobile technology used to create interactive communications allowing the creation and exchange of user-generated content.[51] They include blogs, wikis, networks such as Facebook, and LinkedIn, microsharing sites such as Twitter, and shared media such as YouTube. Social media can be useful for:

- Providing links to resources such as webinars, videos, and articles related to new learning content
- Helping determine future training needs and issues by using tagging capabilities
- Reinforcing and sustaining learning
- Being used as a coaching and mentoring tool
- Linking learners before, during, and after a formal training event
- Engaging Generation X and millennial employees
- Providing content before a face-to-face learning event

A **blog** refers to a webpage where an author posts entries and readers often can comment. There are many different types of blogs, including personal blogs written by one person, company blogs used for marketing and branding purposes, topic blogs focusing on a specific topic area, and blogs based on media (video blogs) and devices (mobile device blog). There are several considerations for effectively using blogs in training.[52] For a blog to be useful for training, it should be related to the learning objectives; otherwise, trainees will find it to be "busy work" and fail to see its benefits. Blogs can be especially useful for trainees to analyze and synthesize information, for learners to reflect on the lesson or course content, and to share ideas and applications of learning content. Instructors need to provide timely and relevant feedback on blog entries. Also, instructors must provide guidelines regarding how blog entries will be evaluated or what types of blog entries are desired (e.g., new ideas, application-related, "what did I learn?"). Blogs can also be useful for training courses involving group work such as projects and cases. Blogs provide a way for team members to share comments, insights, and even get involved in brainstorming.

A **wiki** refers to a website that allows many users to create, edit, and update content and share knowledge. A **microblog or microsharing** refers to software tools such as Twitter that enable communications in short bursts of text, links, and multimedia either through stand-alone applications or through online communities or social networks. **Shared media** refers to audio or video such as YouTube that can be accessed and shared with others.

How are social media being used for learning, training, and development? Many companies are using social networking tools to help employees learn informally and share knowledge both on an as-needed basis and as part of formal training courses.

Consider the following companies and nonprofit organizations' use of social networking tools.[53] Humana, a health-care company, has a social learning platform, known as the Knowledge Exchange, which is designed to build online communities to help employees learn from one another. For example, one hundred employees from different departments, business units, and jobs interacting with each other using Knowledge Exchange identified data visualization as an interest and common learning need. They collaborated, identified learning resources, and learned from each other about data visualization. They used the skills they learned to develop a data visualization product that used the group members' survey results about the effectiveness of the course. Every new employee at Cisco is trained about the appropriate use of social media. Cisco's employees have several tools they can use to interact. An internal WebEx Social platform allows employees to collaborate in teams and get feedback from experts throughout the company. Employees can access a dashboard that lets them check newsfeeds, check meetings and calendars, and review work. General Electric Company created an internal social media platform called GE Collab that allows employees to follow each other, add hashtags to comments so they can be found in searches, and link discussions to documents.

Advantage Sales and Marketing (ASM), a sales and marketing agency based in Irvine, California, added social networking to its sales training program (Accelerated Career Excellence in Sales—ACES), which teaches individuals to become business development managers. The five-month learning program involves participants meeting face to face for a two-day training session and then returning to their home sales markets. The remaining time in the program is spent working in the field with mentors and completing online training modules. During the program, employees have access to the ACES workplace community online for interaction with senior sales leaders, peers, mentors, and other sales persons in the program. Adding the social networking platform to the training program has encouraged employees to share knowledge. For example, one learner in the program contacted all of the ACES mentors to identify best practices on a specific topic. He compiled this information into a document that he shared with the entire learner community. Verizon uses social networking tools to train employees to support new products and devices. Device Blog, Device Forum, and Learning Communities help ensure that employees are ready to support customers when new products and devices are introduced to the market, engages Verizon's multigenerational workforce, and facilitates peer-to-peer learning. Device Blog makes available information and updates on wireless devices (such as the Droid), frequently asked questions (FAQs), how-to videos, and troubleshooting tips. Device Forums enable retail employees to learn from peers and product manufacturers. Employees can ask each other questions, share issues, post tips, make suggestions, and access product experts. Learning communities are accessed through the Device Blog. They include video blogs, message boards, links to online training modules, and product demonstrations. In addition to these tools, employees have access to My Network for collaborating with their peers, knowledge and document sharing, and creating working groups. Some instructors also use it for posting supplemental content for learners' use.

IBM uses social media to connect its employees around the world. IBM's site, known as w3, contributes to the global integration of the company. The w3 On Demand Workplace is a powerful productivity and collaboration tool for 400,000 IBM employees in seventy-five countries. The w3 can be used by employees to find resources and knowledge from peers around the world to help clients innovate and succeed. Employees can create personal profiles, bookmark websites and stories that they are interested in, comment on company blogs, contribute to wikis, share files, and read and review position papers, videos, and podcasts.

Special People in Northeast, Inc. (SPIN), a nonprofit organization that provides services to individuals with disabilities, makes webcasts as well as videos, how-to manuals, and process flowcharts electronically available to employees to ensure that knowledge of key employees is documented and current practices and procedures are available and shared. Intel encourages informal learning two ways: through knowledge sharing and providing employees with "performer support." Both knowledge sharing and performer support are part of Planet Blue, a social media platform for Intel employees. Employees also have access to Intelpedia, an internal wiki that employees can edit. Intelpedia has millions of pages, and thousands of employees have contributed to it. Intelpedia helped create a culture for using technology-based information-sharing solutions at Intel.

How would you determine if social media would be an effective learning tool in a company? Table 8.7 shows the questions to ask to address this issue. The more "yes" answers to these questions, the more likely that social media will be an effective learning solution. The most important consideration is whether social media is already being used in the company, which would make it easier to determine how it fits into the company's learning strategy and how easily it could be adapted to training.

It is important to support the use of social media and to consider if the ideas, content, and recommendations provided in social media are high quality and match company priorities: At Evans Analytical Group (EAG), a high-tech analytical services company, is using social media to reduce the time it takes to locate subject-matter experts and to connect its globally dispersed employees.[54] This is important because EAG's eight hundred employees might not know about possible topic experts because the company has completed over twenty-five mergers and acquisitions during the past several years. Employees use Twitter, LinkedIn, or the company's intranet to find and collaborate with subject-matter experts and acquire and contribute knowledge. Social media usage is also encouraged to reinforce knowledge and skills learned in training programs.

EAG supports the use of social media tools in several different ways. Employees are encouraged to use blogs and wikis by linking their usage to their performance appraisals, weekly recognition of employees with the highest weekly usage rates of social media tools is publicly done on the company's intranet, and the CEO endorses using the tools at company meetings. To help employees understand how to use social media tools and their potential value, EAG provides training videos, tutorials, and frequently asked questions (FAQs) that employees can access on the intranet. To ensure that the tools are effective an employee steering committee conducts interviews and gathers survey data. For example, they compared knowledge retention between two groups of employees who collaborated after the received training. One group used blogs and wikis and the other group used

TABLE 8.7
Factors to Consider in Deciding to Use Social Media for Training and Learning

Sources: Based on T. Bingham and M. Conner, *The New Social Learning* (Alexandria, VA: American Society for Training and Development, 2010); M. Derven, "Social networking: A force for development?" *T+D* (July 2009): 59–63.

Are social networks already being used in the company?
Does social networking fit into the company's learning strategy?
Are employees geographically dispersed?
Does the learning strategy support on-the-job learning?
Is there is a need to foster collaboration?
Are a significant number of employees from the millennial generation or Generation X?
Are employees comfortable using social networks?
Does the business require substantial teamwork?
Does knowledge need to be shared quickly?
Does the company value innovation?
Does the culture support decentralized decision making?

Chatter, a social collaboration tool. The knowledge retention scores did not differ between the two groups. However, 90 percent of the employees found the tools useful. IBM conducts expertise assessment to ensure the quality of the recommendations.[55] All employees conduct an annual self-evaluation that defines their skill level and ability to serve clients. The skills level choices include entry, foundational, experienced, expert, and thought leader. These rankings help employees find those who have the knowledge and experience that they need for a particular skill or solution. Self-evaluations of "thought leader" and "expert" are verified by a second line manager and SMEs. Also, it may also be necessary to have an editor monitor online postings to ensure that they reflect how the company wants to be perceived. The tradeoff of quality evaluations and monitoring is that they may inhibit collaboration and networking.

BLENDED LEARNING

Because of the limitations of online learning related to technology (e.g., insufficient bandwidth and lack of high-speed web connections), trainee preference for face-to-face contact with instructors and other learners, and employees' inability to find unscheduled time during their workday to devote to learning from their desktops, many companies are moving to a hybrid, or blended, learning approach. **Blended learning** combines online learning, face-to-face instruction, and other methods for distributing learning content and instruction. Blended learning courses provide learners with the positive features of both face-to-face instruction and technology-based delivery and instructional methods (such as online learning, distance learning, or mobile technologies like tablet computers or iPhones), while minimizing the negative features of each.[56] In comparison to classroom delivery, blended learning provides increased learner control, allows for self-directedness, and requires learners to take more responsibility for their learning—all factors consistent with the recommendations of adult learning theory discussed in Chapter Four.[57] In comparison to pure online learning, blended learning provides more face-to-face social interaction and ensures that at least some of the instruction is presented in a dedicated learning environment. Blended learning uses the classroom to allow learners to learn together and to discuss and share insights, which helps bring learning to life and make it meaningful. Live feedback from peers is preferable to feedback received online.[58]

One popular application of blended learning is the flipped classroom. The **flipped classroom** blends online and face-to-face instruction. Learners watch lectures, complete online simulations, read books and articles, take quizzes to assess their knowledge and skills, and come to class to work on projects and cases, hear speakers, and interact with faculty.[59] The flipped classroom recognizes that face-to-face instruction using lectures can be effective when it is delivered to individual learners rather than to group of learners in the classroom. Lectures can be captured on video and delivered online. This frees up face-to-face classroom time for reinforcing and applying knowledge and skills. For example, consider how stylists are trained when a new product is introduced. Now, during a one-day training program, the morning is spent with a trainer presenting the features of the product followed by a demonstration of how to apply the product using a model. During the afternoon the stylists practice applying the product. Using a flipped classroom, stylists would view videos before coming to training. The training session would begin with a question-and-answer session and then stylists would have the remaining day to work on the models with trainers and facilitators available to help. This would provide the stylists with more time to practice, observe other stylists and exchange ideas, and get feedback than in the traditional classroom training program. One of the keys for success of the flipped classroom is that learners must understand and complete the assigned content prior to coming to class. Although learners work by themselves online, it is important that the trainer be available via phone, e-mail, or chat room to answer the learners' questions. Also, learners should be required to complete quizzes or exams and earn above a passing score before they can attend the classroom session. Blended learning has been found to be more effective than face-to-face instruction for motivating trainees to learn and for teaching declarative knowledge or information about ideas or topics.[60] It appears that blended learning capitalizes on the positive learning features inherent in both face-to-face and web-based instruction. Interestingly, learners react more favorably toward classroom instruction than blended learning. This may be because blended learning courses are more demanding, requiring a greater time commitment because of the use of two learning approaches. Research suggests that the most significant issues or problems with blended learning are fast-changing technology, insufficient management support and commitment to blended learning, and a lack of understanding of what blended learning really is and how to implement it.[61]

The Water Quality Association (WQA) uses a blended learning approach to enable member companies to train and certify their employees, which include installers, service technicians, and sales representatives.[62] The competency-based system includes learning paths that employees can follow to earn badges demonstrating they have attained competencies. The learning paths include structured on-the-job experiences using a mobile performance support knowledge base, coaching, self-study readings, and mini-tutorials. WQA tracks on-the-job experiences using a mobile e-portfolio that employees can use to complete a task checklist, take a photo of their work, and tag its locations.

The pharmaceutical and life sciences company Novartis has the Digital Acceleration Workshop, which is a blended learning program that includes three parts.[63] First, employees complete four online self-study modules covering marketing and digital solutions for the pharmaceutical industry. Next, they attend two face-to-face sessions that use a case study to apply digital marketing opportunities. The last part of the program focuses on employees' involvement sharing best practices using online learning site to ensure that employees engage in continuous learning about digital marketing. This allows Novartis to build its experience base across different markets, project teams, and brands. To help ensure that the program is successful, employees are quizzed one month after they attend the program to assess retained knowledge. Also, employees complete an action plan at the end of the program. The action plan is shared with their managers, who are asked to follow up with the employees to see if they are applying what they learned to their job.

SIMULATIONS AND GAMES

Simulations and games were introduced as a traditional training method in Chapter Seven. This chapter discusses how development in software and computer technology has improved the learning and transfer that can result from simulators and games. Simulation and games that can be delivered via a personal computer (or gaming technology such as an Xbox immerse trainees in decision-making exercises in an artificial yet realistic environment that allow them to learn the consequences of their decisions. Simulation games are widely popular—one estimate is that 53 percent of adults play video games![64] **Serious games** refer to games in which the training content is turned into a game but has business objectives.[65] "Gamification" means that game-based strategies are applied to e-learning programs. The key is to use the fun and motivational aspects of games to help employees acquire knowledge and skills. Table 8.8 shows four different types of simulations and games. Some simulations include virtual reality or take place in virtual worlds. **Virtual reality** is a computer-based technology that provides trainees with a three-dimensional learning experience. This allows simulations to become even more realistic. Using specialized equipment or viewing the immersive model on the computer screen, trainees move through the simulated environment and interact with its components.[66] Simulations allow the trainees to experience **presence**, which refers to perceptions of actually being in a particular environment. Presence is influenced by the amount of sensory information available to the trainee, control over the environment, and the ability to modify the environment. In simulations, presence can include trainees feeling a sense of motion or experiencing emotions such as anger from a customer or colleague. Poor presence may result in trainees experiencing vomiting, dizziness, headaches (simulator sickness), and frustration because senses are inappropriately distorted. Simulations can also take place in a virtual world. **Virtual worlds** refer to the computer-based, simulated online three-dimensional representation of the real world where learning programs can be hosted. Second Life, ProtoSphere, Forterra, and Virtual Heroes are examples of providers of virtual worlds.[67] In virtual worlds, trainees use avatars to interact with each other in the classroom, webinars, or role-play exercise. An **avatar** refers to computer depictions of humans that are used as imaginary coaches, coworkers, customers, and instructors.[68] Virtual worlds allow employees to learn alone, with their peers, or in teams. Virtual worlds such as Second Life can be used to create virtual classrooms, but their strength is its ability to get the learner actively involved in working with equipment, peers, or customers. For example, British Petroleum (BP) uses Second Life to train new gas station employees in the safety features of gasoline storage tanks and piping systems.[69] BP's virtual world includes three-dimensional replicas of the tank and pipe system at a gas station. Trainees are able to "see" the underground storage tanks and piping systems and observe how safety devices control gasoline flow—something they could never do in real life.

TABLE 8.8
Types of Simulations

Sources: Based on C. Cornell, "Better than the real thing?" *Human Resource Executive* (August 2005): 34–37; S. Boehle, "Simulations: The next generation of e-learning," *Training* (January 2005): 22–31.

Type of Simulation	Description
Branching story	Trainees are presented with a situation and asked to make a choice or decision. Trainees progress through the simulation on the basis of their decisions.
Interactive spreadsheet	Trainees are given a set of business rules (usually finance-based) and asked to make decisions that will affect the business. The decisions are entered into a spreadsheet that shows how the decisions affect the business.
Game-based	Trainees play a video game on a computer.
Virtual	Trainees interact with a computer representation of the job for which they are being trained.

The U.S. Army uses a three-dimensional virtual simulation to help soldiers correctly identify social networks and norms in an area of operations.[70] The simulations reinforce classroom training. Participating in the simulation helps soldiers develop their critical thinking and cultural awareness skills by asking them to identify leaders and evaluate the area for criminal activities such as drug smuggling or human trafficking. The simulation is also based on local and cultural norms such as teenagers carrying assault rifles or perceptions that people outside of the ethnic or religious group are inferior. The simulation helps reduce the soldiers' culture shock and perform more effectively when they are involved in actual operations. The simulation can include up to six square kilometers and thirty players. For example, a group of soldiers can enter a virtual village and, based on their interactions with the villagers, they draw a map of family, friends, foes, and personal and work relationships. Flight simulators including full motion and high-resolution graphics are recent additions to pilot training in the commercial helicopter industry.[71] The simulators are intended to improve helicopters' safety record. On average more than one major helicopter accident occurs each day somewhere in the world. Training accidents using actual helicopters account for approximately one-fourth of all commercial crashes. Buying or leasing a simulator can cost millions of dollars while contracting costs range between $1,000 and $1,500 per hour. But the cost is much less than the hourly cost of taking helicopters out of service to teach pilots. Also, in addition to cost savings, the simulators allow pilots to focus on important safety issues and emergency procedures that are impossible to replicate in an actual helicopter.

Many companies are using games and gamification. An ATD survey of learning professionals found that 25 percent of companies use gamification in learning and 20 percent use serious games.[72] IBM uses simulation games to develop employees' skills in information technology, architecture and infrastructure, finance, project management, and business process management.[73] In the game for business process management the player takes the role of a consultant in a call center. Players have to walk around the space, conduct interviews, and make decisions. The game is supported by a chat room, library, help videos, and leaderboards, which assist the social and competitive nature of the game. Ford of Canada uses gamification to train dealership salespersons.[74] The Professional Performance Program (p^2p) is an online program where sales and service staff from Ford stores in Canada can access online product and service training, sales resources, and certification. The Ford p^2p Cup is a professional auto racing–themed program that includes videos, product information, and web courses. Trainees can earn points and advance to higher levels, work on their personal goals, earn badges that are shown in a trophy case, compete against their peers on a leaderboard, compete against other dealerships, and receive feedback. Allstate Insurance uses the "PII Protectors" game for employees to review their knowledge on privacy protection, that is, how to make sure client's information is safe.[75] The game begins with a video showing the player being declined for a mortgage because their identity was stolen. The player then joins an agency to fight an evil company trying to steal other people's data. They choose to take one of four alter egos, such as Captain Confidential or Firewall. Next, players are faced with solving dilemmas by answering questions based on Allstate's privacy policy. The more problems they solve, the less data their character stops leaking outside the company.

At NetApp Inc., twenty-five managers participated in a game in which they played the role of top executives in an imaginary company modeled after their employer.[76]

The managers worked in five-person teams and competed to produce the strongest sales and operating profit. They were faced with challenges such as balancing long-term investments against short-term results. Managers received information including market analyses based on actual NetApp data and a menu of strategic initiatives such as improving college recruiting. The teams had to choose strategies and allocate employees and money. They were given scenarios such as an important customer seeking to add last-minute product features; in responding, they had to decide whether to add the features (which included determining their related costs) or refuse and risk angering an important client. The teams saw the consequences of their decisions. For example, one team declined to add the product features, which resulted in a decline in customer satisfaction and market share. At the end of the simulation, the sales and total profits of each team, as well as the effects of their strategies, were discussed.

PPD is a global contract research organization that is involved in drug discovery, development, lifecycle management, and laboratory services. PPD's clients and partners include pharmaceutical, biotechnology, medical device, academic, and government organizations. PPD has offices in forty-six countries with more than thirteen thousand employees, making it critical that effective training could be delivered without travel and time demands. PPD used a virtual three-dimensional learning environment to deliver its Clinical Foundations Program.[77] PPD created a virtual doctor's office, as well as reception, training, and conference rooms. Both trainees and instructors communicate and interact using avatars. Excel, PowerPoint, and video can also be used along with the virtual universe. PPD found that the virtual training improved the cost-effectiveness, speed, and employees' accessibility to training. Eighty percent of trainees who participated in virtual programs prefer it to classroom training and 95 percent felt they were more engaged than in traditional instruction.

As you can see from these examples, simulations can be effective for several reasons.[78] First, trainees can use them on their desktop or notebook computer, eliminating the need to travel to a central training location. Second, simulations are meaningful, they get trainees involved in learning, and they are emotionally engaging (they can even be fun!). This increases employees' willingness to practice, encourages retention, improves their skills, and enhances transfer of training. Third, simulators provide a consistent message of what needs to be learned; trainees can work at their own pace; and, compared to face-to-face instruction, simulators can incorporate more situations or problems that a trainee might encounter. Simulators can be used for training interpersonal skills, and how to use equipment. Fourth, simulations can safely put employees in situations that would be dangerous in the real world. Trainees can learn and practice dangerous tasks without putting themselves or others in danger. Fifth, simulations have been found to result in such positive outcomes as shorter training times and increased return on investment.

Simulations do have some disadvantages. The use of simulations has been limited by their development costs. Games and simulations are useful for practicing skills, but trainees must first acquire knowledge and then apply it while playing the game.[79] Debriefing learners after a game is useful for helping trainees understand how their simulation experience relates to their work. A customized simulation can cost between $200,000 and $300,000, while a simulation purchased from a supplier without any customization typically costs $100 to $200 per trainee.[80] The cost to rent space from a virtual-world

TABLE 8.9
Questions to Consider About Serious Games

Source: Based on C. Balance, "Strategic ways to develop game-based learning for high ROI," *T+D* (September 2013): 76–77; B. Roberts, "Gamification: Win, lose or draw," *HR Magazine* (May 2014): 28.35; R. Paharia, *Loyalty 3.0* (New York: McGraw-Hill Education, 2013).

- What is the business objective?
- What behavior or tasks will be learned?
- How many levels and players should it include?
- Will everyone playing the game have access to the same technology?
- Is the game fun and does it drive engagement in learning?
- Does the game provide feedback and elements such as leaderboards, meters, or badges to motivate friendly competition between employees or teams?

program's campus within a public space is $200–$300 per day; it costs $1,000 to $2,000 for a customized simulation within the space.[81] The average cost for a basic fifteen minute game is $20,000 to $30,000 but games can range from $5,000 to $250,000.[82] Leased space in a virtual world is expensive. It can range from $5,000 to $100,000 annually, depending on the size and type of the space leased ($10,000–$20,000 is required for a private space on a public server or a private, customized island). However, although they continue to be an expensive training method, development costs for simulations continue to decrease, making them a more popular training method. Also, the use of simulations as a training method is likely to increase as technology development allows more realism to be built into simulations. The novelty of the experience of a simulation may help trainees recall the experience, but they may also interfere with retention and transfer of the training content to the job.[83] Learners may not take a simulation seriously. Learning in a simulation may be better for those who already have some job experiences because for learners, simulations may confuse and overwhelm them. Finally, trainees may not be comfortable in learning situations that lack human contact.

We all know that games can be fun, but what questions should you consider in purchasing or building a serious game for training? Table 8.9 shows the questions you should consider. It is important to establish the purpose of the game and its relationship to the business. Games can be used for several business-related purposes, including safety training, product training, team building, and new employee orientation. It is also necessary to determine what behaviors or tasks trainees should be able to perform as a result of playing the game. The business purpose and behavior and skills should be included in the game's learning objectives. Learners should be engaged through meaningful game scenarios, narratives, and problems. Feedback, competition, and incentives can enhance the "fun" aspect of the game. Trainees should be able to easily access and see their score and the scores of all players (leaderboard) and have the opportunity to earn badges. Games should be tested (recall our discussion of formative evaluation in Chapter Six) to ensure that they are easy to use and logical, and that technology problems are minimized.

MOBILE TECHNOLOGY AND LEARNING

Mobile technology allows learning to occur anywhere, at any time. Mobile technology consists of[84]

- Wireless transmission systems such as Wi-Fi and Bluetooth that allow transmission of data without the need for physical connections between devices or between a device and an Internet connection.

- Mobile devices such as smartphones, tablet computers, iPods, iPads, global positioning system (GPS) devices, and radio frequency identification (RFID) chips.
- Software applications related to processing audio files, word processing, spreadsheets, Internet, e-mail, and instant messaging.

GPS and RFID devices are used for tracking customers, employees, and property. For example, many cars and trucks are equipped with GPS devices to allow operators to locate drivers. Trucking companies use GPS devices to track loads and to determine expected arrival times. RFID chips are embedded in products to track their movement and to help in inventory control. Hotels are providing mobile devices to allow customers to access information about guest services, dining, entertainment, and accommodations anywhere on the hotel property. Airlines are providing pilots with iPads they can use while in the cockpit.[85] The iPads give the pilots easy access to airport runway approaches, real-time weather updates, and runway diagrams. Before the iPads were available, pilots had to carry heavy flight bags (some weighed thirty-five pounds) with all of the necessary navigation charts and manuals. Besides giving pilots easier access to the information they need, replacing the flight bags with the iPads has resulted in the airlines saving on fuel costs. American estimates that removing the flight bags saved about 400,000 gallons of fuel, which is close to a $1 million savings in fuel costs!

Mobile learning refers to training delivered using a mobile device such as a smartphone, netbook, notebook computer, or iPad. One estimate is that 17 percent of U.S. companies use mobile learning.[86] Mobile learning can involve both formal and informal learning. Formal learning might include e-learning courses, podcasts, or videos on the mobile device. Informal learning includes engaging in communication and messaging with other employees or experts via Twitter, blogs, or Facebook. The advantages of mobile learning include that it is an easy way to get up-to-date information to employees; it can be useful for enhancing transfer of training through providing follow-up; it brings training to employees who are constantly traveling, are out of the office visiting customers or clients, or don't have the time to attend a face-to-face course or program (such as salespeople or executives); and learners can complete training on their own time and pace. Mobile learning allows employees to generate content by creating video, taking photos, or recording an interview and sharing it with others. Also, using mobile devices for learning appeals to millennials. Mobile devices can also provide RSS feeds, shared media (such as YouTube), and podcasts. **Podcasts** are audio or video program content distributed in episodes using software such as RSS. The best use of podcasts is for narrative-based content that inspires the user's imagination using music and sound effects.[87] Podcasts are great for sharing expertise of SMEs using interviews, stories, and role-plays. It is cheap and easy to produce using a microphone, computer with audio software, portable digital recorder, Skype phone recorder, headphones, or speakers. An advantage of podcasts is that learners can listen at any time or place using many different mobile devices such as iPhones, iPads, or notebook computers. Through mobile technologies, training and learning can occur naturally throughout the workday or at home, employees can be connected to communities of learning, and employees are given the ability to learn at their own pace by reviewing material or skipping over content that they already know.[88]

For example, Farmers Insurance Group supplies smartphones to its claim representatives.[89] They can use the smartphone to access product cards to learn about insurance policies, review requirements for settling atypical insurance claims, or learn about changes in policies. At Sonic, the fast-food restaurant, recipes and employee activities are constantly changing due to a rotating menu.[90] At Sonic, managers can use their smartphone to review food preparations with a team member, view a video, access store reports, contact experts, and post questions and answers to an online learning community.

Many companies are using tablets such as the iPad for training because of their ease of use, colorful, easy-to-read display, ability to connect to the web, and availability of powerful apps. **Apps** refer to applications designed specifically for smartphones and tablet computers. Apps are primarily being used to supplement training, manage the path or sequence of training, and to help employees maintain training records.[91] An app for the U.S. military combat medical teams provides details on specific medical procedures such as controlling bleeding. The American Ophthalmological Society (AOS) is using apps in its continuous medical education courses to supplement training. Courses are provided online, but learning tips and techniques are provided as mobile apps.

Some companies are beginning to use apps as primary training. To ensure that learning and transfer of training occurs using these apps, they are designed to catch the learner's attention by incorporating attention-getting videos, stories, and interactions. Sales representatives at Coca-Cola Bottling Company Consolidated (CCBCC) are responsible for business development and customer relationships.[92] Most of their time is spent traveling to meet customer needs or visiting prospects for new business. To help sales reps better manage their workload and meet their sales quotas, CCBCC developed an online learning program. Sales reps can use an iPad to access an app that links to the program's content as well as videos on key concepts and action planning templates. The program's content covers how to get work done, how to work smart, and how to handle information overload. The app also includes editable PDF files that allow sales reps working with their and their managers during on-the-job coaching sessions to create and update action plans. The app is frequently used by sales reps and its use has contributed to a 20 percent increase in daily sales calls. Watson Pharmaceuticals has developed an app for its corporate university, allowing pharmaceutical representatives to access videos and product knowledge from their iPhones. Unisys Corporation offers employees both an e-learning and mobile version of a compliance training program.[93] The mobile version includes four 20 minute segments compared to the one-and-one-half-hour e-learning program. The mobile version also has less content on each screen and limited use of video. Unisys is also providing samples of e-learning or face-to-face programs on mobile devices to entice learners to get involved in other training courses. Northrop Grumman, a defense contractor, is developing games for tablets and iPads that train users on information technology security using an interface that looks like a motherboard. Learners move around the game board in their "truck" and are presented with questions about information technology security. Correctly answering all of the questions earns them the opportunity to play an action game in which they shoot down logic bombs, malicious code, and Trojan horses.

For mobile learning to be effective, it needs to be short, easy to use, and meaningful.[94] One estimate is that the course length should not exceed ten minutes because users likely do not have long periods of time for learning, and attention spans are limited when looking at the small screens on many mobile devices. The screen layout should work with or without graphics. Images should be used only where relevant to the content because download time may be slow due to bandwidth limitations. Images used should be sized so that the user can see them without scrolling horizontally or vertically. Technical requirements due to screen size, web browsers, and mobile operating systems need to be considered, as well as the availability and ability to use plug-ins such as Flash, Java, and Portable Document Format (PDF). Also, simply repurposing lectures by digitizing them and distributing them to employees will not facilitate learning. For example, Capital One creates simulated radio shows with phone-in questions and answers given by announcers to create an audio learning environment that is enjoyable and interesting. As with e-learning, training that uses mobile technology may be most effective if it is part of a blended learning approach that involves face-to-face interaction among trainees as well as audio learning.

ADAPTIVE TRAINING

Adaptive training refers to training that customizes or adapts the content presented to the trainee based on their learning style, ability, personality, or performance.[95] These adaptations include the variety, difficulty, and sequencing of content as well as practice problems. In adaptive training, instruction changes based on trainees scores on tests or quizzes completed either before training or at various times as they experience training. This assessment results in adaptations of the content to best help the trainee learn. Although trainers strive to meet the needs of learners, it is very difficult using face-to-face training methods. Online training makes it easier to use ongoing assessments to identify the most effective instructional pathways for learners. The major challenge in developing adaptive training is to ensure that the different content customizations match the learner needs and help them attain the learning objectives. For example, LearnSmart is an interactive and adaptive study tool that is used in some college courses.[96] Based on their performance on quizzes throughout the course, students are directed to practice exercises and sections of online textbooks they need to read. LearnSmart is designed to help students better use their study time, as well as improve their retention, recall of the material, and their grades. Another example of adaptive training is an intelligent tutoring system. An intelligent tutoring system (ITS) is an instructional system that uses artificial intelligence.[97]

ITS has been used by the National Aeronautics and Space Administration (NASA) in astronaut training.[98] For example, the Remote Maneuvering System ITS was used to teach astronauts how to use the robotic arm on the space shuttle. Astronauts had to learn to complete tasks and procedures related to grappling a payload. The ITS generated processes that were matched to individual astronauts. Feedback was matched to each astronaut's pattern of success and failure in learning the tasks. The system recorded performance data for each astronaut, made decisions regarding the student's level of understanding, and used those decisions to provide appropriate feedback.

DISTANCE LEARNING

Distance learning is used by geographically dispersed companies to provide information about new products, policies, or procedures, as well as deliver skills training and expert lectures to field locations.[99] Distance learning can include virtual classrooms, which have the following capabilities: projection of still, animated, and video images;

instructor-participant audio discussion; sharing of computer software applications; interactions using instant polling technology; and whiteboard marking tools.[100] Distance learning features two-way communications between people, and it currently involves two types of technology.[101] The first technology is teleconferencing. **Teleconferencing** refers to synchronous exchange of audio, video, and/or text between two or more individuals or groups at two or more locations. Trainees attend training programs in training facilities in which they can communicate with trainers (who are at another location) and other trainees using the telephone or personal computer. The second type of distance learning also includes individualized, personal computer–based training.[102] Employees participate in training anywhere they have access to a personal computer. This type of distance learning may involve multimedia training methods, such as web-based training. Course material and assignments can be distributed using the company's intranet, video, or DVDs. Trainers and trainees interact using e-mail, bulletin boards, and conferencing systems.

Teleconferencing usually includes a telephone link so that trainees viewing the presentation can call in questions and comments to the trainer. Also, satellite networks allow companies to link up with industry-specific and educational courses for which employees receive college credit and job certification. IBM, Hewlett-Packard, and Milliken. Corporation are among the many firms that subscribe to the National Technological University (now part of Walden University), which broadcasts courses throughout the United States that technical employees need to obtain advanced degrees in engineering.[103]

A **virtual classroom** refers to using a computer and the Internet to distribute instructor-led training to geographically dispersed employees. The potential advantages of the virtual classroom include its cost savings and convenience: geographically dispersed employees can be brought together for training for several hours each week, and content experts can be brought into the classroom as needed. However, the training delivered using a virtual classroom is not the same as the training delivered face to face by an instructor. There are a number of guidelines for developing effective training in the virtual classroom:[104]

- Design short modules and follow up with an assignment that applies the learning to the job.
- Make learning interactive and interesting, such as modeling the program after a phone-in radio show.
- Include media such as video and audio.
- Limit classroom size to no more than twenty-five learners.
- Offer learners multiple ways of interacting with each other and the instructor, including webinars, e-mail, discussion rooms, message boards, and blogs.
- Test the technology before the first class to ensure it's ready.

Interactive distance learning (IDL) refers to the latest generation of distance learning, which uses satellite technology to broadcast programs to different locations and allows trainees to respond to questions posed during the training program using a keypad.[105] IDL is being used by companies that have employees in many different locations and who lack computers or online access. IDL allows employees in different locations to see behaviors and how to get things done rather than just read or hear about them. For example, JCPenney Company, which produces more than 200 different IDL programs each year, uses distance learning to reach every associate. Each store has a training room where up to twelve employees can sign in to the program and watch on a large television screen. Each employee has his or her own keypad to interact with the program. Employees are able to watch the satellite broadcast live or view a tape of the program later. Regardless of whether watching the program live or via tape, employees can answer questions such as, "How many square feet does your store have for lingerie?" At the end of the program, managers and trainers can access a report on how every store answered. Evaluations of the interactive distance learning program have been positive. IDL has allowed JCPenney to deliver training to every employee in the company, and 86 percent of its employees report that they have the training needed to perform their jobs effectively.

An advantage of distance learning is that the company can save on travel costs. It also allows employees in geographically dispersed sites to receive training from experts who would not otherwise be available to visit each location. Intuit finds that a traditional classroom environment is good for introducing software and providing trainees with the opportunity to network. Virtual classroom training is used for courses on special software features, for demonstrations, and for troubleshooting using application-sharing features. General Mills uses virtual classrooms at smaller plants where offering a class on site is not cost effective.[106] Employees have access to courses in product-specific knowledge (e.g., cereal production), general technical skills (e.g., food chemistry), and functional-specific knowledge (e.g., maintenance). FileNeT Corporation was concerned with how its sales force was going to keep up with new software and software updates.[107] FileNeT tried self-paced online learning but discovered that salespeople did not like to read a lot of material about new products on the web. Enrollment in online courses dwindled, and salespeople flooded the company's training department with requests for one-on-one assistance. To solve the training problem, the company decided to use webcasting. **Webcasting,** or **web conferencing,** involves instruction that is provided online through live broadcasts. Webcasting helped spread the sales force training throughout the year rather than cramming it into twice-a-year sales meetings. Webcasting also helped ensure that the salespeople all received the same information. The salespeople liked the webcasts because of the timely information that helped them have conversations with customers. The live sessions were also popular because participants could ask questions. Webcasting has not replaced face-to-face training at FileNeT; classroom training is still about 80 percent of training, but that percentage has decreased from 90 percent. Webcasting has also resulted in savings of $500,000 annually (because one of the twice-yearly sales meetings was canceled).

The major disadvantages of distance learning are the lack of interaction between the trainer and the audience, technology failures, and unprepared trainers. A high degree of interaction among trainees or between the trainees and the trainer is a positive learning feature that is missing from distance learning programs that use the technology only to broadcast a lecture to geographically dispersed employees. All this does is repurpose a traditional lecture (with its limitations for learning and transfer of training) for a new training technology. To engage trainees in a distance learning environment, it is useful to limit online sessions to sixty to ninety minutes in length, maintain a good instructional pace, avoid presenting unnecessary text, use relevant and engaging visuals (e.g., graphs and animation), and allow trainees to participate using polling devices and small-group breakout rooms for discussion and projects.[108] A group spokesperson can be assigned to summarize and communicate the group's ideas. Weather conditions and satellite glitches can occur at any time, disconnecting the instructor from the audience or making it difficult to show video or other multimedia presentations. Instructors need backup plans for dealing with technical issues. Because many instructors have difficulty speaking to trainees in another location without a live group of trainees in front of them, it is important to prepare instructors for distance delivery. For example, a producer who is familiar with the technology can work with the instructor and help facilitate the training session.

TECHNOLOGIES FOR TRAINING SUPPORT

Technologies such as expert systems, groupware, and electronic support systems are being used to support training efforts. Training support means that these technologies are helping to capture training content so that it is available to employees who may not have attended training. Training support also means that these technologies provide information and decision rules to employees on an as-needed basis (i.e., they are job aids). Employees can access these technologies in the work environment.

Table 8.10 shows when training support technologies are most needed. Many conditions shown in the table relate to characteristics of the task or the environment that can inhibit transfer of training. For example, employees may work some distance away from their manager, the manager may be difficult to contact, or employees may need special expertise that the manager lacks. These situations make it difficult for employees to find answers to problems that arise on the job. Training support technologies can assist in transfer of training by helping employees generalize training content to the work environment and by providing employees with new information (not covered in training).

Expert Systems

Expert systems refer to technology that organizes and applies the knowledge of human experts to specific problems.[109] Expert systems have three elements:

1. A knowledge base that contains facts, figures, and rules about a specific subject
2. A decision-making capability that, imitating an expert's reasoning ability, draws conclusions from those facts and figures to solve problems and answer questions
3. A user interface that gathers and gives information to the person using the system

Expert systems are used as a support tool that employees refer to when they have problems or decisions that they feel exceed their current knowledge and skills. They can also be used to help employees make sense of different conditions and problems and keep track of tasks that need to be completed. For example, at Johns Hopkins Medical Center's data from patient records and monitoring equipment is integrated and available to intensive

TABLE 8.10 Conditions When Training Support Technologies Are Most Needed

Source: Based on A. Rossett, "Job Aids and Electronic Performance Support Systems." In *The ASTD Training and Development Handbook*, 4th ed., ed. R. L. Craig (New York: McGraw-Hill, 1996): 554–577.

- Performance of task is infrequent.
- The task is lengthy, difficult, and information intensive.
- The consequences of error are damaging.
- Performance relies on knowledge, procedures, or approaches that frequently change.
- There is high employee turnover.
- Little time is available for training, or there are few resources for training.
- Employees are expected to take full responsibility for learning and performing tasks.

care unit staff on a tablet computer.[110] The system shows staff what tasks need to be done and when to perform preventative measures for surgical complications and alerts the staff to situations when patients may be at risk such as when drugs may interact to cause medical problems. Color coding alerts the user to whether an urgent action needs to take place (red), a task needs to be performed soon (yellow), or a necessary task has been completed (green).

Although expert systems are discussed as a technology that supports training, expert systems can also be used as a delivery mechanism. Expert systems can be used to train employees in the decision rules of the experts. For example, a financial company dramatically increased the portfolio of products that it offered to customers.[111] The sales force needed to be prepared to introduce these products to clients and to make sales. The company developed an expert system to capture the sales processes used by top sales performers. This web-based expert system allowed salespersons to access information on each financial product, alerted salespersons to information they needed from the customer, and used expert logic to identify opportunities to introduce new products to customers based on data entered by the salesperson (the expert system matches general client characteristics with specific customer characteristics).

Expert systems can deliver both high quality and lower costs. By using the decision processes of experts, the system enables many people to arrive at decisions that reflect experts' knowledge. An expert system helps avoid the errors that can result from fatigue decision biases, and the inability to make sense of large amounts of information. The efficiencies of an expert system can be realized if it can be operated by fewer or less skilled (and likely less costly) employees than the company would otherwise require.

Electronic Performance Support Systems (EPSSs)

An **electronic performance support system (EPSS)** is an electronic infrastructure that captures, stores, and distributes individual and corporate knowledge assets throughout an organization to enable individuals to achieve required levels of performance in the fastest possible time and with a minimum of support from other people.[112] An EPSS includes all the software needed to support the work of individuals (not just one or two specific software applications).

EPSS can be used to help transfer of training and provide just-in-time performance support that substitutes for training. Microsoft's Office software has "wizards," a help function that recognizes the task that the user is starting to perform (e.g., writing a letter) and offers information related to that task. Also, retailers such as Sephora are supplying employee with iPads that they can use as a product-reference guide (a performance support tool). Both Coca-Cola Sabco and SNI use performance support as a means to help transfer of training.[113] Coca-Cola Sabco, a South African bottling company, provides on-demand learning materials using YouTube videos accessible on phones and tablet computers that focus on tasks such as the way to correctly stack products inside coolers. SNI, a company that supplies negotiations skills training, provides its clients with a checklist of seven negotiating tactics they can pull up on their smartphones. Although these tactics are covered in training, the checklist is available to aid clients' recall and transfer of skills to real negotiation situations. Rather than train employees on infrequently performed tasks, ADP provides employees with "Learning Bytes" two-minute learning solutions demonstrating how to perform these tasks. The Learning Bytes have helped reduce calls into ADP's service center.

To use EPSS as a substitute for training, trainers must determine whether problems and tasks require employees to actually acquire knowledge, skill, or ability (learned capability) and whether periodic assistance through an EPSS is sufficient.

LEARNING MANAGEMENT SYSTEMS: SYSTEMS FOR TRAINING DELIVERY, SUPPORT, AND ADMINISTRATION

A **learning management system (LMS)** refers to a technology platform that can be used to automate the administration, development, and delivery of all of a company's training programs. LMSs can provide employees, managers, and trainers with the ability to manage, deliver, and track learning activities. Some of the features of LMSs are shown in Table 8.11. LMSs provide the ability for users to search the database and their company's intranet simultaneously for information on training courses, contact experts who are identified by the company as topic experts, enroll in all courses related to a certification or particular training topic at one time, and use simulations to determine whether employees are complying with ethical standards and skills that they have been trained in using by the LMS.[114]

There are a number of reasons LMSs are being used. An LMS can help a company reduce travel and other costs related to training, reduce time for program completion, increase employees' accessibility to training across the business, and provide administrative capabilities to track program completion and course enrollments. LMSs allow companies to track all learning activity in the business.

TABLE 8.11
Features of LMSs

Source: Based on S. Castellano, "The evolution of the, LMS;" *T+D* (November 2014): 14; "Learning management systems: An executive summary," *Training* (March 2002): 4.

Trainee management and reporting	Track and report on trainee progress and activity.
Training event and resource management	Organize courses and learning events in catalogs; manage and track course resources such as classrooms and instructors; support communications among administrators and students.
Online course delivery infrastructure	Deliver online courses; register and track trainees.
Authoring tools	Create new courses; promote consistency in courses.
Skill assessment	Create, edit, distribute, and deliver assessment tests; review trainee achievements.
Professional development management	Track and compare trainee learning against goals, based on the trainee's job or function.
Knowledge bases	Integrate links to learning references that supplement online learning.
Personalization	Engage employees in learning through the use of target courses, references, and e-mails.
Link to human capital management systems	Link to performance management, career development, and talent management systems.

LMS is also important for human capital management. **Human capital management** integrates training with all aspects of the human resource function (e.g., performance evaluation, human resource planning) to determine how training dollars are spent and how training expenses translate into business dollars for the company. Some of the reasons that companies adopt an LMS are to centralize management of learning activities, track regulatory compliance, measure training usage, measure employee performance and help in talent management.[115]

LMSs are also important for companies to be able to track the number of employees who have completed courses that are required to meet state, federal, or professional regulations (compliance training).[116] These courses cover a wide range of topics, including financial integrity, health and safety, environmental protection, and employee rights. For example, various regulations mandate that companies be able to prove that employees have completed courses in sexual harassment or defensive driving. Employees from a variety of for-profit businesses, including financial services, oil refining, and pharmaceuticals, as well as employees in nonprofit organizations such as government agencies and hospitals, have to complete certain required courses. The Gunderson Lutheran Health System includes hospitals, community clinics, nursing homes, home care, pharmacies, ambulances, mental health services, and vision centers.[117] Employees are required to take courses to comply with national standards on protecting patient privacy, as well as courses related to providing a safe and healthy work environment. Gunderson developed an LMS that includes all mandatory compliance courses, as well as other courses. Employees can access courses on the LMS through computers located at their desks, in computer labs, or at health sciences libraries. Gunderson has realized many benefits from the LMS. The LMS has been useful in reducing the time employees spend on compliance courses (e.g., safety courses now take twenty minutes compared to the two hours required for classroom training). The online courses provide employees with flexibility to fit learning into their schedules. For example, nurses can leave their online course to visit patients and then return to continue learning right where they left off. The online courses offer more interactivity through the use of exercises, assessments, and role-plays than did the classroom training, and such interactivity holds employees' interest. Finally, since the LMS was developed, the demand for learning has increased: Departments want more classroom courses to be converted to online courses.

An LMS can help companies understand the strengths and weaknesses of their employees, including where talent gaps exist.[118] Also, an LMS can be linked to other human resource systems, such as performance management or employee development systems, to identify learning opportunities for employees to strengthen their performance weaknesses. Turner Construction has a competency model that divides jobs into nine job families and divides the families into job levels (senior management, administrative/clerical, and management). Employees receive an online performance evaluation of their skills based on their job family and level. The performance management system links to the company's LMS. The LMS analyzes the employees' skill weaknesses and provides recommendations of courses that can improve those skills. The LMS system allows Turner Construction to identify skill gaps for entire levels, job families, or business units. The results can be used to identify where to spend monies allocated for training to develop new courses.

To maximize its effectiveness, an LMS should be integrated with talent management systems. The interfaces between the systems will provide basic employee information such as business unit, geographic location, and job title. Information about which courses employees have completed and are eligible to complete should also be stored in the LMS. Consider how VCA Animal Hospitals, Vanguard, and MasTec Utility Services Group contributes to the business, encourage employee participation in training, and integrate talent management practices and systems.[119] VCA Animal Hospitals has a geographically dispersed workforce with 13,000 workers in over 500 animal hospitals across forty states. It used to rely on training based on Microsoft PowerPoint presentations with audio narration but recognized that it had to improve the quality of its courses. VCA Animal Hospitals purchased a new LMS that now allows more engaging training methods, including video clips of veterinarians discussing medical practices, simulations, online collaboration between learners and learners and between learners and the instructors, and safety inspection checklists. The LMS is used for online courses, registering veterinarians for classroom-based courses, and tracking who has completed training and how well they scored on post-training tests. Vanguard, the financial services firm, uses an LMS that allows its employees, known as crew members, to get learning recommendations from Vanguard's University based on their career interests, development goals, and relevant content for their current jobs. It also makes it easier for crew members to find and access videos, audio clips, interactive flash demonstrations, and articles, as well as enrolling in classes. The LMS categorizes informal learning sources, such as podcasts, articles, and video clips, with formal learning solutions, including online and classroom-based courses. Informal and formal learning solutions as well as outside courses offered by vendors can also be found using a key work search. MasTec Utility Services Group, a utility company, uses an LMS to help manage its training programs. MasTec wanted to be able to make training content available to employees who work in rural areas as well as in cities. Also, they wanted to make it easier for employees to register for training and managers to approve their enrollment, and to see training requirements, participation rates, and training completion. Using MasTec's online LMS, employees can log in and view training courses and curriculum, access e-learning and videos, and schedule instructor-led courses. Employees can also access company safety bulletins and enroll in U.S. Department of Labor apprenticeship programs. Managers can request reports that show training requirements and which employees have met them. They can display course completion dates, training quiz scores, and expiration dates for compliance training that employees may have completed.

CHOOSING NEW TECHNOLOGY TRAINING METHODS

Table 8.12 compares technology-based training methods based on the same characteristics used to compare traditional training programs in Chapter Seven. Several trends are apparent in this table. First, these methods require considerable investment in development. Development costs are related to purchasing hardware and software, as well as developing programs and transferring programs to new media (e.g., smartphones using apps). However, although development costs are high, costs for administering the program are low. Advantages of these methods include (1) cost savings due to training being accessible to employees at their home or office, (2) reduced number of trainers needed, and (3) reduced costs associated with employees traveling to a central training location (e.g., airfare, food, and lodging). Moreover, with the exception of distance learning and mobile learning, most

TABLE 8.12   Comparison of Technology-Based Training Methods

	Online E-learning Web Based Computer-Based	Computer-Based (No Internet)	Distance Learning	Adaptive Training	Simulations and Games	Mobile Learning	Social Media	MOOC
Learning Outcome								
Verbal information	Yes	Yes	Yes	Yes	Yes	Yes	Yes	Yes
Intellectual skills	Yes	Yes	Yes	Yes	Yes	Yes	No	Yes
Cognitive strategies	Yes	Yes	Yes	Yes	Yes	No	Yes	Yes
Attitudes	Maybe	No	No	No	Yes	No	No	No
Motor skills	No	No	No	Yes	Yes	No	No	No
Learning Environment								
Objective	High	High	High	High	High	High	Medium	High
Practice	High	High	Low	High	High	Low	Medium	Medium
Meaningfulness	High	High	Medium	High	High	Medium	Medium	Medium
Feedback	High	High	Low	High	High	Low	High	Medium
Interaction								
Learner-Content	High	High	Medium	High	High	Medium	High	High
Learner-Instructor	Medium	Low	Medium	High	Medium	Low	Medium	Medium
Learner-Learner	Medium	Low	Medium	Low	High	Low	High	Medium
Transfer of Training	High	Medium	Medium	High	High	Medium	Medium	Medium
Cost								
Development	High	High	Medium	High	High	Medium	Medium	High
Administrative	Low	Low	Low	Low	Low	Low	Medium	Low
Effectiveness	High	Medium	Medium	?	High	?	?	?

of the important characteristics needed for learning to occur (practice, feedback, etc.) can be built into these methods. Note that only a limited number of studies of the effectiveness of several methods (e.g., mobile learning, social networks, adaptive training, and MOOCs) are available because companies are just starting to use these technologies for training.

Recall the discussion in Chapter Six of how to determine the costs and benefits of training programs. Caterpillar found that it spent approximately one-third as much for e-learning as for classroom instruction because of the reduced number of instructors, the lower costs associated with course materials, and the reduced travel expenses.[120] For a one-hour course with a class size of 100 trainees, e-learning was 40 percent less expensive than classroom training ($9,500 versus $17,062, or $76 per trainee). As the number of trainees increases to, for example, 40,000 trainees (Caterpillar has more than 70,000 employees worldwide), the company's cost savings are 78 percent ($1.1 million versus $5 million, or $99 per trainee).[121]

You might assume that e-learning is superior to other methods, but this is not necessarily the case. Its major advantage is that web-based programs can offer collaboration and sharing (connecting trainees to other trainees, experts, and chat rooms) and links to resources available on the web. Web-based training also allows the learner to be given assignments requiring open-ended responses (e.g., write a report on a customer's needs) rather than only yes/no or multiple-choice responses. In web-based training, the instructor can read the assignment and provide detailed feedback. However no training method is inherently superior to other methods. Rather, for any method to be effective it has to create a positive learning environment and aid in training transfer. Face-to-face classroom instruction can be ineffective for the same reasons as online learning, or distance learning. For example, the material is not meaningful, there are limited opportunities for practice, and managers don't support use of training content on the job.

How do new technology training methods relate to traditional training methods discussed in Chapter Seven? Simulations and games and adaptive training are best suited for teaching complex processes related to operating machinery, tools, and equipment. These technological methods are extensions of role-plays, business games, experiential learning, and team training. Online training and MOOCs are best suited for teaching facts, figures, cognitive strategies (e.g., how to hold an effective meeting), and interpersonal skills (e.g., closing a sale). These are technological extensions of lectures and role-plays. Both online training and simulations can be useful for training interpersonal skills if the content and interactions are realistic. However, it is important that simulations, games, and online learning are used together with face-to-face instruction to ensure skills are learned and practiced in real work situations. Mobile learning is probably best suited for teaching facts given the limited personal interaction, and interaction with the content using many mobile devices. Currently, mobile learning and social media are best used as supplements to face-to-face instruction to facilitate learning and transfer of training. Social media are also good tools for knowledge management because they facilitate collaboration on documents, reports (wikis), and personal interaction (blogs, Twitter, and Facebook). Although traditional training methods can be effective, managers and trainers should consider using new technology training methods under certain conditions:[122]

1. Sufficient budget and resources will be provided to develop and support the purchase and use of new technology.
2. Trainees are geographically dispersed, and travel costs related to training are high.
3. Trainees are comfortable using technology, including the Internet, web, iPads, and smartphones.
4. The increased use of new technology is part of the company's business strategy. New technology is being used or implemented in manufacturing of products or service processes.
5. Employees have limited or no time for training.
6. Current training methods allow limited time for practice, feedback, and assessment.
7. Use of new technology fits into the organizational culture or business strategy.

The best uses for classroom instruction may be when trainees need face-to-face interaction, instructor support, or visual cues. It is important to note that many companies recognize the strengths and weaknesses of both traditional training methods and technology-based training methods and are using both in a blended learning approach. Technology-based training methods including MOOCs can be used to provide consistent delivery of training content involving transfer of information (knowledge and skills) to geographically dispersed employees who work at their own pace, practice, and collaborate with the trainer and other trainees online. Then trainees can be brought to a central location for face-to-face training using traditional methods (classroom, action learning, games, and role-plays) that emphasizes through the use of cases and problems the application of the knowledge and skills. Face-to-face instruction is also more useful for facilitating inter-action among trainees as well as collaboration, networking, and discussion. For example, at Pitney Bowes, a mailing equipment provider, e-learning is used for content that many geographically dispersed employees must know, such as legal compliance requirements or new product training.[123] Learning that requires interaction with others—such as leader-ship management training, problem solving, or decision making—requires face-to-face classroom instruction or a blended learning approach.

Summary

This chapter provided an overview of the use of new technologies in training delivery, support, and administration. Many new technologies have features that help ensure learn-ing and transfer of training (e.g., e-learning). If designed correctly these technologies can create a positive learning environment by appealing "to multiple senses and allow" employees to pace themselves, receive feedback and reinforcement, and find informa-tion from experts on an as-needed basis. Mobile learning methods (such as iPads) allow employees to participate in training from home or work on a twenty-four-hour basis. Employees control not only the presentation of training content but also when and where they participate in training. Simulations and virtual reality also can create a more realistic training environment, which can make the material more meaningful and increase the probability that training will transfer to the job. Expert systems and electronic support sys-tems are tools that employees can access on an as-needed basis to obtain knowledge and information. Social media help capture the knowledge that employees gain from training and facilitate their sharing of information. Learning management systems make it easier to store and record training information such as course enrollments and employee train-ing records. This makes it easier for employees to participate in training and to retrieve training-related information for managerial decision making.

Most new technology training methods are superior to traditional methods in one way because they allow trainees to participate in courses at any time or place. However, similar to traditional training methods, technology-based training methods will be ineffective if they do not include interaction, feedback, practice, and other features of a positive learning environment. Considerations in choosing a training method include monies for develop-ment, geographic dispersion of employees, employees' difficulty in attending training, and whether new technologies are part of the company's business strategy. Rather than choosing between face-to-face and technology-based training methods, companies are often choosing to use both in a blended learning approach.

Key Terms

digital collaboration, *335*

synchronous communication, *337*

asynchronous communication, *337*

Web 2.0, *338*

learner control, *338*

computer-based training (CBT), *340*

online learning, *340*

e-learning, *340*

web-based training, *340*

bandwidth, *346*

plug-in, *347*

Discussion Questions

1. Explain how technology has changed the learning environment.
2. What types of learning outcomes are best suited for mobile learning? Explain.
3. What are the differences between expert systems and electronic performance tools?
4. Why are MOOCs a promising way to deliver learning? What are their limitations?
5. Discuss how new technologies make it easier to learn. How do they facilitate transfer of training?
6. Is all Internet training the same? Explain.
7. What are some potential problems with using games and gamification for training?
8. What is social media? Explain how it can be used for training.
9. Explain learner control, sharing, and linking. How do they contribute to the effectiveness of e-learning?
10. What is repurposing? How does it affect the use of new technologies in training?
11. Distance learning can be used to deliver a lecture to geographically dispersed trainees. How might distance learning be designed and used to avoid some of the learning and transfer of training problems of the traditional lecture method?
12. Why would a company use a combination of face-to-face instruction and web-based training?
13. What conditions are best for the use of social media tools as part of a learning solution?
14. What is the most important way adaptive training differs from other training methods?

Application Assignments

1. Using only the web, further investigate any training technology discussed in this chapter. With any search engine on the web (e.g., Google, Yahoo), conduct a search for information about the technology that you have chosen. Find information describing the technology, hints for developing or purchasing the technology, and examples of companies marketing and/or using the technology. Include web addresses in your summary.

2. Watch the video about MD Anderson's Oncology Expert Advisor at http://www .youtube.com/watch?v=CtyYI7ou2B0. What are the benefits of such an expert system to oncology doctors? Are there any disadvantages? What benefits of expert systems are highlighted in this example?

3. Go to *www.inspiredelearning.com*, website for inspired eLearning, a company that provides training solutions. Click on "courses." Under "Course Catalog," choose one of the following: (a) Go to the Skills Library. View the library for the Business and Leadership Skill courses. View the course demos; or (b) Go to Workplace Harassment and view the e-learning format Workplace Harassment Prevention demos. Based on your review of the demos, discuss the features the courses include that help facilitate learning. Provide your ideas for how this online course could be paired with face-to-face instruction to create an effective blended learning approach. Discuss the activities you would include in the face-to-face part of the course.

4. Go to *www.mzinga.com*. Mzinga provides software solutions for learning. Under "Products." Review Omni Social Learning and Omni Social Content. Do you believe that these solutions are effective? Why?

5. Go to *www.capellauniversity.edu*, the website for Capella University—a university that offers online courses. Click on "About Capella," and then "Online Learning." Read "How Online Learning Works" and watch the video on the course room tour.

6. Go to *www.youtube.com*. Search for "Training in Second Life" or "Training Simulations in Second Life." Choose and review a video of one of the many different types of training offered in Second Life (e.g., medicine, nursing, or management). Provide a brief description of the training and the Universal Resource Locator (URL) for the video. Discuss the strengths and weaknesses of the training. Based on the video you reviewed, do you think that companies, interest in Second Life for training will increase or decrease in the future? Why?

7. Go to *www.edx.org*, the website for edX, a MOOC provider that offers interactive online courses. Watch "How It Works" video and review the demo course. How is edX using technology to facilitate learning? What are the strengths and weaknesses of these technologies? Why do you think the completion rate for MOOC courses is very low?

8. Go to http://www.halogensoftware.com website for Halogen Software. Click on "Tours" and then click on "Halogen Learning." Review and watch the demo under "Managing the Learning Offering." This is an example of an LMS. How can a company benefit from this LMS? Can employees benefit, too? Explain.

Case: *Training Jiffy Lube Service Technicians on New Products*

Jiffy Lube International, the vehicle maintenance company, is committed to providing a fast, high-quality, worry-free service experience for its customers. Jiffy Lube's technicians provide a number of services, including changing a vehicle's oil, tire balancing, flushing cooling systems, and replacing worn-out windshield wipers. Jiffy Lube's service technicians need to be up to date on the latest products and service requirements for cars and trucks and provide consistent, excellent, customer service. As a result, training is critical for Jiffy Lube's success a top company priority for achieving continued operational excellence. One new product that has been introduced for cars and vehicles is synthetic motor oil, which is required by many new models but can benefit the engines of older models too. Although many car and truck manufacturers recommend that vehicle owners use specialty oils such as synthetic and high-mileage motor oils, Jiffy Lube found that the proportion of specialty oils sold was low. A needs assessment showed that service technicians were not knowledgeable about or effectively communicating the benefits of specialty motor oils. This suggested that training was necessary. It is difficult for Jiffy Lube's service technicians, many who work for franchised stores, to attend face-to-face classes, making technology-delivered training a realistic learning solution.

What knowledge, skills, or behaviors should the training focus on? What technology training method would you recommend for training the technicians on specialty oils? Why? Briefly describe the learning features you would include in the program and discuss why you recommend including them.

Source: Based on L. Freifeld, "Jiffy Lube revs up to no. 1," *training* (January/February 2014): 30–38; *www.jiffylube.com*, website for Jiffy Lube.

Endnotes

1. S. Banchero, "Today's lesson: Calculate the acceleration of an Angry Bird," *The Wall Street Journal* (October 9, 2013): R5.

2. J. Bellini, "Teaching anatomy in a digital age," *The Wall Street Journal* (October 9, 2013): R6.

3. P. Ketter "2010: Six trends that will change workplace learning forever," *T+D* (December 2010): 34–40; T. Bingham and M. Conner, *The New Social Learning* (Alexandria, VA: American Society for Training and Development, 2010).

4. L. Patel, "The rise of social media," *T+D* (July 2010): 60–61.

5. B. Mirza, "Social media tools redefine learning," *HR Magazine,* December 2010, 74; L. Patel, "The rise of social media," *T+D*, (July 2010), 60–61; J. Meister, E. Kaganer, and R. Von Feldt, "2011: The year of the media tablet as a learning tool," *T+D*, (April 2011), 28–31.

6. P. Shank, "When to use instructional technology," *T+D* (September 2004): 30–37; S. E. O'Connell, "New technologies bring new tools, new rules," *HR Magazine* (December 1995): 43–48; S. E. O'Connell, "The virtual workplace moves at warp speed," *HR Magazine* (March 1996): 51–57.

7. K. Kraiger, "Transforming our models of learning and development: Web-based instruction as enabler of third-generation instruction," *Industrial and Organizational Psychology: Perspectives on Science and Practice*, 1 (2008): 454–457; K. Kraiger, "Third-generation instructional models: More about guiding development and design than selecting training methods," *Industrial and Organizational Psychology: Perspectives on Science and Practice*, 1 (2008): 501–507.

8. J. Salopek, "Digital collaboration," *Training and Development* (June 2000): 39–43.

9. V. Beer, *The Web Learning Fieldbook* (New York: John Wiley, 2000); A. Chute, P. Sayers, and R. Gardner, "Network learning environments," *New Directions for Teaching and Learning* 71 (1997): 75–83.

10. "Qualcomm, Inc: Learning 2.0," *training* (February 2009): 100.

11. *www.farmers.com*, website for Farmers Insurance; M. Weinstein, "Farmers' comprehensive training policy," *training* (January/February 2013): 42–44; L. Freifeld, "Farmers' premier position," *training* (January/February 2011): 26–31; J. Salopek, "Thriving through change, cultivating growth," *T+D* (October 2010): 53–54.

12. M. Rosenberg, *E-Learning: Strategies for Delivering Knowledge in the Digital Age* (New York: McGraw-Hill, 2001); "What Is Web-Based Training?" (from *www.clark.net/pub/nractive/fl.html*); R. Johnson and H. Gueutal, *Transforming HR through Technology* (Alexandria, VA: SHRM Foundation, 2010).

13. P. Harris, "Where innovative learning is the norm," *T+D* (October 2011): 61–62.

14. "Project leadership," *Human Resource Executive* (2000): A16.

15. "Discover financial services," *training* (January/February 2014): 110.

16. M. Moore, "Three types of interaction," *American Journal of Distance Education* 3(2) (1989): 1–6.

17. L. Freifeld, "Online versus in-class success," *training* (September/October 2014): 19–25.

18. P. Galagan, "The e-learning revolution," *Training and Development* (December 2000): 24–30; D. Khirallah, "A new way to learn," *Information Week Online,* May 22, 2000; G. Wang, R. Von Der Linn, D. Foucar-Szocki, O. Griffin, and E. Sceiford, "Measuring the business impact of e-learning—An empirical study," *Performance Improvement Quarterly* 16 (2003): 17–30.

19. L. Freifeld, "Online versus in-class success," *training* (September/October 2014): 19–25; L. Cypher, "Taming online training at the San Diego Zoo," *Chief Learning Officer* (April 2014): 42–48.

20. G. Wright, "Retailers buy into e-learning," *HR Magazine* (December 2010): 87–90.

21. Shared learning demo, January 24, 2001 (from the CCH website, *hr.cch.com*).

22. K. Brown, "Using computers to deliver training: Which employees learn and why?" *Personnel Psychology* 54 (2001): 271–296; E. T. Welsh et al., "E-learning: Emerging uses, empirical results, and future directions," *International Journal of Training and Development* 7(4) (2003): 245–258; T. Sitzmann et al., "The comparative effectiveness of web-based and classroom instruction: A meta-analysis," *Personnel Psychology* 59 (2006): 623–624.

23. M. Mihelich, "Allied Bank," *Workforce* (December 2014): 40.

24. L. Freifeld, "Online versus in-class success," *training* (September/October 2014): 19–25.

25. K. Kraiger, "Transforming our models of learning and development: Web-based instruction as enabler of third-generation instruction," *Industrial Organizational Psychology,* 1(4) (December 2008): 454–467.

26. B. Roberts, "Hard facts about soft-skills e-learning," *HR Magazine* (January 2008): 76–78.

27. L. Freifeld, "Online versus in-class success," *training* (September/October 2014): 19–25.

28. G. Anders, "Companies find on-line training has its limits," *The Wall Street Journal* (March 26, 2007): B3.

29. E. T. Welsh et al., "E-learning: Emerging uses, empirical results, and future directions," *International Journal of Training and Development* 7(4) (2003): 245–258.

30. K. Kiser, "10 things we know so far about online training," *training* (November 1999): 66–70; R. Wells, "Back to the (Internet) classroom," *training* (March 1999): 50–54; L. Martins and F. Kellermans, "A model of business school students' acceptance of a Web-based course management system," *Academy of Management Learning and Education* 3 (2004): 7–26; H. Klein, R. Noe, and C. Wang, "Motivation to learn and course outcomes: The impact of delivery mode, learning goal orientation, and perceived barriers and enablers," *Personnel Psychology* 59 (2006): 665–702; M. Allen, "The return of serious design," *Chief Learning Officer* (July 2014): 31–33.

31. B. Neal, "e-Addie!" *T+D* (March 2011): 76–77.

32. D. Schaaf, "Bandwidth basics," *training* (September 1999): OL23–OL37; J. Adams, "Rapid talent development," *T+D* (March 2008): 68–73.

33. S. Gale, "Making e-learning more than 'pixie dust,'" *Workforce* (March 2003): 58–62.

34. B. Neal, "e-Addie!" *T+D* (March 2011): 76–77; N. Miner and J. Hofman, "It's not the technology, stupid," *T+D* (February 2009): 30–32; E. Edwards, "Quick draw," *T+D* (August 2009): 92–93; S. Putman, "Prototyping an e-learning interface," *T+D* (May 2014): 26–28.

35. K. Brown and J. Ford, "Using Computer Technology in Training: Building an Infrastructure for Active Learning." In *Creating, Implementing, and Managing Effective Training and Development,* ed. K. Kraiger (San Francisco: Jossey-Bass, 2002): 192–233.

36. B. Neal, "e-Addie!" *T+D* (March 2011): 76–77; N. Miner and J. Hofman, "It's not the technology, stupid," *T+D* (February 2009): 30–32; E. Edwards, "Quick draw," *T+D* (August 2009): 92–93.

37. S. Boehle, "Putting the learning back in e-learning," *training* (January 2006): 29–35; K. Brown, "Using computers to deliver training: Which employees learn and why?"

38. R. DeRouin, B. Fritzsche, and E. Salas, "Learner control and workplace learning: Design, person, and organizational issues." In *Research in Personnel and Human Resource Management,* vol. 24, ed. J. Martocchio (New York: Elsevier, 2005): 181–214; T. Sitzmann, B. Bell, K. Kraiger, and A. Kanar, "A multilevel analysis of the effect of prompting self-regulation in technology-delivered instruction." *Personnel Psychology* 62 (2009): 697–734; T. Sitzmann and K. Ely, "Sometimes you need a reminder: The effects of prompting self-regulation on regulatory processes, learning, and attrition," *Journal of Applied Psychology* 95 (2010): 132–144.

39. D. Zielinski, "The lie of online learning," *training* (February 2000): 38–40; D. Zielinski, "Can you keep learners on-line?" *training* (March 2000): 65–75.

40. K. Brown, "A field study of employee e-learning activity and outcomes," *Human Resource Development Quarterly* (Winter 2005): 465–80.

41. S. Chyung and M. Vachon, "An investigation of the profiles of satisfying and dissatisfying factors in e-learning," *Performance Improvement Quarterly* 18 (2005): 97–113.

42. C. Pollack and R. Masters, "Using Internet technologies to enhance training," *Performance Improvement* (February 1997): 28–31.

43. D. Zielinski, "Can you keep learners on-line?" *training* (March 2000): 65–75; K. Brown and J. Ford, "Using Computer Technology in Training: Building an Infrastructure for Active Learning." In *Creating, Implementing, and Managing Effective Training and Development,* ed. K. Kraiger (San Francisco: Jossey-Bass, 2002): 192–233.

44. G. Fowler, "An early report card on MOOCs," *Wall Street Journal* (October 9, 2013): R1–R2; D. Belkin, "Former Yale president to lead Coursera," *Wall Street Journal* (March 25, 2014): B3; D. Belkin, "What role will large online courses play in the future of higher education?" *Wall Street Journal* (May 12, 2014): R3; G. Fowler, "Most online course users well-educated," *Wall Street Journal* (November 21, 2013): A3.

45. L. Fleisher, "Time to test your knowledge," *Wall Street Journal* (October 8, 2013): R6.

46. D. Belkin and C. Porter, "Job market embraces massive online courses," *Wall Street Journal* (September 27, 2013): A3; C. Proulx, "You'll never guess who's disrupting online learning," *Forbes* (December 5, 2013), from *www.forbes.com*, accessed December 10, 2013.

47. S. Herring, "MOOCs come of age," *T+D* (January 2014): 46–49.

48. F. Kalman, "Here come the MOOCs," *Chief Learning Officer* (January 2014): 37–48; M. Fitzgerald, "Companies create MOOCs to fill skill gaps," *www.informationweek.com* (May 28, 2013), accessed September 3, 2013.

49. M. Chafkin, "Uphill climb," *Fast Company* (December 2013/January 2014): 146–156; F. Kalman, "Here come the MOOCs," *Chief Learning Officer* (January 2014): 37–48; T. Lewin, "Master's degree is new frontier of study online," *New York Times* (August 17, 2013) from *www.nytimes.com*, accessed August 20, 2013.

50. M. Weinstein, "Managing MOOCs," *training* (September/October 2014): 26–28; R. Grossman, "Are massive open online courses in your future," *HR* Magazine (August 2013): 30–36; J. Meister, "How MOOCs will revolutionize corporate learning and development," *www.forbes.com* (August 13, 2013), accessed August 20, 2013; C. Straumsheim, "MOOC research conference confirms commonly held beliefs about the medium," from *www.insidehighered.com* (December 6, 2013), accessed January 3, 2014; K. Jordan, "MOOC completion rates: The data," http://www.katyjordan.com/MOOCproject.html (2013) accessed (July 29, 2015); M. Chafkin, "Uphill climb," *Fast Company* (December 2013/January 2014): 146–156.

51. M. Derven, "Social networking a force for development," *T+D* (July 2009): 58–63; A. Kaplan and M. Haenlein, "Users of the world unite! The challenges and opportunities of social media," *Business Horizons* 53 (2010): 59–68.

52. B. Livingston "Harnessing blogs for learning," *T+D* (May 2011): 76–77.

53. T. Bingham, M. Connor, and M. Weinstein, "Netting know-how," *training,* September/October 2010, 26–29; J. Roy, "Transforming informal learning into a competitive advantage," *T+D,* (October 2010), 23–25; P. Galagan, "Unformal, the new normal?," *T+D,* (September 2010), 29–31; M. Weinstein, "Verizon connects to success," *training,* January/February 2011, 40–42; R. Emelo, "Social, informal learning can be measured," *Chief Learning Officer* (February 2014): 18–21; S. Gale, "Still afraid to jump in?" *Workforce Management* (May 2013): 24–29; C. Tate, "Mobile masters", *T+D* (April 2013): 22-24..

54. J. Thomas, "At EAG, learning's all about the chatter," *Chief Learning Officer* (February 2015): 42–43, 49.

55. M. Derven, "Social networking: A force for development?" *T+D* (July 2009): 59–63.

56. S. J. Hysong and L. M. Mannix, "Learning Outcomes in Distance Education versus Traditional and Mixed Environments" (paper presented at the annual conference of the Society for Industrial and Organizational Psychology, Orlando, FL, 2003).

57. M. Knowles, *The Adult Learner,* 4th ed. (Houston, TX: Gulf Publishing, 1990).

58. M. Weinstein, "Got class," *training* (December 2005): 29–32.

59. J. Bergmann and A. Sams, "Flipped learning: Maximizing face time," *T+D* (February 2014): 28–31.

60. T. Sitzmann et al., "The comparative effectiveness of web-based and classroom instruction: A meta-analysis," *Personnel Psychology* 59 (2006): 623–624; H. Klein, R. Noe, and C. Wang, "Motivation to learn and course outcomes: The impact of delivery mode, learning goal orientation, and perceived barriers and enablers," *Personnel Psychology* 59 (2006): 665–702.

61. K. Kim, C. Bonk, and E. Oh, "The present and future of blended learning in workplace settings in the United States," *Performance Improvement* (September 2008): 5–14.

62. M. Resenheck, "Harnessing the 90%," *T+D* (September 2013): 54–59.

63. F. Waltmann, "Honing the digital edge in China," *training* (September/October 2013): 26–27.

64. A. Lenhart, S. Jones, and A. Macgill, "Adults and video games" (December 7, 2008), from *www.pewinternet.org*, accessed March 28, 2015.

65. B. Roberts, "Gamification: Win, lose or draw," *HR Magazine* (May 2014): 28–35.

66. N. Adams, "Lessons from the Virtual World," *training* (June 1995): 45–48.

67. H. Dolezalek, "Virtual vision," *training* (October 2007): 40–46.

68. J. Borzo, "Almost human," *The Wall Street Journal,* May 24, 2004: R1, R10; J. Hoff, "My virtual life," *BusinessWeek,* May 1, 2006: 72–78.

69. P. Galagan, "Second that," *T+D* (February 2008): 34–37.

70. G. Dutton, "U.S. Army: Teaching peacekeepers to ID social networks," *training* (September/October 2013): 40–41.

71. A. Pasztor, "Chopper simulators take off," *Wall Street Journal* (Saturday/Sunday July 12–13, 2014): B4.

72. ASTD Research, "Playing to win: Gamification and serious games in organizational learning" (February 2014), from *www.astd.org*, accessed March 28, 2015.

73. G. Dutton, "IBM helping growth markets hone business process management skills," *training* (September/October 2013): 42.

74. R. Paharia, *Loyalty 3.0* (New York: McGraw-Hill Education, 2013).

75. K. Everson, "Allstate is in gamification's hands," *Chief Learning Officer* (July 2014): 42–43, 48.

76. P. Dvorak, "Theory and practice: Simulation shows what it is like to be the boss; middle managers at NetApp receive useful taste of reality," *The Wall Street Journal* (March 31, 2008): B7.

77. P. Harris, "Avatars rule," *T+D* (October 2013): 60–61; *www.ppdi.com*, website for PPD.

78. C. Cornell, "Better than the real thing?" *Human Resource Executive* (August 2005): 34–37; E. Frauenheim, "Can video games win points as teaching tools?" *Workforce Management* (April 10, 2006): 12–14; S. Boehle, "Simulations: The next generation of e-learning," *training* (January 2005): 22–31; J. Borzo, "Almost human," *The Wall Street Journal,* May 24, 2004: R1, R10.

79. T. Sitzmann, "A meta-analytic examination of the instructional effectiveness of computer-based simulation games," *Personnel Psychology* 64: 489–528.

80. L. Freifeld, "Solid Sims," *training* (October 2007): 48.

81. "What does it cost to use a virtual world learning environment?" *T+D* (November 2008): 88.

82. C. Balance, "Strategic ways to develop game-based learning for high ROI," *T+D* (September 2013): 76–77.

83. K. Taylor and S. Chyung, "Would you adopt Second Life as a training and development tool?" *Performance Improvement* (September 2008): 17–25.

84. D. Gayeski, "Goin' mobile," *T+D* (November 2004): 46–51; D. Gayeski and M. Petrillose, "No strings attached," *Performance Improvement* (February 2005): 25–31; D. Hartley, "Pick up your PDA," *T+D* (February 2004): 22–24.

85. S. Carey, "Airlines jettison a costly load of paper," *Wall Street Journal* (June 27, 2013): B6.

86. K. Kuehner-Hebert, "Go mobile?" *Chief Learning Officer* (March 2014): 18–21.

87. J. Halls, "Give learning a listen: Audio podcasting and learning," *T+D* (October 2010): 92–93.

88. E. Wagner and P. Wilson, "Disconnected," *T+D* (December 2005): 40–43; J. Bronstein and A. Newman, "IM learning," *T+D* (February 2006): 47–50.

89. K. Kuehner-Hebert, "Go mobile?" *Chief Learning Officer* (March 2014): 18–21.

90. B. Hall, "Go slow, quickly: Make the move to mobile," January 22, 2013, from *Chief Learning Officer* at http://clomedia.com, accessed January 30, 2013.

91. G. Dutton, "There's an app for that!" *training* (September/October 2011): 36–37.

92. C. Tate, "Mobile masters," *T+D* (April 2013): 22–24.

93. L. Stevens, "Up close and insightful," *Human Resource Executive* (September 16, 2011): 24–29.

94. E. Wagner and P. Wilson, "Disconnected," *T+D* (December 2005): 40–43; J. Brink, "M-learning: The future of training technology," *T+D* (February 2011): 27–29; G. Woodill, "Getting started with mobile learning," *T+D* (December 2010): 76–77; A. Ahmad and P. Norton, "Smartphones make IBM smarter, but not as expected," *T+D* (January 2010): 46–50.

95. C. Landsberg, R. Astwood, Jr., W. Van Buskirk, L. Townsend, N. SteinHauser, and A. Mercado, "Review of adaptive training systems," *Military Psychology*, 29 (2012): 96–113; R. Spain, H. Priest, and J. Murphy, "Current trends in adaptive training with military applications: An introduction," *Military Psychology*, 29 (2012): 87–95; T. Poeppelman, E. Lobene, and N. Blacksmith, "Personalizing the learning experience through adaptive training," *The Industrial-Organizational Psychologist* (April 2015), from *www.siop.org*.

96. From http://learnsmartadvantage.com/students/benefits/, accessed March 30, 2015.

97. D. Steele-Johnson and B. G. Hyde, "Advanced Technologies in Training: Intelligence Tutoring Systems and Virtual Reality." In *Training for a Rapidly Changing Workplace,* ed. M. A. Quinones and A. Ehrenstein (Washington, D.C.: American Psychological Association, 1997): 225–248.

98. D. Steele-Johnson and B. G. Hyde, "Advanced Technologies in Training: Intelligence Tutoring Systems and Virtual Reality." In *Training for a Rapidly Changing Workplace,* ed. M. A. Quinones and A. Ehrenstein (Washington, D.C.: American Psychological Association, 1997): 225–248.

99. "Putting the distance into distance learning," *training* (October 1995): 111–118.

100. R. Clark, "Harnessing the virtual classroom," *T+D* (November 2005): 40–45.

101. D. Picard, "The future is distance training," *training* (November 1996): s3–s10.

102. A. F. Maydas, "On-line networks build the savings into employee education," *HR Magazine* (October 1997): 31–35.

103. J. M. Rosow and R. Zager, *Training: The Competitive Edge* (San Francisco: Jossey-Bass, 1988).

104. M. Lewis, "Moving into the live virtual classroom," *T+D* (July 2011): 76–77; R. Ubell, "How to run a virtual classroom," *T+D* (October 2011): 92–93; T. Byham and A. Lang, "Avoid these 10 pitfalls of virtual classrooms," *Chief Learning Officer* (May 2014): 18–21.

105. M. Weinstein, "Satellite success," *training* (January 2007): 36–38.

106. "Training Top 100 Best Practices 2006: General Mills," *training* (March 2006): 61.

107. S. Alexander, "Reducing the learning burden," *training* (September 2002): 32–34.

108. R. Clark, "Harnessing the virtual classroom," *T+D* (November 2005): 40–45; R. Clark and R. Mayer, *E-Learning and the Science of Instruction* (San Francisco: John Wiley, 2003; 2d ed. published in 2008 by Jossey-Bass/Pfeiffer); C. Huggett, "Make virtual training a success," *T+D* (January 2014): 40–45.

109. W. Hannum, *The Application of Emerging Training Technologies* (Alexandria, VA: The American Society for Training and Development, 1990).

110. L. Landro, "Hospitals make intensive care friendlier with new apps," *Wall Street Journal* (March 17, 2015): D3.

111. "Module Example: Financial Products Sales Applications," from PortBlue website, *www.portblue.com/pub/solutions-sales-marketing* (April 24, 2006).

112. S. Caudron, "Your learning technology primer," *Personnel Journal* (June 1996): 120–136; A. Marquardt and G. Kearsley, *Technology-Based Learning* (Boca Raton, FL: St. Lucie Press, 1999).

113. P. Harris, "Relying on street smarts," *T+D* (October 2014): 92–93; M. Weinstein, "Just-in-time technology solutions," *training* (September/October 2014): 36–39.

114. S. Boehle, "LMS leaders," *training* (October 2008): 30–34.

115. "LMS Survey Results," from *www.learningcircuits.org/2005/jun2005/LMS_survey.htm* (July 7, 2006), S. Castellano, "The evolution of the LMS," *TD* (November 2014): 14.

116. K. Oakes, "Mission critical," *T+D* (September 2005): 25–28; D. Sussman, "The LMS value," *T+D* (July 2005): 43–45; H. Johnson, "Prescription for success," *training* (October 2003): 52.

117. H. Johnson, "Prescription for Success."

118. J. Barbian, "Great expectations," *training* (September 2002): 10–12; D. Sussman, "The LMS value," *T+D* (July 2005): 43–45.

119. "LMS goes to the dogs," *training*, (September/October 2010): 8; L. Freifeld, "LMS lessons," *training* (September/October 2010): 20–24; R. Shand, S. Long, M. Mitchell-Norman, R. Rector, A. Delima, & J. Muma, "A new lease on learning," *training* (October 2009): 44–46; J. Congemi, "MasTec tackles the LMS," *training* (July/August 2014): 52–54.

120. I. Speizer, "Value-minded," *Workforce Management* (July 2005): 55–58.

121. M. Weinstein, "Got class," *training* (December 2005): 29–32.

122. P. Shank; "When to use instructional technology," *T+D* (September 2004): 30–37; H. Dolezalek, "Dose of reality," *training* (April 2004): 28–34; E. Salas, R. DeRouin, and L. Littrell, "Research-Based Guidelines for Designing Distance Learning." In *The Brave New World of eHR,* eds. H. Gueutal and D. Stone (San Francisco: Jossey-Bass, 2005): 104–137; G. Piskurich, "E-learning: Fast, cheap, good," *Performance Improvement* (January 2006): 18–24.

123. M. Weinstein, "Got class," *training* (December 2005): 29–32.

Chapter **Nine**

Employee Development and Career Management

Objectives

After reading this chapter, you should be able to:

1. Discuss the steps in the development planning process.
2. Explain the employees' and company's responsibilities in planning development.
3. Discuss current trends in using formal education for development.
4. Relate how assessment of personality type, work behavior, and job performance can be used for employee development.
5. Explain how job experiences can be used for development and suggest a job experience to match an employee's development goal or need.
6. Identify the characteristics of an effective mentoring program.
7. Describe the succession planning process and how the nine-box grid is used.
8. Design an effective on-boarding process.

Development Helps ESPN Remain a Sports Dynasty

Entertainment and Sports Programming Network, known as ESPN, is one of the leading companies in the global multimedia sports and entertainment business. Over thirty years ago ESPN became the first sports network to televise complete sports coverage. Today, ESPN, headquartered in Bristol, Connecticut, has over 7,000 employees and includes eight U.S. cable networks, over 300 radio affiliates, and other multimedia and business companies. Its businesses include television networks (ESPN), audio (ESPN Radio, ESPN Deportes Radio), digital (WatchESPN), publishing (*ESPN The Magazine*), event management (X games, ESPYs, college bowls and basketball games), locations (ESPN ZONE at Disney), and corporate outreach (The V Foundation for Cancer). It televises sixty-five sports in sixteen languages in more than two hundred companies. In 2014, ESPN produced more than 47,000 hours of live event/studio programming. In the past several years ESPN has reached several significant industry milestones, including ESPN OnDemand Audio being recognized as the most downloaded radio app (215.6 million downloads) and the opening of Digital Center2, the new home of *SportsCenter* and one of the most sophisticated production centers in the world.

To remain in its leadership role in the sports and entertainment business, ESPN needs to continue to provide the best live sports programming as well as expand and develop its digital presence through social media. To do so, ESPN recognizes the importance of creating exceptional employee experiences through its commitment to people, partnerships, culture, and excellence. Employee development plays a key role in helping create exceptional employee experiences at ESPN. But employee development at ESPN faces several challenges. One challenge is the speed at which the global news, broadcasting, and entertainment business operates. This can make it difficult for employees to take the time away from activities such as producing and delivering programming to focus on development activities. Another challenge is that ESPN is growing its business in global markets such as Latin America. This adds a layer of complexity to building a development culture and career management tools because they must align with local culture and norms in order to be effective.

ESPN has taken several steps to ensure that its development efforts overcome these challenges and support employees' career interests and goals, enhance their skills, and grow top leadership talent. ESPN requires every employee to complete an individual development plan (IDP). The IDP helps employees consider where they currently are in their careers, their career goals, and how they plan to reach their career goals. The learning function at ESPN reviews and supports the IDP, which have been completed by over 95 percent of employees. Similar to other companies, ESPN uses the 70-20-10 approach for development. This means that most of employee development occurs on the job, while 20 percent comes from relationships and informal learning, and 10 percent from formal courses targeted at specific skills. For example, ESPN has a Leadership GPS, which is a tool used by employees to track their development progress. The Leadership GPS helps employees set development goals. It also provides advice on which types of development activities (such as courses, job shadowing, or experiences) are available and will help them meet their goals. ESPN The University offers courses related to different business areas. The courses are taught by executives and business leaders. This is important because it gets company leaders from different business areas involved in developing employees. It also helps provide employees with a greater understanding of the different aspects of ESPN's business such as production, programming, and HR and how they fit together. ESPN Center Court is a development program targeted exclusively to high-potential employees who are on the fast track to future leadership roles in the company. Center Court uses job rotations to give high-potential employees the opportunity to experience different aspects of the business. They also interact with the company's president and top executives. To facilitate development through relationships, ESPN has a mentoring program known as Open Access that is available to all employees. The only requirements are that employees desire to learn from others and want to build relationships to achieve their development goals.

To ensure that development activities support business needs, ESPN has a learning and advisory board, which includes senior leaders and vice presidents from its different businesses. Every major initiative is reviewed and has to receive support from the board before it is implemented. Also, the Employee Learning Council, which includes employees from each of ESPN's business units, provides feedback and helps plan development programs.

Source: Based on F. Kalman, "ESPN's top play: Learning," *Chief Learning Officer* (March 2013): 22–25, 47; "Learning and development" at http://espncareers.com/working_here/learning_development, accessed April 2, 2015; "ESPN Inc. fact sheet," from http://espnmediazone.com/, accessed April 2, 2015.

INTRODUCTION

As the ESPN example illustrates, employee development is a key contributor to a company's competitive advantage by helping employees understand their strengths, weaknesses, and interests and by showing them how new jobs and expanded job responsibilities are available to them to meet their personal growth needs. This helps retain valuable managers who might otherwise leave to join clients or competitors. Employee development is a necessary component of a company's talent management efforts. The attention that ESPN senior leaders pay to development emphasizes that employee development is key to ensuring that employees have the competencies necessary to serve customers and create new products and customer solutions. Regardless of the business strategy, development is also important for retaining talented employees. As we noted in Chapter One, "Introduction to Employee Training and Development," employee engagement is directly related to how employees are treated by their managers. Employee development can help increase employee engagement by (1) showing employees that the company is interested in their skill development and (2) developing managers who can create a positive work environment that makes employees want to come work and contribute to company goals.

This chapter begins by discussing the relationship between development, training, and careers. Choosing an approach is one part of development planning. Second, before employees choose development activities, the employee and the company must have an idea of the employee's development needs and the purpose of development. Identifying the needs and purpose of development are part of its planning. The second section of the chapter describes the steps of the development planning process. Employee and company responsibilities at each step of the process are emphasized. Third, we look at development approaches, including formal education, assessment, job experiences, and interpersonal relationships. The chapter emphasizes the types of skills, knowledge, and behaviors that are strengthened by each development method. The chapter concludes with a discussion of special issues in employee development, including succession planning, developing dysfunctional managers, and on-boarding.

THE RELATIONSHIP AMONG DEVELOPMENT, TRAINING, AND CAREERS

Development and Training

Development refers to formal education, job experiences, relationships, and assessment of personality and skills that help employees prepare for the future. The ESPN example illustrates that although development can occur through participation in planned programs, it often results from performing different types of work. Because it is future-oriented, it

TABLE 9.1
Comparison
Between
Training and
Development

	Training	Development
Focus	Current	Future
Use of work experiences	Low	High
Goal	Preparation for current job	Preparation for changes
Participation	Required	Voluntary

involves learning that is not necessarily related to the employee's current job.[1] Table 9.1 shows the differences between training and development. Traditionally, training focuses on helping employees' performance in their current jobs. Development prepares them for other positions in the company and increases their ability to move into jobs that may not yet exist.[2] Development also helps employees prepare for changes in their current jobs that may result from new technology, work designs, new customers, or new product markets. Development is especially critical for talent management, particularly for senior managers and employees with leadership potential (recall our discussion of attracting and retaining talent in Chapter One). Companies report that the most important talent management challenges they face include developing existing talent and attracting and retaining existing leadership talent.[3] Chapter Two, "Strategic Training," emphasized the strategic role of training. As training continues to become more strategic (i.e., related to business goals), the distinction between training and development will blur. Both training and development will be required and will focus on current and future personal and company needs.

Development and Careers

Traditionally, careers have been described in various ways.[4] Careers have been described as a sequence of positions held within an occupation. For example, a university faculty member can hold assistant, associate, and full professor positions. A career has also been described in the context of mobility within an organization. For example, an engineer may begin her career as a staff engineer. As her expertise, experience, and performance increase, she may move through advisory engineering, senior engineering, and senior technical positions. Finally, a career has been described as a characteristic of the employee. Each employee's career consists of different jobs, positions, and experiences.

Today's careers are known as protean careers.[5] A **protean career** is based on self-direction, with the goal of psychological success in one's work. Employees take major responsibility for managing their careers. For example, an engineer may decide to take a sabbatical from her position to work in management at the United Way Agency for a year. The purpose of this assignment could be to develop her managerial skills, as well as help her evaluate if she likes managerial work more than engineering.

The protean career has several implications for employee development. The goal of the new career is **psychological success**: the feeling of pride and accomplishment that comes from achieving life goals that are not limited to achievements at work (such as raising a family and having good physical health). Psychological success is more under the employee's control than the traditional career goals, which were not only influenced by employee effort but were controlled by the availability of positions in the company. Psychological success is self-determined rather than solely determined through signals the employee receives from the company (like salary increase and promotion). For example, a 52-year-old woman comanaged a real estate business in California with her husband.[6]

She always wanted to work in medicine or health care and took health science classes in college but decided to work in real estate because it provided a good income and flexibility when raising her children. After working in real estate for twenty-five years, she pursued her passion by taking prerequisite classes and applying to nursing school. Unfortunately, her husband suffered a debilitating stroke, making her the sole provider for the family. She sold the real estate business, applied and was accepted to nursing school, and managed her husband's care. At age 57 she graduated from nursing school, but was unable to find a job in California. She eventually found a job in a hospital in Oklahoma and moved there with her husband. After gaining valuable experience, she moved back to California and now works in a facility for developmentally disabled adults. She is passionate about her new job despite its long and inflexible working hours, and the physical and emotional demands of staying on your feet all day and helping people with many needs.

It is important for employees to develop new skills rather than rely on a static knowledge base. This has resulted from companies' need to be more responsive to customers' service and product demands. As we emphasized in Chapter One, learning is continuous, often informal, and involves creating and sharing knowledge. The emphasis on continuous learning has altered the direction and frequency of movement within careers (career pattern).[7] Traditional career patterns consisted of a series of steps arranged in a linear hierarchy, with higher steps related to increased authority, responsibility, and compensation. Expert career patterns involve a lifelong commitment to a field or specialization (such as law, medicine, or management). These types of career patterns will not disappear. Rather, career patterns involving movement across specializations or disciplines (a spiral career pattern) will become more prevalent. These new career patterns mean that developing employees (as well as employees taking control of their own careers) must be provided with the opportunity to (a) determine their interests, skill strengths, and weaknesses; and (b) based on this information, seek appropriate development experiences that will likely involve job experiences and relationships as well as formal courses.

The most appropriate view of today's careers is that they are "boundaryless and often change."[8] It includes movement across several employers (also known as job hopping) or even different occupations. Job hopping is discussed in Chapter Ten, "Social Responsibility: Legal Issues, Managing Diversity, and Career Challenges." Studies have found that 25 percent of employees have held five jobs or more by age 35 and for employees 55 and older, 20 percent have held ten jobs or more.[9] One-third of employers expect job hopping to occur, especially among new college graduates, but 40 percent of employers believe it becomes less acceptable when employees are in their mid-30s. The reality is that employees will be unlikely to stay at one company for their entire or even a significant part of their career. This means that companies and employees should add value to each other.[10] That is, regardless of how long employees stay, developing them can help the company adapt to changing business conditions and strategies by providing new skill sets and managerial talent. Development helps enhance employees' employability with their current and potential future employers. Development can facilitate employee engagement with the company and helps, but does not guarantee that employees will stay with the company. Development can potentially reduce employees' job hopping because they feel they need to change employers to build their skill sets or gain valuable job experiences.

"Boundaryless" means that careers may involve identifying more with a job or profession than with the present employer. A career can also be considered boundaryless in the sense that career plans or goals are influenced by personal or family demands and values, passion, and purpose. One way that employees cope with changes in their personal lives, as well as in employment relationships, is to rearrange and shift their roles and responsibilities. Employees can change their careers throughout their life based on awareness of strengths and weaknesses, perceived need to balance work and life, and the need to find purposeful and exciting work.[11] Career success may not be tied to promotions but to achieving goals that are personally meaningful to the employee rather than those set by parents, peers, or the company. As we discuss later in the chapter, careers are best managed through partnerships between employees and their company that create a positive relationship through which employees are committed to the organization but can take personal control for managing their own careers to benefit themselves and the company.

As this discussion shows, to retain and motivate employees, companies need to provide a system to identify and meet employees' development needs. This is especially important to try to retain good performers and employees who have potential for managerial positions. **Development planning or career management system** refers to a system to retain and motivate employees by identifying and helping to meet their development needs. We discuss these systems next.

DEVELOPMENT PLANNING SYSTEMS

Companies' development planning systems (also known as development planning processes) vary in the level of sophistication and the emphasis they place on different components of the process. Steps and responsibilities in the development planning system are shown in Figure 9.1.

FIGURE 9.1   **Steps and Responsibilities in the Development Planning Process**

	Self-Assessment	Reality Check	Goal Setting	Action Planning
Employee responsibility	Identify opportunities and needs to improve.	Identify what needs are realistic to develop.	Identify goal and method to determine goal progress.	Identify steps and timetable to reach goal.
Company responsibility	Provide assessment information to identify strengths, weaknesses, interests, and values.	Communicate performance evaluation, where employee fits in long-range plans of the company, changes in industry, profession, and workplace.	Ensure that goal is SMART (specific, measurable, attainable, relevant, and timely); commit to help employee reach the goal.	Identify resources employee needs to reach goal, including additional assessment, courses, work experiences, and relationships.

Self-assessment refers to the use of information by employees to determine their career interests, values, aptitudes, and behavioral tendencies. It often involves psychological tests such as the Myers-Briggs Type Indicator (MBTI, a type of personality assessment described later in the chapter), the Strong-Campbell Interest Inventory, and the Self-Directed Search. The Strong-Campbell helps employees identify their occupational and job interests; the Self-Directed Search identifies employees' preferences for working in different types of environments (like sales, counseling, and landscaping). Tests may also help employees identify the relative values they place on work and leisure activities.

Through the assessment, a development need can be identified. This need can result from gaps between current skills and/or interests and the type of work or position the employee wants. For example, employees at PEMCO Mutual Insurance Company use online self-assessments to assess their current skills and identify the skills and competencies they want to acquire.[12] Employees use information obtained from this assessment to meet with managers of the departments that need the skill sets the employees intend to acquire to discuss how they will get the skills.

Reality Check

Reality check refers to the information employees receive about how the company evaluates their skills and knowledge and where they fit into the company's plans (potential promotion opportunities, lateral moves). Usually, this information is provided by the employee's manager as part of the performance appraisal. Some companies also use the 360-degree feedback assessment, which involves employees completing a self-evaluation of their behaviors or competencies and their managers, peers, direct reports, and even customers also providing evaluations of them. The concept of 360-degree feedback is discussed later in the chapter.

It is not uncommon for managers to hold separate performance appraisals and development discussions. This is done because performance appraisal and development discussions have different objectives. Discussing performance and development in the same meeting is difficult because they have different objectives. Performance appraisal discussions are focused on an employee's job performance during a defined period of time (such as six months or a year) and usually involve a discussion of what financial incentives or pay increases the employee can expect to receive as a result of performance. Development discussions do not involve pay or rewards. They focus on the employee's skill set or competencies, how to develop them, and the manager and the employee identifying and agreeing on realistic short- and long-term development goals (responsibilities or positions that the employee can achieve).

For example, at BKD, an accounting and consulting firm, employees frequently move between tax, auditing, and consulting projects.[13] They need a way to track their skills so that they could determine how to achieve their career goals such as moving from a generalist to becoming a tax expert for the health-care industry. To provide feedback on their skills, project leaders use behavioral checklists that provide ratings such as "exceptional," "needs improvement," or "developing." The checklists are given to employees who can then schedule a meeting with the project leader to get more specific feedback about the ratings as well as development recommendations. The development recommendations might include taking a course, seeking a coach or mentor, or networking with managers in areas the employee is interested in working in.

Goal Setting

Goal setting refers to the process of employees developing short- and long-term development objectives. These goals usually relate to desired positions (such as becoming sales manager within three years), level of skill application (use one's budgeting skills to improve the unit's cash flow problems), work setting (move to corporate marketing within two years), or skill acquisition (learn how to use the company's human resource information system). These goals are usually discussed with the manager and written into a development plan. A development plan for a product manager is shown in Figure 9.2. Development plans usually include descriptions of strengths and weaknesses, career goals, and development activities for reaching the career goal. An effective development plan focuses on development needs that are most relevant to the organization's strategic objectives.

Consider Just Born's Career Development Process (CDP), which is used by employees to identify their career path within the company and ready themselves for their next position.[14] The development plan involves identifying both short- and long-term career goals. Employees commit to two goals to help them progress in their career. Just Born provides a competency dictionary on the company's intranet that can be used for identifying development needs. The CDP gives both employees and their managers the opportunity to discuss future career plans and becomes a reality check by raising expectations and increasing performance standards. Employees initiate the CDP by first defining future job interests, identifying work experiences that help prepare for the future job, and establishing the long-term career goal. The CDP is discussed with the employee's manager. The manager can support the CDP or suggest changes. If employees' future job interests are outside their current department, the interests are communicated to the manager of that department.

Action Planning

During this phase, employees complete an action plan. An **action plan** is a written strategy that employees use to determine how they will achieve their short- and long-term career goals. Action plans may involve any one or combination of development approaches discussed later in the chapter (such as enrolling in courses and seminars, getting additional assessment, obtaining new job experiences, or finding a mentor or coach).[15] The development approach used depends on the needs and developmental goal.

Examples of Career Management and Development Systems

Effective career development systems include several important features (see Table 9.2). Also, companies are using technology to provide employees with greater access and give them more responsibility for managing their own careers. Consider career management and development systems at General Mills, Xerox, Genentech, White Lodging Services, and IBM.[16] General Mills's development plan is similar to the one shown in Figure 9.2. Each employee completes a development plan that asks employees to consider four areas:

- *Professional goals and motivation:* What professional goals do I have? What excites me to grow professionally?
- *Talents or strengths:* What are my talents and strengths?
- *Development opportunities:* What development needs are important to improve?

FIGURE 9.2   Development Plan

Name: _____   **Title:** Project Manager   **Immediate Manager:** _____

Competencies
Please identify your three greatest strengths and areas for improvement.
Strengths
- Strategic thinking and execution (confidence, command skills, action orientation)
- Results orientation (competence, motivating others, perseverance)
- Spirit for winning (building team spirit, customer focus, respect colleagues)

Areas for Improvement
- Patience (tolerance of people or processes and sensitivity to pacing)
- Written communications (ability to write clearly and succinctly)
- Overly ambitious (too much focus on successful completion of projects rather than developing relationships with individuals involved in the projects)

Development Goals
Please describe your overall career goals.
- **Long-term:** Accept positions of increased responsibility to a level of general manager (or beyond). The areas of specific interest include but are not limited to product and brand management, technology and development, strategic planning, and marketing.
- **Short-term:** Continue to improve my skills in marketing and brand management while utilizing my skills in product management, strategic planning, and global relations.

Next Assignments
Identify potential next assignments (including timing) that would help you develop toward your goals.
- Manager or director level in planning, development, product, or brand management. Timing estimated to be spring 2017.

Training and Development Needs
List both training and development activities that will either help you develop in your current assignment or provide overall development.
- Master's degree classes will allow me to practice and improve my written communications skills. The dynamics of my current position, teamwork, and reliance on other individuals allow me to practice patience and to focus on individual team members' needs along with the success of the projects.

Employee _____   Date _____
Immediate Manager _____   Date _____
Mentor _____   Date _____

- *Development objectives and action steps:* What will be my objective for this plan? What steps can I take to meet the objective?

Every year, managers and employees are expected to have a development discussion and create an individual development plan. Speakers, online tools, and workshops to help employees complete the development plan and prepare for a development discussion with

TABLE 9.2
Design Factors of Effective Development Systems

Sources: Based B. Conaty and R. Charan, *The Talent Masters* (New York: Crown Business, 2010); D. Hall, *Careers In and Out of Organizations* (Thousand Oaks, CA: Sage, 2002).

1. The system is positioned as a response to a business need or to support the business strategy.
2. Employees and managers participate in developing the system.
3. Employees are encouraged to take an active role in career management and development.
4. Evaluation is ongoing and used to improve the system.
5. Business units can customize the system for their own purposes (with some constraints).
6. Employees have access to development and career information sources (including advisors and positions available).
7. Senior management and the company culture support the development system.
8. The development system uses competencies, skills, and behavior that are common to the company's other human resource practices, including performance management, training, and recruiting.
9. The development system is linked to other human resource practices, such as performance management, training, and recruiting systems.
10. A large, diverse talent pool is created.
11. Development plans and talent evaluation information are available and accessible to all managers.

their manager increase the visibility and emphasize the importance of the development planning process. Evaluation data showed that more than 80 percent of employees report having an effective and motivating development plan. Also, annual survey results show that General Mills ranks 20 percent to 30 percent higher on continued improvement and impact of learning and growth compared to companies it is benchmarked against.

Xerox Services University (XSU) provides an opportunity for employees to develop their skills. At XSUs website, employees have access to different schools, each of which provides a unique development path. Each development path provides recommendations about courses, experiences, and social learning (mentoring, peer coaching) facilitated through social media. The five XSU schools focus on creativity and innovation, operational excellence, leadership, people management, and business foundations. As employees use the system, provide their skill strengths and weaknesses, and identify areas of interest, the social learning software generates personalized and specific recommendations for development opportunities. Genentech Inc., a biotechnology company, developed CareerLab to help perform well in their current job and provide opportunities for job enrichment and lateral career moves. CareerLab is a physical and virtual place where employees can consider their skill strengths, weaknesses, and interests, and take ownership of their development. CareerLab provides several services. Career consultants are available to meet employees in person, over the phone, or using Skype. Learning Labs are webinars and class sessions that cover different topics, including networking for career growth, managing your personal brand, and leveraging strengths for career growth. Mentoring Services helps employees form mentorships. Employees can access online assessments that cover personal style, values, skills, strengths, and interests. Through CareerLab, employees can access short videos designed to get employees to seriously consider their careers, blogs written by career development experts, and animated podcasts. Genentech also offers employees three career development workshops (Growing Your Career, Growing Careers for Managers, and Personal Mastery: Developing Your Full Potential). CareerLab has helped Genentech maintain a lower than industry average turnover rate (6.2 percent) and increased levels of employee engagement (17 percent) since CareerLab was introduced. Employees who have used CareerLab report they are more likely to remain with the company and are satisfied with the future of their careers. White Lodging Services, a hospitality service company, provides each leader with a career steward, who provides mentoring and coaching needed for the person's success. Each leader has a "2 Sheet," which is an online dashboard that provides a snapshot of the leader's performance over time based on the company's balanced scorecard, presents their short- and long-term goals and actions to reach the goals, and identifies the training they have completed and what types of training they will need to achieve their goals.

The Role of the Manager @ IBM is an expert system that provides a customized learning portfolio for each manager based on their background, training, and management style. The expert system guides managers through prework that has to be completed prior to attending learning labs. Learning is reinforced through the use of a knowledge management system that allows managers to post suggestions and store ideas. Managers who have completed the Role of the Manager @ IBM program have created action plans that have generated revenues of $184 million.

APPROACHES TO EMPLOYEE DEVELOPMENT

Four approaches are used to develop employees: formal education, assessment, job experiences, and interpersonal relationships.[17] Many companies use a combination of these approaches. Figure 9.3 shows the frequency of use of different employee development practices. Larger companies are more likely to use leadership training and development planning more frequently than smaller companies. In its Frontline Investment in Growing High-Potential Talent (FLIGHT) program, Asurion, a device insurance company, uses six-month rotational assignments to provide employees with an overall understanding of supply chain operations, mentoring and coaching opportunities with key leaders, and on-the-job and classroom training.[18]

Regardless of the approach used to ensure that development programs are effective, the programs should be developed through the same process used for training design: assessing needs, creating a positive development environment, ensuring employees' readiness for development, identifying the objectives for development, choosing a combination of development activities that will help achieve the objectives, ensuring that the work environment supports development activities and the use of skills and experiences acquired, and evaluating the program. To determine the development needs of an individual, department, or company, an analysis of strengths and weaknesses needs to be completed so that appropriate development activities can be chosen. Many companies have identified key competencies for successful managers. Recall from the discussion in Chapter Three, "Needs Assessment," that competencies are areas of personal capability that enable employees to

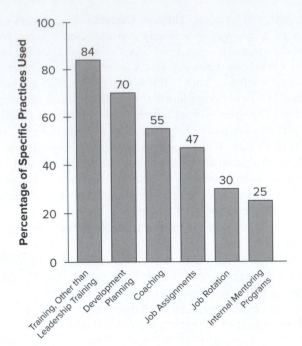

FIGURE 9.3
**Frequency
of Use of
Employee
Development
Practices**

Source: Based
on E. Esen and
J. Collison, *Employee
Development*
(Alexandria, VA:
SHRM Research,
2005).

successfully perform their jobs. Competencies can include knowledge, skills, abilities, or personal characteristics.

IBM's leadership development program focuses on nine practices that relate to three values, dedication to client success, innovation that matters for the company and the world, and trust and personal responsibility in all relationships.[19] The nine practices include sharing expertise, listening for need, putting the client first, restlessly reinventing, daring to create original ideas, and uniting to get it done. Prior to participating in a development program designed specifically for their level of management, aspiring managers complete an online self-assessment, as well as simulations and structured interviews to determine their development needs and readiness for a management role.

Keep in mind that although much development activity is targeted at managers, all levels of employees may be involved in development. For example, most employees typically receive a performance appraisal (an activity that can be used for assessment) at least once per year. As part of the appraisal process, they are asked to complete individual development plans outlining (1) how they plan to change their weaknesses and (2) their future plans (including positions or locations desired and education or experience needed). Next, we explore each type of development approach.

Formal Education

Formal education programs include off-site and on-site programs designed specifically for the company's employees, short courses offered by consultants or universities, executive MBA programs, and university programs in which participants actually live at the university while taking classes. These programs may involve lectures by business experts, business games and simulations, adventure learning, and meetings with customers.

Formal Education Programs

Employee development programs include short courses offered by consultants or universities, executive MBA programs, and university programs.

Many companies rely primarily on in-house development programs offered by training and development centers or corporate universities, rather than sending employees to programs offered by universities.[20] Companies rely on in-house programs because they can be tied directly to business needs, can be easily evaluated using company metrics, and can get senior-level management involved.

Most formal education programs actively involve the employees in learning. Separate programs are usually offered for supervisors, middle managers, and executives. Special programs for particular jobs (such as engineer) are also available. At Raytheon, a leader in the defense industry, leadership development focuses on high-potential early-career leaders from different functional areas, including information technology, human resources, supply chain, engineering, and business development.[21] The program includes rotational assignments, and functional and cross-functional learning opportunities that are related to the company's competency model. The program includes more than one hundred employees in each class. The learning environment is team-based and problem-focused to develop critical knowledge sharing, business acumen, and team leadership that are needed by Raytheon's managers. The capstone event for the program is a simulation that mirrors real market share and profit challenges faced by Raytheon's leaders. Twenty-five-person teams participate in the challenge. Each team has two engineers and the other three team members are from other business functions. The simulation is a test of how well the participants can apply what they learned in the program. To succeed in the simulation, the teams have to be able to draw upon the functional expertise of all members. The simulation requires participants to use tools and processes that the company uses to manage costs, execute projects, and measure success. Teams need to balance both long- and short-term goals to ensure they can successfully compete against each other. There are multiple rounds of competition with information provided on each team's effectiveness. This information is used to inform the next decisions the team needs to make.

Samsung, a leading company in the electronics industry, has three different development programs, each focused on employees at different levels.[22] SVP is a mandatory program for all employees that emphasizes Samsung's core values, culture, and unique way of working, and inspires a sense of pride as Samsung employees. SLP is focused on developing the competencies for the next generation of company leaders. It includes executive and senior executive courses intended to strengthen global management and leadership skills and strategic problem-solving skills. The courses include coaching, assessment, and action learning. As discussed in Chapter Seven, "Traditional Training Methods," action learning involves assigning a real problem that Samsung is facing to program participants who present their recommendations to top company executives. SGP is specifically targeted to developing global talent through courses provided to regional specialists, expatriates (managers working in a country different from their home country), and new global executives. Development includes foreign language courses and global experiences involving managers taking a leave of absence from their current job and moving to one of eighty-eight different countries.

General Electric (GE) has one of the oldest and most widely known management development centers in the world. GE invests approximately $1 billion each year for training and education programs for its employees.[23] GE develops managers at the John F. Welch Leadership Center at Crotonville, New York.[24] The facility has residence buildings where participants stay while attending programs, as well as classrooms for courses, programs, and seminars. Each year, GE employees chosen by their managers based on their performance and potential attend management development programs. The programs include professional skills development and specialized courses in areas such as risk analysis and loan structuring. All of the programs emphasize theory and practical application. Course time is spent discussing business issues facing GE. The programs are taught by in-house instructors, university faculty members, and even CEO Jeff Immelt. Examples of management development programs available at GE are shown in Table 9.3. As you can see, GE uses a combination of coursework and job experiences to develop entry-level and top levels of management. Other programs such as the Business Manager Course and the Executive Development Course involve action learning. Besides programs and courses for management development, GE also holds seminars to better understand customer expectations and leadership conferences designed specifically for African-American, female, and Hispanic managers to discuss leading and learning.

Executive Education

A number of institutions in the United States and abroad provide executive education, including Harvard, Stanford, Columbia, INSEAD, and Ohio State University. Executive education includes executive MBA programs, as well as specialized curriculum on topics such as leadership, entrepreneurship, change, innovation, and global business.[25] Executive education programs typically involve a blended learning approach (blended learning

TABLE 9.3   **Examples of Leadership Development Programs at General Electric**

Program	Summary	Qualifications to Attend
Early Career Program: Communications Leadership Development Program	Formal courses to develop leadership, communications, and business skills. Three eight-month rotations in one of GE's businesses. Challenging assignments in public relations and communications roles (marketing, communications, employee communications, executive communications).	Bachelor's degree with communication-related courses and a minimum 3.0 GPA; prior internship or co-op experience, willingness to relocate.
Experienced Commercial Leadership Program (ECLP) Sales and Marketing	Receive at least six weeks of training to develop marketing and sales capabilities, strengthen leadership skills, foster ECLP culture. Three eight-month business rotations within a GE business; the rotations are marketing focused and sales focused. Every four months, review self-assessment and manager evaluations to identify accomplishments, development needs, and career interests. Training includes classroom and online training and in-residence symposiums at the John F. Welch Learning Center.	MBA; five to eight years' marketing or sales experience; demonstrated achievement and leadership in sales or marketing communications, and analytical skills; willingness to relocate; expertise aligned with a GE business

Source: Based on http://www.ge.com/careers/culture/university-students/communications-leadership-development-program/united-states and http://www.ge.com/careers/culture/university-students/experienced-commercial-leadership-program/program-details#structure, accessed April 3, 2015.

was discussed in Chapter Eight, "Technology-Based Training Methods"). This means that managers visit campus for face-to-face instruction and, between sessions, work online on assignments such as team projects, cases, or reading assignments. For example, Goodyear North America, a manufacturer of tires and related products, used Harvard Business Publishing for designing and implementing a leadership development program.[26] The curriculum includes both face-to-face and virtual sessions. Each course module begins with a face-to-face meeting, followed by virtual learning led by Harvard Business School professors. Participants access course content, including readings, business cases, discussion boards, and webinars, using Harvard's electronic platform. Each program participant has an individual development plan focused on developing their leadership and management skills. The program also includes action learning projects, and job experiences, known as "stretch" assignments, based on the individual development plans that help participants grow and develop their skill sets. For example, one job experience involved moving a manager from the consumer products business unit to the commercial unit to get the manager involved in a strategic change project. To reinforce the importance of the program, Goodyear's executive management team participates as discussion board moderators and determines the participant's career moves to open positions, and stretch assignments.

In addition to blended learning, business schools or other educational institutions have begun offering companies in-house, customized programs to help managers gain real-world skills and study problems in real-world environments—without requiring the managers to disrupt their work by requiring them to travel to campus. These programs supplement formal courses from consultants or university faculty with other types of development activities. For example, Duke Corporate Education developed a custom program for Thomson Reuters to increase their managers' skills related to thinking innovatively to help the company grow.[27] The Thomson Reuters program sponsor encouraged each participant to identify an opportunity or problem with their business that would require innovative thinking. To help the managers develop innovative thinking, Duke used an experiential exercise designed to help managers to consider how different global markets can impact their strategies and understand how consumers' tastes can shift according to where they are located. In the experiential exercise, participants are immersed in a local market to learn how to think about and do business differently. Programs were offered in New York, London, and Shanghai and involved trips to neighborhoods, businesses, and museums and meetings with local leaders to understand the distinctive features of each business market. As a result of the program, participants increased their awareness of how they could be more innovative in their jobs and lead diverse teams. They also gained insights they could directly apply to their business such as how to use brainstorming techniques to quickly integrate knowledge and ideas.

Managers who attend a Center for Creative Leadership development program take psychological tests; receive feedback from managers, peers, and direct reports; participate in group-building activities (like adventure learning, discussed in Chapter Seven); receive counseling; and set improvement goals and write development plans.[28]

Tuition Reimbursement

Enrollment in executive education programs or MBA programs may be limited to managers or employees identified to have management potential. As a result, many companies also provide tuition reimbursement as a benefit for all employees to encourage them to develop on their own. **Tuition reimbursement** refers to the practice of reimbursing employees' costs for college and university courses and degree programs. One estimate is that 60 percent of employers offer a tuition benefit for undergraduate and graduate courses.[29] Typically, the courses or program of study has to relate to the employee's job, employees have to stay with the company for a certain time period after completing the course or risk having to repay all or some of the reimbursed tuition, and the percentage of reimbursed tuition is based on the grade the employee receives (e.g., for a B grade an employee receives 90 percent reimbursement).[30] Companies spend about $10 billion on tuition reimbursement for courses offered by nonprofit colleges and universities, as well as for-profit universities like Capella University.[31] These courses include face-to-face classroom instruction, online learning, and blended learning. Companies that have evaluated tuition reimbursement programs have found that the programs increase employee retention rates and readiness for promotion, and improve job performance.[32] Verizon Wireless invests $26 million annually in tuition assistance program participated in by 23,000 of its employees.[33] Employees can receive tuition assistance for attending a university or college or for the costs of the company's on-site program conducted at call centers and corporate offices. The on-site program classes, taught by university faculty, help employees earn degrees by attending classes where they work and when they have free time in their work schedules. They are eligible for tuition reimbursement from the day they are hired and have to make no commitment to stay employed with the company. Their expenses are limited to $8,000 per year for full-time employees and $4,000 for part-time employees. This exceeds the $5,250 annual reimbursement limit that most companies use based on the tax-free maximum established by the Internal Revenue Service (IRS). To be eligible for reimbursement, coursework has to relate to an employee's current job or career path within Verizon Wireless. Evaluation of the program has shown that it has resulted in increased morale and helped attract new and retain current employees.

Assessment

Assessment involves collecting information and providing feedback to employees about their behavior, communication style, or skills.[34] The employees, their peers, managers, and customers may provide information. Assessments are used for several reasons. First, assessment is most frequently used to identify employees with managerial potential and to measure current managers' strengths and weaknesses. Assessment is also used to identify managers with the potential to move into higher-level executive positions, and it can be used with work teams to identify the strengths and weaknesses of individual team members and the decision processes or communication styles that inhibit the team's productivity. Assessments can help employees understand their tendencies, needs, the type of work environment they prefer, and the type of work they might prefer to do.[35] This information, along with the performance evaluations they receive from the company, can help employees decide what type of development goals might be most appropriate for them (e.g., leadership position, increase scope of their current position). Popular assessment tools include personality test and inventories, assessment centers, performance appraisal, and 360-degree feedback systems.

Personality Tests and Inventories

Tests are used to determine if employees have the personality characteristics necessary to be successful in specific managerial jobs or jobs involving international assignments. They are used to help employees gain self-awareness of how they respond to conflict, what motivates them, how they solve problems, and how they react to stress. Some personality tests such as the NEO Personality Inventory (or the NEO-PI) measure openness to new experiences, conscientiousness or dependability, emotional stability, assertiveness, and the ability to get along with other people. For example, Carmeuse North America uses personality tests in its leadership development program. The personality tests for employees who have been identified as having high potential for top management positions will be used to guide employees into development activities including coaching and formal courses.[36] Starwood Vacation Ownership, a subsidiary of Starwood Hotels and Resorts, uses several assessment tools to determine if its top managers value the commercial success of the business, as well as tolerance for ambiguity, the ability to create and communicate a business strategy, the ability to build business partnerships, and the ability to develop staff. The assessment identifies managers who are ready for international assignments, may not fit their current position, or need coaching to better understand the company culture.[37] CareSource, a Medicaid-managed care provider in Dayton, Ohio, has a defined process for identifying and developing employees who have the potential to be strong leaders and effective managers.[38] Assessment of fit with the organizational values and culture, which emphasize serving the underserved, begins with the recruiting process. The company uses multiple assessment tools to evaluate managers' competencies (recall our discussion of competencies in Chapter Three). These assessments include the Myers-Briggs Type Indicator (MBTI; discussed next), the Gallup's Strength Finder to identify managers' strengths and develop plans for using their strengths with their employee team, and the Leadership Practices Inventory, which provides managers with an idea of their leadership skills as evaluated by peers, their boss, and their own self-assessment, and is used to build a personal leadership development plan. Also twice a year, using the performance management system, they are evaluated on competencies and behavior that CareSource believes are characteristics of an effective leader and manager: service orientation, organizational awareness, teamwork, communications, and organizational leadership. Based on the assessment results, managers with high leadership potential are encouraged to participate in a variety of development activities.

Two popularly used assessment tools are DiSC and the MBTI. Both of these tools can be used to help employees better understand how to adapt and change their behavior to be a more effective leader or team member. These tools can be used to place employees in job experiences they will be most successful in, give them experiences requiring them to adapt their behavior or personality, or assign a mentor or coach who can help them learn how to adapt to different situations. The DiSC measures personality and behavioral style, including dominance (direct, strong-willed, forceful), influence (sociable, talkative), steadiness (gentle, accommodating) and conscientiousness (private, analytical).[39] See *www.discprofile.com* for more information on DiSC. The **Myers-Briggs Type Inventory (MBTI)** refers to an assessment that is based on Carl Jung's personality type theory. This theory emphasizes that we have a fundamental personality type that shapes and influences how we understand the world, process information, and socialize. The assessment determines which one of sixteen personality types fits best. The sixteen unique personality types are based on preferences for introversion (I) or extraversion (E), sensing (S) or intuition (N), thinking (T) or feeling (F), and judging (J) or perceiving (P). The assessment tool identifies an individual's preferences for energy (introversion versus extroversion), information gathering (sensing versus intuition), decision making (thinking versus feeling), and lifestyle (judging versus perceiving).[40] Each personality type has implications for work habits and interpersonal relationships. For example, individuals who are introverted, sensing, thinking, and judging (known as ISTJs) tend to be serious, quiet, practical, orderly, and logical. These persons can organize tasks, be decisive, and follow through on plans and goals. ISTJs have several weaknesses, however, because they do not tend to use the opposite preferences: extroversion, intuition, feeling, and perceiving. These weaknesses include problems dealing with unexpected opportunities, appearing too task-oriented or impersonal to colleagues, and making overly quick decisions. Visit the website *www.cpp .com* for more information on the personality types.

Hallmark Cards has helped people express their feelings and celebrate important events and occasions for over 100 years.[41] Hallmark executives want to change the company's culture from that of a manufacturing company focused on developing products to a consumer-based company focusing on engaging its key customers. It recognizes the importance of developing leaders that can view situations from different perspectives, provide support to each other and work together, inspire employees, and efficiently implement new ideas. To help make this cultural shift, Hallmark Cards is using the MBTI to help managers increase their self-insight into how their actions and communications are perceived by other employees and managers, as well as how they tend to interact in teams, and their work and leadership styles.

Hallmark Cards has realized several positive results from using the MBTI. The speed of managers' decision making and clarity of communications to employees have improved. There has been a noticeable improvement in employees feeling comfortable expressing their thoughts and managers communicating in ways that appeal to all employee types.

Assessment Center

At an **assessment center,** multiple raters or evaluators (assessors) evaluate employees' performance on a number of exercises.[42] An assessment center is usually an off-site location such as a conference center. Six to twelve employees usually participate at one time. Assessment centers are primarily used to identify if employees have the personality characteristics, administrative skills, and interpersonal skills needed for managerial jobs. They are also increasingly being used to determine if employees have the necessary skills to work in teams.

The types of exercises used in assessment centers include leaderless group discussions, interviews, in-baskets, and role-plays.[43] In a **leaderless group discussion,** a team of five to seven employees is assigned a problem and must work together to solve it within a certain time period. The problem may involve buying and selling supplies, nominating a subordinate for an award, or assembling a product. In the **interview,** employees answer questions about their work and personal experiences, skill strengths and weaknesses, and career plans. An **in-basket** is a simulation of the administrative tasks of the manager's job. The exercise includes a variety of documents that may appear in the in-basket, e-mail, or on a manager's desk. The participants read the materials and decide how to respond to them. Responses might include delegating tasks, scheduling meetings, writing replies, or completely ignoring the memo! Role-plays refer to the participant taking the part or role of a manager or other employee. For example, an assessment center participant may be asked to take the role of a manager who has to give a negative performance review to a subordinate. The participant is told about the subordinate's performance and is asked to prepare for and actually hold a forty-five-minute meeting with the subordinate to discuss the performance problems. The role of the subordinate is played by a manager or other member of the assessment center design team or company. The assessment center might also include interest and aptitude tests to evaluate an employee's vocabulary, general mental ability, and reasoning skills. Personality tests may be used to determine if employees can get along with others, their tolerance for ambiguity, and other traits related to success as a manager.

Assessment center exercises are designed to measure employees' administrative and interpersonal skills. Skills typically measured include leadership, oral and written communication, judgment, organizational ability, and stress tolerance. Table 9.4 shows an example of the skills measured by the assessment center. As we see, each exercise gives participating employees the opportunity to demonstrate several different skills. For example, the exercise requiring scheduling to meet production demands evaluates employees' administrative and problem-solving ability. The leaderless group discussion measures interpersonal skills such as sensitivity toward others, stress tolerance, and oral communication skills.

Managers are usually used as assessors. The managers are trained to look for employee behaviors that are related to the skills that will be assessed. Typically, each assessor observes and records one or two employees' behaviors in each exercise. The assessors review their notes and rate each employee's level of skills (e.g., 5 = high level of leadership skills, 1 = low level of leadership skills). After all employees have completed the exercises, the assessors discuss their observations of each employee. They compare their ratings and try to agree on each employee's rating for each of the skills.

Research suggests that assessment center ratings are related to performance, salary level, and career advancement.[44] Assessment centers may also be useful for development because employees who participate in the process receive feedback regarding their attitudes, skill strengths, and weaknesses.[45] For example, Steelcase, the office furniture manufacturer based in Grand Rapids, Michigan, uses assessment centers for first-level managers.[46] The assessment center exercises include in-basket, interview simulation, and a timed scheduling exercise requiring participants to fill positions created by absences. Managers are also

TABLE 9.4   **Examples of Skills Measured by Assessment Center Exercises**

Skills	Exercises				
	In-Basket	**Scheduling Exercise**	**Leaderless Group Discussion**	**Personality Test**	**Role-Play**
Leadership (dominance, coaching, influence, resourcefulness)	X		X	X	X
Problem solving (judgment)	X	X	X		X
Interpersonal (sensitivity, conflict resolution, cooperation, oral communication)			X	X	X
Administrative (organizing, planning, written communications)	X	X	X		
Personal (stress tolerance, confidence)			X	X	X

X indicates a skill measured by the exercise.

required to confront an employee on a performance issue, getting the employee to commit to improve. Because the exercises relate closely to what managers are required to do at work, feedback given to managers based on their performance in the assessment center can target specific skills or competencies that they need to be successful managers.

Performance Appraisals and 360-Degree Feedback Systems

Performance appraisal is the process of measuring employees' performance. Performance appraisal information can be useful for employee development under certain conditions.[47] The appraisal system must tell employees specifically about their performance problems and how they can improve their performance. This includes providing a clear understanding of the differences between current performance and expected performance, identifying causes of the performance discrepancy, and developing action plans to improve performance. Managers must be trained in frequent performance feedback. Managers also need to monitor employees' progress in carrying out action plans.

Consider how Just Born, the company that makes Mike and Ike, Hot Tamales, and Peeps, uses performance appraisals for evaluation and development.[48] The appraisal starts with a planning meeting between employee and manager. The strategic initiatives of the department are discussed along with the employee's role. The employee and manager agree on four personal objectives that will help the department reach its goals, as well as key performance outcomes related to the employee's job description. Competencies that the employee needs to reach the personal objectives are identified. The manager and employee jointly develop a plan for improving or learning the competencies. During the year, the manager and employee monitor the progress toward reaching the performance and personal objectives and achievement of the learning plan. Pay decisions made at the end of each year are based on the achievement of both performance and learning objectives.

Upward feedback and 360-degree feedback are popular tools for development, particularly for managers. **Upward feedback** refers to appraisal that involves collecting subordinates' evaluations of managers' behaviors or skills. The 360-degree feedback process is a special case of upward feedback. In **360-degree feedback systems,** employees' behaviors or skills are evaluated not only by subordinates but by peers, customers, their bosses, and themselves. The raters complete a questionnaire asking them to rate the person on a number of different dimensions. Table 9.5 provides an example of the types of skills related to management success that are rated in a 360-degree feedback questionnaire. Typically, raters are asked to assess the manager's strength in a particular item or whether development is needed. Raters may also be asked to identify how frequently they observe a competency or skill (e.g., always, sometimes, seldom, never).

The results of a 360-degree feedback system show how the manager was rated on each item. The results also show how self-evaluations differ from evaluations from the other raters. Table 9.6 shows the type of activities involved in using 360-degree feedback for development.[49] Typically, managers review their results, seek clarification from the raters, and set specific development goals based on the strengths and weaknesses identified.[50]

The benefits of 360-degree feedback include collecting multiple perspectives of managers' performance, allowing employees to compare their own personal evaluations with the views of others, and formalizing communications about behaviors and skill ratings between employees and their internal and external customers. Several studies have shown that performance improves and behavior changes as a result of participating in upward

TABLE 9.5   Skills Related to Managerial Success

Resourcefulness	Can think strategically, engage in flexible problem solving, and work effectively with higher management
Doing whatever it takes	Has perseverance and focus in the face of obstacles
Being a quick study	Quickly masters new technical and business knowledge
Building and mending relationships	Knows how to build and maintain working relationships with co-workers and external parties
Leading subordinates	Delegates to subordinates effectively, broadens their opportunities, and acts with fairness toward them
Compassion and sensitivity	Shows genuine interest in others and sensitivity to subordinates' needs
Straightforwardness and composure	Is honorable and steadfast
Setting a developmental climate	Provides a challenging climate to encourage subordinates' development
Confronting problem subordinates	Acts decisively and fairly when dealing with problem subordinates
Team orientation	Accomplishes tasks through managing others
Balance between personal life and work	Balances work priorities with personal life so that neither is neglected
Decisiveness	Prefers quick and approximate actions to slow and precise ones in many management situations.
Self-awareness	Has an accurate picture of strengths and weaknesses and is willing to improve
Hiring talented staff	Hires talented people for the team
Putting people at ease	Displays warmth and a good sense of humor
Acting with flexibility	Can behave in ways that are often seen as opposites

Source: Adapted with permission from C. D. McCauley, M. M. Lombardo, and C. J. Usher, "Diagnosing management development needs: An instrument based on how managers develop," *Journal of Management* 15 (1989): 389–403.

TABLE 9.6 Activities in Using 360-Degree Feedback for Development

1. **Understand strengths and weaknesses.**
   Review ratings for strengths and weaknesses.
   Identify skills or behaviors where self-ratings and others' (manager, peer, customer) ratings agree and disagree.

2. **Identify a development goal.**
   Choose a skill or behavior to develop.
   Set a clear, specific goal with a specified outcome.

3. **Identify a process for recognizing goal accomplishment.**
   Identify a timeframe for achieving the development goal.
   Identify development goal outcomes that can be measured and tracked.

4. **Identify strategies for reaching the development goal.**
   Establish strategies such as reading, job experiences, courses, and relationships.
   Establish strategies for receiving feedback on progress.
   Establish strategies for reinforcing the new skill or behavior.

feedback and 360-degree feedback systems.[51] The most change occurs in individuals who receive lower ratings from others than they gave themselves (overraters).

Potential limitations of 360-degree feedback include the time demands placed on the raters to complete the evaluations, managers seeking to identify and punish raters who provided negative information, the need to have a facilitator help interpret results, and companies' failure to provide ways that managers can act on the feedback they receive (development planning, meeting with raters, taking courses, etc.).

Effective 360-degree feedback systems include several factors. The system must provide reliable or consistent ratings and competencies, raters' confidentiality is maintained, the behaviors or skills assessed are job-related (valid), the system is easy to use, and managers receive and act on the feedback.[52]

Technology allows 360-degree questionnaires to be delivered online to the raters. This increases the number of completed questionnaires returned, makes it easier to process the information, and speeds feedback reports to managers.

Regardless of the assessment method used, the information must be shared with the employee for development to occur. Along with assessment information, the employee needs suggestions for correcting skill weaknesses and using skills already learned. These suggestions might be to participate in training courses or develop skills through new job experiences. Based on the assessment information and available development opportunities, employees should develop action plans to guide their self-improvement efforts.

At AlliedBarton Security Systems, its 360-degree feedback report maps onto the company's core values and what it calls its Leadership Non-Negotiables.[53] The process is linked to an online talent tool kit, which gives managers leadership tips based on their 360-degree feedback. The CEO of Food 4 Less sought 360-degree feedback from his executive team on his leadership skills.[54] After receiving the report of his results, he met with his executive team to share what he learned, to thank them for their feedback, and to publically commit to working on several key areas identified in the assessment. Following the CEO's lead, each member of his executive team also participated in a 360-degree assessment of their leadership skills. St. Joseph's Hospital and Medical Center is a nonprofit hospital that provides a wide range of health, social, and support services.[55] St. Joseph's has transitioned from a local community hospital to a research-based hospital with nationally recognized programs in selected fields of medicine. This meant recruiting and adding new physicians, some of whom have significant leadership responsibilities over departments, faculty, and resident physicians. St. Joseph's used 360-degree feedback to identify, measure, and emphasize those competencies necessary for these leaders. St. Joseph's developed the 360-degree assessment with a consulting firm. Based on the 360-degree assessments, one-on-one coaching was provided to give the hospital leaders insights into how to develop their competencies.

Job Experiences

Most employee development occurs through **job experiences:**[56] relationships, problems, demands, tasks, or other features that employees face in their jobs. A major assumption of using job experiences for employee development is that development is most likely to occur when employees are given stretch assignments. **Stretch assignments** refer to assignments in which there is a mismatch between the employee's skills and past experiences and the skills required for success on the job. To succeed in their jobs, employees must stretch their skills—that is, they are forced to learn new skills, apply their skills and knowledge in a new way, and master new experiences.[57] New job assignments help take advantage of employees' existing skills, experiences, and contacts, while helping them develop new ones.[58] General Electric uses experienced managers to integrate newly acquired companies. The Rainforest Alliance, an international nonprofit organization with 300 employees that helps product makers employ sustainable land practices, is challenged by quick growth and the need it created to identify and develop managerial staff.[59] The Rainforest Alliance gives many junior employees the chance to lead research and other initiatives and, if they are successful, promotes them to manage the initiatives. For example, one employee, who started with the company as an administrative assistant, was asked to take on more responsibilities, including researching climate change, and she is now the coordinator of a new climate initiative. Junior employees also can take part in internship programs in foreign offices to learn more about the organization and work on the "front lines" in implementing sustainable land practices.

Most of what we know about development through job experiences comes from a series of studies conducted by the Center for Creative Leadership.[60] Executives were asked to identify key career events that made a difference in their managerial styles and the lessons they learned from these experiences. The key events included those involving the job assignment (such as fixing a failing operation), those involving interpersonal relationships (getting along with supervisors), and the specific type of transition required (situations in which the executive did not have the necessary background). The job demands and what employees can learn from them are shown in Table 9.7.

One concern in the use of demanding job experiences for employee development is whether they are viewed as positive or negative stressors. Job experiences that are seen as positive stressors challenge employees to stimulate learning. Job challenges viewed as negative stressors create high levels of harmful stress for employees exposed to them. Recent research findings suggest that all of the job demands, with the exception of obstacles, are related to learning.[61] Managers reported that obstacles and job demands related to creating change were more likely to lead to negative stress than the other job demands. This suggests that companies should carefully weigh the potential negative consequences before placing employees in development assignments involving obstacles or creating change.

Although the research on development through job experiences has focused on executives and managers, line employees can also learn from job experiences. As we noted earlier, for a work team to be successful, its members now need the kinds of skills that only managers were once thought to need (such as dealing directly with customers, analyzing data to determine product quality, and resolving conflict among team members). Besides the development that occurs when a team is formed, employees can further develop their skills by switching work roles within the team.

Figure 9.4 shows the various ways that job experiences can be used for employee development. These include enlarging the current job, job rotation, transfers, promotions, downward moves, and temporary assignments. For companies with global operations (multinationals), it is not uncommon for employee development to involve international assignments that require frequent travel or relocation.

Enlarging the Current Job

Job enlargement refers to adding challenges or new responsibilities to employees' current jobs. This could include special project assignments, switching roles within a work team, or researching new ways to serve clients and customers. For example, an engineering employee may join a task force developing new career paths for technical employees.

TABLE 9.7   **Job Demands and the Lessons Employees Learn from Them**

Making transitions	*Unfamiliar responsibilities:* The manager must handle responsibilities that are new, very different, or much broader than previous ones. *Proving yourself:* The manager has added pressure to show others that they can handle the job.
Creating change	*Developing new directions:* The manager is responsible for starting something new in the organization, making strategic changes in the business, carrying out a reorganization, or responding to rapid changes in the business environment. *Inherited problems:* The manager has to fix problems created by a former incumbent or take over handling problem employees. *Reduction decisions:* Decisions about shutting down operations or staff reductions have to be made. *Problems with employees:* Employees lack adequate experience, are incompetent, or are resistant.
Having a high level of responsibility	*High stakes:* Clear deadlines, pressure from senior managers, high visibility, and responsibility for key decisions make success or failure in this job clearly evident. *Managing business diversity:* The scope of the job is large with responsibilities for multiple functions, groups, products, customers, or markets. *Job overload:* The sheer size of the job requires a large investment of time and energy. *Handling external pressure:* External factors that affect the business (e.g., negotiating with unions or government agencies, working in a foreign culture, coping with serious community problems) must be dealt with.
Being involved in nonauthority relationships	*Influencing without authority:* Getting the job done requires influencing peers, higher management, external parties, or other key people over whom the manager has no direct authority.
Facing obstacles	*Adverse business conditions:* The business unit or product line faces financial problems or difficult economic conditions. *Lack of top management support:* Senior management is reluctant to provide direction, support, or resources for current work or new projects. *Lack of personal support:* The manager is excluded from key networks and gets little support and encouragement from others. *Difficult boss:* The manager's opinions or management style differs from those of the boss, or the boss has major shortcomings.

Source: C. D. McCauley, L. J. Eastman, and J. Ohlott, "Linking management selection and development through stretch assignments," *Human Resource Management* 84 (1995): 93–115. Copyright © 1995 Wiley Periodicals, Inc., a Wiley Company.

Through this project work, the engineer may lead certain aspects of career path development (such as reviewing the company's career development process). As a result, the engineer not only learns about the company's career development system, but also uses leadership and organizational skills to help the task force reach its goals. Some companies are enlarging jobs by giving two managers the same responsibilities and job title and allowing them to divide the work (two-in-a-box).[62] This helps managers learn from a more experienced employee, helps companies fill jobs that require multiple skills, and, for positions requiring extensive travel, ensures that one employee is always on site to deal with work-related issues. For example, at Cisco Systems, the head of the Cisco routing group, who was trained as an engineer but now works in business development, shared a job with an engineer. Each employee was exposed to the other's skills, which has helped both perform their jobs better.

FIGURE 9.4
How Job Experiences Are Used for Employee Development

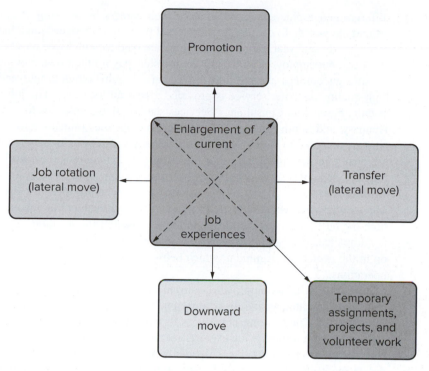

Job Rotation and Lateral Moves

Moving up the career ladder is not always possible for a number of reasons, including the lack of opportunities due to flatter company structures and employees not retiring or staying longer in their positions. As a result, companies are using lateral moves and job rotation for employee development. **Job rotation** and lateral moves give employees a series of job assignments in various functional areas of the company or movement among jobs in a single functional area or department. Job rotation involves a planned sequence of jobs that the employee is expected to hold while lateral moves may not necessarily involve a predetermined sequence of jobs or positions. For example, at AT&T, 40 percent of the company's managers made a lateral move in 2013.[63] In her eleven-year career at AT&T, one manager has held six different positions and she never had the same title for more than three years. In her last position she was in charge of hiring, reporting to executives, training and supporting all sellers located in her region. Now, she has taken a position as a director of call centers. This position has a greater scope and more responsibilities than her previous position (she oversees about 1,700 employees). At Stryker Orthopaedics, the sales department allows employees the opportunity to experience five different functional areas with sales so that employees can decide which areas they might be most interested working in.[64] The Four Seasons, a company with luxury hotel chains located in ninety properties around the world, has employees working in some of the world's great cities such as Toronto, Canada, or at destination resort locations such as Orlando, Florida, or in Seychelles.[65] Regardless of where they work, Four Seasons has a common service culture guided by one rule: Treat others as you would like to be treated. Employees at the Four Seasons can pursue internal transfers. Employees like having the opportunity to explore different geographic areas and advance their careers by working at different properties around the world. To qualify for an internal transfer, employees must have been with the company for one year. Relocation benefits are paid for employee moves requested by the company, but employees who apply for transfers pay for their own moving costs. The Four Seasons encourages internal transfers because it helps retain employees and ensure that high-quality customer service is provided across all locations. The job rotation program at India-based Tata Consultancy Services sends native employees to operations in China, Hungary, and South America.[66] The program helps the company have skilled employees who are prepared to work in any of the company's offices in forty-two countries. Employees also gain an understanding of the culture of the country they work in. It also helps improve customer service because the company can draw on the strength of its entire workforce, rather than just relying on employees who are located close to the customer. The assignments typically last eighteen to twenty-four months, involving learning from both the customers and the local employees based at the location. After the assignment is completed, the employee usually works on the same kinds of projects they worked on in the overseas assignment, which helps transfer the knowledge gained to their home operations.

Job rotation helps employees gain an overall appreciation of the company's goals, increases their understanding of different company functions, and develops a network of contacts.[67] Encouraging employees to move laterally helps companies retain talented employees who want new job experiences and opportunities. It also helps identify employees' strengths and weaknesses, especially related to determining if they might be a candidate for leadership positions in the future. Employees get the opportunity to work on new projects and problems, develop new skills, and apply their current skills in a new way. Also, employees learn about different aspects of the business that are important for future promotion opportunities. A lateral move can involve physically relocating to a new office in the same building or moving across the country or internationally. Because lateral moves can create confusion and stress, it is important for companies to reimburse the employees for moving and relocation expenses, provide orientation to the new job and location, and encourage managers and peers to provide coaching and emotional support. To attract and retain millennials, General Motors uses internships, and functional job rotation programs to give them responsibility for real jobs and projects and to help them explore career paths.[68] At TJX, retailer of off-price clothes and home fashions, buyers need to understand consumer and fashion trends and develop relationships with vendors.[69] Buyers' training includes classroom instruction on topics such as finance so they understand the results of their buying decisions and mentoring with more experienced buyers. After completing the training, they spend time in the planning organization, which allocates merchandise to stores. The last step in becoming a buyer is to move between departments, brands, and locations, which exposes them to different parts of the business. The moves include both U.S. and international locations, which help them gain global experience. Working in different parts of the business helps the buyers develop their communication and negotiation skills and gain confidence in their buying decisions, which can involve hundreds or millions of items. Despite its advantages, there are several potential problems with job rotation for both the employee and the work unit. The rotation may create a short-term perspective on problems and solutions in rotating employees and their peers. Employees' satisfaction and motivation may be adversely affected because they find it difficult to develop functional specialties and they don't spend enough time in one position to receive a challenging assignment. Productivity losses and workload increases may be experienced by both the department gaining a rotating employee and the department losing the employee due to training demands and loss of a resource.

Table 9.8 shows characteristics of effective job rotation systems. Effective job rotation systems are linked to the company's training, development, and career management systems. Also, job rotation is used for all types of employees, not just those with managerial potential.

Transfers, Promotions, and Downward Moves

Upward, lateral, and downward mobility is available for development purposes in most companies.[70] In a **transfer,** an employee is assigned a job in a different area of the company. Transfers do not necessarily increase job responsibilities or compensation. They are likely lateral moves (a move to a job with similar responsibilities). **Promotions** are advancements into positions with greater challenges, more responsibility, and more authority than in the previous job. Promotions usually include pay increases.

Transfers may involve relocation within the United States or to another country. This can be stressful not only because the employee's work role changes, but if the employee is in a two-career family, the spouse must find new employment. Also, the family has to join a new community. Transfers disrupt employees' daily lives, interpersonal relationships, and work habits.[71] People have to find new housing, shopping, health care, and leisure facilities, and they may be many miles from the emotional support of friends and family. They also have to learn a new set of work norms and procedures; they must develop interpersonal relationships with their new managers and peers; and they are expected to be as productive in their new jobs as they were in their old jobs, even though they may know little about the products, services, processes, or employees for whom they are responsible.

Because transfers can provoke anxiety, many companies have difficulty getting employees to accept them. Research has identified the employee characteristics associated with a willingness to accept transfers:[72] high level of career ambition, a belief that one's future with the company is promising, and a belief that accepting a transfer is necessary for success in the company. Employees who are not married and not active in the community are generally most willing to accept transfers. Among married employees, the spouse's willingness to move is the most important influence on whether an employee will accept a transfer.

TABLE 9.8
Characteristics of Effective Job Rotation Systems

1. Job rotation is used to develop skills, as well as give employees experience they will need for managerial positions.
2. Employees understand specific skills that will be developed by rotation.
3. Job rotation is used for all levels and types of employees.
4. Job rotation is linked with the career management process so that employees know the development needs addressed by each job assignment.
5. Benefits of rotation are maximized and costs are minimized through timing the rotations to reduce work load costs and help employees understand the job rotation's role in their development plans.
6. All employees have equal opportunities for job rotation assignments, regardless of their demographic group.

Sources: Based on L. Cheraskin and M. Campion, "Study clarifies job rotation benefits," *Personnel Journal* (November 1996): 31–38; M. Fiester, A. Collis, and N. Cossack, "Job rotation, total rewards, measuring value," *HR Magazine* (August 2008): 33–34.

A **downward move** occurs when an employee is given less responsibility and authority.[73] This may involve a move to another position at the same level (lateral demotion), a temporary cross-functional move, or a demotion because of poor performance. Temporary cross-functional moves to lower-level positions, which give employees experience working in different functional areas, are most frequently used for employee development. For example, engineers who want to move into management often take lower-level positions (like shift supervisor) to develop their management skills.

Because of the psychological and tangible rewards of promotions (such as increased feelings of self-worth, salary, and status in the company), employees are more willing to accept promotions than lateral or downward moves. Promotions are more readily available when a company is profitable and growing. When a company is restructuring or experiencing stable or declining profits—especially if numerous employees are interested in promotions and the company tends to rely on the external labor market to staff higher-level positions—promotion opportunities may be limited.[74]

Unfortunately, many employees have difficulty associating transfers and downward moves with development. They see them as punishment rather than as opportunities to develop skills that will help them achieve long-term success with the company. Many employees decide to leave a company rather than accept a transfer. Companies need to successfully manage transfers not only because of the costs of replacing employees but because of the relocation costs such as home sales and purchases directly associated with them. One challenge that companies face is learning how to use transfers and downward moves as development opportunities—convincing employees that accepting these opportunities will result in long-term benefits for them.

To ensure that employees accept transfers, promotions, and downward moves as development opportunities, companies can provide

- Information about the content, challenges, and potential benefits of the new job and location
- Involvement in the transfer decision by sending the employees to preview the new location and giving them information about the community
- Clear performance objectives and early feedback about their job performance
- A host at the new location to help them adjust to the new community and workplace
- Information about how the job opportunity will affect their income, taxes, mortgage payments, and other expenses
- Reimbursement and assistance in selling and purchasing or renting a place to live
- An orientation program for the new location and job
- Information on how the new job experiences will support employees' career plans
- Assistance for dependent family members, including identifying schools and child care and elder care options
- Help for the spouse in identifying and marketing skills and finding employment[75]

Temporary Assignments, Projects, Volunteer Work, and Sabbaticals

Temporary assignments refer to job tryouts such as employees taking on a position to help them determine if they are interested in working in a new role, project work, employee exchanges, sabbaticals, and voluntary assignments. All temporary assignments have a predetermined ending date after which the employee returns to their permanent position. For example, Mondelēz International, a snack company with 100,000 employees, wanted to help its managers learn about how to market its products using mobile devices. For several days, they sent their managers to nine small mobile-technology companies to help them gain an understanding of their entrepreneurial spirit and how quickly these companies generated ideas and built and tested prototypes of new marketing efforts.[76] An Associate Brand Manager from PepsiCo's New York headquarters spent a week at Airbnb, a San Francisco–based start-up travel rental business with only two hundred employees. Managers from the two companies hoped to learn from each other's brand management practices. Both companies have casual, collaborative work environments. But compared to PepsiCo, brand management at Airbnb is based more on instinct than on data analysis and the ideas of marketing agencies. Marketing managers at Airbnb were interested in learning about how PepsiCo built data sets of market research. To develop a broad understanding of the business, directors at Genentech Inc. spend 10 percent of their time over six to nine months in a different function working on special projects, participating in task forces, and shadowing business leaders.[77]

Employee exchange is another type of temporary assignment. Procter & Gamble (P&G) and Google have started to swap employees.[78] Employees from the two companies participate in each other's training programs and attend meetings where business plans are discussed. Both companies hope to benefit from the employee swap. P&G is trying to increase its understanding of how to market laundry detergent, toilet paper, and skin cream products to a new generation of consumers, who spend more time online than watching television. Google wants to gain more ad revenue by persuading companies to shift from showcasing their brands on television to video-sharing sites such as YouTube. The idea of the employee swap occurred when P&G recognized that a switch to a smaller Tide laundry soap bottle with a more concentrated formula did not include an online campaign, where buyers could find answers as to why the bottle decreased in size. Employees of both companies have benefited from the swap. Google employees have learned that Tide's bright orange packaging is a critical part of the brand and have adopted P&G's marketing language, and P&G employees have recognized that online ad campaigns can increase brand awareness, even for products such as diapers that are not purchased online. P&G has invited mommy-bloggers to visit their baby division to better understand how their diapers can meet their needs.

Temporary assignments can include a **sabbatical** (a leave of absence from the company to renew or develop skills). Employees on sabbatical often receive full pay and benefits. Sabbaticals improve employee well-being through reducing stress and burnout and helping them acquire new skills and perspectives.[79] Sabbaticals also allow employees more time for personal pursuits such as writing a book or spending more time with young children. Sabbaticals are common in a variety of industries ranging from consulting firms to the fast-food industry.[80] Despite their benefits, employees are reluctant to take sabbaticals because they fear it will damage their careers.[81] As a result, companies are offering short sabbaticals. At Deloitte LLP, employees can avoid burnout by taking an extended leave after six months. Ruby Receptionist, a virtual receptionist company, has a five-week leave program, which provides employees with three life-coaching sessions and $1,000 if they let the company publicize their experience. Birchbox Inc., an online beauty business, gives employees a three-week sabbatical after they work for the company for three years.

Birchbox employees have an unlimited vacation policy, but they were reluctant to take off work for more than one week. After taking the three-week sabbatical, employees returned to work refreshed and less-experienced employees learned new skills filling in for them.

Volunteer assignments can also be used for development. **Volunteer assignments** refer to employees serving their local community and its members. Volunteer assignments may give employees opportunities to manage change, teach, have a high level of responsibility, and be exposed to other job demands shown earlier in Table 9.7. For General Mills, volunteer assignments and involvement with community projects is one of the ways the company lives its corporate values.[82] Employees work in a wide variety of charities, with duties ranging from serving meals to the homeless, painting child care center rooms, or serving as corporate board members. Besides providing valuable services to community organizations, General Mills believes volunteer assignments help employees improve team relationships and develop leadership and strategic thinking skills. Lawyers at Sidley Austin, a legal firm, do pro bono work in which they work for free to serve disadvantaged clients.[83] Pro bono work is especially valuable for developing the firm's associates because they get to work through an actual case from the beginning to the end, participating in each step. For example, junior associates can get experience putting witnesses on the stand or cross-examining them. Also, they can expand their personal network and the firm's knowledge by working on immigration or custody cases, which the firm doesn't typically deal with in its for-profit business. The firm tracks each associate's skills and experiences regardless of whether they were developed in a pro bono case or a client paying regular fees. Besides developing skills, working on pro bono cases helps associates feel satisfied with their work because they have made a difference in their client's lives and the firm gets positive recognition for supporting the community. The pro bono casework often motivates associates to become board members or fund-raisers for the community service organizations whose clients it represents.

How to Match Job Experiences to Employees' Development Needs and Goals

Job experiences are used for development in companies of all sizes, but their type and availability vary.[84] Large companies, such as HCA, Inc., with 195,000 employees in the health care business, have the ability to provide high-potential employees with many different kinds of developmental experiences. For example, an administrator can begin working in a position in a smaller health-care facility, and then move to a larger facility, including a hospital or health-care business. Smaller companies might not have the same type or number of development experiences at work, but can encourage employees to get relevant experiences outside of work. For example, Murray Martin, the CEO at Pitney Bowes, learned a lot about conflict management through his role as vice president of his homeowners' association. Regardless of the size of the company, for job experiences to be an effective development activity, they should be tailored to employees' development needs and goals. Table 9.9 shows which job experiences are most appropriate for different types of employee development needs or goals.

Interpersonal Relationships

Employees can also develop skills and increase their knowledge about the company and its customers by interacting with a more experienced organization member. Mentoring and coaching are two types of interpersonal relationships that are used to develop employees.

TABLE 9.9
Matching Job Experiences to Employees Development Needs

Source: Based on B. Kaye, "Up is not the only way . . . really!" *T+D* (September 2011): 41–45.

Job Experience	Employee Development Need or Goal
Job enlargement	Interested in developing new skills, would like to continue in their current position, and their position has opportunities for skill development
Job rotation or transfer	Desire a job with similar responsibilities to their current position but assignments requiring new skills, interest in learning about another function, division, or product of the organization
Promotion	Want and are ready to assume more responsibility, accountability for other employees and projects, and desire to influence business decisions
Downward move	Considering changing or trying out a new profession or career and needs to acquire new skill, wants to reduce job stress or achieve better work and nonwork balance, prefers a previous job
Temporary assignments, project work, volunteer work, sabbatical	Want a new understanding or perspective of customers, products, community issues, obtain job experiences and develop skills in jobs not available in the company, use and develop current skills in a new context, avoid burnout and alleviate stress

Mentoring

A **mentor** is an experienced, productive senior employee who helps develop a less experienced employee (the protégé). Because of the lack of potential mentors and recognizing that employees can benefit from relationships with peers and colleagues, some companies have initiated and supported group and peer mentoring. In **group or peer mentoring programs,** a successful senior employee is paired with a group of four to six less experienced protégés. One potential advantage of peer mentoring is that protégés are encouraged to learn from each other, as well as from a more experienced senior employee. Also, group mentoring acknowledges the reality that it is difficult for one mentor to provide an employee with all the guidance and support he or she needs. Group mentoring provides a development network for employees: a small group that an employee can use for mentoring support and also can rely on to take an interest in his or her learning and development. The leader helps protégés understand the organization, guides them in analyzing their experiences, and helps them clarify career directions. Each member of the group may complete specific assignments, or the group may work together on a problem or issue.[85]

Most mentoring relationships develop informally as a result of interests or values shared by the mentor and protégé. Research suggests that employees with certain personality characteristics (like emotional stability, the ability to adapt their behavior based on the situation, and high needs for power and achievement) are most likely to seek a mentor and be an attractive protégé for a mentor.[86] Mentoring relationships can also develop as part of a formal mentoring program (i.e., a planned company effort to bring together successful senior employees with less experienced employees). Table 9.10 shows examples of how companies are using formal mentoring programs. Mentoring programs have many important purposes, including socializing new employees, developing managers, and providing opportunities for women and minorities to share experiences, and gain the exposure and skills needed to move into management positions.

TABLE 9.10
Examples of Mentoring Programs

Sources: Based on *www.sodexousa.com*, the website for Sodexo, Inc.; "Training top 125 Aditya Birla Minacs," *training* (January/ February 2014): 101. "Best practices and outstanding initiatives," *training* (January/February 2011): 94–98; "Training top 125," *training* (January/ February 2011): 54–93; R. Emelo, "Conversations with mentoring leaders," *T+D* (June 2011): 32–37.

SCC Soft Computer—Every new hire is assigned a mentor. The mentor creates a personalized learning passport, including the new employee's photo, and identifies the competency areas that the new hire needs to develop. After identifying the competency the mentor is responsible for, the mentor follows up with the employee regularly. When the employee's personal learning passport is complete, he or she is eligible for advancement.

Microsoft—The mentoring program includes career development mentoring and peer mentoring. Career development mentoring focuses on career and professional development through structured, yearlong, cross-group mentoring. Peer mentoring is less structured and focuses on transfer of work-related knowledge among members of the same work team.

Sacramento Municipal Utility District (SMUD)—Includes a one-year mentoring program in its Building Leadership Talent program. The program matches protégés with mentors who are outside their business unit. SMUD provides an orientation and half-day session for the mentors that includes skill building, role-playing, a process model for effective mentoring, templates for documenting goals and progress toward meeting the goals, skill practice, and web-based training.

Sodexo—Peer-to-peer mentoring is a program managed directly by Sodexo's Network Groups. Networks are organized around a common dimension of diversity and are created by employees who want to raise awareness in Sodexo of their identity groups. They include network groups based on national orientation, race, sexual preference, military service, and employees from mixed generations. The Spirit of Mentoring Bridge Programs are informal divisional pairings in which newly hired employees and front-line managers come together to expand professional development opportunities and increase the depth and diversity of Sodexo's management.

Agilent Technologies—The Next Generation Leadership Program accelerates development for top talent by matching senior executives with high potential.

McDonalds—Offers a virtual online mentoring program that employees can use to build their skill sets and develop relationships.

Aditya Birla Minacs—The Altitude program is a career progression program designed to support frontline staff transition to a team leader role. Program outcomes include self-identified action items that the staff intends to complete to aid their career progression. Mentor Magic is a program in which successful supervisors, based on their experience and performance, mentor frontline staff on the action items.

Developing Successful Mentoring Programs   One major advantage of formalized mentoring programs is that they ensure access to mentors for all employees, regardless of gender or race. An additional advantage is that participants in the mentoring relationship know what is expected of them.[87] One limitation of formal mentoring programs is that mentors may not be able to provide counseling and coaching in a relationship that has been artificially created.[88] To overcome this limitation, it is important that mentors and protégés spend time discussing work styles, their personalities, and their backgrounds, which helps build the trust needed for both parties to be comfortable with their relationship.[89] Toshiba America Medical Systems doesn't have a formal mentoring program. However, Toshiba encourages informal mentoring from the first day employees are hired. Both managers and

HR business partners take the time to help new employees meet their colleagues and show them around the workplace.[90]

Table 9.11 presents the characteristics of a successful formal mentoring program. Mentors should be chosen based on interpersonal and technical skills. They also need to be trained.[91] For mentors, protégés, and the company to get the most out of mentoring, tools and support are needed.[92] For example, at the University of New Mexico Hospitals (UNMH), a "Mentorship Program Partnering Guide" provides information on the mentor and protégé roles, monthly meeting structure, and ideas for development activities and how to build relationships. Yum! Brands provides goal sheets, discussion guides, websites, books, and self-guided e-learning modules.

A key to successful mentoring programs is that the mentor and protégé are well matched and can interact with each other face to face or virtually using video-conferencing. American Fidelity Assurance Company created a specialized mentoring program for developing leaders.[93] Current leaders serve as mentors but also can serve as protégés. In the program, participants are paired based on assessment results and mentee goals and objectives. Paying attention to mentor–protégé pairings has paid off: 88 percent of protégés indicated that their mentors played a key role in reaching their goals, and 88 percent plan to continue the

TABLE 9.11
Characteristics of Successful Formal Mentoring Programs

1. Mentor and protégé participation is voluntary. The relationship can be ended at any time without fear of punishment.
2. The mentor–protégé matching process does not limit the ability of informal relationships to develop. For example, a mentor pool can be established to allow protégés to choose from a variety of qualified mentors.
3. Mentors are chosen on the basis of their past record in developing employees, willingness to serve as a mentor, and evidence of positive coaching, communication, and listening skills.
4. Mentor–protégé matching is based on how the mentor's skills can help meet the protégé's needs.
5. The purpose of the program is clearly understood. Projects and activities that the mentor and protégé are expected to complete are specified.
6. The length of the program is specified. The mentor and protégé are encouraged to pursue the relationship beyond the formal period.
7. A minimum level of contact between the mentor and protégé is specified. Mentors and protégés need to determine when they will meet, how often, and how they will communicate outside the meetings.
8. Mentors and protégés need to determine the mechanics of the relationship: when they will meet, how often, and how they will communicate outside of the meetings.
9. Protégés are encouraged to contact one another to discuss problems and share successes.
10. The mentor program is evaluated. Interviews with mentors and protégés give immediate feedback regarding specific areas of dissatisfaction. Surveys gather more detailed information regarding benefits received from participating in the program.
11. Employee development is rewarded, which signals to managers that mentoring and other development activities are worth their time and effort.

mentoring relationship. At UNMH, quarterly "Speed Networking" sessions are an important part of the mentoring program. These sessions provide the opportunity for up to fifteen mentors to meet and interact with fifteen protégés. These sessions provide the protégé with exposure to the guidance and tips of multiple leaders and the opportunity to network. Microsoft provides an online portal that provides assistance in matching mentors and protégés and a social networking function that helps employees connect with each other.

Web-based matching systems are also available to help match mentors and protégés. Mentors enroll themselves into a database of experts. Similar to the results of a Google search, the program provides a list of mentors with a percentage indicator that helps identify mentors whose skills and expertise best match the protégés' development needs. Protégés can then choose the mentor who they believe can best further their development. Software is also available to track mentor's and protégé's work, help build development plans, and schedule mentor and protégé meetings.[94] At Cartus, a relocation company, employees who are interested in being either a mentor or protégé can apply to participate in a mentoring program. Employees provide a profile of their interests, expertise, and experiences. Software matches mentors and protégés based on the profiles. Six months after the mentoring relationship is started, the software prompts them to report their progress.

A mentoring program for new regional sales managers at SAP, a global business software company, has many characteristics of a successful mentoring program.[95] The mentoring program helps new sales managers understand company resources, identify experts to add to their sales network, assimilate into the company culture, and practice discovering clients, account plans, and presentations. Mentors track protégés' progress on sales plans, customer and prospective customer meetings, and closed deals. Mentors first interact with their protégés, new regional sales managers, when they accept their employment offer. The six-month mentoring program initially focuses on support for using sales tools and processes and learning the company culture. Next, territory planning, account prioritization, and internal and external network building are emphasized. Mentors are certified by the International Coaching Federation. They use a learning path designed to direct the new manager to training courses, job experience, and informal learning opportunities that match their needs. The mentors and new managers use social collaboration tools to share best practices, discuss challenges, and provide support to each other. Mentors use different types of data so they are prepared to meet each new manager's needs. They review their résumé to determine the types of courses or personal support that may be helpful. Also, mentors review customer reports for each manager to track their progress and identify points of emphasis during their weekly discussions. A study comparing new sales managers who were mentored with those who were not found that mentored managers have more than a 300 percent improvement in closed sales deals, more than three times made quota, and turnover was down 80 percent.

Benefits of Mentoring Relationships   Both mentors and protégés can benefit from a mentoring relationship. Research suggests that mentors provide career and psychosocial support to their protégés. **Career support** includes coaching, protection, sponsorship, and providing challenging assignments, exposure, and visibility. **Psychosocial support** includes serving as a friend and a role model, providing positive regard and acceptance, and creating an outlet for the protégé to talk about anxieties and fears. Additional benefits for the protégé include higher rates of promotion, higher salaries, and greater organizational influence.[96]

Mentoring relationships provide opportunities for mentors to develop their interpersonal skills and increase their feelings of self-esteem and worth to the organization. For individuals in technical fields such as engineering or health services, the protégé may help them gain knowledge about important new scientific developments in their field (and therefore prevent them from becoming technically obsolete). Tamara Trummer summarizes some of the benefits she gained from mentoring relationships: "I found mentors in two of my earlier companies, both male and female managers who 'taught me the ropes' in an informal sense by giving me inside information about the company, certain executives—and even such practical things as how to conduct business travel and handle an expense account."[97] One mentor arranged for her to travel from the remote manufacturing plant where she worked to the corporate office and set up meetings to meet key employees she would have to work with. Her mentors have also included co-workers, peers, and even subordinates who have taught her computer software skills. As a result of her positive experiences as a protégé Trummer now mentors others employees. Protégés can also help mentors learn about how to use social media such as Twitter and Facebook and to understand the needs and motivations of younger employees.[98] This is especially the case in reverse mentoring programs. **Reverse mentoring** refers to mentoring in which younger employees mentor more senior employees.

For example, approximately one hundred employees have been involved in reverse mentoring at MasterCard.[99] In one of the relationships, a 24-year-old with two years' experience in digital communications was paired as a mentor with a 50-year-old executive. The executive wanted to learn how to use social media to relate better to MasterCard's millennial employees and customers and to refocus the company's image to a technology company rather than a credit card company. A reverse mentoring program at Hartford Financial Services Group led benefits for mentors, protégés, and the company. The program led to changing rules to allow employees to use social media for work and more executives using an internal social network. Mentors filed a patent application on how online public safety data might be used by insurance underwriters to assess risks. Also, within a year of participating in the program almost all of the mentors were promoted.

Mentoring can also occur between mentors and protégés from different organizations. Websites such as Everwise are available to help find online mentors. For example, Amy Dobler wanted to enhance her career at Jive Software, so she went online and was matched with Edel Keville, a human resources vice president at Levi Strauss & Company.[100] Using Everwise, she completed an online questionnaire about her personality, education, career path, and personal goals. Both women had similar personalities and career paths in human resources and technology. After the online match, an Everwise relationship manager personally introduced the two women. The advice, guidance, and support that Dobler received from Keville in the mentoring relationship over a few months helped her gain confidence needed to present to senior managers, to lead international training sessions, and to improve her delegation skills.

Mentoring programs can also help encourage women and minorities who tend to be underrepresented in leadership positions to develop management skills and move into management positions.[101] The Economical Insurance Group (TEIG), one of the largest property and casualty insurance groups in Canada, is focused on women's leadership development. TEIG's women's leadership development program includes an instructor-led workshop focusing on the fundamentals of achievement, leadership, and legacy specific to women in the company. Following the workshop female leaders were invited to participate in the TEIG Women's Leadership Network, held quarterly. The network meetings use the company's virtual classroom to discuss business ideas and challenges unique to women and to share leadership experiences.

Coaching

A **coach** is a peer or manager who works with employees to motivate them, help them develop skills, and provide reinforcement and feedback. There are three roles that a coach can play.[102] The main reasons that coaches are used include developing high-potential managers, acting as a sounding board for managers, or specifically trying to change behaviors that are making managers ineffective.[103] Part of coaching may be one-on-one with an employee (such as giving feedback). Another role is to help employees learn for themselves. This involves helping them find experts who can assist them with their concerns and teaching them how to obtain feedback from others. Third, coaching may involve providing resources such as mentors, courses, or job experiences that employees may not be able to gain access to without the coach's help. Consider how Walgreens, Capital BlueCross, PricewaterhouseCoopers (PwC), and University Hospitals use coaching.[104] Coaching sessions are part of Walgreens executive development program. Executives meet for nine days of formal learning that includes face-to-face instruction, discussion, team-building exercises, and action learning projects. They also are encouraged during and after the program to share ideas and get involved in discussions on Walgreens social collaboration site. Each executive is involved in six coaching sessions, which reinforce learning and support their individual development. Capital BlueCross plans to provide a certified coach to employees after they complete training courses to discuss and reinforce the learning that occurred. The coach will also work with employees to identify their strengths, weaknesses, and development activities matched to their current and future career needs. PwC's leadership development program, "Discover," focuses on newly promoted senior associates increasing their skills in making effective decisions. Senior associates are typically struggling to balance careers with family, community, and personal choices. The goals of the program are to help participants maximize their personal energy, clarify their values, identify their focus, and make conscious rather than reactive decisions. In the Explore phase of the program, participants complete prework assignments such as "Discover Your Values" and discuss the results with life coaches. Participants work with the coaches to create "Who Am I?" stories. At University Hospitals, coaching is used as part of an executive development program designed for physician and functional leaders. The participants receive one-on-one coaching and also become certified coaches themselves. This allows them to serve as formal coaches for other potential leaders in the future. The one-on-one coaching they receive emphasizes discovering their ideal self, understanding their real self, creating a learning agenda, experimenting with new behaviors, and leveraging trusting relationships. It uses 360-degree feedback to help them recognize differences between their real self and ideal self and prepare a learning agenda to narrow this gap using new behaviors and personal relationships. Research suggests that coaching improves managers' use of 360-degree feedback by helping them set specific improvement goals and solicit ideas for improvement, which results in improved performance.[105]

PG&E, an energy company, hired a coach to work with a skilled manager whose brash personality was hurting her relationships with her associates and her career.[106] The coach videotaped her as she role-played an actual clash that she had had with another manager over a new information system. During the confrontation (and the role-play), she was aloof, abrasive, cold, and condescending. The coach helped her see the limitations of her approach. She apologized to colleagues and listened to their ideas. Coaching helped this manager learn how to maintain her composure and focus on what is being said rather than on the person saying it, or the way it made her feel.

The best coaches should be empathetic, supportive, practical, and self-confident, but not appear as someone who knows all the answers or wants to tell others what to do.[107] Employees who are going to be coached need to be open-minded and interested, not defensive, closed-minded, or concerned with their reputation. Both the coach and the employee to be coached take risks in the relationship. Coaches use their expertise and experiences to help an employee. Employees are vulnerable by honestly communicating about their weaknesses.

To develop coaching skills, training programs need to focus on four issues related to managers' reluctance to provide coaching.[108] First, managers may be reluctant to discuss performance issues even with a competent employee because they want to avoid confrontation. This is especially an issue when the manager is less of an expert than the employee. Second, managers may be better able to identify performance problems than to help employees solve them. Third, managers may also feel that the employee interprets coaching as criticism. Fourth, as companies downsize and operate with fewer employees, managers may feel that there is not enough time for coaching.

Special Topics in Employee Development: Succession Planning, Developing Dysfunctional Managers, Onboarding

Succession Planning

Succession planning refers to the process of identifying, evaluating, developing, and tracking high-potential employees who are capable of moving into different positions in the company, resulting from planned or unplanned job openings due to turnover, promotion, or business growth. Succession planning is often discussed when considering company's managers or top leaders but it is an important consideration for any job. Succession planning helps organizations in several different ways. It identifies and prepares future company leaders, helps ensure that the company runs smoothly when key employees and managers leave, and creates opportunities for development and promotion. It provides a set of development experiences that managers must complete to be considered for top management positions: This avoids the premature promotion of managers who are not ready to move into leadership positions. Succession planning also helps attract and retain managerial employees by providing them with development opportunities that they can complete if upper management is a career goal for them. Succession planning often focuses on high-potential employees. **High-potential employees** are those people that the company believes are capable of being successful in higher-level managerial positions, such as general manager of a strategic business unit, functional director (such as director of marketing), or CEO.[109] High-potential employees typically complete an individual development program that involves education, executive mentoring and coaching, and rotation through job assignments. Job assignments are based on the successful career paths of the managers whom the high-potential employees are being prepared to replace. High-potential employees may also receive special assignments, such as making presentations and serving on committees and task forces.

Despite the importance of succession planning, many companies do not do it well. A recent survey found that a approximately one-third of senior-level executives were satisfied or very satisfied with their company's succession planning programs and less than one-quarter believed their company had developed a strong pool of candidates ready to fill top leadership positions.[110] The dissatisfaction with succession planning may result from the tendency to focus only on managers at the vice president level or above, failing to identify successors because they don't want to risk potential leaders leaving the company because they are discouraged and disappointed, and a short-term focus on succession planning only when vacancies occur rather than a long-term process designed to develop "bench strength." **Bench strength** refers to having a pool of talented employees who are ready when needed.

Process of Developing a Succession Plan

Table 9.12 shows the process used to develop a succession plan.[111] The first step is to identify what positions are included in the succession plan, such as all management positions or only certain levels of management. The second step is to identify which employees are part of the succession planning system. For example, in some companies, only high-potential employees are included in the succession plan. Third, the company needs to identify how positions will be evaluated. For example, will the emphasis be on competencies needed for each position or on the experiences an individual needs to have before moving into the position? Fourth, the company should identify how employee potential will be measured. That is, will employees' performance in their current jobs as well as ratings of potential be used? Will employees' position interests and career goals be considered? Fifth, the succession planning review process needs to be developed. Typically, succession planning reviews first involve employees' managers and human resources. A talent review could also include an overall assessment of leadership talent in the company, an identification of high-potential employees based on their performance and potential, and a discussion of plans to keep key managers from leaving the company. Sixth, succession planning depends on other HR systems, including compensation, training and development, and staffing. Incentives and bonuses may be linked to completion of

TABLE 9.12
The Process of Developing a Succession Plan

Sources: Based on W. Rothwell, "The future of succession planning," *T+D* (September 2010): 51–54; B. Dowell, "Succession Planning." In *Implementing Organizational Interventions,* eds. J. Hedge and E. Pulaskos (San Francisco: Jossey-Bass, 2002): 78–109; R. Barnett and S. Davis, "Creating greater success in succession planning," *Advances in Developing Human Resources* 10 (2008): 721–739.

1. Identify what positions are included in the plan.
2. Identify the employees who are included in the plan.
3. Develop standards to evaluate positions (e.g., competencies, desired experiences, desired knowledge, developmental value).
4. Determine how employee potential will be measured (e.g., current performance and potential performance).
5. Develop the succession planning review.
6. Link the succession planning system with other human resource systems, including training and development, compensation, performance management, and staffing systems.
7. Determine what feedback is provided to employees.
8. Measure the effectiveness of the succession plan.

development opportunities. Activities such as training courses, job experiences, mentors, and 360-degree feedback can be used to meet development needs. Companies need to make decisions (such as will they fill an open management position internally with a less experienced employee who will improve in the role over time, or will they hire a manager from outside the company who can immediately deliver results?). Seventh, employees need to be provided with feedback on future moves, expected career paths, and development goals and experiences. Finally, the succession planning process needs to be evaluated. This includes identifying and measuring appropriate results outcomes (such as reduced time to fill manager positions, increased use of internal promotions) as well as collecting measures of satisfaction with the process (reaction outcomes) from employees and managers. Also, modifications that will be made to the succession planning process need to be identified, discussed, and implemented.

Assessing and Making Development Plans Using the Nine-Box Grid

Many companies use the nine-box grid for conducting the succession planning review. The **nine-box grid** is a three-by-three matrix used by groups of managers and executives to compare employees within one department, function, division, or the entire company.[112] The nine-box grid is used for analysis and discussion of talent, to help formulate effective development plans and activities, and to identify talented employees who can be groomed for top-level management positions in the company. As shown in Figure 9.5, one axis of the matrix is based on an assessment of job performance. The other axes are typically labeled "potential" or "promotability." The manager's assessment of performance and potential influences employees' development plans. For example, as shown in Figure 9.5, high-potential employees who are high performers are found in the top-right corner of the matrix. These are employees who should be developed for leadership positions in

FIGURE 9.5
Example of a Nine-Box Grid

Sources: Based on K. Tyler, "On the grid," *HR Magazine* (August 2011): 67–69; D. Day, *Developing Leadership Talent* (Alexandria, VA: SHRM Foundation, 2007).

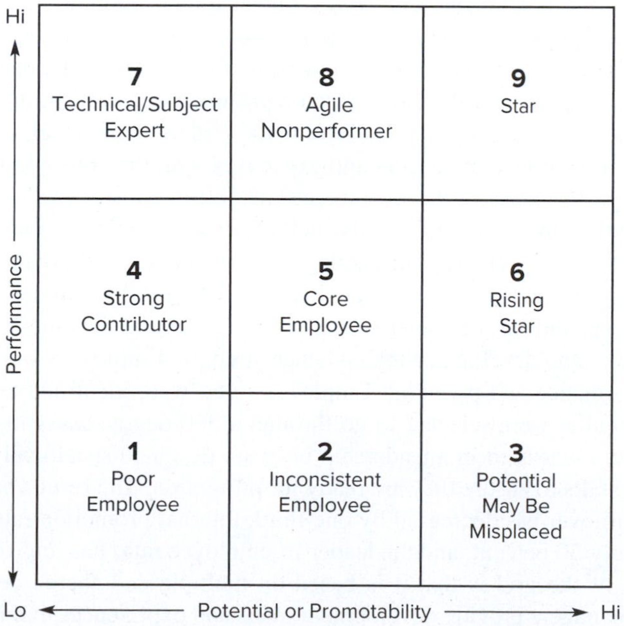

7 Technical/Subject Expert	**8** Agile Nonperformer	**9** Star
4 Strong Contributor	**5** Core Employee	**6** Rising Star
1 Poor Employee	**2** Inconsistent Employee	**3** Potential May Be Misplaced

Hi (Performance axis, vertical)
Lo ← Potential or Promotability → Hi

the company. Contrast the development plans of high-potential, high-performance employees with employees in the other areas of the grid. The development plans for employees with low potential and low performance emphasize performance improvement in their current position, rather than finding them challenging new job experiences. If they do not improve in their current position, they are likely to be fired. Employees in the top-left corner of the grid are outstanding performers but have low potential. These employees are likely experts in their field of expertise. Their development plans likely emphasize keeping their knowledge, skills, and competencies current and finding them experiences that will continue to motivate them and facilitate creativity and innovation. Employees who are low performers with high potential (located in the bottom-right corner of the grid) may have just taken a new position and haven't had the time to demonstrate high performance or these employees' knowledge, skills, or competencies might not match their job requirements. Development plans for these employees might emphasize moving them to a position that best matches their skill set, or, if they have just moved to the job, ensuring that they get the training and development opportunities and resources necessary to help them attain high performance levels. Employees in the middle of the grid, core employees, are solid but not outstanding performers who have moderate potential. Development plans for these employees will include a mix of training and development designed to help ensure that their solid performance continues. Also, core employees' development plans likely include some development experiences that can help grow their skills and determine their interest and ability to perform in positions requiring different skills and/or more responsibility.

How can companies use the nine-box grid? The process begins by clearly defining each box (e.g., what does a star performer look like?) and provides examples of desirable behavior to managers. Next, managers categorize their direct reports on the grid and then meet with other managers to compare, discuss, and defend their categorizations (a process often referred to as *calibration meeting*). Managers use the nine-box grid to determine the development plans for their direct reports and to decide who to recommend for high-potential leadership positions or development programs. Typically, each manager's grid is consolidated into an overall grid that can represent a department, division, geographic area, and even the entire company. Collapsing the grid to higher levels of the organization provides HR and top-level managers and executives with the ability to see the mix of the potential and performance of the workforce. This information can be used to determine if the talent exists to meet strategic needs such as growing the business, where talent gaps and excesses exist, and changes in employees performance and potential over time. For example, CHG Healthcare Services' goal was to increase the number of company leaders by 15 percent and reduce leader's turnover.[113] CHG used the nine-box grid to identify potential leaders and develop leadership bench strength. Employees were evaluated based on their performance and potential. Employees who were identified as high performers with high potential were selected to go through a 360-degree assessment of their skills. This assessment was used in a leadership program designed specifically to develop their potential and skills to ensure they are ready for promotion. The results have been positive. Leadership turnover has decreased by one-third, internal promotion rates for leader have increased nearly 50 percent, and the leader-to-employee ratio has improved 24 percent.

The value of the grid is that it is based on multiple and shared perspectives of talent, it helps managers provide development plans and experiences that best fit employees based on their performance and potential (such as mentorships, job rotations, training opportunities), and it provides a snapshot of the company's talent. For the nine-box grid to be effectively used for development and talent management, the process must include a frank and honest discussion of employees by their managers, the information gathered from the process is discussed with employees and helps form their development plans, and employees are identified and placed in key job roles and experiences needed to best use their skills in the company.

Examples of Succession Planning

Turnover is common in Valvoline Instant Oil Change's industry.[114] This means that succession planning and developing bench strength is critical for all employees. Each month managers rate all their employees on their readiness for promotion to their next job level and provide an overall evaluation of when they are ready, such as "today" or "within six months." Managers work with employees on development plans designed to get them to be ready today. The development plans and evaluations are entered into an online system that allows higher-level managers to identify stores and areas where talent is not available in order to improve succession plans. Managers can identify employees, known as "blockers," who are not willing or able to develop further but are in positions that would be considered as a promotion for other employees. Succession planning has initiated a demand for training across the entire career path to ensure that assistant managers are developed, as well as senior technicians who might take their jobs and new technicians who need to be ready to take on more responsibilities. Top-level managers use the online system to identify if talent is available to expand stores in a geographic area. Also, the company includes the number of managers available for promotion on their balanced scorecard, which measures company performance.

Miami Children's Hospital succession planning involves company leaders and managers at all levels.[115] Miami Children's Hospital's CEO has conversations with other executive team members to develop the learning and development plans of leaders in key positions as well as identify succession plans. They discuss the gaps in talent and develop solutions to ensure executive-level talent is available when needed. The performance and potential of managers at all levels of the company are discussed. The CEO leads discussions for executive-level leaders and other members of the executive team lead discussions for managers working at lower levels. All managers are asked to complete development plans and identify their preferred career path.

Blue Cross Blue Shield of Michigan (BCBSM) identifies and develops the company's next generation of leaders as well as talented employees.[116] Members of the executive team have formed succession plans. BCBSM conducts company-wide talent reviews to identify current and future skill strengths and weaknesses. BCBSM uses a nine-box grid to assess performance and potential. Management teams meet to discuss the nine-box results for their employees individually and as a group. Part of the meeting is devoted to ensuring that managers are using similar standards for evaluating employee performance and likelihood of future advancement. After the talent reviews are completed, BCBSM holds talent summits to ensure that managers across all division understand the company's talent and their development needs, and are aware of cross-division job openings and talent strengths and weaknesses. Supporting this process, BCBSM conducts an annual talent inventory. Employees are asked to identify their career interests and skills. This information is used in manager-employee discussions of BCBSM talent needs and their individual development plans, career goals, and development activities.

Paychex bases succession planning on its leadership competency model.[117] Paychex uses the nine-box grid to identify leaders with high performance and potential. Potential evaluations are based on agility, ability, and aspiration. Succession candidates participate in two leadership development programs. Each succession candidate develops an individual development plan. The individual development plans are designed to meet business needs and competency gaps through development activities that are known at Paychex as the 3Es: education, exposure, and experience. A dedicated "leadership developer" works with the employee and their manager to provide coaching, help with the individual development plan, and monitor progress. Last year, over 1,700 executives, senior executives, managers, and supervisors completed assessment of their leadership competencies, performance, and potential. The succession planning process has resulted in over 25 percent of senior managers, managers, and supervisors identified as ready for a promotion to the next level within one to two years, succession plans for all officer and senior manager positions at Paychex, and an increase of 18 percent increase in open senior management positions filled with internal candidates.

Issues in Succession Planning

One of the important issues in succession planning is deciding whether to tell employees if they are on or off the list of potential candidates for higher-level manager positions.[118] There are several advantages and disadvantages that companies need to consider. One advantage to making a succession planning list public or telling employees who are on the list is that they are more likely to stay with the company because they understand they likely will have new career opportunities. Another is that high-potential employees who are not interested in other positions can communicate their intentions. This helps the company avoid investing costly development resources in them and allows the company to have a more accurate idea of its high-potential managerial talent. The disadvantages of identifying high-potential employees are that those not on the list may become discouraged and leave the company, or changes in business strategy or employees' performance could take them off the list. Also, employees might not believe they have had a fair chance to compete for leadership positions if they already know that a list of potential candidates has been established. One way to avoid these problems is to let employees know they are on the list but not discuss a specific position that they will likely reach. Another is to review the list of candidates frequently and clearly communicate plans and expectations. Managers at Midmark Corporation, a medical equipment manufacturer based in Versailles, Ohio, identify successors every six months as part of the company's performance review process and produce a potential list of candidates. Some employees are labeled as "high professionals." "High professionals" are employees who are strong performers, happy in their current position, and unlikely or not interested in more demanding leadership positions. Other employees are identified as having high potential for leadership positions. Employees with high potential for leadership positions are considered for challenging development assignments involving overseas relocation. Using interviews, the company determines if employees on the succession list are interested and qualified for leadership positions.

Developing Managers with Dysfunctional Behaviors

A number of studies have identified managerial behaviors that can cause an otherwise competent manager to be a "toxic" or ineffective manager. These behaviors include insensitivity and aggressiveness toward others, inability to be a team player, arrogance, poor conflict-management skills, inability to meet business objectives, and inability to change or adapt during a transition.[119] For example, a skilled manager who is interpersonally abrasive, aggressive, and autocratic may find it difficult to motivate subordinates, may alienate internal and external customers, and may have trouble getting their ideas accepted by superiors. These managers are in jeopardy of losing their jobs and have little chance of future advancement because of their dysfunctional behavior. Typically, a combination of assessment, training, and counseling is used to help managers change dysfunctional behavior. For example, a chief technical officer at TaylorMade-adidas Golf (TMaG), a golf equipment company and U.S.-based subsidiary of the Adidas Group, had decades of experience, and his education and technical abilities were sufficient to effectively manage the more than 100 engineers and other staff who reported to him.[120] However, his people skills needed improvement. In meetings, he made cynical comments and quickly reviewed technical information with his staff, not taking time to answer their questions. His lack of people skills caused a high turnover rate in his department. To improve his people skills, the manager began working with a coach to help him identify his strengths and weaknesses. Now he meets his coach twice a month to develop his people skills based on a set of clearly defined improvement objectives that they developed together. As a result of the coaching, employees now come to him first with their issues and problems because he is a good listener.

One example of a program designed specifically to help managers with dysfunctional behavior is the Individual Coaching for Effectiveness (ICE) program.[121] Research suggests that managers' participation in these programs results in skill improvement and reduced likelihood of termination.[122] The ICE program includes diagnosis, coaching, and support activities. The program is tailored to the manager's needs. Clinical, counseling, or industrial/organizational psychologists are involved in all phases of the ICE program. They conduct the diagnosis, coach and counsel the manager, and develop action plans for implementing new skills on the job.

The first step in the ICE program, diagnosis, involves collecting information about the manager's personality, skills, and interests. Interviews with the manager and the manager's supervisor and colleagues plus psychological tests are used to determine whether the manager can actually change the dysfunctional behavior. For example, personality traits such as extreme defensiveness may make it difficult for the manager to change the problem behavior. If it is determined that the manager can benefit from the program, then typically the manager and the manager's supervisor set specific developmental objectives tailored to the manager's needs.

In the coaching phase of the program, the manager is first presented with information about the targeted skills or behavior. This information may be about principles of effective communication or teamwork, tolerance of individual differences in the workplace, or methods for conducting effective meetings. The second step is for the manager to participate in behavior-modeling training, which was discussed in Chapter Seven. The manager also receives psychological counseling to overcome beliefs that may inhibit learning the desired behavior.

Onboarding

Onboarding or socialization refers to the process of helping new hires adjust to social and performance aspects of their new jobs.[123] This is important to help employees adjust to their jobs by establishing relationships to increase satisfaction, clarifying goals and expectations to improve performance, and providing feedback, coaching, and follow-up activities to reduce turnover. There is wide variation in the types of onboarding programs across companies. However, effective onboarding involves the four steps shown in Figure 9.6. Effective onboarding includes understanding mundane tasks, such as completing tax forms and knowing how to complete time sheets or travel reimbursement forms. But it goes beyond compliance to include enhancing new hires' self-confidence, feeling socially comfortable and accepted by their peers and manager, understanding their role and job expectations, responsibilities, and performance requirements, and helping them "fit" into and understand the company culture. Effective onboarding is related to many important outcomes for the employee and the company, including higher job satisfaction, organizational commitment, lower turnover, higher performance, reduced stress, and career effectiveness.[124]

Table 9.13 shows the characteristics of effective orientation programs. Effective onboarding programs actively involve the new employee. Several companies offer onboarding programs that include the characteristics shown in this table. New hires at Sierra Nevada Corporation, a company in the defense and aerospace industry, are contacted by the company's talent acquisition and training teams before orientation.[125] The program includes a review of the company's history, culture, vision, and values. On their first day on the job, new hires have a meet-and-greet lunch date with their manager. Employees continue onboarding for ninety days, which includes e-learning, mentoring, on-the-job training,

FIGURE 9.6
The Four Steps in Onboarding

Sources: Based on T. Bauer, *Onboarding New Employees: Maximizing Success* (Alexandria, VA: SHRM Foundation, 2010); G. Chao et al., "Organizational socialization: Its content and consequences," *Journal of Applied Psychology*, 79 (1994): 730–743.

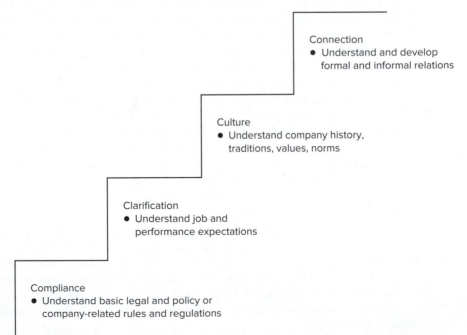

TABLE 9.13
Characteristics of Effective Onboarding Programs

Employees are encouraged to ask questions.
The program includes information on both technical and social aspects of the job.
The employee's manager has some onboarding responsibility.
Debasing or embarrassing new employees is avoided.
Employees learn about the company culture, history, language, products, services, and customers.
Follow-up of employee progress occurs at different points up to one year after joining the company.
The program involves participation, active involvement, and formal and informal interaction between new hires and current employees.
Relocation assistance is provided (such as house hunting or information sessions on the community for employees and their significant others).

and a performance review. Booz Allen, a strategy and technology consulting company, revised its onboarding program to reduce the time that it took for new employees to become productive, support their decision to join the company, and develop knowledge regarding the company culture and core values.[126] The onboarding programs involve face-to-face and online activities to enhance the effectiveness of their process. The new program, which spans twelve months, includes learning activities and events organized into three phases. The first phase, known as "Engage," is designed to motivate and prepare new hires for their first year. Engage spans two to three weeks. It includes learning activities that actively involve the new hires in working in cross-functional teams with members from different offices and levels. New hires can use their laptops to explore online resources for career planning and development. Teams of three new hires each begin to compete in a simulated yearlong client project. They have access to an experienced employee who can provide insights and examples of how they have worked with clients during their career. Also, senior company leaders deliver welcome messages and lead discussions of how to succeed at the company. The second phase of the onboarding program, "Equip," begins in the new hire's second week and continues through their first six months. "Equip" provides employees with the skills, behaviors, and tools that they need for success at the company. It includes thirty-, sixty-, and ninety-day meetings with their manager, a series of e-newsletters, and detailed onboarding tool kit designed to reinforce and build on what they learned in the first phase of the program. The third and final phase, "Excel," emphasizes professional development, relationship building, and acceptance of the company's values. "Excel" involves the seven-month period through the end of the new hires' first year of employment. The employees' first annual performance review occurs at the end of "Excel." In addition to the three phases, new hires have access to and are encouraged to use the company's social media and knowledge management tool, known as the Onboarding Community, to discover and share information via blogs and take part in online activities and resources that support the onboarding program.

The results of the program have been positive. More than 8,000 new employees have completed the program. Over 95 percent report that the program had a positive impact on their decision to join and stay at the company and improved their job readiness. Turnover for new employees who have been with the company six months or less has been reduced by 4 percent. New employees' time to productivity has been reduced, saving the company millions of dollars in lost revenue.

Shape Corp. designs, engineers, manufactures, and tests metal and plastic products that absorb impact energy and protect vehicles, their occupants, and pedestrians.[127] Shape's employees work with cutting torches, welders, grinders, and other machinery. This makes it critical that Shape's orientation program focuses on safety as well as onboarding. Based on a needs assessment using employee focus groups, Shape found that many new employees had little experience working in manufacturing and had begun working prior to any training or orientation. As result, the orientation was changed from one day to four days for all new employees, followed by a six-day manufacturing technician training course for employees working in manufacturing. The new orientation includes speakers, plant tours, introduction to the company's mentoring program, and the employee's mentor, web-based training, and instructor-led safety training. If employees fail the manufacturing technology training course, they are not allowed to work in manufacturing and may be terminated. The orientation program has been implemented globally to 1,800 employees in their native languages. Shape constantly revises the program content based on focus groups who meet semiannually. As a result of the new orientation program, injury rates have decreased 75 percent among employees who have worked one year or less at Shape. The program provides employees with the knowledge they need to perform their jobs, improves their safety awareness, and helps them develop relationships at work that enhance their socialization.

Summary

This chapter emphasized the various development methods that companies use: formal education, assessment, job experiences, and interpersonal relationships. Most companies use one or more of these approaches to develop employees. Formal education involves enrolling employees in courses or seminars offered by the company or educational institutions. Assessment involves measuring the employee's performance, behavior, skills, or personality characteristics. Job experiences include job enlargement, rotating to a new job, promotions, or transfers. Involvement in mentoring and reverse mentoring can help employees better understand the company, how to use new technology, and gain exposure and visibility to key persons in the organization. Part of a manager's job responsibility may be to coach employees. Regardless of the development approaches used, employees should have a development plan to identify (1) the type of development needed, (2) development goals, (3) the best approach for development, and (4) whether development goals have been reached. For development plans to be effective, both the employee and the company have responsibilities that need to be completed. The chapter concluded by discussing important issues in employee development including succession planning, dealing with dysfunctional manger, and onboarding.

Key Terms

development, *385*

protean career, *386*

psychological success, *386*

development planning or career management system, *388*

self-assessment, *389*

reality check, *389*

goal setting, *390*

action plan, *390*

formal education programs, *394*

tuition reimbursement, *398*

assessment, *398*

Myers-Briggs Type Inventory (MBTI), *399*

assessment center, *400*

leaderless group discussion, *400*

interview, *400*

in-basket, *400*

Discussion Questions

1. How could assessment be used to create a productive work team?

2. List and explain the characteristics of effective 360-degree feedback systems.

3. Why do companies develop formal mentoring programs? What are the potential benefits for the mentor? For the protégé?

4. Your boss is interested in hiring a consultant to help identify potential managers among current employees of a fast-food restaurant. The manager's job is to help wait on customers and prepare food during busy times, oversee all aspects of restaurant operations (including scheduling, maintenance, on-the-job training, and food purchase), and help motivate employees to provide high-quality service. The manager is also responsible for resolving disputes that might occur between employees. The position involves working under stress and coordinating several activities at one time. She asks you to outline the type of assessment program that you believe would do the best job of identifying employees who will be successful managers. What will you tell her?

5. Many employees are unwilling to relocate because they like their current community, and their spouses and children prefer not to move. Yet employees need to develop new skills, strengthen skill weaknesses, and be exposed to new aspects of the business to prepare for management positions. How could an employee's current job be changed to develop management skills without having to relocate them?

6. What is coaching? Is there one type of coaching? Explain.

7. Why should companies be interested in helping employees plan their development? What benefits can companies gain? What are the risks?

8. What are the manager's roles in a development system? Which role do you think is most difficult for the typical manager? Which is the easiest role? List the reasons why managers might resist involvement in career management.

9. What should be included in a development plan? What do you think is the most important part of the plan for ensuring that employees develop? Explain your choice.

10. Should a company identify and formally acknowledge its high-potential managers or should it be kept secret? Should managers know they are considered high-potential managers? Explain your positions.

11. Nationwide Financial, a 5,000-employee life insurance company based in Columbus, Ohio, uses the nine-box grid for its succession review. What type of development plans and activities would you recommend for solid but not outstanding performers

with moderate leadership potential? How would these plans differ from employees with high potential and high performance (stars)? Explain.

12. Explain the four steps in on-boarding. What should new hires learn at each step? How might social media or the Internet aid the on-boarding process?

13. What is bench strength? Is it important for companies to have bench strength? Why? How does succession planning influence a company's bench strength?

Application Assignments

1. Your manager wants you to create a one-page form for development planning. Create the form, and provide a rationale for each category you include on it.

2. Go to *www.shrm.org/foundation*; under "Complimentary Resources," click on "DVD series". Watch the video *Seeing Forward: Succession Planning at 3M*.

   Answer the following questions:

   a. Why is development important at 3M?

   b. How does 3M develop employees?

   c. In addition to development activities, what else is necessary for effective employee development?

3. Watch the YouTube video about one employee's experience working at Dow Chemical at https://www.youtube.com/watch?v=ERvag-Z7VdU. How were his job experiences developmental? Besides job experiences what other things might Dow consider to help employees develop?

4. Read about how United Parcel Service uses volunteer assignments for management development at http://www.responsibility.ups.com/committed-to-more/diversity-and-inclusion/. What skills might managers develop by participating in the Community Internship program? What other development opportunities should UPS and other companies consider to contribute to both their diversity and inclusion goals and to develop employees?

5. Watch the YouTube video about ABB company at https://www.youtube.com/watch?v=ih6Au7sjOz8. Why is employee development important at ABB? How does ABB help employees develop?

6. Watch the YouTube video about the employee training and development plan used by the State of North Carolina Department of Transportation (NCDOT) at https://www.youtube.com/watch?v=yKFta1zfC8o. What parts of their process contribute to the effectiveness of the development plan? What else might they consider for improving the planning process?

7. Go to *www.keirsey.com*, the website for Keirsey.com, an organization offering publications, assessments, and professional services for employee and leadership development. Complete the Keirsey Temperament Sorter by clicking on "Take the KTS-II." This is an example of an assessment instrument that can be used for development. What did you learn about yourself? How could this instrument be useful for management development? What might be some disadvantages of using this instrument?

8. Go to *www.dukece.com*, a provider of custom corporate education programs. Under "Clients," click on "Client Stories" and read one of the client success stories. Prepare a brief summary of the business issue, approach, learning experience, execution, and outcome. Why do you think the program was successful?

Case: *Onboarding at MGM Resorts*

MGM Resorts International owns and operates hotels and casino properties such as the MGM Grand, Mandalay Bay, and Bellagio. Guest experience is the key performance indicator. This is assessed by asking guests how satisfied they were during their current stay as well as whether they would return to the property and how likely they are to recommend it to friends and family. MGM's values include:

- Value Others—Acknowledge and value the contributions of all people.
- Be Respectful—Everyone is worthy of your respect.
- Be Inclusive—Treat one another with openness and acceptance; leave no one behind.
- Be Understanding—Understand and appreciate the differences of co-workers and guests.
- Be Considerate—Use tact in dealing with everyone.
- Be First and Best—Your actions make MGM Resorts International a stronger company.

MGM Resorts plans to open new properties in National Harbor, Maryland; Toronto, Ontario, Canada; and Macau, China. This means that new employees will need onboarding.

1. What topics should be included in MGM Resorts onboarding program for hotel front desk staff? The job description for front desk staff includes:
   - Assist guests at the front desk by checking them in and out.
   - Responsible for registering and assigning rooms to guests.
   - Provide quotes for room rates and up-sell the guest when possible.
   - Control and issue keys to rooms and assist in coordinating of the Front Desk and the House-keeping Department.
   - Determine if the guest is eligible for credit.
   - Verify that the correct charges and credits are posted to the corresponding guest folio.
   - Collect payment for charges on the guest folio.
   - Ensure all cash and cash equivalents are accounted for and balanced at the beginning and end of each work shift.
   - Respond to guest inquiries.
   - Resolve guest complaints within scope of authority; otherwise refer the matter to the Front Desk Supervisor.
   - Notify his/her supervisor and/or security of all unusual events, circumstances, missing items, or alleged thefts.
   - Complete all duties in accordance with the standards and procedures.
   - Perform all other job-related duties as requested.

2. If you were asked to develop the onboarding program, explain what content and activities you would include in the program, who would be involved, and the length of the program. Provide a rationale for your recommendations.

3. What data or outcomes should be collected to monitor the effectiveness of the onboarding program? Explain the business reasons for your choice of data.

Source: Based on J. Salopek, "Showstopping Learning," *TD* (October 2014): 56–59; *www.mgmresortscareers.com*, website for MGM Resorts International, accessed April 7, 2015.

Endnotes

1. D. Day, *Developing Leadership Talent* (Alexandria, VA: SHRM Foundation, 2007); M. London, *Managing the Training Enterprise* (San Francisco: Jossey-Bass, 1989); C. McCauley and S. Heslett, "Individual Development in the Workplace." In *Handbook of Industrial, Work, and Organizational Psychology*, Vol. 1, eds. N. Anderson et al. (London: Sage Publications, 2001), 313–335.

2. R. W. Pace, P. C. Smith, and G. E. Mills, *Human Resource Development* (Englewood Cliffs, NJ: Prentice Hall, 1991); W. Fitzgerald, "Training versus development," *Training and Development Journal* (May 1992):

81–84; R. A. Noe et al., "Employee Development: Issues in Construct Definition and Investigation of Antecedents." In *Improving Training Effectiveness in Work Organizations*, ed. J. K. Ford (Mahwah, NJ: Lawrence Erlbaum, 1997), 153–189.

3. Towers-Perrin HR Services, *Talent Management: The State of the Art* (Chicago, IL: Towers Perrin, 2005). Available at *www.towersperrin.com*.

4. J. H. Greenhaus and G. A. Callanan, *Career Management*, 2nd ed. (Fort Worth, TX: Dryden Press, 1994); D. C. Feldman, *Managing Careers in Organizations* (Glenview, IL: Scott Foresman, 1988); D. Hall, *Careers In and Out of Organizations* (Thousand Oaks, CA: Sage, 2002); M. Wang, D. Olson, and K. Shultz, *Mid and Late Career Issues* (New York: Routledge, 2013); J. Greenhaus, G. Callanan, and V. Godshalk, *Career Management* (4th ed.) (Thousand Oaks, CA: Sage Publications, Inc., 2010).

5. D. T. Hall, "Protean careers of the 21st century," *Academy of Management Executive* 11 (1996), 8–16; D. Hall, *Careers In and Out of Organizations*; S. Sullivan and Y. Baruch, "Advances in career theory and research: A critical review and agenda for future exploration," *Journal of Management,* 35 (2009): 1542–1571; M. Gubler, J. Arnold, and C. Coombs, "Reassessing the protean career concept: Empirical findings, conceptual components, and measurement," *Journal of Organizational Behavior*, 35 (2014): 23–40.

6. K. Essick, "From a job to a calling," *Wall Street Journal* (March 16, 2015): R4.

7. K. R. Brousseau et al., "Career pandemonium: Realigning organizations and individuals," *Academy of Management Executive* 11 (1996), 52–66.

8. M. B. Arthur, "The boundaryless career: A new perspective of organizational inquiry," *Journal of Organization Behavior* 15 (1994): 295–309; P. H. Mirvis and D. T. Hall, "Psychological success and the boundaryless career," *Journal of Organization Behavior* 15 (1994): 365–380; M. Lazarova and S. Taylor, "Boundaryless careers, social capital, and knowledge management: Implications for organizational performance," *Journal of Organizational Behavior* 30 (2009): 119–139; D. Feldman and T. Ng, "Careers: Mobility, embeddedness, and success," *Journal of Management* 33 (2007): 350–377; S. Tams and M. Arthur, "New directions for boundaryless careers: Agency and interdependence in a changing world," *Journal of Organizational Behavior*, 31 (2010), 629–646; M. Wang, D. Olson, and K. Shultz, *Mid and Late Career Issues* (New York: Routledge, 2013).

9. "Nearly one-third of employers expect workers to job-hop," May 15, 2014, from *www.careerbuilder.com*, accessed April 2, 2015; "Is Job Hopping the New Normal?" *T+D* (August 2014): 20.

10. R. Hoffman, B. Casnocha, and C. Yeh, "Tours of duty: The new employer-employee compact," *Harvard Business Review* (June 2013): 48–58.

11. L. Mainiero and S. Sullivan, "Kaleidoscope careers: An alternative explanation for the "opt-out" revolution," *Academy of Management Executive* 19 (2005), 106–23; S. Sullivan and L. Mainiero, "Benchmarking ideas for fostering family-friendly workplaces," *Organizational Dynamics* 36 (2007), 45–62; N. Craig and S. Snook, "From purpose to impact," *Harvard Business Review* (May 2014): 104–111.

12. L. Stevens, "Customizing their career," *Human Resource Executive* (November 2013): 18–20.

13. Ibid.

14. M. Sallie-Dosunmu, "Born to grow," *T+D,* May 2006, 34–37.

15. D. T. Jaffe and C. D. Scott, "Career Development for Empowerment in a Changing Work World." In *New Directions in Career Planning and the Workplace,* ed. J. M. Kummerow (Palo Alto, CA: Consulting Psychologists Press, 1991), 33–60; L. Summers, "A logical approach to development planning," *Training and Development* 48 (1994), 22–31; D. B. Peterson and M. D. Hicks, *Development First* (Minneapolis, MN: Personnel Decisions, 1995).

16. K. Ellis, "Individual development plans: The building blocks of development," *training*, December 2004, 20–25; "Training Top 10 Hall of Fame," *training*, February 2010, 60, 62; R. Emlo, "The power of discovery," *Chief Learning Officer* (January 2015): 38–48; "Genentech, Inc.: Career lab," *training* (January/February 2015): 102–103; K. Kuehner-Herbert, "Career advice key to post-growth development," *Chief Learning Officer* (November 2014): 50–51, 56; "Lessons from the best," *Human Resource Executive* (May 2014): 48–50.

17. T. Shawel, "Homegrown career development," *HR Magazine*, April 2011, 36–38; "Training top 125," *training*, January/February 2011, 54–93; T. Barron, "IBM's new fangled, old-fashioned pep," *T+D*, April 2004, 64–65; D. Robb, "Succeeding with succession," *HR Magazine*, January 2006, 89–92; N. Lewis and

P. Orton, "The five attributes of innovative e-learning," *Training and Development*, June 2000, 47–51; N. Davis, "One-on-one training crosses continents," *HR Magazine*, November 2007, 54–56.

18. "Leaders take flight," *T+D* (February 2014): 72.

19. L. Freifeld, "Leadership leaders," *training* (May/June 2014): 32–36.

20. C. Waxer, "Course review," *Human Resource Executive* (December 2005): 46–48.

21. M. Teeley, "Raytheon challenges high-tech talent," *training* (May/June 2014): 12–13.

22. D. Chung, "A management 180," *T+D* (July 2013): 56–59.

23. GE website: *www.ge.com/company/culture/leaderhip_learning.html*, accessed February 2, 2012.

24. R. Knight, "GE's corporate boot camp cum talent spotting venue," *Financial Times Business Education*, March 20 (2006) 2; J. Durett, "GE hones its leaders at Crotonville," *training* (May 2006): 25–27.

25. J. Bolt, *Executive Development* (New York: Harper Business, 1989); M. A. Hitt et al., "Understanding strategic intent in the global marketplace," *Academy of Management Executive* 9 (1995), 12–19; G. Gloeckler, "The best business schools of 2013," Bloomberg BusinessWeek. March 20, 2013 from www.bloomberg.com, accessed June 3, 2015.

26. G. VanderLind and A. Alexy, "All for tomorrow's leaders," *HR Magazine* (August 2013): 26–28.

27. Duke Corporate Education (2012), "Thomson Reuters case study: Innovation," from http://www.dukece.com/clients/documents/ThomsonReutersCaseStudy.pdf, accessed April 3, 2015.

28. Center for Creative Leadership, "Develop a pipeline of successful leaders at all levels," from http://www.ccl.org/leadership/pdf/programs/LDR.pdf, accessed April 3, 2015.

29. Society for Human Resource Management, *2013 Employee Benefits* (Alexandria, VA, Society for Human Resource Management, 2013).

30. S. Carliner and M. Savard, "Top 125 in-tuition," *training* (March/April 2014): 32–35; T. Cherry, "Rejuvenating tuition reimbursement programs," *HR Magazine* (June 2014): 79–85.

31. C. Waxer, "Course review," *Human Resource Executive* (December 2005): 46–48.

32. R. Johnson, "The learning curve: The value of tuition reimbursement," *training* (November 2005): 30–33; G. Benson, D. Finegold, and S. Mohrman, "You paid for the skills, now keep them: Tuition reimbursement and voluntary turnover," *Academy of Management Journal* 47 (2004): 315–331.

33. P. Babcock, "Always more to learn," *HR Magazine* (September 2009): 51–56. "Top 125 hall of fame, Verizon," *training* (January/February 2014): 58–59; "Tuition assistance," from http://www.verizon.com/about/tuition-assistance, accessed April 3, 2015.

34. D. Day, *Developing Leadership Talent* (Alexandria, VA: SHRM Foundation, 2007).

35. M. Weinstein, "Personalities and Performance," *training* (July/August 2008): 36–40.

36. E. Krell, "Personality counts," *HR Magazine* (November 2005): 47–52.

37. C. Cornell, "The Value of values," *Human Resource Executive* (November 2004): 68–72.

38. M. Weinstein, "The X factor," *training* (May/June 2011): 65–67.

39. From *www.discprofile.com*, the website for DiSc, accessed February 1, 2012.

40. S. K. Hirsch, *MBTI Team Member's Guide* (Palo Alto, CA: Consulting Psychologists Press, 1992); A. L. Hammer, *Introduction to Type and Careers* (Palo Alto, CA: Consulting Psychologists Press, 1993); J. Llorens, "Taking inventory of Myers-Briggs," *T+D* (April 2010): 18–19.

41. J. Overbo, "Using Myers-Briggs personality type to create a culture adapted to the new century," *T+D* (February 2010): 70–72.

42. G. C. Thornton III and W. C. Byham, *Assessment Centers and Managerial Performance* (New York: Academic Press, 1982); L. F. Schoenfeldt and J. A. Steger, "Identification and Development of Management Talent." In *Research in Personnel and Human Resource Management*, eds. K. N. Rowland and G. Ferris (Greenwich, CT: JAI Press, 1989), Vol. 7, 151–181.

43. Thornton and Byham, *Assessment Centers and Managerial Performance*.

44. B. B. Gaugler, D. B. Rosenthal, G. C. Thornton III, and C. Bentson, "Metaanalysis of assessment center validity," *Journal of Applied Psychology* 72 (1987), 493–511; D. W. Bray, R. J. Campbell, and D. L. Grant, *Formative Years in Business: A Long-Term AT&T Study of Managerial Lives* (New York: Wiley, 1974).

45. R. G. Jones and M. D. Whitmore, "Evaluating developmental assessment centers as interventions," *Personnel Psychology* 48 (1995), 377–388.

46. J. Schettler, "Building bench strength," *training* (June 2002): 55–58.

47. S. B. Silverman, "Individual development through performance appraisal," *Developing Human Resources*, 5 (1991), 120–151.

48. M. Sallie-Dosunmu, "Born to grow," *T+D* (May 2006): 34–37.

49. Center for Creative Leadership, *Skillscope for Managers: Development Planning Guide* (Greensboro, NC: Center for Creative Leadership, 1992); G. Yukl and R. Lepsinger, "360-degree feedback," *Training* (December 1995): 45–50.

50. J. S. Lublin, "Turning the tables: Underlings evaluate bosses," *The Wall Street Journal* (October 4, 1994): B1, B14; D. O'Reilly, "360-degree feedback can change your life," *Fortune* (October 17, 1994): 93–100; J. F. Milliman et al., "Companies evaluate employees from all perspectives," *Personnel Journal* (November 1994): 99–103.

51. L. Atwater, P. Roush, and A. Fischthal, "The influence of upward feedback on self- and follower ratings of leadership," *Personnel Psychology* 48 (1995), 35–59; J. F. Hazucha, S. A. Hezlett, and R. J. Schneider, "The impact of 360-degree feedback on management skill development," *Human Resource Management* 32 (1993), 325–351; J. W. Smither et al., "An examination of the effects of an upward feedback program over time," *Personnel Psychology* 48 (1995), 1–34; J. Smither and A. Walker, "Are the characteristics of narrative comments related to improvements in multirater feedback ratings over time?" *Journal of Applied Psychology* 89 (2004), 575–581; J. Smither, M. London, and R. Reilly, "Does performance improve following multisource feedback? A theoretical model, meta-analysis, and review of empirical findings," *Personnel Psychology* 58 (2005), 33–66.

52. D. Bracken, "Straight talk about multirater feedback," *Training and Development* (September 1994): 44–51; K. Nowack, J. Hartley, and W. Bradley, "How to evaluate your 360-feedback efforts," *Training and Development* (April 1999): 48–52; M. Levine, "Taking the burn out of the 360-degree hot seat," *T+D* (August 2010): 40–45.

53. "Training top 125," *training* (January/February 2011): 54–93.

54. "Case study: Seek employee feedback for improvement opportunities," from http://www.talentsmart.com/case-studies/kroger.php, accessed April 3, 2015.

55. "St. Joseph's Medical Center uses 360-degree feedback and coaching to develop lead physicians and healthcare leadership," from https://www.decision-wise.com/case-study/360-feedback-and-coaching-for-physicians/, accessed April 3, 2015.

56. M. W. McCall Jr., M. M. Lombardo, and A. M. Morrison, *Lessons of Experience* (Lexington, MA: Lexington Books, 1988); L. Dragoni et al., (2009). "Understanding managerial development: integrating developmental assignments, learning orientation, and access to developmental opportunities in predicting managerial competencies," *Academy of Management Journal* 52 (2009): 731–43.

57. R. S. Snell, "Congenial ways of learning: So near yet so far," *Journal of Management Development* 9 (1990): 17–23. M. Weinstein, "Paths to success: Responsibility vs. promotion," *training* (July/August 2014): 26–29.

58. R. Morrison, T. Erickson, and K. Dychtwald, "Managing middlescence," *Harvard Business Review* (March 2006): 78–86.

59. K. Spors, "Top small workplaces 2008: Rainforest Alliance," *The Wall Street Journal* (October 13, 2008): R9. The Rainforce Alliance at http://www.rainforest-alliance.org, accessed April 6, 2015.

60. M. McCall, M. Lombardo, and A. Morrison, *Lessons of Experience*; M. W. McCall, "Developing executives through work experiences," *Human Resource Planning* 11 (1988), 1–11; M. N. Ruderman, P. J. Ohlott, and C. D. McCauley, "Assessing Opportunities for Leadership Development." In *Measures of Leadership*, 547–562; C. D. McCauley, L. J. Estman, and P. J. Ohlott, "Linking management selection and development through stretch assignments," *Human Resource Management* 34 (1995), 93–115.

61. C. D. McCauley et al., "Assessing the developmental components of managerial jobs," *Journal of Applied Psychology* 79 (1994), 544–560; J. LePine, M. LePine, and C. Jackson, "Challenge and hindrance stress: Relationships with exhaustion, motivation to learn, and learning performance," *Journal of Applied Psychology* 89 (2004): 883–891. S. Courtright, A. Colbert, and D. Choi, "Fired up or burned out? How developmental challenge differentially impacts leader behavior," *Journal of Applied Psychology*, 99 (2014): 681–696.

62. S. Thurm, "Power-sharing prepares managers," *The Wall Street Journal* (December 5, 2005): B4.

63. E. Short, "Move around before moving up," *Chief Learning Officer* (July 2014): 19–21.

64. B. Ware, "Stop the Gen Y revolving door," *T+D* (May 2014): 58–63.

65. R. Hackett, "A globe of opportunity," *Fortune* (February 1, 2015): 22.

66. M. Weinstein, "Foreign but familiar," *training* (January 2009): 20–23.

67. M. London, *Developing Managers* (San Francisco: Jossey-Bass, 1985); M. A. Campion, L. Cheraskin, and M. J. Stevens, "Career-related antecedents and outcomes of job rotation," *Academy of Management Journal* 37 (1994), 1518–1542; M. London, *Managing the Training Enterprise* (San Francisco: Jossey-Bass, 1989); E. Short, "Move around before moving up," *Chief Learning Officer* (July 2014): 19–21.

68. R. Hackett, "A globe of opportunity," *Fortune* (February 1, 2015): 22.

69. C. Meyrowitz, "The CEO of TJX on how to train first-class buyers," *Harvard Business Review* (May 2014): 45–48.

70. D. C. Feldman, *Managing Careers in Organizations* (Glenview, IL: Scott Foresman, 1988); D. Hall, *Careers In and Out of Organizations* (Thousand Oaks, CA: Sage, 2002).

71. J. M. Brett, L. K. Stroh, and A. H. Reilly, "Job Transfer." In *International Review of Industrial and Organizational Psychology: 1992*, eds. C. L. Cooper and I. T. Robinson (Chichester, UK: John Wiley and Sons, 1992); D. C. Feldman and J. M. Brett, "Coping with new jobs: A comparative study of new hires and job changers," *Academy of Management Journal* 26 (1983), 258–272.

72. R. A. Noe, B. D. Steffy, and A. E. Barber, "An investigation of the factors influencing employees' willingness to accept mobility opportunities," *Personnel Psychology* 41 (1988), 559–580; S. Gould and L. E. Penley, "A study of the correlates of willingness to relocate," *Academy of Management Journal* 28 (1984): 472–478; J. Landau and T. H. Hammer, "Clerical employees' perceptions of intraorganizational career opportunities," *Academy of Management Journal* 29 (1986): 385–405; R. P. Duncan and C. C. Perruci, "Dual-occupation families and migration," *American Sociological Review* 41 (1976): 252–261; J. M. Brett and A. H. Reilly, "On the road again: Predicting the job transfer decision," *Journal of Applied Psychology* 73 (1988): 614–620.

73. D. T. Hall and L. A. Isabella, "Downward moves and career development," *Organizational Dynamics* 14 (1985): 5–23.

74. H. D. Dewirst, "Career Patterns: Mobility, Specialization, and Related Career Issues." In *Contemporary Career Development Issues*, ed. R. F. Morrison and J. Adams (Hillsdale, NJ: Lawrence Erlbaum, 1991), 73–108.

75. J. M. Brett, "Job transfer and well-being," *Journal of Applied Psychology* 67 (1992): 450–463; F. J. Minor, L. A. Slade, and R. A. Myers, "Career Transitions in Changing Times." In *Contemporary Career Development Issues*, 109–120; C. C. Pinder and K. G. Schroeder, "Time to proficiency following job transfers," *Academy of Management Journal* 30 (1987), 336–353; G. Flynn, "Heck no—We won't go!" *Personnel Journal*, March 1996, 37–43.

76. R. Silverman, "Field trip: Learning from startups," *Wall Street Journal* (March 27, 2013): B8.

77. C. McCauley, "Make experience count," *Chief Learning Officer* (May 2014): 50.

78. E. Byron, "A new odd couple: Google, P&G swap workers to spur innovation," *The Wall Street Journal* (November 19, 2008): A1, A18.

79. O. Davidson et al., "Sabbatical leaves: Who gains and how much?" *Journal of Applied Psychology* 95 (2010): 953–964.

80. C. J. Bachler, "Workers take leave of job stress," *Personnel Journal* (January 1995): 38–48.

81. R. Feintzeig, "A cure for office burnout: Mini sabbaticals," *Wall Street Journal* (October 29, 2014): B7.

82. M. Weinstein, "Charity begins @ work," *training* (May 2008): 56–58; K. Ellis, "Pass it on," *Training* (June 2005): 14–19. "Volunteerism" from http://www.generalmills.com/en/Responsibility/Communities/volunteerism, accessed April 6, 2015.

83. K. Everson, "Sidley Austin harnesses pro bono experience," *Chief Learning Officer* (December 2014): 64–65.

84. R. Grossman, "The care and feeding of high-potential employees," *HR Magazine* (August 2011): 34–39.

85. B. Kaye and B. Jackson, "Mentoring: A group guide," *Training and Development* (April 1995): 23–27.

86. D. B. Turban and T. W. Dougherty, "Role of protégé personality in receipt of mentoring and career success," *Academy of Management Journal* 37 (1994), 688–702; E. A. Fagenson, "Mentoring: Who needs it?

A comparison of protégés' and nonprotégés' needs for power, achievement, affiliation, and autonomy," *Journal of Vocational Behavior* 41 (1992), 48–60.

87. A. H. Geiger, "Measures for mentors," *Training and Development Journal* (February 1992): 65–67.

88. K. E. Kram, *Mentoring at Work: Developmental Relationships in Organizational Life* (Glenview, IL: Scott Foresman, 1985); K. Kram, "Phases of the mentoring relationship," *Academy of Management Journal* 26 (1983), 608–625; G. T. Chao, P. M. Walz, and P. D. Gardner, "Formal and informal mentorships: A comparison of mentoring functions and contrasts with nonmentored counterparts," *Personnel Psychology* 45 (1992), 619–636; C. Wanberg, E. Welsh, and S. Hezlett, "Mentoring Research: A Review and Dynamic Process Model." In *Research in Personnel and Human Resources Management*, eds. J. Martocchio and G. Ferris (New York: Elsevier Science, 2003), 39–124.

89. E. White, "Making mentorships work," *The Wall Street Journal* (October 23, 2007): B11; E. Holmes, "Career mentors today seem short on advice but give a mean tour," *The Wall Street Journal* (August 28, 2007): B1; J. Sandberg, "With bad mentors it's better to break up than to make up," *The Wall Street Journal* (March 18): 2008, B1.

90. M. Weinstein, "Please don't go," *training* (May/June 2011): 28–34.

91. L. Eby, M. Butts, A. Lockwood, and A. Simon, "Protégés' negative mentoring experiences: Construct development and nomological validation," *Personnel Psychology* 57 (2004), 411–447; M. Boyle, "Most mentoring programs stink—but yours doesn't have to," *training* (August 2005): 12–15.

92. R. Emelo, "Conversations with mentoring leaders," *T+D* (June 2011): 32–37.

93. M. Weinstein, "Please don't go," *training* (May/June 2011): 28–34; "Training top 125," *Training* (January/February 2011): 54–93.

94. M. Weinstein, "Tech connects," *training* (September 2008): 58–59; L. Francis, "Mentoring makeover," *T+D* (July 2007): 53–57. "Training top 125 Cartus," *training* (January/February 2015): 87; J. Alsever, "Looking for a career mentor you love? Let cold data be your guide" (July 14, 2014), from www.fastcompany.com, accessed July 22, 2014.

95. J. Dearborn, "Sinking fast," *T+D* (December 2013): 44–47.

96. G. F. Dreher and R. A. Ash, "A comparative study of mentoring among men and women in managerial, professional, and technical positions," *Journal of Applied Psychology* 75 (1990), 539–546; T. D. Allen et al., "Career benefits associated with mentoring for protégés: A meta-analysis," *Journal of Applied Psychology* 89 (2004), 127–136; R. A. Noe, D. B. Greenberger, and S. Wang, "Mentoring: What We Know and Where We Might Go." In *Research in Personnel and Human Resources Management*, eds. G. Ferris and J. Martucchio (New York: Elsevier Science, 2002), 129–174; R. A. Noe, "An investigation of the determinants of successful assigned mentoring relationships," *Personnel Psychology* 41 (1988): 457–479; B. J. Tepper, "Upward maintenance tactics in supervisory mentoring and nonmentoring relationships," *Academy of Management Journal* 38 (1995): 1191–205; B. R. Ragins and T. A. Scandura, "Gender differences in expected outcomes of mentoring relationships," *Academy of Management Journal* 37 (1994): 957–971.

97. S. Wells, "Tending talent," *HR Magazine* (May 2009): 53–60.

98. L. Kwoh, "Reverse mentoring cracks workplace," *The Wall Street Journal* (November 28, 2011): B7.

99. S. Shellenbarger, "Tech-impaired? Pair up with a younger mentor," *Wall Street Journal* (May 28, 2014): D3.

100. J. Alsever, " Looking for a career mentor you love? Let cold data be your guide" (July 14, 2014), from *www.fastcompany.com*, accessed July 22, 2014.

101. "TEIG locks in on leadership," *training* (January/February 2011): 34–39.

102. D. B. Peterson and M. D. Hicks, *Leader as Coach* (Minneapolis, MN: Personnel Decisions, 1996).

103. D. Coutu and C. Kauffman, "What coaches can do for you," *Harvard Business Review* (January 2009): 91–97; J. Ehrlich and K. Holt, "Global support," *T+D* (July 2014): 44–49.

104. "Walgreens: Leading well at Walgreens," *training* (January/February 2015): 104; L. Freifeld, "Capital BlueCross thinks big," *training* (January/February 2015): 40–42; "PwC: Discover," *training* (January/February 2014): 62–63; J. Marques, "Coaching," *training* (May/June 2014): 76.

105. J. Smither et al., "Can working with an executive coach improve multisource ratings over time? A quasi-experimental field study," *Personnel Psychology* 56 (2003), 23–44.

106. J. Lublin, "Did I just say that?! How you can recover from foot-in-mouth," *The Wall Street Journal* (June 18, 2002): B1.

107. J. Toto, "Untapped world of peer coaching," *T+D* (April 2006): 69–71.

108. R. Zemke, "The corporate coach," *training* (December 1996): 24–28.

109. C. B. Derr, C. Jones, and E. L. Toomey, "Managing high-potential employees: Current practices in thirty-three U.S. corporations," *Human Resource Management* 27 (1988), 273–290.

110. "Comprehensive global korn ferry study shows only one third of executives are satisfied with succession management outcomes," from *www.businesswire.com*, accessed April 7, 2015; B. Leonard, "Some executives doubtful succession plans really work," (February 18, 2015), from *www.shrm.org* website for Society for Human Resource Management, accessed April 7, 2015.

111. D. Sims, "Five ways to increase success in succession planning," *TD* (August 2014): 60–63; W. J. Rothwell, *Effective Succession Planning* (4th ed.) (New York: AMACOM, 2010); N. Davis and W. Pina-Ramirez, "Essential continuity," *TD* (March 2015): 45–47.

112. K. Tyler, "On the grid," *HR Magazine* (August 2011): 67–69; D. Day, *Developing Leadership Talent* (Alexandria, VA: SHRM Foundation, 2007).

113. M. Weinstein, "The heart of CHG Healthcare Services," *training* (January/February 2015): 44–48.

114. "Valvoline instant oil change: Bench planning," *training* (January/February 2014): 108.

115. "Training top 125 Miami Children's Hospital," *training* (January/February 2014): 64–103.

116. M. Weinstein, "BCBSM empowers employees," *training* (January/February 2015): 50–53.

117. J. Grenzer, "Succession planning," *training* (May/June 2014): 74–75.

118. M. Steen, "Where to draw the line on revealing who's next in line," *Workforce Management* (June 2011): 16–18; "Should you tell employees they're part of a succession plan," *HR Magazine* (January/February 2015): 26–27.

119. M. W. McCall, Jr., and M. M. Lombardo, *Off the Track: Why and How Successful Executives Get Derailed*, Technical Report No. 21 (Greensboro, NC: Center for Creative Leadership, 1983); E. V. Veslor and J. B. Leslie, "Why executives derail. Perspectives across time and cultures," *Academy of Management Executive* 9 (1995): 62–72.

120. S. Boehle, "Crafting a coaching culture," *training* (May 18, 2007): 22–24. M. Kets de Vries, "Coaching the toxic leader," *Harvard Business Review* (April 2014): 100–109.

121. L. W. Hellervik, J. F. Hazucha, and R. J. Schneider, "Behavior Change: Models, Methods, and a Review of Evidence." In *Handbook of Industrial and Organizational Psychology*, 2d ed., eds. M. D. Dunnette and L. M. Hough (Palo Alto, CA: Consulting Psychologists Press, 1992), 3: 823–899.

122. D. B. Peterson, "Measuring and Evaluating Change in Executive and Managerial Development." Paper presented at the annual conference of the Society for Industrial and Organizational Psychology, (Miami, FL, 1990).

123. T. Bauer, *Onboarding New Employees: Maximizing Success* (Alexandria, VA: SHRM Foundation, 2010); T. Bauer and B. Erdogan, "Delineating and reviewing the role of newcomer capital in organizational socialization," *Annual Review of Organizational Psychology and Organizational Behavior*, 1 (2014): 439–457.

124. H. Klein and N. Weaver, "The effectiveness of organizational-level orientation program in the socialization of new hires," *Personnel Psychology*, 23 (2000): 47–66; C. Wanberg and J. Kammeyer-Mueller, "Predictors and outcomes of proactivity in the socialization process," *Journal of Applied Psychology*, 85 (2000): 373–385; T. Bauer et al., "Newcomer adjustment during organizational socialization: A meta-analytic review of antecedents, outcomes, and methods," *Journal of Applied Psychology* 92 (2007): 707–721; D. Allen, "Do organizational socialization tactics influence newcomer embeddedness and turnover? *Journal of Management*, 32 (2006): 237–256. J. Kammeyer-Mueller, C. Wanberg, A. Rubenstein, and Z. Song, "Support, undermining, and newcomer socialization: Fitting in during the first 90 days," *Academy of Management Journal*, 56 (2013): 1104–1124.

125. "Training top 125," *training* (January/February 2011): 91.

126. D. Milliken, "Poised for discovery," *T+D* (August 2011): 70–71.

127. R. Weiss, "Inside story: A new orientation program for new employees" (January 21, 2013), from *www.astd.org*, the website for the Association for Talent Development, accessed April 7, 2015.

Development Is Served 24/7 in InterContinental Hotel Group's Leaders Lounge

Intercontinental Hotel Group (IHG), an Atlanta-based company, operates by a simple strategy: "Great hotels guest's love." IHG operates brands such as InterContinental, Crowne Plaza, Hotel Indigo, Holiday Inn, Holiday Inn Express, Staybridge Suites, and Candlewood Suites. These brands include 4,400 hotels, with 652,000 rooms, in more 100 countries around the world. The company believes that how its employees feel about its brands and how they deliver the guest experience is what distinguishes it from the competition. "Winning Ways," IHG's core values, help guide and motivate employees to improve their personal and professional lives, take ownership, work together, and engage in responsible behavior. IHG makes four promises to employees:

- Room to Have a Great Start
- Room to Be Involved
- Room to Grow
- Room for You

The "Room to Grow" promise means that employees are given support for development opportunities and encouraged to pursue a rewarding career. "Room to Grow" ensures that employees know what success means for their job, they receive regular, high-quality feedback, they have opportunities to develop in their current and future roles, and they are aware of career opportunities within IHG around the world.

In keeping with its "Room to Grow" promise, IHG wanted to create a way to respond to the needs of many of its global corporate and hotel-level managers, who had indicated in surveys that they did not feel connected to each other and senior management. To develop managers' leadership skills, IHG created a virtual leadership development community called the Leaders Lounge, for the general managers in its hotels, as well as for employees holding corporate director or higher-level positions. The Leaders Lounge features short and concise information on leadership, which is provided in articles, tips, videos, downloadable tools, and best practices within IHG. Employees who access the site can use social networks to post tips and react to the leadership content. There are several dedicated areas within the Leaders Lounge, including the "Leadership Gym," which features assessment tools designed to help employees identify their leadership strengths and weaknesses; and "Problem Solver," which asks employees for input on leadership issues. Also included is a section known as "The Academy," for users to access e-learning opportunities on business topics including finance, customer service, and coaching skills. Use of "The Academy" also allowed IHG to move several modules of its Senior Leadership Program online, generating cost savings resulting from reducing travel costs related to global managers having to travel to the training site.

There is compelling evidence that the Leaders Lounge has been effective for developing managers. The Lounge costs 5 percent of the costs for a typical three-day on-site leadership workshop. More than 70 percent of Lounge members use it in any one month, averaging six times per year. More than 3,000 leadership tools have been downloaded and shared with leadership teams around the world. Lounge members across the globe have taken content from the Lounge and used it to build local learning workshops and training sessions. Surveys for hotel general managers (who make up 75 percent of the Leaders Lounge membership) show that their engagement scores increased approximately 3 percent.

Sources: Based on *www.ihgplc.com*, the website for Inter Continental Hotels Group; P. Harris, "Where people power makes the difference," *T+D* (October 2010): 32–34; "Best practices and outstanding initiatives: InterContinental Hotels Group Leaders Lounge," *training* (January/February 2011): 96–97.

Questions

1. What are the advantages and disadvantages of IHG's virtual leadership development program for the company? For employees?

2. Many companies are using a blended approach for employee development. That is, they are using both face-to-face and technology-aided training and development activities for leadership development. What more traditional development activities would you recommend the IHG include in the development program to make it more effective? Explain how these development activities will enhance the program's effectiveness.

3. Do you think that IHG's evaluation of the program makes a strong business case for it? Why or why not? What other metrics or outcomes would you suggest that IHG include to improve its overall evaluation of the effectiveness of the virtual leadership program for employees and the business? What other outcomes or metrics should IHG use to determine whether the program contributes to the "Winning Ways" core values?

Part **Four**

Social Responsibility and the Future

Chapter Ten, "Social Responsibility: Legal Issues, Managing Diversity, and Career Challenges," focuses on how training contributes to a company's social responsibility through partnerships with unions, community colleges, and other educational institutions. Also, socially responsible companies take steps to manage diversity and help employees work effectively in different cultures, as well as preparing employees to cope with career challenges like balancing work-life, coping with career breaks, recycling their careers, dealing with job loss, and preparing for retirement.

Chapter Eleven, "The Future of Training and Development," discusses how training and development will evolve in the future. Many factors will influence the future of training and development, including the development of new technology, which can affect how training is delivered and the quality and realism of instruction; the increased emphasis on just-in-time learning; and the increased value placed on intellectual capital, which can be developed through social relationships and networks.

Part Four concludes with a case that explores how companies are changing their vacation policy to encourage employees to use their vacation time.

Chapter Ten

Social Responsibility: Legal Issues, Managing Diversity, and Career Challenges

Objectives

After reading this chapter, you should be able to

1. Discuss the role of training partnerships in developing skills and contributing to local communities.

2. Discuss the potential legal issues that relate to training.

3. Develop a program for effectively managing diversity.

4. Design a program for preparing employees for cross-cultural assignments.

5. Discuss the importance of career paths and dual career paths for employees and companies.

6. Develop policies to help employees achieve work-life balance.

7. Describe how companies are helping veterans develop skills and get employment.

8. Explain the value of phased retirement programs for older employees.

Eliminating the Skills Gap and Reducing Unemployment Through Job Training Programs

Both workers and companies are suffering from a skills gap. Millions of Americans are searching for work, but companies are struggling to find employees who have the skills necessary for the job openings they have. For example, despite the estimated loss of thousands of jobs as the manufacturing sector shrinks in the next ten years, it will still experience a shortage of skilled labor as manufacturing workers retire and few are available to replace them. Companies, job seekers, and federal and local government are hoping that training programs can help the unemployed get jobs, the underemployed get jobs that better match their skills, and prepare the workforce with the skills necessary for the jobs that will be added when the economy recovers.

Consider one example of many job training programs funded by the Workforce Innovation and Opportunity Act of 2013, which is responsible for providing the majority of federal funding, approximately $3 billion, for job training. The Machinist Training Institute (MTI) is a program run by a Detroit, Michigan–based nonprofit organization called Focus: HOPE. Focus: HOPE is an organization dedicated to solving the problems of hunger, economic disparity, inadequate education, and racial divisiveness. Since the 1980s, Focus: HOPE has trained 12,000 people, and MTI has trained 3,000 people and helped diversify the machinist trades. Many graduates were the first African Americans or female machinists hired by companies.

Focus: HOPE offers several different education and training programs that have been developed through partnerships with employers to ensure students develop marketable skills. Youth education programs focus on high school and middle school students. They can pursue job training and basic college courses on a part-time basis while finishing high school; enroll in specialized programs focusing on developing leadership, software programming, photography, media production, and other skills; or attend camps that include activities designed to pique their interest and understanding of science, technology, engineering, and math (STEM) topics. A skill enhancement program, Ready, Set, Go! focuses on improving math, reading, study, and work readiness skills of adults with a high school diploma or GED through small classes, tutoring, and personal attention. Earn+Learn is designed to help young minority males between the ages of 18 and 24 obtain work skills, set and achieve education goals, and gain work experience. The focus is on skills necessary to find jobs in health care, logistics, information technology, and advanced manufacturing. After successfully completing four weeks of job readiness training, students are ready for advanced education or placement in jobs, or job training programs. Focus: HOPE also offers certificate and college degree programs. For example, information technology (IT) certificate programs such as Microsoft Office specialist or Cisco-Certified Network administrator help individuals start careers in IT industries. The Machinist Training Institute (MTI) provides machinist training to prepare individuals to become machine operators. The MTI program is a twenty-week program in which students are in "class" five days each week. The current MTI class includes both older and younger students who come from a variety of backgrounds. Some students have been laid off from their high-paying jobs, have dropped out of community college, or have been unable to get employment due to criminal backgrounds. MTI includes classroom instruction but also requires students to practice and gain experience working in its labs and shops, both with conventional equipment used in skilled trades such as metalworking lathes and newer, computer-controlled versions that are used in many of today's manufacturing operations. These require students to have high levels of literacy and numerical and computer skills needed to program the equipment. Focus: HOPE takes many steps to help the students succeed. They find scholarships for students to cover tuition costs, offer subsidized child care, give them free bus tickets so they can get to class, and have a credit union that is open to all students, regardless of their credit rating.

Through various programs students can earn college degrees that lead to good jobs. For example, the Center for Advanced Technologies students can earn a college degree in engineering working with university and industry partners. Android

Industries leases space in the Center for Advanced Technologies to assemble headliners and suspension modules for the Chevrolet Volt automobile, providing over 130 new jobs. Oakland University is moving two of its nursing programs to Focus: HOPE's Detroit campus to train students to become licensed practical nurses and certified nurse assistants, which are jobs in demand across the country.

Both the public and private sector recognize the value of Focus: HOPE for the positive impact it has on the lives of those who attend its programs and the local community and economy. In 2014 Focus: HOPE was funded with $4.5 million in federal funds and over $2 million from state and local funds. Individual and corporate contributors provided $9 million. Recently, JP Morgan Chase provided a $1.2 million donation targeted specifically to Focus: HOPE's workforce development and education programs.

Sources: Based on "2014 Annual Report & Honor Roll of Donors" from *www.focushope.edu*, accessed April 9, 2015; D. Bennett, "Do the unemployed get a second act?" *Bloomberg Business Week* (September 19–25, 2011): 64–70; *www.focushope.edu*, the website for Focus: HOPE.

INTRODUCTION

Training and development should help companies achieve their business goals, resulting in profits and, for publicly traded companies, positive returns to stockholders. But stockholders represent only one of the parties (or stakeholders) that have an interest in a company's success. Other important stakeholders include the local community and employees who can also benefit from training and development. Companies have a social responsibility to help improve the communities where they are located by protecting the environment, supporting cultural activities, and helping reduce poverty and unemployment. For example, companies can develop partnerships with schools, community colleges, and universities to design programs that can increase the skills of the workforce. These partnerships benefit the company because they provide a source of skilled employees. They also contribute to the local community because they improve the skill level of the local labor market. This helps keep employers from moving to other locations in the United States and abroad to find the skills they need and can help attract new employers. This chapter's opening vignette highlights a federally funded program that helps the unemployed find jobs and provides companies with a source for skilled workers. Focus: HOPE is one example of a nontraditional source that companies are using as they struggle to find workers with skill sets needed for many jobs (recall the discussion in Chapter One, "Introduction to Employee Training and Development," of the mismatch between the skills available in the workforce and skills that companies need). The first section of this chapter discusses the different types of training partnerships that companies are participating in with schools, unions, and nonprofit organizations to provide them with skilled workers.

Social responsibility also means that companies need to comply with laws and regulations but perhaps more importantly, take actions and create conditions to help all employees grow, develop, and contribute to company goals, regardless of their background and career issues they are facing. The second section of the chapter discusses how laws and regulations influence training and development and how to ensure the talents and skills of a diverse workforce are best used. This includes managing diversity and inclusion, melting the glass ceiling that women face in trying to achieve higher-level management positions, and preparing employees to work in cross-cultural assignments. The final section of the chapter discusses specific career challenges that employees face and what employees can do to help them manage and cope with them. These challenges include balancing work and life, career breaks, coping with job loss, job hopping and recycling careers, and retirement.

Training Partnerships

Government agencies, trade groups, foundations, and companies are working with schools to develop employee skills and provide jobs. **Sector partnerships** refer to government agencies and industry trade groups that help identify the skills that local employers require and work with community colleges, universities, and other educational institutions to provide qualified employees. Sector partnerships can focus on jobs that require more than a high school diploma but less than a four-year college degree, and some provide skills that are needed for professional employees such as engineers. Through such partnerships, workforce skill needs can be met faster than if individual employers worked alone. Job Corps is a career and technical training program funded by Congress and administered by the U.S. Department of Labor.[1] Job Corps trains young people between the ages of 16 and 24 in academic, information technology, and vocational skills needed in jobs such as masonry, carpentry, and nursing. Education, training, and support services are provided to students at 125 Job Corps center campuses located throughout the United States and Puerto Rico and through private contractors. Troy Carter dreamed of becoming a music industry success and received his GED from a Job Corps center in Maryland. He became the CEO of Coalition Media Group, a Beverly Hills, California, artist management and digital marketing company that has worked with Sean "Diddy" Combs, Nelly, and Will Smith and include Lady Gaga among his clients.

Some programs are specifically directed at helping the hard-to-employ, such as low-income or homeless people or individuals with a criminal record, escape the poverty cycle through learning marketable skills and helping them get a job. For example, The Center for Energy Workforce Development (CEWD) received a grant of more than $1 million from the Bill and Melinda Gates Foundation to work with low-income young adults to help them find careers in the energy industry.[2] Youths will be placed in jobs in natural gas and electrical utilities, construction, and manufacturing. CEWD was formed to help utilities work together to develop solutions to the coming workforce shortage in the utility industry due to retirement or employees leaving the industry. One estimate is that over 40 percent of the U.S. workforce in energy will be eligible for retirement in the next five years. It is the first partnership between utilities, their associations, contractors, and unions to focus on the need to build a skilled workforce pipeline that will meet future industry needs.

The federal government created manufacturing institutes in Chicago and Detroit that are designed to stimulate advanced manufacturing and create jobs.[3] Alcoa is a member of the Detroit-based institute called the American Lightweight Materials Manufacturing Innovation Institute (LM3I). It includes sixty companies, nonprofit organizations, and universities. Alcoa hopes to benefit from the institute by gaining a better understanding of advanced manufacturing technologies and lightweight materials, forecast engineering and manufacturing talent needs, and get involved in programs to prepare new employees and enhance the skills of current employees. Michigan Technological Institute, an academic partner in LM3I, houses the Enterprise Program in which students and faculty work on company-sponsored projects. This helps the students develop skills and companies identify and connect with graduates who can be hired for hard-to-fill skilled manufacturing jobs.

Founded by CEO Gerald Chertavian, Year Up's mission is to create opportunities for low-income youth aged 18 to 24 by providing them with the skills, experience, and support that will help them to reach their potential through professional careers and higher education.[4] Year Up has locations across the United States, including Buffalo, Philadelphia, Boston, and San Francisco. Year Up has been recognized by various publications and groups as one of the best organizations for using business excellence to create social change. Year Up is an intensive one-year training and education program that admits students into the program who are motivated to achieve. Six months after they are admitted to the program, students complete skills training programs in areas with high demands for jobs, including information technology helpdesk/desktop support, financial operations, software quality assurance, or project management. Also, they are trained in important soft skills such as business communications and customer service skills. Then they are placed in a six-month internship in one of Youth Up's 250 diverse partner companies, including American Express, NASA, LinkedIn, and T-Mobile. They receive coaching, feedback, and guidance from advisors, mentors, and internship managers. The interns are screened using interviews, reference checks, and testing. Over 250 companies have employed one or more of Year Up's 8,500 alumni. In 2013, over 80 percent of Year Up alumni went on to find employment or pursue higher education within four months of graduation.

Federal legislation encourages partnerships between educational institutions, employers, and labor unions. The **School-to-Work Opportunities Act** is designed to assist the states in building school-to-work systems that prepare students for high-skill, high-wage jobs or future education. The act encourages partnerships between educational institutions, employers, and labor unions. The act requires that every school-to-work system include work-based learning, school-based learning, and connecting activities that match students with employers and bring classrooms and workplaces together. Wisconsin has one of the most fully developed school-to-work programs. Apprenticeships are offered in thirteen fields ranging from tourism to engineering. Committees of employers and educators developed the skill sets to be covered and identified appropriate classroom and work experiences. For example, the Wisconsin Health Science Youth Apprenticeship Program focuses on different paths in health sciences, including therapeutic services (dental, nursing, medical assistant), informatics (patient data management), and ambulatory/support services (dietary, laboratory, optometry).[5] The program provides high school juniors or seniors with skills and knowledge needed for these careers through integrating classroom and on-the-job learning.

The **Workforce Innovation and Opportunity Act (WIOA)** signed into law by President Obama in 2014 is designed to help job seekers access employment, education, training, and support services to succeed in the labor market and to match employers with the skilled workers.[6] WIOA is an amendment and reauthorization of the Workforce Investment Act of 1998. WIOA received bipartisan support in Congress and is the first legislative reform in 15 years of the public workforce system. WIOA streamlines workforce development systems by eliminating existing programs, it established a common set of metrics for evaluating remaining programs, it provides states with the flexibility to direct funds to develop skills needed in their region and workforce, and it supports access to on-the-job training and development opportunities. Also, it ensures that individuals with disabilities have the necessary skills to be successful in employment and it improves outreach to out-of-school youth and high school dropouts. The cornerstone of the system is One-Stop service delivery, which unifies numerous training, education, and employment programs into a single, customer-friendly system in each community. The underlying notion of One-Stop is the coordination of programs, services, and governance structures so that customers have access to a seamless system of workforce investment services. It is envisioned that a variety of programs could use One-Stop's common intake, case management, and job development services in order to take full advantage of One-Stop's potential for efficiency and effectiveness. A wide range of services, including training and employment programs, are available to meet the needs of employers and job seekers. The challenge in helping One-Stop live up to its potential is to make sure that the state and local boards can effectively coordinate and collaborate with the network of other service agencies, including Temporary Assistance for Needy Families (TANF) agencies, transportation agencies and providers, metropolitan planning organizations, child care agencies, nonprofit and community partners, and the broad range of partners who work with youth.

O*NET, the Occupational Information Network, is a unique, comprehensive database and directory of occupational titles, worker competencies, and job requirements and resources.[7] O*NET, which supports One-Stop service delivery, is the primary source of occupational information in the United States. The O*NET database includes information on skills, abilities, knowledge, work activities, and interests associated with occupations. O*NET information can be used to facilitate career exploration, vocational counseling, and a variety of human resource (HR) functions, such as developing job orders, creating position descriptions, and aligning training with current workplace needs. Job seekers can use O*NET to find out which jobs fit with their interests, skills, and experience and to identify the skills, knowledge, and abilities needed for their dream job.

Joint Union-Management Programs

The initial goal of these programs was to help displaced employees find new jobs by providing skill training and outplacement assistance. Currently, **joint union-management training programs** provide a wide range of services designed to help employees learn skills that are directly related to their jobs and also develop skills that are "portable"—that is, valuable to employers in other companies or industries.[8] Both employers and unions contribute money to run the programs, and both oversee their operation. The National Coalition for Telecommunications Education and Learning (NACTEL) is a partnership between telecommunications companies, including AT&T, Century Link, Frontier, and Verizon, and labor unions, including the Communication Workers of America (CWA) and International Brotherhood of Electrical Workers (IBEW), that has developed online education programs.[9] NACTEL includes courses that allow employees to work toward associate degrees (e.g., in telecommunications) and certificate programs (e.g., Introduction to Telecommunications). The NACTEL programs are offered by Pace University's School of Computer Science and Information Systems.

Chrysler implemented the World Class Manufacturing (WCM) process, designed to improve quality, reduce costs, and empower employees. The process saved Fiat from going out of business by improving the quality of its cars and making production more efficient.[10] Chrysler worked with the United Auto Workers (UAW) to renovate its training center in Warren, Michigan, and introduce technology-based training methods to teach problem-solving skills that employees use in their plant jobs. Chrysler wants to have more than 1,200 hourly and salaried employees attend the WCM Academy each year to create a culture of continuous improvement and learning. The UAW was initially resistant to supporting WCM but is now supportive because of the high level of employee involvement. The UAW labor agreement provides a $500 annual bonus, which can increase to $1,000 for each employee if a plant reaches WCM goals. Also, UAW members understand that WCM and the Academy are important for driving changes needed in the plants to maintain Chrysler's competitiveness and keep manufacturing jobs.

Unlike previous training, only 30 percent will involve classroom instruction. A total of 70 percent of the training at the Academy involves hand-on training activities, including high-tech simulations and games designed to focus on the specific needs of manufacturing facilities. For example, at a simulated work station, employees put on a special suit containing motion detectors. While employees work at the station, the system identifies stressful actions and provides diagnostic feedback designed to help them use more safe and efficient motions. Three-dimensional goggles allow employees to become immersed in a plant full of unsafe behaviors and working conditions. Employees watch videos emphasizing unsafe conditions and identify potential risks and solutions within the three-dimensional plant environment. Workers train on a simulated door line that helps them learn how to create kits that reduce inventory and materials handling. After spending two days at the Academy, workers return to their plants to work with a trainer on applying what they have learned. Workers return to the Academy at a later time to share best practices and how they have applied what they have learned to project assignments. This enables workers to share their knowledge and expertise and provides ideas for trainers about how to improve the Academy experience.

LEGAL ISSUES AND MANAGING A DIVERSE WORKFORCE AT HOME AND ABROAD

Legal Issues

Table 10.1 shows potential training activities and situations that can make an employer vulnerable to legal actions and harm the company's reputation. The following sections describe each situation and potential implications for training.[11]

Failing to Provide Training or Providing Inadequate Training

To comply with a wide range of laws and regulations, companies are required to show that employees not only have completed training programs, but also are applying their new knowledge on the job. Most companies provide training to reduce the potential for a hostile work environment for employees protected by Title VII of the Civil Rights Act (covering race, color, gender, religion, nationality, and national origin), the Age Discrimination in Employment Act (ADEA; covering age), or the Americans with Disabilities Act (ADA; covering disability).[12] For example, the U.S. Supreme Court considers sexual harassment training to be an important factor for companies that wish to avoid punitive damages in

TABLE 10.1
Situations That May Result in Legal Action

- Failing to provide required training or providing inadequate training
- Incurring employee injury during a training activity
- Incurring injuries to employees or others outside the training session
- Breach of confidentiality or defamation
- Reproducing and using copyrighted material in training classes without permission
- Excluding women, minorities, and older Americans from training programs
- Failing to ensure equal treatment while in training
- Requiring employees to attend training programs that they may find offensive
- Revealing discriminatory information during a training session
- Not accommodating trainees with disabilities
- Incorrectly reporting training as an expense, or failing to report training reimbursement as income

sexual harassment cases. Employers must also train employees to comply with practices designed to prevent harassment of any class protected by Title VII.

Federal laws may require a certain number of training hours and types of training for employees in certain industries. For example, initial training for flight attendants must include how to handle passengers, use galley equipment, evacuate the airplane, and use the public address system. The safe landing of U.S. Airways Flight 1549 on the Hudson River in 2009 was one of the rare moments when a U.S. passenger plane completed a forced landing without loss of life of passengers or crew. As a result, the Federal Aviation Administration (FAA) implemented new training regulations and rules for airlines, calling for hands-on drills on the use of emergency equipment and procedures for all flight attendants.[13]

The FAA has also introduced training standards requiring scenario-based simulations to help pilots operate today's new aircraft, which have integrated systems, greater speed, range, and altitude, and new multifunctional flight displays.[14]

Companies in health care are required to comply with the Health Insurance Portability and Accountability Act (HIPAA); companies in finance are required to comply with the Bank Secrecy Act; and companies in the gaming industry (such as casinos) are required to train employees on how to handle money and report suspicious activity.[15] The increase in the number of incidents in the United States in which the use of force by police officers has been questioned has resulted increased scrutiny of their training. For example, a murder charge brought against a police officer in the shooting of a fleeing man has resulted in examining whether the twelve weeks of basic training for officers is long enough and whether enough attention is given to when and how to use force and deal with the public.[16] Legislation can also require training that is related to providing a drug-free workplace (e.g., training about drug abuse and making counseling available) and a safe workplace (e.g., training about the handling of hazardous materials and the use of safety equipment as dictated by the Occupational Safety and Health Act/OSHA).

Incurring Employee Injury During a Training Activity

OJT and simulations often involve the use of work tools and equipment (e.g., welding machinery, printing press) that could cause injury if incorrectly used. Workers' compensation laws in many states make employers responsible for paying employees their salary and/or providing them with a financial settlement for injuries received during any employment-related activity such as training. Managers should ensure that (1) employees are warned of potential dangers from incorrectly using equipment and (2) safety equipment is used.

Incurring Injuries to Employees or Others Outside a Training Session

Managers should ensure that trainees have the necessary level of competence in knowledge, skills, and behaviors before they are allowed to operate equipment or interact with customers. Even if a company pays for training to be conducted by a vendor, it is still liable for injuries or damages resulting from the actions of poorly, incorrectly, or incompletely trained employees. A company that contracts out training to a vendor or consultant should ensure that the vendor has liability insurance, be sure that the trainers are competent, and determine if there has been previous litigation against the trainer or the vendor providing the training. Also, trainers should be sure to keep copies of notes, activities, and training manuals that show that training procedures were correct and followed the steps provided by licensing or certification agencies (if appropriate).

Incurring Breach of Confidentiality or Defamation

Managers should ensure that information placed in employees' files regarding performance in training activities is accurate. Also, before discussing an employee's performance in training with other employees or using training performance information for promotion or salary decisions, managers should tell employees that training performance will be used in that manner.

Reproducing and Using Copyrighted Material in Training Classes Without Permission

Copyrights protect the expression of an idea (e.g., a training manual for a software program) but not the ideas that the material contains (e.g., the use of help windows in the software program).[17] Copyrights also prohibit others from creating a product based on the original work and from copying, broadcasting, or publishing the product without permission.

The use of videotapes, learning aids, manuals, and other copyrighted materials in training classes without obtaining permission from the owner of the material is illegal. Managers should ensure that all training materials are purchased from the vendor or consultant who developed them, or that permission to reproduce materials has been obtained. Material on Internet sites is not necessarily free from copyright law.[18] Many websites and published material are governed by the fair use doctrine, which means that you can use small amounts of copyrighted material without asking permission or paying a fee so long as the use meets four standards. The standards relate to (1) the purpose for which the copyrighted materials are being used, (2) what the copyrighted work is, (3) the proportion of the copyrighted material you are using, and (4) how much money the copyright owner can lose as a result of the use. Republishing or repackaging under your own name material that you took from the Internet can be a violation of copyright law. For example, Crisp Learning, a small training company, frequently finds itself in court defending copyright issues. Crisp Learning develops and sells video and training courses that deal with skills such as business report writing and time management. The series of courses, known as the Fifty-Minute series, is popular because it is easily applied and can be completed in a short period of time. Crisp Learning has found that copyright violators have actually retyped its books and sold them as their own work.

Violating copyright can be expensive. Copyright violators can end up paying expensive legal fees and paying damages that are more expensive than what it would have cost to legally purchase the training materials. To obtain copyright permission, you need to directly contact the owners of the material and explain how the material will be used and how ownership will be cited. Another way to get copyright permission is to seek permission from organizations such as the Copyright Clearance Center (*www.copyright.com*) or iCopyright.com.

Excluding Women, Minorities, and Older Employees from Training Programs

Two pieces of legislation make it illegal for employers to exclude women, minorities, or older persons from training programs. **Title VII of the Civil Rights Act** (amended in 1991) makes it illegal to deny access to employment or deprive a person employment because of the person's race, color, religion, gender, or national origin. The **Age Discrimination in Employment Act (ADEA)** prohibits discrimination against persons who are aged 40 or older. The **Equal Employment Opportunity Commission (EEOC)** is responsible for enforcing both the Civil Rights Act and the ADEA.

Although these two pieces of legislation have existed for several years, a study by the U.S. Department of Labor found that training experiences necessary for promotion are not as available or accessible to women and minorities as they are to white males.[19] Women, minorities, and older employees sometimes are illegally excluded from training programs, either by not being made aware of opportunities for training or by purposeful exclusion from enrollment in training programs. Denial of training opportunities and better treatment of younger employees can be used to support claims of age discrimination.[20] Older employees may bring lawsuits against companies based on a denied promotion or discharge. As evidence for age discrimination, the courts will investigate whether older workers were denied training opportunities that were provided to younger workers. To avoid age discrimination in training, managers and trainers need to ensure that the organization's culture and policies are age-neutral. Decisions about training and development opportunities should not be made on the basis of stereotypes about older workers and should take into account job-relevant factors such as performance. Managers should be held accountable for fair training and development practices and for ensuring that all employees have development plans. Finally, all employees should receive training on the ADEA and on how age stereotypes can affect treatment of older employees. Stereotypes such as "Older workers are resistant to change" may result in exclusion of older workers from training and development programs.

The University of Phoenix had to pay over $1 million for demonstrating a religious bias against non-Mormon employees who worked as enrollment counselors in the university's Online Division.[21] The religious bias occurred when tuition waivers for non-Mormon employees were denied for failing to meet student registration goals, yet waivers were provided to Mormon employees who failed to meet the same goals.

New Prime, Inc., a large trucking company, violated federal law by discriminating against female truck driver job applicants when it required that they be trained only by female trainers.[22] Training was provided for male job applicants with no delay, but female job applicants were put on a waiting list, resulting in delaying or denying them jobs.

Not Ensuring Equal Treatment of All Employees While in Training

Equal treatment of all trainees means that conditions of the learning environment, such as opportunities for practice, feedback, and role-playing, are available for all trainees regardless of their background. It also means that all trainees are given similar physical and financial resources necessary to be successful. Also, trainers should avoid jokes, stories, and props that might create a hostile learning environment. For example, because of claims that female employees were being harassed at air traffic control centers, the FAA required employees to attend diversity training where male employees were made to experience what it felt like to be taunted and jeered at as they walked down the aisle in an air traffic control facility (known as "walking the gauntlet"). One of the male employees found the experience to be distasteful and psychologically stressful, sued the FAA, and won.

Merrill Lynch was sued by an African American broker for race discrimination.[23] Only 2 percent of its financial advisors were African Americans and were less likely than white brokers to be top producers. The case was settled for $160 million, which was distributed to 1,400 black brokers. Although Merrill ran several programs designed to help black brokers succeed by bringing in clients, black brokers were less likely to be asked to join teams, which limited their sales. Also, the average account asset transferred to them as trainees for their first twenty-eight months of employment was significantly less compared to white brokers.

Requiring Employees to Attend Programs That Might Be Offensive

Allstate Insurance has been the focus of several religious discrimination lawsuits brought by insurance agents. Some agents charged that the principles emphasized in training programs were based on Scientology and were offensive and counter to their religious beliefs. For example, the training program taught concepts such as the "tone scale" which catalogs emotions and Scientologists believe can influence behavior.[24]

Revealing Discriminatory Information During a Training Session

At Lucky Store Foods, a California supermarket chain, notes taken during a diversity training program were used as evidence of discrimination.[25] In the training session, supervisors were asked to verbalize their stereotypes. Some comments ("Women cry more," "Black women are aggressive") were derogatory toward women and minorities. The plaintiff in the case used the notes as evidence that the company conducted the training session. To avoid an investigation by the EEOC, the case was settled out of court.

Not Accommodating Trainees with Disabilities

The **Americans with Disabilities Act (ADA)** prohibits individuals with disabilities from being discriminated against in the workplace. The ADA prohibits discrimination based on disability in employment practices, including hiring, firing, compensation, and training. The ADA defines a disability as a physical or mental impairment that substantially limits one or more major life activities, a record of having an impairment, or being regarded as having such an impairment. This includes serious disabilities such as epilepsy, blindness, or paralysis, as well as persons who have a history of heart disease, mental illness, or cancer that is currently in remission.

The ADA requires companies to make "reasonable accommodation" to the physical or mental condition of a person with a disability who is otherwise qualified, unless doing so would impose an "undue hardship" on the organization's operations. Determination of undue hardship is made by analyzing the type and cost of the accommodation in relation to the company's financial resources. Even if the undue hardship can be justified, the ADA requires that the person with the disability be provided the option of paying the part of the cost that causes the undue hardship.

In the context of training, **reasonable accommodation** refers to making training facilities readily accessible to and usable by individuals with disabilities. Reasonable accommodation may also include modifying instructional media, adjusting training policies, and providing trainees with readers or interpreters. Employers are not required to make reasonable accommodation if the person does not request them. Employers are also not required to make reasonable accommodation if persons are not qualified to participate in training programs (e.g., they lack the prerequisite certification or educational requirements).

One example of how the ADA might influence training activities involves adventure learning. Some adventure learning experiences demand a high level of physical fitness. Employees who have a disability cannot be required to attend adventure learning training programs.[26] If it does not cause an undue hardship, employees should be offered an alternative program for developing the learned capabilities emphasized in the adventure learning program.

It is impossible to give specific guidelines regarding the type of accommodations that trainers and managers should make to avoid violating the ADA. It is important to identify if the training is related to "essential" job functions. That is, are the tasks or knowledge, skills, and abilities that are the focus of training fundamental to the position? Task analysis information (discussed in Chapter Three, "Needs Assessment") can be used to identify essential job functions. For example, tasks that are frequently performed and critical for successful job performance would be considered essential job functions. If training relates to a function that may be performed in the job but does not have to be performed by all persons (a marginal job function), then a disability in relation to that function cannot be used to exclude that person from training. To the extent that the disability makes it difficult for the person to receive the training necessary to complete essential job functions, the trainer must explore whether it is possible to make reasonable accommodations.

Incorrectly Reporting Training as an Expense Failing to Report Training Reimbursement as Income, or Failing to Pay Employees for Attending Training

The cost of training is covered by the Internal Revenue Code. Companies can often deduct the cost of training provided to employees as a business expense. The Employer Assistance Program, part of the IRS Code, allows an employer to pay an employee up to $5,250 per year for certain educational expenses. This amount can be deducted by the employer as a business expense without adding the payment to the employee's yearly gross income. In other programs (e.g., the Educational Reimbursement Program), the employer can decide which training is paid for and how it is funded. Reimbursement for training expenses that an employee incurs may be considered part of the employee's taxable income. Employees may be able to deduct work-related educational expenses as itemized deductions on their income taxes. To be deductible, the expenses must be for training that maintains or improves skills required in the job or that serves a business purpose of the company and is required by the company, or by law or regulations, in order for employees to keep their present salary, status, or job. See *www.irs.gov* for more information about business and individual reporting of educational expenses.

The Fair Labor Standards Act requires employees to receive compensation for all hours worked. However, it is unclear whether the time employees spend at training programs whether they use online or face-to-face methods are considered as hours worked. The time that employees spend in training should be considered working time, which means they should be paid unless four conditions are met.[27] The conditions are training is outside of the employee's regular working hours, training is voluntary, the training is not directly related to the employee's job, and the employee does not perform any productive work during training.

Managing Workforce Diversity and Inclusion

Diversity can be considered any dimension that differentiates a person from another.[28] For example, at Verizon, diversity means embracing differences and variety, including age, ethnicity, education, sexual orientation, work style, race, gender, and more. **Inclusion** refers to creating an environment in which employees share a sense of belonging, mutual respect, and commitment from others so they can perform their best work.[29] Inclusion allows companies to capitalizing not only on the diversity of employees but also customers, suppliers, and community partners.

Diversity training refers to learning efforts that are designed to change employee attitudes about diversity and/or develop skills needed to work with a diverse workforce. The goals of diversity training are (1) to eliminate values, stereotypes, and managerial practices that inhibit employees' personal development; and therefore (2) to allow employees to contribute to organizational goals regardless of their race, sexual orientation, gender, family status, religious orientation, or cultural background.[30] Equal Employment Opportunity (EEO) laws help ensure that women and minorities are adequately represented in a company's labor force. That is, companies have focused on ensuring equal access to jobs. However, diversity training and a focus on EEO laws are insufficient for a company to truly capitalize on the value of a diverse workforce. They are one part of a larger emphasis on managing diversity and inclusion.

Research shows that diversity training has a small to medium effect on affective (attitudes), cognitive (acquiring knowledge), and behavioral outcomes.[31] Greater benefits were found for diversity training using training design features that created a positive learning environment. That is, the training program was sufficient length for trainees to learn (four hours or more), managers were used as trainers, and trainees interacted face to face with the instructor, the content, and other learners using cases and exercises. The most common area addressed through diversity training is the pervasiveness of stereotypes, assumptions, and biases.[32] For example, BAE Systems requires that middle managers and executives take a two-hour class on unconscious bias.[33] Unconscious bias means that based on their background and experiences managers might unintentionally make employment decisions that give preference to individuals with certain characteristics such as the color of their skin, age, body type, or personality. Trainees watch videos, participate in exercises, and discuss research to help them understand why unconscious bias occurs and how to overcome it.

Managing diversity and inclusion involves creating an environment that allows all employees to contribute to organizational goals and experience personal growth. This environment includes access to jobs, as well as fair and positive treatment of all employees. The company must develop employees who are comfortable working with people from a wide variety of ethnic, racial, and religious backgrounds. Managing diversity may require changing the company culture. It includes the company's standards and norms about how employees are treated, competitiveness, results orientation, innovation, and risk taking. The value placed on diversity is grounded in the company culture.

Managing diversity and inclusion can provide companies with a competitive advantage in several different ways. It helps a company develop a reputation as a favorable employer, which attracts talent, women and minority employees. Women and minority employees will feel valued and free to contribute their insights, which can help develop new products and improve marketing efforts focused on specific consumer segments such as Hispanics.

For example, in addition to training managers to reduce their unconscious bias, BAE Systems also takes steps to manage diversity and inclusion.[34] One step was that BAE changed the composition of the interview panels used to hire middle managers. The interview panels now include women and people of color as well as white males. As a result, the number of women and people of color in managers' roles increased about 10 percent.

Diversity may enhance performance when organizations have an environment that promotes learning from diversity.[35] There is no evidence to support the direct relationship between diversity and business.[36] Rather, a company will see the success of its diversity efforts only if it makes a long-term commitment to managing diversity and has a zero tolerance policy toward discrimination. Successful diversity requires that it be viewed as an opportunity for all employees to (1) learn from each other how to better accomplish their work, (2) be provided with a supportive and cooperative organizational culture, and (3) be taught leadership and process skills that can facilitate effective team functioning. Diversity is a reality in labor and customer markets and is a social expectation and value. Managers should focus on building an organizational environment, on HR practices, and on managerial and team skills that all capitalize on diversity. As you will see in the discussion that follows, managing diversity requires difficult cultural change, not just slogans on the wall.

Table 10.2 shows the characteristics associated with the long-term success of diversity programs. It is critical that a diversity program be tied to business objectives. Measuring the effectiveness of managing diversity helps ensure that it is treated as important as other business outcomes such as productivity or customer satisfaction. Diversity and inclusion goals are included in managers' performance objectives and they are expected to be actively involved in promoting diversity. For example, when asked why advancing diversity in his company was important to him, the CEO of Merisant emphasized that employees with different lifestyles and backgrounds challenge each other and create disagreement, which is necessary for business innovations and creativity.[37] Bank of America includes questions about diversity and inclusiveness on its employee engagement survey. They use these results to understand if employees feel they are treated fairly. AT&T senior executives have regular meetings to discuss diversity objectives and part of their compensation is based on meeting those objectives. Top management support can be demonstrated by creating a structure to support the initiative.

Consider Sodexo's diversity effort.[38] Sodexo is the leading food and facilities management company in the United States, Canada, and Mexico, daily serving 10 million customers. With employees in 80 countries representing 128 nationalities connecting with customers on a daily basis, a policy of inclusion is not an option or a choice—it is a business

TABLE 10.2   Characteristics Associated with Diversity Programs' Long-Term Success

- Top management provides resources, personally intervenes, and publicly advocates diversity.
- The program is structured.
- Capitalizing on a diverse workforce is defined as a business objective.
- Capitalizing on a diverse workforce is seen as necessary to generate revenue and profits.
- The program is evaluated using metrics such as sales, retention, and promotion rates.
- Manager involvement is mandatory.
- The program is seen as a culture change, not a one-shot program.
- Managers and demographic groups are not blamed for problems.
- Behaviors and skills needed to successfully interact with others are taught.
- Managers are rewarded on progress toward meeting diversity goals.
- Management collects employee feedback and responds to it.
- Create a safe and open culture that all employees want to belong to, in which employees can discover and appreciate differences and where the benefits of diversity are recognized by all employees.

Sources: B. Groysberg and K. Connolly, "Great leaders who make the mix work," *Harvard Business Review* (September 2013): 68–76; K. Bezrvkova, K. Jehn, and C. Spell, "Reviewing diversity training: Where we have been and where we should go," *Academy of Management Learning and Education* 11 (2012): 207–227; S. Rynes and B. Rosen, "A field survey of factors affecting the adoption and perceived success of diversity training," *Personnel Psychology* 48 (1995): 247–270; R. Anand and M. Winters, "A retrospective view of corporate diversity training from 1964 to the present," *Academy of Management Learning and Education* 7 (2008): 356–372; C. Chavez and J. Weisinger, "Beyond diversity training: A social infusion for cultural inclusion," *Human Resource Management* 47 (2008): 331–350.

necessity. Sodexo is focused on gender representation, generational opportunities in the workplace, people with disabilities, and ethnic minority representation. As a result, diversity and inclusion are core elements of the business strategy. Sodexo believes that diversity and inclusion is a fundamental business objective focused on employees (e.g., work culture, recruitment, talent development, work-life effectiveness), customers, clients, and shareholders (e.g., supplier diversity, cross-market diversity council, diversity consulting), and communities (e.g., Sodexo Foundation and Community Partners). For example, some of the objectives include understanding and living the business case for diversity and inclusion; increasing awareness of how diversity relates to business challenges; creating and fostering a diverse work environment by developing management practices that drive hiring, promotion, and retention of talent; engaging in relationship management and customer service to attract and retain diverse clients and customers; and partnering with women and minority businesses to deliver food and facility management services. Diversity and inclusion are core competencies at Sodexo. Diversity and inclusion are part of employees' training and managers' annual performance review; new employee orientation emphasizes Sodexo's values and expectations regarding diversity and inclusion.

Sodexo separates Equal Employment Opportunity (EEO) and legal compliance training from diversity training. At Sodexo, diversity training is part of the managing diversity strategy. Every three years, employees are required to take EEO and affirmative action refresher courses. Top management is also involved in and committed to managing diversity. The senior executives program includes ongoing classroom training that is reinforced with community involvement, sponsoring employee groups, and mentoring diverse employees. Executives are engaged in learning the business case for diversity and are personally held accountable for the company's diversity agenda. Every manager takes an eight-hour introductory class (called Spirit of Diversity). Sodexo's diversity training involves learning labs focused on skill building and diversity awareness. Examples of these learning labs include Generations in the Workplace, Disability Awareness Training, Cross-Cultural Communications, and Improving Team Effectiveness Through Inclusion. The company's learning and development team develops customized learning solutions for different functions and work teams. For example, a course related to selling to a diverse client base was developed and offered to the sales force, and a cross-cultural communications program was provided for recruiters.

In addition to diversity training activities, Sodexo has many employee network groups—such as the African American Leadership Forum, People Respecting Individuality, Diversity, and Equality (PRIDE), Honoring Our Nation's finest with Opportunity and Respect (HONOR), and the Intergenerational Network Group (IGEN). These network groups provide forums for helping employees feel a sense of community, learn from each other, develop their careers, and share input and ideas to support the companys' diversity efforts. Sodexo's "Champions of Diversity" program rewards and recognizes employees who advance diversity and inclusion.

To emphasize the importance of diversity for the company, at Sodexo, each manager has a diversity scorecard that evaluates his or her success in recruitment, retention, promotion, and development of all employees. The scorecard includes both quantitative goals and evaluation of behaviors such as participating in training, mentoring, and doing community outreach. A proportion of their pay bonuses is determined by success in these areas.

Sodexo has found that its diversity training and efforts to manage diversity are having a positive impact on business results. Its mentoring program has led to increased productivity, engagement, and retention of women and people of color. There was an estimated ROI of $19 for every dollar spent on the program. Sodexo also has been awarded several new business contracts and retained clients because of its involvement in managing diversity. Sodexo has also been recognized for its diversity and inclusion efforts, which help attract talented employees by signaling that the company cares about the well-being of all of its employees. Sodexo was ranked number 5 on the 2015 Diversity Inc Top 50 Companies for Diversity list. This marks the tenth consecutive year that the company has been recognized by Diversity Inc for the success of its diversity efforts. Sodexo is also recognized as a top company for executive women and ranked among the top ten companies for Latinos, blacks, global diversity, and people with disabilities. Most effective programs to manage diversity, such as Sodexo's diversity program, include the key components shown in Table 10.3.

As should be apparent from this discussion, successful diversity programs involve more than just an effective training program. They require an ongoing process of culture change that includes top management support, as well as diversity policies and practices in the areas of recruitment and hiring, training and development, and administrative structures, such as conducting diversity surveys and evaluating managers' progress on diversity goals.[39] They also focus on enhancing diversity and inclusion with suppliers, vendors, and in the communities where the company conducts business. One way that top management is supporting the management of diversity and reinforcing its importance for the business is by creating Chief Diversity Officer executive positions. ABB North America recently created a chief diversity and inclusion officer position reporting directly to the CEO.[40] This sends a message that diversity is supported and creates a position responsible for managing diversity and inclusion and establishing metrics to track progress.

TABLE 10.3   Key Components of Effective Managing Diversity Programs

Top Management Support
- Make the business case for diversity.
- Include diversity as part of the business strategy and corporate goals.
- Participate in diversity programs, and encourage all managers to attend.
- Ensure that the composition of the executive management team mirrors the diversity of the workforce.

Recruitment and Hiring
- Ask search firms to identify wider arrays of candidates.
- Enhance the interviewing, selection, and hiring skills of managers.
- Expand college recruitment at historically minority colleges.

Identifying and Developing Talent
- Form a partnership with internship programs that target minority students for management careers.
- Establish a mentoring process.
- Refine the company's global succession planning system to improve identification of talent.
- Improve the selection and development of managers and leaders to help ensure that they are capable of maximizing team performance.
- Ensure that all employees, especially women and minorities, have access to management development and leadership programs.

Employee Support
- Form resource groups or employee network groups, including employees with common interests, and use them to help the company develop business goals and understand the issues they are concerned with (e.g., Asian Pacific employees, women, gays, lesbians, transgenders, Native Americans, veterans, Hispanics).
- Celebrate cultural traditions, festivities, and holidays.
- Make work-life balance initiatives (such as flextime, telecommuting, elder care) available to all employees.

Ensuring Fair Treatment
- Conduct extensive diversity training.
- Implement an alternative dispute resolution process.
- Include women and minorities on all human resources committees throughout the company.

Holding Managers Accountable
- Link managers' compensation to their success in meeting diversity goals and creating openness and inclusion in the workplace.
- Use employee attitude or engagement surveys to track employees' attitudes about such things as inclusion, fairness, opportunities for development, work-life balance, and perceptions of the company culture.
- Implement 360-degree feedback for all managers and supervisors.

Improving Relationships with External Stakeholders
- Increase marketing to diverse communities.
- Provide customer service in different languages.
- Broaden the company's base of suppliers and vendors to include businesses owned by minorities and women.
- Provide scholarships and educational and neighborhood grants to diverse communities and their members.

Sources: Based on B. Groysberg and K. Connolly, "Great leaders who make the mix work," *Harvard Business Review* (September 2013): 68–76; R. Anand and M. Winters, "A retrospective view of corporate diversity training from 1964 to the present," *Academy of Management Learning and Education* 7 (2008): 356–372; C. Chavez and J. Weisinger, "Beyond diversity training: A social infusion for cultural inclusion," *Human Resource Management* 47 (2008): 331–350; "Diversity & Inclusion." Verizon's diversity program available at the company website, *www.verizon.com*, accessed April 13, 2015.

Melting the Glass Ceiling

A major development issue facing companies today is how to get women and minorities into upper-level management positions—how to break the glass ceiling. The **glass ceiling** refers to a barrier to advancement to higher-level jobs in the company that adversely affects women and minorities. Surveys show that in Fortune 500 companies, women represent less than 4 percent of CEOs and approximately 18 percent of executive officers.[41] Two-thirds of these companies lack specific programs targeted at the needs of women leaders, and 23 percent offer some activities or programs targeted to the needs of women. These activities include flexible scheduling, diversity recruiting, and coaching and mentoring. One of the dilemmas is that companies may be reluctant to treat women any differently than men from a leadership development perspective despite acknowledging that women lack executive sponsors or mentors, have insufficient experience, and need better work-life balance. This barrier may be due to stereotypes or company systems that adversely affect the development of women or minorities.[42] The glass ceiling is likely caused by lack of access to training programs, appropriate developmental job experiences, and developmental relationships (such as mentoring).[43] For example, Mary Barra made history when she became the first woman chief executive officer of General Motors, a global carmaker.[44] Prior to becoming CEO, Barra was in a product development job, an operational job critical to the company's success. But 55 percent of women are in functional roles such as lawyers, chief of finance, or human resources, which may not put them in the career path needed to become a CEO. Women and minorities often have trouble finding mentors because of their lack of access to the "old-boy network," managers' preference to interact with other managers of similar status rather than with line employees, and intentional exclusion by managers who have negative stereotypes about women's and minorities' abilities, motivation, and job preferences.[45] Research has found no gender differences in access to job experiences involving transitions or creating change.[46] However, male managers receive significantly more assignments involving high levels of responsibility (high stakes, managing business diversity, handling external pressure, etc.) than female managers of similar ability and managerial level. Also, female managers report experiencing more challenges due to lack of personal support (which makes it more difficult to cope with stress) and appreciation for their contributions than male managers. Career encouragement from peers and senior managers does help women advance to higher management levels.[47] Managers making developmental assignments need to carefully consider whether gender biases or stereotypes are influencing the types of assignments given to women versus men.

AstraZeneca, a biopharmaceutical company, helps develop women leaders through providing workshops, formal mentoring programs, and leadership courses. In its commercial operations an eighteen-month development program is available for mid-level employees. Fifty percent of those enrolled in the development program are female.[48] Johnson & Johnson (J&J) has more than doubled women at the corporate executive level to 33 percent and seen a 29 percent increase in the number of women senior managers. J&J has taken steps to get women into important positions they need to grow and develop to meet their career goals and to position them for top management and executive positions.[49] J&J is willing to take risks on employees wanting to develop skills and their careers through providing stretch assignments, mentoring, and coaching. For example, early in her career

TABLE 10.4 Recommendations for Melting the Glass Ceiling

Source: Based on B. Groysberg and K. Connolly, "Great leaders who make the mix work," *Harvard Business Review* (September 2013): 68–76; D. McCracken, "Winning the talent war for women," *Harvard Business Review* (November–December 2000): 159–167.

Make sure senior management supports and is involved in the program.
Make a business case for change.
Make the change public.
Gather data on problems that cause the glass ceiling using task forces, focus groups, and questionnaires.
Create awareness of how gender attitudes affect the work environment.
Force accountability through reviews of promotion rates and assignment decisions through stretch assignments, mentoring, and networking.
Promote development for all employees.
Support work-life balance and continue to offer employees development opportunities after they return from sabbaticals and parental leave.

a woman who is now a vice president at J&J was sent to Switzerland as part of a team to launch a new business. She also spent nine years working in manufacturing, supply chain, and planning before switching to marketing based on the support of J&J's vice president for marketing who had recognized her skills and potential. J&J also supports women's career progress by allowing them to turn down an opportunity for a leadership position, promotion, or other opportunity if other priorities, such as family, are more important at that point in time in their career. Women are not seen as disinterested in their career as a result of turning down such opportunities but are considered again when they are available. The Economical Insurance Group (TEIG), one of the largest property and casualty insurance groups in Canada, women's leadership development program includes an instructor-led workshop focusing on the fundamentals of achievement, leadership, and legacy specific to women in the company.[50] Following the workshop, female leaders are invited to participate in the TEIG Women's Leadership Network, held quarterly. The network meetings use the company's virtual classroom to discuss business ideas and challenges unique to women and to share leadership experiences. Table 10.4 provides recommendations for melting the glass ceiling and helping retain talented women.

CROSS-CULTURAL PREPARATION

As we mentioned in Chapter One, companies today are challenged to expand globally. Because of the increase in global operations, employees often work outside their country of origin or work with employees from other countries. An **expatriate** works in a country other than his or her country of origin. The most frequently selected locations for expatriate assignments include the United States, China, Africa, and India. At Ernst & Young, about 2,600 of over 167,000 employees are on an international assignment at any one time, including 270 Americans in thirty countries including Brazil, China, India, Russia, and South Africa.[51] Many U.S. companies are using expatriate assignments as a training tool. For example, employees who want top management positions, such as chief financial officer, need to understand how cultural norms and the political environment influence the movements in currencies and commodities in order to build effective global financial plans.[52] Guardian Industries, a glass manufacturer in Michigan, has expats in eighteen different countries.[53] Guardian's expat retention rate is close to 90 percent, which is likely due to how it treats the expats during and after their assignments. Guardian values expat experience by looking at these employees first when considering who to fill open positions. While on their assignments, Guardian stays in contact with the expats. Expat assignments can be of varying lengths depending on business needs. One former expat spent thirteen years in Saudi Arabia and Thailand, moving from department head to plant manager. The expat and his family asked to return to the United States, but the company had no plant manager openings. The expat was willing to take a lower-level position to learn things he didn't yet know about the business. When a plant manager position became available, it was offered to him.

Cross-cultural preparation educates employees (expatriates) and their families who are to be sent to a foreign country. To successfully conduct business in the global marketplace, employees must understand the business practices and the cultural norms of different countries.

Steps in Cross-Cultural Preparation

To prepare employees for cross-cultural assignments, companies need to provide cross-cultural preparation. Most U.S. companies send employees overseas without any preparation. This has resulted in failed overseas assignments, which means companies don't fully capitalize on business opportunities and incur costs for replacing employees who leave the company after returning to the United States.[54] Cross-cultural preparation is especially important because North American companies plan to increase the length of expatriate assignments from two to five years.[55]

To succeed overseas, expatriates (employees on foreign assignments) need to be

1. Competent in their areas of expertise
2. Able to communicate verbally and nonverbally in the host country
3. Flexible, tolerant of ambiguity, and sensitive to cultural differences
4. Motivated to succeed, able to enjoy the challenge of working in other countries, and willing to learn about the host country's culture, language, and customs
5. Supported by their families[56]

One reason for U.S. expatriates' high failure rate is that companies place more emphasis on developing employees' technical skills than on preparing them to work within other cultures. Research suggests that the comfort of an expatriate's spouse and family is the most important determinant of whether the employee will complete the assignment.[57] Studies have also found that personality characteristics are related to expatriates' desire to terminate the assignment and performance in the assignment.[58] Expatriates who were extroverted (outgoing), agreeable (cooperative and tolerant), and conscientious (dependable, achievement-oriented) were more likely to want to stay with the assignment and perform well. This suggests that cross-cultural preparation may be effective only when expatriates' personalities predispose them to be successful in assignments in other cultures.

The key to a successful foreign assignment is a combination of training and career management for the employee and family. Cross-cultural preparation involves three phases: predeparture, on-site, and repatriation (preparing to return home).

Predeparture Phase

Before departure, employees need to receive language training and training focused on the new country's culture and customs.[59] English is the common language at many multi-national companies. But failing to speak the native language can cause employees to risk being misinterpreted or fail to understand informal conversations. Speaking and under-standing the local language can help employees avoid misunderstandings and gain greater respect from business partners, subordinates, and customers. For example, at Intel, employ-ees with a business need can take classes in Mandarin, Japanese, and Spanish at various offices throughout the United States, free of charge.[60] Also, it is critical that the family be included in orientation programs.[61] Expatriates and their families need information about housing, schools, recreation, shopping, and health care facilities in the areas where they will live. Expatriates also must discuss with their managers how the foreign assignment fits into their career plans and what types of positions they can expect upon their return.

Cross-cultural training methods include presentational techniques, such as lectures that expatriates and their families attend on the customs and culture of the host country, e-learning, immersion experiences, or actual experiences in the home country in cultur-ally diverse communities.[62] Experiential exercises, such as miniculture experiences, allow expatriates to spend time with a family in the United States from the ethnic group of the host country. For example, an Indian trainer took twenty managers from Advanced Micro Devices on a two-week immersion trip during which the group traveled to New Delhi, Bangalore, and Mumbai, meeting with businesspersons and government officials.[63] The program required six months of planning, including providing the executives with infor-mation on foods to eat, potential security issues, and how to interact in business meetings. For example, Indians prefer a relatively indirect way into business discussions, so the man-agers were advised to discuss current events and other subjects before talking business.

VF Asia Limited is a Hong Kong–based unit of VF Corporation. VF Corporation is the world's largest apparel company and the owner of many brands, including Nautica, Wrangler, Jansport, and North Face.[64] VF Asia's Self-Enhancement Learning Fundamen-tals (SELF) program is an online customer training program that includes instruction on topics that help employees understand and communicate with individuals from the diverse cultures throughout Asia with whom they do business. Course topics include business eti-quette, holding successful meetings, and negotiations. VF Asia's training team maintains a partnership with the VF Corporation development team. Both teams work together to develop and implement global initiatives to ensure that they are customized to local needs and requirements.

Research suggests that the degree of difference between the United States and the host country (cultural novelty), the amount of interaction with host country citizens and host nationals (interaction), and the familiarity with new job tasks and work environment (job novelty) all influence the "rigor" of the cross-cultural training method used.[65] Hands-on and group-building methods are most effective (and most needed) in assignments with a high level of cultural and job novelty that require a good deal of interpersonal interaction with host nationals.

On-Site Phase

On-site training involves continued orientation to the host country and its customs and cultures through formal programs or through a mentoring relationship. Expatriates and their families may be paired with an employee from the host country, who helps them understand the new, unfamiliar work environment and community.[66] Additionally, expatriates should be encouraged to develop social relationships both inside and outside the workplace.[67] Companies are also using websites and social media to help employees on expatriate assignments get answers to questions such as, "How do I conduct a meeting here?" or "What religious or business philosophy might have influenced today's negotiation behavior?"[68] Companies also are using websites and social media to help employees who are not expatriates but interact with clients around the world or who work on cross-cultural teams requiring limited travel. IBM uses social networking tools to connect its employees around the world. IBM's site, known as w3, contributes to the global integration of the company. The w3 On Demand Workplace is a powerful productivity and collaboration tool for 400,000 IBM employees in seventy-five countries. The w3 can be used by employees to find resources and knowledge from peers around the world to help clients innovate and succeed. Employees can create personal profiles, bookmark websites and stories they are interested in, comment on company blogs, contribute to wikis, share files, and read and review position papers, videos, and podcasts.

A major reason that employees refuse expatriate assignments is that they can't afford to lose their spouse's income or are concerned that their spouse's career could be derailed by being out of the workforce for a few years.[69] Some "trailing" spouses decide to use the time to pursue educational activities that could contribute to their long-term career goals. But it is difficult to find these opportunities in an unfamiliar place. GlaxoSmithKline's International Service Center, which handles all of its relocations from or to the United States, offers a buddy system for spouses to connect with others who have lived in the area for the past several years.[70] General Motors (GM) offers career continuation services that reimburse spouses $2,500 each year during the expatriate assignment for maintaining professional licenses or certifications. The World Bank manages an Internet site dedicated to expatriates, where spouses can post résumés and ask for job leads.

Repatriation Phase

Repatriation prepares expatriates for return to the parent company and home country from the foreign assignment. Expatriates and their families are likely to experience high levels of stress and anxiety when they return because of changes that have occurred since their departure. Employees should be encouraged to self-manage the repatriation process.[71] Before they go on the assignment, they need to consider what skills they want to develop and the types of jobs that might be available in the company for an employee with those skills. Because the company changes and colleagues, peers, and managers may leave while the expatriate is on assignment, they need to maintain contact with key company and industry contacts. Otherwise, on return, the employees' reentry shock will be heightened when they have to deal with new colleagues, a new job, and a company culture that may have changed. This includes providing expatriates with company newsletters and community newspapers and ensuring that they receive personal and work-related mail from the United States while they are on foreign assignment. It is also not uncommon for employees and their families to have to readjust to a lower standard of living in the United States than they had in the foreign country, where they may have enjoyed maid service, a limousine, private schools, and clubs. Salary and other compensation arrangements should be worked out well before employees return from overseas assignments.

Aside from reentry shock, many expatriates decide to leave the company because the assignments they are given upon returning to the United States have less responsibility, challenge, and status than their foreign assignments.[72] As noted earlier, career planning discussions need to be held before the employees leave the United States to ensure that they understand the positions they will be eligible for upon repatriation. For example, after completing five overseas assignments in operations and human resources positions in Indonesia and China, a manager for Walmart Stores left the company because he missed the responsibility and authority he had in these assignments.[73] He couldn't find a similar position with Walmart when he completed his last international assignment. As a result, he took a job at Kimberly-Clark's international division as vice president of human resources.

Royal Dutch Shell, a joint Dutch and British oil and gas company, has one of the world's largest expatriate workforces. To avoid expatriates who feel undervalued and leave the company, Royal Dutch Shell gets involved with expatriates and their careers. Resource planners track workers abroad, helping identify their next assignment. Most expatriates know their next assignment three to six months before the move, and all begin the next assignment with a clear job description. Expatriates who have the potential to reach top-level management positions are placed in the home office every third assignment to increase their visibility to company executives. Expatriates are also assigned technical mentors who evaluate their skills and help them improve their skills through training at Royal Dutch Shell's training center. At Xerox, expatriates are assigned a sponsor who helps ensure the assignment is a good fit and helps them transition back to the United States.[74]

CAREER CHALLENGES FACING A MULTIGENERATIONAL WORKFORCE

Employees' careers involve four stages: exploration, establishment, maintenance, and decline.[75] In the exploration stage, employees attempt to identify the type of work that interests them. They consider their interests, values, and work preferences and begin pursuing the type of education and training they need. Establishment involves finding employment, making an independent contribution, achieving more responsibility and financial success, and establishing a suitable lifestyle. In the maintenance stage, individuals are concerned with keeping their skills up to date and being perceived as someone who are still contributing to the company. They have many years of experience, much job knowledge, and an in-depth understanding of how business is conducted. The last stage, disengagement, involves individuals preparing to phase out of work and retire. Although individuals can go through these stages in a linear fashion and at certain ages (e.g., exploration typically occurs before age 30), most individuals do not because today's careers are boundaryless and often change.[76] This means that careers may involve identifying more with the profession than the present employer, resulting in job changes. Also, at different times in their lives, individuals reconsider their interests, values, and how to best use their skills, resulting in one or more career changes.

It is important to recognize that there are likely generational differences in what employees want in their career. Generation Xers (Gen Xers), more than previous generations, appear to place higher importance on work-life balance, opportunities for growth, and good work relationships.[77] Millennials and Gen Xers are more used to change and job insecurity than baby boomers, and as a result, they are more likely to leave jobs to develop their skills. Baby boomers tend to be loyal to one company and therefore willing to relocate for a promotion or new assignment than Gen Xers, who want to stay in an area where they have formed social and work relationships. Although there are generational differences, similarities also exist. All generations share similar values related to family, respect, and trust.[78] Regardless of potential generational differences affecting employees' career needs, the reality is that most companies' workforce includes four or five generations of employees. As a result, to attract, motivate, and retain a talented multigenerational workforce companies need to understand and manage career challenges and help employees deal with career issues. These career challenges and issues include balancing work-life needs, providing career ladders, career recycling, understanding job hopping, helping employees return to work after career breaks, helping employees deal with job loss, and meeting the needs of older employees, including retirement. These career challenges and issues are discussed next.

Work-Life Balance

Maintaining a healthy work-life balance is a concern for all employees, regardless of whether they have families, significant others, or dependents. It is difficult for employees to maintain work-life balance due to long work hours, night shift work, travel, and tethered to smartphones, notebook computers, and i-watches that bombard employees on a 24/7 basis with work demands and family member requests. One study found that 67 percent of employers think their employees have work-life balance but 45 percent of employees feel they don't have enough time each week for personal, social, and recreational activities.[79] **Work-life balance** refers to helping employees deal with the stresses, strains, and conflicts related to trying to balance work and nonwork demands. Work-life conflict has been found to be related to increased health risks, decreased productivity, tardiness, turnover, and poor mental health.[80] Work-life conflict occurs due to competing time demands, the stress of work and life roles, and when employees behavior in their work roles is not appropriate for their behavior in nonwork roles (such as when a manager has to be logical and impartial at work, but they are expected to be warm, emotional, and friendly with family members and friends).

Social legislation has been approved to help employees balance work and family. The **Family and Medical Leave Act (FMLA)** is a federal law that provides up to twelve weeks of unpaid leave in a one-year period for parents with new infants or newly adopted children.[81] The FMLA also covers employees who must take a leave of absence from work to care for a family member who is ill or to deal with their own personal illness. Employees can also take twenty-six workweeks of leave during a single twelve-month period to care for a service member with a serious injury or illness if the eligible employee is the service member's spouse, son, daughter, parent, or next of kin (military caregiver leave). Companies are required to provide employees with health care benefits during their leave of absence.

Men are often reluctant to take advantage of the FMLA or work-life balance programs for fear that they will dead-end their careers. For example, at Ernst & Young, about six hundred men take parental leave every year, but only 90 percent use two weeks, although the company offers six weeks with pay.[82] Some employers still assume that men's first priority is work over other aspects of their lives. But both men and women need support for their parenting roles. Several companies are providing and supporting programs specifically targeted at fathers.[83] American Express offers a Fatherhood Breakfast Series that encourages men to talk about issues related to blending career and family. Deloitte Dads is an employee group in which working fathers can network and share ideas about balancing work, making partners, and how to have a great family life. Additionally, Deloitte has adopted the concept it calls "work-life fit," which allows employees to take sabbaticals, adopt a compressed workweek, work virtually, and provide adoption services and even offers discounted pet health insurance! Bandwith.com Inc., a telecommunications company with 425 employees, provides new fathers with one week of paid leave, flexible work arrangements, and additional perks such as taking ninety-minute lunch and exercise breaks every day.

Many companies have gone beyond relying on the FMLA to help employees balance work and family life. Work-family programs include paid/unpaid elder care leave, flexible spending accounts for dependent care, elder care resources and referrals, flexible spending accounts for elder care, and on-site child care. Research has found that employees working at companies that offer these programs believe that the organization supports their family and this leads to more positive job attitudes and better job performance.[84] Also, employees who use work-family programs have less work-family conflict than employees who do not. Additionally, companies are recognizing the benefits that can be gained by providing all employees, regardless if they have a spouse, children, or elders, with work-life balance through flexible work schedules, protecting their free time, and more productively using work time.[85] The benefits include the ability to have an advantage in attracting and retaining talented employees and reduced stress, resulting in healthier employees and a rested workforce that can maximize the use of their skills. As a result, typically companies provide programs and practices that assist employees in coping with both family and broader non work-life demands. Table 10.5 shows examples of work-life balance practices.

Consider the following examples of work-family and work-life balance practices and programs.[86] Amerisure Mutual Insurance in Farmington Hills, Michigan, built a work environment and provides flexible programs designed to increase employee retention and engagement. A new computer system makes it easier for employees to work at home by giving them access to work files using their home computers. **Telecommuting** refers to a work arrangement that gives employees flexibility in both work location and hours. Employees meet with their managers to discuss the feasibility of working off site and how

TABLE 10.5
Examples of Work-Life Balance Practices

Flexible work schedules
Job sharing
Child care
Eldercare
Personal leave
Telecommuting
Reduced meeting times
Reduced work hours
Adoption support
Paid vacation time
Personal services (supply meals, purchase gifts, arrange home and auto services)

their performance will be evaluated. Amerisure also allows employees to take days off each year for volunteer work, and provides five paid days each year for family commitments related to medical care, such as caring for ill grandparents and immediate family members. The company's turnover rate has dropped from 18 percent to 10 percent, and employee engagement survey scores have increased. Hourly employees at health care provider Kaiser Permanente can get paid time off for several hours during the workday so they can manage doctor or school appointments without having to miss an entire day's work. They are also providing employees with more flexibility on when they want to start and end work. This helps employees more easily accommodate dropping off kids at school or running errands for elderly parents. At Marriott International, 87 percent of its employees are hourly workers. To help keep hourly workers at their best at work, the company offers many different flexibility options, including compressed workweeks, shift swapping, and work-at-home positions. A **compressed workweek** refers to a work schedule that allows employees to work fewer days but with longer hours, for example, four days, ten hours each day. Also, Marriott offers a cross-training program that allows employees such as housecleaners to get trained in a different unit (such as catering), which will give them more opportunities to choose to work when they are available. Employee survey results suggest that over 75 percent of employees with access to flexible scheduling options report that it is a major reason that they intend to remain employed at Marriott. Some companies, particularly those in the software industry, offer cutting-edge benefits that help attract new employees and make it easier for current employees to stay productive.[87] Asana gives employees a $10,000 allowance for computers and office décor, which employees can use to purchase mini-refrigerators, headphones, and ergonomic chairs. Asana also offers free yoga classes and in-house chefs. Google provides employees with food service, fitness centers, bicycle repairs, and napping pods.

Unilever's Agile Working Program is used by 80 percent of salaried employees at thirty-seven company locations around the world.[88] Agile Working allows employees to work any hours, anywhere they want to. Office cubicles have been replaced with collaborative workspaces with small shared work pods. The new work areas are designed to provide a comfortable environment by including televisions, foosball tables, and treadmills. Agile Working has benefited Unilever in several ways. Unilever has seen a reduction in real estate and travel costs. The program helps Unilever meet diversity goals because it allows working mothers and employees with disabilities to work at home. Banana Republic, known for its stylish, yet affordable, fashions, has implemented a results-oriented work environment (ROWE) at its San Francisco and New York headquarters offices. ROWE gives employees the opportunity to decide how and where they work according to the deliverables and results that they are accountable for achieving.[89] RSM McGladrey, a consulting firm in Rochester, Minnesota, gives employees several flextime options, including FlexYear, which provides a schedule similar to a teacher (work nine months with pay distributed over the entire year), and FlexCareer, which enables employees to take up to five years off for personal reasons and provides resources such as training to keep employees connected with the firm and the industry so they can more easily transition back to work at the end of their sabbaticals. **Flextime** refers to giving employees the option of choosing when to work during the workday, workweek, or work year. Flexible work arrangements focused on the workweek usually give employees the choice as to how they want to arrange their start and ending time, so long as they work a total of eight hours each day.

They also require employees to work during certain core hours (such as 9 A.M. to 3 P.M.). At Bon Secours Health System employees can work compressed workweeks, with options including four ten-hour shifts or three twelve-hour shifts per week. They can also choose other options, such as working weekends only, four- and eight-hour shifts, and seven consecutive workdays followed by seven days off. At U.S. Bank, tellers can choose to job-share. **Job sharing** refers to having two employees divide the hours, the responsibilities, and the benefits of a full-time job. Companies may also use two job-sharing employees to fill one full-time position.

There are several challenges with the use of work-life balance policies. The first challenge is using them to help employees achieve work-life balance without hurting business needs such as customer service and productivity. Second, managers need to understand and accept the idea that employees should not be punished for use of work-life balance policies. Employees' performance and development should be based on what they accomplish and how they do it, not whether they are seen around the office or put in "face time" with their manager. Third, it is important to ensure that work-life balance practices are accessible to everyone and meet the needs of all employees, not just those with families. Consider how Medtronic, a company that makes medical devices, addresses these challenges.[90] One hundred fifty of its one thousand employees in Santa Rosa, California, are home-office workers. They come into the office once or twice a week. Medtronic took several steps to ensure that its program was successful. It allowed employees to work at home only if they had jobs in which most of their work was being done through the computer. This eliminated research-and-development jobs and other jobs requiring face-to-face social interaction. It provided both managers and employees with guidelines for telecommuting. These guidelines included emphasizing the importance of managers setting specific performance targets and requiring employees to respond to e-mails by the end of the day. Medtronic also provides rooms that home-office workers can use for meetings when they are in Santa Rosa. The program has saved Medtronic over $1 million in office space costs and improves productivity. Also, it helps Medtronic attract employees from San Francisco (an hour away) who want to continue to live there but avoid commuting and daycare expenses and hassles.

CAREER PATHS AND DUAL CAREER PATHS

A **career path** is a sequence of job positions involving similar types of work and skills that employees move through in the company.[91] Career paths help companies offer career options to their employees that help them make job choices that best fit their life situations. Providing career paths and making sure employees understand them is especially important because lack of career opportunities ranks after pay as the major reason employees leave companies. One survey showed that less than 50 percent of employees believe their organization provides useful career planning tools and opportunities to advance their careers.[92] Also, career paths help companies build employees' skills through a series of jobs or roles. This maximizes their value to the company and shows employees that they don't have to leave the company to move to new positions with different responsibilities and skill requirements. Figure 10.1 shows examples of vertical, horizontal, and cross-functional career paths at Whirlpool. To move along the vertical career path

FIGURE 10.1   Examples of Career Paths at Whirlpool

Vertical Career Path

Category Marketing Director
(Directs, plans, and evaluates the marketing activities of several products or product lines)

↑

Category Senior Manager
(Manages the planning and direction of all marketing programs for a specific product and product line)

↑

Category Manager
(Assists in the development, execution, and tracking of marketing programs for a specific product or program line by collecting, analyzing, and reporting marketing data)

↑

Category Marketing Analyst
(Conducts marketing under supervision. Audits data, performs gap analysis, and proofs creative products)

Horizontal Career Path

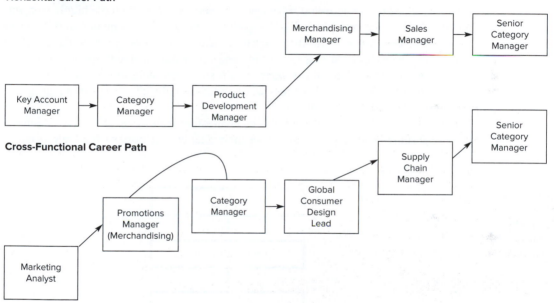

Cross-Functional Career Path

Source: Based on "Mapping Out Your Career," from http://us.whirlpoolcareers.com, accessed April 14, 2015.

requires the employees to be promoted to new jobs, which require taking on managerial responsibilities. The horizontal career path shows that an employee can move from Key Account Manager to jobs that differ because they focus on a category or a product but have similar managerial responsibilities. From Product Development the employee needs to be promoted into the Merchandising Manager role, which requires additional responsibilities such as developing plans and strategies. The cross-functional career path involves moving from a Marketing Analyst job to a Promotion Manager role in a specific function (merchandising). From that job an employee can move into a Category Manager job and Global Consumer Design Lead. Then, the employee can again move cross-functionally to a job as a Supply Chain Manager.

Developing career paths involves analyzing work and information flows, important development experiences, qualifications and the types of tasks performed across jobs, similarities and differences in working environments, and the historical movement patterns of employees into and out of jobs (i.e., wherein the company employees come from and what positions they take after leaving a job).[93]

Dual Career Path

For companies with professional employees such as engineers and scientists, an important issue is how to ensure that they feel valued. Many companies' career paths are structured so that the only way engineers and scientists (individual contributors) can advance and receive certain financial rewards (such as stock options) is by moving into managerial positions. Figure 10.2 shows examples of traditional career paths for scientists and managers. Advancement opportunities within a technical career path are limited. Individual contributors who move directly into management may lack the experience and/or competencies needed to be successful. Managerial career paths may be more highly compensated than technical career paths. A career path system such as the one in Figure 10.2 can have negative consequences for the company. Scientists may elect to leave the company because they have lower status, less salary, and fewer advancement opportunities than managers enjoy. Also, if scientists want to gain status and additional salary, they must choose to become managers. Scientists who cannot meet the challenges of a managerial position may leave the company.

Many companies are using multiple- or dual-career-path systems to give additional career opportunities to scientists and other individual contributors such as salespersons.

FIGURE 10.2
Traditional Career Paths for Scientists and Managers

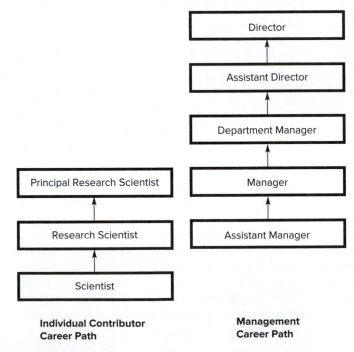

Individual Contributor Career Path

Management Career Path

A **dual-career-path system** enables employees to remain in a technical or sales career path or move into a management career path.[94] Figure 10.3 shows a dual-career-path system. Research scientists have the opportunity to move into three different career paths: a scientific path and two management paths. It is assumed that because employees can earn comparable salaries and have similar advancement opportunities in all three paths, they will choose the path that best matches their interests and skills. For example, Toshiba Medical Systems is reconsidering its retention strategies as baby boomers retire and Gen Xers move into leadership positions in the company.[95] Recognizing that baby boomers may tend to judge the success of their careers based on promotions, but younger employees place less value on level, title, and money, Toshiba has developed both technical and managerial career ladders. The technical career ladders allow employees to continue to perform hands-on work in areas they enjoy, but still allow them to move up in the company.

FIGURE 10.3
Example of a Dual-career Path System

Source:
Z. B. Leibowitz,
B. L. Kaye, and
C. Farren, "Multiple career paths," *Training and Development Journal* (October 1992): 31–35.

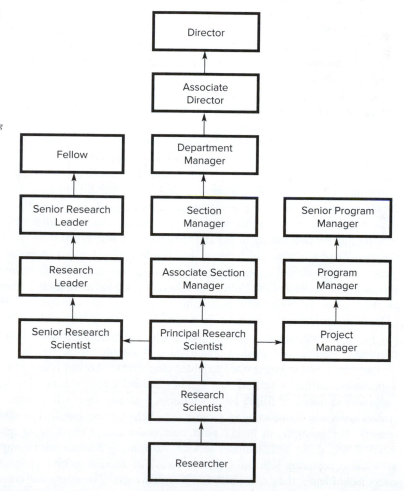

Effective dual-career paths have several characteristics:[96]

- Salary, status, and incentives for technical employees compare favorably with those of managers.
- Individual contributors' base salaries may be lower than that of managers, but they are given opportunities to increase their total compensation through bonuses (e.g., for patents and developing new products).
- The individual contributor career path is not used to satisfy poor performers who have no managerial potential. The career path is for employees with outstanding technical skills.
- Individual contributors are given the opportunity to choose their career path. The company provides assessment resources (such as psychological tests and developmental feedback, as discussed in Chapters Nine and Eleven). Assessment information enables employees to see how similar their interests, work values, and skill strengths are to those of employees in technical and managerial positions.

CAREER RECYCLING

Recycling involves changing one's major work activity after having been established in a specific field. Recycling is accompanied by a re-exploration of values, skills, interests, and potential employment opportunities. Kirk Rademaker has an art degree and worked as a carpenter and a project manager for a cabinet company.[97] He liked his work but was emotionally drained from it as well from a divorce. To relieve his stress, he would often drive to a beach to spend time making sandcastles. He kept sculpting sand, entered competitions, and began winning awards for his sculptures. He made a decision to do work he enjoyed, not just for the money. He quit his job and decided to start a professional sand-sculpting business. His first clients were companies that hired him to lead team-building events on local beaches. He also worked creating sand sculptures for corporate events such as a motorcycle rising from the sand for Harley-Davidson Motor Company. He was making just enough money to pay his bills. Then he was asked if he would take a part in the show *Sand Masters*, which ran on the Travel Channel for two years. Being on the show gave him international exposure to clients, which helped grow his business, Sand Guys International. A dean of the College of Liberal Arts at Portland State University took a job as chief executive officer of a continuing care retirement community.[98] He had no plans to leave the academic world but enjoyed building relationships with the local community. His job at the retirement community allows him to help the organization by utilizing his lifetime of experiences, wisdom, and training as a gerontologist.

Recycling is not just limited to older employees who are nearing retirement. Many companies that face a serious shortage of qualified employees are developing retraining programs in hopes of filling labor shortages with employees from other fields.[99] Companies are using these training programs to help recycle employees into new jobs and careers. For example, in the IT field, companies face a shortage of qualified staff for internal help desks and customer service. Also, many persons with computer skills who seek these positions lack the interpersonal skills needed to give counsel and advice to users of software, databases, and company intranets. The computer consulting industry is training former stockbrokers, flight attendants, and bank tellers to work at help desks. These training programs are referred to as "boot camps" because the training emphasizes total immersion in the job, one-on-one supervision, and cramming into a short training program what knowledge and skills the employee needs to have.

It is also not uncommon for employees who are considering recycling to conduct **informational interviews** with managers or other employees who hold jobs in functional areas that they believe may be congruent with their interests and abilities, to gather information about the skills, job demands, and benefits of their jobs. For example, a manager at Level 3 Communications received strong performance evaluations and earned awards in her eleven years at the company.[100] She was so effective at streamlining customer service departments after they were acquired by Level 3 and training new hires that she was always assigned those tasks. Because she felt bored and not challenged in her role, she took a new job managing a design team who was responsible for disconnecting unneeded sections of fiber-optic cable. However, she soon found herself training new hires and again felt a lack of challenge in her work. Based on the recommendations she took away from a leadership training program for women that she attended, she planned to have a conversation with her boss to ask for a chance to contribute more. Part of her conversation with her boss included a presentation about her experiences, her progress toward her career goals, and her reflections on staying in her current job, moving up to a new position, or leaving Level 3. As a result, her manager agreed he would try and help her find a mentor and look for other job opportunities. The manager got her a job involving partnering with Google to provide broadband services to U.S. Starbucks stores. She took the job and was promoted ten months later to account manager. She feels that her new job is the ideal job for her. She enjoys her job and feels challenged. Her new boss really likes her motivation, attitude, and commitment to her work.

Job Hopping

Job hopping refers to employees changing jobs, usually between companies, every two to three years. Job hopping is prevalent today, especially among Gen Xers and millennials, as more employees view themselves as "free agents" who must actively manage their own careers. It is estimated that employees in all age groups are staying at jobs for a shorter period of time compared to the 1980s. They recognize that they have a protean career, which means they have to take responsibility for their own careers because companies may lay them off if business declines or changes in the business strategy make them expendable. Loyalty does not guarantee job security. Employees recognize that their employability and economic well-being depends on their personal growth and pay, and as a result, they will leave for another job offer if the company offers more learning opportunities or better compensation.[101] Although job hopping was once considered damaging to an employee's career, today, companies are more used to the practice. This is especially true in high-technology industries, where talented employees are in demand and new start-ups offer stock options that can result in substantial financial gains if the company grows.

Is job hopping good for companies and employees? There are advantages and disadvantages to it, for both employees and companies.[102] For companies, job hopping results in a loss of talent and productivity that results from turnover, retraining, and recruitment costs. Also, job hopping makes it difficult to create and sustain a culture that supports relationships between employees or continuity in employee-customer relationships.

Job hopping does provide companies with the opportunity to hire employees who have a variety of experiences in different companies, which can allow the company to understand and implement best practices. Hiring employees who job hop may increase company's flexibility and adaptability because these employees are capable of quickly learning different jobs. Also, employees who job hop likely do not need or have high expectations for job security, making it easier for the company to downsize if necessary. For employees, in addition to better pay and growth opportunities, job hopping can provide opportunities to work in a variety of industries, in different-sized companies, and to gain new skills, experiences, and personal contacts. The downside of job hopping for employees is that they may not be staying in any one job long enough to complete important projects, develop personal networks, or gain relevant experiences. This may hurt their opportunity to obtain attractive job and career opportunities in the future.

Companies are unlikely to eliminate job hopping. However, companies can reduce job hopping and attract and retain talented employees by creating conditions for employee engagement, providing employees with growth opportunities, and offering incentives and rewards for good performance.

COPING WITH CAREER BREAKS

Both men and women face major problems in trying to return to work after taking several months or years off for family-related or other reasons.[103] This is especially the case for returning troops from Iraq and Afghanistan, who often have difficulty returning to their jobs and finding employment. The unemployment rate for veterans tends to be higher than the rate for the overall labor force, with the unemployment rate for those aged 22 to 24 more than three times as high as for non veterans of the same age.[104] Returning troops face many obstacles to finding employment or returning to their jobs, including lack of experience in the workplace, incomplete skill sets and education credentials, difficulty to work in less structured situations without clear-cut guidelines and expectations, and psychological and physical challenges. But veterans are known to have many characteristics and skills that are valuable for employers including attention to detail, self-discipline, problem solving, decision making in stressful situations, and teamwork.

Both the federal government and companies are involved in helping veterans return to work or find new jobs.[105] The **Uniformed Services Employment and Reemployment Rights Act** covers deployed employees' rights, such as guaranteeing jobs when they return except under certain circumstances. However, the job a service member returns to may be different from the one he or she left, and it could require new skills or be in a different location. Also, veterans who return to work have to prove themselves all over again, and some may have received disabling physical or psychological injuries from their military service. At Booz Allen Hamilton, about 28 percent of its employees have a military background. The company recruits veterans, makes accommodations based on their physical needs, works with organizations that help them transition between military and civilian life, and offers them onboarding programs and mentoring. Aon, an insurance and consulting company, offers a peer mentoring program that matches veterans with managers who can help them address their job skills and knowledge needs. Aon has worked with other companies and the Wounded Warrior Project to identify disabled veterans who need help. They have provided training for job interviews and networking and résumé development. American Electric Power, one of the largest electric utilities in the United States, is one of four U.S. electric companies participating in the Troops to Energy Jobs program. The Troops to Energy Jobs Program, developed under CEWD, provides training in community and technical colleges and four-year universities to help veterans complete and finish their education in order to complement their current skill sets. The program helps veterans get placed in internships and permanent jobs, including engineering, security, line workers, and technicians. The United Association of Plumbers, Pipefitters, and Sprinkler Fitters partnered with the U.S. military to create a program that provides veterans with two weeks of transitional training to help them adjust to civilian life, followed by sixteen weeks of accelerated technical training in topics such as welding, piping, and heating and ventilation, and then a four-year apprenticeship. Veterans are paid during the training and apprenticeship and are guaranteed employment when they complete the program. The Department of Defense and the Department of Energy will work together in the Solar Energy Vets Program to help veterans learn skills that can prepare them for careers in the solar energy industry.[106] The program will be offered at ten U.S. military bases.

COPING WITH JOB LOSS

Coping with job loss is a major career issue because of the increased use of downsizing to deal with excess staff resulting from corporate restructurings, mergers, acquisitions, and takeovers. Research suggests that layoffs do not result in improved profits, they have mixed effects on productivity, and they have adverse effects on the morale, workload, and commitment of employees who remain with the company.[107] Job loss also causes stress and disrupts the personal lives of laid-off employees.[108] Because of the potential damaging effects of downsizing, companies should first seek alternative ways to reduce head count (the number of employees) and lower labor costs. These alternatives may include asking employees to work fewer hours, offering early retirement plans, delaying wage increases, and deciding not to fill position openings created by turnover and retirements. However, job loss may be inevitable in the case of mergers or acquisitions (which may create redundant positions and an excess of employees with similar skills) or downturns in business that force the company to reduce labor costs by eliminating employees in order to survive.

Job loss is especially traumatic for older workers. They may find it difficult to find a job because of their age. For example, a sixty-two-year-old middle manager who had been making $65,000 a year was laid off from his job at Boston Mutual Life Insurance Company.[109] He and his wife are down to their last $2,500 after using up all his unemployment benefits. He now finds himself standing on a street corner with a sign that says "I need a job . . . 36 yrs exper; Insur/mngmnt" and includes his phone number. He has no pension, and he cannot live on the $1,200 per month that Social Security would pay.

Pillowtex Corporation, a North Carolina–based textile company, laid off 5,500 employees.[110] One of them was Ruth Jones, an 83-year-old employee with over 50 years of service at Pillowtex, and she doesn't know how she will meet her expenses. She gets unemployment benefits and Social Security benefits, but because the company is bankrupt, she is unlikely to get severance pay from Pillowtex. She does get two small pensions from two companies that preceded Pillowtex (Cannon Mills and Fieldcrest Cannon), and her home is paid off. She plans to seek other jobs at the local grocery store or the gas station.

From a career management standpoint, companies and managers have two major responsibilities. First, they are responsible for helping employees who will lose their jobs. Second, steps must be taken to ensure that the "survivors" of the layoff (the remaining employees) remain productive and committed to the organization.

To prepare employees for layoffs and reduce their potential negative effects, companies need to provide outplacement services. Outplacement services should include:[111]

- Advance warning and an explanation for the layoff
- Psychological, financial, and career counseling
- Assessment of skills and interests
- Job seeking services, such as résumé-writing assistance and interview training
- Job banks where job leads are posted and where out-of-town newspapers, phones, and books regarding different occupations and geographic areas are available
- Electronic delivery of job openings, self-directed career management guides, and values and interest inventories

Some companies provide training and education to assist outplaced employees. Ford Motor Company closed several of its North American factories and cut more than 34,000 jobs.[112] Ford offered its Educational Opportunity Program to laid-off workers at these factories. Under the program, Ford paid as much as $15,000 per year in tuition for UAW members who go to school full time to earn a degree, certificate, or license. Employees received half their usual hourly salary plus medical benefits. Boeing, the aircraft manufacturer in Washington, worked with Washington State and local business and government officials to offer a small business training program to outplaced employees.[113] Selection for the program—which involved classes, reviews of business plans, and consultation—was rigorous. Applicants had to have a viable business idea, identify competitors and customers, and indicate how they would support themselves until the business made a profit. Laid-off workers started such businesses as restaurants, bookstores, and accounting offices. Besides helping former employees, the program allowed Boeing to hold down its unemployment insurance contributions and improve its image in the community.

Many laid-off workers, frustrated by long job searches and craving independence, have started their own businesses despite high odds against success.[114] For example, Julie Ganong and Alan Mons were laid off from their jobs in the finance sector.[115] They used their severance pay (pay provided by companies to employees when they are terminated) to open a baking company and café. Julie never imagined baking for a living but had trouble finding a job after she was laid off during the recession. Alan had always wanted to run a food business, and when he lost his job, the couple decided it was time to do so. Their business, Chococoa, has a website, ten employees, and sells about 10,000 whoopie pies, its specialty (made of frosting between two pieces of cake) each week.

Typically, companies devote more resources to outplacing employees who have lost their jobs than to employees who remain. Employees in upper-level managerial and professional positions typically receive more personalized outplacement services (e.g., office space, a private secretary) than do lower-level employees.[116] Although losing a job causes grief and denial in employees, once employees have worked through their emotions, they are capable of carrying on a campaign to find a new job. Laid-off employees are certain of their future, in that they know that they need to seek alternative employment. However, for the **survivors** (employees who remain with the company following a downsizing), uncertainty about their future remains. Survivors feel some sense of gratification because they have kept their jobs. However, they do not know how safe their current job is, nor do they know in what direction the company is heading. Also, in many cases, survivors are expected to perform the work of the laid-off employees as well as their own. As a result, survivors experience considerable anxiety, anger toward top-level managers, cynicism toward reorganization and new business plans, resentment, and resignation.[117]

Survivors are more likely to view layoffs as fair if employees are asked to cut costs to avoid layoffs, if the factors used to decide whom to lay off (e.g., performance, seniority) are applied equally to individual contributors and management employees, if advance notice is provided, and if clear and adequate explanations are given for the layoffs.[118] Survivors need to be trained to deal with increased workloads and job responsibilities due to the consolidation and loss of jobs. The company also needs to provide survivors with realistic information about their future with the company.

MEETING THE NEEDS OF OLDER WORKERS

As was discussed in Chapter One, there is a shortage of talented employees in many industries. As a result, companies are trying to keep talented older employees working. Many potential retirees plan to cut back on work but not completely quit working. For example, one study found that 80 percent of baby boomers plan to work at least part time during their retirement.[119] This is due to both personal preferences and economic reasons. Because of the stock market plunge and the decrease in home values during the last economic recession, many recent retirees are finding themselves low on money and looking to reenter the workforce. To meet the needs of older workers and to avoid skill shortages, companies are offering alternative work schedules and arrangements, including part-time work, rehiring of retirees, and phased retirement programs in which employees gradually reduce their work hours.

When are employees considered "older" employees? As discussed earlier in the chapter, the ADEA begins protecting employees at age 40. This includes denying access for training programs and forcing employees to retire (without a legitimate reason) who are covered by the act. Mandatory retirement ages vary according to occupation: for air traffic controllers, it is 56; for pilots, it is 65; and for federal law enforcement officers, it is 57. Professional football players and other professional athletes are considered "old" at age 30. Older employees do not have higher absenteeism rates and are not more likely to put less effort into work as they approach retirement. However, they do likely require more help in learning new technology, prefer hands-on practice during training, and enjoy training programs that involve social interaction and collaboration.[120] Older employees are as productive and customer-savvy as younger employees, and they have valuable experience.

Companies can take several actions to meet the needs of older employees.[121] First, flexibility in scheduling allows older employees to take care of sick spouses, go back to school, travel, or work fewer hours. CVS Caremark learned that many customers prefer to discuss their health issues with an older, more experienced pharmacist. As a result, to retain older pharmacists, Caremark has a program that allows them to work in the northern U.S. states in the summer and in the warmer, southern states in the winter.[122] Michelin North America has over nineteen thousand retirees and 37 percent of Michelin employees are 50 years of age or older.[123] The company stays connected with its older employees by providing them with ongoing access to retirement planning workshops and information, and by formally acknowledging employees upon their retirement. Retirees are offered temporary work assignments, consulting or contract work, telecommuting, as well as full- and part-time work.

At the National Institutes of Health (NIH), 47 percent of employees are 50-plus, and the average older worker has been with the NIH for more than 18 years.[124] Many NIH employees are researchers with advanced degrees who are working in scientific careers. Helping older employees is fundamental because scientific research often takes a long time before results are known and solutions and cures for diseases are provided. At NIH, older employees are valued for their knowledge and experience, which they are encouraged to pass along by mentoring less experienced and younger scientists. Also, NIH actively recruits older scientists to join the organization.

NIH offers personal finance seminars on topics such as estate planning and social security, investment funds that reallocate assets depending on your age, on-site child and grandchild care, contract and part-time work for its retirees, telecommuting, anniversary parties for its long time worker and a "Fit Plus Program," a health initiative. Second, research suggests that the probability of receiving company-sponsored training peaks at age 40 and declines as an employee's age increases.[125] Companies need to ensure that older employees receive the training that they need to avoid obsolescence and to be prepared to use new technology. Third, older employees need resources and referral help that address long-term health care and elder care. Fourth, assessment and counseling are necessary to help older employees recycle to new jobs or careers, or transition to less secure positions whose responsibilities are not as clearly defined. Fifth, it is important to recognize that as older employees' physical and mental abilities decline, they can rely on experience and motivation to avoid poor performance. Companies should consider moving valuable older employees who are suffering skill deterioration to other jobs. Bon Secours Health System in Richmond, Virginia, credits the company's success to its older employees. Because 30 percent of Bon Secours's employees are over 50, the company tries to accommodate them. For example, a licensed practical nurse at Bon Secours found the physical aspects of her job (walking, lifting, and helping patients to stand up) too demanding. In response, the company moved her to the employee wellness program, where she gives inoculations and performs less strenuous duties.[126] Finally, companies need to ensure that employees do not hold inappropriate stereotypes about older employees (e.g., that they fear new technology or cannot learn new skills).

Preretirement Socialization

Preretirement socialization is the process of helping employees prepare to exit from work. It encourages employees to learn about retirement life; plan for adequate financial, housing, and health care resources; and form accurate expectations about retirement. Employees' satisfaction with life after retirement is influenced by their health, their feelings about their jobs, and their level of optimism. Employees who attend preretirement socialization programs have fewer financial and psychological problems and experience greater satisfaction with retirement compared to employees who do not attend these programs. These programs typically address the following topics:[127]

- Psychological aspects of retirement, such as developing personal interests and activities
- Housing, including a consideration of transportation, living costs, and proximity to medical care
- Health during retirement, including nutrition and exercise
- Financial planning, insurance, and investments
- Health care plans
- Estate planning
- The collection of benefits from company pension plans and Social Security

Preretirement socialization or retirement planning can help employees avoid being forced to return to work because of poor financial planning. For example, a 58-year-old retiree took an early retirement package from GTE, the telecommunications company.[128] He accepted a buyout from GTE after its merger talks with Bell Atlantic. Stock market losses and his decision to withdraw $2,000 from his retirement account each month have made it necessary for him to seek employment again. He now works for $10.50 an hour at a car dealership chain, loading and delivering car parts. After paying his bills, he is able to save $100 per week in a savings account. He is considering retirement again at age 60, when he will begin collecting his military pension. But the turbulence in the stock market and rising health insurance expenses (which have increased between $150 and $450 per quarter) may make it difficult for him to retire until he reaches age 62, when he can collect Medicare and Social Security benefits.

Many companies are also using phased retirement and alternative work arrangements such as rehiring retired employees to help employees make the transition into retirement while at the same time continuing to use their talents. **Phased retirement** involves employees transitioning from full-time employment to full-time retirement by working part time. Phased retirement can benefit both companies and their employees. It can help companies cope with the shortages of skilled employees in the labor market. It provides a source of income for employees who have seen the value of their retirement funds decrease during the economic recession. There are several different passed retirement plans. An employee can retire and return as an independent contractor, consultant, or part-time worker. The use of phased retirement plans is complicated by regulations regarding taxation of retirement benefits and concerns about continued health care coverage (e.g., there is no legal definition of phased retirement, and the tax code has few regulations for how to offer phased retirement within a defined retirement benefits plan). Consider the programs that several companies are offering to capitalize on older employees' skills and accommodate their needs.[129] At Herman Miller, the Michigan-based furniture manufacturer, employees can begin the retirement process two years ahead of their actual retirement date by working fewer hours. This helps ease their transition out of their job and workplace and provides them time to share their knowledge and help train other employee to take their job. NIH has two phased-retirement programs that allow employees to choose to gradually transition to retirement by reducing hours or a trial retirement program that allows retirees to return to work within one year of retiring in case they decide they aren't ready to leave the workforce.

Formal preretirement socialization programs are primarily for employees who are considering retirement, but financial planning, estate planning, and purchasing insurance need to be done much earlier in their careers to ensure that employees will have the financial resources necessary to live comfortably during retirement.

Retirement

Retirement involves leaving a job and a work role and making a transition into life without work. For some employees, retirement involves making a transition out of their current job and company, seeking full- or part-time employment elsewhere, or recycling into another career.

By 2022, one out of four employees of the U.S. labor force will be over 55 years old. Recent changes in the Social Security system have led to no mandatory retirement age for most jobs, and financial needs suggest that employees may elect to work longer for whatever reason.[130] The oldest members of the baby boom generation should be retiring soon because they are reaching age 62, the earliest age for collecting Social Security benefits.

Historically over half of all employees retire before age 63, and 80 percent leave by the time they are 70. This may be because employees accept companies' offers of early retirement packages, which usually include generous financial benefits. Also, employees may find work less satisfying and be interested in pursuing primarily non work activities as a source of satisfaction.

The aging workforce and the use of early retirement programs (discussed next) to shrink companies' workforces have three implications. First, companies must meet the needs of older employees. Second, companies must take steps to prepare employees for retirement. Third, companies must be careful that early retirement programs do not unfairly discriminate against older employees.

Early Retirement Programs

Early retirement programs offer employees financial benefits to leave the company. These programs are usually offered when companies are trying to reduce labor costs without having to lay off employees. Financial benefits usually include a lump sum of money and a percentage of salary based on years of service. These benefits can be quite attractive to employees, particularly those with long tenure with the company. Eligibility for early retirement is usually based on age and years of service. For example, the United States Postal Service (USPS) offered voluntary early retirement to postal employees working in mail processing plants scheduled to close.[131] To be eligible for the early retirement, employees needed to be at least 50 years of age with at least twenty years of service, or any age with at least twenty-five years of service, and at least five years was required to be creditable civilian service, not military service. Additionally, about three thousand eligible postmasters at post offices slated for cutbacks in business hours under organizational changes laid out in the U.S. Postal Service's new strategy have the opportunity to accept a voluntary early retirement offer. USPS is offering a $10,000 voluntary separation incentive payment for affected postmasters who qualify for voluntary early retirement. The voluntary early retirement allows employees to receive their retirement income (a defined benefit) years before they otherwise would be eligible to receive it.

Early retirement programs have two major problems. First, employees who may be difficult to replace may elect to leave the company. Second, older employees may believe that early retirement programs are discriminatory because they feel they are being forced to retire. To avoid costly litigation, companies need to make sure that their early retirement programs contain the following features:[132]

- The program is part of the employee benefit plan.
- The company can justify age-related distinctions for eligibility for early retirement.
- Employees are allowed to choose early retirement voluntarily.

Eligibility requirements should not be based on stereotypes about ability and skill decrements that occur with age. Research suggests that age-related declines in specific abilities and skills have little effect on job performance.[133] Employees' decisions are considered voluntary if they can refuse to participate, if they are given complete information about the plan, and if they receive a reasonable amount of time to make their decisions.

Training plays an important role in early retirement programs. Companies teach employees to understand the financial implications of early retirement. Training programs are also used to help employees understand when and in what forms health benefits and retirement savings can be received. For example, retirement savings can often be distributed to retirees either as a one time lump sum of money or as a payout of a specific amount of money each month, quarter, or year.

Summary

Public and privately held companies are in business to use tax dollars wisely and to create financial returns. But they also have a social responsibility to improve the communities where they are located by helping reduce poverty and unemployment, comply with laws and regulations, and help all employees contribute to company goals by helping them grow, develop, and address their career challenges. This directly benefits the local community and the workforce, but it also enhances the company's reputation, which helps attract, motivate, and retain talented employees. Through partnerships with government agencies, trade groups, labor unions, and foundations, a company's training and development function can develop the skills of the labor force to improve their employability and attract jobs to the local community. Also, being socially responsible means that training and development practices are accessible to all employees, they are treated appropriately during training activities, and copyright laws are followed (i.e., credit is given and payment is provided for materials used in courses). Today's workforce is not only diverse in race, gender, and national origin, but it is also multigenerational. To fully capitalize on the competitive advantage of diversity and meet social responsibility goals, companies need to proactively manage diversity and inclusion. This means going beyond diversity training to ensure that top management support diversity, managers are held accountable for diversity goals, employees are supported, and recruitment, hiring, and development are focused on identifying and nurturing the talent of all employees. Finally, companies need to help employees manage career challenges to increase their engagement, productivity, and reduce stress. The chapter discusses these challenges and the types of policies and programs that can help employees cope with them. The career challenges include balancing work and life, career breaks, coping with job loss, job hopping, recycling careers, and retirement.

Key Terms

sector partnerships, *445*
School-to-Work
Opportunities Act, *446*
Workforce Innovation and
Opportunity Act, *446*
joint union-management
training programs, *447*
copyrights, *450*
Title VII of the Civil
Rights Act *451*
Age Discrimination in
Employment Act
(ADEA), *451*
Americans with Disabilities
Act (ADA), *452*
reasonable
accommodation, *453*

inclusion, *454*
diversity training, *454*
managing diversity and
inclusion, *454*
glass ceiling, *459*
expatriates, *460*
cross-cultural
preparation, *461*
repatriation, *463*
work-life balance, *465*
Family and Medical Leave
Act (FMLA), *465*
telecommuting, *466*
compressed workweek,
467
flextime, *467*
job sharing, *468*

career path, *468*
dual-career path
system, *471*
recycling, *472*
informational
interviews, *473*
job hopping, *473*
Uniformed Services
Employment and
Reemployment Act, *474*
survivors, *477*
preretirement
socialization, *478*
phased retirement, *479*
retirement, *480*
early retirement
programs, *480*

Discussion Questions

1. What is a sector partnership? Why is it important? Provide an example of a sector partnership.

2. Assume you were asked to investigate whether or not a police officer training program adequately covered use of force. What would you review? Would you look at any data?

3. Explain the relationship between "managing diversity and inclusion" and "diversity training." Which is most effective? Why?

4. How would you prepare a team of three managers to go to Warsaw, Poland, to oversee the operations of a recently acquired financial services firm? They will be leaving in one month, and the assignment lasts two years.

5. What should companies do to develop talented women to take top management positions? Provide support for your recommendations.

6. How are career paths useful for employees? How can they contribute to company effectiveness?

7. What is job hopping? Which career challenges might a company focus on to reduce job hopping?

8. What advantages and disadvantages might a company gain by using phased retirement?

9. What are work-life programs? How are they related to work-family programs? What are some of the challenges in developing and using work-life programs?

10. How could you help the survivors of a downsizing remain motivated and productive? Which of your recommendations is most important? Explain why.

Application Assignments

1. Read Verizon's Corporate Responsibility Supplement at http://www.verizon.com/ about/sites/default/files/2014_Verizon_Corporate_Social_Responsibility_Report.pdf. Why is managing diversity important to Verizon? What are the strengths and weaknesses of Verizon's approach for managing diversity? What role does learning, training, and development play in managing diversity at Verizon?

2. Go to *www.workingmother.com*, the website for *Working Mother* magazine. Search for and review any five of the "2014 Working Mother Best Companies." What practices do they use to help employees balance work-life and work-family? What types of outcomes or metrics would you collect to see if these practices were effective?

3. Go to http://fairuse.stanford.edu, a website called Copyright and Fair Use created by Stanford University's library system. How does work fall in the public domain? That is, how can you use someone else's work without having to obtain permission to use it?

4. Go to *www.aep.com*, the website for American Electric Power. Click on "Careers," then click on "A Military-Friendly Employer." Watch the videos and review the Troops to Energy Website. What are the steps that an interested veteran would take to get started in the program? Explain why each of the steps is important from a career or developmental perspective.

5. Go to *www.youtube.com*, and search for "World Manufacturing Academy." Watch the video *Chrysler World Class Manufacturing Academy Feature*. What is the purpose of the Academy? What type of training is used? What are the learning advantages of the training shown in the video compared to classroom instruction?

6. Watch the YouTube video about millennials' career expectations at https://www .youtube.com/watch?v=oN009pksHas. How are their career expectations similar or different from your career expectations? Based on what you read in the chapter, what do you think companies should do to help manage and meet millennials' career expectations?

7. Go to http://www.ibm.com/ibm/responsibility/corporateservicecorps/ the website for IBM's Corporate Service Corps. Watch one of the videos highlighting the different assignments employees have had in the Corporate Service Corp. How does the assignment help IBM? The local community where the assignment takes place? The employee who is sent on the assignment?

8. Watch the SHRM Foundation DVD "Ernst & Young: Creating a Culture of Flexibility," online at http://www.shrm.org/about/foundation/products/pages/shrmfoundationdvds .aspx. What are the major challenges to creating a culture of flexibility? How does Ernst & Young manage those challenges?

Case: *Successful Management Requires International Experience*

As companies become more global, economic patterns and business practices in one area of the world can determine the success of a company on the other side of the world. At P&G, being a successful global leader requires an international background. A majority of P&G's 140,000 employees work outside the United States. P&G uses international assignments for employees to learn how business is conducted in another country so that lessons learned there can be applied at home or in another region. Only a quarter of relocations originate in the United States; the majority are from place to place across the world. An important goal of employees who receive international assignments is to develop local talent to replace themselves.

For example, a manager who is being prepared to take over a top finance position in Russia might go to Britain to gain experience working in a more structured and complex market. P&G managers in Europe must learn to keep the company's products on big-box-store shelves such as Carrefour, the European supermarket and discount chain and one of the largest retailers in the world. P&G might send junior U.S. managers to work with European managers who are responsible for products at Carrefour, expecting that they will transfer skills learned in these assignments to dealing with product placement in big-box

retailers such as Walmart and Costco. P&G also partners with UNICEF to offer P&G employees in Europe, the Middle East, and Africa the opportunity to take a three-month sabbatical to work with UNICEF. The program is aimed at employees who have always wanted to undertake humanitarian work but have not had the chance before. UNICEF benefits from the diverse backgrounds of P&G employees as they apply communications, promotion, leadership training, and supply chain management skills.

What steps should P&G take to prepare employees for international assignments to help them succeed? Should P&G also include spouses and family members in preparation for international assignments? Why or why not?

Source: Based on M. Schoeff, "P&G places a premium on international experience," *Workforce Management* (April 10, 2006): 28; "Partnering for Healthy Babies," from *www.pg.com*, accessed April 14, 2015.

Endnotes

1. "Workforce readiness programs prepare future workforce," *T+D* (December 2010): 23; *www.cewd.org*, the website for Center for Energy Workforce Development; *www.jobcorps.gov*, the website for Job Corps.

2. Ibid.

3. M. McGraw, "Manufacturing talent," *Human Resource Executive* (November 2014): 44–46.

4. From http://www.yearup.org, website for Year Up and "Making Change Happen: 2013 Annual Report," accessed from *www.yearup.org*, April 9, 2015.

5. "Caring for Wisconsin, Health Science YA," from http://dwd.wisconsin.gov/dwd/publications/dws/youthapprenticeship, accessed April 9, 2015.

6. "United States Department of Labor, Workforce Innovation and Opportunity Act," from http://www.doleta.gov/WIOA/, accessed April 9, 2015.

7. See http//online.onetcenter.org/. the website for the Occupational Information Network (O*NET), U.S. Department of Labor, accessed August 22, 2015.

8. M. Hequet, "The union push for lifelong learning," *training* (March 1994): 26–31; S. J. Schurman, M. K. Hugentoble, and H. Stack, "Lessons from the UAW-GM Paid Education Leave Program." In *Joint Training Programs,* eds. L. A. Ferman et al. (Ithaca, NY: ILR Press, 1991): 71–94. See also *www.nactel.org*, the website for the National Coalition for Telecommunications Education and Learning, accessed August 22, 2015.

9. See *www.nactel.org*, the website for the National Coalition for Telecommunications Education and Learning, accessed April 9, 2015. L. Schroeder, "Agree to degrees," *Chief Learning Officer* (March 2015): 42–45.

10. "Chrysler Group LLC opens state-of-the-art world class manufacturing academy in Warren, Michigan," from http://www.media.chrysler.com/newsrelease.do;jsessionid=E0906FFBCF81B726FAC396C65DCDA070?&id=11917&mid=9, accessed August 22, 2015. B. Snavely, "High-tech retraining," *Columbus Dispatch* (February 4, 2012): A1, A9.

11. J. Sample, *Avoiding Legal Liability for Adult Educators, Human Resource Developers, and Instructional Designers* (Malabar, FL: Krieger Publishing, 2007); A. Cardy, "The legal framework of human resource development: Overview mandates, structures, and financial implications," *Human Resource Development Review* 2 (2003): 26–53; A. Cardy, "The legal framework of human resource development, Part II: Fair

employment, negligence, and implications for scholars and practitioners," *Human Resource Development Review* 2 (2003): 130–154; A. Cardy, "Reputation, goodwill, and loss: Entering the employee training audit question," *Human Resource Development Review* (September 2005): 279–304.

12. W. Turner and C. Thrutchley, "Employment Law and Practices Training: No Longer the Exception—It's the Rule," in *Legal Report* (Alexandria, VA: Society for Human Resources Management, July–August 2003): 1–4.

13. A. Pasztor and S. Carey, "Rescue renews focus on training," *The Wall Street Journal* (January 17–18, 2009): A3.

14. Federal Aviation Administration, "FAA-Industry Training Standards (FITS)" from www.faa.gov, accessed August 22, 2015.

15. D. Zielinski, "A closer look," *training* (November 2005): 16–22.

16. Z. Elinson, "Length of basic training in South Carolina's police academy is too short, experts say," *The Wall Street Journal* (April 9, 2015): A4.

17. G. Kimmerling, "A licensing primer for trainers," *Training and Development* (January 1997): 30–35; M. Partridge, "Copyrights and wrongs," *HR Magazine* (November 2008): 101–104; T. Hill, "Use it or lose it," *training* (March/April 2015): 30–31.

18. R. Ganzel, "Copyright or copywrong?" *training* (2002): 36–44.

19. U.S. Department of Labor, *A Report on the Glass Ceiling Initiative* (Washington, D.C.: U.S. Government Printing Office, 1991); C. Petrini, "Raising the ceiling for women," *Training and Development* (November 1995): 12.

20. T. Maurer and N. Rafuse, "Learning, not litigating: Managing employee development and avoiding claims of age discrimination," *Academy of Management Executive* 15 (2001): 110–121.

21. "University of Phoenix to Pay $1,875,000 for Religious Bias Against Non-Mormons," November 10, 2008, press release from www.eeoc.gov, the website for the Equal Employment Opportunity Commission (EEOC).

22. "EEOC Brings Class Lawsuit Against New Prime Trucking for Sex Discrimination," September 22, 2011, press release from *www.eeoc.gov*, accessed August 22, 2015.

23. K. Weise, "The man who took on Merrill," *Bloomberg BusinessWeek* (November 27, 2013), from http://www.bloomberg.com/bw/articles/2013-11-27/merrill-lynchs-racial-bias-settlement-vindicates-george-mcreynolds, accessed April 9, 2015.

24. R. Sharpe, "In whose hands? Allstate and Scientology," *The Wall Street Journal* (March 22, 1995): A1, A4.

25. Bureau of National Affairs, "Female grocery store employees prevail in sex-bias suit against Lucky Stores," *BNAs Employee Relations Weekly* 10 (1992): 927–938; *Stender v. Lucky Store Inc.,* DCN California, No. C-88-1467, 8/18/92.

26. J. Sample and R. Hylton, "Falling off a log—and landing in court," *training* (May 1996): 67–69.

27. E. Green and J. Schwartz, "Are your employees being compensated correctly for training time?" (January 10, 2014), from *www.lexology.com*, accessed August 22, 2015.

28. H. Dolezalek, "The path to inclusion," *training* (May 2008): 52–54.

29. E. McKeown, "Quantifiable inclusion strategies," *T+D,* October 2010): 16.

30. S. E. Jackson et al., *Diversity in the Workplace: Human Resource Initiatives* (New York: Guilford Press, 1992).

31. Z. Kalinoski, D. Steele-Johnson, E. Payton, K. Leas, J. Steinke, and N. Bowling, "A meta-analytic evaluation of diversity training outcomes," *Journal of Organizational Behavior,* 34 (2013): 1076–1104.

32. S. Rynes and B. Rosen, "A field study of factors affecting the adoption and perceived success of diversity training," *Personnel Psychology* 48 (1995): 247–270.

33. J. Lublin, "Do you know your hidden work biases?" *The Wall Street Journal* (January 10, 2014): B1, B4.

34. Ibid.

35. For example, see P. McKay, D. Avery, and M. Morris, "A tale of two climates: Diversity climate from subordinates' and managers' perspectives and their role in store unit sales performance," *Personnel Psychology,* 62 (2009): 767–791; M. Triana, M. Garcia, and A. Colella, "Managing diversity: How organizational efforts to support diversity moderate the effects of perceived racial discrimination on affective commitment," *Personnel Psychology* 63 (2010): 817–844.

36. T. Kochan et al., "The effects of diversity on business performance: Report of the Diversity Research Network," *Human Resource Management* 42 (2003): 8–21; F. Hansen, "Diversity's business case just doesn't add up," *Workforce* (June 2003): 29–32; M. J. Wesson and C. I. Gogus, "Shaking hands with the computer: An examination of two methods of newcomer socialization," *Journal of Applied Psychology* 90 (2005), 1018–1026; H. J. Klein and N. A. Weaver, "The effectiveness of an organizational-level orientation training program in the socialization of new hires," *Personnel Psychology* 53 (2000): 47–66. K. Jones, E. King, J. Nelson, D. Geller, and L. Bowes-Sperry, "Beyond the business case: The ethical perspective on diversity training," *Human Resource Management* (January–February 2013): 55–74.

37. B. Groysberg and K. Connolly, "Great leaders who make the mix work," *Harvard Business Review* (September 2013): 68–76.

38. R. Anand and M. Winters, "A retrospective view of corporate diversity training from 1964 to the present," *Academy of Management Learning and Education,* 7 (2008), 356–372; H. Dolezalek, "The path to inclusion," *training* (May 2008): 52–54; "Sodexo 2010 Diversity and Inclusion Annual Report," from *www.sodexousa.com*, the website for Sodexo USA, accessed June 20, 2011. "Diversity & inclusion," from http://sodexousa.com, accessed April 13, 2015; M. Landel, "How we did it . . . SODEXO's CEO on smart diversification," *Harvard Business Review* (March 2015): 41–44; R. Emelo, "Peer collaboration enhances diversity and inclusion," *TD* (December 2014): 48–52.

39. K. Bezrvkova, K. Jehn, & C. Spell, "Reviewing diversity training: Where we have been and where we should go," *Academy of Management Learning and Education* 11 (2012): 207–227; C. T. Schreiber, K. F. Price, and A. Morrison, "Workforce diversity and the glass ceiling: Practices, barriers, possibilities," *Human Resource Planning* 16 (1994): 51–69.

40. "Most Employers Lacking a Strategy for Developing Women Leaders," press release from October 25, 2010, at *www.mercer.com*, the website of Mercer, a global provider of consulting, outsourcing, and investment services; R. Pyrillis, "Programs that help women take the lead," *Workforce Management,* January 2011, 3–4.

41. B. Groysberg and K. Connolly, "Great leaders who make the mix work," *Harvard Business Review* (September 2013): 68–76.

42. U.S. Department of Labor, *A Report on the Glass Ceiling Initiative* (Washington, D.C.: U.S. Department of Labor, 1991).

43. P. J. Ohlott, M. N. Ruderman, and C. D. McCauley, "Gender differences in managers' developmental job experiences," *Academy of Management Journal* 37 (1994): 46–67; D. Mattioli, "Programs to promote female managers win citations," *The Wall Street Journal,* January 30, 2007, B7; B. Groysberg and K. Connolly, "Great leaders who make the mix work," *Harvard Business Review* (September 2013): 68–76.

44. J. Green, "This is not a trend," *Bloomberg BusinessWeek* (September 1–7, 2014): 19–20.

45. U.S. Department of Labor, *A Report on the Glass Ceiling Initiative* (Washington, D.C.: U.S. Government Printing Office, 1991)*;* R. A. Noe, "Women and mentoring: A review and research agenda," *Academy of Management Review* 13 (1988): 65–78; B. R. Ragins and J. L. Cotton, "Easier said than done: Gender differences in perceived barriers to gaining a mentor," *Academy of Management Journal* 34 (1991): 939–951.

46. L. A. Mainiero, "Getting anointed for advancement: The case of executive women," *Academy of Management Executive* 8 (1994): 53–67; J. S. Lublin, "Women at top still are distant from CEO jobs," *The Wall Street Journal* (February 28, 1995): B1,B5; P. Tharenov, S. Latimer, and D. Conroy, "How do you make it to the top? An examination of influences on women's and men's managerial advancement," *Academy of Management Journal* 37 (1994): 899–931.

47. P. Tharenou, "Going up? Do traits and informal social processes predict advancement in management?" *Academy of Management Journal* 44 (2001): 1005–1017; P. Cappelli, M. Hamori, and R. Bonet, "Who's got those top jobs?" *Harvard Business Review* (March 2014): 74–79.

48. "The 2015 National Association for Female Executives top 50 companies for executive women: AstraZeneca," from *www.workingmother.com*, accessed April 13, 2015.

49. K. Bowers, "Change the ratio," *www.workingmother.com*, accessed April 13, 2015.

50. L. Freifeld, "TEIG locks in on leadership," *training* (January/February 2011): 34–39.

51. S. Ladika, "Lost in translation," *Workforce Management* (May 2013): 30–33.

52. K. Johnson, "Career Builders: A stint abroad," *The Wall Street Journal* (February 10, 2015): B7.

53. A. Andors, "Happy returns," *HR Magazine* (March 2010): 61–62.

54. R. L. Tung, "Selection and training of personnel for overseas assignments," *Columbia Journal of World Business* 16 (1981): 18–78; R. Feintzeig, "After stints abroad, re-entry can be hard," *The Wall Street Journal* (September 18, 2013): B6.

55. W. A. Arthur Jr. and W. Bennett Jr., "The international assignee: The relative importance of factors perceived to contribute to success," *Personnel Psychology* 48 (1995): 99–114; G. M. Spreitzer, M. W. McCall Jr., and J. D. Mahoney, "Early identification of international executive potential," *Journal of Applied Psychology* 82 (1997): 6–29.

56. J. S. Black and J. K. Stephens, "The influence of the spouse on American expatriate adjustment and intent to stay in Pacific Rim overseas assignments," *Journal of Management* 15 (1989): 529–544; M. Shaffer and D. A. Harrison, "Forgotten partners of international assignments: Development and test of a model of spouse adjustment," *Journal of Applied Psychology* 86 (2001): 238–254.

57. M. Shaffer et al., "You can take it with you: Individual differences and expatriate effectiveness," *Journal of Applied Psychology* 91 (2006): 109–125; P. Caligiuri, "The big five personality characteristics as predictors of expatriate desire to terminate the assignment and supervisor-rated performance," *Personnel Psychology* 53 (2000): 67–88.

58. H. Ren, M. Shaffer, D. Harrison, C. Fu, and K. Fodchuk, "Reactive adjustment or proactive embedding? Multistudy, multiwave evidence for dual pathways to expatriate retention," *Personnel Psychology* 67 (2014): 203–239.

59. G. Weber, "Intel's internal approach," *Workforce Management* 83 (2004): 49.

60. E. Dunbar and A. Katcher, "Preparing managers for Foreign assignments," *Training and Development Journal* (September 1990): 45–47.

61. J. S. Black and M. Mendenhall, "A Practical but Theory-Based Framework for Selecting Cross-Cultural Training Methods." In *Readings and Cases in International Human Resource Management,* eds. M. Mendenhall and G. Oddou (Boston: PWS-Kent, 1991): 177–204.

62. P. Tam, "Culture course," *The Wall Street Journal* (May 25, 2004): B1,B12.

63. "Success is in the details," *T+D* (October 2009): 37–38; D. Zielinski, "Training game," *HR Magazine* (March 2010): 64–66.

64. S. Ronen, "Training the International Assignee," in *Training and Development in Organizations,* ed. I. L. Goldstein (San Francisco: Jossey-Bass, 1989), 417–453.

65. P. R. Harris and R. T. Moran, *Managing Cultural Differences* (Houston: Gulf, 1991); S. Ladika, "Socially evolved," *Workforce Management* (September 2010): 18–22.

66. H. Ren, M. Shaffer, D. Harrison, C. Fu, and K. Fodchuk, "Reactive adjustment or proactive embedding? Multistudy, multiwave evidence for dual pathways to expatriate retention," *Personnel Psychology* 67 (2014): 203–239.

67. J. Carter, "Globe trotters," *training* (August 2005): 22–28.

68. C. Solomon, "Unhappy trails," *Workforce* (August 2000): 36–41.

69. C. Patton, "Coming to America," *Human Resource Executive* (January/February 2012): 22, 26–29.

70. H. Lancaster, "Before going overseas, smart managers plan their homecoming," *The Wall Street Journal* (September 28, 1999): B1; A. Halcrow, "Expats: The squandered resource," *Workforce* (April 1999): 42–48.

71. P. R. Harris and R. T. Moran, *Managing Cultural Differences* (Houston: Gulf, 1991).

72. R. Feintzeig, "After stints abroad, re-entry can be hard," *The Wall Street Journal* (September 18, 2013): B6.

73. Ibid.

74. J. H. Greenhaus, G. Callanan, and V. Godshalk, *Career Management,* 4th ed. (Sage Publications, 2010).

75. M. Wang, D. Olson, and K. Shultz, *Mid and Late Career Issues: An Integrative Perspective* (New York: Routledge, 2013.)

76. S. Hewlett, L. Sherbin, and K. Sumberg, "How Gen Y and boomers will reshape your agenda," *Harvard Business Review* (July–August 2009): 71–76; A. Fox, "Mixing it up," *HR Magazine* (May 2011): 22–27; K. Ball and G. Gotsill, *Surviving the Baby Boomer Exodus* (Boston: Cengage, 2011). "Millennials: From generational differences to generating growth," from Development Dimensions Inc., http://www.ddiworld.com/DDI/media/trend-research/glf2014-findings/millennials_glf2014_ddi.pdf, accessed February 20, 2015;

"Millennials at work: Reshaping the workplace in Financial Services," from *www.pwc.com/ financial services*, accessed February 26, 2015; Sinar, E. "Perspective: Are millennials ready to lead," *GOMagazine*, http://www.ddiworld.com/go/archive/2012-issue-1/perspective-millennials-are-ready-to-lead, accessed February 20, 2015.

77. Society for Human Resource Management, *Generational Differences: Myths and Realities* 4 (Alexandria, VA: Society for Human Resource Management, 2007).

78. Career Arc, "2015 workplace flexibility study," from http://www.careerarc.com/, accessed April 13, 2015.

79. J. H. Greenhaus and N. Beutell, "Sources of conflict between work and family roles," *Academy of Management Review* 10 (1985): 76–88; J. H. Pleck, *Working Wives/Working Husbands* (Newbury Park, CA: Sage, 1985); R. Kelly and P. Voydanoff, "Work/family role strain among employed parents," *Family Relations*, 34 (1985): 367–374; J. Quick, A. Henley, and J. Quick, "At work and at home," *Organizational Dynamics* 33 (2004): 426–438.

80. Family and Medical Leave Act; from U.S. Department of Labor, Wage and Hour Division website, *www .dol.gov/whd/fmla/index.htm*, accessed August 22, 2015.

81. L. Weber and J. Lublin, "The daddy juggle: Work, life, family and chaos," *The Wall Street Journal* (June 13, 2014): B1–B2; L. Weber, "Why dads don't take paternity leave," *The Wall Street Journal* (June 13, 2013): B1, B7.

82. L. Weber, "Why dads don't take paternity leave," *The Wall Street Journal* (June 13, 2013): B1, B7; S. Kolhatkar, "Alpha dads: Men get serious about work-life balance," *Bloomberg Businessweek* (May 30, 2013): 58–63; "Deloitte benefits and rewards," from *www2.deloitte.com/us/en/pages/about-deloitte/articles/ inclusion-work-life-fit.html*, accessed April 13, 2015; M. Ramsey, "Not your father's workplace," *HR Magazine* (November 2014): 30–35.

83. W. Casper and M. Butts, *Is There a Business Case for Work-Family Programs*? (Alexandria, VA: SHRM Foundation Research Report); J. Wayne, W. Casper, R. Matthews, and T. Allen, "Family supportive organization perceptions and organizational commitment: The mediating role of work-family conflict and enrichment and partner attitudes," *Journal of Applied Psychology* 98 (2013): 606–622.

84. A. Fox, "Achieving integration," *HR Magazine*, April 2011: 42–47. T. Allen, R. Johnson, K. Kiburz, and K. Shockley, "Work-family conflict and flexible work arrangements: Deconstructing flexibility," *Personnel Psychology* 66 (2103): 345–376.

85. R. Silverman, "For manual jobs, white collar perks," *The Wall Street Journal* (October 3, 2011): B8; M. O'Brien, "Balancing work/life by the hour," *Human Resource Executive* (July/August 2011): 40–42; Families and Work Institute, *2009 Guide to Bold Ideas for Making Work Work* (New York: Families and Work Institute, 2009); S. Shellenberger, "Time-zoned: Working round the clock workforce," *The Wall Street Journal* (February 15, 2007): D1; D. Meinert, "The gift of time," *HR Magazine* (November 2011): 37–41.

86. R. Feintzeig, "Meet Silicon Valley's 'Little Elves'," *The Wall Street Journal* (November 21, 2014): A1, A10.

87. W. Bunch, "Unleashing the workforce," *Human Resource Executive* (November 2012): 14–17.

88. B. Ware, "Stop the Gen Y revolving door," *T+D* (May 2014): 58–63.

89. E. Frauenheim, "Reflecting re:flexing," *Workforce Management* (June 2013): 28–37.

90. G. Carten, K. Cook, and D. Dorsey, *Career Paths* (Chichester, U.K., 2009); J. Greenhaus, G. Callanan and V. Godshalk, *Career Management*, 4th ed. (Thousand Oaks, CA: SAGE Publications, 2010).

91. Towers Watson, "Career management: Making it work for employees and employers," 2014, from *www .towerswatson.com*, accessed April 14, 2015.

92. R. H. Vaughn and M. C. Wilson, "Career management using job trees: Charting a path through the changing organization," *Human Resource Planning* 17 (1995): 43–55.

93. H. D. Dewirst, "Career Patterns: Mobility, Specialization, and Related Career Issues." In *Contemporary Career Development Issues,* eds. R. F. Morrison and J. Adams (Hillsdale, NJ: Lawrence Erlbaum, 1991): 73–107.

94. M. Weinstein, "Please don't go," *training* (May/June 2011): 28–34.

95. Z. B. Leibowitz, B. L. Kaye, and C. Farren, "Multiple career paths," *Training and Development Journal* (October 1992): 31–35.

96. K. Essick, "He found his footing in the sand," *The Wall Street Journal* (December 12, 2013): R3.

97. J. Tergesen, "The case for quitting your job—Even if you still love it," *The Wall Street Journal* (October 13, 2014): R1–R2.

98. S. Shellenbarger, "Some employees begin to find what helps shiftworker families," *The Wall Street Journal* (September 20, 2000): B1.

99. S. Shellenbarger, "Break the competency curse: Try something new at work," *The Wall Street Journal* (August 27, 2014): D1–D2.

100. I. DeBare, "Keeping a bag packed at work: Employees today are more apt to job hop than ever before," *San Francisco Chronicle*, accessed from website for Integral Talent Systems, *www.itsinc.net/job-hop.htm* on October 7, 2011; M. Korn, "The young are happy at work," *The Wall Street Journal* (October 17, 2011): B7; R. Hoffman, B. Casnocha, and C. Yeh, "Tours of duty: The new employer-employee compact," *Harvard Business Review* (June 2013): 48–58.

101. T. Khadder, "Job-hopping: Career killer or savior?" *Excelle* (June 25, 2009), accessed at http://excelle .monster.com on October 7, 2011; A. Balderrama, "Is job hopping the new normal?" February 2, 2011, accessed at *www.azcentral.com* on October 7, 2011; "Nearly one-third of employers expect workers to job-hop," May 15, 2014, from *www.careerbuilder.com*, accessed April 2, 2015; "Is job hopping the new normal?" *TD* (August 2014): 20.

102. A. Chaker and H. Stout, "After years off, women struggle to renew their careers," *The Wall Street Journal* (May 4, 2004): A1,A8; S. Shellenbarger, "Rewriting the rule book on when mothers work," *The Wall Street Journal*; E. Simon, "Smoothing war-to-work shift takes care," *Columbus Dispatch* (October 21, 2007): D3.

103. L. Freifeld, "Warriors to workers," *training* (September/October 2010): 14–18; E. Glazer, "Vets join tough job market," *The Wall Street Journal* (November 21, 2011): B7.

104. S. Greengard, "When Johnny or Janey comes marching home," *Workforce Management* (June 2011): 3–4; Troops to Energy Jobs Program at *www.cewd.org*, the website for Center for Energy Workforce Development; T. Ridout, "AEP to Attract Military Veterans Through Troops to Energy Jobs Pilot Program," AEP Press Releases, accessed from *www.aep.com* on August 22, 2015; L. Freifeld, "Warriors to workers," *training* (September/October 2010): 14–18.

105. B. Tau, "Veterans to be offered training in solar industry," *The Wall Street Journal* (April 4–5, 2015): A4.

106. W. Cascio, *Responsible Restructuring: Creative and Profitable Alternatives to Layoffs* (San Francisco: Berrett-Koehler, 2002).

107. J. Brockner, "The Effects of Work Layoffs on Survivors: Research, Theory, and Practice," in *Research in Organizational Behavior,* Vol. 10, eds. B. M. Staw and L. L. Cummings (Hillsdale, NJ: Lawrence Erlbaum, 1988): 45–95; L. Greenhalgh, A. T. Lawrence, and R. I. Sutton, "Determinants of workforce reduction strategies in declining organizations," *Academy of Management Review* 13 (1988): 241–254; J. Nocera, "Living with layoffs," *Fortune* (April 1, 1996): 69–71; J. Martin, "Where are they now?" *Fortune* (April 1, 1996): 100–108.

108. J. Pereira, "A worker's quest for a job lands on a street corner," *The Wall Street Journal* (March 5, 2003): A1, A7.

109. D. Morse, "Older workers in the lurch," *The Wall Street Journal* (August 20, 2003): B1, B10.

110. J. C. Latack and J. B. Dozier, "After the ax falls: Job loss as career transition," *Academy of Management Review* 11 (1986): 375–392; J. Brockner, "Managing the effects of layoffs on survivors," *California Management Review* (Winter 1992): 9–28; S. L. Guinn, "Outplacement programs: Separating myth from reality," *Training and Development Journal* 42 (1988): 48–49; D. R. Simon, "Outplacement: Matching needs, matching services," *Training and Development Journal* 42 (1988): 52–57; S. Rosen and C. Paul, "Learn the inner workings of outplacement," *The Wall Street Journal* (July 31, 1995): editorial page; S. Spera, E. D. Buhrfeind, and J. P. Pennebaker, "Expressive writing and coping with job loss," *Academy of Management Journal* 37 (1994): 722–733.

111. J. McCracken and J. White, "Ford will shed 28% of workers in North America," *The Wall Street Journal* (January 24, 2006): A1, A16; J. McCracken, "To shed idled workers, Ford offers to foot the bill for college," *The Wall Street Journal* (January 18, 2006): B1, B3.

112. J. Cole, "Boeing teaches employees how to run small business," *The Wall Street Journal* (November 7, 1995): B1–B2.

113. K. Dunham, "Frustrated laid-off workers take risk of entrepreneurship," *The Wall Street Journal* (July 8, 2003): B10.

114. K. Essick, "Couple's second career means new start for New England treat," *The Wall Street Journal* (October 13, 2014): R2.

115. E. B. Picolino, "Outplacement: The view from HR," *Personnel* (March 1988): 24–27.

116. H. M. O'Neill and D. J. Lenn, "Voices of survivors: Words that downsizing CEOs should hear," *Academy of Management Executive* 9 (1995): 23–34.

117. J. Brockner, "Managing the effects of layoffs on survivors," *California Management Review* (Winter 1992): 9–28; J. Brockner et al., "Interactive effects of procedural justice and outcome negativity on victims and survivors of job loss," *Academy of Management Journal* 37 (1994): 397–409.

118. S. Brown, "Staying ahead of the curve 2003: The AARP Working in Retirement Study," American Association for Retired Persons (September 2003). Available in the "Policy and Research" section of the AARP website at *www.aarp.org*.; H. Dolezalek, "Boomer reality," *training* (May 10, 2007): 16–21.

119. R. Grossman, "Mature workers: Myths and realities," *HR Magazine* (May 2008): 40–41; G. Callahan and J. Greenhaus, "The Baby boomer generation and career management: A call to action," *Advances in Developing Human Resources* 10 (2008): 70–85; A. Gegenfurtner and M. Vauras, "Age-related differences in the relation between motivation to learn and transfer of training in adult continuing education," *Contemporary Educational Psychology* 37 (2012): 33–46.

120. C. Paullin, *The Aging Workforce: Leveraging the Talents of Mature Employees* (Alexandria, VA: SHRM Foundation, 2014); P. Garber, "Older and wiser," *T+D* (December 2013): 48–53; S. Boehm, F. Kunze, and H. Bruch, "Spotlight on age-diversity climate: The impact of age-inclusive HR practices on firm-level outcomes," *Personnel Psychology* 67 (2014): 667–704.

121. C. Leahey, "What—me retire?" *Fortune* (January 16, 2012): 56.

122. "AARP 2013 best employers to work for over fifty," from www.aarp.org, accessed April 14, 2015.

123. R. Harris, "Is this America's best employer for older workers?" from *www.huffingtonpost.com*, June 17, 2014, accessed April 14, 2015; "AARP 2013 best employers to work for over fifty," from *www.aarp.org*, accessed April 14, 2015.

124. C. A. Olson, "Who Receives Formal Firm-Sponsored Training in the U.S.?" October 15, 1996, National Center for the Workplace, Institute of Industrial Relations, University of California (Berkeley). Document at http://violet.lib.berkeley.edu/-iir/.

125. R. Grossman, "Keep pace with older workers," *HR Magazine* (May 2008): 38–46.

126. A. L. Kamouri and J. C. Cavanaugh, "The impact of preretirement education programs on workers' preretirement socialization," *Journal of Occupational Behavior* 7 (1986): 245–256; N. Schmitt and J. T. McCune, "The relationship between job attitudes and the decision to retire," *Academy of Management Review* 24 (1981): 795–802; N. Schmitt et al., "Comparison of early retirees and non-retirees," *Personnel Psychology* 32 (1981): 327–340; T. A. Beehr, "The process of retirement," *Personnel Psychology* 39 (1986): 31–55; S. M. Comrie, "Teach employees to approach retirement as a new career," *Personnel Journal* 64(8) (1985): 106–108; L. Grensing-Pophal, "Departure plans," *HR Magazine* (July 2003): 83–86.

127. K. Greene, "Back on an early shift, but at half the pay," *The Wall Street Journal* (March 5, 2003): B1, B2.

128. S. Mulligan, "Wisdom of the ages," *HR Magazine* (November 2014): 23–27; V. Giang, "The fifty best employers for older workers," June 17, 2013 from *www.businessinsider.com*, accessed April 14, 2015.

129. K. Greene, "Many older workers to delay retirement until after age 70," *The Wall Street Journal* (September 23, 2003): D2; C. Leahey, "What—me retire?" *Fortune* (January 16, 2012): 56.

130. "Guide to early-out retirement offers for federal and postal employees," from http://www.myfederalretirement.com, accessed April 14, 2015.

131. M. L. Colusi, P. B. Rosen, and S. J. Herrin, "Is your early retirement package courting disaster?" *Personnel Journal* (August 1988): 60–67.

132. B. Rosen and T. Jerdee, "Managing Older Workers' Careers." In *Research in Personnel and Human Resources Management,* Vol. 6, eds. G. Ferris and K. Rowland (Greenwich, CT: JAI Press, 1998): 37–74.

Chapter **Eleven**

The Future of Training and Development

Objectives

After reading this chapter, you should be able to

1. Identify the future trends that are likely to influence training departments and trainers.
2. Discuss how these future trends may affect training delivery and administration, as well as the strategic role of the training department.
3. Discuss how rapid instructional design differs from traditional training design.
4. Discuss the advantages of embedded learning.
5. Discuss how training can contribute to a company's sustainability initiative.
6. Discuss the implications of cloud computing for learning, training, and development.

Welcome to the Office of the Future!

What might the office of the future look like? Physically, it will look the same as today's offices. Employees still will have desks, meet in conference rooms, and eat in the cafeteria. There likely will be new technology, such as smaller tablet computers. Teleconferences will provide instantaneous language translations, making it easier for employees who do not speak each other's language to talk to each other. "Tables" will be able to make three-dimensional holograms of real-world objects without requiring special glasses to see them. Holographic technology (like that used to have such late entertainers as rapper Tupac Shakur or Frank Sinatra "appear" at parties and music festivals) can be used for CEOs to communicate messages to a global company "in person," employees to virtually appear in meetings, and learners to interact with complex products and equipment in a way that makes it easier to understand how they work. Offices will have special window glass that can change from a solar panel to a multimedia screen to a frosted privacy shade. Technology like that found in game consoles will allow employees to navigate computer screens just by moving their wrists. Computer programs will be available to tell employees who they should work with on their next project. People will also work with computers that capitalize on the innate strengths of humans—computers are strong on routine processing, repetitive arithmetic, and error-free consistency, while at least for now we humans are better at complex communications, pattern matching, intuition, and creativity. For example, consider two examples of how people and computers can capitalize on each other's strengths to help make the workplace more efficient and effective. In 2011, Watson, a specially programmed computer, was able to beat the best human *Jeopardy!* players (including Ken Jennings, who won more consecutive episodes of the game show than anyone in history) by quickly extracting the correct answer from huge datasets of information. Watson can understand natural language, including puns, slang, and jargon. It "learns" by reprogramming itself as more information is presented and it makes mistakes. Watson provides not one but multiple answers ranked by the probability they are correct. A pop-up window provides support for each answer. Since its debut in 2011, Watson has slimmed down in size and increased it capacity. It once took up the space of a large room. Now, Watson fits into a computer server the size of four pizza boxes and it is 240 times faster! Watson was the first step in the development of "Search bots," which can be used to review the web to find information that fits a profile provided by employees. This will include major developments, news feeds and alerts, and searches of relevant professional publications. For example, Watson helped IBM develop an adviser for oncologists who treat lung cancer. Watson was given more than 600,000 medical files and 2 million pages of medical journals and results of clinical drug trials. Doctors can ask Watson a question and Watson will provide treatment recommendations. The search bot will improve with feedback telling it that you like some content but not other content.

Keep in mind that regardless of current advances in computer pattern recognition and complex communication, human skills in applied math and statistics, negotiation and group dynamics, writing, solving open-ended problems, persuasion, nurturing, and interaction cannot be replaced by a computer and will remain in demand. For example, driverless cars, self-driving trucks at iron ore mines that need no human operators, and computers that perform legal research are recent advances in automation. But computing technology has been unable to replicate human skills and abilities used to fold laundry! Unlike humans, robots have been unable to make the distinctions between fabric types and weights and irregular clothes sizes that are needed to neatly fold clothes. Researchers are working to narrow the gap between the human mind and the robot mind. Cyberconsciousness, an awareness of feelings, caring, and living, is being developed for software. Cyberconsciousness will allow us to download our brains to create virtual people and "mindclones." For example, the Siri app on i-Phones is a crude version of a virtual person. The development of virtual people is currently limited because of the lack of power of software, but research is under way to develop virtual versions of historical people. Cyberconsciousness will allow robots to take over jobs and become our workplace partners. For example, Sophie, a robot developed jointly by NEC Corporation in Japan and La Trobe University Business School in Australia, is intended to be used to interview job candidates. Sophie can ask and respond to questions, assess a candidate's physiological responses, and compare their results with the top 10 percent of the existing workforce.

Nanotechnology advances will be available to help us enhance our learning and computational skills. Three-atom-wide nanobots injected into the brain could assist in memory and cognition. We may also pop ampakine pills to enhance our attention spans and aid learning and memory without experiencing the side effects of sleeplessness. Learning will likely occur 24/7 using mobile devices such as smart phones, tablets such as the iPad, and netbooks. This learning will be brief and available wherever we need it. Using global positioning system (GPS) sensitivity, we will be able to set our social networking profile to alert us when topic experts are available and tell us their physical proximity from our location. Social learning via shared workspaces, social networks, and wikis (learning from others) will supplement traditional training, encouraging employees to learn from each other, from trainers and instructors, and from other work experts.

Sources: Based on J. Faragher, "Could holographic technology revolutionize training and development?" *Personnel Today* (February 14, 2013), from *www.personnelltoday.com*, accessed February 21, 2013; M. Mihelich, "Welcome to cyberia," *Workforce* (January 2015): 40–43, 49; G. Colvin, "In the future, will there be any work left for people to do?" *Fortune* (June 2, 2014), from *www.fortune.com*, accessed April 21, 2015; J. Hempel, "IBM's massive bet on Watson," *Fortune* (October 7, 2013): 81–88; T. Aeppel, "Jobs and the clever robot," *The Wall Street Journal* (February 25, 2015): A1, A10; G. Colvin, "Brave new work: The office of tomorrow," *Fortune* (January 16, 2012): 34–41; 49–54; P. Galagan, "How would you train a transhuman?" *T+D* (January 2012): 27–29; P. Ketter, "2010 six trends that will change workplace learning forever," *T+D* (December 2010): 34–40; E. Brynjolfsson and A. McAfee, "Winning the race with ever-smarter machines," *MIT Sloan Management Review* (Winter 2012): 53–60.

INTRODUCTION

The previous ten chapters discussed training design and delivery, development and career management, and training's role in contributing to social responsibility through managing diversity and inclusion and helping the multigenerational workforce prepare and successfully deal with career challenges. This chapter takes a look at what the future of training and development might look like. The chapter opener highlights how technological advancements will shape where and how we work and learn. Technological advances represent one trend that is likely to influence the future of training and development and your future as a trainer. Table 11.1 shows the future trends discussed in this chapter that will influence training.

TABLE 11.1
Future Trends That Will Affect Training

- Need to contribute to sustainability
- Use of new technologies for training delivery at instruction
- Breakthroughs in neuroscience about learning
- Greater emphasis on speed in design, focus on content
- Increased emphasis on capturing and sharing intellectual capital and social learning
- Increased use of just-in-time learning and performance support
- Increased emphasis on performance analysis, Big Data, and learning for business enhancement
- Increased use of stakeholder-focused learning, training partnerships, and outsourcing training

Training for Sustainability

Sustainability refers to a company's ability to make a profit without sacrificing the resources of its employees, the community, or the environment. A growing number of companies have made sustainability an important part of their business strategy. Training and development can contribute to companies' sustainability initiatives by providing learning opportunities for employees in organizations in developing countries that lack the resources, providing development experiences for employees in poor and emerging countries that benefit the local community, and teaching employers to protect the environment. Consider how training at Novartis and Ingersoll Rand is helping these companies reach their sustainability goals.[1]

Novartis, the pharmaceutical company, is actively involved in improving health care in Africa by helping the fight against infectious diseases that have made life expectancy in Africa fifteen years less than the global average.[1] The Novartis Malaria Initiative has delivered more than 500 million free treatments. To support health professionals working with sick children, Novartis worked with the World Health Organization to develop e-learning for managing childhood illnesses. Alcon, the eye division of Novartis, has trained eye care professionals in Sierra Leone. Also, Novartis supports the Regional Psychosocial Support Initiative (REPSSI), an African-based philanthropic organization that provides emotional and psychological support to children affected by the HIV/AIDS epidemic. The company's trainers provide REPSSI's employees with leadership development training. To help meet the organization's goal of helping children and youth so that they can live with hope and dignity, REPSSI managers need training in communication skills, providing feedback, intercultural skills, and project management. Novartis has transformed its corporate training programs into a form useful for REPSSI. The training content is delivered through instructor-led courses and e-learning. Novartis and training vendor partners, including business schools, send speakers at their own expense to Africa. Instructors are also available for follow-up after each course is completed.

Ingersoll Rand, a global industrial company, wanted employees to understand how to reduce energy consumption and waste and to lower emissions. The company has several target goals for becoming more sustainable by 2020, including reducing greenhouse gas emissions of its operations 35 percent and a 50 percent reduction in the greenhouse gases produced by its heating, ventilation, air-conditioning, and refrigeration products. To accomplish these goals, Ingersoll Rand developed the Design for Sustainability training program. The training emphasizes understanding sustainability and incorporating it in product design and how to analyze and communicate the value of sustainability in product markets. Employees can receive two levels of credentials in the program. The silver level requires seven hours of self-paced online learning and focuses on understanding why Ingersoll Rand focuses on design sustainability. The gold level includes ten hours of self-paced online learning. It also includes three ninety-minute sessions led by a virtual instructor from UL Environment, a consulting firm. To receive either the silver- or gold-level certification requires employees to pass an exam. The first participants in the program included design and manufacturing engineers, product managers, and other employees working in product development. To evaluate the program, Ingersoll Rand is collecting data on the number of new products developed using materials to reduce greenhouse gases, the use of new material to reduce product weight (which reduces shipping costs and increases fuel efficiency), and employee engagement. Based on the positive feedback it received from the first participants in the program, Ingersoll Rand is planning to offer it to all employees.

INCREASED USE OF NEW TECHNOLOGIES FOR TRAINING DELIVERY AND INSTRUCTION

The use of social media, smartphones, and other new technologies will likely increase in the future for several reasons. First, the cost of these technologies will decrease. Second, companies can use technology to better prepare employees to serve customers and generate new business. Third, use of these new technologies can substantially reduce the training costs related to bringing geographically dispersed employees to one central training location (e.g., travel, food, and housing). Fourth, these technologies allow trainers to build into training many of the desirable features of a learning environment (e.g., practice, feedback, reinforcement). Fifth, as companies employ more contingent employees (e.g., part-timers and consultants) and offer more alternative work arrangements (e.g., flexible work schedules and working from home), technology will allow training to be delivered to any place and at any time. Sixth, new technologies will make it easier for training and performance support to be accessible to learners anytime and anyplace.

Table 11.2 shows technological advances that will likely influence training delivery and instruction. Wearable technology is being used for consumer applications. For example, guests at Walt Disney World wear MagicBands that substitute for their park tickets, charge cards, and hotel room keys.[2] MagicBands link to a phone app (My Disney Experience), which tracks groups visiting the park, allowing them to see the location of others in their group in order to arrange meeting places. Wearable bands such as FitBits allow us to track how many steps we walk each day; our heart rate before, during, and after exercise; and how many calories we burned. Smart eyewear allows images to be projected directly onto the retina of the eye. The technology takes what can be shown on a computer screen, reduces it, and projects it on the retina where it can be seen in full color. Wearables are just beginning to be developed and used for training and performance support solutions. Wearable Intelligence provides smart eyewear technology and camera technology that gives employees hands-free, voice-activated access to procedures and checklists; live access to experts using tablet computers that allow data and live video sharing; the opportunity to review best-practice videos before or during the performance of complex procedures

TABLE 11.2

New Technological Advances That Will Influence Training

Source: Based on K. Everson, "Special report: Learning is all in the wrist," *Chief Learning Officer* (March 15, 2015), from *www.clomedia.com*, accessed March 18, 2015; "Overview Tin Can API," *www.tincanapi.com/overview*, accessed April 20, 2015; J. Ford and T. Meyer, "Advances in training technology: Meeting the workplace challenges of talent development, deep specialization, and collaborative learning." In *The Psychology of Workplace Technology*, eds. M. Coovert and L. Thompson, (New York: Routledge, 2014): 43–76.

Wearables (smartwatches, bands, smart eyewear)
Gamification
Wireless Tablet-Based Technology
Mobile Learning
Augmented Reality
Virtual Communications
Tin Can API (or Experience API)
Learning Records Store (LRS)
Artificial Intelligence

and operations; and real-time notifications and alerts.[3] The technology is currently being used in energy and health care. An operator who might be working on a remote oil rig or a surgeon in a sterile operating room can share live video with experts and get their advice needed to fix a broken valve or complete a medical procedure, while remaining focused on the equipment or patient. Wearable technologies can also potentially be used to provide useful needs assessment data by tracking what tasks employees perform the most. For example, a health club could track how much time fitness trainers spend in their offices, working in the gym providing personal training, or conducting group exercise classes. This helps managers and trainers identify how frequently tasks are performed, which is useful information for determining what tasks and skills should receive the most attention in training programs. Also, this information could be useful for evaluating if fitness trainers are spending too much time performing certain tasks, for example, administrative tasks in their offices. This could trigger further needs assessment to determine if this is a training problem. That is, fitness trainers may be spending more time on administrative tasks because they lack the sales and interpersonal skills needed to interact with customers and convince them to sign up for personal training. Smartwatches, such as the Apple Watch, could be used to provide training and help make sure employees complete it.[4] For example, an employee's smartwatch can deny them access to certain areas of a manufacturing plant until they successfully complete a required safety compliance course.

PlayerLync, a training and development software company, has developed wireless tablet–based technology.[5] This technology shrinks video and documents with integrated, interactive messaging to miniscule sizes and delivers them quickly and automatically, even in low-bandwidth environments. Professional and college sports teams have used the tablet-based technology to develop digital playbooks and game preparation video, including the coaches' comments. This technology is beginning to be used in companies for training retail, construction, and restaurant teams.

Augmented reality refers to a live direct or indirect view of a physical, real-world environment whose elements are supplemented by computer-generated sound, video, graphics, or GPS data. Augmented reality can allow a learner to enter books, magazines, and training rooms and experience them in three-dimensional form as in real life. An intelligent agent such as Apple's Siri can help the learner navigate their learning experience.

On-demand learning and message boards allow employees to choose what they want to learn and to interact with their peers and experts. Employees will be able to see job openings and career paths and have the freedom to choose courses to develop the skills and knowledge required for these opportunities. They can share and communicate with peers about what they find fun and challenging in their positions.

Artificial intelligence will become even more humanlike and accessible at a lower cost. Amelia is a computer who learns from textbooks, transcriptions of conversations, e-mail chains, and other texts.[6] As long as the answer is in the data she receives, she can solve problems. She also has the ability to learn. Programmers have tried to provide her with the human ability to think. Amelia is already being tested at working in customer call centers. Customer service depends on providing the right answer to the same question, regardless of who calls. Amelia can provide the correct answer because prior to working on her own, she has worked alongside a human customer service rep, listening to every support request received and the answers given. Amelia helps automate tasks but she is not alive. However, she does have three emotional states—arousal, dominance, and pleasure—that are influenced by how customers communicate with her. These emotions affect her decision making in dealing with customers. Robots with artificial intelligence such as Amelia will likely provide performance support increasingly in the future or entirely replace employees in nonexpert repetitive jobs.

The **Tin Can API** (or **Experience API**) is a specification for learning technology that makes it possible to collect data about an employee's or a team's online and face-to-face learning experiences.[7] The Tin Can API allows the collection of data based in the reality that learning occurs everywhere using different tools and methods, including simulations, virtual worlds, serious games, social collaboration, and through real-world experiences and formal training programs. When an employee engages in learning, the Tin Can API sends statements in the form of a learner, an action, and an activity such as "I did this" to a Learning Records Store. The **Learning Records Store (LRS)** collects and stores all of the learning experiences in the form of statements that can be organized and presented in a meaningful way. LRSs can communicate with each other, allowing data about learning activities to be easily shared across organizations. Also, LRSs can be accessed by learning management systems and reporting tools. Employees can have their own "personal lockers," which include their personal learning history. Enabled devices can automatically send Tin Can API statements when learning is ongoing and completed. The LRS can be used to show the relationship between learning experiences and business outcomes such as sales, revenue, customer satisfaction, safety, and employee engagement (recall our discussion of Big Data in Chapter Six, "Training Evaluation"). For example, Devereux is a nonprofit behavioral health-care organization that provides services for individuals with emotional, developmental, and educational disabilities.[8] Devereux wanted to improve treatment outcomes for individuals served by enhancing employee performance. An LRS developed by Watershed allowed this by tracking the experiences that happen to employees during training as well as during performance monitoring on the job, and correlating that experience data to the real-world outcomes of individuals served.

The use of games and mobile learning is likely to increase as companies seek to make training fun, maximize the learning experience, and appeal to millennials' and other learners' expectations that learning is quick, includes short interactive lessons, is available at their fingertips, and allows them to ask their peers questions, share experiences, and seek advice.[9] Several surveys of business and learning leaders have found that companies not currently using games for training are considering using them in the next few years and mobile learning is expected to contribute significantly to how their organizations learn in the future.[10] The gamification experience might include advanced simulations that learners can explore in a three-dimensional environment.

BREAKTHROUGHS IN NEUROSCIENCE ABOUT LEARNING

Advances in neuroscience are increasing researchers' ability to study the brain and its functioning.[11] This is leading to a better understanding of how we learn which can be used to design more effective training and development programs. For example, researchers have shown that whether an idea can be easily recalled is linked to the strength of activating the hippocampus, located in the lower section of the brain, during a learning task. The stronger the hippocampus is stimulated during learning, the greater the recall of the idea.

Further research on the hippocampus has identified the conditions that are necessary for learning to occur (attention, generation, emotion, and spacing). From a training design perspective, this means that learners have to eliminate distractions, they need to make their own connections to new ideas, they need some but not overwhelming emotional stimulation, and long-term recall of learning is better when we learn information over several different time periods rather than all at once. Time Warner Cable Enterprises applied results of the hippocampus research to a leadership development program that included weekly videos, practice exercises, and a two-hour webinar. Learning in short, engaging bursts held managers' attention. Immediate, one-page practice tools were provided to help managers use what they saw in the videos. The entire program was spaced out over thirty days. The managers' emotions were stimulated by the communications about the sense of urgency for the program and the realization that thousands of their peers were participating in the program at the same time. There are many other areas of ongoing neuroscience research that can potentially influence training and development program design. For example, research is helping us understand the conditions that are necessary for learners to make creative insights between learning content and its application to work issues and problems. Other research is investigating the biological markers of cognitive processes that are known to accelerate learning (e.g., self-explanation or other meaning-based processing methods), which can help us understand how feedback can be provided to learners to help them consistently use the most effective cognitive processes for learning.[12]

INCREASED EMPHASIS ON SPEED IN DESIGN, FOCUS ON CONTENT, AND USE OF MULTIPLE DELIVERY METHODS

Because of new technology, trainers are being challenged to find new ways to use instructional design.[13] Shifts are taking place in who is leading the learning (from the instructor to the employee), as well as where learning is taking place (from workplace to mobile learning). For example, trainers need to determine the best way to design an effective training course for a smartphone. Despite the use of new technology for learning, the fundamental questions remain: Why is training occurring? Who is the audience? What resources are necessary so that employees can learn what they need to know?

As discussed in Chapter One, "Introduction to Employee Training and Development," the traditional training design model has been criticized for several reasons. First, it is a linear approach driven by subject-matter experts (SMEs). Second, the instructional system design model uses a rational, step-by-step approach that assumes that the training content is stable. Third, given the accelerated demand for training to be delivered just in time, traditional training takes too long. **Rapid instructional design (RID)** is a group of techniques that allows training to be built more quickly. RID modifies the training design model, which consists of needs analysis, design, development, implementation, and evaluation (recall the discussion of training design in Chapter One). There are two important principles in RID.[14] One is that instructional content and process can be developed independently of each other. The second is that resources that are devoted to design and delivery of instruction can be reallocated as appropriate. *Design* includes everything that happens before the training experience; *delivery* is what happens during the training experience. For example, if a company has limited resources for training delivery, such as large groups of trainees and a tight schedule, extra time should be allocated to the design process. Table 11.3 lists RID strategies. For example, learning preferences make it difficult to develop a training program that maximizes learning for all employees. As a result, if possible, training content can be offered through books, manuals, audiotapes, videotapes, and online learning. It may also be possible to combine some steps of the design process, such as analyses and evaluation. For example, knowledge tests and other evaluation outcomes may be based on task analysis and other needs analysis results. There is no need to conduct separate analyses of training needs and learning outcomes. If the client is convinced that there is a training need and if the trainer can quickly confirm this need, then there is no reason to conduct a full needs analysis (e.g., new regulations that affect business transactions in financial services, or product changes). Job aids such as checklists, worksheets, and performance support tools can be provided to employees based on the results of a task analysis to identify activities and decisions needed to complete a procedure. Job aids can be chosen to help employees complete the procedure, and training can be provided to teach employees how to use the job aid. The point to keep in mind is that use of a training design process (or instructional design process), as discussed in Chapter One, should not be abandoned. Rather, in the future, trainers will further develop RID techniques to reduce the time and cost and to increase the efficiency of training design in order to better meet business needs.

Managers are demanding training courses that are shorter and that focus only on the necessary content.[15] Training departments will be expected to reduce the number of courses and programs that are offered without directly addressing a business issue or performance problem. SMEs used as trainers will be expected to focus their presentations on information that is directly relevant to trainees. Seminars and classes that take place over several days or half-days will have to be retooled to be more accessible and individualized. Bass & Associates, P.C., is a law firm that specializes in debt recovery. In the debt recovery business, employees spend much of the time on the phone. Bass provides employees with Bits, mini-training videos that take three to twelve minutes to watch.[16] The videos are available to employees on demand. After they complete the videos, employees take short quizzes to assess their learning. Other companies are asking trainees to complete more pre class assignments and are using more post course job aids. The development of focused content will become easier because of blogs and podcasts that allow training content to be developed without programming languages such

TABLE 11.3
Examples of RID Strategies

Source: Based on S. Thiagarajan, "Rapid Instructional Development." In *The ASTD Handbook of Training Design and Delivery,* ed. G. Piskurich, P. Beckschi, and B. Hall (New York: McGraw-Hill, 2000): 54–75.

Focus on accomplishment and performance.
Develop a learning system instead of an instructional system.
Use shortcuts (e.g., use existing records for needs assessment; conduct focus groups).
Combine different steps of the instructional design process.
Implement training and continuously improve it.
Skip steps in the instructional design process.
Use existing course materials that can be customized with examples, exercises, and assignments.
Develop instruction around job aids and performance support.
Use recording equipment, Internet, and e-mail to collect data and exchange information with SMEs.

as Hypertext Markup Language (HTML). Content-developed authoring tools will likely continue to become more user-friendly. More companies will consider using massive open online courses (MOOCs) for training (MOOCs are discussed in Chapter Eight, "Technology-Based Training Methods.").[17] MOOCs are an attractive training delivery method because they provide consistent learning and allow employees to learn through collaboration, observing through videos, and listening to subject experts. Learning can occur anytime or anyplace employees can access the online course; credentials, certificates, or digital badges can be used as incentives for completing the course.

Given the increased popularity of notebooks and tablets, new types of apps for learning will continue to be developed. These likely will include apps related to locating experts, the training scheduler, retirement planners, and the development activities chooser. For example, the Assessment and Development Group International has developed apps to help increase coaching success and facilitate behavioral change, engage and retain employees, and improve sales and customer relationships.[18] Using a smartphone, the Coach app allows users to identify their interaction style (driver, analytical, expressive, and supportive). A graph of team members' interaction styles is generated, and coaching tactics specific to each style are provided. The app also suggests how to modify behavior and be more responsive to team members and a question-and-answer exercise to help address specific issues that may occur during coaching.

INCREASED EMPHASIS ON CAPTURING AND SHARING INTELLECTUAL CAPITAL AND SOCIAL LEARNING

Companies that recognize the strategic value of becoming a learning organization and are concerned about the loss of valuable knowledge because their baby boomer employees are retiring (see the discussions in Chapters One and Five) will continue to seek ways to turn employees' knowledge (human capital) into a shared company asset. As emphasized in Chapter Two, "Strategic Training," training functions will focus on learning, with an emphasis on employee training and development and the management and coordination of organizational learning. Sharing knowledge and contributing to the company's intellectual capital is going to become more common as collaborative social networking technology and Web 2.0 tools make this simpler to implement. The rise of intelligent tutors and on-demand learning technologies will make connections to information faster, more current and accurate, and more easily customizable to employees' needs and work. More teams and groups of employees will make use of social media and Web 2.0 tools to share links and content with each other, participate in discussions, collaborate, and create learning content.

Social learning refers to learning with and from others. We can learn from others in face-to-face interactions occurring in classrooms, conferences, and group meetings, as well as online using social media such as Twitter, blogs, and social networks such as Facebook. Potentially, through sharing ideas, information, and experiences, we can learn more with others than we can alone.[19] For example, EMC upgraded its collaboration platform and integrated its intranet to help employees learn, share, and access company news.[20] Within two weeks of the upgrade, twenty thousand more employees used the platform. Also, the number of documents created has increased over 500 percent, 200 percent more discussions were created, and there has been over 100 percent increase in replies to discussion. Tata Consultancy Services Limited provides employees with a social learning application known as Knome. Nearly half of Tata Consultancy employees actively participate on Knome, forming communities to get work done and discussing ideas.[21]

The increasing use of new technologies to deliver training and to store and communicate knowledge means that trainers must be technologically literate. That is, they must understand the strengths and weaknesses of new technologies and implementation issues such as overcoming users' resistance to change (which is discussed later in this chapter). Also, many companies have created positions such as knowledge manager or chief information officer, whose job is to identify reliable knowledge and make sure it is accessible to employees.

INCREASED USE OF JUST-IN-TIME LEARNING AND PERFORMANCE SUPPORT

Companies are moving away from courseware and classes as a performance improvement method and are instead adopting true performance support that is available during the work process.[22] **Just-in-time learning** (or **embedded learning**) refers to learning that occurs on the job as needed; it involves collaboration and nonlearning technologies such as microblogs, and it is integrated with knowledge management.[23]

Embedded learning may become increasingly prevalent in the future because companies can no longer have employees attend classroom instruction or spend hours on online learning that is not directly relevant to their current job demands. Formal training programs and courses will not disappear but will focus more on the development of competencies that can benefit the employee and the company over the long term, whereas embedded learning will focus on providing the learning that the employee needs to complete key job tasks. Embedded-learning products include task-specific, real-time content and simulation that are accessible during work, as well as real-time collaboration in virtual workspaces. Recent, rapid adoption of wireless technology is connecting employees directly to business processes. For example, radio frequency identification chips are implanted in products such as clothing, tires, and mechanical parts. These chips contain information that is beamed via radio waves to employees processing handheld wireless devices. The device, the task context, and the performance environment are incompatible with classroom or courseware-based learning but with performance support. Learning is a business process that is integrated with several other business processes. Learning is expected as a result of collaboration with employees and machines in the work process. Employees can be provided with real-time performance support through communications with experts and through automated coaching.

More learning will become just-in-time, using mobile devices such as notebooks and tablets such as the iPad. As a result, instead of having to complete specific training classes, learning functions will focus on setting standards required to achieve accreditation, create systems to allow employees to meet accreditation standards, and track completion of standards.[24] To achieve accreditation may involve having specific job experiences, observing a expert-level employee, contributing content for helping peers and less experienced employees learn, and passing a test.

There is a new type of learner emerging, the "social cyborg," who integrates social networks into the way they think, learn, and solve problems.[25] As Facebook and other social networking sites and smartphones with communications and Internet access continue to spread and evolve, employees will spend more time on computers and online playing games, working, and connecting to friends and work associates using e-mail and text. "Social cyborgs" are already prevalent among the millennial generation who expect companies to accommodate their need to access the latest tools and technologies at work including tablets and mobile devices, Really Simple Syndication (RSS) feeds, and social networking sites. This means that training, development, and learning functions will need to adjust their assumptions about how and where we learn. Design and development strategies based on individual learners who learn alone and without technology will continue to become obsolete. Employees will expect training and development to include simulations, games, and virtual reality, which will become more realistic than they are today. For example, researchers are developing wearable devices that allow the use of hand gestures to interact with environment and contact lenses that act as a computer display. Also, learners will expect training and development to use social media, as well as learning that is delivered when it is needed rather than during a scheduled course.

A new set of learning strategies will be need to be adopted, including learning environments that include online mentoring and collaborative learning platforms. This means that companies will need to consider how, when, and for which employees to use social media such as Facebook and Twitter, as well as mobile devices for learning. Social networking platforms will be part of learning management systems. This will allow managers to determine which learning content is in most demand and take content developed by social network contributors and use it in formal training courses. Not using or forbidding the use of social media will no longer be an option to attract, motivate, and retain talented employees (and customers!). Instead, companies will need to establish policies regarding the use of social media.

INCREASED EMPHASIS ON PERFORMANCE ANALYSIS: BIG DATA AND LEARNING FOR BUSINESS ENHANCEMENT

Because of an increasing focus on contributing to the company's competitive advantage, training departments will have to ensure that they are seen as both helping the business functions (e.g., marketing, finance, production) meet their needs and contributing to overall business goals and the "bottom line."[26]

This means that you understand the business enough to ask the right questions to develop an appropriate learning solution (recall the discussion of needs assessment in Chapter Three, "Needs Assessment"). Such questions might include how success will be measured and why the company has not thus far seen desired results. The role of the learning professional is to understand business challenges and consistently work to fill employee performance gaps. To enhance the business means that learning professionals have to be aligned with the business and take responsibility for the relationship and the business outcomes from learning solutions, have an agreed-upon business outcome that is included in the learning function and business performance plan, attend business staff meetings and network with internal customers, and identify as a partner with the business with the joint goal of improving performance.

Consider how companies in three different industries expect training to influence their bottom line.[27] The training offered at TRX, a company that provides transaction processing and data integration services, is expected to have a direct influence on boosting customer satisfaction scores and agents' productivity. Metrics such as hours of training delivered are not as important as showing how training is contributing to customer service, productivity, and profitability. Supply-chain training for Coca-Cola must be tied in some way to the company's three-year business plan or it will not be supported. At Ho-Chunk Casino in Wittenberg, Wisconsin, the director of training spends time educating managers on how the training unit adds value to the business. One of the director's biggest challenges is convincing first-line supervisors to support transfer of training. The training director has found that explaining Kirkpatrick's evaluation model (reaction, learning, behavior, results) to the supervisors helps them understand that training is a process, not an event, and that they play an important role in determining the success or failure of training. (Kirkpatrick's model is discussed in more detail in Chapter Six.)

Training departments must shift the focus from training as *the* solution to business problems to a performance analysis approach. A **performance analysis approach** involves identifying performance gaps or deficiencies and examining training as one possible solution for the business units (the customers). Training departments will need to continue instructing managers to consider all potential causes of poor performance before deciding that training is the solution. Poor employee performance may be due to poor management, inefficient technologies, or outdated technology rather than deficiencies in skill or knowledge (recall the discussion of person analysis in Chapter Three). Three ways that training departments will need to be involved are (1) focusing on interventions related to performance improvement, (2) providing support for high-performance work systems, and (3) developing systems for training administration, development, and delivery that reduce costs and increase employees' access to learning.

Training departments' responsibilities will likely include a greater focus on systems that employees can use for information (such as expert systems or electronic performance support systems) on an as-needed basis. This need is driven by the use of contingent employees and the increased flexibility necessary to adapt products and services to meet customers' needs. For example, companies do not want to spend money to train employees who may be with the company only a few weeks. Instead, through temporary employment agencies, companies can select employees with the exact skill set needed. Training departments need to provide mechanisms to support the temporary employees once they are on the job and encounter situations, problems, rules, and policies they are unfamiliar with because they are not yet knowledgeable about the company.

As was discussed in Chapter One, more companies are striving to create high-performance workplaces because of the productivity gains that can be realized through this type of design. High-performance work requires that employees have the interpersonal skills necessary to work in teams. High-performance work systems also require employees to have high levels of technical skills. Employees need to understand statistical process control and the Total Quality Management (TQM) philosophy. Employees also must understand the entire production and service system so that they can better serve both internal and external customers. As more companies move to high-performance work systems, training departments will need to be prepared to provide effective training in interpersonal, quality, and technical skills, as well as to help employees understand all aspects of the customer-service or production system.

Business competitiveness can be realized by quick change, speed in delivery, and reductions in costs and time constraints. LPL Financial uses a talent development council, composed of company leaders from across the company's functional areas, to evaluate new learning and requested learning based on its talent strategy.[28] The group meets once a month to ensure that learning is provided by the learning department only when it is necessary. Because the council includes only senior-level managers, it helps align learning with the business strategy and outcomes. For learning to be approved, it has to support both the business and the employees. Establishing the talent council has helped get company leaders more involved in developing an overall business learning strategy and managers encourage employees to use available learning resources and programs for development.

Just-in-time learning is many companies' answer to quick learning and the quick application of learning to the business.[29] La Quinta's Q-Tubes are short, e-learning courses. The Q-Tubes use conversational language to make trainees feel as if they are being trained by their peers or a team leader. Each Q-Tube includes a knowledge check and provides feedback. Training completion rates have increased 92 percent for general managers and 484 percent for team members since the Q-Tubes were introduced. American Express designs its learning paths around behavioral outcomes and emphasizes the importance of how learners engage in learning, not just what they are supposed to learn. A learning path usually includes workshops, peer learning, and on-the-job learning. Also, American Express emphasizes teaching employees how to best participate in activities to maximize their learning.

Because the direction in training is away from learning as the primary outcome and more toward learning as a way to enhance business performance, companies will continue to purchase learning management systems (LMSs) that provide training administration, development tools, and online training. (LMSs are discussed in Chapter Eight.) LMS is moving from its historical emphasis on providing and track training to a broader focus on talent management.[30] This means that LMS will include more career planning tools that will connect employees with many different development resources, including mentors, skills requirements for jobs, potential mentors, and competency models. LMS can also include performance evaluations that can be used by employees and managers to identify skill gaps. Also there will be increased demand for LMS software that includes learning analytics, or analysis tools, that can track learning activity and costs and can relate learning results to product revenues or sales goals.[31]

Today, most companies own their own software and hardware and keep them on site in their facilities. However, cloud computing allows companies to lease software and hardware, and employees don't know the location of computers, databases, and applications that they are using (this is known as being in the "cloud"). **Cloud computing** refers to a computing system that provides information technology infrastructure over a network in a self-service, modifiable, and on-demand.[32] Clouds can be delivered on-demand via the Internet (public cloud) or restricted to use by a single company (private cloud). Cloud computing gives companies and their employees access to applications and information from smartphones and tablets rather than relying solely on personal computers. It also allows groups to work together in new ways, can make employees more productive by allowing them to more easily share documents and information, and provide greater access to large company databases. From a learning perspective, this means that tools for conducting workforce analytics using metrics on learning, training and development programs, and social media and collaboration tools such as Twitter, blogs, Google documents, and YouTube videos will be more easily accessible and available for use. Cloud computing also can make it easier for employees to access formal training programs from a variety of vendors and educational institutions. Finally, the cloud can be used to store learning data in a "warehouse" (such as Redshift), which makes it easily available for analysis of trends and predictions of business outcomes. In the future the emerging interest in collecting and using big data related to learning, training, and development will continue to grow. As we discussed in Chapter Six, big data involves collecting data about users activities, analyzing or mining the data to identify patterns and trends, and understanding how these patterns and trends link to business goals and outcomes. Big data can be useful for understanding what training methods best deliver what needs to be taught and identifying how employees learn, who the experts and leaders are in social networks, and what type of instruction will lead to positive reactions from learners and results. For example, Intrepid Learning's e-learning programs include a "tile." The "tile" is provided at the beginning of the program to explain how the different parts of the e-learning module fit together. Through tracking who has read the tile, Intrepid was able to determine that 80 percent of learners who read the "tile" completed the program, compared to a 10 percent completion rate for learners who did not read it.[33] Saba's data analytics platform tracks performance ratings, succession planning activities, and learning data.[34] It tracks what information employees are accessing, identifies the topics they are posting, and identifies who they are connecting with. It provides social graphs that visually display employees who are the center of social networks and most influential. The system is linked to an intelligent search engine that recommends learning activities. The system can also be linked to financial systems and other business data. JPMorgan Chase is including employee attendance at compliance training as one of several factors (the other factors include violating personal trading rules and going over market-risk limits) used in trying to predict which employees may be likely to violate government regulations or company policy.[35] The increased use of big data will be aided by the development of more user-friendly ways for data to be accessed, analyzed, and the results displayed. For example, Looker is a start-up company that provides web-based business intelligence platform presenting data in a dashboard format.

INCREASED USE OF STAKEHOLDER-FOCUSED LEARNING, TRAINING PARTNERSHIPS, AND OUTSOURCING TRAINING

Chapter Two discussed the importance of making learning, training, and development strategic by ensuring that it supports the business strategy and the needs of different stakeholders, including managers, employees, and customers. The emphasis on strategic learning influencing different stakeholders will continue in the future as learning professionals and companies recognize that competitive advantage can come from developing internal human capital and providing learning services to customers. This helps develop and retain a satisfied, skilled, and innovative workforce and attract, keep, and satisfy customers.

For example, STIHL produces outdoor power equipment including chain saws, blowers, trimmers, and edgers.[36] STIHL has manufacturing facilities for its equipment, which are sold through over eight thousand power equipment retailers. STIHL only sells its products through dealers, so helping them satisfy customers is critical for the business. Customers include homeowners , professionals, landscaping and utility companies, the military, government agencies such as the U.S. Forest Service, and emergency first responders. This means that learning programs need to include not only STIHL's employees, but also retail dealers and their customers. STIHL provides its employees learning programs in technical areas such as manufacturing and engineering as well as leadership development. If there are open seats in its training courses, STIHL's training and development department allows smaller companies to send their employees to its technical and leadership courses at a low cost. The fees help reduce some of the expenses of STIHL's training department. At the retail level, STIHL provides training programs that help dealers understand how to sell and service the equipment. For example, STIHL has a certification program for service technicians, which must be renewed every three years. The certification focuses on training the technicians to diagnose problems, provide the correct repairs, and communicate to customers how to care for their equipment. STIHL iCademy is a web-based program that dealers can access. It covers topics such as troubleshooting, in-store marketing, selling skills, and customer service. STIHL also has a training seminar for high school and college instructors of small engine repair classes, which teaches students how to service products. In addition, to ensure that customers correctly and safely use equipment, STIHL provides training programs for professional landscaping tree services, public utilities, first responders, and the military. Also, consumers who use STIHL equipment can access blogs and YouTube videos on the company's website.

As discussed in Chapter One, the demographic, global, and technological changes are creating a skills gap that presents challenges for companies in the United States and around the world. Also, the current education-to-employment system is not preparing students and adults for the twenty-first-century economy. Barriers between business and educational institutions make it difficult for many employees to update their skills and knowledge that they need for their current jobs or preparation for jobs in another career. Recall our discussion of business and education partnerships in Chapter Ten, "Social Responsibility: Legal Issues, Managing Diversity, and Career Challenges." To cope with the skills gap, we will likely see more business, education, and community partnerships working on rebuilding education to employment systems.[37] The goal of these partnerships is to help individuals prepare for higher-skill and higher-wage jobs and attract new companies to the area by integrating employee retraining, elementary through high school career education programs, career academies, and higher education programs into a lifelong learning system. A lifelong learning system can provide better opportunities for more people to develop the talent needed to suit multiple jobs and careers that they will likely hold during their lifetimes.

Also, due to an increased urgency to find ways to eliminate unemployment, underemployment, and meet skill gaps, federal, state, and local governments probably will provide more economic incentives for retraining employees, including tax credits and tax breaks for companies to invest in training and the spread of lifelong learning accounts.

Lifelong Learning Accounts (LiLAs) refer to an account for education to which both the employee and company contribute. The employee keeps the account even if they leave the company to pay for additional education at vocational schools and colleges and universities.

For example, Walmart Stores donated $16 million in grants to seven nonprofit groups (Achieving the Dream, The ACT Foundation, Dress for Success, Goodwill Industries, Jobs for the Future, McKinsey Social Initiative, and the National Able Network) to try to improve the skills of more than twelve thousand entry-level workers in retail and related industries such as transportation and distribution.[38] The nonprofits will work with government agencies and employers to develop training programs. For example, Achieving the Dream will use its grant to create training programs at four community colleges.

The Brose Group, a German manufacturer of systems such as seat structures for car makers and suppliers, is actively involved in the Michigan Advanced Technical Training Program.[39] The program uses classroom learning and on-the-job training to prepare students for jobs in mechatronics, which requires electrical, mechanical, and electronic competencies. The program is a partnership between the Michigan Economic Development Corporation, two community colleges, and eleven businesses located in Michigan. Brose partnered with the community to identify the necessary skills and competencies, create courses that would develop the competencies, and build a course curriculum. Program applicants are required to provide a résumé and complete a test designed to measure their skills in reading, writing, math, and English as a second language. Most participants are from high schools and colleges, but the program is open to all Michigan residents. Brose, like the other companies who are participating in the program, pay for students' full cost of tuition and an hourly wage for time they are working on the job. Brose sponsors four students who will rotate between jobs and all three of the company's Michigan locations. After successfully completing the program, participants receive an advanced associate's degree and a guaranteed job. They are required to work for two years at their sponsoring company.

Chapter Two discussed several reasons for companies to outsource their training. Two main reasons were that employees need to learn specialized new knowledge and that companies want to gain access to best practices and cost savings. External suppliers may be consultants, academics, graduate students, or companies in the entertainment and mass communications industries. External suppliers can be partners or be sole providers of training services. The key decision for companies will not be whether to outsource but rather how much training to outsource.

Trainers and other learning professionals will need to identify outsource providers who can deliver effective training solutions, particularly in technology-based learning solutions in which they lack the internal expertise to develop in house. McKesson, a health-care services company, was providing customers with face-to-face instructor-led training on one of its products, an evidence-based clinical decision support system.[40] However, customers began to negotiate to remove training from their contracts. They were dissatisfied with the quality of the program and lost productivity and disruption that occurred because their employees had to leave their jobs to attend training. McKesson recognized that the training was important, but that changes were necessary. McKesson could not redesign the program in-house because it lacked a centralized learning function with all of the skills necessary to do so. They outsourced most of the design of the new training to Aptara, a training provider specializing in content development, learning strategies, and digital conversion.

TABLE 11.4
Skills for Future Trainers

Source: Based on C. Malamed, "What will your training role be in the future?" (February 13, 2012), from *www.astd .org*, accessed April 24, 2015; M. Laff, "Trainers skills 2020," *T+D* (December 2008): 42; P. Galagan, "New skills for a new work reality," *T+D* (November 2011): 26–29.

- Matching training content and methods to the local culture of the workforce
- Designing learning space, as well as content in technology-driven learning environments
- Use of multimedia tools, including audio, video, webcasts, and live action
- Delivering and packaging training in different formats for beginners and experts
- Use of assessments to determine trainees' learning styles
- Developing search-and-identify techniques so employees can find information and training when they need it
- Be a change agent: Facilitating learning and staying in touch with employees, managers, and business units to identify what they need and making suggestions regarding tools, processes, or procedures that could help them work more effectively
- Developing and delivering learning that is integrated with the job
- Understand how social media can be used for learning, the limitations of social media, and ability to make a business case for it
- Identify the root cause of job and business problems

Aptara worked with McKesson's instructional designers to develop new training that included self-paced web-based training combined with the option to have either an instructor-led classroom instruction or a virtual instructor-led session. The new web-based course engaged learners using assessments, role plays, and simulations. Since the introduction of the new blended learning program, customer training purchases and satisfaction have increased. Also, McKesson has benefited, too. They can now deliver more training requiring less staff; the program is easy to change and add new content; and it allows them to work with their customers to choose the blended learning approach that is best for them.

Implications of Future Trends for Trainers' Skills and Competencies

A recent study found that the competencies and expertise included in the ASTD competency model (see Figure 1.4 in Chapter One) are likely to be needed in the future. However, increased emphasis will also be placed on the ability of trainers to more effectively use technology. Also, as companies become more global, they will need to adapt training methods and content to local cultures.[41] Table 11.4 shows the skills that trainers will need to develop in the future.

Summary

This chapter discussed future trends that are likely to influence training and development. These trends relate to training delivery and structure of the training function. Training will contribute to a company's sustainability goals. Trainers will be asked to design focused content more quickly and to deliver training using multiple methods. New technology will have a growing impact on training delivery in the future. Also, new technology will allow training departments to store and share human capital throughout the company. There will be an increased emphasis on integrating training with other human resource functions and showing how training helps the business. Training departments are more likely to develop partnerships with vendors and other companies in the future.

Key Terms

sustainability *494*

augmented reality, *496*

Tin Can API, *497*

Learning Records Store (LRS), *497*

rapid instructional design (RID), *498*

social learning, *500*

just-in-time learning, *501*

performance analysis approach, *503*

cloud computing, *504*

Lifelong Learning Accounts (LiLAs), *507*

Discussion Questions

1. Do you think this will lead to more (or less) effective training/learning? Explain your perspective.

2. What new skills will trainers need to be successful in the future?

3. What is rapid instructional design? How does it differ from the traditional training design process discussed in Chapter One? (See Figure 1.1.)

4. How does the use of a learning management system better link training to business strategy and goals?

5. What is cloud computing? How does it enable just-in-time training delivery?

6. How will social learning and social networks influence employee expectations about learning, training, and development?

7. Explain the excitement about using big data related to learning, training, and development. What's the usefulness of big data?

8. How can training contribute to a sustainability initiative?

9. How is program design being influenced by neuroscience research?

10. What are wearables? How might they be useful for learning and training?

Application Assignments

1. Interview a manager. Ask this person to evaluate his or her company's training department in terms of training delivery, service, expertise, and contribution to the business. Ask him or her to explain the rationale for the evaluation. Summarize this information. Based on the information you gathered, make recommendations regarding how the training department can be improved.

2. This chapter discussed several trends that will influence the future of training. Based on future social, economic, political, or technological factors, identify one or two additional trends that you think will influence training. Write a two- to three-page paper summarizing your ideas. Make sure you provide a rationale for your trends. Many organizations are moving from a training perspective to a performance perspective. That is, they are interested in performance improvement, not training just for the sake of training.

3. Go to http://2oms.com/apps/ website for the Assessment and Development Group International. Click on "Mobile Apps." Read about and install on your smartphone either Performance Coach or Super Manager. What are the strengths and weaknesses of the app?

4. Go to *www.youtube.com* website. First, watch the video "IBM's Watson Supercomputer Destroys All Humans on Jeopardy." Then watch the video *IBM Watson: Watson After Jeopardy!* How can Watson and the technology that it uses help make us "smarter" and improve performance?

5. Go to YouTube at *www.youtube.com*. Watch the video "10 Amazing Robots That Will Change the World." What are the advantages and disadvantages of using these robots in the workplace? What types of training will human employees need to work alongside robots?

6. What cost and benefits would you use to make the business case for replacing face-to-face instructor-led training with virtual instructor-led training in order to contribute to a sustainability goal of reducing training's carbon footprint? Explain.

7. There are many different training providers that companies can use. Review one of the training providers listed below:

Aptara (*www.aptaracorp.com*)

GP Strategies (*www.gpstrategies.com*)

Intrepid Learning (*www.intrepidlearning.com*)

Skillsoft (*www.skillsoft.com*)

Why might a company choose to contract with a training provider? What services are provided by the training provider you chose to review?

Case: *Work Styles Promotes Flexible Work at TELUS*

TELUS, a telecommunications company, is a Canadian company spread across several time zones. TELUS's Work Styles program was started to enhance employee productivity, help employees stay happy by promoting practices that enhance their work-life balance, and support TELUS's commitment to environmental sustainability. Work Styles allows employees to choose to work away from the office—at home or on the road. Part of the Work Styles program includes providing employees with technology that can help them meet their job responsibilities and allow them to work when and where they can be most effective. Because many employees work at home or on the road, TELUS provides mobile devices including smartphones and notebook and tablet computers. These devices include teleconferencing and video conferencing capabilities and cloud-based networking applications, which help employees collaborate and interact with their peers. TELUS provides training courses that help employees work effectively in such a flexible work environment. These courses cover how to lead effective meetings, establish and sustain team norms, and lead and succeed in high-performing Work Styles teams. Also, employees can participate in weekly one-hour webinars during which the philosophy of the Work Styles program is discussed, and they can ask questions and share success stories. TELUS's goal is to have 70 percent of employees working on the road or at home, rather than in office buildings across Canada.

If you were asked to evaluate the effectiveness of Work Styles, what outcomes or data would you collect? How would you collect your data or outcomes? What are the challenges of delivering learning to employees who work on the road or at home? What should be included in mobile-delivered training courses to ensure that employees learn?

Source: "Working in style," *TD* (April 2015): 112; *www .telus.ca*, the website for TELUS (accessed April 23, 2015); J. Salopek, "Getting social to create transparency," *T+D* (October 2011): 68–70.

Endnotes

1. M. Weinstein, "Charity Begins @ Work," *training* (May 2008): 56–58; "Corporate responsibility performance report 2013" and "Improving healthcare in Africa," from http://www.novartis.com, accessed April 22, 2015; D. Parrey, "The employees are greener at Ingersoll Rand," *Chief Learning Officer* (March 2015): 46–53; H. Dolezalek, "Good news: Training can save the world," *training* (May 2006): 28–33.

2. K. Everson, "Special report: Learning is all in the wrist," *Chief Learning Officer* (March 15, 2015), from *www.clomedia.com*, accessed March 18, 2015.

3. "About" and "Products," from *www.wearableintelligence.com*, the website for Wearable Intelligence, accessed April 21, 2015.

4. K. Everson, "In the know, in the now," *Workforce* (January 2015): 44–47.

5. From *www.playerlync.com*, website for PlayerLync.

6. C. Mims, "Amelia, a machine, thinks like you," *The Wall Street Journal* (September 28, 2014): B1–B2; M. Rundle, "Amelia: IPSoft's new artificial intelligence can think like a human and wants your job" (March 4, 2014), from *www.huffingtonpost.co.uk*, accessed April 21, 2015.

7. "Overview Tin Can API," *www.tincanapi.com/overview*, accessed April 20, 2015.

8. J. Horne, "Devereux," from http://site.watershedlrs.com/six-watershed-first-organizations/, accessed April 21, 2015; J. Salopek, "Digital collaboration," *Training and Development* (June 2000): 38–43.

9. S. Castellano, "Innovations in learning technology," *T+D* (March 2015): 64–66; J. Veloz, "Old tactics are kryptonite for today's attention spans," from *www.adweek.com*, accessed April 20, 2015; J. Ford and T. Meyer, "Advances in training technology: Meeting the workplace challenges of talent development, deep specialization, and collaborative learning." In *The Psychology of Workplace Technology*, eds. M. Coovert and L. Thompson, (New York: Routledge, 2014): 43–76; J. Bersin, "What's in store for HR in 2015," *HR Magazine* (January/February 2015): 33–51.

10. L. Miller, *Playing to Win* (Alexandria, VA: American Society for Training & Development, 2014); C. Morrison, *Going Mobile: Creating Practices That Transform Learning* (Alexandria, VA: American Society for Training and Development, 2013).

11. D. Rock, "Your brain on learning," *Chief Learning Officer* (April 13, 2015), from http://www.clomedia .com, accessed April 22, 2015; D. Rock, "The 'aha' moment," *T+D* (February 2011): 45–49.

12. Learning Research Development Center, University of Pittsburgh, from http://www.lrdc.pitt.edu/schunn /research/neurolearning.html, accessed April 22, 2015.

13. H. Dolezalek, "Who has the time to design?" *training* (January 2006): 24–28.

14. S. Thiagarajan, "Rapid Instructional Development." In *The ASTD Handbook of Training Design and Delivery*, eds. G. Piskurich, P. Beckschi, and B. Hall (New York: McGraw-Hill, 2000): 54–75.

15. M. Weinstein, "Six for '06," *training* (January 2006): 18–22.

16. "Bass & Associates, P.C.," *TD* (October 2014): 96.

17. M. Plater, "Three trends shaping learning," *Chief Learning Officer* (June 2014): 44–47; S. Castellano, "MOOCs in the workplace," *T+D* (September 2014): 16.

18. "Manage employees and clients like a hero," *T+D* (February 2012): 17.

19. T. Bingham and M. Conner, *The New Social Learning* (American Society for Training and Development: Alexandria, VA, 2010); R. Landers and A. Goldberg, "Online social media in the workplace: A conversation with employees." In *The Psychology of Workplace Technology*, eds. M. Coovert and L. Thompson (New York: Routledge, 2014): 284–304.

20. "Training top 125, EMC Corporation," *training* (January/February 2015): 85.

21. "Training top 125, Tata Consultancy Services," *training* (January/February 2015): 99.

22. S. Adkins, "The brave new world of learning," *T+D* (June 2003): 28–37.

23. M. Littlejohn, "Embedded learning," *T+D* (February 2006): 36–39.

24. J. Meister and K. Willyerd, "Looking ahead at social learning: 10 predictors," *T+D* (July 2010): 34–41.

25. J. Campbell and W. Finegan, "Dawn of the social cyborg," *training* (September/October 2011): 20–27; J. Meister and K. Willyerd, *The 2020 Workplace* (Harper Business: New York, 2010); A. Thompson, "Delivering meaningful outcomes for your organization," *T+D* (February 2012): 38–41; J. Meister and K. Willyerd, "Looking ahead at social learning: 10 predictors," *T+D* (July 2010): 34–41.

26. E. Salas, S. Tannenbaum, K. Kraiger, and K. Smith-Jentsch, "The science of training and development in organizations: What matters in practice," *Psychological Science in the Public Interest* 13 (2012): 74–101; A. Thompson, "Delivering meaningful outcomes for your organization," *T+D* (February 2012): 38–41.

27. D. Zielinski, "Wanted: Training manager," *training* (January 2006): 36–39.

28. T. Handcock, W. Howlett, and J. Martin, "The future of the learning function," *Chief Learning Officer* (April 13, 2015): 26–47.

29. "Training top 125, La Quinta Holdings," *training* (January/February 2015): 75; T. Handcock, W. Howlett, and J. Martin, "The future of the learning function," *Chief Learning Officer* (April 13, 2015): 26–47.

30. S. Castellano, "The evolution of the LMS," *T+D* (November 2014): 14.

31. M. Hequet, "The state of the e-learning market," *training* (September 2003): 24–29.

32. A. McAfee, "What every CEO needs to know about the cloud," *Harvard Business Review* (November 2011): 124–132; B. Roberts, "The grand convergence," *HR Magazine* (October 2011): 39–46; M. Paino, "All generations learn in the cloud," *Chief Learning Officer* (September 28, 2011), accessed from http://blog.clomedia.com, October 11, 2011.

33. K. Everson, "In the know, in the now," *Workforce* (January 2015): 44–47.

34. B. Hall, "Will big data equal big learning?" *Chief Learning Officer* (March 2013): 16.

35. "Markets/finance," *Bloomberg Businessweek* (April 13–19, 2015): 34.

36. T. Bingham and P. Galagan, "Training powers up at STIHL," *T+D* (January 2014): 29–33; C. Gambill, "Creating learning solutions to satisfy customers," *T+D* (January 2014): 35–39.

37. E. Gordon, "Talent challenge: Renewing the vision," *T+D* (June 2010): 42–47.

38. K. Whitney, "Wal-Mart puts up cash to close skills gap," *Chief Learning Officer* (March 2, 2015), from *www.clomedia.com*, accessed March 6, 2015.

39. J. Ramirez, "Stemming the tide," *Human Resource Executive* (September 2014): 27–31.

40. Aptara, "Making customer self-service a reality: Fast forwarding content development," from http://www.aptaracorp.com/why-aptara/success-story/mckesson, accessed April 23, 2015.

41. P. Galagan, "New skills for a new work reality," *T+D* (November 2011): 26–29; J. Salopek, "Keeping it real," *T+D* (August 2008): 42–45; C. Malained, "What will your training role be in the future?" (February 13, 2012), from *www.astd.org*, accessed April 24, 2015.

Case 4

Learning in Practice

Working at Home: A Bad Idea?

Yahoo's CEO Marissa Mayer decided as one part of her plan to revitalize the company that she wanted to end the company's work-from-home policy. In an internal memo from Yahoo's executive vice president of people and development, working at the office rather than at home was necessary because of the need for employees to communicate and collaborate and to reduce the chance that speed and quality would be diminished. Criticism of Yahoo's policy change focused on the message that not allowing home work sends to employees: We can't trust you to get the work done.

Many employees want to work at home so companies are using working at home as a benefit that helps recruit and retain talented employees. Several studies have demonstrated benefits from working at home. Cisco Systems found that employees who could work remotely from home experienced an increase in their quality of life. This could result from reducing the hassles of commuting to work and allowing employees to better balance work and life responsibilities such as childcare, running errands, or dealing with a sick child, spouse, or family member. Another study showed that when employees of a Chinese travel agency were allowed to work from home, they were more productive, resulting in cost savings of $2,000 per employee each year. Finally, a study found that office employees who work from home may work fifty-seven hours each week before they feel as if their work-life is out of balance, compared to thirty-eight hours for employees who work at their office.

Working at home also may have significant disadvantages. The disadvantages include employees taking advantage of the policy to extend their weekends by not working in the office on Fridays or Mondays, and loss of the potential benefit from having face-to-face interactions with colleagues that are useful for sharing knowledge and generating creative solutions to product or service problems. Being in the office is especially important today because many jobs require close collaboration with peers or working on team projects. Also, unplanned personal interactions occurring at the office can lead to new ideas or working relationships. The biggest problems for employees working from home is overcoming other employees' and managers' perceptions that they are not as productive as they could be, that they lack focus, and that they lose "face-time," which leads to fewer opportunities for promotions.

Questions

1. Do you think that companies should have a policy that allows all employees to work at home? Why or why not? How would you determine which jobs are best suited for working at home?

2. What role can technology play in allowing employees to work at home? Do you believe that interaction using technology can replace interpersonal face-to-face interaction between employees or between employees and their manager?

3. Some employees don't take advantage of flexible work options such as working at home because they believe it hurts their career. Why might they feel this way?

Sources: Based on B. Goldsmith, "Yahoo's work-from-home ban stirs backlash," *The Columbus Dispatch* (February 27, 2013): A5; P. Marinova, "Who works from home and when" (February 28, 2013), from *www.cnn.com*, accessed February 28, 2013; C. Suddath, "Work-from-home truths, half-truths, and myths," *Bloomberg Businessweek* (March 4–10, 2013): 75; R. Silverman and Q. Fottrell, "The home office in the spotlight," *The Wall Street Journal* (February 27, 2013): B6; N. Shah, "More Americans working from home remotely," *The Wall Street Journal* (April 6, 2013): A3.

Glossary

360-degree feedback   A special case of the upward feedback system. Here employees' behaviors or skills are evaluated not only by subordinates but also by peers, customers, bosses, and employees themselves via a questionnaire rating them on a number of dimensions.

70-20-10 model   A common learning model that assumes that 70 percent of learning occurs on the job, 20 percent occurs socially through coaching and mentoring, and 10 percent through formal classroom instruction.

ability   The physical and mental capacity to perform a task.

action learning   A training method that involves giving teams or work groups a problem, having them work on solving it and committing to an action plan, and then holding them accountable for carrying out the plan.

action plan   A written document detailing steps that a trainee and the manager will take to ensure that training transfers to the job.

adaptive training   Training that customizes or adapts the content presented to the trainee based on their learning style, ability, personality, or performance.

advance organizers   Outlines, texts, diagrams, and graphs that help trainees organize information that will be presented and practiced.

adventure learning   A training method focusing on developing teamwork and leadership skills using structured outdoor activities.

affective outcomes   Outcomes including attitudes and motivation.

Age Discrimination in Employment Act   A federal law that prohibits discrimination against individuals 40 years of age or older.

alternative work arrangements   Independent contributors, on-call workers, temporary workers, and contract company workers.

Americans with Disabilities Act (ADA)   A 1990 act prohibiting workplace discrimination against people with disabilities.

andragogy   The theory of adult learning.

application assignments   Assignments that require trainees to identify work problems or situations and to apply training content to solve them.

application planning   The preparing of trainees to use key behaviors on the job.

apprenticeship   A work-study training method with both on-the-job and classroom training.

apps   Applications designed specifically for smartphones and tablet computers that are being used to supplement training, manage the path or sequence of training, and to help employees maintain training records.

assessment   The collecting of information and providing of feedback to employees about their behavior, communication style, or skills.

assessment center   A process in which multiple raters or evaluators (also known as assessors) evaluate employees' performances on a number of exercises.

asynchronous communication   A non real-time interaction in which people cannot communicate with each other without a time delay.

attitude   Combination of beliefs and feelings that predispose a person to behave in a certain way.

audiovisual instruction   Media-based training that is both watched and heard.

augmented reality   A live direct or indirect view of a physical, real-world environment whose elements are supplemented by computer-generated sound, video, graphics, or GPS data

automatization   Making performance of a task, recall of knowledge, or demonstration of a skill so automatic that it requires little thought or attention.

avatars   Computer depictions of humans that are used as imaginary coaches, co-workers, and customers in simulations.

balanced scorecard   A means of performance measurement that allows managers to view the overall company performance or the performance of departments or functions (such as training) from the perspective of internal and external customers, employees, and shareholders.

bandwidth The number of bytes and bits (information) that can travel between computers per second.

basic skills Skills necessary for employees to perform their jobs and learn the content of training programs.

behavior modeling A training method in which trainees are presented with a model who demonstrates key behaviors to replicate and provides them with the opportunity to practice those key behaviors.

benchmarking The use of information about other companies' training practices to help determine the appropriate type, level, and frequency of training.

bench strength A pool of talented employees who are ready to move to new jobs or positions when they are needed.

benefits The value company gains from a training program.

big data Complex data sets characterized by volume, variety, and velocity that are developed by compiling data across different organizational systems, including marketing and sales, human resources, finance, accounting, customer service, and operations.

blended learning Learning that involves a combination of online learning, face-to-face instruction, and other methods.

blog A webpage where an author posts entries and readers can comment.

boosters Short multiple-choice, short-answer quizzes, or other activities that can help learners consider training information as important and help retain it.

brand The look and feeling of the training function that is used to create expectations for its customers.

business-embedded training Training that aligns closely with the company's business strategy and that is characterized by five competencies: strategic direction, product design, structural versatility, product delivery, and accountability for results.

business game A training method in which trainees gather information, analyze it, and make decisions.

business process outsourcing The outsourcing of any business process, such as human resource management, production, or training.

business strategy A plan that integrates a company's goals, policies, and actions.

career path A sequence of job positions involving similar types of work and skills that employees move through in a company.

career support Coaching, protection, sponsorship, and provision of challenging assignments, exposure, and visibility to an employee.

case study A description of how employees or an organization dealt with a situation.

centralized training Organizing the training department so that training and development programs, resources, and professionals are primarily housed in one location and decisions about training investment, programs, and delivery are made from that department.

change The adoption of a new idea or behavior by a company.

chief learning officer (CLO) A leader of a company's knowledge management efforts (also called *knowledge officer*).

climate for transfer Trainees' perceptions about a wide variety of characteristics of the work environment; these perceptions facilitate or inhibit use of trained skills or behavior.

closed skills Training objectives that are linked to learning specific skills that are to be identically produced by the trainee on their job.

cloud computing A computing system that provides information technology infrastructure over a network in a self-service, modifiable, and on-demand.

coach A peer or manager who works with employees to motivate them, help them develop skills, and provide reinforcement and feedback.

cognitive ability Verbal comprehension, quantitative ability, and reasoning ability.

cognitive outcomes Outcomes that are used to measure what knowledge trainees learned in a training program.

cognitive strategies Strategies that regulate the learning processes; they relate to the learner's decision regarding what information to attend to, how to remember, and how to solve problems.

community of practice (COP) A group of employees who work together, learn from each other, and develop a common understanding of how to get work accomplished.

comparison group A group of employees who participate in an evaluation study but do not attend a training program.

competency An area of personal capability that enables employees to perform their job.

competency model A model identifying the competencies necessary for each job as well as the knowledge, skills, behavior, and personal characteristics underlying each competency.

competitive advantage An upper hand over other firms in an industry.

competitiveness A company's ability to maintain and gain market share in an industry.

compressed workweek A work schedule that allows employees to work fewer days but with longer hours, for example, four days ten hours each day.

computer-based training (CBT) An interactive training experience in which the computer provides the learning stimulus, the trainee must respond, and the computer analyzes the responses and provides feedback to the trainee.

concentration strategy A business strategy that focuses on increasing market share, reducing costs, or creating a market niche for products and services.

consequences Incentives that employees receive for performing well.

continuous learning A learning system in which employees are required to understand the entire work system including the relationships among their jobs, their work units, and the company. Also, employees are expected to acquire new skills and knowledge, apply them on the job, and share this information with fellow workers.

control A manager's or employee's ability to obtain and distribute valuable resources.

coordination training Training a team in how to share information and decision-making responsibilities to maximize team performance.

copyright Legal protection for the expression of an idea.

corporate university A centralized training organization in which learning is provided to not only company employees and managers but also stakeholders outside the company.

cost-benefit analysis The process of determining the economic advantages of a training program using accounting methods.

course or program Includes units or lessons that are smaller sections or modules covering different topics that can involve several hours, half-days, full days or even weeks.

criteria Measures or outcomes that trainer and the company use to evaluate training programs.

criteria relevance The extent to which training outcomes relate to the learned capabilities emphasized in training.

criterion contamination When a training program's outcomes measure inappropriate capabilities or are affected by extraneous conditions.

criterion deficiency The failure to measure training outcomes that were emphasized in training objectives.

cross-cultural preparation The education of employees (expatriates) and their families who are to be sent to a foreign country.

cross training A training method in which team members understand and practice each other's skills so that members are prepared to step in and take another member's place should someone temporarily or permanently leave the team; also, more simply, training employees to learn the skills of one or several additional jobs.

crowdsourcing Asking a large group of employees (the crowd) using social media or the web to help provide information for needs assessment.

curriculum An organized program of study designed to meet a complex learning objective such as preparing a learner to become a salesperson, certified computer network technician or a licensed nurse.

curriculum road map A figure showing all of the courses in a curriculum, the paths learners can take through it, and the sequences in which courses have to be completed.

customer capital The value of relationships with persons or other organizations outside a company for accomplishing the goals of the company (e.g., relationships with suppliers, customers, vendors, government agencies).

dashboards A computer interface designed to receive and analyze the data from departments within the company to provide information to managers and other decision makers.

detailed lesson plan The translation of the content and sequence of training activities into a guide used by the trainer to help deliver training.

development Formal education, job experiences, relationships, and assessments of personality and abilities that help employees prepare for the future.

development planning or career management system A system to motivate and retain employees by identifying and meeting their career and development needs.

digital collaboration An interaction between two or more people mediated by a computer; the use of technology to enhance and extend employees' ability to work together regardless of their geographic proximity.

direct costs Costs that are actually connected to training, including the salaries and benefits of all employees involved, program supplies, equipment and classroom rental or purchase, and travel costs.

discrimination   The degree to which trainees' performances on an outcome actually reflect true differences in performance.

disinvestment strategy   A business strategy that emphasize the liquidation and divestiture of businesses.

distance learning   Training method in which geographically dispersed companies provide information about new products, policies, or procedures as well as skills training and expert lectures to field locations.

diversity training   Training programs designed to change employees' attitudes about diversity and/or to develop skills needed to work with a diverse work force.

downward move   The reduction of an employee's responsibility and authority.

dual-career-path system   A career path system that enables technical employees to either remain in a technical career path or move into a management career path.

early retirement program   A system of offering (usually older) employees financial benefits to leave a company.

elaboration   A learning strategy requiring the trainee to relate the training material to other more familiar knowledge, skills, or behavior.

e-learning   Instruction and delivery of training by computer online through the Internet or web.

electronic performance support system (EPSS)   A computer application that can provide, as requested, skills training, information access, and expert advice.

employee engagement   The extent to which employees are fully involved in their work and the strength of their commitment to their job and the company.

error management training   Training in which trainees are given opportunities to make errors, which can aid in learning and improve trainees' performance on the job.

evaluation design   Designation of what information is to be collected, from whom, when, and how to determine the effectiveness of training.

expatriate   A person working in a country other than his or her nation of origin.

expectancy   The belief about the link between trying to perform a behavior (or effort) and actually performing well; the mental state that the learner brings to the instructional process.

experiential learning   A training method in which participants (1) are presented with conceptual knowledge and theory, (2) take part in a behavioral simulation,

(3) analyze the activity, and (4) connect the theory and activity with on-the-job or real-life situations.

expert systems   Technology (usually software) that organizes and applies human experts' knowledge to specific problems.

explicit knowledge   Knowledge that can be formalized, codified, and communicated.

external analysis   Examining the company's operating environment to identify opportunities and threats.

external conditions   Processes in the learning environment that facilitate learning.

external growth strategy   A business strategy emphasizing acquiring vendors and suppliers or buying businesses that allow the company to expand into new markets.

external validity   The generalizability of study results to other groups and situations.

Family and Medical Leave Act (FMLA)   A federal law that provides for up to 12 weeks of unpaid leave for parents with new infants or newly adopted children; also covers employees who must take a leave of absence from work to care for a family member who is ill or to deal with a personal illness.

far transfer   Trainees' ability to apply learned capabilities to the work environment even though it is not identical to the training session environment.

feedback   Information that employees receive while they are performing about how well they are meeting objectives.

fidelity   The extent to which a training environment is similar to a work environment.

flextime   Providing employees with the option of choosing when to work during the workday, workweek, or work year.

flipped classroom   A type of blended learning in which learners online watch lectures, complete simulations, read books and articles, take quizzes to assess their knowledge and skills, then come to class to work on projects, cases, hear speakers, and interact with instructors.

focus group   A face-to-face meeting with subject-matter experts (SMEs) in which specific training needs are addressed.

formal education program   An off-site or on-site program designed for a company's employees, a short course offered by a consultant or school, an executive MBA program, or a university program in which students live at the university while taking classes.

formal training and development   Training and development programs, courses, and events that are developed and organized by the company.

formative evaluation   Evaluation conducted to improve the training process; usually conducted during program design and development.

gap analysis   Determining the difference between employees' current and expected performance.

generalization   A trainee's ability to apply learned capabilities to on-the-job work problems and situations that are similar but not identical to problems and situations encountered in the learning environment.

generalizing   Adapting learning for use in similar but not identical situations.

glass ceiling   A barrier to advancement to an organization's higher levels.

goal   What a company hopes to achieve in the medium- to long-term future.

goal orientation   A trainee's goals in a learning situation.

goal setting   An employee's process of developing short- and long-term career objectives.

goal setting theory   A theory assuming that behavior results from a person's conscious goals and intentions.

gratifying   The feedback that a learner receives from using learning content.

group building methods   Training methods designed to improve team or group effectiveness.

group mentoring program   A program in which a successful senior employee is paired with a group of four to six less experienced protégés to help them understand the organization, guide them in analyzing their experiences, and help them clarify career directions.

guided team self-correction   Training that emphasizes continuous learning and knowledge sharing in teams through team members observing each other's behavior and giving and receiving performance feedback.

hands-on method   A training method in which the trainee is actively involved in learning.

Hawthorne effect   A situation in which employees in an evaluation study perform at a high level simply because of the attention they are receiving.

high-potential employee   An employee who the company believes is capable of succeeding in a higher-level managerial position.

human capital   The sum of the attributes, life experiences, knowledge, inventiveness, energy, and enthusiasm that a company's employees invest in their work.

human capital management   The integration of training with other human resource functions so as to track how training benefits the company.

human resource development   The integrated use of training and development, organizational development, and career development to improve individual, group, and organizational effectiveness.

human resource management   The policies, practices, and systems that influence employees' behavior, attitudes, and performance.

human resource management (HRM) practices   Management activities relating to investments in staffing, performance management, training, and compensation and benefits.

human resource planning   The identification, analysis, forecasting, and planning of changes needed in a company's human resources area.

hyperlinks   Links that allow a user to easily move from one web page to another.

in-basket   A training exercise involving simulation of the administrative tasks of the manager's job.

inclusion   Creating an environment in which employees share a sense of belonging, mutual respect, and commitment with others so they can perform their best work.

indirect costs   Costs not related specifically to a training program's design, development, or delivery.

informal learning   Learning that is learner initiated, involves action and doing, is motivated by an intent to develop, and does not occur in a formal learning setting.

informational interview   An interview an employee conducts with a manager or other employee to gather information about the skills, job demands, and benefits of that person's job.

input   Instructions that tell employees what, how, and when to perform; also, the resources that employees are given to help them perform their jobs.

instruction   The characteristics of the environment in which learning is to occur.

Instructional System Design (ISD)   A process for designing and developing training programs.

instrumentality   In expectancy theory, a belief that performing a given behavior is associated with a particular outcome.

intellectual capital   The codified knowledge that exists in a company.

intellectual skills   The mastery of concepts and rules.

interactive distance learning (IDL) The use of satellite technology to broadcast programs to different locations, allowing trainees to respond to questions posed during the training program using a keypad.

internal analysis Identifying the company's strength and weaknesses based on examining the available quantity and quality of financial, physical, and human capital.

internal conditions Processes within the learner that must be present for learning to occur.

internal growth strategy A business strategy focusing on new market and product development, innovation, and joint ventures.

internal validity Establishing that a treatment (training) made a difference.

interview Employees answer questions about their work and personal experiences, skill strengths and weaknesses, and career plans.

ISO 10015 A quality management tool designed to ensure that training is linked to a company's needs and performance.

ISO 9000:2000 A family of standards developed by the International Organization for Standardization that includes 20 requirements for dealing with such issues as how to establish quality standards and document work processes.

job A specific position requiring completion of certain tasks.

job analysis The process of developing a description of a job (duties, tasks, and responsibilities) and the specifications (knowledge, skills, and abilities) that an employee must have to perform it.

job enlargement The adding of challenges or new responsibilities to an employee's current job.

job experience The relationships, problems, demands, tasks, and other features that an employee faces on the job.

job hopping The practice of employees changing jobs usually between companies every two to three years.

job incumbent An employee currently holding a particular job.

job rotation Assigning employees a series of jobs in various functional areas of a company or movement among jobs in a single functional area or department.

job sharing A work situation in which two employees divide the hours, responsibilities, and benefits of a full-time job.

joint union-management training program A program created, funded, and supported by both union and management to provide a range of services to help employees learn skills that are directly related to their jobs and that are "portable" (valuable to employers in other companies or industries).

Just-in-time (embedded learning) Learning that occurs on the job as needed.

kaizen Practices in which employees from all levels of the company focus on continuous improvement of business processes.

key behaviors A set of behaviors that is necessary to complete a task; an important part of behavior modeling training.

knowledge Facts or procedures that individuals or teams of employees know or know how to do (human and social knowledge); also a company's rules, processes, tools, and routines (structured knowledge).

knowledge management The process of enhancing company performance by designing and implementing tools, processes, systems, structures, and cultures to improve the creating, sharing, and use of knowledge.

knowledge officer A leader of a company's knowledge management efforts (also called a *chief learning officer*).

knowledge workers Employees who own the means of producing a product or service. These employees have a specialized body of knowledge or expertise that they use to perform their jobs and contribute to company effectiveness.

lapse Situation in which a trainee uses previously learned, less effective capabilities instead of trying to apply capabilities emphasized in a training program.

leaderless group discussion A training exercise in which a team of five to seven employees must work together to solve an assigned problem within a certain time period.

lean thinking Doing more with less effort, equipment, space, and time, but providing customers with what they need and want. Part of lean thinking includes training workers in new skills or how to apply old skills in new ways so that they can quickly take over new responsibilities or use new skills to help fill customer orders.

learner control A trainee's ability to learn actively through self-pacing, selecting how content is presented, exercises, exploring links to other material, and conversations with other trainees and experts.

Learning Records Store (LRS) A technology that collects and stores employees' learning experiences in the form of statements that can be organized and presented in a meaningful way.

learner-content interaction   The learner interacts with the training content such as reading text on the web or in books, listening to multimedia modules and in activities that require the manipulation of tools or objects such as writing and completing case studies.

learner-instructor interaction   Discussion between the learner and the expert (trainer).

learner-learner interaction   Discussion between learners with or without an instructor.

learning   The acquisition of knowledge by individual employees or groups of employees who are willing to apply that knowledge in their jobs in making decisions and accomplishing tasks for the company; a relatively permanent change in human capabilities that does not result from growth processes.

learning management systems (LMS)   A system for automating the administration of online training programs.

learning organization   A company that has an enhanced capacity to learn, adapt, and change; an organization whose employees continuously attempt to learn new things and then apply what they have learned to improve product or service quality.

learning orientation   Learners who try to increase their ability or competence in a task.

lecture   A training method in which the trainer communicates through spoken words what trainees are supposed to learn.

lesson plan overview   A plan that matches a training program's major activities to specific times or time intervals.

Lifelong Learning Account (LiLA)   An account for adult education to which both the employee and the company contribute and the employee keeps—even if he or she leaves the company.

logical verification   Perceiving a relationship between a new task and a task that has already mastered.

maintenance   The process of continuing to use newly acquired capabilities over time.

Malcolm Baldrige National Quality Award   A national award created in 1987 to recognize U.S. companies' quality achievements and to publicize quality strategies.

managing diversity and inclusion   The creation of an environment that allows all employees (regardless of their demographic group) to contribute to organizational goals and experience personal growth.

massed practice   A training approach in which trainees practice a task continuously without resting.

massive open online courses (MOOCs)   Learning that is designed to enroll large number of learners (massive)—it is free and accessible to anyone with an Internet connection (open); it takes place online using videos of lectures, interactive coursework including discussion groups and wikis (online); and it has specific start and completion dates, quizzes and assessment, and exams (courses).

mental requirements   The degree to which a person must use or demonstrate mental skills or cognitive skills or abilities to perform a task.

mentor   An experienced, productive senior employee who helps develop a less experienced employee (a protégé).

metacognition   A learning strategy whereby trainees direct their attention to their own learning process.

metrics   Business-level outcomes chosen to measure the overall value of training or learning initiatives.

micro blogs or micro sharing   Software tools such as Twitter that enable communications in short bursts of text, links, and multimedia either through stand-alone applications or through online communities or social networks.

mission   A company's long-term reason for existing.

mobile learning   Refers to informal or formal learning delivered using a mobile device such as a smartphone, netbook, notebook computer, or i-Pad.

modeling   Having employees who have mastered the desired learning outcomes demonstrate them for trainees.

modeling display   A training method in which trainees are shown key behaviors, which they then practice; often done by videotape or computer.

motivation to learn   A trainee's desire to learn the content of a training program.

motor skills   Coordination of physical movements.

Myers-Briggs Type Inventory (MBTI)   A psychological test for employee development consisting of over 100 questions about how the person feels or prefers to behave in different situations.

near transfer   A trainee's ability to apply learned capabilities exactly to the work situation.

need   A deficiency that a person is experiencing at any point in time.

needs assessment The process used to determine if training is necessary; the first step in the Instructional System Design (ISD) model.

nine-box grid A three-by-three matrix used by groups of managers and executives to compare employees within one department, function, division, or the entire company for analysis and discussion of talent, to help formulate effective development plans and activities, and to identify talented employees who can be groomed for top-level management positions in the company.

norms Accepted standards of behavior for work-group members.

objective The purpose and expected outcome of training activities.

offshoring The process of moving jobs from the United States to other locations in the world.

onboarding The orientation process for newly hired managers.

online learning Instruction and delivery of training by computer online through the Internet or web.

on-the-job training (OJT) Training in which new or inexperienced employees learn through first observing peers or managers performing a job and then trying to imitate their behavior.

open skills Training objectives linked to general learning principles.

opportunity to perform The chance to use learned capabilities.

organizational analysis A training analysis that determines the appropriateness of training, considering the context in which training will occur.

organizing A learning strategy that requires the learner to find similarities and themes in training materials.

other In task analysis, a term referring to the conditions under which tasks are performed; for example, physical condition of the work environment or psychological conditions, such as pressure or stress.

output A job's performance standards.

outsourcing The acquisition of training and development activities from outside a company.

overall task complexity The degree to which a task requires a number of distinct behaviors, the number of choices involved in performing the task, and the degree of uncertainty in performing the task.

overlearning Employees' continuing to practice even if they have been able to perform the objective several times.

part practice A training approach in which each objective or task is practiced individually as soon as it is introduced in a training program.

past accomplishments A system of allowing employees to build a history of successful accomplishments.

perception The ability to organize a message from the environment so that it can be processed and acted upon.

performance analysis approach An approach to solving business problems that identifies performance gaps or deficiencies and examines training as a possible solution.

performance appraisal The process of measuring an employee's performance.

performance orientation A learner's focus on task performance and how the learner compares to others.

person analysis Training analysis that involves (1) determining whether performance deficiencies result from lack of knowledge, skill, or ability or else from a motivational or work-design problem, (2) identifying who needs training, and (3) determining employees' readiness for training.

person characteristics An employee's knowledge, skill, ability, behavior, or attitudes.

phased retirement A phase during which older employees gradually reduce their hours, which helps them transition into retirement.

physical requirements The degree to which a person must use or demonstrate physical skills and abilities to perform and complete a task.

pilot testing The process of previewing a training program with potential trainees and managers or other customers.

plug-in Extra software that needs to be loaded on a computer, for example, to listen to sound or watch video.

post-test only An evaluation design in which only post-training outcomes are collected.

post-training measure A measure of outcomes taken after training.

power The ability to influence others.

practicality The ease with which outcome measures can be collected.

practice An employee's demonstration of a learned capability; the physical or mental rehearsal of a task, knowledge, or skill to achieve proficiency in performing the task or skill or demonstrating the knowledge.

preretirement socialization   The process of helping employees prepare for exit from work.

presence   In training, the perception of actually being in a particular environment.

presentation methods   Training methods in which trainees are passive recipients of information.

pretest/post-test   An evaluation design in which both pretraining and post-training outcome measures are collected.

pretest/post-test with comparison group   An evaluation design that includes trainees and a comparison group. Both pretraining and post-training outcome measures are collected.

pretraining measure   A baseline measure of outcomes.

program design   The organization and coordination of a training program.

project management   The skills needed to manage a team of people and resources to create a learning solution.

promotion   An advancement into a position with greater challenges, more responsibility, and more authority than the previous job provided; usually includes a pay increase as well.

protean career   A career that is frequently changing based on changes in the person's interests, abilities, and values as well as changes in the work environment.

psychological success   A feeling of pride and accomplishment that comes from achieving life goals.

psychosocial support   Serving as a friend and role model to an employee; also includes providing positive regard, acceptance, and an outlet for the protégé to talk about anxieties and fears.

random assignment   The assignment of employees to training or a comparison group on the basis of chance.

rapid instructional design (RID)   A group of techniques that allow training to be built more quickly; the two principles of RID are that instructional content and process can be developed independently of each other and that resources devoted to design and delivery of instruction can be reallocated as appropriate.

rapid needs assessment   A needs assessment that is done quickly and accurately but without sacrificing the quality of the process or the outcomes.

rapid prototyping   An iterative process used in designing e-learning in which initial design ideas are proposed and provided in rough form in an online working prototype that is reviewed and refined by design team members.

reaction outcomes   A trainee's perceptions of a training program, including perceptions of the facilities, trainers, and content.

readability   Written materials' level of difficulty.

readiness for training   The condition of (1) employees having the personal characteristics necessary to learn program content and apply it on the job, and (2) the work environment facilitating learning and not interfering with performance.

realistic job preview   Stage in which a prospective employee is provided accurate information about attractive and unattractive aspects of a job, working conditions, company, and location to be sure that the employee develops appropriate expectations.

reality check   The information employees receive about how the company evaluates their skills and knowledge and where they fit into the company's plans (potential promotion opportunities, lateral moves).

reasonable accommodation   In terms of the Americans with Disabilities Act (ADA) and training, making training facilities readily accessible to and usable by individuals with disabilities; may also include modifying instructional media, adjusting training policies, and providing trainees with readers or interpreters.

recycling   Changing one's major work activity after having been established in a particular field.

reflection   Trainees spend a short amount of time, such as fifteen minutes, reviewing and writing about what they learned and how they performed.

rehearsal   A learning strategy focusing on learning through repetition (memorization).

reinforcement theory   A theory emphasizing that people are motivated to perform or avoid certain behaviors because of past outcomes that have resulted from those behaviors.

reliability   The degree to which outcomes can be measured consistently over time.

repatriation   Preparing expatriates for return to the parent company and country from a foreign assignment.

repurposing   Directly translating a training program that uses a traditional training method onto the web.

request for proposal (RFP)   A document that outlines for potential vendors and consultants the requirements for winning and fulfilling a contract with a company.

resistance to change   Managers' and/or employees' unwillingness to change.

results   Outcomes used to determine a training program's payoff.

retirement   The leaving of a job and work role to make the transition into life without work.

retrieval   The identification of learned material in long-term memory and use of it to influence performance.

return on expectations (ROE)   The process through which evaluation demonstrates to key business stakeholders, such as top level managers, that their expectations about training have been satisfied.

return on investment (ROI)   A comparison of a training program's monetary benefits and costs.

reversal   A time period in which training participants no longer receive training intervention.

role-play   A training exercise in which the participant takes the part or role of a manager or some other employee; training method in which trainees are given information about a situation and act out characters assigned to them.

sabbatical   A leave of absence from the company to renew or develop skills.

scenario-based training   Training that places team members in a realistic context while learning.

School-to-Work Opportunities Act   A federal law designed to assist states in building school-to-work systems that prepare students for high-skill, high-wage jobs or future education.

sector partnerships   Government agencies and industry trade groups that help identify the skills that local employers require and work with community colleges, universities, and other educational institutions to provide qualified employees.

self-assessment   An employee's use of information to determine career interests, values, aptitudes, and behavioral tendencies.

self-evaluation   Learners' estimates of how much they know or have learned from training.

self-directed learning   Training in which employees take responsibility for all aspects of their learning (e.g., when it occurs, who is involved).

self-efficacy   Employees' belief that they can perform their job or learn the content of a training program successfully.

self-management   A person's attempt to control certain aspects of his or her decision making and behavior.

self-regulation   Learners' involvement with the training material and assessing their progress toward learning.

semantic encoding   The actual coding process of incoming memory.

serious games   Games in which the training content is turned into a game but has business objectives.

shared media   Audio or video such as YouTube that can be accessed and shared with others.

simulation   A training method that represents a real-life situation, with trainees' decisions resulting in outcomes that mirror what would happen if they were on the job.

situational constraints   Work environment characteristics that include lack of proper equipment, materials, supplies, budgetary support, and time.

Six Sigma process   A process of measuring, analyzing, improving, and then controlling processes once they have been brought within the Six Sigma quality tolerances or standards.

skill   Competency in performing a task.

skill-based outcomes   Outcomes used to assess the level of technical or motor skills or behavior; include skill acquisition or learning and on-the-job use of skills.

social capital   The value of relationships among employees within a company.

social learning   Learning with and from others.

social learning theory   A theory emphasizing that people learn by observing other persons (models) who they believe are credible and knowledgeable.

social media   Online and mobile technology used to create interactive communications allowing the creation and exchange of user-generated content

social network analysis   A map of employee relationships that can be used to help identify informal employee communications and information- and knowledge-sharing patterns.

social support   Feedback and reinforcement from managers and peers.

Solomon four-group   An evaluation design combining the pretest/post-test comparison group and the post-test-only control group designs.

spaced practice   A training approach in which trainees are given rest intervals within the practice session.

staffing strategy   A company's decisions regarding where to find employees, how to select them, and the mix of employee skills and statuses.

stakeholders   Company leaders, top-level managers, mid-level managers, trainers, and employees who are end users of learning who have an interest in training and development and their support is important for determining its success (or failure).

storyboard   A group of pictures created using pencil-and-paper or markers on notebooks, erasable marker boards, flip charts, or PowerPoint slides that tell a story.

strategic choice   The strategy believed to be the best alternative to achieve the company goals.

strategic training and development initiatives Learning-related actions that a company takes to achieve its business strategy.

strategic value   Employees' potential to improve company effectiveness and efficiency.

stretch assignments   Job assignments that help employees develop because there is a mismatch between the employee's skills and past experiences and the skills required for success on the job.

STEM skills   Science, technology, engineering, and math skills that U.S. employers need and value, but employees lack.

subject-matter expert (SME)   A person who knows a great deal about (1) training issues, (2) the knowledge, skills, and abilities required for task performance, (3) necessary equipment, and (4) the conditions under which tasks have to be performed.

success cases or stories   Concrete examples of the impact of training that show how learning leads to results that the company finds worthwhile and the managers find credible.

succession planning   The process of identifying and tracking high-potential employees for advancement in a company.

summative evaluation   Evaluation of the extent that trainees have changed as a result of participating in a training program.

support network   A group of two or more trainees who agree to meet and discuss their progress in using learned capabilities on the job.

survivor   An employee remaining with a company after downsizing.

sustainability   The ability of a company to make a profit without sacrificing the resources of its employees, the community, or the environment.

SWOT analysis   An identification of a company's operating environment as well as an internal analysis of its strengths and weaknesses. SWOT is an acronym for Strengths, Weaknesses, Opportunities, and Threats.

synchronous communication   Communication in which trainers, experts, and learners interact with each other live and in real time in the same way that they would in face-to-face classroom instruction.

tacit knowledge   Personal knowledge that is based on individual experience and that is difficult to explain to others.

talent management   The process of attracting, retaining, developing, and motivating highly skilled employees and managers.

task   A statement of an employee's work activity in a specific job.

task analysis   Training analysis that involves identifying the tasks and knowledge, skills, and behaviors that need to be emphasized in training for employees to complete their tasks.

task redefinition   Changes in managers' and/or employees' roles and methods.

team leader training   Training that a team manager or facilitator receives.

team training   A training method that involves coordinating the performances of individuals who work together to achieve a common goal.

telecommuting   Working in a remote location (distant from a central office), where the employee has limited contact with peers but can communicate electronically (also called *teleworking*).

teleconferencing   The synchronous exchange of audio, video, and/or text between two or more individuals or groups at two or more locations.

temporary assignments   Job tryouts including employee exchanges and volunteer assignments in which employees take on a position to help them determine if they are interested in working in a new role.

threats to validity   Factors that lead one to question either (1) the believability of a study's results or (2) the extent to which evaluation results are generalizable to other groups of trainees and situations.

time series   An evaluation design in which training outcomes are collected at periodic intervals pre- and post-training.

Tin Can API (or experience API)   A specification for learning technology that makes it possible to collect data about an employee or a team's online and face-to-face learning experiences.

Total Quality Management (TQM)   A style of doing business that relies on the talents and capabilities of both labor and management to build and provide high-quality products and services and continuously improve them.

traditional training methods   Training methods requiring an instructor or facilitator and involve face-to-face interaction between trainees.

training   A company's planned effort to facilitate employees' learning of job-related competencies.

training administration   Coordination of activities before, during, and after a training program.

training context   The physical, intellectual, and emotional environment in which training occurs.

training design process   A systematic approach to developing training programs. Its six steps include conducting needs assessment, ensuring employees' readiness for training, creating a learning environment, ensuring transfer of training, selecting training methods, and evaluating training programs.

training effectiveness   The benefits that a company and its trainees receive from training.

training evaluation   The process of collecting the outcomes needed to determine whether training has been effective.

training outcomes (criteria)   Measures that a company and its trainer use to evaluate training programs.

training site   The place where training is conducted.

transfer   Giving an employee a different job assignment in a different area of the company.

transfer of training   Trainees' applying to their jobs the learned capabilities gained in training.

tuition reimbursement   The practice of reimbursing employees the costs for college and university courses and degree programs.

Uniformed Services Employment and Reemployment Rights Act   An act that covers deployed employees' rights, such as guaranteeing jobs when they return, except under special circumstances.

uniqueness   The extent to which employees are rare and specialized and not highly available in the labor market.

upward feedback   An appraisal process involving the collection of subordinates' evaluations of managers' behaviors or skills.

utility analysis   A cost-benefit analysis method that involves assessing the dollar value of training based on estimates of the difference in job performance between trained and untrained employees, the number of individuals trained, the length of time a training program is expected to influence performance, and the variability in job performance in the untrained group of employees.

valence   The value that a person places on an outcome.

values   Principles and virtues that symbolize the company's beliefs.

verbal information   Names or labels, facts, and bodies of knowledge.

verbal persuasion   Offering words of encouragement to convince others that they can learn.

vicarious reinforcement   A situation in which a trainee sees an example of someone being reinforced for using certain behaviors.

virtual classroom   Using a computer and the Internet to distribute instructor-led training to geographically dispersed employees.

virtual reality   A computer-based technology often used in simulations that provides trainees with a three-dimensional learning experience that approximates reality.

virtual team   A team that is separated by time, geographic distance, culture, and/or organizational boundaries and that relies almost exclusively on technology to interact and complete projects.

virtual work arrangement   A work arrangement (including virtual teams as well as teleworking) in which location, organization structure, and employment relationship are not limiting factors.

virtual worlds   Computer-based, simulated online three-dimensional representation of the real world where learning programs can be hosted.

vision   The picture of the future that a company wants to achieve.

volunteer assignments   Employees develop their skills through serving the community by taking positions in community organizations.

Web 2.0   User-created social networking features on the Internet, including blogs, wikis, and Twitter.

Web-based training   Training delivered on public or private computer networks and displayed by a web browser (also called *Internet-based training*).

webcasting   Classroom instructions that are provided online through live broadcasts.

whole practice   A training approach in which all tasks or objectives are practiced at the same time.

wiki   A website that allows many users to create, edit, and update content and share knowledge.

workforce analytics   The practice of using quantitative methods and scientific methods to analyze data from human resource databases, corporate financial statements, employee surveys and other data sources to make evidence-based decisions and show that human resource practices (including training, development, and learning) influence important company metrics.

Workforce Innovation and Opportunity Act   A 2014 federal law that created a new, comprehensive work force investment system that is customer focused, that provides Americans with career management information and high-quality services, and that helps match U.S. companies with skilled workers.

working storage   The rehearsal and repetition of information, allowing it to be coded for memory.

work-life balance   Helping employees deal with the stresses, strains, and conflicts related to trying to balance work and non-work demands.

work team   A group of employees with various skills who interact to assemble a product or produce a service.

Name Index

Company Index

Subject Index

Transfer of training *(Continued)*
  training administration and, 186–187
  training content to memory,
    182–184
  in training design process, 11
  training effectiveness and, 159
  training outcomes and, 263
  work environment and, 188–190
Transfer of training theories
  cognitive theory of transfer, 173
  implications for training design, 170
  stimulus generalization approach,
    172–173
  theory of identical elements,
    170–172
Troops to Energy Jobs program, 475
True performance support, 501
TSpace, at AT&T, 75
Tuition reimbursement, 397–398
Turkey, 16
Twitter, 336, 339, 353, 362, 417
  customers sharing experiences on,
    19
  informal learning through, 8
  for training and development, 35–36

U

Unemployment
  for older workers, 475
  reducing through job training
    programs, 442–444
  of veterans, 474
Unemployment rate, 14, 474
  impact of, 14
Unified Learning Kit (ULK), 340
Uniformed Services Employment and
    Reemployment Act, 474–475
Unionization, 88
Uniqueness, 87
Universities, corporate, 93–97
University of Excellence, 97
Unstructured on-the-job training, 300
Upper-level managers, needs assessment
    and, 122
Upward feedback, 402
US Airways Flight 1549, 6, 449
U.S. Army, 235, 359
U.S. Bureau of Labor Statistics, 22, 38
U.S. Department of Labor, 303, 305,
    445, 451
U.S. Supreme Court, 448
Utility analysis, 277–278
Utility companies, 235–236

V

Valence, 167
Validity
  external, 264
  internal, 263–264
  threats to, 263–266
Values, 69
Vendor, training service, 224–226
Verbal comprehension, 133
Verbal information, 160, 192, 320
Verbal persuasion, 163
Veterans returning to work, 474–475
The V Foundation for Cancer, 383
Vicarious reinforcement, 310
Vice president for human resources, 113
VideoCafe, 21
Videos, 298–299
Vietnam, 16
Vietnam War, 24
Violating copyright, 450–451
Virtual classrooms, 333, 336, 337, 339,
    364, 365
Virtual Heroes, 358
Virtual reality, 358
  networked, 37
Virtual teams, 40
Virtual worlds, 358
Visas, H-1B, 16–17
Vision, company, 69
Visuals, 209
Volunteer assignments, 412

W

W3 On Demand Workplace, 463
Wages
  offshoring and, 17
  of training professionals, 14, 16–17
Wall covering, in training room site, 205
WALL-E (film), 67
Walls, in training room site, 205
Watson (computer), 492
Wearable technology, 495
Web 2.0 technologies, 338, 500
Web-based training programs, 13, 340–
    341. *see also* E-learning Webcasting,
    366
Webcasts, 336
Web conferencing, 366
Webinars, 336
Who is involved, in design document,
    219
Whole practice, 182

Wi-Fi, 361
Wikis, 5, 8, 22, 35, 334, 336, 338, 353
Wireless communication, 37, 501
Wisdom, conventional, 180
Women
  excluded from training programs,
    451
  glass ceiling, 459–460
  labor force participation, 22
Women of color, 26
Work at home for employees, 513
Work-at-home positions, 467
Work environment
  facilitating learning and transfer of
    training, 176
  of the future, 491–493
  not identical to training session, 170
  obstacles that inhibit transfer of
    training, 188
  supporting learning and transfer,
    188–190
  transfer of training and, 188–190
Workforce. *see also* Employees
  aging, 23
  changing demographics and
    diversity in, 22–23
  expatriate, 460–464
  forces affecting training at, 4–6
  generational differences in, 23–26
  increase in civilian, 22
  managing diversity, 454–458
  managing diversity and inclusion of,
    454–458
  skills deficit in, 29
Workforce analytics, 281
Workforce Investment Act (1998), 446
Workforce Management (magazine), 50
Working storage, 173
Work-life balance, 465–468
Work-related attitudes, 161
Work teams, 39
World Class Manufacturing (WCM)
    process, 447

X

Xbox, 358

Y

Year Up's mission, 446
"You Matter" social network, 75
YouTube, 334, 353